CHRISTIANIZATIO]
CHRISTIAN

MW01011601

This is the first comparative, interdisciplinary analysis of one of the most fundamental stages in the formation of Europe. Leading scholars explore the role of the spread of Christianity and the formation of new principalities in the birth of Denmark, Norway, Sweden, Bohemia, Hungary, Poland and Rus' around the year 1000. Drawing on history, archaeology and art history, and emphasizing problems related to the sources and historiographical debates, they demonstrate the complex interdependence between the processes of religious and political change, covering conditions prior to the introduction of Christianity, the adoption of Christianity and the development of the rulers' power. Regional patterns emerge, highlighting both the similarities in ruler-sponsored cases of Christianization, and differences in the consolidation of power and in the use made of institutions introduced by Christianity. The essays reveal how local societies adopted Christianity; medieval ideas of what constituted the dividing line between Christians and non-Christians; and the connections between Christianity and power.

NORA BEREND is Senior Lecturer in Medieval History at the University of Cambridge.

CHRISTIANIZATION AND THE RISE OF CHRISTIAN MONARCHY

Scandinavia, Central Europe and Rus' c. 900–1200

EDITED BY

NORA BEREND

CAMBRIDGE UNIVERSITY PRESS

CAMBRIDGE UNIVERSITY PRESS
Cambridge, New York, Melbourne, Madrid, Cape Town, Singapore,
São Paulo, Delhi, Dubai, Tokyo, Mexico City

Cambridge University Press
The Edinburgh Building, Cambridge CB2 8RU, UK

Published in the United States of America by Cambridge University Press, New York

www.cambridge.org
Information on this title: www.cambridge.org/9780521169301

First published 2007
First paperback edition 2010

A catalogue record for this publication is available from the British Library

ISBN 978-0-521-87616-2 Hardback
ISBN 978-0-521-16930-1 Paperback

Contents

Contributors

PROF. SVERRE BAGGE (Centre for Medieval Studies, University of Bergen)

PROF. ROBERT BARTLETT (University of St Andrews)

DR NORA BEREND (University of Cambridge)

PROF. NILS BLOMKVIST (Gotland University, Visby)

PROF. STEFAN BRINK (University of Aberdeen)

DR MICHAEL H. GELTING (Danish National Archives, Copenhagen)

PROF. JÓZSEF LASZLOVSZKY (Central European University, Budapest)

PROF. THOMAS LINDKVIST (Göteborg University)

DR SÆBJØRG WALAKER NORDEIDE (Centre for Medieval Studies, University of Bergen)

DR ZOË OPAČIĆ (Birkbeck College, London)

DR STANISŁAW ROSIK (Institute of History, Wrocław University)

DR JONATHAN SHEPARD (formerly University of Cambridge)

DR PETR SOMMER (Centre for Medieval Studies, Prague)

DR BÉLA ZSOLT SZAKÁCS (Central European University and Pázmány Péter Catholic University, Budapest)

DR DUŠAN TŘEŠTÍK (Centre for Medieval Studies, Prague)

PROF. PRZEMYSŁAW URBAŃCZYK (Institute of Archaeology and Ethnology, Polish Academy of Sciences, Warsaw)

PROF. JOSEF ŽEMLIČKA (Centre for Medieval Studies, Prague)

Maps

Acknowledgements

Our work would have been impossible without funding, and I thank the AHRC for its 'Innovation Award', as well as the Centre for Medieval Studies at the University of Bergen, Norway, and the Trevelyan Fund at the University of Cambridge, for additional financial help. I am also indebted to the Centre for Research in the Arts, Social Sciences and Humanities at Cambridge for organizational assistance.

I am grateful to Sverre Bagge for his help with organizing the project and hosting one of our workshops in Voss; and to Susan Reynolds for reading the manuscript. My thanks also go to Zoë Opačić, who was a part-time research assistant on the project, for her work on Bohemia, and to Philip Stickler who drew the maps.

Note

Because many names have no English equivalent, we used the local forms of names. We chose the term central Europe to designate Bohemia, Moravia, Poland and Hungary; others may prefer central-eastern, east-central or eastern Europe for these polities. Central-eastern Europe designates central Europe and Rus'.

Our bibliographies are severely curtailed because of limitations of space, and do not include all the works we drew on, nor are we able to give a full list of all the editions of the primary sources. We created a web site at http://christianization.hist.cam.ac.uk which contains images, bibliographies and more details on some of the issues discussed in the chapters.

Common abbreviations

AQ *Ausgewählte Quellen zur deutschen Geschichte des Mittelalters*

MGH *Monumenta Germaniae Historica*

  SRG *Scriptores rerum Germanicarum in usum scholarum separatim editi*

    n.s. nova series

  SS *Scriptores*

MPH *Monumenta Poloniae Historica*

    n.s. nova series

1. Europe at the time of the Ottonians

2. Europe in the late twelfth century

CHAPTER I

Introduction[1]

Nora Berend

1. THE PROJECT

This book is the product of a year-long research project I organized, conducted in collaboration with the Centre for Medieval Studies at the University of Bergen, and with scholars from several countries. Together, we agreed on a set of questions to be addressed, read each other's rough drafts and held a series of workshop discussions in common, so that the book is not a collection of articles, but a coherent whole where all chapters address the same issues. We worked as a team and all the participants contributed more than their particular chapter in this volume; in a way the entire book, including this introduction, is the result of our common work.

The extension of Christendom's frontiers by the Christianization of Scandinavia and central-eastern Europe, a process also linked to the formation of new principalities and kingdoms, was one of the most fundamental stages in the formation of Europe. It resulted in the incorporation of large swaths of land into a political system that eventually gave rise to the European states as we know them. In the medieval 'making of Europe', one can distinguish between several regions: areas that joined Christian Europe under the leadership of their own elite, and those that either remained outside Christendom or were subjugated by force. We focused on the first, where two developments coincided in time: as Christianity was introduced, local rulers also consolidated their power over these areas. Thus we set out to investigate the relationship between religious change and political change, Christianization and the rise of Christian monarchy, around the year 1000 in an interdisciplinary and comparative framework. In order to highlight the specificity of these developments, other patterns of Christianization and political control will be discussed below in section 3.

Denmark, Norway and Sweden in Scandinavia, and Bohemia, Hungary and Poland in central Europe joined Latin Christendom in roughly the

[1] I thank the members of the project, and Susan Reynolds and David d'Avray for their suggestions.

I

century and a half between the late ninth century and the middle of the eleventh century. Rus' in the same period adopted Byzantine Christianity. This dating is derived from the conversion of rulers. These 'official' conversions did not immediately entail the Christianization of the population even in an institutional sense, let alone in the sense of an internalization of beliefs. Nor, however, did they necessarily mean the forced conversion of the population. In some cases before, while in others after, the ruler's conversion, Christians and pagans coexisted in more or less easy or uneasy ways for a while. These official conversions however signal what in these cases turned out to be the point of no return, after which, despite pagan revolts in some of the areas, religious change progressed in one direction only, towards Christianization. They also indicate the linking of Christianity and princely power.

The scholars who worked on this project included historians, archaeologists and art historians. This interdisciplinary approach prevented us from either simply using the findings of art and archaeology as illustration or ignoring them entirely in an interpretive framework that hinges on texts alone. The comparative nature of our undertaking questions explanatory frameworks whose perspective is either exclusively national or western European. Causality and historical processes are seen in a new light when viewed across northern and central-eastern Europe as a whole, highlighting the inadequacies of purely local explanations. Regional patterns emerge, within which similarities and differences can be closely analysed. Although on the surface similar processes took place in all these areas, a closer comparison reveals many significant differences. Thus in the interlinked process of the adoption of Christianity and political consolidation, we investigated the relationship between borrowing (especially from western Europe), adaptations and local specificities. Some aspects were common to the whole area, others were specific to particular regions or countries. When local variations are explored in depth, it becomes clear that the process of Christianization and political consolidation cannot be equated with the adoption of a western European blueprint.

Both Christianization and the consolidation of polities are topics with a venerable past in scholarship. I shall not reiterate terminological debates, but use conversion to denote individual religious change and Christianization to refer to the process of the penetration of Christianity into society and accompanying societal change.[2] Sociological studies of religion inform our

---

[2] Russell 1994, 26–30; Sawyer, Sawyer and Wood 1987, 1–22; Sanmark 2004, 13–14. On the contrary, conversion as possible synonym of Christianization: Rambo 1993, 172.

understanding of religious change.[3] Sociologists, however, have primarily analysed modern and most often individual conversions: the sources and the psychological insights available for such studies differ widely from those available to medievalists.[4] Cultural anthropology, with more research on the conversion of communities and whole societies, provides helpful analogies, as do some sociohistorical studies of the Christianization of societies.[5] Pierre Hadot drew attention to how conversion is specific to religions of 'rupture', entailing absolute faith in the word of God.[6] Scholars, however, have access only to the accounts and interpretations of conversion, not to the experience itself.[7] In our case, we have little data even of views expressed on the individual feelings accompanying conversion. Texts mention a few cases of individual conversions, but we have no evidence matching that on Augustine of Hippo, or Herman-Judah, however riddled they be with difficulties, such as the relationship between literary construct and experience.

Conversion, even in well-documented individual cases, was not simply an individual matter; scholars of all fields emphasize that conversion is contingent on the social context.[8] A greater degree of instability, sociocultural crisis and a discontinuity of old explanatory structures have been linked to the likelihood of group conversion.[9] In our context, however, we cannot attribute religious change to dissatisfaction with existing explanatory structures. In order to understand the religious change that took place we must look at a combination of factors, including political motivations and coercion. Our primary concern is religious change as introduced by a ruler and its impact on society.[10] In the societies under investigation, conversion was a question of collective identity, as religion both before and after Christianization was central to social life. Religious change entails the transfer of feelings of awe and reverence to another source and a change in rituals. In our cases, the distinction between the sacred and the profane existed both before and after Christianization, but the content of each changed: for example sacred trees ceased to be accepted as sacred. As Émile Durkheim pointed out long ago, religion does not simply consist of belief;

[3] Especially Weber 1969; Durkheim 1965; Berger 1973; Stark and Bainbridge 1987. Cf. Geertz 1966.
[4] Kilbourne and Richardson 1989; Stark and Bainbridge 1987, 195–202; Snow and Machalek 1984; Rambo 1993, esp. 30–3, 48–65, 81–6, 160–2; Rambo 1999.
[5] Tippett 1992; Kraft 1992; several studies in Buckser and Glazier 2003; Russell 1994; Stark 1996. Cf. also Cusack 1999.
[6] Hadot 1981. [7] Morrison 1992, 4–5; Rambo 1993, 171.
[8] Malony and Southard 1992; Rambo 1993; Buckser and Glazier 2003.
[9] Berger 1973, 54–9; Rambo 1993, 46–7.
[10] Urbańczyk 2003 provides a schematic overall analysis without reflecting on changes in Christianity.

collective ceremonial and ritual activities, carried out in order to create or reinforce group solidarity, are key elements of religion.[11] The latter was a paramount issue in early medieval Christianity, with its focus on public rituals and the close association of religion and secular power, as cogently demonstrated by Mayke de Jong's analysis.[12] Christianization meant that one set of rituals was exchanged for another; and this was accompanied by the imposition of new religious specialists who were initially outsiders, immigrants. Individual conversions mean leaving one social milieu in order to become part of another; collective conversion means a transformation of the social milieu itself. For example, certain social practices including those involving marriage or infanticide were not accepted under the new dispensation.

The more specific meanings of Christianization in our period and area will be discussed below. First, it is crucial to address the key issues concerning definitions of being a 'Christian' and Christianization. Modern studies emphasize the multiple meanings and different types of conversion, and the negotiated nature of Christian commitment.[13] The definition of who is 'religious' is difficult even for students of modern religiosity: for example different results have been reached by focusing on church attendance or on particular beliefs as constituting religiousness.[14] It is clear that one must avoid defining 'authentic' religiosity by motivation, thus for example denying that behaviour which aims at securing safety, status or good luck is religious, as such an attitude precludes the examination of the meaning of religiosity.[15] Robert Markus demonstrated the need to focus on a given period's own conception of Christianity, and showed how Christianity itself changed during the first few centuries.[16] In the same way, modern definitions of Christianity in the period under investigation need to be based on the medieval understanding of what constituted a Christian, in order to avoid anachronism. Belief, religious practice (rituals and devotion), the experience of the ultimate nature of reality, knowledge about faith and its consequences in one's behaviour have all been cited as parameters of religiosity; but the question is what was crucial at the time in determining the dividing line between Christians and non-Christians.

---

[11] Durkheim 1965, bk 3. Also Turner 1969.
[12] de Jong 2001; others have drawn similar conclusions but often with a negative judgement on the meaning of medieval Christianity, summarized in Sanmark 2004, 31–2.
[13] Summary in Rambo 1993; Mills and Grafton 2003.
[14] E.g. Stark and Glock 1968, 11–21.
[15] As opposed to the classification by Allport 1960, 33; criticism Stark and Glock 1968, 18–19.
[16] Markus 1990. Also Fletcher 1997.

Medieval ideas of conversion themselves were not static, and by the eleventh–twelfth centuries monastic theological circles developed sophisticated ideas, which, however, were not common to all members of society. Underpinning medieval understandings of conversion were two key issues: conversion as redemption, and the implementation of conversion, which meant joining a group, the Church. The first notion entailed that conversion led to truth and life, that it was a turning of the heart to God. Two possible conclusions, however, followed from this. One was that because it was not due to human endeavour but only to God's grace, conversion could not be imposed but only voluntary.[17] A different view, however, was advocated by some, and became significant by the thirteenth century (despite contemporary critics), which permitted the use of pressure and even force, because the ultimate aim, the salvation of souls, was seen as justifying such intervention: just as medical procedures causing pain led to healing, pain could be imposed by force to cure the soul, turning military threat and warfare into acceptable means to bring about conversion.[18] The second issue concerned the nature of conversion. Both medieval commentators and modern scholars have been divided in their opinions about whether conversion is an event, a turning point (in this case baptism) or a process, which can even last a lifetime; current consensus tends towards the latter.[19] Although K. Morrison has shown how eleventh- and twelfth-century writers understood conversion in the sense of the self-perfection of Christians (the imitation of Christ), as a process ending only in death, it is equally clear that many missionaries followed a policy of 'baptize first, teach later' when it came to the mass-conversion of pagans.[20] The hardening of papal policy in the thirteenth century on baptism as irrevocable even in the case of Jews baptized under duress similarly indicates that baptism was seen as a crucial milestone that had irrevocable consequences.[21] Baptism, one act, may only be a part of the process of conversion, but in our period and geographical area, baptism was clearly a crucial element of conversion. It is significant that while in the eleventh and especially twelfth century medieval authors were preoccupied by internalized self-perfection, a constant seeking of God, the conversion of northern and central Europe took a radically different form. Breaking down the old and assuming the

---

[17] Morrison 1992, 81.

[18] Morrison 1992, 81, 79; Duggan 1997; Urban 1989b. Case-studies on the significance of military pressure e.g. Bartlett 1985; Karras 1986 (also discusses contemporary critics); Jensen 2001.

[19] Nock 1933; Hadot 1981; Snow and Machalek 1984; Kilbourne and Richardson 1989; Rambo 1993; Morrison 1992; Russell 1994; Sanmark 2004, 13–14; Rambo 1992, 160; Buckser and Glazier 2003.

[20] Cf. similar policies elsewhere Ryan 1997; Sanmark 2004, 43–5.

[21] First formulated at Toledo IV (633). Ravid 2000.

new man was a standard part of understandings of conversion – in our case this was to be a lengthy process *after*, rather than before, baptism. We do not, however, engage in charting the internalization of Christianity: this would necessitate another research project and the establishment of exact criteria to avoid an implicit dismissal of certain forms of religiosity, and value-judgements inherent in seeking to distinguish a stage when the population became 'truly' Christian.

Christianization in these areas was linked to the rise of polities. Although initially our working title included 'state formation', we decided not to engage in argument over whether the emerging units were 'states', as it would lead us far from our purpose. Yet, because the wider problem of the formation of states and their characteristics has a bearing on discussions of power and political consolidation, it is worth pointing out where our topic is situated within such a framework. Divergent views are held on the beginnings of states among both social scientists and medievalists. Many argue that it is misleading to call only the modern national state (where government has sovereign power over the citizens of a defined territorial area) and its direct antecedents (which according to some go back to the medieval period) 'state', and the word has been applied to the Greek polis, the Roman Empire, Italian city-states and other units. Theories of state formation abound, prioritizing causes as diverse as for example irrigation agriculture, warfare, voluntary subordination or economic exchange.[22] Sociologists have argued about the characteristics of states and their differences from other political units. The distinction has been drawn between political centralization without fully developed states, where a warrior- or priest-chief ruled with a council, and people owed allegiance to him; and states, where the ruler had a court and controlled the armed force, and full-time officials carried out administration and justice.[23] Stephen K. Sanderson distinguished between chiefdom and state, defining the former as a form of sociopolitical organization that is an essential precursor to the state. Despite many similarities between states and chiefdoms, he saw a crucial qualitative distinction: the state has a monopoly of violence, whereas the chiefdom does not.[24]

Not everyone follows such a classification, however. Because states themselves have been defined in different ways, whether a particular polity will be categorized as a state will depend on the definition used. Max Weber saw a state as a compulsory association claiming monopoly of the legitimate use

[22] E.g. Tilly 1985; Sanderson 1999, 70–82.
[23] Giddens 2001, chap. 14 (more details in 1993, chap. 10); Mann 1986, chap. 1.
[24] Sanderson 1999, 55–7.

of physical force within its territories; Charles Tilly as a coercion-wielding organization that exercises a clear priority in some respects over all other organizations within substantial territories; Anthony Giddens as a political apparatus of government ruling over a territory, with a legal system and the ability to use force to buttress its power; and Joseph Strayer used a simple set of 'signs' to detect the existence of states: the long-term geographic stability of a human group, the existence of impersonal and relatively permanent political institutions with political power, and people's loyalty to these.[25] Some scholars stress that many different types of states have existed, including ones with little durable state apparatus.[26] It is not surprising therefore that, although no one denies that during the medieval period personal bonds and cross-cutting jurisdictions were important, and that exclusive territorial sovereignty was not the form medieval power took, both sociologists and medievalists have proposed different starting dates for the development of European (usually meaning west European) states. One finds views on the existence of states in the seventh century, on the emergence of states in the period 1000–1300 or in the twelfth century, or the birth of the 'modern state' in the fourteenth and fifteenth centuries, to name but a few positions on the issue.[27] Others prefer to speak of stateless or polycentric societies for the medieval period.[28] Recent criticism of using the concept of 'state' for the medieval period suggested that it obscures the complexity of the power structure, the fact that other sources of power existed apart from the king and imposes a false image of delegated authority.[29]

This is not a debate we wish to engage in; clearly, depending on the definition one chooses, these polities can or cannot be defined as states. For example, major administrative structures and complex institutions only came into being later than our period in the areas under discussion; the beginnings of institutions of rule such as chanceries and courts, or ideologies of rulership, on the other hand, emerged during the period we are analysing. Whether or not one decides to call the emerging political units states, they are clearly situated on a continuum of political centralization. Therefore some conclusions from sociologists are worth mentioning here, as they are particularly pertinent to our investigations. Several scholars have emphasized how the development of states can only be understood

[25] Weber 1968, vol. I, chap. 1, concept of state at 56 (I was unable to consult the 1979 edition); Tilly 1992; Giddens 2001, 421; Strayer 1970. Cf. Axtmann 1993; Reynolds 1997a.

[26] Tilly 1992, 21.

[27] Thacker 2000; Strayer 1970; Mann 1986; Zmora 2001 respectively. For a critical discussion, Reynolds 1997a. The entire 2002, vol. 15, no. 1 issue of the *Journal of Historical Sociology* is dedicated to discussion concerning the definition of states.

[28] Listed in Davies 2003.   [29] Davies 2002; 2003; response: Reynolds 2003.

in relation to other states.[30] The need to view the historical developments of political units treated here in terms of interaction and not in the isolation of modern national boundaries is clear. Norbert Elias underlined the long-term nature of state-formation processes and posed the question of why parts of society became more integrated and functionally more interdependent over the centuries (with each move towards closer integration engendering tension and conflict).[31] Our project fits into this analytical framework, with its focus on the growing consolidation of the ruler's power and of polities without engaging with the issue of when exactly political centralization turns into a state. The polities that came into being eventually all became 'regnal communities' as defined by Susan Reynolds.[32]

Christianization and the rise of polities could be studied independently. However, we are interested in the intersection of the two, and the relationship between them. To what extent were these two processes interconnected, Christianization helping in the consolidation of political units, and/or political consolidation facilitating Christianization? What were the connections between the two in terms of personnel, methods of control and communication (including the use of writing), institutions and structures? Our work offers a detailed comparative study that has hitherto been absent from the scholarship. Although in the extensive national historiographies Christianization and the beginnings of the state take pride of place, comparative work is rare and does not focus on local variations. Thus the analysis of the history of central and northern Europe's conversion has been affected by two separate trends. On the one hand, competing national myths have long held sway over this area of research. On the other hand, medievalists from outside the countries in question primarily studied the process as the expansion of western Europe, be it primarily through the agency of the aristocracy (Robert Bartlett) or missionaries (Richard Fletcher).[33] Scandinavia's Christianization overall has been studied, although most work deals with individual countries, but there is no in-depth analysis of this topic for central and eastern Europe, nor, apart from brief overviews, of all these regions in a comparative perspective.[34]

The changes in northern and central-eastern Europe were part of long-term processes that resulted in, on the one hand, the rise of Christianity as the dominant religion of European societies, and, on the other hand,

---

[30] E.g. Skocpol 1985; Tilly 1992; Mann 1986; Anderson 1974, esp. 37–8; Elias 2000, esp. 262–4.
[31] Elias, 2000, 257–362; 1972.   [32] Reynolds 1997b.   [33] Bartlett 1993; Fletcher 1997.
[34] Scandinavia: Sawyer, Sawyer and Wood 1987; Sanmark 2004; Kattinger, Olesen and Wernicke 2004, with a list of previous volumes. Overview notably Kłoczowski 1993, positing the link between state and Christianization.

the development of a system of states as the political structure of these societies. The process started well before the period we are focusing on, and in some respects continued after it. But the transformations we discuss were crucial in the creation of 'Europe'. Constantine's conversion to Christianity and introduction of single dynastic rule started the political ascendancy of the religion and forged the link between Christianity and power, although the connection was played out in a variety of ways over the centuries. The subsequent spread of Christianity entailed compromises and accommodations at every stage, as eloquently analysed by Peter Brown.[35] Among a series of turning-points, the eighth century was significant in the rise of political systems that were no longer linked to the ancient world, with aristocracies that had no knowledge of Latin, and the establishment of ties between the Franks and the popes. This local Christendom was then expanded, first along its peripheries through the Christianization of Frisia and Saxony, entailing submission to the Frankish rulers. Christianity and kingship were associated, as were paganism, brutishness and a kingless society. Missionaries under the patronage of rulers started to go out, first to put an end to the coexistence of Christian and pagan practices, and eventually to persuade pagans to convert. It was the time of 'the emergence of a distinctive Christianity in the west . . . characterized . . . by the alliance of a substantially new Church with a new political system',[36] both intent on their further expansion. The spread of Christianity involved serious education in the core areas, but quick baptisms along the frontiers; 'Christianity had become part of the language of power throughout north-western Europe.'[37] The conversion of northern and central-eastern Europe was the last step in this 'rise of Western Christendom'.

The development of Christendom consisted of more than the spread of a new religion. Numerous scholars have pointed out that the ninth to the eleventh or twelfth centuries was the period of the 'birth of Europe': the political units that took shape then continued with some variations to become the Europe as we know it.[38] Our investigations fall into the period that R. I. Moore calls the 'first European revolution',[39] laying the foundations of the ancien régime. It was an era of significant new developments in western Europe itself: the development of papal power, of parishes, of monastic orders. Some of these innovations rapidly arrived in the newly joined lands. The period of the 'expansion of Europe' was not simply one of adding new territories, however. It meant further diversification, bringing

---

[35] Brown 1997; also Herrin 1989; Fletcher 1997.   [36] Brown 1997, 275.
[37] Brown 1997, 306.   [38] Bartlett 1993; Fried 1991; Leyser 1994a; Le Goff 2005.
[39] Moore 2000 (for the period 970–1215).

about even more variety in religious practices and increasing the number
of political players.

2. SCANDINAVIA AND CENTRAL-EASTERN EUROPE:
A COMPARATIVE ANALYSIS

The following chapters discuss the same set of issues linked to Christianization and the rise of Christian polities country by country. Each of us
is bound by our particular expertise, and therefore the only way to produce a comparative analysis was to rely on a framework based on modern
nation-states. Readers can draw their own conclusions from the material
presented in the chapters; here I present key comparisons and overall considerations.[40] Open questions remain of course, and further research may
shed light on issues of pagan religion or the importance of missionary
centres for example, leading to new answers.

The nature of our sources, whether written, archaeological or artistic,
poses particular problems. They often provide only fragmentary evidence
which is open to conflicting interpretations. The biases of the written
sources and the problems of interpretation relating to archaeological finds
need to be weighed constantly. Wherever possible, comparing the testimony
of different sources can offer clearer insights; for example, when analysing
the Scandinavian pantheon of gods, the place names give a different picture
of locally important gods than the narratives constructed during Christian
times. However, such comparisons are not always possible; for example,
archaeology provides the only evidence in many cases. Similarly, what is
reliable and what is later invention in the Christian narrative sources often
remain a matter of guesswork. In the same way, the linking of artistic
influences to political or religious impact is often speculative. By laying bare
the source-base of our work, and indicating doubts, problems, uncertainties
and rival interpretations, instead of creating a smooth narrative, we aim to
demonstrate how we know what we know, admit what we do not know
and signal the possibilities in between.

A). Pre-Christian religions and the first contacts with Christianity

Looking at Christianization and the rise of Christian monarchies in a
comparative perspective, it is clear that striking similarities and equally

---

[40] I shall not footnote the material that can be found in the individual chapters; references will only
be included to primary and secondary sources I have drawn on for this section.

conspicuous differences cut across the boundaries of polities. My analysis will proceed in the order of the main thematic issues we chose, the first of which is pagan religion.[41] Much more is known of Scandinavia's indigenous beliefs and practices than those of central and eastern Europe. In Scandinavia pre-Christian cult seems to have continued longer, at least in some places, and Snorri Sturluson in the early thirteenth century wrote at length about pre-Christian mythology. In central Europe and Rus', local cults were forbidden, suppressed and written out of the sources. Yet problems relating to the written and archaeological sources are not dissimilar; they are analysed by Robert Bartlett. Already in the fourth century paganism (the word *paganus* itself circulated from the late fourth century) was equated to empty illusions by Christians, rather than to a form of religion. For our period, the extent to which Christian authors writing after, and sometimes long after, conversion recast indigenous beliefs according to classical and/or Christian models is still debated. Material evidence of local pre-Christian religions is much richer in Scandinavia, pointing to differences in the expression of indigenous beliefs. Yet some of this evidence is also controversial in many areas, for example the distinction between pagan and Christian burials is often unclear. In terms of beliefs and practices, in all regions under investigation we have no or little evidence of a separately organized religion with doctrine and gods, but rather of local populations with practices linked to natural features such as sacred trees or springs, divination of different sorts and sacrifice. The lack or role of cult buildings and priests is a much debated topic. Where they certainly existed, among the eleventh–twelfth-century Polabian Slavs, and in parts of Scandinavia, were they imitations of Christian practice?

Second, we analysed contacts with and knowledge of Christianity before the formal Christianization of a polity. Most of the populations under investigation encountered Christianity (and sometimes other monotheistic religions as well) sometime before their conversion. Naturally, traders and raiders who penetrated into Christian lands – Scandinavians, Rus' and Hungarians – had more such contacts than members of sedentary societies – Poles and Bohemians. However, sedentary elites also interacted with the elites of powerful Christian neighbours, particularly the Franks, through diplomacy and alliances, and this could result in cultural borrowing. Burial evidence shows the use of Christian objects in otherwise non-Christian graves, for example as jewellery. Contact sometimes but

---

[41] 'Pagan' in origin is a Christian term with negative connotations, but it has often been used in scholarship to denote 'pre-Christian' and I shall use it that way.

not always resulted in individual conversions. We know of Scandinavians (especially Svears and Norwegians), Rus' and Hungarian chieftains who were prime-signed or baptized.[42] The nature of such conversion is sometimes an open question: prime-signing or baptism could be a resort for those seeking trade advantages, or used as a diplomatic strategy. Christian sources complain of 'fake' conversions (their stance is similar to Nock's concept of adhesion[43]). At other times a more sustained effort followed, thus Norway's rulers between the mid-tenth and early eleventh century were converted abroad in the context of political alliances and then spread Christianity in their lands; a Byzantine missionary bishop was installed in eastern areas of the Hungarians after the mid-tenth-century baptism of one of their chieftains. In some cases, notably Denmark and Birka in Sweden, Frankish missions were present generations before the official conversion. Rus' provides a case of mission at the insistence of a female member of the dynasty, Olga, *c.* 960 (preceded by a German mission), which however encountered the resistance of locals. The knowledge of Christianity could also produce a reaction against it: Vladimir of Rus' at first tried to introduce a compulsory pagan cult; some of the Slavic people gave a sharper definition to pagan religion.

To what degree were local societies influenced by Christianity before the formal imposition of that religion? Material culture demonstrates the presence of Christian cult in Scandinavia prior to the official introduction of Christianity. At times it is impossible to determine whether there was insignificant Christianization or simply no (or inconclusive) evidence remains of Christianization: in the Hungarian case, pectoral crosses in graves and the possibility of the survival of a pre-conquest Christian population are insufficient to show whether or not there were conversions within Hungary in the tenth century, although there is written evidence of evangelization. When both written and archaeological sources are silent, however, as in the case of Poland, one may draw a firmer conclusion concerning the lack of Christianization. Ninth-century Birka is an interesting example of abortive Christianization: although Christianity took hold in the trade emporium for about two decades, it then disappeared, perhaps linked to a shift in trade. Bohemian princes also experimented with Christianity in the mid-ninth century and then renounced it; probably both events were due to political strategy. Christian influences seem to have been strongest in Rus' where part of the Rus' elite was Christianized prior to Vladimir's

[42] Recently Coviaux 2005.   [43] Nock 1933, 7.

conversion, and in parts of Scandinavia prior to rulers' decisions to convert. Yet Christianity did not become dominant anywhere before the official conversion: there was no Christian majority to influence the course of events. The study of early medieval conversions drew attention to a period of awareness prior to conversion.[44] Sociological and anthropological studies also highlight such a period, which may be accidental or intentionally stimulated, of variable length and which could involve external or internal pressures, simple interaction or direct missionary advocacy.[45] In our cases, it seems that while many areas were indeed in contact with Christianity for a while prior to conversion, not all were. The real impact of Christianity in most cases was linked to the decision of rulers to convert: Christian cult became significant in Bohemia in the late ninth century, in Norway from the mid-tenth century, although perhaps earlier in limited areas, in Rus', Poland, Denmark and Sweden in the late tenth century (except Birka), in Hungary in the early eleventh century (in eastern areas in the late tenth century).

B). *Rulers' conversions and their consequences*

Third, we analysed the rulers' decision to convert and its consequences. Rulers sought to control the sacred in order to legitimize their power both before and after Christianity.[46] The link between rulers' power and Christianization needs to be addressed; what did rulers gain by converting?[47] Both real and literary precedents convey some answers. Early medieval conversions established a link to the Roman world and also conferred a political identity. A long literary tradition existed on royal decisions to convert, from Constantine onwards. Early medieval rulers are presented by the sources as making such decisions in consultation with their people, witness Gregory of Tours's account of Clovis, or Bede's of Æthelberht of Kent and Edwin of Northumbria.[48] These were seen as the act through which new Christian peoples emerged. These patterns only partially applied to the conversions analysed here. The answer usually supplied for the period under consideration consists of two elements: building strong power at

---

[44] Wood 2001, 265–6; also Cusack 1999, 20.   [45] Tippett 1992, 195.

[46] Garnsey and Humfress 2001, 25–51.

[47] Russell 1994, 50; Strzelczyk 2001. Summary on motives to convert to world religions (not limited to rulers): Hefner 1993, Introduction. Kłoczowski 1993, 873–4 takes the advantages for rulers as granted.

[48] Bede I.25–6 (at 72–8); II.9–14 (at 162–88) (I was unable to consult the 1991 edition); Gregory of Tours II.29–31 (at 90–3).

home and avoiding external threat, especially conquest by the German Empire. Neither, however, is unproblematic. Many men sought to establish their power over society or against rivals by conversion to Christianity, often in the hope of military assistance from a Christian power, usually the Franks/Germans. This was by no means a foolproof method, as is demonstrated by the case of the Danish Harald Klak, who was baptized in 826 in Mainz and returned to rule Denmark but was quickly overthrown. Other conversions of rulers did not lead to Christianization either. The conversion of Bohemian princes in 845 was not rejected by the population; rather, it was soon repudiated by the princes themselves. Sweden had several Christian kings without this resulting in the official Christianization of the polity. Conversion, therefore, was not necessarily a road to power. In all the cases treated here, however, rulers who succeeded in promoting Christianity also further consolidated their power.

As far as we can determine from the sources, initially patchworks of local communities with no overarching political authority or many local strongmen (chieftains) existed everywhere. Rulers emerged from among local leaders with varying degrees of authority over territories. Looting raids and trade were ways to gain part of the wealth and prestige of western Europe; so was conversion. In every case, rulers had some role in Christianization. They all imported Christianity, although their own conversion followed two paths: some rulers were converted abroad, while others were baptized 'at home'. The Christianizing rulers established their power over larger areas than their predecessors, except probably in Sweden, where, however, the lack of sources precludes any certainties. Yet this surface similarity masks significant differences. The extent of the change varied widely between the different areas: in some, a strong pre-existing power was now extended; elsewhere, centralizing power was established for the first time. In some cases rulers first established strong power and then advocated or forced the acceptance of Christianity, such as Vladimir of Rus' or Mieszko of Poland; in other cases, they accomplished the consolidation of power and Christianization in parallel, such as Bořivoj and his son in Bohemia. What Christianity therefore brought the rulers could differ: prestige, legitimacy and a possible rise of status in the first case, often material help in consolidating rule, accompanied by prestige in the second. Consolidation of power, which eventually led to monarchy, was well underway before initial Christianization in Denmark, started a short time before such Christianization in Norway (with Harald Hårfagre in the late ninth and early tenth centuries) and Poland (with Mieszko before his conversion), was more or less parallel to it in Bohemia (*c.* 884–after 935) and Hungary (Géza and István) and continued significantly after the introduction of Christianity in Sweden (where the consolidation of kingship was accomplished in the thirteenth century). Rus' is an exception, where the introduction of Christianity coincided with individual rule but where such rulership did not become the norm.

Secular rule and Christianity were interlinked in many ways after the ruler's conversion, a connection that goes back to the Christianization of the Roman Empire.[49] Key examples for the medieval period are: the rulers' control over the Church and its personnel; the territorial and administrative organization, taxation and literacy that Christianity could bring; and the use of ecclesiastics in administration. Differences also existed: for example in Sweden, Cistercians, not secular clerics, played an important role in royal government. The significant exception was Rus', where rulers did not rely on ecclesiastics in governing their polity. Christianity also brought ideological legitimacy, especially in its emphasis on kingship. Christian rhetoric provided a model of power for kings, creating a political context for Christianity from Late Antiquity. Kingdoms became the archetype of political unit, and kingship, drawing on the Bible, conferred prestige which was unavailable through other means.[50] We should not assume, however, that one could not be a powerful ruler without a royal title: in Bohemia, a permanent royal title was introduced only at the end of the twelfth century, and most Polish rulers were not kings. Many ways of displaying power and finding legitimation existed, reflecting different influences and needs, and not necessarily the different strength of a ruler's power. Moreover, although Christianization was an opportunity for legitimacy and prestige, Christianity's contribution to royal power often only developed fully *after* Christian polities were firmly established. A Christian royal ideology gained prominence often generations after the initial Christianization: in Scandinavia in the late twelfth century, with the first coronations taking place then or even in the thirteenth century. Thus we need to distinguish between motives for introducing Christianity and the later role of Christianity after the permanent establishment of both the new religion and monarchy.[51] In addition, wealth, alliances and personal networks were all important in the consolidation of power, which could not be achieved by Christianization alone.

[49] Garnsey and Humfress 2001, chap. 3 esp. 28–9; Brown 1992, esp. 152–8.
[50] Reynolds 1997b, 259.
[51] Cf. cumulative long-term consequences of conversion: Rambo 1993, 145–64.

C). The geopolitical context

Rulers' decisions to convert were not taken in a vacuum; and therefore it is important to consider the links to contemporary Christian powers, the German and Byzantine empires and the Anglo-Saxon kingdoms. Newly Christianized lands themselves could export the new faith, and thus relations to immediate neighbours were also significant. The Anglo-Saxon kingdoms never had the power or possibility to threaten; their role was restricted in the conversion process. They provided opportunity, especially for kings of Denmark, to draw on missionaries and even on the ecclesiastical structure for their own ends; and influences emanated from them through missionaries. On the contrary, Frankish military power may have played a role in Christianization since Charlemagne. The role of the German Empire in the creation of new Christian polities has been the most contested, and in particular the role of Emperor Otto III (king 983–, emperor 996–1002). Debate concerning Otto's personality and his alleged policy (or unrealistic dream) for the renovation of the ancient Roman Empire has been ongoing. According to one interpretation, Otto, together with Pope Sylvester II, planned to implement policies according to the Roman renewal ideology, albeit the judgement of historians on such a plan varied between detractors and admirers.[52] According to another interpretation, there was no underlying ideological motivation to Otto's actions and no 'policies'.[53] For the proponents of the *renovatio imperii Romanorum*, the creation of new archbishoprics in Poland and Hungary, and the elevation of István to kingship and Bolesław Chrobry to a (controversial) special status, are parts of Otto's grand scheme for a family of kings around the emperor. Although the details are much debated, Otto's significant role in the emergence of the new ecclesiastical provinces and polities is not. According to Gerd Althoff's view, however, renewal should be understood in the context of medieval calls for improvement rather than a specific political ideology. How important was the role of German rulers then in the conversions and creation of polities? That they were definitely one of the powers to be taken into account is shown by the fact that the Bohemian Boleslav, Polish Mieszko and Abodrite Mistui initially supported Henry the Quarrelsome against Otto III; the first two then appeared at the Easter celebrations of Otto at Quedlinburg following Henry's acknowledgement of Otto. Boleslav and Mieszko in their own conflicts drew on Liutizi and Ottonian military backing respectively. Friendship with the emperor could

---

[52] Fried 1989; Gieysztor 1997; and overview of scholarship in Althoff 2003, 1–16, 81–9.
[53] Althoff 2003.

mean an elevation of rank and prestige. Otto seems to have supported the elevation of the ruler of Hungary to kingship and the creation of the independent church provinces there and in Poland, but what his role was exactly remains an unsolvable problem. According to one hypothesis, his actions at Gniezno may have been a response to the Byzantine–Rus' partnership.[54] Otto III's actions, rather than being the main explanatory factor, were perhaps confined to a response to local aspirations for royal status and the establishment of an ecclesiastical hierarchy.[55] To what extent did military pressure, and the threat of military subjection, motivate rulers to convert? Pressure to convert certainly existed especially on Germany's neighbours in periods when the Empire was strong. Rulers equally imposed Christianity without outside threat, however, as in Norway. German victories over the Hungarians (933, 955) may have contributed to the latter's conversion a generation later, yet German armies attacked Christian Poles and Hungarians as well. Conversion was no guarantee of peace, nor German attack the synonym of conquest and incorporation. Pressure or fear alone cannot explain conversions, although in some cases probably contributed to this choice.[56]

The Byzantine role in conversion has also been interpreted in radically different ways, from the idea that Byzantine missionaries were agents of imperial foreign policy, attempting to draw various countries into a 'commonwealth', rivalling German power, to the notion that Byzantium did not have a missionary policy towards non-Christian lands in general.[57] According to the latter, Byzantine emperors partly responded, as and when local rulers demanded baptism and/or missionaries, and partly took advantage of some of the opportunities; Christianity also spread through unofficial channels, notably the endeavours of individual monks.[58] Just like the German emperor, the Byzantine one led military campaigns into regions seen as crucial for the Empire's security and even annexed them. Yet, although the rhetoric of expanding the Empire's frontiers was strong, in reality territorial expansion was rarely a main aim in the period we discuss. Policies towards peoples settled within the Empire differed from those towards peoples on the other side of the frontier. In the latter cases diplomacy as a means of dealing with 'barbarians', potential enemies or allies, often played a more significant role than war, including grants of titles, access to trade

---

[54] Shepard 2001b.   [55] Shepard 2001a, 242. On the interactive nature of the process Wolfram 2001.
[56] Overview of German–central European relations: Higounet 1989.
[57] Obolensky 1994, chaps. 1, 9; 2000, 73, 79–80, 84, 272–5; Shepard 2002; Hannick 2004. Cf. Noonan 2000.
[58] Shepard 2002.

and payment of tribute, although diplomacy could be more flexible than the description in the contemporary Byzantine sources would suggest.[59] Such interaction at times included the recognition of the barbarians' own terms; for example, when swearing an alliance with the Bulgarians, the emperor took an oath over slaughtered dogs. Baptism of local leaders was also part of this diplomatic strategy of gaining loyalty through grants of status and gifts. The current consensus tends more towards seeing Byzantine involvement as mainly responding to local initiatives, albeit exploiting possibilities to ensure the Empire's stability through putting pressure on key rulers at times. Byzantine Christianity certainly expanded rapidly in the 860s (Moravia, Bulgaria, the Serbs, Rus'), whether through a more active Byzantine missionary activity linked to diplomacy or through responding to local initiatives.

The role of all three Christian polities was restricted to certain regions. Lands neighbouring the German Empire had to face German pressure or influence. Byzantine influence extended to Moravia and, through Old Church Slavonic literacy and liturgy, to Bohemia only in the early part of our period, to Rus' and to Hungary throughout the period, and perhaps reached parts of Scandinavia through Northmen in the Byzantine guard (Varangians) or Rus', but only as cultural rather than political influence. Anglo-Saxon influences played a role in Scandinavia. In analysing decisions to convert therefore, one needs to weigh the geopolitical situation, the immediate political context and the relative strength of the king.

Another international player needs to be considered, the papacy. Exceptionally, early medieval popes such as Gregory the Great took the initiative in sending out missions, but mostly such matters were left to rulers and other churchmen, with popes at most playing a subsidiary role giving advice or approval.[60] Between 900 and 1050, popes intervened more, but still in response to queries and anxieties. However, the range of areas encompassed by papal responses grew dramatically, and most of the new polities had some dealings with the popes.[61] Some, however, developed close ties through paying Peter's pence or being vassals of the papacy: Moravia, Denmark, Poland and perhaps Hungary. The list suggests a link between the sphere of German power and ties to the papacy, either because these polities used the papacy to counterbalance German power or because of the cooperation between German emperors and popes. Pope Gregory VII sent letters to all of the

---

[59] Obolensky 1994, chap. 1; Shepard 1992; Stephenson 2000.
[60] Addison 1936, chap. 4; de Jong 2001, 138; Wood 2001, 178–9, 257–8; Markus 2002 with further bibliography; Sanmark 2004, 53–8.
[61] Strzelczyk 2001, 46.

new polities; the reform papacy's promotion of papal power involved the strengthening of ties to these regions.

D). *The process of Christianization*

Fourth, we looked at the process of Christianization in its various aspects: methods and progress of Christianization, interaction between pagans and Christians, and the erection of ecclesiastical structures.[62] In the texts, baptism to Christianity is not defined as entailing an intellectual or spiritual understanding of the content of the faith (unlike in the case of some other medieval converts). One should note, however, that even modern social science emphasizes that people often become attached to doctrines of a new faith after, rather than before, conversion.[63] The main stumbling block to conversion, if presented, is not a disagreement about the nature of God or the Trinity; rather, it was disquiet about abandoning the laws and customs of one's fathers and being divided from them in the afterlife, and inviting the revenge of the old gods in the form of bad harvests or other catastrophes for deserting them.[64] That is why military defeat by Christians or victory in the sign of the cross was a most powerful inducement to convert: it demonstrated the superior power of the new god. Anthropological studies of group conversions in Samoa and the Americas reached similar conclusions.[65] One solution to the problem of pagan forefathers was to include ancestors posthumously, by Christianizing them: in Denmark Harald Bluetooth's father Gorm perhaps had a Christian reburial; in Rus' some pagan princes were baptized posthumously and reburied in church; in Hungary a church was built next to the alleged grave of Árpád, the dynasty's pagan ancestor.[66]

The methods of Christianization included evangelization, but more commonly after baptism, and forms of coercion; much of the process was 'top down' similar to early medieval western Europe.[67] The central role of kings in the success of Christianization has often been highlighted.[68] Missionaries were sometimes active prior to the official conversion, and were then called in by rulers to spread the new religion, which was linked to the power of rulers to shape communities.[69] We can cite some important

[62] Articles on related issues in Armstrong and Wood 2000.   [63] Stark 1996, chap. 1.
[64] E.g. on Pomeranians: Bartlett 1985, 190; Scandinavians: *Heimskringla*, 165; Rimbert, 100 and cf. 86. More cases: Fletcher 1997, 239–40; Strzelczyk 2001, 62–3.
[65] Kraft 1992.   [66] Similar in an earlier period: Brown 1997, 164–5.
[67] Fletcher 1997, 97–130, 236–40; Sanmark 2004, 39–43.
[68] E.g. Addison 1936, chap. 2; Kłoczowski 1993; Padberg 1998, 206–9; Obolensky 2000, 281–2; Sanmark 2004, 34–9, 75–83; Brown 1997, 224; Cusack 1999, 175–8; Strzelczyk 2001, 54–8; Lindkvist 2004.
[69] Corradini, Diesenberger and Reimitz 2003.

and influential figures, such as Methodius and Constantine, sent in 863–4 at the ruler's request to Moravia, whose work had an impact on central and eastern European Christianity through the creation of Old Church Slavonic. The role of missionaries, however, has undergone a complete re-evaluation, from the idea that heroic missionary figures effectively spread Christianity, to the notion of a gradual penetration of Christianity, with the later elaboration of the role of a few individuals for very specific purposes. It has been demonstrated that many instances of missionaries' *Lives* are not narrative accounts of events but rather expressions of claims by bishoprics to territories that the authors maintain were converted by missionaries from that centre.[70] This also applies to the areas we cover. Missionary centres, such as the archbishopric of Hamburg-Bremen were furthering their own aims, and not necessarily in areas that were unacquainted with Christianity. In this they followed early medieval bishops who extended their own power through organizing missions. In this way, Adam of Bremen in his narrative obscured earlier influences and the presence of Christianity in the lands claimed as mission-fields of Hamburg-Bremen.[71] Another example is Adalbert of Prague who was turned into the main evangelizer of Hungary in order to hide the politically more charged activity of German missionaries. Although the heroic missionary may often be a rhetorical device, priests and monks did have to baptize and teach the population: in general, baptism was given after minimal or no instruction, and the teaching of the basic Christian tenets followed afterwards.[72] Monasticism was in some places an agent of Christianization, notably in Rus' and Hungary, which might be due to Byzantine influence, although Latin monks as well as Greek ones were active in both polities, and until at least the tenth century monasteries were key centres of Christianization and pastoral care in the west as well. The role of women in spreading Christianity in Scandinavia has been highlighted; no substantial evidence of such activity exists from our other areas apart from female members of dynasties, for example Olga in Rus', or Ludmila in Bohemia.[73]

Coercion of various degrees could play a role in Christianization, although we have more data on dramatic opposition from elites than on the processes affecting the entire population. Although it was possible to justify the use of force in Christianization,[74] we must distinguish between the use

---

[70] Wood 2001.   [71] Wood 2001, chap. 6.

[72] Cf. Sanmark 2004, 43–6, 91–100. Similar pattern in Lithuania: Kłoczowski 1989; Rabikauskas 1989b.

[73] Scandinavia: e.g. Staecker 2003; Gräslund 2003. Central-eastern Europe: Homza 1997.

[74] Hadot 1981 on links between doctrine and the use of force; Duggan 1997. A case of justification in medieval sources: Timonen 1996.

of violence in the consolidation of power and its employment against the population at large in order to make them convert. The first, war against rivals, some of whom were pagan, in order to establish or strengthen a ruler's power, was prevalent. The latter did not often occur in these areas, except perhaps in Norway and Hungary if we are to believe the sagas and later hagiographical accounts. Nonetheless an element of compulsion was frequently present. An example is legislation issued in the formative period of the Christian polity; we have evidence from Norway, although debated,[75] Hungary and to some extent Bohemia. Laws prohibited and prescribed a number of practices. According to the sources, punishments equally existed for certain deeds in Rus' and Poland. Prohibited practices included pagan burial and cult, polygamy, adultery and other practices contrary to Christian ideas of marriage. Legislation also introduced new compulsory elements of cult related to Christianity, such as the building of churches, fasts and observing the feasts of saints and Sunday, and attendance at church on Sundays; and transformed certain existing practices, such as turning drinking parties in honour of gods into drinking parties in honour of Christ and the Virgin in Norway.

Compulsion alone, however, does not explain Christianization, which was played out on many levels, including voluntary acceptance of the new religion. 'Top-down' Christianization did not necessarily mean Christianization by force; political and cultural factors determined its process. The type of power wielded in a society was crucial; anthropologists have called attention to the role of 'opinion leaders' in society, whose example was widely followed.[76] The ruler's role as 'opinion leader', in many areas in consultation with the elite, probably played a significant part in conversion to Christianity as well. Social scientists and historians have highlighted reasons for the appeal of world religions such as Christianity in traditional societies. The study of early medieval Christianization as well as the spread of Christianity in modern times demonstrated the importance of social and family networks, sociocultural cohesion, the nature of the prevailing world-view, the level of development, and of associations of the new religion with the political aims or with the grandeur of already Christian societies as influencing the acceptance of the new religion.[77]

Once Christianity arrived, there was a period of interaction between pagans and Christians before and/or after the ruler's conversion; this was of a variable length of time.[78] Mutual influence and pagan resistance both

---

[75] Summary of views: Sanmark 2004, 133–45.   [76] Kraft 1992, 272–3.
[77] E.g. Hefner 1993; Russell 1994; Cusack 1999; Stark 1996; Rambo 1993.
[78] Overview Strzelczyk 2001, although some of our interpretations diverge.

characterized such interaction. The self-definition of Christianity in theory entailed a complete divide between Christians and pagans, and often a learned construction of paganism rather than observations of real practices formed the basis of such definitions.[79] In reality a series of adaptations and compromises were worked out. Missionary strategies and their impact on conversion have been thoroughly studied, although there is much more modern than medieval evidence.[80] The religious fluidity that accompanied the introduction of Christianity and the first phase of Christianization is equally attested from Late Antiquity, the early Middle Ages and any subsequent period of Christianization. The introduction of Christianity as the official religion triggered an increase in religious diversity; paganism itself evolved into new forms and Christians created syncretist practices;[81] boundaries between licit and illicit belief and practice were often blurred and crossed by both Christians and pagans.[82] Fourth- and fifth-century Christians of the Roman Empire acknowledged the influence of the lower Powers in everyday matters; Christian priests in mid-eighth-century German lands ate sacrificial meats; King Rædwald of East Anglia erected two adjacent altars, one to Christ, one to pagan gods; Pomeranians continued the cult of the old gods next to that of the 'German god'.[83] The post-conversion period is thus representative of both 'religious fusion' and of 'localised reinterpretations of . . . the Christian paradigm'.[84] Similar developments have been highlighted by modern cultural anthropological studies of conversion of small communities.[85] In areas where Christianity was not imposed by sheer force, where missionaries were not backed by military power, or where the new religion was adopted through consensus, clerics had to adapt to local customs, and could only promote Christianity if they made it acceptable to the local population: the latter accepted Christ only if he was useful, and had something to offer. They often saw Christ as a stronger god, rather than as part of a different, monotheistic, religion.[86]

---

[79] Brown 1997, 35–6; Wood 2001, chap. 12.   [80] Rambo 1993, chaps. 5–6.

[81] The term has been criticized for denying the inherent capacity of religions to evolve. It is, however, useful in our context provided it is not used to denote deviations from an ideal-type of Christianity, but the combining into one system of elements attested in the separate religious systems that meet (as opposed to other forms of coexistence such as dualism): Carver 2003, 30–1; Colpe 1987; Saler 2000, 36–8.

[82] Garnsey and Humfress 2001, 132–69.

[83] Brown 1997, 37, 267; Bede II.15 (at 188–90); Bartlett 1985, 190. Changes in Christianity due to the Christianization of Germanic peoples: Karras 1986; Russell 1994.

[84] Pluskowski and Patrick 2003, 46.   [85] Tippett 1992; Kraft 1992, 271.

[86] Addison 1936, chap. 5; Brown 1995, 67; Russell 1994, 212; Padberg 1998, 211; Sanmark 2004, 97. E.g. Rimbert, 54, 62, 64, 98.

In our cases, the characteristics of relations between, and possible syncretist mixture of, paganism and Christianity were linked to varying levels and combinations of social consent and royal coercion in the introduction of Christianity. In Denmark after the official conversion amulets and crosses were made from the same mould, whereas in Norway, pagans and Christians lived geographically separately. Burial practices attest a period of simultaneous reliance on both religious systems at least at the level of grave goods (including crosses as well as amulets for example) in all of the polities. The local meaning of Christianity, discussed below, took shape through such processes. A final reinterpretation of paganism occurred long after the introduction of Christianity: with the latter's consolidation, the pagan past, often radically transformed, was incorporated into Christian learned culture, through ecclesiastics who wrote of pagan ancestors of the kings or peoples. A confident inclusion of the pagan past is more characteristic of Scandinavia.[87]

Pagan–Christian interaction had another side – confrontation. Narrative accounts, all written from a Christian and often ecclesiastical perspective, often emphasize confrontation and hide the fact of coexistence detectable through archaeological research. For example, according to Snorri Sturluson, Olav Tryggvason (995–1000) of Norway offered the choice of conversion or being sacrificed to ancient gods to a group of chieftains; and changed his mind about marrying Queen Sigrid of Sweden when she refused to abandon her own religion. In response, he struck her in the face with his glove saying 'Why should I wed you, you heathen bitch?'[88] Confrontation broke out in pagan reactions or rebellions in Bohemia, Hungary, Poland and Sweden. Anthropologists have linked peaceful and consensual conversion – which entailed the moulding of the new religion to the culture of the receiving society – to the stability of the new religion, and connected the imposition of a new religion to its instability.[89] In our cases the lack of such rebellions could signal either consensus or the ruler's strong power, and a consequent fear of resistance. Pagan rebellions combined political and religious opposition: to a new form of rule or the person of the ruler, and to a change in cult practices. It has been shown that resistance to proselytizing, when no other factors are present, is the typical response of the majority of people faced with a new religion.[90] In addition,

---

[87] Cf. Ireland: Brown 1997, 206. Traditions affirmed after consolidation of new religion across cultures: Rambo 1993, 101.

[88] *Heimskringla*, 169, 165. Morrison 1992, 44, 1.

[89] Tippett 1992, 197.   [90] Rambo 1993, 35–6, 87.

in our cases members of the old elite or the dynasty who were excluded from power or were threatened by such a development tried to maintain or regain their power this way. Thus there was a rebellion in Bohemia after Bořivoj's conversion, put down with help from the Great Moravian ruler Svatopluk who controlled Bohemia. In Poland, a long pagan revolt (1032–8) led to the complete destruction of ecclesiastical structures, and was defeated by the ruler with outside help. In Hungary, we find a conspiracy against King István, and revolts in 1046 and 1060–1, entailing the deposition of a ruler, Peter, the killing of clerics and destruction of churches, and a wish to return to pagan customs. In Sweden, pagan reaction first affected one locality alone, Birka, the centre of early medieval conversions. Later, uprisings were linked to Svealand, and to rivalry for power with the Götar in 1080, and the 1120s: while Christian monarchy was well established in the Götaland provinces, in Svealand resistance recurred against centralizing Christian kings and the ecclesiastical organization they represented. Possible triggers of such revolts could include a lack of familiarity with Christianity through contacts before the official conversion of polities; coercive Christianization from above, and thus a more abrupt religious change; radical change in the form of rulership (the establishment of sole power), or political rivalry. Pagan resistance could also take other forms, such as instances of pagan burials which made exceptionally lavish use of traditional forms, or even incorporated desecrated Christian objects.

The baptism of rulers is relatively easy to pinpoint, but the progress of Christianization among the population is difficult to map, and its chronology is usually complex. Narrative models of conversion have been available since Late Antiquity, both of Christianization as instantaneous, because God-given, and of a long fight against pagan superstitions, which is also adopted by modern historians when they talk about a slow Christianization as an ongoing struggle. Late-antique authors created the explanatory narratives of both Christian triumph and lurking pagan practices ('superstitions') hard to eradicate; neither were descriptions of reality, as the Christianization of the Roman Empire did not happen in a unified way.[91] Similarly in our cases, neither the stereotype of quick conversion due to a ruler's decision nor that of gradual slow penetration of the new religion fits; the variety of processes must be emphasized.[92] Changes in burial practices, especially the disappearance of pagan graves, rune-stones in Scandinavia, the evidence of art as well as written texts help in piecing together the puzzle. It emerged

[91] Brown 1995, xii, 4–8, 25–6.   [92] Similarly by anthropologists: Tippett 1992, 198–9.

clearly from our investigation that everywhere the areas most firmly under the rulers' power were the first to become Christian, such as coastal areas in Norway, towns in Rus' and the western part of Hungary. Areas peripheral to the rulers' power also resisted Christianity longer, such as the north-east forest regions of Rus' with their *volkhvy* (wizards) or northern Norway, which was not under the effective power of Norwegian kings until the twelfth century.[93] Christianization was never an instantaneous event, but its length varied greatly, not simply between polities, but within them as well. Regional differences in the penetration of Christianity existed everywhere, the greatest discrepancy being in Norway, where the Saami in the north were Christianized mainly from the seventeenth century on. Within roughly 50 to 100 years after the reign of the first baptized ruler, most polities' populations (with the exception of those living in areas peripheral to the ruler's power in some cases) were Christian. The exception is Sweden where in many regions the process took longer, stretching into the twelfth century. The recurring notion of Sweden's 'late' Christianization, however, does not entirely match the historical record. The first royal baptism and the establishment of the first bishoprics (early eleventh century) were not later than in Norway; but pagan revolts lasted much longer than elsewhere. The answer to the Swedish difference lies in power structures. What took longer in Sweden than elsewhere was the consolidation of power: the end of pagan rebellions and of the possibility to turn away from Christianity were linked to the establishment of the Sverker dynasty in the 1130s. Once converted, areas became exporters of Christianity: the Scandinavian polities to Baltic areas, and central European countries towards their northern and eastern pagan neighbours.

Part of the process of Christianization was the building of ecclesiastical structures after the ruler's decision to convert. The establishment of permanent ecclesiastical structures began with the dioceses, which often started in the area under the direct control of the ruler. In most cases this was initiated by the first Christian rulers (in Poland in the late tenth century, in Hungary in the early eleventh century, in Denmark in the second half of the tenth century, in Sweden in the mid-eleventh century although only from the twelfth century in Svealand, in Rus' in the late tenth century), but in Bohemia (973) and Norway (after 1075) began only after the reign of several Christian rulers. In Denmark (*c.* 1021) the initial structure was entirely replaced and in Poland it had to be renewed (late eleventh century).

---

[93] On the latter: Urbańczyk 1992.

Everywhere, new dioceses continued to be added for generations and some-times centuries after the erection of the first ones: that is, ecclesiastical structures were not implanted in a short period, but developed over time. Whereas Hungary and Poland quickly gained separate archbishoprics, this was the exception. An independent ecclesiastical province was not granted to Denmark until 1103 (though the ruler relied on the archbishopric of Canterbury until 1043), to Norway until 1152–3, to Sweden until 1164 and to Bohemia until 1344. It is therefore clear that although the existence of an independent archbishopric was doubtless significant symbolically, judging from the efforts in many polities to acquire one, practically, the lack of an archbishopric did not diminish monarchical power or autonomy. Rulers controlled ecclesiastics in their realms, and most of the time ensured the de facto independence of their church.

The introduction of other ecclesiastical institutions, buildings and per-sonnel was of equal importance to the implantation of dioceses. Churches were built from the time of the rulers' conversion, often initially in wood, which played an especially important role in Scandinavia, but also in stone. Rulers often played a key role in founding these churches. Monasteries were introduced soon after the conversion of the ruler in Bohemia, Hungary and Rus'. In Poland over thirty years, in Denmark, Norway and Sweden even a century elapsed between the two events. This notable difference between central-eastern Europe and Scandinavia would merit further study. As a consequence monasteries also played different roles: in Hungary and Rus', for example, they participated in Christianization and the care of souls; in Sweden, they were important in royal administration and ideology. Begin-ning in the mid-twelfth century, however, the newly established religious orders arrived very quickly in these polities after their foundation in west-ern Europe (except in Rus' which did not belong to the sphere of Latin Christianity), showing that by that time all of the countries had become an integrated part of Christendom. Collegiate churches and cathedral chap-ters were also founded, mostly beginning in the late eleventh and twelfth centuries. Clerics and monks initially arrived from abroad; for example Moravians went to Bohemia, Germans to Bohemia and Hungary, Bohemi-ans to Poland and Hungary, Italians to Poland and Hungary, English to Norway, with locals increasingly taking over significant roles within one or two generations. The tithe was introduced, in most areas not imme-diately after conversion. The pattern of parishes developed only gradually and patchily, but this was true of western Europe as well. Ecclesiastical divisions, perhaps 'large parishes', characterized a number of areas from the eleventh century on, but parish structures developed from the late twelfth and especially during the thirteenth century, sometimes continuing into the fourteenth.

E). The meaning of Christianization

Fifth, the meaning of Christianization in the period needs to be explored. What had to change with conversion, what could remain the same was redefined in each context; the focus was on practices in this respect. Rival definitions of what it meant to be a Christian were propounded already in Late Antiquity: according to one, it was enough to avoid certain key pagan rites such as blood-sacrifice, whereas many social customs could continue. According to the other, put forward by Augustine, many forms of behaviour were not appropriate for a Christian.[94] Papal and Byzantine views famously clashed over the possible acceptance of social customs in the case of Bulgaria in 866.[95] It has often been shown that conversion was a matter of behaviour and practice in the Middle Ages; but even in modern times, conversion narratives provide frameworks into which individual converts must fit, so that practice and outward conformity remain key elements of religious conversion.[96] The definition of sets of practices as pagan or Christian to some extent depended on Christian learned culture, and to some extent on the social customs prevalent in an area, leading missionaries to see them as pagan. In the polities under investigation, we do not have such detailed accounts on the local meaning of Christianity as contained in Pope Nicholas I's response to the Bulgarians. Laws, however, allow us glimpses into the meaning of Christianity, together with providing lists of customs Christianizing rulers were trying to suppress.[97] They placed an emphasis on adhesion to Christian rituals (such as baptism, attendance at church, observance of fasts, Christian burial) and a strict renunciation of pagan cult. Practices singled out as pagan that were to be avoided did not exclusively focus on matters of cult: they included infanticide, forms of burial, marriage customs and the eating of horsemeat. There was concerted effort to change these practices. Sex and marriage were regulated, abortion and infanticide prohibited (the circumstances of the latter in some cases initially only modified). The teaching of faith was not important in the laws; when it is present, the tenets mentioned are the very basics only. Finally, there was another aspect to the meaning of Christianization: the physical taking over of pagan space, the best example of which is the building of

---

[94] Brown 1995, 15, 21–2.   [95] Fine 1983, 120–1; Obolensky 2000, 87–93; Hannick 2004.
[96] Hadot 1981, 179; Kilbourne and Richardson 1989, 15.
[97] Padberg 1998, 216–25. Parallels in Saxony: Karras 1986.

Christian churches over pagan cult sites as in Mære, Trøndelag in Norway.[98]
The introduction of stone architecture itself in many places was linked to
the arrival of Christianity.

On a different plane, Christianity gained local meaning through particular influences and adaptations. Saints' cults are a good indicator. Although
some major cults, such as those of the Virgin and the apostles, were
imported everywhere, other saints attest to stimuli from particular areas,
such as Anglo-Saxon influences in Denmark, Bavarian ones in Bohemia and
Hungary, and Byzantine in Rus', Bohemia and perhaps Hungary. All polities developed cults of their own local saints as well, mostly starting during
the eleventh century (Bohemia already in the tenth century). Liturgy is a
similar indicator: liturgical manuscripts were initially imported from different centres, and then the production of local liturgical texts and objects
began (although importation also continued), in many cases within about a
century of the introduction of the new religion, although sometimes later.
The importation of liturgical texts shows a wide range of influence: for
example English ones in Norway, Denmark and western Sweden; German
ones in Norway and Hungary; the Slavonic liturgical language in Rus' and
Bohemia. Christian terminology, laws, architectural styles and art all convey
information, albeit often open to conflicting interpretations, on the areas
from which Christian influence reached each polity. The variety in the local
production and adaptation of saints, liturgy and artistic styles marks a proliferation of local Christianities (Peter Brown's 'micro-Christendoms').[99]

Sixth, Christianity affected the new or developing polities in a variety of ways. We chose a representative sample to analyse the impact of
Christianity: writing, laws and coinage. Writing in Latin was introduced
through Christianity, but the different areas had diverse backgrounds in literacy, and the impact of Latin literacy itself varied. In Scandinavia, where
runes had been used for centuries before the introduction of Christianity, although not extensively in administration, they continued as a major
form of written communication in all three polities for centuries after
Christianization. The impact of Christianity probably triggered a more
widespread and practical use of runes in Norway. Reliance on Latin varied
between the three kingdoms: it was the language of charters and hagiography from the late eleventh century and of chronicles from the twelfth
in Denmark, but started to be used in Sweden only in the second half of
the twelfth century for royal charters. Latin did not become the exclusive

---

[98] Cf. Howe 1997; instances collected in Sanmark 2004, 101–2.
[99] Brown 1997. Local meanings and variations also the focus of Mills and Grafton 2003; Carver 2003.
On local adaptations by converts Rambo 1993, 99–101.

language of government in any of the three kingdoms, and vernacular was used in an especially large range of writing in Norway, from homilies to laws, chronicles and royal charters. In central and eastern Europe, on the other hand, where there was either no indigenous writing at all (Bohemia, Poland) or at most a very limited presence of runes probably restricted to some groups in the population (Hungary, Rus'), the introduction of literacy by Christianity made a large difference in administration. In Bohemia, Poland and Hungary, Latin was quickly exploited for ecclesiastical needs and to a lesser degree for royal administration, with Old Church Slavonic also used in Bohemia for the former purpose, while lay literacy remained non-existent.[100] In Rus', however, where literacy was also linked to the arrival of Christianity, widespread lay literacy and a flourishing religious culture developed from the early eleventh century on. There was thus a large divide between Scandinavia and Rus' on the one hand and central Europe on the other, with a lack of indigenous and lay literacy in the latter region. The late use of Latin in Sweden is linked to the development of the monarchy rather than to the introduction of Christianity, and suggests that without the needs of royal power, ecclesiastical needs did not provide sufficient impetus for the development of Latin literacy there. Overall, the traditional ideas concerning the assimilative powers of Latin Christianity and a common Latin culture connecting all of Christendom should be nuanced. Ecclesiastical elites of course knew Latin but in other respects local languages and Old Church Slavonic made the picture much more diverse; in Norway Old Norse was used extensively even for ecclesiastical administration.

Written legislation was everywhere a result of the introduction of Christianity, but it did not start in most places at the time of the establishment of Christian polities. Thus laws could be a means of Christianization, or simply one of its long-term results. Pre-Christian societies had their legal systems, often as part of their religious life, but we know nothing or next-to-nothing about them, so that it is impossible to tell how much was changed by Christian legislation, except by inference from the prohibitions of Christian laws themselves. Written legislation in the service of royal power and for the regulation of ecclesiastical matters developed in all areas, but usually centuries after the introduction of Christianity, with the notable exception of Norway and Hungary. Whether written laws existed did not depend on general literacy: for example Denmark with its indigenous runic script predating Christianization had laws only in the second

[100] Adamska 1999.

half of the twelfth century, while Hungary, where there was no lay literacy, had its first laws in the early eleventh century.

Coinage was also a sign of Christian rulership. The early Christianizing rulers, sometimes the first one, but often, as in Norway and Poland, only one of his successors, many decades after the introduction of Christianity, introduced minting; the coins contained symbols and inscriptions referring to Christianity and royal power. The types of coinage again reflected specific influences, and were modelled on, for example, Anglo-Saxon or Bavarian types. However, whereas in Bohemia, Hungary, Poland and Denmark coinage was continuous after the first coins were minted, in Norway, Sweden and Rus' coinage ceased for a long period after its first introduction.

We can see therefore that Christianization provided the same impulses in each newly converted land, but the socio-economic context, local conditions and needs determined the vitality of newly introduced elements. Thus for example Latin literacy was introduced, but its use varied between the different polities; coins were introduced between 995–1030 everywhere (and somewhat earlier in Bohemia), but then were not used until the second half of the twelfth century in Sweden whereas they were used continuously in Bohemia. That Christianization led to a normative integration into Europe through a common civilization of Latin Christendom and sense of belonging[101] must be qualified when looking at the immense variety in the localities of the different liturgies, saints, languages used and so on.

3. OTHER PATHS OF CHRISTIANIZATION

Christianization, linked to the consolidation of power and the rise of Christian polities, was one path in the last stage of the medieval making of Europe. If we compare the seven polities considered here to the rest of northern Europe and the Balkans, it is clear that many areas around and after 1000 followed different routes. A brief comparison between the development of the regions we covered and these other areas is significant in order to situate our project, although what follows did not form part of our investigations, and simply draws on available secondary works. One can distinguish several types of development in these areas Christianized during or after the period we dealt with. First, those where local rulers emerged and converted to Christianity but an instability of rule, a fragmented and shifting territorial power base and the international situation led to outcomes that differed from the one analysed in our project: Bulgaria, the

---

[101] Axtmann 1993, 27.

Serbian lands and Croatia all became Christian and experienced periods of local rule but succumbed to mighty neighbours. Second, territories in the Baltic that did not voluntarily (led by their own ruler) convert to Christianity, and did not have a strong local ruler or elite, thus falling prey to their neighbours, being subjugated, conquered and converted by force. A significant sub-type here consists of lands whose rulers converted without their people following suit, and where a local elite accepted submission to stronger Christian neighbours. Third, Lithuania, that did not convert but did have strong local leadership, and developed into a pagan polity. Fourth, Iceland, that converted but had no single ruler.

The Bulgarian case exhibits the most similarities to the seven polities analysed in our project: the centralization of power from the early ninth century, coupled with religious experimentation, followed by the ruler Khan Boris's conversion to Christianity in 863 and the imposition of Christianity from above.[102] This entailed the suppression of rebellions, including a pagan one. Negotiations with both Rome and Constantinople finally resulted in the reception of a separate archbishopric from the Byzantine emperor. Bulgaria became an Orthodox Christian polity (using the Slavonic rite), emulating Byzantium, for example in Greek inscriptions and court acclamations. It was also a strong polity, especially under Symeon (893–927), who tried to extend his hegemony over the Balkans and took tribute from Byzantium. However, repeated wars with Byzantium from the tenth century onward culminated in 1018 in the subjugation and annexation of Bulgaria. An independent polity was only established after a victorious rebellion led by Peter and Ivan Asen in 1185–7.

The rest of the Balkans consisted of unstable political organizations; the Southern Slavs lived under fragmented political authority: Duklja (or Dalmatia Superior, later Zeta), Zahumlje, Travunija, Dalmatia Inferior, Croatia, Raška and Rama (Bosna) each consisted of a number of lands ruled by *župans*.[103] Most of the Balkans converted to Orthodox Christianity although Croatia to Latin Christianity. Although some Christian rulers emerged, notably in Croatia and the Serbian lands, overall political structures were weaker or developed later than in Bulgaria, and the problems posed by strong neighbours were more dominant. At first the Southern Slavs were subject to a degree of Byzantine control, which worked through local power structures using Byzantine titles and gifts that benefited the local elite, although rebellions elicited a military response. Bulgarians vied

---

[102] Fine 1983; Mayr-Harting 1994; Obolensky 2000; Shepard 1999; Stephenson 2000; Sullivan 1994; Wasilewski 1997.
[103] Fine 1983; Obolensky 2000; Stephenson 2000.

with Byzantium to control some local rulers; then Venetians and from the end of the eleventh century onward Hungarians also participated in the struggles to extend their political control to parts of the Balkans. This led to wars, domination and annexation.

In the Balkans, then, the establishment of Christian rulership was plagued by political fragmentation, and vulnerability to mighty neighbours, resulting in interventions and subjugation. Although local leaders became Christian rulers, more permanent Christian polities were only established in the period from the end of the twelfth century, when Byzantine power was weak, highlighting how the link between Christianity and rulership was not enough in itself. Most of the Balkans did not coalesce into consolidated stable polities, and even the areas, notably Bulgaria, which did, could not survive in the context of contemporary 'international relations'.

Apart from Denmark, Norway and Sweden, the rest of Baltic Europe, although frequented by missionaries and German merchants, became a fighting ground between various expanding powers. In 1000, the conquest and settlement of these areas was not a foregone conclusion, and a variety of power and religious structures developed. The late twelfth century, however, was a crucial turning point; most European regions that were not Christianized by then were conquered.

Among the Polabian Slavs,[104] paganism and traditional political organization with no homogeneous political units and no central authority dominated until the twelfth century. Although relations with the Frankish Empire in the ninth and tenth centuries triggered a centralization of authority, especially for the princes of Brandenburg, Mecklenburg and Oldenburg, they lacked a strong permanent retinue and sufficient power to create permanent centralized monarchies. The leading power in the region shifted as regional groups formed, broke up and re-formed in new constellations. The Ottonians, according to some, were interested in the conquest and incorporation of Slav lands east of the Elbe. According to another interpretation, there was no plan of conquest, only opportunistic frontier warfare for tribute, booty and revenge, often led by key local players (Saxons), some of whom changed sides, rather than by the ruler.[105] The foundation of bishoprics by Otto I (936–73) are thus either seen as part of a larger plan of territorial expansion, or as independent evangelization perhaps at

---

[104] Lübke 1984–8 on sources; 1997a; 1997b; 2000; 2001; 2002; Łowmiański 1993, 136–61, 261–315; Higounet 1989 on relations to Germans. Even the names used by modern historians to describe them vary: Wends, north-western Slavs, Western Slavs, Slavs along the Elbe and Oder rivers, and Polabians (not an ethnonym).
[105] Althoff 1999, 96; one example: Thietmar of Merseburg IV.22 (at 138).

most aimed at establishing regular tribute payments. In 983 a pagan Slav uprising put an end to Ottonian aspirations in the territories east of the Elbe.

More is known of Polabian paganism than of the Slavic beliefs elsewhere, thanks to both written Christian sources and archaeology, as analysed in the appendix to the chapter on Poland. Pagan cult evolved, with new elements appearing in the late tenth century, probably influenced by contacts with and opposition to Christianity. The building of shrines, the worship of named gods (even though in the form of polytheism), the use of sacred banners and the statue of a goddess in warfare mirrored Christian practices. So did the destruction of Christian cult places. The Christian God was seen as the God of the Germans. Thus a Polabian alternative to Christian states emerged, based on organized pagan cult and warfare as uniting factors rather than on monarchy. Some rulers, however, became Christian: a Christian dynasty ruled over the Hevellians, with its seat at Brandenburg, by the beginning of the tenth century. The Abodrites, whose prince was a significant power by the end of the tenth century, came under Christian rule when Godescalc (c. 1043–66), educated in Saxony, returned from exile in Denmark and consolidated central power. Despite a pagan uprising in 1066, the crusade of 1147 and Henry the Lion's offensives between 1160–6, native rulers continued to wield power. The first Pomeranian duke known by name, Wartislav I in 1121–2, was also a Christian whose dynasty continued to rule over western Pomerania until 1637.

Poles, Scandinavians and Germans competed for the conquest of Polabian Slav lands. From the twelfth century on, German and Scandinavian warfare intensified, often in the guise of crusades. In 1147 the crusade against Wends, with German, Danish, Czech and Polish participants, was the beginning of major successes. From this time on both conquest and mission continued, increasingly relentlessly, with Polish suzerainty established over eastern Pomerania, and Danish and German conquests of other Polabian Slav lands.

From the end of the twelfth century, Christianization was linked to military conquest. Finland was incorporated and Christianized by Sweden from the second half of the twelfth century, although in south-western Finland Christian burials from the eleventh–twelfth centuries signal that the region's Christianization was not simply by conquest. The conquest, settlement and forced conversion of the north (Estonia, Livonia, Semgallia, Lettgallia, Samogitia, Kurland and Prussia) was completed in the thirteenth century, according to the interests of Christian merchants, rulers, missionaries and crusaders, and accompanied by fights for territories between some of the conquerors.[106] Thus most of north-eastern Europe was subjugated by force and Christianized, with Germans settling throughout the region. The period between the official introduction of the new religion and the conformity of burials to Christian customs however lasted for centuries: it was only between the seventeenth and twentieth centuries that Baltic burials ceased to include pre-Christian elements.[107]

Lithuania, inhabited by Baltic peoples, the Lithuanians and Samogitians, constitutes a significant exception to both patterns discussed so far: it became a powerful pagan polity.[108] However, it is in a way less of an exception than is apparent at first glance: here, political centralization was linked to a pagan cult rather than to Christianity. As the evidence is scarce and mainly archaeological for the period prior to the thirteenth century, there are competing opinions about the origins of the Lithuanian state, dating it as early as the eleventh century or as late as the middle of the thirteenth. The most convincing interpretation is that a loose confederation of warrior duchies of the late twelfth and early thirteenth centuries was welded into one polity through the development of the grand ducal office. Plundering raids were a key to Lithuanian power. Although not without reverses, political consolidation continued and culminated in a strong expanding pagan polity in the fourteenth century, with a grand ducal clan exercising collective rule under one ruler. Lithuania avoided the fate of conquest in the twelfth and thirteenth centuries, therefore making the development of a polity under native rulers possible due to a combination of reasons: its relative isolation provided protection; a militarized society, with effective techniques of guerrilla warfare and helped by the influx of warriors from neighbours conquered by Germans could fight against potential conquerors; trade and eventually expansion strengthened the polity. Lithuanian rulers also skilfully made use of promises of baptism in diplomatic negotiations with western and eastern Christians alike, and adapted their negotiating procedures to the Christian practices they encountered.

Religion played a role in the political construction of more centralized power.[109] No uniformity existed in indigenous Baltic beliefs. Cult and funerary practices varied geographically and chronologically. Mindaugas

[106] Higounet 1989; Blomkvist 1998; 2005; Carver 2003; Christensen 1997; Murray 2001; Jensen 2001 questions traditional division between early peaceful mission and later crusade; Urban 1989a; 1994; 2000; 2003; 2004. Example of local variations in conversion even in areas of conquest: Mägi 2004.
[107] Valk 1998.
[108] Baranauskas 2000; Łowmiański 1993, 201–32; Mažeika 1989; 1994; 1997; Rowell 1992; 1994; Urban 1989b.
[109] Rowell 1994, chap. 5; Gimbutas 1989; Kajackas 1989; Mažeika 1997; 2001; Rabikauskas 1989a.

experimented with conversion to Christianity circa 1251. Soon Pope Innocent IV granted him a crown as king of Lithuania (1253), brought him and his kingdom under papal protection and authorized the consecration of a bishop of Lithuania. Instead of becoming Lithuania's Olav or István, however, Mindaugas turned away from his short-lived experiment, and reverted to paganism in 1261. From 1263 (the death of Mindaugas) to 1386 (the conversion of Jogaila) although Lithuania tolerated Christianity within its borders, it maintained a pagan cult. Vilnius became a cult centre and burial place of grand dukes. A pagan temple was built in the ruins of Mindaugas's cathedral, probably in the first half of the fourteenth century by Grand Duke Gediminas. Cult and rulership were associated through the grand duke being both military leader and priest. The attempt to centralize religious practice through the creation of a temple and link it to the growth of ducal power was a result of contact with Christianity. Lithuania was the last European area to join Christendom, and the decision to convert was due to political reasons. In 1386, Jogaila (Jagiełło) accepted baptism in order to marry Jadwiga (Hedwig), queen of Poland, and create a personal union of Poland and Lithuania. Lithuania's case indicates that some form of political unity and military power was the determinant factor in the formation of independent polities rather than Christianity, although religion (be it Christian or pagan) was given a role in centralization. Despite western stereotypes, political consolidation was not dependent on Christianization.

Finally, we must consider the case of Iceland,[110] which has been used to suggest that voluntary Christianization of an entire population was possible, without any link to a central power. Icelandic society was to some extent different from the societies of Scandinavia and central-eastern Europe covered in our book. Settled by Norsemen, Iceland was extremely poor in natural resources. The chieftains' power, the nature and extent of which varied, was exercised through gatherings in chieftains' halls. This personal power, which depended on connections and wealth, was not necessarily passed down in the family. In such a decentralized society, which lacked executive power, dispute-settlement techniques were crucial.

The only account of the conversion is by the chronicler Ari fróði, whose *Íslendingabók* (1122–33) and other writings are the first existing written sources for Icelandic history. According to this account, in 999–1000 King Olav Tryggvason of Norway sent two baptized chieftains to invite the Icelanders to convert, threatening them with violence if they refused. The

---

[110] Divergent explanations: Byock 1993, chap. 7; Jochens 1999; Vésteinsson 2000.

general assembly debated this request, at first splitting into two opposing camps; finally the pagans were willing to embrace Christianity provided that they could continue various pagan customs (including infanticide, eating horsemeat and sacrifice to pagan gods in private). The decision was taken in the interest of political unity, as a measure of 'crisis management' to save Iceland from a bitter split. Iceland is often hailed as an impressive 'democratic' example of conversion, a voluntary common decision taken in 1000, importing Christian institutions and doctrines but adjusting them to Icelandic customs. Providing an alternative and much more convincing interpretation, Orri Vésteinsson argues that the chieftains of the south, allied with the Church, created power bases that ensured the survival of their family power. The basis for territorial power was created with the introduction of ecclesiastical divisions of tithe areas and ministries; the rise of local leaders was interconnected with Christianization. We do not know what significance, if any, Icelanders at the time attributed to the adoption of Christianity. Foreign missionary bishops were present in Iceland from the early eleventh century and in 1056 an Icelander was consecrated missionary bishop. Two sees were established in the late eleventh century and the tithe was introduced (1097). The Christianization of the population through the introduction of Christian customs, such as attending mass and learning the basic prayers, continued in the twelfth century. Christianization in Iceland therefore was also linked to increasing centralization of power, even if this centralization did not mean the rise of monarchical power.

What this comparative survey suggests is that power-relations rather than the espousal of Christianity explain the rise of autonomous polities. The possibility for a local military leader to build and consolidate centralized rule internally through plunder, trade, war or other means ensured the rise of polities in Scandinavia and eastern and central Europe (as earlier in western Europe), and its lack led to the conquest of the Baltic. This possibility always depended both on the immediate domestic political context and on the geopolitical balance of power: the rulers' authority was not simply a question of territorial domination, nor did it depend on conversion alone, as for example the fate of Christian polities in the Balkans demonstrates. Centralizing rulers ensured the survival of Lithuania without Christianization: organized pagan cult could strengthen the ruler's power internally, fulfilling a role similar to Christianity. At the same time conversion to Christianity was no guarantee of independence, although it could serve as a means to buttress a ruler's power, or to draw on help in its name against internal enemies. Proximity to strong Christian neighbours provided significant impetus for conversion. Chronology was also important:

most areas that did not convert by the twelfth century (or where despite Christian rulers there were no recognized Christian polities), and lay in the path of Scandinavian and German interests, were conquered and subjugated. As it often happens, the eventual losers such as the Abodrites or Kurs were largely written out of history; but we should not forget that in 950 or 1000 central and northern European rulers made decisions in a world that was very far from decisively Christian.

4. CONCLUSION

Although we do not lay claim to our conclusions being definitive, we hope that others may find both our methods and our analyses stimulating. Our collaboration, setting research questions together and discussing our findings, was thought-provoking for all participants, partly because of the interdisciplinary nature of the project and partly because we could evaluate our data in the light of material concerning countries other than the one(s) we were familiar with, and compare the work done in different national traditions on the same issues. Our project concentrated on the relationship between Christianity and secular power. We did not analyse economic and social change that also took place at the time; the period we studied was one of many changes, and we do not claim that all were related to Christianization and the rise of Christian rulership. Our work suggests ways of interrelationship between religion and power and indicates how the boundary of Latin Christendom shifted.

The similarity between medieval Latin Christendom and modern Europe (recently the European Union) is often highlighted.[111] Our project questions this equation in a number of ways. No sharp dividing line existed from the beginning between the region that came to constitute Latin Christendom and the area of Byzantine Christianity. Byzantine influences penetrated central Europe and were significant in Hungary for centuries.[112] As the case of Rus' demonstrates, similarities in Christianization (although not in political structures) cut across the divide between Latin and Byzantine Christendom,[113] while differences within Latin Christendom should not be minimized. It is true that in medieval texts one finds the terminology of Christendom and occasionally of 'Europe' denoting a unity to defend and enlarge, and providing a common purpose. From the late eighth century the classical geographical term *Europa* was used by the clerical elite to designate dominions of Charlemagne, soon to become a term of panegyric

---

[111] Most recently Le Goff 2005, esp. 1–5, 48, 197–8.   [112] Patlagean 2000.   [113] Cf. Lind 2004.

associated to rulers' power as well as to papal supremacy.[114] Viking and
Magyar attacks led to the association of Europe with common values and
defence in the face of an enemy. From the thirteenth century it became a
synonym of Christendom.[115] *Christianitas* and *Europa*, however, projected
a notional, rhetorical unit and unity, linked to papal and royal agendas and
ideology, rather than reality, masking the variety of practices and institutions that evolved locally.[116] If there is a similarity between medieval Latin
Christendom and the modern European Union, it is in the discrepancy
between the ideology of unity and local diversity.

Some of the most interesting issues that emerged from comparing the
material from the different countries could become topics for further studies. These include the contrast between the long continuation of pagan cult
and the relatively early incorporation of pagan myths into Christian written
sources in Scandinavia on the one hand, and the suppression and writing
out of paganism from sources (or at most its much later incorporation)
in central-eastern Europe on the other hand. Or, to give another example, the complexity of the link between contacts with Christianity and the
subsequent process of Christianization after the ruler's conversion: early
extensive contacts sometimes facilitated the more peaceful spread of the
new religion but this was not necessarily the case, as knowledge of Christianity could also trigger opposition and lead to the formation of opposing
factions within society. A final example is the period of religious experimentation that often preceded the ruler's decision to convert, which sometimes
entailed the organization of pagan cult.

Our research highlights that the real turning point was the ruler's conversion and the imposition of Christianity, although voluntary conversions
occurred in many areas prior to the ruler's decision. The link between the
support of local rulers and successful Christianization is evident. The benefits of Christianity to rulers (for example in prestige, or new techniques),
however, often developed over a longer period of time, fully by the twelfth
century. Conversion to Christianity was not necessarily a road to power,
but ultimately in all the regions under investigation rulers consolidated
their power and promoted Christianity. Some, however, established centralizing power first and converted afterwards; elsewhere the two processes
were parallel or conversion preceded centralization. Therefore the relationship between Christianization and royal power differed markedly in the
various polities. Regional differences in the speed of Christianization are

---

[114] Leyser 1994b.   [115] Berend 2003; Hay 1968; Paravicini Bagliani 1994.
[116] In favour of 'Europe' denoting a sense of community during the Middle Ages: Le Goff 2005, 48.
     Radical criticism rejecting the use of the term Europe for the medieval period: Urbańczyk 2004.

remarkable, with areas under the rulers' power Christianized first. The development of ecclesiastical structures was similar everywhere with the establishment of dioceses first and parishes last, but also entailed many differences, for example in the introduction of monasticism, which was much later in Scandinavia than in central-eastern Europe. Integration into Christendom by the mid-twelfth century is clear, but did not mean uniformity: particular influences and local adaptations are noticeable in liturgy, saints' cults, art and architectural styles. Although Christianity introduced similar impulses in the fields of writing, laws and coinage, local responses differed greatly in the use of writing, in recourse to Latin or the vernacular and in the continuity of coinage. Christianization in these lands was no mop-up operation; Christianity kept changing through adaptation.

REFERENCES

Adamska, A. 1999, 'The Introduction of Writing in Central Europe (Poland, Hungary and Bohemia)', in *New Approaches to Medieval Communication*, ed. M. Mostert, Turnhout, 165–90.

Addison, J. T. 1936, *The Medieval Missionary: A Study of the Conversion of Northern Europe, AD 500–1300*, New York and London.

Allport, G. W. 1960, *Religion in the Developing Personality*, New York.

Althoff, G. 1999, 'Saxony and the Elbe Slavs in the Tenth Century', in *The New Cambridge Medieval History*, vol. III, ed. T. Reuter, Cambridge, 267–92.

Althoff, G. 2003, *Otto III*, Eng. tr. University Park, PA (original Darmstadt 1996).

Anderson, P. 1974, *Lineages of the Absolutist State*, London, repr. 1979.

Armstrong, G. and I. N. Wood, eds. 2000, *Christianizing Peoples and Converting Individuals*, Turnhout.

Axtmann, R. 1993, 'The Formation of the Modern State: The Debate in the Social Sciences', in *National Histories and European History*, ed. M. Fulbrook, London, 21–45.

Baranauskas, T. 2000, *Lietuvos valstybės ištakos*, Vilnius, Eng. summary 245–72.

Bartlett, R. 1985, 'The Conversion of a Pagan Society in the Middle Ages', *History* 70, 185–201.

Bartlett, R. 1993, *The Making of Europe: Conquest, Colonization and Cultural Change 950–1350*, London, repr. 1994.

Bede, *Bede's Ecclesiastical History of the English People*, ed. B. Colgrave and R. A. B. Mynors, Oxford Medieval Texts, Oxford, 1969.

Berend, N. 2003, 'Défense de la Chrétienté et naissance d'une identité: Hongrie, Pologne et péninsule Ibérique au Moyen Âge', *Annales HSS* (septembre octobre 2003/5), 1009–27.

Berger, P. L. 1973, *The Social Reality of Religion*, Harmondsworth (first published in 1967 as *The Sacred Canopy*).

Blomkvist, N. ed. 1998, *Culture Clash or Compromise? The Europeanisation of the Baltic Sea Area 1100–1400 AD*, Visby.

Blomkvist, N. 2005, *The Discovery of the Baltic: The Reception of a Catholic World System in the European North (AD 1075–1225)*, Leiden and Boston.

Brown, P. 1992, *Power and Persuasion in Late Antiquity: Towards a Christian Empire*, Madison, WI.

Brown, P. 1995, *Authority and the Sacred: Aspects of the Christianisation of the Roman World*, Cambridge.

Brown, P. 1997, *The Rise of Western Christendom*, Malden, MA and Oxford.

Buckser, A. and S. D. Glazier, eds. 2003, *The Anthropology of Religious Conversion*, New York, Toronto and Oxford.

Byock, J. L. 1993, *Medieval Iceland: Society, Sagas, and Power*, Enfield Lock.

Carver, M. ed. 2003, *The Cross Goes North: Processes of Conversion in Northern Europe, AD 300–1300*, York.

Christensen, E. 1997, *The Northern Crusades: The Baltic and the Catholic Frontier 1100–1525*, 2nd edn, London.

Colpe, C. 1987, 'Syncretism', in *The Encyclopedia of Religion*, ed. M. Eliade, vol. XIV, London and New York, 218–27.

Corradini, R., M. Diesenberger and H. Reimitz, eds. 2003, *The Construction of Communities in the Early Middle Ages: Texts, Resources and Artefacts*, Leiden and Boston.

Coviaux, S. 2005, 'Baptême et conversion des chefs scandinaves du IXe au XIe siècle', in *Les Fondations scandinaves en Occident et les débuts du duché de Normandie: Colloque de Cerisy-la-Salle (25–29 septembre 2002)*, ed. P. Bauduin, Caen, 67–80.

Cusack, C. M. 1999, *The Rise of Christianity in Northern Europe, 300–1000*, London and New York (first published in 1998 as *Conversion among the Germanic Peoples*).

Davies, R. 2002, 'The State: Tyranny of a Concept?', *Journal of Historical Sociology* 15/1, 71–4.

Davies, R. 2003, 'The State: Tyranny of a Concept?', *Journal of Historical Sociology* 16/2, 280–300.

Duggan, L. G. 1997, '"For Force is Not of God"? Compulsion and Conversion from Yahweh to Charlemagne', in Muldoon 1997, 49–62.

Durkheim, E. 1965, *The Elementary Forms of the Religious Life*, London (first published 1912).

Elias, N. 1972, 'Processes of State Formation and Nation Building', in *Transactions of the 7th World Congress of Sociology 1970*, vol. III, Sofia, 274–84.

Elias, N. 2000, *The Civilizing Process: Sociogenetic and Psychogenetic Investigations*, rev. edn, Oxford and Malden, MA (first published in two separate volumes, *The History of Manners* 1978 and *State Formation and Civilization* 1982; first combined edn 1994).

Fine, J. V. A. Jr 1983, *The Early Medieval Balkans: A Critical Survey from the Sixth to the Late Twelfth Century*, Ann Arbor.

Fletcher, R. 1997, *The Conversion of Europe: From Paganism to Christianity 371–1386AD*, London.

Fried, J. 1989, *Otto III und Boleslaw Chrobry. Das Widmungsbild des Aachener Evangeliars, der 'Akt von Gnesen' und das frühe polnische und ungarische Königtum. Eine Bildanalyse und ihre historischen Folgen*, Stuttgart.

Fried, J. 1991, *Die Formierung Europas 840–1046*, Munich.

Garnsey, P. and C. Humfress 2001, *The Evolution of the Late Antique World*, Cambridge.

Geertz, C. 1966, 'Religion as a Cultural System', in *Anthropological Approaches to the Study of Religion*, ed. M. Banton, London, 1–46.

Giddens, A. 2001, *Sociology*, 4th rev. edn, Cambridge (1993 2nd rev. edn).

Gieysztor, A. 1997, *L'Europe nouvelle autour de l'an mil: la papauté, l'empire et les 'nouveaux venus'*, Rome.

Gimbutas, M. 1989, 'The Pre-Christian Religion of Lithuania', in Rabikauskas 1989a, 13–25.

Gräslund, A.-S. 2003, 'The Role of Scandinavian Women in Christianisation: The Neglected Evidence', in Carver 2003, 483–96.

Gregory of Tours, *Gregorii episcopi Turonensis historia Francorum*, ed. W. Arndt, *MGH Scriptorum rerum Merovingicarum*, vol. I/1, Hanover, 1884, 1–450.

Hadot, P. 1981, 'Conversion', in *Exercices spirituels et philosophie antique*, Paris.

Hannick, C. 2004, 'Les Enjeux de Constantinople et de Rome dans la conversion des Slaves méridionaux et orientaux', in *Cristianità d'Occidente e cristianità d'Oriente (secoli VI–XI), Settimane di studio della Fondazione Centro Italiano di studi sull'alto medioevo* 51, Spoleto, 171–204.

Hay, D. 1968, *Europe: The Emergence of an Idea*, 2nd rev. edn, Edinburgh.

Hefner, R. W. ed. 1993, *Conversion to Christianity: Historical and Anthropological Perspectives on a Great Transformation*, Berkeley, Los Angeles and Oxford.

Heimskringla, or The Lives of the Norse Kings by Snorre Sturlason, ed. and tr. E. Monsen and A. H. Smith, New York, 1990 (repr. of Cambridge, 1932).

Herrin, J. 1989, *The Formation of Christendom*, rev. edn, Princeton.

Higounet, C. 1989, *Les Allemands en Europe centrale et orientale au Moyen Âge*, Paris.

Homza, M. 1997, 'The Role of Saint Ludmila, Doubravka, Saint Olga and Adelaide in the Conversions of their Countries (The Problem of Mulieres Suadentes, Persuading Women)', in Urbańczyk 1997, 187–202.

Howe, J. M. 1997, 'The Conversion of the Physical World: The Creation of a Christian Landscape', in Muldoon 1997, 63–78.

Jensen, C. S. 2001, 'The Nature of the Early Missionary Activities and Crusades in Livonia 1185–1201', in *Medieval Spirituality in Scandinavia and Europe: A Collection of Essays in Honour of Tore Nyberg*, ed. L. Bisgaard, C. S. Jensen, K. V. Jensen and J. Lind, Odense, 121–37.

Jochens, J. 1999, 'Late and Peaceful: Iceland's Conversion through Arbitration in 1000', *Speculum* 74/3, 621–55.

de Jong, M. 2001, 'Religion', in *The Early Middle Ages: Europe 400–1000*, ed. R. McKitterick, *Short Oxford History of Europe*, Oxford, 131–64.

Kajackas, A. 1989, 'History and Recent Investigation of Vilnius Cathedral', in Rabikauskas 1989a, 263–84.

Karras, R. M. 1986, 'Pagan Survivals and Syncretism in the Conversion of Saxony', *The Catholic Historical Review* 72/4, 553–72.

Kattinger, D., J. E. Olesen and H. Wernicke, eds. 2004, *Der Ostseeraum und Kontinentaleuropa 1100–1600. Einflußnahme, Rezeption, Wandel*, Culture Clash or Compromise VIII, Schwerin.

Kilbourne, B. and J. T. Richardson 1989, 'Paradigm Conflict, Types of Conversion, and Conversion Theories', *Sociological Analysis* 50/1, 1–21.

Kłoczowski, J. 1989, 'La Pologne et la christianisation de la Lituanie', in Rabikauskas 1989a, 137–57.

Kłoczowski, J. 1993, 'La Nouvelle Chrétienté du monde occidental: la christianisation des Slaves, des Scandinaves et des Hongrois entre le IXe et le XIe siècles', in *Histoire du Christianisme des origines à nos jours*, vol. IV, *Évêques, moines et empereurs (610–1054)*, ed. G. Dagron et al., Paris, 869–908.

Kraft, C. H. 1992, 'Conversion in Group Settings', in Malony and Southard 1992, 259–75.

Le Goff, J. 2005, *The Birth of Europe*, Oxford.

Leyser, K. 1994a, 'The Ascent of Latin Europe', in *Communications and Power in Medieval Europe: The Carolingian and Ottonian Centuries*, ed. T. Reuter, London, 215–32.

Leyser, K. 1994b, 'Concepts of Europe in the Early and High Middle Ages', in *Communications and Power in Medieval Europe: The Carolingian and Ottonian Centuries*, ed. T. Reuter, London, 1–18.

Lind, J. H. 2004, 'The Concept of "Europeanisation" on the Baltic Rim as Seen from the East', in *The European Frontier: Clashes and Compromises in the Middle Ages*, ed. J. Staecker (International symposium of the Culture Clash or Compromise project and the Department of Archaeology, Lund University, held in Lund, 13–15 October 2000), Lund, 41–4.

Lindkvist, T. 2004, 'Christianization and State-Building in the Baltic Sea Area', in Kattinger, Olesen and Wernicke 2004, 127–30.

Łowmiański, H. 1993, *Les Slaves et leurs voisins dans l'Antiquité et au Moyen Âge*, Wrocław, Warsaw and Cracow.

Lübke, C. 1984–8, *Regesten zur Geschichte der Slaven an Elbe und Oder (vom Jahr 900 an)*, 5 vols., Giessener Abhandlungen zur Agrar- und Wirtschaftsforschung des europäischen Ostens 131, 133, 134, 152, 157, Berlin.

Lübke, C. 1997a, 'Forms of Political Organisation of the Polabian Slavs (until the 10th Century AD)', in *Origins of Central Europe*, ed. P. Urbańczyk, Warsaw, 115–24.

Lübke, C. 1997b, 'Heidentum und Widerstand. Elbslawen und Christliche Staaten im 10.–12. Jahrhundert', in Urbańczyk 1997, 123–8.

Lübke, C. 2000, 'Die Elbslaven – Polens Nachbarn im Westen', in *The Neighbours of Poland in the 10th Century*, ed. P. Urbańczyk, Warsaw, 61–77.

Lübke, C. 2001, 'The Polabian Alternative: Paganism between Christian Kingdoms', in Urbańczyk 2001, 379–89.

Lübke, C. 2002, 'Zwischen Polen und dem Reich. Elbslawen und Gentilreligion', in *Polen und Deutschland vor 1000 Jahren. Die Berliner Tagung über den 'Akt von Gnesen'*, ed. M. Borgolte, Europa im Mittelalter. Abhandlungen und Beiträge zur historischen Komparatistik 5, Berlin, 91–110.

Mägi, M. 2004, 'From Paganism to Christianity: Political Changes and their Reflection in the Burial Customs of 12th–13th Century Saaremaa', in Kattinger, Olesen and Wernicke 2004, 27–34.

Malony, H. N. and S. Southard, eds. 1992, *Handbook of Religious Conversion*, Birmingham, AL.

Mann, M. 1986, *The Sources of Social Power*, vol. I, *A History of Power from the Beginning to AD 1760*, Cambridge.

Markus, R. A. 1990, *The End of Ancient Christianity*, Cambridge.

Markus, R. A. 2002, 'The Papacy, Missions and the Gentes', in *Integration und Herrschaft. Ethnische Identitäten und soziale Organisation im Frühmittelalter*, ed. W. Pohl and M. Diesenberger, Österreichische Akademie der Wissenschaften, Philosophisch-Historische Klasse, Denkschriften 301; Forschungen zur Geschichte des Mittelalters 3, Vienna, 37–42.

Mayr-Harting, H. 1994, *Two Conversions to Christianity: The Bulgarians and the Anglo-Saxons*, The Stenton Lecture 1993, Reading.

Mažeika, R. 1989, 'The Relations of Grand Prince Algirdas with Eastern and Western Christians', in Rabikauskas 1989a, 63–84.

Mažeika, R. 1994, 'Of Cabbages and Knights: Trade and Trade Treaties with the Infidel on the Northern Frontier, 1200–1390', *Journal of Medieval History* 20, 63–76.

Mažeika, R. 1997, 'Bargaining for Baptism: Lithuanian Negotiations for Conversion, 1250–1358', in Muldoon 1997, 131–45.

Mažeika, R. 2001, 'When Crusader and Pagan Agree: Conversion as a Point of Honour in the Baptism of King Mindaugas of Lithuania (*c.* 1240–63)', in Murray 2001, 197–214.

Mills, K. and A. Grafton, eds. 2003, *Conversion in Late Antiquity and the Early Middle Ages: Seeing and Believing*, Rochester, NY.

Moore, R. I. 2000, *The First European Revolution c. 970–1215*, Malden, MA and Oxford.

Morrison, K. F. 1992, *Understanding Conversion*, Charlottesville and London.

Muldoon, J. ed. 1997, *Varieties of Religious Conversion in the Middle Ages*, Gainesville, FL.

Murray, A. V. ed. 2001, *Crusade and Conversion on the Baltic Frontier 1150–1500*, Aldershot.

Nock, A. D. 1933, *Conversion: The Old and the New in Religion from Alexander the Great to Augustine of Hippo*, Oxford.

Noonan, T. S. 2000, 'Why Orthodoxy Did Not Spread among the Bulgars of the Crimea during the Early Medieval Era: An Early Byzantine Conversion Model', in Armstrong and Wood 2000, 15–24.

Obolensky, D. 1994, *Byzantium and the Slavs*, Crestwood, NY.

Obolensky, D. 2000, *The Byzantine Commonwealth: Eastern Europe 500–1453*, 2nd edn, London.

Padberg, L. E. von 1998, *Die Christianisierung Europas im Mittelalter*, Stuttgart.

Paravicini Bagliani, A. 1994, 'Il papato medievale e il concetto di Europa', in P. Anderson, M. Aymard, P. Bairoch, W. Barberis and C. Ginzburg, dir., *Storia d'Europa*, vol. III, *Il Medioevo (secoli V–XV)*, ed. G. Ortalli, Turin, 819–45.

Patlagean, É. 2000, 'Les États d'Europe centrale et Byzance, ou l'oscillation des confins', *Revue Historique* 302/4, 827–68.

Pluskowsi, A. and Ph. Patrick 2003, '"How to Pray to God?" Fragmentation and Variety in Early Medieval Christianity', in Carver 2003, 29–57.

Rabikauskas, P. ed. 1989a, *La Cristianizzazione della Lituania*, Vatican City.

Rabikauskas, P. 1989b, 'La Cristianizzazione della Samogizia', in Rabikauskas 1989a, 219–33.

Rambo, L. R. 1992, 'The Psychology of Conversion', in Malony and Southard 1992, 159–77.

Rambo, L. R. 1993, *Understanding Religious Conversion*, New Haven and London.

Rambo, L. R. 1999, 'Theories of Conversion: Understanding and Interpreting Religious Change', *Social Compass* 46/3, 259–72.

Ravid, B. 2000, 'The Forced Baptism of Jews in Christian Europe: An Introductory Overview', in Armstrong and Wood 2000, 157–67.

Reynolds, S. 1997a, 'The Historiography of the Medieval State', in *Companion to Historiography*, ed. M. Bentley, London and New York, 117–38.

Reynolds, S. 1997b, *Kingdoms and Communities in Western Europe 900–1300*, Oxford.

Reynolds, S. 2003, 'There were States in Medieval Europe: A Response to Rees Davies', *Journal of Historical Sociology* 16/4, 550–5.

Rimbert, 'Vita Anskarii', ed. W. Trillmich, in *Quellen des 9. und 11. Jahrhunderts zur Geschichte der Hamburgischen Kirche und des Reiches*, Darmstadt, 1961 (*AQ* XI), 1–133.

Rowell, S. C. 1992, 'A Pagan's Word: Lithuanian Diplomatic Procedure 1200–1385', *Journal of Medieval History* 18, 145–60.

Rowell, S. C. 1994, *Lithuania Ascending: A Pagan Empire within East-Central Europe, 1295–1345*, Cambridge.

Russell, J. C. 1994, *The Germanization of Early Medieval Christianity: A Sociohistorical Approach to Religious Transformation*, New York and Oxford.

Ryan, J. D. 1997, 'Conversion vs. Baptism? European Missionaries in Asia in the Thirteenth and Fourteenth Centuries', in Muldoon 1997, 146–67.

Saler, B. 2000, *Conceptualizing Religion: Immanent Anthropologists, Transcendent Natives, and Unbounded Categories*, 2nd edn, New York and Oxford.

Sanderson, S. K. 1999, *Social Transformations: A General Theory of Historical Development*, expanded edn, Lanham, MA, Boulder, CO, New York and Oxford.

Sanmark, A. 2004, *Power and Conversion: A Comparative Study of Christianization in Scandinavia*, Uppsala.

Sawyer, B., P. Sawyer and I. Wood, eds. 1987, *The Christianization of Scandinavia: Report of a Symposium Held at Kungälv, Sweden, 4–9 August 1985*, Alingsås.

Shepard, J. 1992, 'Byzantine Diplomacy, AD 800–1204: Means and Ends', in *Byzantine Diplomacy: Papers from the Twenty-Fourth Spring Symposium of Byzantine*

Studies, Cambridge, March 1990, ed. J. Shepard and S. Franklin, Aldershot, 41–71.

Shepard, J. 1999, 'Bulgaria: The Other Balkan "Empire"', in *The New Cambridge Medieval History*, vol. III, *c. 900–c. 1024*, ed. T. Reuter, Cambridge, 567–85.

Shepard, J. 2001a, 'Europe and the Wider World', in *The Early Middle Ages: Europe 400–1000*, ed. R. McKitterick, *Short Oxford History of Europe*, Oxford, 201–42.

Shepard, J. 2001b, 'Otto III, Boleslaw Chrobry and the "Happening" at Gniezno, AD 1000: Some Possible Implications of Professor Poppe's Thesis Concerning the Offspring of Anna Porphyrogenita', *Byzantina et Slavica Cracoviensia* 3, Cracow, 27–48.

Shepard, J. 2002, 'Spreading the Word: Byzantine Missions', in *The Oxford History of Byzantium*, ed. C. A. Mango, Oxford, 230–47.

Skocpol, T. 1985, 'Bringing the State Back In: Strategies of Analysis in Current Research', in *Bringing the State Back In*, ed. P. B. Evans, D. Rueschemeyer and T. Skocpol, Cambridge.

Snow, A. and R. Machalek 1984, 'The Sociology of Conversion', *Annual Review of Sociology* 10, 167–90.

Staecker, J. 2003, 'The Cross Goes North: Christian Symbols and Scandinavian Women', in Carver 2003, 463–82.

Stark, R. 1996, *The Rise of Christianity: A Sociologist Reconsiders History*, Princeton.

Stark, R. and W. S. Bainbridge 1987, *A Theory of Religion*, New York, Berne, Frankfurt a/M and Paris.

Stark, R. and C. Y. Glock 1968, *American Piety: The Nature of Religious Commitment*, Berkeley and Los Angeles, repr. 1970.

Stephenson, P. 2000, *Byzantium's Balkan Frontier: A Political Study of the Northern Balkans*, Cambridge.

Strayer, J. 1970, *On the Medieval Origins of the Modern State*, Princeton.

Strzelczyk, J. 2001, 'The Church and Christianity about the Year 1000 (the Missionary Aspect)', in Urbańczyk 2001, 41–67.

Sullivan, R. E. 1994, 'Khan Boris and the Conversion of Bulgaria: A Case Study of the Impact of Christianity on a Barbarian Society', in *Christian Missionary Activity in the Early Middle Ages*, Aldershot, no. IV.

Thacker, A. 2000, 'Peculiaris Patronus Noster: The Saint as Patron of the State in the Early Middle Ages', in *The Medieval State: Essays Presented to James Campbell*, ed. J. R. Maddicott and D. M. Palliser, London and Rio Grande, 1–24.

Thietmar of Merseburg, *Chronicon*, ed. W. Trillmich, Berlin, 1957 (*AQ* IX).

Tilly, C. 1985, 'War Making and State Making as Organized Crime', in *Bringing the State Back In*, ed. P. B. Evans, D. Rueschemeyer and T. Skocpol, Cambridge, 169–91.

Tilly, C. 1992, *Coercion, Capital, and European States, AD 990–1992*, 2nd rev. edn, Cambridge, MA and Oxford.

Timonen, A. 1996, 'Saint Olaf's "Cruelty": Violence by the Scandinavian King Interpreted over the Centuries', *Journal of Medieval History* 22/3, 285–96.

Tippett, A. R. 1992, 'The Cultural Anthropology of Conversion', in Malony and Southard 1992, 192–205.
Turner, V. W. 1969, *The Ritual Process: Structure and Anti-structure*, London (repr. Harmondsworth, 1974).
Urban, W. 1989a, *The Samogitian Crusade*, Chicago.
Urban, W. 1989b, 'The Teutonic Order and the Christianization of Lithuania', in Rabikauskas 1989a, 105–35.
Urban, W. 1994, *The Baltic Crusade*, 2nd rev. edn, Chicago.
Urban, W. 2000, *The Prussian Crusade*, 2nd rev. edn, Chicago.
Urban, W. 2003, *The Teutonic Knights: A Military History*, London.
Urban, W. 2004, *The Livonian Crusade*, 2nd edn, Chicago.
Urbańczyk, P. 1992, *Medieval Arctic Norway*, Warsaw.
Urbańczyk, P. ed. 1997, *Early Christianity in Central and Eastern Europe*, Warsaw.
Urbańczyk, P. ed. 2001, *Europe around the Year 1000*, Warsaw.
Urbańczyk, P. 2003, 'The Politics of Conversion in North Central Europe', in Carver 2003, 15–27.
Urbańczyk, P. 2004, '"Europe" around the Year 1000 as Seen from the Papal, Imperial and Central-European Perspectives', in *The European Frontier: Clashes and Compromises in the Middle Ages*, ed. J. Staecker (International symposium of the Culture Clash or Compromise project and the Department of Archaeology, Lund University, held in Lund, 13–15 October 2000), Lund, 35–9.
Valk, H. 1998, 'About the Transitional Period in the Burial Customs in the Region of the Baltic Sea', in Blomkvist 1998, 237–50.
Vésteinsson, O. 2000, *The Christianization of Iceland: Priests, Power, and Social Change 1000–1300*, Oxford, repr. 2003.
Wasilewski, T. 1997, 'L'Église de la Bulgarie Danubienne en 863–1082', in Urbańczyk 1997, 47–52.
Weber, M. 1968, *Economy and Society: An Outline of Interpretive Sociology*, 3 vols., New York.
Weber, M. 1969, *The Sociology of Religion*, 5th printing, Boston.
Wolfram, H. 2001, 'New Peoples around the Year 1000', in Urbańczyk 2001, 391–408.
Wood, I. 2001, *The Missionary Life: Saints and Evangelisation of Europe 400–1050*, London and New York.
Zmora, H. 2001, *Monarchy, Aristocracy, and the State in Europe, 1300–1800*, London and New York.

CHAPTER 2

From Paganism to Christianity in medieval Europe

Robert Bartlett

Between the tenth and the twelfth centuries new Christian monarchies were established throughout northern and central Europe.[1] By the year 1200 Scandinavia was divided between the kingdoms of Denmark, Norway and Sweden, still today features of the political map of Europe, while in central Europe the Magyars, the pagan nomadic raiders of the tenth century, now ruled a large Christian monarchy, which was bordered on the north by the new Christian states of Bohemia, Poland and Rus'. In contrast to the expansion of Christianity into the eastern Baltic region in the thirteenth century (and also into Saxony in the ninth), the new religion was not imposed by invaders from outside but adopted by native elites.

When we use the term 'Christianization' as a label for this process, we seek to designate a transformation and hence imply a 'before' and an 'after'. In the context of northern and central Europe, the 'before' is the world of indigenous European paganism, the 'after' is medieval Christian Europe. We know a lot more about the 'after' than the 'before'. The Christian kingdoms and principalities of Scandinavia or central Europe, with their monarchical dynasties, ecclesiastical hierarchies and Latin learning, are known and recognizable parts of a Latin Christian world. There is plenty of room for more research into that world, but there is also a fair amount of evidence on which to base the research. When we turn to the 'before', the situation is quite different.

SOURCES AND THEIR PROBLEMS

Sources of information on the non-Christian indigenous religions of northern and central Europe (the simplest definition of 'paganism' in this context) fall into three basic categories: the writings of contemporary Christian

---

[1] This chapter aims at a general and synthetic view of European paganism. Some of the themes discussed here are developments of ideas in Bartlett 1985; 1998.

observers, the material remains (whether uncovered by archaeological excavation or in the form of standing monuments) and, especially for the
Scandinavian world, post-conversion indigenous literature.

Contemporary Christian observers

Among the most important Christian authors who wrote about the paganism of northern and central Europe are:

Thietmar of Merseburg, who wrote in the years 1013–18. Thietmar was
from the Saxon high nobility (his family were counts of Walbeck), was
born in 975, as he himself records, served in the church of Magdeburg for
many years and was bishop of Merseburg 1009–18. He was deeply hostile
to the alliance with the pagan Liutizi entered into by the emperor Henry II
in his campaigns against Bolesław Chrobry of Poland but this fortunately
stimulated a long account of their religious practices. He is a contemporary,
well placed on a frontier diocese and with good sources of information (e.g.
he knew a former chaplain of the duke of the Abodrites). Both Magdeburg
and Merseburg were frontier bishoprics, the former founded explicitly for
'all the people of the Slavs beyond the Elbe and Saale, lately converted and
to be converted to God'.[2]

Adam of Bremen, writing 1074–80. Adam came from Upper Germany,
arrived in Bremen in 1066–7 and served as a canon in the cathedral there.
He described his work as a record of the deeds (*gesta*) of 'the most holy
fathers, through whom the church was exalted and Christianity spread
among the pagans'. Filial devotion to Hamburg-Bremen and the centrality
of mission are prominent features of his approach. His sources included
both earlier written materials and oral informants, notably Sven Estridson,
king of Denmark (1047–74/6).

The hagiographers of Otto of Bamberg, who composed their works in
the 1140s and 1150s. Otto's two missions to the Pomeranians in the years
1124–5 and 1128 are described by three monastic writers: an anonymous
monk of Prüfening, who produced the so-called *Vita Prieflingensis*, and
two monks of St Michael's in Bamberg, Ebo and Herbord. The last is
generally considered the most tendentious, but all three drew on eyewitness
testimony. They present Otto's missionary activities as part of a wider
career as an active prelate and monastic founder. Otto was canonized in
1189.

---

[2] *Diplomata . . . Ottonis I*, no. 366.

Helmold of Bosau, author of the *Chronica Slavorum*, which dates to 1163–72. Helmold was schooled in Brunswick, had become a deacon by 1150 and was subsequently parish priest of Bosau in Holstein. He accompanied Bishop Gerold of Oldenburg-Lübeck (1154–63) during his missionary activities among the Slavs. He explicitly describes the theme of his work as 'the conversion of the Slavic people'.

Saxo Grammaticus, who wrote 1185–*c*. 1215. Saxo came from the Danish island of Seeland, his father and grandfather fought for King Valdemar I (1157–82) and he was a clerk and companion of Absalon, archbishop of Lund (1178–1201). Warlike activities in the Baltic, and Absalon's prominent role in them, have a large place in his history.

Of these writers, all except Saxo were Germans and several of them had first-hand experience of the Christian–pagan frontier and the mission field. Thietmar was bishop of the border see of Merseburg and Helmold was priest of Bosau in the recently conquered area of eastern Holstein. It is worth noting that the information these authors give on Slavic paganism is much fuller than that on Scandinavian paganism and that, moreover, their accounts of the Slavs between Elbe and Oder (i.e. those who did *not* form medieval Christian monarchies) are fullest of all. We thus have far more detailed accounts of the religious practices of such peoples as the Liutizi, Rani and Pomeranians than of the Poles or Bohemians.

The problems in dealing with Christian authors on pagan topics are well known. First is their hostility. Some Christian writers were so hostile that they even refused to discuss pagan times and pagan princes. A pioneer in this conspiracy of silence was the Venerable Bede. Writing of the pagan reaction in northern England under kings Osric and Eanfrith in 633–4, he says, 'It has pleased all those who compute the reigns of kings to sweep away the memory of these perfidious kings and to assign that year to the reign of their successor, that is Oswald, a man loved by God.'[3] Such casualness about the chronology of pagans is echoed at the other end of the Middle Ages by the Bohemian chronicler Neplach of Opatovice: '894 AD: here begin the acts and deeds of the dukes and kings of Bohemia, but since some of them were pagans there is no need to worry when or how long they reigned'.[4]

Writers such as Thietmar, Adam and the others listed above, were not as dismissive as this of the pagan practices they encountered, but there are always certain doubts that arise when reading their accounts. They write in Latin, which was neither their own vernacular nor that of the pagans

---

[3] Bede III.1 (at 214).   [4] Neplach, 460.

they are describing; they had a classical education, which might intrude elements of classical paganism into the picture; they had a long tradition of stereotypes inherited from patristic authors. And, of course, in many cases their personal knowledge was very limited.

It is very natural to have doubts about the accuracy of Christian reports of pagan cult behaviour, but it is possible for scepticism to go too far. A curious instance that reveals some of the problems, but also some of the possibilities, of Christian accounts of contemporary pagan practice, concerns a custom of the pagan Slavs of Arkona on the island of Rügen, attested by Saxo. Their idol of the god Svantevit held a great horn filled with drink. Each year, after the harvest, the priest would inspect this and, depending on the level of the liquid, would predict that either a good or a bad year for crops was coming.[5] Now contact between the Danes and the Slavs of Rügen was often close, uncomfortably close in many cases, for there is good evidence for the kidnapping and enslavement of Danes by Slavs, as well as recurrent warfare. Nor were linguistic difficulties insuperable. In the decisive campaign of 1168, which saw the destruction of Svantevit's shrine, the Danish leader Archbishop Absalon was accompanied by 'Gottschalk, his interpreter among the Slavs'.[6] Hence Christian Danes had both the chance to observe and the chance to understand local practice. It looks as if the account of the predictive rite associated with the god's drinking horn is as good as we could hope to get.

At first glance a text from another twelfth-century historian would seem only to strengthen the point. William of Malmesbury, an English monk writing in the 1120s, and very far from the Baltic, commented, in his discussion of the achievements of the Emperor Henry III (1039–56), that 'he subjugated the Wends and Liutizi . . . who, to the present day, alone among mortals cling to pagan superstitions . . . The Wends worship Fortune, whose idol they place in an eminent place; they fill the horn in its right hand with the drink of water and honey . . . on the last day of November they sit in a circle around it and drink in common; if they find the horn full, they applaud with a great noise, because abundance, with her full horn, will answer to them in everything in the coming year; if not, they groan.'[7] The most recent editors of William of Malmesbury comment, with justice, 'It is hard to imagine how William obtained this information.'[8] The impossibility of mutual influence or common source requires that Saxo and William

---

[5] Saxo XIV.39.3.5 (vol. II, 495) (fol. 167).
[6] Saxo XIV.39.29 (vol. II, 505) (fol. 169v); cf. XIV.37.1–3; 42.20 (vol. II, 489, 527) (fols. 165v, 175).
[7] William of Malmesbury II.189 (vol. I, 338–40); see now Slupecki and Zaroff 1999.
[8] William of Malmesbury vol. II, 181.

be treated as two independent witnesses and their agreement, despite the
lifetime and the North Sea that lay between them, naturally encourages
us to think we have here dependable contemporary information on pagan
cultic practice.

And yet . . . How, we may ask, does William know that the Slavs worship *Fortuna*? Is it simply a deduction from the nature of the augury, for
who else gives good and bad harvests? And what was the name of the deity
in William's source, oral or written? William himself gives us some further help. Such an annual prognostication, he writes, has been widespread
among pagans: 'St Jerome, in the eighteenth book of his Commentary on
Isaiah, confirms that the Egyptians and almost all eastern peoples did the
same.' Jerome is here commenting on Isaiah 65: 11, where the prophet – as
so often – is threatening terrible judgement on those who follow false gods,
here, in particular, 'you who have abandoned the Lord, who have forgotten
my sacred mountain, who place a table for *Fortuna*, and pour out libations
upon it'. 'It is an old custom of idolatry', comments Jerome, '. . . that on
the last day of the year they place a table full of dishes of various kinds
and a drinking vessel mixed with honey, as auguries of the fertility of the
past or coming year.'[9] The deity *Fortuna* holding the mead-filled horn may
indeed be from a good ethnographic report on the Wends, but biblical and
patristic echoes from Jerome's Vulgate and commentary are also part of the
picture and, when analysing the Latin sources on European paganism, we
must always keep an ear open for such echoes.

Material remains

Scandinavia offers a very rich iconography from the pre-Christian period:
gold bracteates in their hundreds, small gold foils (especially from
Bornholm) in their thousands and over 400 picture stones from Gotland.
This material, dating from the fifth to the twelfth century, offers an enormous corpus of images, some abstract, some figural. The later material
is clearly from the Christian period but some of the earlier pieces have
scenes that can be interpreted as mythological (with the aid of the post-
conversion indigenous literature discussed below). In addition, many of
the rune-stones, standing stones with runic inscriptions, date to the pagan

[9] Jerome XVIII.65.11 (at 753–4) *Ponitis, inquit, fortunae mensam, et libatis super eam. Siue iuxta
Septuaginta: Paratis fortunae mensam, et impletis daemoni poculum . . . Est autem in cunctis urbibus, et
maxime in Aegypto, et in Alexandria idololatriae uetus consuetudo, ut ultimo die anni et mensis eorum
qui extremus est, ponant mensam refertam uarii generis epulis, et poculum mulso mixtum, uel praeteriti
anni uel futuri fertilitatem auspicantes.*

period and a few have clearly cultic references. In general, medieval Christianity is loquacious, medieval paganism mute, but these runic inscriptions form an important exception.

Archaeological investigation cannot always clarify the function of the sites and objects it finds, and sites and objects with a cultic or ritual function are perhaps among the more difficult to interpret. Some archaeologists, indeed, regard 'ritual' as a last and desperate classification, tantamount to an admission of ignorance. That may be too harsh, yet there are difficulties in identifying cult sites, difficulties that are acute in northern and central Europe. This is brought out sharply by a comparison with the situation in the ancient Roman or Romanized world. For archaeologists working in that field, there may be some ambiguous cases, but there are also hundreds of extremely well-attested temples and shrines, with sacred areas, votive objects and, in many cases, named deities who were venerated at those sites. There is nothing like this in the Scandinavian world or central Europe, perhaps because the building tradition was largely in wood, perhaps because of more limited literacy, perhaps, it might be argued (see below), because such sites never or scarcely existed.

In the search for cult sites in non-Roman Europe certain diagnostic features are helpful, among them two in particular: (1) large open spaces without the normal evidence of occupation; (2) animal bones, especially if capable of ritual interpretation (e.g. skulls found alone). Both features are found in the supposed temple or cult hall excavated in the 1970s at Gross Raden in Mecklenburg: the building was approximately 11 by 7 metres, showed no signs of domestic use (e.g. there was no hearth) but contained the skulls of several horses. The planks forming the outer wall were shaped into what could be seen as anthropomorphic forms – we might be reminded of the Rus' revering 'a long post of wood fixed in the ground with a face like that of a man', as reported by Ibn Fadlan.[10] It is not unreasonable to conclude that this was a building dedicated to worship and sacrifice, but it is a matter of judgement and lacks the indisputable clarity of Greco-Roman pagan sites.

Nevertheless, the hunt for cult buildings in northern and central Europe continues, and, as is discussed by other contributors to this volume, sometimes produces results. Excavations at Uppåkra in Scania, and at Borg and Sanda in central Sweden, have revealed cult houses, while a recent reinterpretation of excavations at Wrocław in Silesia suggests a rectangular cult building, with anthropomorphic planks, a horse skull and precious

---

[10] Schuldt 1985, 35–49; Slupecki 1994, 95–101; Ibn Fadlan, 120–1.

hangings. To add a final finishing touch, dendrochronological dating places the construction of this building in 1032–3, exactly the time when written sources report a pagan reaction in Poland.

Post-conversion indigenous literature

Scandinavia has by far the richest literary tradition concerning its ancestral paganism, the great bulk of it produced in Iceland, or at least by Icelanders. The writings of Snorri Sturluson (d. 1241), especially the (*Prose* or *Younger*) *Edda* and the early part of the *Heimskringla*, and the ancient mythological poems of the (*Poetic* or *Elder*) *Edda*, a poetic anthology preserved in a manuscript of *c.* 1270, contain stories about gods and heroes and references to pagan religious practices and belief. The existence of such sources means the picture of Scandinavian mythology is far richer and more detailed than that of central Europe. As has been pointed out, 'Although Icelanders do not seem to have been less Christian than other peoples, they pursued the lore of their pre-Christian culture when other Christianized peoples were doing everything they could to forget or disguise theirs.'[11]

Of course, these texts were written down in Christian times, and it has been argued that Christianity has influenced this material, particularly the *Vǫluspá*, the most cosmographical of the Eddic poems, but it is probable that much of the material reflects actual beliefs and practices of the pre-Christian northern world. This is especially true of the skaldic verses (transmitted mainly by Snorri but also in some sagas) which have named authors of the pagan period and tight metrical forms that must have aided oral transmission. Indeed the earliest known skaldic poet, Bragi Boddason, has been dated to the ninth century. Some scholars have understandable doubts that material first extant in manuscripts of the thirteenth century can accurately record verse of the ninth, tenth or eleventh century, but there is a considerable consensus that some skaldic poetry is genuinely from the pagan period, thus joining the runic inscriptions as another exception to the silence of paganism. Those who support this consensus must be aware, however, that they are espousing a very strong theory: that words can be transmitted accurately from mouth to mouth for 400 years.

Clearly, sources for northern and central European paganism are very different: the rune-stones, images and wealth of post-conversion myth and legend make the former much richer than the latter in general, although

---

[11] Tulinius 2002, 66.

there are some exceptions to this rule, notably in the very full accounts of West Slav temples and cultic practices from Christian observers.

CULT

Deities

Such are the sources and some of the problems associated with them. If we turn to the question of what they reveal about European paganism, a natural starting point is cult, that is formal religious activity, and the deities to whom cult was directed. The names of the pagan gods have been transmitted in various ways, through the Latin writers, in runes and skaldic verse, and in the Old Norse literature of the Christian period, even, in the case of Snorri, in mythological treatises. The Old Norse 'Trinity' of Thor, Odin and Frey is particularly prominent, but there are a host of other named deities and supernatural beings.[12] Again, the Scandinavian material is richer than that from central and eastern Europe, although named gods are referred to there too. The *Russian Primary Chronicle* transmits the name Perun, the chief god worshipped in pagan Kiev, while numerous West Slav deities are known from the Latin chroniclers.[13] It is, of course, helpful if more than one source corroborates a particular name. Thus the naming of the Liutizian deity Zuarasi or Zuarasici both by Bruno of Querfurt in a letter of 1008 and by Thietmar in his chronicle of 1013–18 gives us greater confidence that they are accurately transmitting the name of a Slav deity.[14] On balance it seems that female deities are relatively uncommon in sources about the Slavs and more well attested among the Scandinavians.

One area of social life where the pagan pantheon left its imprint was in names, both place names (for instance, the theophorous place names like Odense on Funen) and personal names – and this is true well into the Christian period. Names formed with 'Thor', for example, were extremely common in many areas of Scandinavian settlement or influence. Indeed, Iceland's first saint was Thorlak Thorhallsson (d. 1193), while

---

[12] For Thor, Odin and Frey, see, classically, Adam of Bremen IV.26–7, but the association of the three is brought home even more clearly in a misunderstanding by the twelfth-century Norman chronicler Orderic Vitalis: describing the troops raised by Sven Estridson, king of Denmark, for his invasion of England in 1069, he refers to the levies from the land of the Liutizi – 'a populous people . . . who worship Odin, Thor and Frey'. His ignorance of the situation highlights the strong conventional association of the three gods (vol. II, 226, *Leuticia* there mistakenly translated as 'Lithuania').

[13] *Russian Primary Chronicle*, 65, 74, 77, 90, 93, 116–17; for some of the West Slav deities see the Table, below.

[14] Bruno of Querfurt, *Epistola*, 101; Thietmar of Merseburg VI.23.

3. Northern and eastern Europe: important Christian and pagan sites

the Winchester survey of 1148 shows that in the popular name Turstin (Thorsteinn) the name of the god Thor still echoed, even in this English episcopal city with 500 years of Christianity behind it.[15] As in the case of Late Antiquity, Christianization of the name-hoard was not necessarily a swift consequence of conversion.

The days of the week contain another fossilization of the pantheon, at least among speakers of Germanic and Romance languages, although

[15] Biddle 1976, 175, 187.

Place	Source	Structure	Image	Attributes	Sacrifice	Horse divination	Priests
Riedegost (Liutizi, exact site not identified)	Thietmar VI.23–5	triangular stronghold with three doors, containing elaborate wooden *fanum*, supported by animal horns; exterior carved with images	Zuarasici and other armed gods	banners	'blood of men and beasts'	yes	*ministri*
Uppsala (Sweden)	Adam IV.26–7	*templum*	Thor on throne, Wodan armed, priapic Fricco	see 'Image'	nine male animals; dogs, horses and men suspended in the sacred grove		*sacerdotes*
Szczecin (Pomerania)	*Vitae* of Otto	two wooden *fana* called *continae* (*Vita Prieflingensis*); *delubra* (Ebo); four *continae*, the most important carved with images of men and beasts inside and out (Herbord)	three-headed of Triglav	saddle; drinking horns and vessels	'the sacrifices they offered' (Ebo III.1)	yes	*pontifex* (*Vita Prieflingensis*); *pontifices*/*sacerdotes* (Ebo); *sacerdotes* (Herbord)

	Vitae of Otto	*famum/templum/delubrum*					
Wolgast (Pomerania)							
Arkona (Rügen)	Saxo XIV.39.2–11	elegant wooden *delubrum*; double enclosure, exterior carved with images; one door; red roof	four-headed of Svantevit	golden shield dedicated to Gerovit; horn; bow; bridle and saddle; sword	annual animal after harvest	yes	*sacerdos*, with long hair and beard
Garz (Rügen)	Saxo XIV.39.38–41	three magnificent *fana*	oaken of seven-faced Rugiaevit; five-headed Porevit; four-faced Porenut	swords (of Rugiaevit)			

on occasion uncompromising ecclesiastics might mount campaigns against even these faint echoes of the pagan past. Among the Icelanders, the prohibition of these pagan names and their replacement by the neutral 'second day', 'mid-week day', 'fifth day', etc. was attributed to Bishop Jón Ögmundarson of Hólar (1106–21).[16] He was in a long tradition, going back at least as far as the sixth-century bishop of Braga, Martin, who condemned the 'ignorant rustics' for naming the days of the week after 'demons'.[17]

Christians automatically described pagans as idol-worshippers but the convention appears to have been largely accurate, for anthropomorphic images of the deities were very frequently the focus of devotion, and conversion was often most dramatically signalled by destruction of such images. The *Russian Primary Chronicle* describes the smashing and burning of the 'idols' in Kiev in 988, with that of Perun being dragged behind a horse, beaten and thrown into the Dnieper, while Otto's biographers and Saxo go into some detail about similar destruction and desecration of the images of West Slav gods.[18] A few such images have even survived. Some polycephalic images have been found in excavation of West Slav sites and the dramatic 'Svantevit Stone' now in Kraków indicates that images could be made of stone as well as wood.[19]

Temples and priests

One of the big questions about European paganism is the role of temples and priests. Thietmar, the hagiographers of Otto of Bamberg, and Saxo all describe the temples of the West Slavs between Elbe and Oder, while Adam has a famous – but also very controversial – passage on the temple at Uppsala. The usual terms employed by these authors to designate pagan sacral buildings are *fanum*, *templum* and *delubrum*, although the biographers of Otto of Bamberg also provide the native term *contina*.[20] Many modern scholars prefer the slightly colourless 'cult building', in order to avoid the romantic or hierophantic overtones of 'temple' and 'shrine' (not to mention the archaic 'fane'). The Table presents the information provided by these authors in summary form: details of the structure, the images within and their attributes, the nature of sacrifice, the presence of horse divination

[16] *Jóns saga helga* XI.3 (at 554).   [17] Martin of Braga, chap. 8 (at 189).
[18] *Russian Primary Chronicle*, 116; *Vita Prieflingensis* II.12; Ebo II.13; III.10–11; Herbord II.32; Saxo XIV.39.31–3, 40–4 (vol. II, 505, 509) (fols. 169v, 170v).
[19] Herrmann 1985, 306–7 and pl. 72; Slupecki 1994, chap. 11.
[20] Discussed in Slupecki 1994, 12–13.

(a characteristic feature of West Slav paganism) and the words used to describe the pagan priesthood (if that is what it was).[21]

Interpretative issues that arise from this corpus include the following:

(a) the fact that, with the exception of Uppsala, these descriptions concern a very limited geographical area, in a fairly defined period: temples of the Liutizi, Pomeranians and Rani – i.e. the West Slav peoples between the lower Elbe and lower Oder – in the period *c.* 1010–1170. Naturally there is debate over whether such temples can be generalized to other Slavic or non-Slavic peoples, at other periods.

(b) problems correlating the textual descriptions and the archaeology. It has proved very difficult, for instance, to localize Thietmar's Riedegost, and, while over-enthusiastic excavators in the 1920s thought they had discovered the cult building at Arkona, later archaeologists refuted this claim and concluded that, because of coastal erosion, Svantevit's shrine is now under the waters of the Baltic Sea.[22] On the other hand, attested cult buildings like Gross Raden do not appear in the written sources.

(c) the particular question of whether these eleventh- and twelfth-century temples, with their elaborate structures and priesthoods, can be regarded as pagan imitations of Christian practice. The same issue is sometimes argued for late pagan Scandinavian belief and practice, e.g. 'Christological' aspects of Odin, Thor's hammer as a counterpart to the Christian cross.

(d) the issue of Scandinavian temples, as crystallized by Uppsala. One position, classically argued in Olsen 1966, is that there were no dedicated cult buildings or full-time priests in Scandinavian paganism, and that Adam's account is fictitious – and some would add disproved by archaeological findings. Here Olsen and others echo Tacitus on the ancient Germans – 'they do not judge it right to constrain the gods with walls'.[23]

Clearly, the question whether northern and central European pagan religion was characterized by 'temples' and 'priests' is a fundamental one. A religion with sacral buildings and ritual specialists is very different from one in which religious activity takes place in the same space as ordinary secular life and under the guidance of the ordinary secular leaders. The nature of power and the very meaning of the sacred would be different. The debate

---

[21] Adam of Bremen's account of Rethra has been excluded. He appears to be referring to Thietmar's Riedegost, but, as is pointed out by Slupecki 1994, 62, his description 'differs from Thietmar's in so many points that serious doubts arose whether they referred to the same sanctuary'.

[22] The map in Slupecki 1994, 59, shows the various attempts to localize Riedegost; Slupecki 1994, 34–6, on excavations at Arkona.

[23] *Germania* 9.

about pagan sacral buildings and priesthoods is thus partly a debate about how similar pagan religion was to medieval Christianity.

Divination, sacrifice, cult of natural objects[24]

There is no doubt that in some ways native European paganism was very different from Christianity, for at its heart lay regular public divination and blood-sacrifice (sometimes including human sacrifice), both of them practices that Christianity rejected, condemned or abhorred. In these respects, the pagan practices of northern and central Europe were like those of classical antiquity, when much of religious ritual was concerned with exactly these things, prognostication and sacrifice. Details of divinatory techniques might vary, with the casting of lots important in some regions, the rites of horse divination in others, but the central function of religious activity – to give precise guidance for the future – was clear, and contrasted strongly with the much more diffused providentialism of medieval Christianity.

The two strands of pagan practice – divination and sacrifice – intertwined. Thus, when he was pondering whether to set sail for Iceland in the winter of 873, Ingolfr Arnarson 'made ready a great sacrifice, and enquired of the oracle as to his coming life or fate'.[25] Sometimes sacrificial victims were chosen by lot, as reportedly at Kiev in 983.[26] Sacrifice could be individual and circumstantial, as in the case of Ingolfr, but also communal and regular: both Thietmar and Adam refer to especially important public sacrifices among the Scandinavians that took place every nine years, with animals and men sacrificed in multiples of nine (a well-attested sacred number among the Scandinavians).[27]

Whatever conclusion one comes to about pagan sacral buildings, the evidence is extensive and firm that open-air and natural sites had a far greater significance in pagan than in Christian religion. The veneration of natural objects, especially springs and groves, including sacrifices to them, is recorded among all the pagan peoples of northern and central Europe. Helmold of Bosau gives a long and detailed account of a sacred grove of the West Slavs in what is now eastern Holstein, while the missionary assault on holy trees and recurrent legislation against such veneration among newly converted populations runs from St Martin in the fourth century to Lithuania in the fifteenth. Otto of Bamberg echoed Martin's biographer in

[24] These important themes are only summarized here as they are discussed at length in Bartlett 1998.
[25] *Landnáma-bóc* I.3.5 (at 21).   [26] *Russian Primary Chronicle*, 95.
[27] Thietmar of Merseburg I.17; Adam of Bremen IV.27.

this Christian opposition to pagan reverence for natural objects: 'there is nothing religious in a tree trunk'.[28]

The role of women

There are sufficient hints in the written sources to support the idea that the religious role of women in pagan times was more prominent than after the conversion. These hints are of two basic types: (a) myths and legends of an early period when women were important; (b) recurrent references to the role of female seers or diviners (*phitonissae* in the Latin sources). Sometimes these two kinds of evidence overlap. The legendary prehistory of the Bohemians, as narrated by their first Latin historian, Cosmas of Prague, involves rule by three sisters, one of whom, Lubossa, is a *phitonissa* especially responsible for giving legal judgements. In her time young women bore arms and were not yet 'in the power of men'.[29] In the Eddic poem *Vǫluspá*, a seeress recounts to Odin the whole history of the universe from Creation to Ragnarok, while, according to Snorri, divinatory magic (*seithr*) was taught to the gods by the goddess Freya and was not deemed suitable for manly men, being the preserve of priestesses.[30] Condemnation of *phitonissae* was a prominent part of Otto of Bamberg's evangelization of the Pomeranians and one is reported accompanying a Polish army as late as 1209.[31] The part played by female seers in the saga literature again supports the idea that they were associated with the pagan past.

Additionally, there has been a recent attempt to identify the burials of such 'seeresses' in the graveyards of Viking Age Scandinavia. Several unusual or elaborate burials (or occasionally cremations) from the eighth to tenth century have been claimed as the last resting places of *volur*, the female divinatory specialists referred to in later Old Norse texts. A particular diagnostic feature has been the presence in these graves of 'staffs of sorcery' (the term *volur* means 'staff-bearers'), although it should be pointed out that some archaeologists prefer to see these items as meat spits![32]

SOCIAL PRACTICES

If one turns from the strictly cultic, that is the rites and ceremonies of pagan religion, to the more general social practices of pagan societies, it

[28] Sulpicius Severus XIII.1 (vol. I, 280); *Vita Prieflingensis* III.11.   [29] Cosmas I.3–9.
[30] Snorri Sturluson, *Heimskringla, Ynglingatal*, 4 and 7.
[31] *Vita Prieflingensis* II.21; Ebo II.12; *Chronicon Montis Sereni*, 176.
[32] There is a recent discussion in English in Price 2002, 112–204.

is clear that some of these were of much more concern to Christian missionaries and observers than others. This was because some customs were
not religiously neutral, but had acquired an association with either pagan
or Christian cult, even though not cultic themselves. This definition of
a set or bundle of practices as essentially Christian was the outcome of a
long process, partly shaped by the Judaic roots of Christianity, partly by the
accidental and contingent decisions of the mission field. Christian social
practice was often at variance with that of the pagan peoples and that variance could be interpreted as religiously significant. Three examples that
were of great importance in northern and central Europe were ways of
disposing of the dead, family structure and diet. Methods of disposal of
the dead, although highly variable between cultures, usually appear fundamental and self-evident to their various practitioners. The Greek historian
Herodotus, for example, tells how the great Persian king Darius brought
together some Greeks from one end of his empire and some Indians from
the other. The Greeks were disgusted when they learned that the Indians
disposed of their dead by eating them. But the Indians were equally horri-
fied when they heard that the Greeks actually burned their dead relatives.[33]
Similar vital divergences characterized the world of northern and central
Europe as it shifted from pagan to Christian practice. In his preface to the
Heimskringla, Snorri Sturluson actually divided human history into different epochs according to the prevalent method of disposing of the dead: first
is the age of cremation, then the age of burial mounds, before the adoption
of Christian inhumation. Archaeologists are usually less schematic. While
assuming that evidence of cremation is evidence of paganism, or at least of
only superficially assimilated Christianity, they are wary of assuming that
inhumation and absence of grave goods are themselves compelling evidence
for Christianity. Indeed, in some of the most intriguing cases a shift from
cremation to inhumation occurs without reason to believe this is part of
Christianization. In any event, it is clear that Christian missionaries were
insistent that the dead be buried, not cremated, in cemeteries, not in woods
or fields, and without grave goods or accompanying sacrifices.

Family structures likewise vary from society to society. Christianity had
its own model of the family, especially a model of marriage, that was clear
and distinctive. It did not always match that found in the societies under-
going conversion. Polygamy, recognition of illegitimate children as equal
to legitimate children, the practice of female infanticide – these are a few of
the customs found in some or all of the peoples of Scandinavia or central

---

[33] Herodotus III.38.

Europe prior to their conversion. Thorough Christianization meant their elimination. When Otto of Bamberg preached to the Pomeranians in the 1120s, his programme involved not only the demand 'let them not bury dead Christians among the pagans, in woods and fields, but in cemeteries', but also the requirements 'let them not kill their daughters' and 'let each man be content with one wife only'.[34] A century later the pope himself was condemning female infanticide among the pagan Prussians.[35] These are, of course, unfriendly Christian voices, but clearly the practice of infanticide could be identified with pagan religion not only by hostile missionaries but also by members of pagan societies themselves, for one of the exclusions negotiated by pagan Icelanders upon the conversion to Christianity in the year 1000 was that, as far as infanticide was concerned, 'the old laws should stand'.[36]

Another opt-out clause allowed to the Icelanders at this time was the eating of horsemeat, and this introduces a final topic to be considered in this discussion of how social practices and cultic loyalty could interweave. Diet is an important issue for most religions, with taboos on certain kinds of food being among the most common and defining features of religious communities. Unlike Judaism and Islam, Christianity did not have as a starting point scriptural prohibitions against named items of food. Indeed, an important part of the story of the Acts of the Apostles is Peter's education in the lesson that the universal mission of the Church – to Gentiles and Jews alike – involves recognition that the old dietary laws are superseded. Nevertheless, by the early Middle Ages it is clear that certain foods were being prohibited by the Christian authorities. 'The Lord' may have 'restored freedom in matters of food when he freed the world from the Law,'[37] in the words of one medieval theologian, but Christian authorities had reimposed them quite strictly. Horsemeat was among the important issues.

There is clear evidence of a Christian campaign against the eating of horsemeat, going back at least to the eighth century. Boniface's mission in Germany in the first half of that century involved an attack on the eating of horsemeat as something that should be shunned by Christians and that Boniface might eventually ban 'with Christ's help'.[38] Later in that same century a papal mission to England condemned the eating of horse-meat among other 'pagan customs' (including sortilege).[39] Irish penitentials

---

[34] *Vita Prieflingensis* II.21; Ebo II.12.   [35] *Monumenta Poloniae Vaticana* 3, no. 10 (at 5–6) (Po. 5793).
[36] *Íslendingabók* chap. 7 (at 298).
[37] Robert Pullen, *Sententiae* VIII.10 (at 974): *Dominus dum mundum a lege liberavit, libertatem quoque ciborum in lege prohibitorum restituit.*
[38] Boniface, ep. 28 and 87 (at 100, 294).   [39] *Councils*, 3, 459.

likewise condemned the practice although there was also room in the penitential literature for a more nuanced view: 'Horsemeat is not prohibited, but
it is the custom not to eat it.'[40] This neutral tone was, however, unusual, for
the killing and eating of horses seems to have been an aspect of Germanic
paganism, identified as an integral part of the religious world both by hostile
Christians and defiant pagans.

The sacred horses of the West Slavs, as described by Thietmar, the biographers of Otto of Bamberg and Saxo, were divinatory rather than sacrificial animals, and the missionaries' tactic was to desacralize them: Bishop
Burchard of Halberstadt rode back home on the sacred horse of the Liutizi
after a successful campaign against them in 1068, while Otto of Bamberg
ordered the sacred horse of the Pomeranians to be sold abroad, saying 'it
was more suitable to pull a cart than to make prophecies'.[41] Scandinavian
practice, however, certainly included horse sacrifice: Thietmar reports the
sacrifice of horses, among other animals (and men) on Seeland, while horses
are also among the sacrifices reported at Uppsala by Adam.[42] Archaeological
findings of horse skulls and horse skeletons support this picture. There is
even some evidence (although the source is regarded by some scholars as a
doubtful one) that the pagan reaction in Hungary in 1046 was marked by
(a return to?) eating of horsemeat.[43] The sacrifice of horses, as disclosed by
these written and archaeological sources, implies the eating of horsemeat,
since sacrificial meat is invariably consumed by the worshippers. Indeed, it
is likely that Christians opposed the eating of horsemeat not because it was
horse but because it was sacrificed. Although the New Testament message
implied a general dispensation from dietary laws, St Paul was still wary of
the dangers of eating sacrificial meat.

The most piquant episode in the religious struggle over horsemeat
involves the tenth-century Norwegian king Håkon Athelstansfostre, who,
as his name suggests, was raised at the court of Athelstan, king of England
(d. 939), before returning to Norway. As a Christian ruler of a mainly
pagan people, he found the eating of horsemeat a vexed issue. The earliest
recorded version of the story, in the twelfth-century historical source *Ágrip*,
explains that Håkon 'bit horse-liver, but wrapped it in cloth so that he
should not bite it directly'. Snorri's elaboration of the tale of this attempted

[40] *Irish Penitentials*, 160, 259; *Canones Theodori*, 241, 267, 279, 325 (variant versions).
[41] *Annales Augustani*, a. 1068 (at 128); Herbord II.33.
[42] Thietmar of Merseburg I.17; Adam of Bremen IV.27.
[43] *Legenda sancti Gerhardi*, 15 (at 501); brief discussion of the debate: Klaniczay and Madas 1996, 113–14, 138–40.

compromise contains the illuminating comment, 'and neither party was satisfied with that'.[44]

The long transition in which northern and central Europe was engaged in this period was thus only partly a matter of cult and high politics; there were also such vital issues as marriage, cremation and horsemeat. Christianity was often termed 'the Christian law (*lex christiana*)', and the phrase usefully conveys the sense that Christianity involved rules of social conduct as well as cultic belief and practice. Exactly the same was true of pagan religion and there are numerous instances in missionary literature when the ancestral and defining nature of paganism is visible. The Pomeranians complained of the difficulty of changing 'the ancient law of our fathers and ancestors'.[45] One West Slav ruler of the late tenth century, who had adopted a pro-German and pro-Christian policy, was accused of 'destroying ancestral laws (*patriis legibus*)'.[46] Echoing this invocation of the forefathers, the twelfth-century *Life of St Olav* presents the Norwegians as being 'unwilling to receive a new religion, contrary to their ancestral laws (*paternis legibus*)'.[47] In the *Livonian Rhymed Chronicle*, the German author pictures the pressure put upon the Lithuanian leader Mindaugas to revert to paganism: 'Be truly sorrowful that a worthy king like yourself . . . has rejected the gods who stood by your parents.'[48]

The accumulation of such evidence, from diverse times and places, suggests the reality of such native responses. One isolated case might be a rhetorical flourish or an imagined retort, but, taking the body of material as a whole, there are sufficient indicators that pagans viewed the complex of cult and practice in which their social world was embodied as ancient and identifying.

Human groups could thus be defined by their paganism. It was a definition, like all social definitions, that not only included but also excluded. The self-awareness of pagan societies could induce in them a defiant hostility towards Christianity. It could also create a defiant hostility towards their own rulers, or those who aspired to become so, especially if those rulers seemed to be favourable towards the new religion and its missionaries. There are many cases of convert rulers of unconverted societies,

---

[44] *Ágrip* 5; Snorri Sturluson, *Heimskringla, Hákonar saga Gótha*, 17.   [45] Ebo II.11.
[46] Helmold 13.   [47] *Passio . . . Olavi*, 73.   [48] *Livländische Reimchronik*, lines 6404–9.

rulers who might seek to further Christianization and make alliances with Christian powers, or sometimes just sit tight, content with a chapel and court priest in the midst of a pagan world – Henry of Old Lübeck (d. 1127), ruler of the Abodrites (living in what is now Mecklenburg), and Pribislav-Henry of Brandenburg (d. 1150) are examples among the West Slavs.[49] The Abodrites especially lived in a constant tension between Christianizing rulers and pagan reactions, such as that of 1066, when Godescalc, the father of Henry of Old Lübeck, 'was killed by the pagans he was striving to convert to Christianity'.[50] Some Scandinavian kings, perhaps including Håkon Athelstansfostre, could be seen in the same light.

The relationship between Christianity and monarchy is one of the main themes explored in this volume. It is a large and complicated subject, but there does seem to be some justification for associating the two. There are numerous cases where conversion and the imposition of a newly powerful monarchy are associated and, conversely, instances where paganism and decentralized rule seem to belong together, one of the most celebrated being that of the pagan Saxons, who had no kings and decided matters in local assemblies in the period before Frankish conquest brought them monarchy, a comital system and Christianity. The Saxon rising of 841–2 pitted the Saxon freemen and freedmen against the new class of lords, and one of their aims was to re-establish 'the law that they had had in the time when they were worshippers of idols'; they wished to expel the lords and 'each man to live by the law he wished, in the old style'.[51] Paganism and a popular constitution are here explicitly connected.

A curious echo of this image of the pagan, freedom-loving Saxons is found in a passage in the earliest Polish chronicle (traditionally known as Gallus Anonymus), dating to the very early twelfth century. The author has occasion to discuss Prussia, the land to the north of the Poles occupied by pagans. This takes him at once back to Charlemagne and the Saxons: 'In the time of Charlemagne, king of the Franks, when the Saxons were in rebellion against him and unwilling to accept the yoke either of lordship or of the Christian faith, this people sailed away from Saxony in their ships and occupied this region [i.e. Prussia] . . . To this day they continue, without a king and without law, nor have they abandoned their original faithlessness and ferocity.'[52] Needless to say, there is no historical content to this myth, but it is very telling that the traditional association of fierce paganism and rejection of monarchical lordship could be exemplified in this way, for the

---

[49] Kahl 1962 is a classic study of this topic.   [50] Adam of Bremen III.50.
[51] Nithard IV.2.   [52] *Gesta principum Polonorum* II.42 (at 194).

Saxons and the Prussians do indeed constitute two of the clearest cases of indigenous peoples stubbornly resisting both monarchy and Christianity.

The resistance to Christianization should thus not be underestimated. Time and again apparent conversions were reversed by pagan reactions. Cases can be found in both Scandinavia and central Europe: Poland 1032–4, Hungary 1046, a 'persecution of the Christians' in Sweden *c.* 1120 according to the *Life of St Botvid*, as well as the perennial resistance of the Slavs between Elbe and Oder. It was the Baltic region, where Scandinavia and eastern Europe merge, that was to be the most loyal bastion of indigenous pagan religion. The Prussians, Estonians, Lithuanians and other peoples of the region fought hard for their religions and clung tenaciously to them. As the author of the *Livonian Rhymed Chronicle* noted, *diu heidenschaft ist hochgemuot* – 'paganism is proud'.[53]

CHRISTIAN INTERPRETATIONS OF PAGANISM

Christians tended to have three basic views of the paganism they encountered (and that they knew they themselves had at one time abandoned): it was devil-worship; it was an ignorant mistake, worshipping natural objects; it was the misapplication of religious reverence to real human beings of the past (Euhemerism).

The speech that Herbord puts into the mouth of Otto of Bamberg, preaching to the Pomeranians in the 1120s, splices together the first two views of pagan worship: it is inane and empty, but it is also devil-worship. Otto refers to 'those deceivers, your deaf-mute gods, graven images (*sculptilia*), and the unclean spirits which are in them'.[54] On the one hand, the pagan 'gods' are deaf and silent, because they are in fact the work of human hands – 'graven images' is the standard Vulgate term for the images of false gods. On the other hand, there are real spirits 'in them' – demonic forces with real powers. The demons are 'the *inhabitants* of your shrines and graven images'. Hence the assault on pagan idols often reflects these two contrary views. Smashing the idols and dragging them out of the town incites the pagans to wonder whether they are really gods, for, if they were, they would defend themselves. The logic is clear: 'If they had any divine power . . . they would defend themselves. But if they cannot defend themselves, how can they defend us?'[55] Yet also, the evil spirits are thus induced to leave the idols. At Gützkow in Pomerania, as the images were hacked to pieces, 'flies of unusual size, never seen in that land, burst out of the

---

[53] *Livländische Reimchronik*, line 327.   [54] Herbord II.30.   [55] Herbord II.31.

shrines of the idols with a great rush'.[56] At Arkona 'a demon in the shape of a dark animal' rushed out of the shrine when the image of Svantevit was being destroyed, while in Kiev Prince Vladimir 'appointed twelve men to beat the idol with sticks, not because he thought the wood was sensitive, but to affront the demon who had deceived man in this guise'.[57]

The pagan gods might be stocks and stones or they might be demons. There was also the euhemeristic approach, the idea that famous men might be mistakenly revered as gods after their death. The most notable exponent of this idea was Snorri, the early passages of the *Heimskringla* giving an account of the ancient warrior chieftain Odin, 'who died in his bed in Sweden', but there is an earlier and remarkable instance, in which the pagan gods themselves seem to espouse the concept. An extraordinary story in the *Life of Anskar* tells how the pagan gods in Sweden, offended at the apparent need of their worshippers for 'another God' (i.e. the Christian God), offered instead to make the dead Swedish king Erik one of them: 'if you desire to have many gods, and we are not enough for you, we all agree to enlist your former king Erik in our fellowship'. So it turned out: 'they established a temple in honour of the recently deceased king and began to offer sacrifices and vows to him as a god'.[58]

Christians could thus identify the objects of pagan worship in a variety of ways. They also often attributed motives for pagan worship. For instance, a story recounted by the biographers of Otto of Bamberg tells how a pagan priest, in order to stir up opposition to the missionaries, disguised himself as a god and appeared to one of the Pomeranians, uttering the following speech: 'I am your god; it is I who clothe the fields with grass and the woods with leaves; the fruits of the fields and trees, the offspring of the flocks, and everything that is of use to human beings, lie in my power. It is my practice to give these things to those who revere me and to take them away from those who despise me.'[59] Clearly the hagiographers have a theory of what pagans thought they were worshipping *for*. Similarly, Adam's trinity of gods at Uppsala dealt with 'weather and harvest', 'courage against enemies' and 'peace and pleasure' respectively. The priest at Arkona prayed for 'good increase in wealth and victories for himself, the country and the people'.[60]

Christians thus had a functional theory of pagan religion: its purpose was to bring earthly prosperity. The point is brought out dramatically on those occasions when Christian missionaries adopted an extreme ascetic pose, as in the case of Bruno of Querfurt, whose bare feet and poor clothing

[56] Ebo III.11.   [57] Saxo XIV.39.32 (vol. II, 505) (fol. 169v); *Russian Primary Chronicle*, 116.
[58] Rimbert, chap. 26 (at 86–8).   [59] Herbord III.4; cf. Ebo III.8.
[60] Saxo XIV.39.5 (vol. II, 497) (fol. 167v).

suggested to his audience not that he was a man of exceptional piety but that he was a cunning beggar.[61] The idiom of ascetic renunciation is here presented as alien and incomprehensible to pagans. Likewise, a century later, the Pomeranians were deeply unimpressed with another barefoot preacher: 'How', they asked, 'can we believe that you are a messenger of the most high god, since he is so glorious and filled with all riches and you are contemptible and so poor that you cannot afford shoes?'[62] A true god was one who brought prosperity to his worshippers.

THE FATE OF PAGANISM

Eventually the pagan past slipped away. There might still be people named after Thor, but no worshippers of the god. When forced by desperation to eat horsemeat, people in the high Middle Ages were struck by the fact that this was unusual and repellent, not that it was a pagan custom. The temples – where there had been temples – were gone. The pagan reactions had failed.

Some aspects of pagan cult slowly dissolved into the amorphous sea of 'superstition', to be criticized by rigorous clerics along with moral failings and abuses of Christian ritual. Hence one encounters recurrent condemnation of sortilege and divination alongside the attack on such practices as dancing and singing at saints' festivals. Official and public pagan cult had disappeared, leaving practices that generations of clerics labelled 'popular' and, eventually, intellectuals dubbed 'folkloric'.

In one society the remembered pagan past achieved new life in the form of a body of extraordinary stories – the Icelandic sagas. Here, writers of the thirteenth and subsequent centuries told long, involved tales, many set in Iceland's pagan past. These are not myths, as preserved by Snorri and the *Edda*, but views of the writers' own societies prior to Christianization. The richness of this imagined pagan past can be called 'novelistic' in a literal sense, for one finds all the features of the bourgeois novel of the nineteenth and twentieth centuries – realistic social settings, imagined dialogue, development of character, etc. Scholars have long been divided about this 'saga world'. Is it a precious window on pre-Christian Europe or does it tell us nothing at all about pagan society, being a mere 'literary paganism'?[63]

The problems of interpretation are clear. For example, the *Saga of Erik the Red* contains a full and dramatically rich account of the activities of a seeress. Her dress, the ritual of her reception, the preparatory chant and her

---

[61] Peter Damian, chap. 27 (at 58); it has been suggested that the 'Russians' mentioned in this passage are a confusion for 'Prussians' (58, n. 3; Wood 2001, 239).
[62] Ebo II.1.   [63] North 1991, title of c. VII.

predictions are all described in detail. The story is set in the late tenth century, the earliest manuscript of the saga is of early fourteenth-century date. Obviously, there is the possibility for a variety of views here: (1) the saga describes ancient pagan practice, as transmitted by oral tradition; (2) the saga is a fictional narrative and the source of the details about divination is the imagination of an author (probably of the thirteenth century); (3) the passage describes contemporary practice, i.e. divinatory ritual among thirteenth-century Scandinavians. It is clear that big issues of orality and literacy, of the nature of literary fiction and the whole question of so-called 'pagan survivals' are involved in interpretation of this one short passage.

Medieval Christians knew they had a pagan past. They responded to it in a variety of ways: we can find antiquarian interest, as notably in Snorri, and much censorious silence. There is occasionally also a hint of poignancy, perhaps most memorably conveyed in the last chapter of the *Saga of Ragnar Lodbrok*. Ragnar was a legendary king of the pagan period, whose sons had taken dramatic revenge for his death. Many years after their time, a Danish ship put in to an anchorage on the island of Samsø off the Jutland coast and the crew went ashore. There they found a huge wooden idol, covered with moss. As they wondered who could have sacrificed to this figure, 'the man of wood' himself gave them the answer:

Lodbrok's sons set me up in the south by the sea; at that time I was worshipped with human sacrifices . . .

There they bade me stand near a thorn-bush, and overgrown with moss, for as long as the coast endures; now the tears of the clouds beat upon me; neither flesh nor cloth protects me.[64]

Abandoned, moss-covered and weather-beaten, the huge idol sings the elegy of European paganism.

REFERENCES

Adam of Bremen, *Gesta Hammaburgensis ecclesiae pontificum*, ed. W. Trillmich, *Quellen des 9. und 11. Jahrhunderts zur Geschichte der Hamburgischen Kirche und des Reiches* (AQ XI), Darmstadt, 1961, 135–503.

Ágrip, ed. M. J. Driscoll, London, 1995.

Annales Augustani, ed. G. Pertz, *MGH SS* III, Hanover, 1839, 124–36.

Bartlett, R. 1985, 'The Conversion of a Pagan Society in the Middle Ages', *History* 70, 185–201.

Bartlett, R. 1998, 'Reflections on Paganism and Christianity in Medieval Europe', *Proceedings of the British Academy* 101 (1998 Lectures and Memoirs), 55–76.

---

[64] McTurk 1991, 23.

Bede, *Bede's Ecclesiastical History of the English People*, ed. B. Colgrave and R. A. B. Mynors, Oxford Medieval Texts, Oxford, 1969.

Biddle, M. ed. 1976, *Winchester in the Early Middle Ages*, Oxford.

Boniface, *Epistolae*, ed. R. Rau (*AQ* IVb), Darmstadt, 1968.

Bruno of Querfurt, *Epistola Brunonis ad Henricum regem*, ed. J. Karwasińska, *MPH* n.s. IV/3, 1973, 85–106.

Die Canones Theodori, ed. P. W. Finsterwalde, Weimar, 1929.

Chronicon Montis Sereni, ed. E. Ehrenfeuchter, *MGH SS* XXIII, Hanover, 1874, 130–226.

Cosmas of Prague, *Chronica Boemorum*, ed. B. Bretholz, *SRG* n.s., Berlin, 1923.

Councils and Ecclesiastical Documents relating to Great Britain and Ireland, ed. A. W. Haddan and W. Stubbs, 3 vols., Oxford, 1869–78.

Diplomata Conradi I, Heinrici I et Ottonis I, ed. T. Sickel, *MGH, Diplomata regum et imperatorum Germaniae* I, Hanover, 1879–84.

Ebo, *Vita sancti Ottonis episcopi Babenbergensis*, ed. J. Wikarjak and K. Liman, *MPH* n.s. VII/2, Warsaw, 1969.

Gesta principum Polonorum, ed. P. Knoll and F. Schaer, Budapest, 2003.

Helmold of Bosau, *Cronica Slavorum*, ed. Heinz Stoob (*AQ* XIX), rev. edn, Darmstadt, 1973.

Herbord, *Dialogus de vita sancti Ottonis episcopi Babenbergensis*, ed. J. Wikarjak and K. Liman, *MPH* n.s. VII/3, Warsaw, 1974.

Herrmann, J. ed. 1985, *Die Slawen in Deutschland. Ein Handbuch*, new edn, Berlin.

Ibn Fadlan, 'La Relation du voyage d'Ibn Fadlân chez les Bulgares de la Volga', ed. M. Canard, *Annales de l'Institut d'Études Orientales (Algiers)* 15, 1957, 41–146.

The Irish Penitentials, ed. L. Bieler, Dublin, 1963.

Íslendingabók, ed. G. Vigfusson and F. York Powell, *Origines Islandicae*, 2 vols., Oxford, 1905, vol. I, 279–306.

Jerome, *Commentariorum in Esaiam libri XVIII*, ed. M. Adriaen, 2 vols. (Corpus Christianorum, series latina 73–73A), 1963.

Jóns saga helga, ed. G. Vigfusson and F. York Powell, *Origines Islandicae*, 2 vols., Oxford, 1905, vol. I, 534–67.

Kahl, H.-D. 1962, 'Heidnisches Wendentum und christliche Stammesfursten', *Archiv für Kulturgeschichte* 44, 72–119.

Klaniczay, G. and E. Madas 1996, 'La Hongrie', in *Hagiographies* II, ed. G. Philippart (Corpus Christianorum), Turnhout, 103–60.

Landnáma-bóc, ed. G. Vigfusson and F. York Powell, *Origines Islandicae*, 2 vols., Oxford, 1905, vol. I, 2–236.

Legenda sancti Gerhardi episcopi, ed. I. Madzsar, in *Scriptores rerum Hungaricarum*, ed. I. Szentpétery, II, Budapest, 1938, 461–506.

Livländische Reimchronik, ed. L. Meyer, Paderborn, 1876.

McTurk, R. 1991, *Studies in Ragnars saga Lodbrókar*, Oxford.

Martin of Braga, *De correctione rusticorum*, ed. C. W. Barlow, *Martini episcopi Bracarensis opera omnia* (Papers and Monographs of the American Academy in Rome 12), 1950, 159–203.

Monumenta Poloniae Vaticana III: *Analecta Vaticana*, ed. J. Ptasnik, Cracow, 1914.

Neplach of Opatovice, *Chronicon*, ed. J. Emler, in *Fontes rerum Bohemicarum* III, Prague, 1882, 451–84.

Nithard, *Historiarum libri IIII*, ed. R. Rau, *Quellen zur karolingischen Reichsgeschichte* I (*AQ* V), Darmstadt, 1955, 383–461.

North, R. 1991, *Pagan Words and Christian Meanings*, Amsterdam.

Olsen, O. 1966, *Hørg, hov og kirke*, Copenhagen.

Orderic Vitalis, *Historia ecclesiastica: The Ecclesiastical History*, ed. M. Chibnall, 6 vols., Oxford, 1968–80.

Passio et miracula Beati Olavi, ed. F. Metcalfe, Oxford, 1881.

Peter Damian, *Vita beati Romualdi*, ed. G. Tabacco (Fonti per la Storia d'Italia 94), Rome, 1957.

PL: Patrologia cursus completus, series latina, ed. J.-P. Migne, 221 vols., Paris, 1844–64.

Price, N. 2002, *The Viking Way: Religion and War in Late Iron Age Scandinavia*, Uppsala.

Rimbert, *Vita Anskarii*, ed. W. Trillmich, *Quellen des 9. und 11. Jahrhunderts zur Geschichte der Hamburgischen Kirche und des Reiches* (*AQ* XI), Darmstadt, 1961, 1–133.

Robert Pullen, *Sententiae*, *PL* CLXXXVI, cols. 639–1010.

The Russian Primary Chronicle, tr. S. H. Cross and O. P. Sherbowitz-Wetzor, Cambridge, MA, 1953.

Saxo Grammaticus, *Gesta Danorum*, ed. E. Christiansen, *Danorum regum heroumque historia, Books X–XVI*, 3 vols. (British Archaeological Reports, International Series 84, 118/1–2), Oxford, 1980–1.

Schuldt, E. 1985, *Groß Raden. Ein slawischer Tempelort des 9./10. Jahrhunderts in Mecklenburg*, Berlin.

Slupecki, L. 1994, *Slavonic Pagan Temples*, Warsaw.

Slupecki, L. and R. Zaroff 1999, 'William of Malmesbury on Pagan Slavic Oracles', *Studia Mythologica Slavica* 2, 9–20.

Snorri Sturluson, *Heimskringla*, tr. L. M. Hollander, Austin, 1964.

Sulpicius Severus, *Vita Sancti Martini*, ed. J. Fontaine, 3 vols. (Sources chrétiennes 133–5), 1967–9.

Thietmar of Merseburg, *Chronicon*, ed. W. Trillmich (*AQ* IX), Darmstadt, 1957.

Tulinius, T. 2002, *The Matter of the North: The Rise of Literary Fiction in Thirteenth-Century Iceland*, Eng. tr. Odense.

Vita Prieflingensis (Sancti Ottonis episcopi Babenbergensis vita Prieflingensis), ed. J. Petersohn (*SRG*), Hanover, 1999.

William of Malmesbury, *Gesta regum Anglorum: The History of the English Kings*, ed. R. A. B. Mynors, R. M. Thomson and M. Winterbottom, 2 vols., Oxford, 1998–9.

Wood, I. 2001, *The Missionary Life: Saints and the Evangelisation of Europe 400–1050*, Harlow.

CHAPTER 3

The kingdom of Denmark

Michael H. Gelting

I. BEFORE CHRISTIANITY: RELIGION AND POWER

If the Danish evidence were considered in isolation, very little would be known of the Danish pagan religion. A few rune-stones carry invocations to the god Thor, and onomastic evidence indicates that Thor was by far the most popular of the gods of the Nordic pantheon. The name of the god Freyr is attested as a component in a few names on rune-stones, but while the names alluding to Thor remained in use after the conversion, the names referring to Freyr did not.[1] Although its philological roots have nothing to do with the pagan god, the name Odinkar seems to have been understood in the eleventh century to be referring to Odin (Wodan).[2] A broader range of the Nordic pantheon is represented in place names; the name of the later episcopal city of Odense is derived from 'Odin's vi', that is, the sacred ground of Odin, indicating that it was a location for pagan cult before the conversion.[3]

Any idea of the myths and beliefs connected with these gods can be obtained only from Icelandic literature; Saxo Grammaticus's heavily reworked and classicizing rendering of the myths (c. 1200) is ultimately derived from Icelandic informants. A few pieces of art can be identified as representations of mythical episodes known from the Icelandic literature.[4] This shows that Danes knew the same gods and at least some of the same myths as the Icelanders, but it is impossible to tell whether there were substantial differences between Danish paganism and the beliefs and customs of pagan Iceland. As in other Germanic languages, the names of the week were named after pagan gods. It is supposed on philological grounds that these names were borrowed from the Anglo-Saxons well before the conversion.[5]

---

[1] Halvorsen *et al.* 1968, cols. 219–20.
[2] Kousgård Sørensen 1974, 110; cf. Adam of Bremen, 97, schol. 25.
[3] Hald 1965, 248–53; map in Nielsen 1991, 250.   [4] E.g. Sawyer 1988, 132–3.   [5] Green 1998, 248.

■	Permanent sees
□	Temporary sees
●	Early towns
◉	Coastal marketplaces
⊕	Viking Age ring-forts
○	Abbeys and priories
✚	Canonized saints centre
✛	Unofficial or uncertain cult centre
×	Possible pagan cult sites
•	Other places

4. Denmark from the tenth to the twelfth century

A few structures excavated in recent years have been interpreted as pagan temples. One of these is located at the site of a large aristocratic residence by Lake Tissø in western Sjælland (Sealand); the site was abandoned in the late eleventh century. The name of the lake is probably derived from the god Tyr.[6] The last of the structures erected on the presumed temple site seems to have been cross-shaped and may have been a Christian chapel.[7] If the identification is correct, it would be a unique case of site continuity from the pagan to the Christian cult.[8] Archaeological finds in the pre-Christian royal residence of Lejre in Sjælland and at Uppåkra in Skåne (Scania) have similarly been interpreted as indicating pagan cultic sites in connection with aristocratic residences.[9] Some titles appearing on rune-stones, especially *gode* and *thul*, have been interpreted to imply cultic functions. Without

---

[6] Hald 1965, 249.   [7] Jørgensen 2002, 234–8, 243–5; cf. Jensen 2004, 300–4.
[8] Cf. Olsen 1966, esp. 275.   [9] Christensen 2004, 192–6; Hårdh 2005, 384–5.

corroborating evidence these interpretations must remain speculative; the case is most convincing for the title *gode*, because of the similar and better documented Icelandic title *goði*. This title designated a chieftain who also exercised cultic functions that would fit the recent archaeological finds at Danish aristocratic residences from the Viking Age.[10] The finds of numerous weapons and other artefacts in Lake Tissø next to the aristocratic residence are likely to represent sacrificial offerings, and both there and at the great hall of Lejre, significant amounts of animal bones and cooking-stones (used for boiling water) witness to great meals that probably had a cultic aspect.[11] In the early eleventh century, Thietmar of Merseburg described gruesome rituals involving large-scale human sacrifices at Lejre in the 930s;[12] his sources for this statement are unknown, and so far it has not been corroborated by archaeological evidence.[13]

The power structures of Denmark in the tenth century are hardly less elusive. A monarchy was already in existence at the time of the first Frankish missionary attempt in the early eighth century (before 714), although our source for this, Alcuin's *Life of St Willibrord*, insists more upon the cruelty of the ruler Ongendus than upon his royal title.[14] An indication of the resources and level of organization of this early Danish monarchy is provided by some substantial works of engineering that have been dated dendrochronologically to the first half of the eighth century: the earliest stages of the Danevirke, the defensive wall across the root of the peninsula of Jylland (Jutland), where the original wall of the late seventh and early eighth centuries was transformed into a much stronger and more sophisticated defensive unit in 737 and strengthened even further later in the eighth century;[15] and a canal for ship haulage across an isthmus on the island of Samsø, dated 726.[16] However, it is impossible to determine the geographical area dominated by the early eighth-century kings. By the late eighth century, the Danish kingdom appears as a consolidated (although unstable) political unit, whose rulers are consistently referred to in Frankish sources as kings (*reges*).[17]

With Charlemagne's conquest of Saxony in the late eighth century, Denmark became the neighbour of the Frankish kingdom. The relationship

[10] Jón Viðar Sigurðsson 1999, 185–94. For *thul*, Meulengracht Sørensen 1991, 237.

[11] Jørgensen 2002, 243; Christensen 2004, 192–6.   [12] Thietmar of Merseburg I.17 (at 20).

[13] Christensen 2004, 195–6.

[14] *De Sancto Willibrordo*, 441 (Alcuin's prose *Life of St Willibrord*), I.9; ibid. (at 453) (Alcuin's metrical *Life of St Willibrord*), II.7. It appears from both versions, I.13 (at 443); II.8 (at 453) that Willibrord's missionary attempt in Denmark took place before Pippin of Herstal's death in 714. However, Lund 2004b, 23, argues for a date between 714 and 719.

[15] Andersen 1998, 10–13.   [16] Christensen 1995, 110–14.   [17] Sawyer 1991a, 283.

between the two realms was tense, and the Danish king Godfred (d. 810) had sufficient military resources at his disposal to be considered a serious threat by the Franks. A man from Skåne is mentioned among the members of one of the diplomatic legations that Godfred sent to negotiate with the Franks. This indicates that his kingdom may have included all the major provinces of medieval Denmark, and that impression is confirmed by the ninth-century descriptions of the sailing routes of the Baltic that are appended to King Alfred's Anglo-Saxon translation of Orosius.[18] Only the island of Bornholm is said there to have had its own king;[19] Bornholm probably did not come under Danish control until the late eleventh century. On the other hand, Frisia was subject to a loose and unstable Danish overlordship for large parts of the ninth century and possibly already in the eighth.[20]

Godfred's death was followed by a period of internal strife between rival claimants to the throne. These claimants belonged to two families which were probably branches of the same royal house; the occurrence among them of the name Angandeo suggests that they were descended from the royal lineage that had governed Denmark in the time of King Ongendus a century earlier.[21] From the middle of the ninth to the middle of the tenth century information on events in Denmark is so sparse that it is not even possible to reconstruct a convincing regnal list.

According to Frankish sources and medieval Danish tradition, the Danish rulers of the pagan age had their main residence in Lejre in Sjælland. This tradition has been borne out by the excavation of the traces of a wooden hall of extraordinary size, surrounded by large stables and numerous smaller buildings.[22] Lejre was abandoned during the tenth century, and the mid-tenth-century kings appear to have had their residence in Jelling in Jylland. This is likely to indicate a change of dynasty, although the evidence is sparse. For some decades in the mid-tenth century Denmark may have been split between a western kingdom ruled by the kings of the Jelling dynasty, the pagan Gorm (d. c. 958) and his son Harald Bluetooth (c. 958–c. 987), and an eastern kingdom, perhaps still under the control of the old Lejre dynasty.[23] The exact nature of the Danish kings' power in the ninth and tenth centuries is unknown, but they were able to muster considerable military force, and their control of the country is shown by the fact that all the Frankish and German missionary ventures of the period were dependent upon the goodwill and authority of the kings. Accounts of these missions indicate

---

[18] Sawyer 1991a, 283–5.   [19] Lund 1991, 167.   [20] Lund 2002.
[21] Sawyer 1991a, 283, 286–7.   [22] Christensen 2004, 191–6.   [23] Sawyer 1991a, 284.

that the Danish kings had officers whom the Frankish sources identify as counts (*comites*);[24] they may have been in charge of regional military commands. In addition to exacting tribute from adjacent regions, the Danish kings undoubtedly derived important resources from protecting, controlling and taxing interregional trade.[25] The city of Ribe on the south-west coast of Jylland was founded *c.* 704–5. In 808, King Godfred forcibly resettled the merchants from the emporium of Reric in the land of the Slavic Obodrites in Haithabu (Hedeby) at the neck of the Jutish peninsula, which was henceforth the most important emporium in the western Baltic. Århus on the east coast of Jylland was founded as a fortified commercial settlement in the early tenth century. These three towns were to become the first episcopal seats in Denmark in the mid-tenth century.[26]

The king's power must have been based upon the allegiance of local aristocrats, whose power in turn rested upon the allegiance of lesser free men. Economically, all of these relied upon agriculture and cattle farming. A substantial part of the workforce may have been slaves; the supply of war captives was plentiful in the centuries of the Viking raids, and Haithabu is mentioned among others as a great slave market.[27] The kingdom's military organization would most likely have been based upon the king's summons to the local aristocrats who would in turn rally their own retainers and clients among the free peasantry. But the kings were also able to extract substantial resources from their dominions, in labour services and in kind.[28]

2. CONTACTS

St Willibrord's attempt to Christianize the Danes in the early eighth century had no immediate sequel, and it was not until Frankish control over Saxony had become reasonably secure in the early ninth century that a concerted effort was undertaken. The Frankish kings interfered in the dynastic struggles in Denmark in order to gain influence on the policies of the Danish kings. Their most promising attempt in this respect was the baptism of the exiled King Harald (Klak) at Mainz in 826, followed by his reinstatement in Denmark; however, he was overthrown the following year.[29] During the following decades, the mission does not appear to have been able to gain a permanent foothold in Denmark. Yet growing Frankish influence raised hopes of converting the Danes in the near future; the creation of the archbishopric of Hamburg in the 830s as a basis for Christian missions in

---

[24] Sawyer 1988, 169–71.   [25] Sawyer 1991a, 285.   [26] Jensen 2004, 234–43, 427–40.
[27] Jankuhn 1986, 141–6.   [28] Sawyer 1991a, 285.   [29] Lund 2004b, 24–5.

Scandinavia and among the Slavs east of the Elbe must be understood in that context. These prospects suffered a severe setback when a Danish fleet destroyed Hamburg in 845;[30] Archbishop Ansgar was given the diocese of Bremen, previously a suffragan of Cologne, as a more secure base for his activities. Ansgar was nevertheless able to resume his missionary activities in Denmark after 845; but as the Frankish realm itself became increasingly disrupted by internal strife, it became an easy prey for Viking armies, probably composed of warriors from all the Scandinavian regions.[31] Missionary efforts in Scandinavia were seriously weakened, not to be resumed until the second third of the tenth century. The East Frankish king Henry the Fowler carried out a military offensive against Denmark in 934, but it is doubtful whether he was able to force the Danish king Gnupa to convert to Christianity, as later chroniclers claimed.[32] At least the expedition did not bring any lasting results. It was during the reign of Otto I that the mission finally succeeded.[33]

Despite the hagiographical nature of the sources, the ninth- and tenth-century German missions to Denmark appear to have been part and parcel of diplomatic moves to obtain peaceful relations or even alliances with Danish kings. Their relative success or failure were thus predicated on the political relationship between the two kingdoms.[34] The missionaries were sometimes allowed to found churches in the major trading centres of Jylland, Haithabu and Ribe. Some missionaries were able to bring home a number of Danish boys for Christian upbringing,[35] but apart from that it is unknown how many Danes were converted. The claim that churches were founded is corroborated by the find of an early (possibly ninth-century) church bell in the port of Haithabu,[36] but probably the churches were mostly used by visiting Christian merchants and, perhaps, by Christian captives among the slaves.

Archaeological evidence of Christian cult or belief earlier than the late tenth century is virtually non-existent. Probably Christian influence accounts in part for a general change in burial customs by the end of the ninth century, when cremation had been replaced by inhumation, mostly without grave goods, without burial mounds, and with a west–east orientation.[37] But without the presence of indisputably Christian artefacts, it is open to doubt whether this indicates widespread conversion. The tenth

---

[30] Lund 2002, 18–20.   [31] Sawyer 1988, 105–25.
[32] Widukind I.40 (at 59); Thietmar of Merseburg I.17 (at 20–2).
[33] See also Wood 2001, 123–5, 136.   [34] Cf. Lund 2002.
[35] De Sancto Willibrordo, 441–2 (Alcuin's prose Life of St Willibrord), I.9.
[36] Drescher 1984.   [37] Eisenschmidt 2004.

century saw a recrudescence of rich pagan burials with burial mounds. In the richest graves, the dead person was buried in a subterranean wooden chamber; one of these, Bjerringhøj by Mammen in Jylland, has been dated dendrochronologically to 970–1, i.e. shortly after King Harald's conversion. Some scholars assume that this type of grave, which has been found mainly in Jylland and Fyn, was a conscious and ostentatious expression of the rejection of Christianity; the type disappeared in the last decades of the tenth century.[38]

If Widukind of Corvey is to be trusted, the missionaries had achieved no more than a syncretistic acceptance of Christ as an addition to the Danish pagan pantheon in the times before Harald Bluetooth's conversion *c.* 963.[39] Possibly this should be understood simply as Widukind's harmonizing of his written sources' reports of successful Christian missions since the early ninth century and the manifest paganism of Denmark until Harald's conversion.[40] Danes participating in Viking raids on western Europe would have been subjected to missionary attempts in the regions upon which they inflicted their presence, particularly in connection with defeat or negotiated settlements. Several sources confirm, however, that baptism was considered by them as a pure formality,[41] and without being followed up by the continuing presence and teaching of missionaries, the effect on the religious beliefs and behaviour of the Vikings must have been minimal.

Contacts with religions other than Latin Christianity cannot be traced. Danes may have served in the Varangian guard of the Byzantine emperors,[42] but there are no records of Byzantine missionary attempts in Denmark. The finds of lead seals of the Byzantine *patrikios* Theodosius in the aristocratic residence at Lake Tissø and in the emporia of Ribe and Haithabu should probably be seen in a political rather than a missionary context; Theodosius visited Venice and the court of Lothar I in Trier in 840–2, and the finds of his seals in important centres of power in Denmark may indicate that he went on an otherwise unrecorded diplomatic visit to Denmark in this connection.[43]

The Arab traveller al-Tartushi visited Haithabu in the early tenth century and included a description of the emporium in his geographical work. This shows that Muslim merchants occasionally reached the western Baltic ports, possibly in connection with the slave trade, but contacts were too sporadic to have had any cultural effect.[44]

---

[38] Jensen 2004, 356–63.   [39] Widukind III.65 (at 140).   [40] Lund 2004b, 20.
[41] Sawyer 1988, 125–6.   [42] Rahbek Schmidt *et al.* 1975, cols. 537–8.
[43] Jørgensen 2002, 241–3.   [44] Jankuhn 1986, 135–6, 145.

Danes would evidently have had regular contacts with other pagan peoples around the Baltic, of which the Slavs and the Baltic and Finnish tribes had different pantheons from the Nordic one. There seem to have been some Slavic settlements on the southern Danish islands of Lolland, Falster and Møn, but'apart from some place names they left no durable cultural impact. Some of these settlements may have originated after the conversion, perhaps as late as the twelfth century. At that time, the 'Wendic' presence especially in Falster was sufficiently strong to cause serious doubts about the island's loyalty to the Danish king during the wars against the Wends under Valdemar I (1157–82).[45] Nevertheless, no syncretism between the Nordic pagan religion and Slavic beliefs is traceable.

3. CHRISTIANIZATION

The conversion of Denmark finally began with the baptism of King Harald Bluetooth a few years after his accession to the throne c. 958. The earliest account of the event is that of Widukind of Corvey, which is also the first description of the ordeal passed by the priest Poppo, whereby he convinced the pagan king of the superiority of Christ. According to Widukind, King Harald thereupon ordered his subjects to adhere to the cult of Christ alone and to abandon the pagan deities.[46] Widukind is likely to have been well informed, since he wrote almost contemporaneously with the event, finishing his chronicle c. 968.[47] The identity of the missionary Poppo has long been a subject of debate, but it has now been established that he was identical with Folkmar, close collaborator and future successor of Archbishop Bruno of Cologne.[48] The conversion is likely to have happened in 963, which is the chronological context of Widukind's account of the event.[49] This means that it occurred at a time when Archbishop Bruno was in charge of much of the German kingdom's foreign relations during Otto I's absence in Italy, and that it should be seen as part and parcel of negotiations over the tense political relationship between Germany and Denmark. At the same time it meant that Denmark was converted from Hamburg-Bremen's most dangerous rival, the metropolitan see of Cologne, which had old claims to the see of Bremen. This explains why Adam of Bremen went out of his way to obfuscate the story of Poppo's ordeal and Harald's conversion,[50]

---

[45] Housted 1994; 2002, 32; Grinder-Hansen 2002, 11–14.
[46] Widukind III.65 (at 140–1). On the complexities of the sources, Bolin 1931b, 63–112; Demidoff 1973, 39–67.
[47] Widukind, xxi–xxx.   [48] Janson 2004, 221.   [49] Widukind III.64–7 (at 139–42).
[50] Adam of Bremen II.3 (at 62–4); II.35 (at 95–6).

thereby creating material for generations of scholarly disagreement in the nineteenth and twentieth centuries.

In 965 the Emperor Otto I issued a charter of privileges in favour of the Danish bishoprics of Schleswig, Ribe and Århus.[51] The three bishops, Liafdag, Hored and Reginbrand, all had German names.[52] They had already been consecrated in 948, probably at the synod of Ingelheim,[53] but it is impossible to say whether they had been able to visit their putative dioceses before King Harald's conversion. The immediate purpose of creating the three Danish sees was probably to bolster Hamburg-Bremen's problematic status as a metropolitan see without suffragans,[54] but it is likely that the act also signalled optimism about the prospects of finally converting the Danish kingdom. Otto I's 965 charter was addressed to Archbishop Adaldag of Hamburg-Bremen, thus confirming his see's metropolitan authority over the new Danish church. According to local tradition in Ribe, known from thirteenth-century sources, the first bishop of that see, Liafdag, suffered martyrdom when preaching to the pagans in Ribe.[55] But Adam of Bremen, otherwise so keen to stress the missionary zeal of the church of Hamburg-Bremen, fails to mention this, and the tale is possibly a twelfth-century fabrication: Bishop Radulf (Ralph) of Ribe (1162–71) made an unsuccessful attempt at canonizing Liafdag; the legend may have been invented for that purpose.[56]

The course of events in Denmark over the following decades is difficult to follow. Adam of Bremen's claim that King Harald was converted as a consequence of military defeat at the hands of Otto I is spurious,[57] and the conversion should rather be understood in the context of Harald's cautious policy towards the German kingdom during the early 960s.[58] But soon the relationship between Denmark and the German kingdom deteriorated. A war between the two realms was already threatening in 968, and Harald Bluetooth strengthened the fortifications on the old border wall towards Germany, the Danevirke.[59] Hostilities broke out after Otto I's death in April 973. King Harald raided southwards the following year, but a German counter-attack resulted in the temporary loss of the southernmost part of Jylland, later called the Mark of Schleswig, including the important

[51] *MGH DO* I, no. 294 (26 June 965).
[52] Gelting 1992b, 67; Radtke 1992, 100–1; Nyborg 1992, 40–1.
[53] Fuhrmann 1964, 163–4.   [54] Gelting 2004b, 172; cf. Nilsson 2004, 12–13.
[55] *Ribe Bispekrønike* (c. 1220), 26; *Annales Sorani*, a. 1268, in *DMA*, 100.
[56] *Ribe Bispekrønike*, 29. Nielsen 1985b, 48–9, suggests that there might be some truth to Liafdag's legend; cf. also Nilsson 2005, 18–19.
[57] Adam of Bremen II.3 (at 62–4); Grund 1871.   [58] Widukind III.64 (at 139).
[59] Widukind III.70 (at 148); Andersen 1998, 13–15.

emporium of Haithabu.[60] However, modern research generally denies that the remaining parts of Harald's realm became tributary to Germany,[61] and in 983 the Danes destroyed one of the fortresses that Otto II had built against them and reconquered Haithabu.[62] The ring forts, Trelleborg in Sjælland, Nonnebakken by Odense in Fyn, and Fyrkat by Hobro and Aggersborg on the Limfjord, both in northern Jylland, as well as an impressive bridge in Ravning Enge by Vejle, also in Jylland, have been dated dendrochronologically to this period (Trelleborg to 980–1, the bridge probably to the 980s, although possibly slightly later).[63] The circular forts are spectacular for the mathematical precision of the master plan that was used for all of them.[64] Yet another ring fort has been found recently in Trelleborg in Skåne; it is likely to be contemporary with the other ring forts, but does not conform to their type in every respect.[65] The forts were no doubt connected to the tensions between Denmark and Germany in these years and were abandoned after having been in use for only a few years, but their exact purpose remains mysterious.[66]

On the greater Jelling rune-stone, Harald Bluetooth stated that he 'won all of Denmark and Norway'. The latter claim probably refers to direct possession of Viken in south-eastern Norway, which was traditionally within the Danish kings' sphere of interest, and an overlordship over the ruler of the rest of the country, Håkon Jarl.[67] As for Denmark, the original creation of bishoprics only for Jylland may indicate that the 'Jelling dynasty' in the mid-tenth century controlled only that province. A fourth see in Odense on the island of Fyn was erected at some point before 988, but there is no mention of dioceses in eastern Denmark in King Harald's time. Combined with Harald's claim on his Jelling stone that he 'won all of Denmark', this suggests that he did not extend his sway to eastern Denmark until the last years of his reign.[68] These provinces (Sjælland and Skåne) were becoming Christianized too by the end of the tenth century. An early church with a surrounding cemetery in Lund in Skåne may be dated to the early 990s. The cemetery remained in use until the mid-eleventh century; the number of burials seems out of proportion to the estimated population of the early town, which suggests that Lund served as burial place for a substantial part

---

[60] Bolin 1931a, 203–5.   [61] Christensen 1969, 232; Sawyer 1988, 224.
[62] Thietmar of Merseburg III.24 (at 112).
[63] Bonde and Christensen 1982, 145–7; Christiansen 1982, 108; Christensen 2003 questions the previous dating of the Ravning Enge bridge to 979–80.
[64] Nørlund 1948 for Trelleborg; Olsen and Schmidt 1977; and Roesdahl 1977 for Fyrkat.
[65] Jacobsson 1995, 45–59.   [66] Jensen 2004, 381–92.
[67] Moseng et al. 1999, 62–3; Sawyer 1988, 253.   [68] Bolin 1931a, 200; Lund 1991, 168–9.

of the surrounding region.[69] In Sjælland, the mighty hall at Lejre with its probable pagan cultic functions was demolished in the late tenth century, and it was succeeded *c.* 1000 by the founding of Roskilde; Roskilde from the outset probably included a royal residence and one or more churches.[70] In eastern Denmark, the shift from pagan to Christian burial customs appears not to have been complete until the early eleventh century.[71]

Harald Bluetooth's reign was brought to an abrupt end by the rebellion of his son Sven Forkbeard, probably in 987.[72] Adam of Bremen claims that the uprising was a pagan reaction against the Christian king,[73] but apart from this statement there is no evidence of an official return to paganism. What is clear is that the four suffragan bishops obeying the archbishop of Hamburg-Bremen were forced to flee. A charter of Emperor Otto III of 988 guaranteed their material support while in exile, thereby indicating that the situation was expected to be of some duration.[74] In their place King Sven relied on Anglo-Saxon missionary bishops without fixed dioceses. According to Adam only a few of Hamburg-Bremen's missionary bishops were able to operate in Denmark, perhaps even only one, Odinkar the Elder, who was a scion of the highest Danish aristocracy and probably related to the royal house.[75] King Sven's move is likely to have been motivated by political considerations: ecclesiastical dependence on the imperial see of Hamburg-Bremen might easily be interpreted as implying political subjection to the German king and emperor. The itinerant, missionary character of Sven's bishops may indicate that Christianity was still mainly an aristocratic concern, closely connected to the constantly travelling royal court.

A new diocesan structure was probably not established until early in the reign of Sven Forkbeard's son Knud (Cnut) the Great, in *c.* 1021. It seems to have consisted of four bishoprics, one for each of the main provinces: Jylland, Fyn, Sjælland and Skåne. Their bishops were consecrated by the primate of Knud's English kingdom, the archbishop of Canterbury, and paid no allegiance to Hamburg-Bremen. However, Knud may for a short time around 1030 have recognized the German metropolitan's authority in connection with negotiations with the German king Conrad II, notably solving the old dispute over the Mark of Schleswig.[76] From then on, Denmark had a stable institutional framework to support the Christian cult. It was probably also in Knud's time that Denmark obtained the privileged relationship

---

[69] Nyborg 2004, 134–5; Cinthio 2004.   [70] Christensen 2004, 196–8.   [71] Nielsen 1991, 253–5.
[72] Refskou 1985, 31–2.   [73] Adam of Bremen II.27 (at 87).   [74] *MGH DO* III, 440, no. 41.
[75] Adam of Bremen II.41 (at 101); II.49 (at 110); cf. Gelting 2004b, 174–7.
[76] For this and the following two paragraphs, Gelting 2004b, 175–87. Somewhat different account in Nilsson 2004, 14–16.

with the papacy that was symbolically expressed by the payment of Peter's pence to Rome.[77]

From 988 to the 1050s, while their authority was not recognized in Denmark, the archbishops of Hamburg-Bremen bolstered their pretensions to metropolitan power over Denmark by maintaining a succession of non-resident bishops of Schleswig. After Conrad II's waiving of his claims to the Mark of Schleswig had removed the legal basis of this fiction, the archbishops still kept a non-resident suffragan vaguely titled 'bishop of the Danes'.

Knud's autonomous Danish church on the Anglo-Saxon pattern was largely glossed over by Adam of Bremen, and surprisingly the Danish historiography that began to develop from the 1130s was almost entirely dependent on Adam's account, including his denigration of Sven Forkbeard as a pagan who was brought to believe in Christ only after suffering a series of defeats at the hands of the Slavs. The only place in Denmark where the historiographical tradition was independent of Adam of Bremen was the see of Ribe. Its short episcopal chronicle from the early thirteenth century related that the first resident bishop, Odinkar (the Younger), who was bishop in his kinsman King Knud the Great's time, left all his wealth to his church with the intention that the see should remain hereditary in his descendants. According to the chronicle he was succeeded by his son Christian. This account is likely to be essentially correct.

Harald Bluetooth claimed for himself the honour of having Christianized the Danes in his self-laudatory inscription on the stone he raised in Jelling in memory of his parents King Gorm and Thyre, and the stone carries a magnificent relief of the crucified Christ.[78] In the archaeological evidence, pagan burials seem to disappear by the end of the tenth century, but no exact date may be derived from the finds.[79] The life of the obscure Danish saint Thøger (Theodgar) recounts that he evangelized the region of Thy in northernmost Jylland after having served a Norwegian king Olav, probably Olav Tryggvason (995–1000),[80] which would imply that Thy had remained pagan until the early eleventh century. Adam of Bremen reports that two fringe areas, Blekinge in present-day southern Sweden and the island of Bornholm, were Christianized through the missionary efforts of Bishop Egino of Dalby in the 1060s;[81] however, it is uncertain whether

---

[77] Nilsson 2004, 15; Nyberg 1979, 128; Seegrün 1967, 63–4.
[78] Sawyer 2000, 158–9.   [79] Eisenschmidt 2004, 136–7.
[80] *VSD*, 14–15, 18–19. Gelting 2004b, 198, erroneously identifies the king as St Olav (d. 1030).
[81] Adam of Bremen IV.8 (at 236).

Blekinge was under Danish control at that time, and Bornholm may have remained autonomous until the late eleventh century.[82] Although Bishop Egino had his seat at the royal palace of Dalby close to Lund, he seems to have worked exclusively as a missionary outside the Danish kingdom until the death of Bishop Henry of Lund (d. 1067–71), when he succeeded the latter in Lund, and the episcopal status of Dalby was discontinued.[83] Adam's account is not necessarily inconsistent with finds of presumably Christian burial areas, characterized by the absence of grave goods and by the west–east orientation of the graves, beginning in the early eleventh century on Bornholm. Topographically such early Christian burial areas did not differ much from their pagan predecessors, and they do not seem to have been connected to church buildings. Christians and pagans may have coexisted for a couple of generations before the island came under direct Danish control.[84]

A period of uneasy coexistence of the old and the new religion is indicated by archaeological finds and by runic inscriptions. Numerous amulets in the shape of the hammer of the pagan god Thor have been found,[85] and one find of a mould for amulets in the shape both of crosses and of Thor's hammers is rather telling.[86] The inscriptions on a few rune-stones end with an invocation of Thor.[87] Just as the amulets are likely to have been a reaction against the Christian mission,[88] these inscriptions are likely to have countered Christian invocations on other rune-stones.[89] In Denmark these Christian invocations are just as rare as those of Thor; only the late rune-stones of Bornholm are an exception.[90] In a final stage, the last pockets of paganism may have been eliminated by making the right to inherit dependent on having been baptized; but since this provision survives only in late twelfth- and early thirteenth-century law texts, where it applied to children who died before baptism,[91] no certain conclusions may be drawn on this point.

---

[82] In the ninth century Blekinge was considered to belong to Sweden, and Bornholm was an independent kingdom; Lund 1991, 167. 'Guests' (*hospites*) from Bornholm were given the same rights as 'guests' from Saxony, Frisia and Iceland in the municipal laws of Schleswig (first half of the thirteenth century, but containing earlier material), suggesting the recent subjection of the island: *DGKL*, 1, Slesvig no. 1, Text I, chap. 29 (at 8).

[83] Gelting 2004b, 190–2.   [84] Wagnkilde and Pind 1996; Wagnkilde 2000.

[85] Staecker 1999, 213–44, esp. 236–9.   [86] Pedersen 2004, 66–9; Jensen 2004, 495.

[87] Moltke 1985, 224–31.   [88] Staecker 1999, 236–9, 382–92.

[89] Moltke 1985, 240–1. On problems of interpretation Øeby Nielsen 2004, 86–8; Lerche Nielsen 2004.

[90] Moltke 1985, 328–40.

[91] The earliest instance is in the 'Book of Inheritance' (*Arvebogen*), probably dating from 1169–70, chap. 53; *DGL*, vol. VII, 39. Gelting 2005, 108–15.

Archaeological traces of wooden stave churches have been found under a substantial number of Romanesque parish churches,[92] and in one case such a church, surrounded by a Christian cemetery, has been found in an eleventh-century seasonal market and artisanal site on the coast (Sebbersund on the Limfjord inlet in northern Jylland).[93] None of these buildings may be dated earlier than the very end of the tenth century, and most belong to the mid- or late eleventh century.[94] The most impressive specimen is the large wooden church built over a chamber grave between the two huge burial mounds in Jelling. According to a controversial hypothesis, the grave contained the remains of Harald Bluetooth's father King Gorm, which would thus have been transferred from his pagan burial mound, dendrochronologically dated c. 958, to a Christian grave after his son's baptism.[95] A less equivocal case of posthumous inclusion in the new faith of a deceased pagan ancestor seems to be represented by the church of Hørning by Randers (eastern Jylland), where a grave mound was razed and a Christian wooden church built in its place, so that the pagan burial – that of an aristocratic woman – was situated under the nave of the church. In this case the pagan burial was probably about a century earlier than the church.[96] Such cases are exceptional, however, and in particular there is no evidence of continuity between pagan and Christian cult sites or cemeteries.[97]

The paucity of evidence of church buildings for almost a century after King Harald's conversion raises the problem of where the Christian cult took place during this period. A possible answer would be that initially the new cult was carried out much as was its pagan predecessor, in the residential halls of the aristocracy.[98] Only from the mid-eleventh century onwards did the Christian cult obtain a separate location in specialized church buildings. The relative frequency of finds of large aristocratic farms next to early churches speaks in favour of such an hypothesis.[99] A particularly telling case is the church of Lisbjerg immediately north of Århus, where a wooden church replaced the main building of such a large aristocratic farm, sometime after the middle of the eleventh century; it is possible that

[92] Nyborg 1986, 28–33; Thaastrup-Leth 2004. Summary of early finds Møller and Olsen 1961.
[93] Nielsen 2004, 105–14; Nyborg 2004, 120–1.   [94] Thaastrup-Leth 2004, cf. Nielsen 2004, 118–19.
[95] Krogh 1993, 233–48. Against this interpretation Andersen 1988; 1995, suggesting (1995, 30–1) that the buried person might be Harald Bluetooth himself.
[96] Krogh and Voss 1961 dated the pagan grave to c. 1000, but it is more likely to be from the mid-tenth century; the wooden church was probably built shortly after the middle of the eleventh century; Roesdahl 2004, 202.
[97] Olsen 1966, esp. 275.   [98] Cf. Iceland: Jón Viðar Sigurðsson 1999, 189–90.
[99] Nyborg 1986, 28–30.

at this time the farm became the main residence of the bishop of Århus after the re-erection of the see *c.* 1059.[100]

The institutional framework for the care of souls in the eleventh century seems to have been based on a few large churches, possibly one by *herred* (a jurisdictional unit roughly comparable to the English 'hundred'), which were invested with full parish rights. Below that level, small chapels were built on some individual farms, but these 'private' chapels did not form a parochial network properly speaking.[101] The economic basis for creating a full-fledged parochial network was created by the introduction of the tithe *c.* 1100; from then on the initiative of building parish churches increasingly passed from individual aristocrats to peasant collectivities, and the ownership of the churches began to be transferred from lay to ecclesiastical hands.[102]

These considerations support the conclusion that for about a century after Harald Bluetooth's conversion, the Christianization of Denmark remained largely a royal and aristocratic affair. Thereby decapitating the old pagan cult, the conversion may have left the majority of the population in a sort of cultural limbo, nominally Christian but only tenuously connected to the new cult. The small dimensions of most of the early wooden churches would have made them more fit for a single aristocratic household than for a wider community.[103] If this was the general situation in the eleventh century, Pope Gregory VII's condemnation of Danes who accused priests of causing bad weather and disease may reflect a conflict between the common people and the aristocracy that was both cultural and social.[104] Conditions would change dramatically with the proliferation of rural parish churches from the end of the eleventh century onwards.

4. ROYAL POWER

It is difficult to assess how and to what extent the exercise of royal power in Denmark was affected by Christianization. The material basis of the kings' wealth and social power was not necessarily transformed substantially by the conversion and the ensuing gradual development of an ecclesiastical institutional apparatus. The only extant survey of the revenues of the Danish

---

[100] Jensen 2004, 298; cf. Jeppesen and Madsen 1991.
[101] Nyborg 1986, 20–30 and 43, n. 24, pointing out the similarities of this organization to the Anglo-Saxon church; Nyborg 2004, 116–17.
[102] Nyborg 1979.   [103] Nyborg 1986, 30.
[104] *DD*, ser. 1, vol. II, 42, no. 20 (19 April 1080, to King Harald Hén of Denmark). Different interpretation: Breengaard 1982, 118–20.

crown in the high Middle Ages is a late thirteenth-century miscellany, 'King Valdemar's Land Register' (*Kong Valdemars Jordebog*), which includes lists of royal properties and revenues.[105] The main list, dated 1231, shows that the king derived substantial revenues from all parts of the kingdom, some from royal manors, but most of it from taxation.[106] This taxation is unlikely to have been a recent innovation,[107] a conclusion supported by the high level of organization and the ability to mobilize the kingdom's resources during the last pre-Christian centuries. The standard formula for the king's public revenue in early Danish royal charters mirrors that of the German kings, and the high medieval unit of evaluation of landed property, *bol*, is also semantically and structurally closely akin to the Carolingian *mansus*. There is no convincing reason for assuming that the Danish kings were unable to copy such profitable institutions before Christianization.[108]

On the ideological level, however, it is evident that Christianization had momentous consequences for conceptions of kingship in Denmark. Royal charters are the main source for reconstructing Danish royal ideology in the twelfth century. They show a conception of monarchy that was closely patterned on European models, emphasizing the king's obligations to preserve internal peace and uphold justice, besides his duty to protect and support the Church. From the beginning of the sole reign of Valdemar I (1157–82), the divine origin of the king's office and power was stressed, at the same time as the charters became strongly influenced by biblical language. In addition, the wording of papal privileges seems to have been used as a source of inspiration for the preambles of the charters of the Valdemarian kings, while there is no traceable influence from the diplomatic style of the imperial chancery.[109]

This new emphasis on the divine authority behind the king's office may give credence to the allegation of the *Continuation of the Chronicle of Roskilde* that Valdemar I was anointed and crowned by Archbishop Eskil in 1157.[110] At least it is certain that Danish kings were crowned with religious ceremonial from the accession of Knud VI as co-regent in 1170 onwards.[111]

The latter event was staged in connection with the translation of Valdemar I's father Knud Lavard (d. 1131), who had just been canonized by the pope. This raises the question of the function of royal saints in Danish royal ideology. One king, Knud IV (1080–6), and the father of another,

---

[105] Edited in *Kong Valdemars Jordebog*; cf. Rasmussen 1975. On the manuscript and its history Kroman 1936.
[106] Ulsig 1991, 66–72; Venge 2002, 48–61.   [107] Ulsig 1981, 159.
[108] Sawyer 1991a, 285; Venge 2002, 46–8, 62–4.   [109] Damsholt 1970, 99–107; Riis 1977, 83–5.
[110] *SM*, vol. I, 33.   [111] Beskow and Swensen 1964, col. 499.

Knud Lavard, were canonized during Denmark's first Christian centuries. In the case of the former, it is likely that the canonization was aimed at stigmatizing regicide and, by implication, rebellion against royal authority, as sacrilege. At the same time, Knud IV's policies were described as carrying out in practice an ecclesiastical policy of peace and protection of the poor and oppressed, including the Church.[112] The canonization of Knud Lavard is more likely to have been designed to enhance the prestige of Knud's descendants, King Valdemar I and his sons, thereby de-legitimizing rival branches of the royal house.[113]

Thus the canonization of the two royal saints should be understood in the context of a policy aimed at providing kingship with a sacred aura that would place the king outside the reach of the dynastic and social struggles that had cost so many Danish kings their lives, both in the twelfth century and earlier. This policy seems to have been pursued fairly consistently by the Danish church and kings in cooperation during the twelfth century.[114] There is no positive evidence of any connection between these canonizations and hypothetical sub-pagan notions of sacral kingship or *Königsheil*. However, when Saxo heaped ridicule at German women and peasants believing in the beneficial effects of the 'royal touch' from Valdemar I, it may have been intended as an oblique criticism of similar beliefs in Denmark.[115]

Danish kings took an active interest in the crusades. In practice, however, this interest was largely shaped by the kings' territorial ambitions. The only Danish king who undertook an expedition to the Holy Land in this period was Erik I (1095–1103/4), whose pilgrimage in 1103 was closely connected with his negotiations with the pope for a Danish metropolitan see.[116] Otherwise, even though the kings approved of aristocratic participation in the crusades, their personal involvement was concentrated on fighting and subjugating the pagan peoples on the southern and eastern coasts of the Baltic, in a problematic and tense partnership with similar endeavours by German lay and ecclesiastical princes. This enabled Valdemar I and Knud VI to establish Danish overlordship over Rügen and Pomerania during the years from 1168 to 1185, although only Rügen remained after the breakdown of the Valdemarian Baltic empire in the 1220s.[117] Lordship over northern Estonia, which was established with some difficulty in the early thirteenth century, was upheld until the mid-fourteenth century.[118]

---

[112] Breengaard 1982, 122–49.   [113] Skyum-Nielsen 1971, 182–3.   [114] Breengaard 1982.
[115] Saxo XIV.28.13 (vol. II, 306).   [116] Lind *et al.* 2004, 26–8; Breengaard 1982, 170–80.
[117] Lind *et al.* 2004, 29–91; Gaethke 1999, esp. 347–93; Skyum-Nielsen 1971, 291.
[118] Lind *et al.* 2004, 199–231, 323–33.

The integration of the Danish monarchy into western Christendom also widened the potential scope of the kings' marital alliances, while such alliances with traditional partners in the nearby Wendish area became impossible as long as they remained pagan. The most signal recognition of the Danish king as an equal of the foremost European rulers was the marriage between King Philip Augustus of France and Valdemar I's daughter Ingeborg in 1193, although the marriage turned into a protracted scandal, as on the day after the wedding Philip demanded a divorce.[119]

Nothing has survived of the Danish royal treasure of the first Christian centuries, and the only direct evidence for the signs and symbols of Christian monarchy consists of the few royal seals that are known from the period.[120] The earliest royal seal is that of King Knud IV, known from seventeenth-century drawings from the king's 1085 charter for Lund cathedral. The king is represented enthroned on the obverse, while the reverse shows him as a falconer on horseback; the legend's artful Latin attests to the presence of well-educated clerics at the royal court.[121] Twelfth-century royal seals followed the usual European pattern of showing the king enthroned; the reverse of Erik III's seal represented him as a lance-wielding warrior on horseback. The royal coat of arms with three lions/leopards rampant is known from *c.* 1194 onwards. It may have been adopted as an implicit reference to the heraldic lion of the Welf dukes of Saxony, as a marker of independence from the Staufen emperors.[122]

From the reign of Sven Forkbeard onwards, kings were also represented on coins; however, the close imitation of foreign coinage makes it difficult to assess the extent to which these pictures may be used as sources for the symbols of specifically Danish monarchy. Sven Forkbeard's coinage followed the Anglo-Saxon pattern, and this was continued during the reign of his son Knud the Great (1018–35), who was king of England (from 1017) as well as of Denmark. However, a rebellion *c.* 1026, during which Knud's son Hardeknud (Harthacnut, king 1035–42) became co-regent, seems to have resulted in a loosening of the connections between the coinages of the two realms.[123] A coin of Hardeknud carries letters that may be expanded into *REX-LEX-LUX-PAX*, indicating that the Christian ideal of the king as upholder of law, the Christian faith and peace had by then become the official ideology of Danish kingship.[124] With the break-up of Knud's North Sea empire, continental models came to dominate the motifs of Danish coinage from Sven Estridson onwards. During Hardeknud's and

[119] Skyum-Nielsen 1971, 235–9.   [120] Petersen 1917, I, nos. 1–5, and pl. 1; Riis 1977, 152–65.
[121] *DD*, ser. I, vol. II, 43–52, no. 21 (21 May 1085).   [122] Bartholdy 1984.
[123] Jensen 1995, 11–12, 22, 36.   [124] Carelli 2001, 212, with different emphasis.

Sven Estridson's reigns a number of coin types were patterned on Byzantine coinage.[125] A peculiar feature of Sven Estridson's minting was the use of runes for the legend of a number of coins.[126]

The coinage of King Niels (Nicholas, 1104–34) includes some remarkable types: one carries the names both of the king and of his queen, Margrethe (Margaret), possibly indicating that Margrethe held a share in the mint as part of her dowry,[127] while another displays the legend *PAX POR[TV]*, literally 'harbour-peace'.[128] The latter might indicate that the coinage was intended for buying the king's peace upon the merchant's arrival to a Danish port or town; in any case it refers ideologically to the king's function as upholder of the peace.[129]

Apart from seals and coins, pictorial representations of Danish kings from the early Christian centuries are essentially restricted to paintings of royal donors in twelfth-century churches. In the church of the Premonstratensian abbey of Vä in Skåne, the most magnificent painted space to have survived from twelfth-century Denmark, a king and a queen, possibly King Niels and Queen Margrethe, are depicted as donors.[130] A damaged early thirteenth-century capital from the church of Dalby in Skåne shows two crowned men, both holding the hilt of a sword that is placed between them. One of them is named in an accompanying legend as *HEINRICVS IMPERATOR*. It is usually assumed that the two men are the Emperor Henry IV and King Sven Estridson,[131] but there is no record of Sven Estridson having considered himself as the German king-emperor's vassal, and even if he had been, it does not seem particularly likely that anybody should have wished to commemorate it in the heyday of the Valdemarian kings.[132] It might conceivably represent the Emperor Henry VI (1190–7), and the king would then be Knud VI. In that case it might suggest that the army Knud VI led to Estonia in 1197 was somehow a joint venture on the emperor's behalf.[133]

No funerary monuments of Danish kings have survived from the time span between Harald Bluetooth's Jelling stone and the second half of the thirteenth century, and the exact burial place of several of the Danish monarchs from the late eleventh to the middle of the twelfth century is

[125] Jensen 1995, 66–7, 80–1. [126] Jensen 1995, 82–5; Nielsen in Page and Nielsen 2003, 552–5.
[127] Cf. coin types with the image of the king and a bishop: Skyum-Nielsen 1971, 171–2; cf. Jensen 1995, 116.
[128] Hauberg 1900, 58 and 230 (*PAX POR* type); 59 and 230 (Margrethe type); Nyborg 2004, 160 and 180, n. 149.
[129] Skyum-Nielsen 1971, 46–7; cf. Carelli 2001, 128–9. [130] Banning 1976–82, vol. IV, 9–11.
[131] Cinthio 1992. [132] Nyborg forthcoming.
[133] *Annales Lundenses*, 1197 (*DMA*, 60), cf. Lind *et al.* 2004, 149 and 169; Heinrich of Latvia, I.11 (at 8).

unknown. When the cathedral of Roskilde was rebuilt, the remains of King Sven Estridson and of a Queen Margrethe *alias* Estrid (probably King Niels's spouse, daughter of King Inge of Sweden[134]) were transferred to secondary graves in walled-up recesses in the pillars of the choir of the new building, probably *c.* 1225. A third wall-grave was alleged to contain the remains of Harald Bluetooth, but while Sven's and Estrid's skeletons could be extracted for analysis in the late nineteenth century, Harald's presumed pillar grave turned out to be empty; probably Adam of Bremen's allegation of his burial in Roskilde was spurious.[135] From Valdemar I until the end of the thirteenth century, the Danish kings and their family were buried in the abbey church of Ringsted, which was the centre of the cult of Valdemar's father Knud Lavard (St Canute *dux*). Valdemar I was buried with a lead plaque whose inscription enumerated the principal achievements of his reign,[136] but nothing has survived of any grave slabs or monuments that might have commemorated the kings above ground, except for wall paintings in memory of some of the thirteenth-century rulers who were entombed in the church.[137]

A new feature of Danish society in the high Middle Ages that was closely connected to royal power was the creation of a network of royal towns. Pre-Christian Denmark had few towns, all of them located in Jylland, and all of them under royal control. From the late tenth century onwards, however, new towns began to be founded: the first of them to take off seems to be Lund in Skåne. It appears to have originated as a royal residence and a religious centre rather than as a mercantile community. In the second half of the eleventh century the settlement pattern of Lund changed, and it developed into a commercial and artisanal centre.[138] A similar origin may be guessed at in the case of the other new episcopal cities of the late tenth and eleventh centuries: Viborg, Odense and Roskilde,[139] and probably also Schleswig on the north side of the Schlei.[140]

Royal control of long-distance trade is also evidenced in the foundation of a kingdom-wide network of merchant guilds devoted to St Canute (*Skt. Knudsgilder*) under the sponsorship and protection of the king. Probably the guild network originated in 1170, in connection with Knud Lavard's canonization in 1169.[141]

[134] Kruse 2004, 14.   [135] Lund 1998.   [136] Worsaae 1856, 5–20.
[137] *DK*, vol. V.1, 137–47 (wall paintings), 162–4 (royal burials).
[138] Carelli 2001, 106–18; Blomqvist 1951, 33–4.
[139] Krongaard Kristensen 1998, 349–54; Christensen 1988, 129–30; Christensen 2004, 196–8.
[140] Radtke 1995, 47–59; cf. Jankuhn 1986, 223.   [141] Anz 1998, 185–95, 235–44.

In tandem with these transformations, a royal administration evolved. It is likely that the age of the North Sea empire of Knud the Great and his sons (*c.* 1018–42) saw the introduction of administrative structures inspired by Knud's Anglo-Saxon kingdom, but apart from coinage, nothing is known thereof. A few royal writs have survived from the reign of King Erik III (1137–46),[142] but it is impossible to tell whether they reflect a tradition dating back to Knud's reign or later influence from Anglo-Norman England. At the central level, the king was assisted by lay dignitaries carrying the title of *staller* (*stabularii*), who may have had positions of authority in the king's military household, but who seem also to have been detached to carry out functions in local administration; they are mentioned from 1085.[143] A chamberlain (*camerarius*) is mentioned early in the reign of King Niels, indicating an incipient specialization of the financial administration.[144] For writing, the king relied upon his chaplains, one of whom carried the title of royal notary.[145] Valdemar I reformed royal administration after 1157 with the help of his Anglo-Norman chancellor, Radulf.[146]

In the eleventh and the first half of the twelfth century, vast regional commands seem to have been entrusted to powerful *jarls* (earls) who were frequently kinsmen of the king, but the exact nature of their functions is unknown.[147] The disappearance of these regional powers in the second half of the twelfth century must have entailed a restructuring of royal representation on the local and regional level. Scattered mentions in earlier sources show that royal officers on the local level, *villici* (*bryder*), were already in existence by the beginning of the twelfth century.[148] According to the early thirteenth-century law books the king had a representative, *ombudsmand*, in each hundred, whose functions included overseeing judicial procedures in the hundred courts.[149]

At the same time, the physical appearance of the sites of royal representation was changing. Eleventh- and early twelfth-century royal and aristocratic residences continued the Viking Age tradition of large, unfortified compounds. After conversion, a church became a frequent element in these compounds; in some instances, such as Dalby near Lund, inspiration from Ottonian and Salian *Pfalz* structures may be discerned.[150] The stimulus to

---

[142] *DD*, ser. 1, vol. II, 137–40, no. 71 (undated); 153–4, no. 79 ((1140) *c.* 7 April); 160, no. 85 (1142–6).
[143] Skyum-Nielsen 1971, 8, 39, 175.
[144] *DD*, ser. 1, vol. II, 76, no. 32 (1104–17); Skyum-Nielsen 1971, 39; Venge 2002, 40–1; but reservations: Hermanson 2000, 65–7.
[145] *DD*, 176, no. 91 (1145 *c.* 1 September).   [146] Gelting 1992b, 73.
[147] Hermanson 2000, 80–8.   [148] Skyum-Nielsen 1971, 178–80; Venge 2002, 41–6.
[149] Skyum-Nielsen 1971, 297–8.   [150] Cinthio 1983; 1966.

building castles on a European model appears to have been the protracted civil wars from 1131 to 1157.[151] The Chronicle of the bishops of Ribe explicitly states that Bishop Helias (1142–62) was the first to fortify the episcopal manors.[152] Most of these structures were earthworks with wooden defences, but some castles were built in stone, such as the formidable Bastrup tower in Sjælland, probably built by Archbishop Absalon's uncle Ebbe Skjalmson, and Absalon's own castle of Havn (København/Copenhagen). The construction of these castles frequently entailed the desertion of earlier 'open' residences. This is particularly clear in the case of Hjulby in Fyn: this apparently unfortified aristocratic site reaching back to the seventh century[153] was still an important royal residence in the early 1180s;[154] by 1193 it had been replaced by a royal castle on the coast, significantly called Nyborg ('Newcastle').[155] The new fortified residences were not a royal monopoly; they were built as well by the highest lay and ecclesiastical aristocracy. But castles were mainly built in strategic locations on the coasts, and unfortified royal and aristocratic residences remained the rule well into the thirteenth century.[156]

5. THE EFFECTS OF CHRISTIANIZATION

The end of the dynastic union between Denmark and England in 1042 cut off the Danish church from access to an archiepiscopal see within the realms of the Danish king. In the long run this made it impossible to ignore Hamburg-Bremen's claim to metropolitan authority over Denmark, especially since this claim was reinforced by new papal privileges at this time. During the 1050s King Sven Estridson reached an understanding with Archbishop Adalbert of Hamburg-Bremen. The Danish church recognized Hamburg-Bremen as its metropolitan see, and in return the number of Danish dioceses was augmented, probably in 1059:[157] the see of Schleswig, which had hitherto existed only in name, its titular bishops serving as coadjutors in various German dioceses, was re-established; and the large Jutish diocese was split into four: Ribe, Århus, Viborg and the diocese of Wendila for the islands north of the Limfjord inlet. Wendila was not named after the site of a cathedral, but after a province, which was at variance with the rule that a bishop should reside in a city (*civitas*). It probably indicates

[151] On Danish twelfth-century castles Olsen 1996, 28–46.
[152] *Ribe Bispekrønike*, 28.   [153] Henriksen 2003.
[154] *DD*, ser. 1, vol. III, 132–5, no. 89 (6 February 1180), and 172–6, no. 111 (21 March 1183).
[155] *DD*, ser. 1, vol. III, 205–7, no. 189 (22 January 1193).
[156] Olsen 1996, 42–3, cf. 28–9.   [157] Gelting 2004b, 187–92.

that the territory of the new diocese as yet lacked important urban centres. Between 1086 and 1103 the bishop obtained the royal manor of Børglum as his residence.[158] For a short while there was also a bishop in Dalby close to Lund in Skåne, but this seems to have been an interim arrangement until the incumbent bishop of Lund should die; as soon as that happened, the bishop of Dalby took over the see of Lund, and Dalby was converted into an Augustinian priory.[159]

Sven Estridson's plan was to create a separate Danish ecclesiastical province, and after having obtained the desired new episcopal sees, the Danish church's contacts with Hamburg-Bremen were reduced to a bare minimum.[160] Archbishop Adalbert tried to counter King Sven's plan by obtaining the patriarchal title for Hamburg-Bremen with authority over the Scandinavian churches.[161] Although King Sven's advances in Rome were supported by the powerful Cardinal Hildebrand,[162] when the latter had become pope as Gregory VII (1073–85), the outbreak of his conflict with the Emperor Henry IV soon made it impossible to carry on with the plans.[163] It was not until 1103 that renewed direct negotiations between the Danish king Erik I and the papacy resulted in the creation of a Danish archbishopric with authority also over the churches in Sweden, Iceland and, at least in theory, in Norway.[164] The new metropolitan see was placed in Lund, which seems to have been favoured by Sven Estridson's sons, while King Sven appears to have planned for making Roskilde the archiepiscopal see.[165] By this act, Denmark's ecclesiastical structures had been established as they were to remain until the Protestant Reformation. Nevertheless, the archbishops of Hamburg-Bremen during the twelfth century repeatedly sought to effect the abolition of the Danish metropolitan see, and even succeeded for a short while in the 1130s; the threat from Hamburg-Bremen did not finally dissolve until the 1160s.[166] Lund's authority over Norway and Sweden was lost with the creation of separate ecclesiastical provinces in those kingdoms in the 1150s, although the archbishop of Lund retained the status of primate of Sweden.[167] In the later twelfth and early thirteenth centuries the archbishops of Lund also had the status of permanent papal legates for Denmark and Sweden. This is likely to have been a product of the popes' intention to use them as mainstays of the efforts to convert

[158] Gelting 1992a, 46–7; Nyberg 1986, 79–89.   [159] Gelting 2004b, 190–2.
[160] Gelting 2004b, 192–3.   [161] Fuhrmann 1955.
[162] *DD*, ser. I, vol. II, 21–4, no. 11.   [163] On papal–Danish relations Nilsson 2004, 20–5.
[164] *DD*, ser. I, vol. II, 62–7, nos. 28–30; Seegrün 1967, 122–4.   [165] Skovgaard-Petersen 1988.
[166] Seegrün 1967, 133–42; Breengaard 1982, 211–23, 237–9, 276–86; Gelting 2004a, 184–97, 214–23.
[167] Seegrün 1967, 146–99.

the pagan peoples of the eastern Baltic. After that function had passed to the newly created archbishopric of Riga, the legatine status of the Danish archbishops lapsed.[168] With the conquest of the Slavic island of Rügen on the southern side of the Baltic in 1168, that island was added to the diocese of Roskilde, although not without some wrangling with the Emperor Frederick Barbarossa and Duke Henry the Lion.[169] The Danish subjugation of northern Estonia in the early thirteenth century entailed the creation of a new diocese in Tallinn (Reval) under the metropolitan authority of Lund.[170]

The bishops were originally appointed by the king, but apparently the Danish kings' status as vassals of the German king from 1131 onwards also meant that the Concordat of Worms was applied in Denmark; the first canonical election of a bishop is recorded in 1137. In practice, however, the king retained a paramount influence upon episcopal elections.[171]

The consolidation of the institutional structures of the Danish church introduced an entirely new social group, the clergy. During the first century or so after Harald Bluetooth's conversion archaeological evidence suggests that the priesthood must have been entirely dependent upon the lay aristocracy and not very numerous. According to the letters of Gregory VII, priests were still looked upon with suspicion or even hostility by the people.[172]

This situation changed as the number of local churches steadily grew during the late eleventh and the twelfth centuries. Adam of Bremen gives rough numbers for each of the major Danish provinces at the time of his writing in the 1070s: 300 in Skåne, 150 in Sjælland, 100 in Fyn; no number is provided for Jylland.[173] Even this modest number was no doubt the result of recent growth. By the end of the following century, it had probably trebled, an expansion linked to the introduction of the tithe. This seems to have occurred c. 1100, but not without difficulties. While the laity accepted to pay the tithe for the church building and to the parish priest, they were reluctant to pay it to the bishop. In the dioceses of Lund, Roskilde and Schleswig the full bishop's tithe was accepted through various compromises in the later twelfth century, but in the rest of Jylland the matter of the bishop's tithe was not settled until the early sixteenth century.[174] The introduction of the tithe must have implied the delimitation of each parish, and during the twelfth and thirteenth centuries the Danish parish network was completed.

Separate ecclesiastical jurisdiction was not fully introduced until the first quarter of the twelfth century. The *Chronicle of Roskilde* states that it

---

[168] Perron 2003.   [169] Gaethke 1999, 347–93.   [170] Christiansen 1997, 109–13; Riis 2003, 65–73.
[171] Gelting 2004a, 189–92.   [172] Breengaard 1982, 118–22.
[173] Adam of Bremen IV.7 (at 235).   [174] Hamre *et al.* 1974, cols. 291–5.

was introduced as a consequence of laymen persecuting married priests in
Sjælland in *c.* 1123–4; an event that in itself shows that by then Denmark was
well integrated into the Latin church, since it can hardly be a coincidence
that it occurred immediately after the First Lateran Council's call for the
enforcement of clerical celibacy.[175] The privilege must have become a general phenomenon by the mid-twelfth century. The procedural forms of the
ecclesiastical courts appear to have caused dissatisfaction among the laity,
and *c.* 1171 a compromise was reached on approximately the same terms
in the dioceses of Lund and Roskilde. The two bishops made a number
of concessions to bring practice in their ecclesiastical courts in line with
the customs of the lay courts by admitting legal proof by ordeal and by
co-jurors; the financial demands of the bishop were also regulated, and
the church owners' right to present priests to parochial benefices was confirmed.[176] In return, the lay community of the diocese agreed to pay the full
bishop's tithe, which they had hitherto refused. The resultant texts, called
the Ecclesiastical Law of Skåne and Sjælland, respectively, are written in
Danish and represent an interesting case of the modification of canon law
to suit local conditions.[177] There is no reason to suppose that similar texts
existed in the rest of the Danish dioceses.

There is no evidence for the foundation of monastic houses during the
first century or so after Harald Bluetooth's conversion. Possibly the structures of power and property in Danish rural society made it difficult to
establish the kind of large-scale estates with tenant farmers that would normally support such institutions. Chapters were founded at the cathedrals
of Roskilde and Lund in the early 1070s and *c.* 1085, respectively,[178] and
the first Benedictine monasteries were founded at about the same time.[179]
A house of Augustinian canons was instituted at the formerly episcopal
church of Dalby in Skåne *c.* 1070.[180] The great surge of monastic foundations, however, did not come until the twelfth century. Benedictine houses
continued to be founded well into the twelfth century, one of the most
important foundations being St Peter's of Næstved in Sjælland, created by
the aristocrat Peder (Peter) Bodilson and his brothers in 1135.[181]

Shortly afterwards, the new reforming orders came into favour. The first
Cistercian abbey was founded at Herrisvad in Skåne by monks from Cîteaux

---

[175] *SM*, vol. I, 26.   [176] Nyborg 1979.
[177] *DGL*, vol. I.2, 821–67 (Skåne); vol. VIII, 445–57 (Sjælland). Cf. Gallén and Iuul 1965, cols. 5–6.
[178] Roskilde: Arhnung 1937, 4–7. Lund: Weibull 1946, 26–8.
[179] Nyberg 2000, 36–67; his attempts (32–5) to date two Benedictine monasteries to the early eleventh
century remain unconvincing.
[180] Nyberg 2000, 44–6.   [181] Hill 1992, 183–93.

in 1144, and many more had followed by the end of the century. Several of the Cistercian abbeys had originally been founded as Benedictine houses and were thus established through reform rather than as new foundations. During the period of Danish overlordship on the southern Baltic coast in the late twelfth century, daughter houses in Pomerania (Colbaz, Dargun and Eldena) were founded from the Cistercian abbey of Esrom in Sjælland, as well as the Cistercian nunnery of Bergen in Rügen, whose mother house was the nunnery of Roskilde.[182] The Premonstratensians probably also made their first entry into Denmark in Skåne, at Tommarp, where a Premonstratensian house was founded in 1155.[183] The Premonstratensians, too, participated in the Danish monastic colonization of Pomerania with the short-lived foundation of Belbuck in 1177.[184] An attempt to introduce the Carthusian order at Asserbo in Sjælland in the 1160s failed, perhaps because of insufficient endowment of the abbey.[185] Archbishop Eskil has traditionally been credited with a paramount role in the introduction of the new orders, but it has been shown that his role has been exaggerated, and that royal patronage was probably more important.[186]

The twelfth century also witnessed the foundation of cathedral chapters at the rest of the Danish sees, beginning with Odense shortly before 1100, unusually founded as a Benedictine house staffed by monks from the English abbey of Evesham,[187] and ending with Århus in 1197.[188] The Benedictine chapter at Odense is testimony to the continuing connections between the Danish church and England, maintaining its fraternity with the English abbey throughout the twelfth century.[189] On the other hand, the second regular cathedral chapter in Denmark, the Premonstratensian house of Børglum in northern Jylland, was founded from Steinfeld in Germany in the mid-twelfth century.[190] Intermediary agents of the bishop in the supervision of the parish churches, titled *prepositi*, are first mentioned in 1140. Their functions at this early stage cannot be determined precisely.[191]

Only one of the military orders, the Knights of St John of Jerusalem, established itself in Denmark. Its house at Antvorskov in Sjælland seems to have been in existence by the 1160s.[192] This might conceivably indicate that

---

[182] McGuire 1982, 37–87.   [183] Skyum-Nielsen 1971, 125–8.   [184] Skyum-Nielsen 1971, 187–8.
[185] Skyum-Nielsen 1971, 128.   [186] Green-Pedersen 1981.
[187] Nyberg 2000, 55–6, dating its founding to 1095. The date can hardly be determined more precisely than 1095–1100; *DD*, ser. 1, vol. II, 55, no. 24.
[188] *DD*, ser. 1, vol. III, 350–1, no. 221.   [189] *DD*, ser. 1, vol. III, 271–3, no. 171 (1191–1205).
[190] The foundation cannot be dated more precisely than before 1178; Skyum-Nielsen 1971, 127–8. However, Nyberg 1986, 79–110, argues from circumstantial evidence that it may have taken place as early as 1139–42.
[191] Dahlerup 1968, 27–37.   [192] Skyum-Nielsen 1971, 128–9.

its foundation was the result of a reorganization, according to an approved rule, of a religious guild created by a certain Wetheman from Roskilde in the early 1150s. This guild of sea-warriors combined fighting against the pagan Wends with pious exercises, and its customs – reported by Saxo Grammaticus – may reflect influence from similar forms of organization on the Christian borders with Muslim Spain.[193]

Denmark participated actively in the crusading movement from the beginning. According to German sources, Sven, one of King Sven Estridson's numerous sons, met his death together with two Danish bishops in Anatolia while on their way to join the crusaders in Jerusalem c. 1101.[194] Large-scale Danish involvement came with the Second Crusade, when warfare against Muslims in Spain and against pagans in the Baltic was formally defined as equally meritorious as expeditions to the Holy Land. In 1147, the rival Danish kings Sven and Knud shelved their enmity for a time in order to join the German crusading expedition against the pagan Slavs.[195] That expedition did not bring substantial gains, but the crusading drive was maintained and finally resulted in the Danish conquest of Rügen in 1168. An attempt by a group of Danish aristocrats to join the Third Crusade ended in disaster.[196]

Remarkably, almost no missionary saints were venerated in medieval Denmark. It was probably for political reasons that there was no important cult of the German missionary saints who visited Denmark during pagan times, notably St Ansgar, the first archbishop of Hamburg,[197] but the lack of indigenous saints from the conversion period is puzzling. It is possible that attempts were made to turn Harald Bluetooth into a missionary royal saint, but if so, nothing came of it.[198] A series of gilded copper plates from c. 1200 from the large and early stone church at Tamdrup in Jylland represents scenes from Harald's conversion, including Poppo's ordeal. They must originally have formed part of an altar or, perhaps more likely, a reliquary.[199] But if this indicates an early cult of either Poppo or Harald at the church, it has not left any trace in the written evidence. By the end of the twelfth century, Harald had ceased to be the ideal convert depicted by Adam of Bremen; both the chronicler Sven Aggeson and Abbot William of Æbelholt thought that he had apostatized towards the end of his life, while his son Sven Forkbeard was credited with carrying through the

---

[193] Møller Jensen 2000, 314–23.   [194] Møller Jensen 2000, 294–9.
[195] Lind et al. 2004, 51–65; cf. Gaethke 1999, 97.
[196] De profectione Danorum in Hierosolymam, SM, vol. II, 443–92; cf. Skovgaard-Petersen 2001.
[197] Jørgensen 1909, 9; Gad 1961, 185.   [198] Sawyer 1988, 245.
[199] DK, vol. XVI.9.52, 5043–6, 5113–35.

Christianization of Denmark.[200] This shift, too, may have had something to do with the desire to minimize Hamburg-Bremen's part in the conversion that is evident in Danish historical writing of the twelfth century. An attempt in the 1160s to canonize the first bishop of Ribe, Liafdag, on the basis of the probably spurious legend of his martyrdom, failed as the relics were destroyed in a fire in the cathedral.[201] The only missionary saint to be officially recognized was finally St Thøger (Theodgar) of Vestervig, whose sanctity was confirmed by the local bishop after an ordeal, probably in the 1060s;[202] his cult does not seem to have reached far beyond the region of Thy.[203]

While the majority of the saints venerated in medieval Denmark belong to the general stock of the standard martyrologies, a few elements may be singled out that point to influences active in the first Christian centuries in Denmark. Runic inscriptions indicate that the Archangel Michael enjoyed particular favour in the conversion period;[204] generally speaking, in the first Christian centuries in Denmark, as in the rest of Scandinavia, saints seem to have been valued as powerful allies, healers and miracle-workers rather than as models of Christian virtue.[205] Due to the influence of Anglo-Saxon missionaries and churchmen, a number of insular saints continued to be venerated in Denmark. The most widespread of these, at least by counting the number of church dedications, was apparently the East Anglian St Botolph, and he remained honoured by a major feast day in the Danish liturgy throughout the Middle Ages.[206] St Alban was also included in the liturgy of all the Danish dioceses until the Reformation; a St Alban's church existed in Odense in 1086. Other Anglo-Saxon saints occur more sporadically. Most of these saints may be assumed to have been introduced during the period of close connections between the Danish and the Anglo-Saxon church in the first half of the eleventh century, but later influences cannot be excluded; thus the inclusion of St Egwin, the founder of Evesham abbey, in the litany of Odense was doubtless due to the monks who were invited from that abbey in the late 1090s.[207] Continuing close connections between Denmark and England in the later twelfth century are witnessed by the swift introduction of the cult of St Thomas Becket, notably commemorated by a series of reliefs on a Romanesque baptismal font in the church of Lyngsjö in Skåne.[208] The persistence of the English influence is also witnessed by the late thirteenth-century martyrology of

---

[200] Christensen 1975, 131–2.   [201] *Ribe Bispekrønike*, 29.   [202] *VSD*, 15–16. Gelting 1992a, 49 n. 40.
[203] Jørgensen 1909, 53–4.   [204] Jørgensen 1909, 6–8; Gad *et al.* 1966, cols. 617–19.
[205] Nilsson 2005, 18–24.   [206] Jørgensen 1909, 17; Jørgensen 1908, 204–5; Odenius 1957.
[207] Jørgensen 1909, 17–19.   [208] Bekker-Nielsen *et al.* 1974, cols. 245–6.

Ribe, which must have been ultimately copied from a model from New Minster in Winchester.[209] It is quite likely that the use of this martyrological tradition dated from the time of Knud the Great; Bishop Odinkar of Ribe (*c.* 1029/32–1043?) was partly educated in England.[210]

The reorganization of the Danish church *c.* 1059 brought a strong influence from the metropolitan see of Bremen, and from Germany in general. The martyrology of Lund, probably written in 1137–8,[211] was based on a model derived from the Carolingian martyrology of Ado. The most recent contribution to the martyrology was Bishop Godehard of Hildesheim, canonized in 1131, which suggests that the martyrology was derived from a German model.[212] Another Lund manuscript from the mid-twelfth century, later brought to the Cistercian abbey of Colbaz in Pomerania, has a calendar whose composition points specifically towards a Benedictine model from the diocese of Freising in southern Germany; it has been suggested that this model might have been brought to Denmark by the future Archbishop Eskil, who was educated in Hildesheim.[213]

Centred on the cathedral of Viborg, the cult of St Willehad was quite popular in Jylland. Viborg had relics of the saint, and early modern sources mention a medieval collection of his miracles, now lost, that was kept there. Willehad, who was especially connected to Bremen, was a missionary saint, but he never evangelized in Denmark; it is likely that his cult was introduced by the first bishop of Viborg, Heribert, who came from Bremen.[214]

During the twelfth century, the obscure St Thøger was joined by a number of more famous native saints. The friendly relationship between Denmark and the papacy that obtained for the last half of the eleventh and most of the twelfth century meant that papal canonization became a rule unusually early, the first instance being St Canute *rex* (King Knud IV, 1080–6), canonized by the pope *c.* 1100.[215] Significantly, the destruction of the relics of Bishop Liafdag of Ribe was apparently understood as a punishment of the initiator of the canonization, Bishop Radulf (1162–71), for not having obtained archiepiscopal and papal authorization of the putative saint.[216] It is symptomatic that it was felt necessary to include a papal authorization of the canonization of St Thøger in his legend; as his canonization otherwise appears in the text as a traditional process conducted by the local bishop, this is likely to be a later interpolation.[217]

---

[209] Jørgensen 1908, 200–1. [210] Gelting 2004b, 175.
[211] Gelting 2004a, 202–14, questioning the generally accepted date of 1145.
[212] Weeke 1884–9, VI–VII; cf. Jørgensen 1908, 201. [213] Jørgensen 1908, 201–2.
[214] Jørgensen 1909, 9–10; Gelting 1992c, 119. [215] Breengaard 1982, 162–70; Gad 1963b, cols. 596–7.
[216] *Ribe Bispekrønike*, 29. [217] Nielsen 1985a, 4–5.

Other officially recognized saints of the period were St Canute *dux* (King Valdemar I's father Knud Lavard, duke of Schleswig, murdered 1131, canonized 1169),[218] the provost of the cathedral chapter of Viborg St Kjeld (*Ketillus*, d. 1150, canonized 1189)[219] and, at the turn of the twelfth century, the French-born abbot of the Augustinian house of Æbelholt, St William (d. 1203, canonized 1224).[220] A son of King Knud Magnusson (murdered 1157), Niels of Århus (d. 1180), had a local reputation for sanctity, but an attempt to obtain his official canonization in 1254–5 failed.[221] There may also have been attempts to consider his murdered father as a saint, but the evidence is inconclusive.[222] Archbishop Absalon tried to make a case for the sanctity of his murdered kinswoman Margrethe (Margaret), but although apparently a local cult existed in the late twelfth and thirteenth centuries, she was never officially recognized as a saint.[223] Thus no Danish women were canonized during the period. Only the two Canutes, as royal saints, gained a widespread cult, due to royal sponsorship and to their connection to the powerful merchant guilds dedicated to St Canute.[224]

As in other European countries, Christianization meant the introduction of a new stock of personal names. In the eleventh and twelfth centuries, at least among the aristocracy, a Christian name seems to have been given at baptism in addition to a traditional name.[225] Thus, King Knud the Great was also called Lambert.[226] King Sven Estridson's Christian name Magnus was sometimes conflated with his traditional name in the form *Swenomagnus*, particularly in Ailnoth's *Gesta Swenomagni regis et filiorum eius et passio gloriosissimi Canuti regis et martyris*, from the beginning of the twelfth century;[227] its Carolingian overtones were hardly coincidental. However, traditional names remained dominant into the thirteenth century, when they began to be superseded by saints' names as in the rest of Europe.[228]

With Christianization came the use of the Latin language and script. As in the rest of Scandinavia this created an interesting cultural situation, since pagan Danes were already in possession of a script of their own, the runes. Runic inscriptions from the pagan centuries mainly fall in two categories: memorial inscriptions on stones, and short inscriptions on artefacts, most often only a name (presumably the owner's), but sometimes more or less incomprehensible words that are usually interpreted as magical

[218] Breengaard 1982, 303–19; Gad 1963c, cols. 600–1.   [219] Gad 1963a, col. 435.
[220] Nielsen 1976, col. 69.   [221] Gad 1967; Paludan 1988.   [222] Sawyer 1991b, 59.
[223] Gad 1966.   [224] E.g.Wallin 1986; Jexlev 1986; Kofod-Hansen 1986.
[225] Steenstrup 1892–4; Meldgaard 2000, 116–18. Sometimes both names might belong to the traditional, pagan name-stock; Halvorsen *et al.* 1968, col. 221.
[226] Adam of Bremen, schol. 37 (at 112).   [227] *VSD*, 77–89.
[228] Halvorsen *et al.* 1968, cols. 224–6; cf. Meldgaard 2000, 121–6.

formulas.[229] The use of runes for letter-writing in pagan times is mentioned by the chronicler Saxo Grammaticus (*c.* 1200),[230] but no specimens of such letters have been identified with certainty among archaeological finds.[231]

The introduction of Christianity and of Latin literacy did not immediately entail the demise of 'runacy'. The sixteen-letter *fuþark* (runic alphabet) of the Viking Age was adapted so that it contained exact equivalents for all Latin letters except *c*, *q*, *x*, *y* and *z*.[232] The custom of raising memorial stones with runic inscriptions had disappeared by the mid-eleventh century except on the island of Bornholm, where it seems to have been introduced only with the coming of Christianity in the 1060s and continued till the end of the century.[233] Despite the end of the custom of raising rune-stones, runes continued to be used for other purposes, and a substantial number of Romanesque gravestones carry runic inscriptions. A few coins issued by King Sven Estridson (1047–76) carry legends in runic script. Runes were also used by artisans to sign their works, both church buildings and liturgical implements; a glass pane with runes from a lost stained-glass window in the church of Give in Jylland is particularly remarkable. Surviving Romanesque church roofs show that the *fuþark* was used by carpenters to mark the beams. Several runic inscriptions have been found scribbled on the surface of church walls. The runes were not abandoned as a common means of communication until the fourteenth century; the last dated inscription is from 1310 or 1311.[234]

It is uncertain whether the use of either script had anything to do with a distinction between lay and clerical culture. A surprising number of runic inscriptions from the Middle Ages are partly or entirely in Latin, indicating that 'runacy' may have been part of the culture of Latinate clerical milieus.[235] The inverse case, texts in Danish with Latin letters, does not occur until the late twelfth century.[236] But by the end of the twelfth century, runes were already regarded with a certain antiquarian veneration as a national heirloom. King Valdemar I sent experts to study a presumed runic inscription in Blekinge that was rumoured to contain a description of a legendary battle of the Iron Age,[237] and Archbishop Absalon raised a

---

[229] Moltke 1985, 284–327, 346–90.   [230] Saxo III.6.16 (vol. I, 228).

[231] For two dubious cases, see Moltke 1985, 151–3, 347–8, 371–3; Sawyer 1988, 12.

[232] Moltke 1985, 30–1.

[233] Sawyer 2000, 10. Moltke 1985, 184, dates the disappearance of the custom to *c.* 1025; with possible exceptions 398–402. Bornholm: Moltke 1985, 328–40.

[234] Moltke 1985, 407–17, 394–7 (also Jensen 1995, 82–5), 417–26, 442–56, 438–40, 426–38, 500 respectively.

[235] Moltke 1985, 407–500.   [236] Lundt Hansen 2001, 61.

[237] Saxo, Præfatio chap. 2.5 (vol. I, 78–80), cf. VII.10.3 (vol. I, 494). On the 'inscription' Ødegaard 1994.

perfectly anachronistic rune-stone by the parish church of Norra Åsum in Skåne, commemorating his and a kinsman's building of the church.[238] Even manuscripts were written in runes; the most famous example is the *Codex runicus* of the *Law of Skåne*, roughly datable on philological grounds to *c.* 1300.[239] However, the extremely few surviving cases of such manuscripts may indicate that these specimens were expressions of antiquarian zeal rather than of common usage.

It was probably the adaptation of Latin writing to the Danish language that ultimately spelled the end of the runes as a common script.[240] The earliest texts in Danish with Latin script that have been preserved are the law books. The first of these, the 'Book of Inheritance' (*Arvebogen*), was probably issued in 1169–70;[241] the oldest surviving manuscripts of the texts are about a century later.[242] By the late thirteenth century, Denmark was divided into three legal provinces: Jylland with Fyn, Sjælland with adjacent islands, and Skåne with Halland, Blekinge and Bornholm. Each of these provinces had its specific set of law books, and this probably reflected ancient differences in legal customs. Nevertheless there are many similarities and loans between the provincial law books, and it has been argued that rather than being codifications of ancient custom, all the law books should be seen as either products of, or preparatory work for, royal legislation at the national level, largely prompted by ecclesiastical influence. The prologue of the *Law of Jylland* of 1241 explicitly mentions that the law was given by the king and agreed upon by the 'land'.[243] As a consequence of the introduction of separate ecclesiastical jurisdiction in the early twelfth century, the Danish law books do not contain any provisions on matters pertaining to canon law, contrary to their Norwegian and Swedish counterparts.

The hypothesis that the law books represent innovative legislation means that we are largely ignorant of the exact nature of Danish law before their enactment. In the twelfth century, the traditional legal order seems to have been referred to as 'the laws of King Harald'. It is not clear whether this referred to Harald Bluetooth (*c.* 958–*c.* 987) or to Harald Hén (1076–80);[244] the *Chronicle of Roskilde* (*c.* 1138) states that the latter had secured the use of the forests for the people against the aristocracy's attempts to monopolize them.[245] According to Ailnoth's life of St Canute (*c.* 1104–17), the people of Jylland assembled every year in Viborg to agree upon the laws and to

---

[238] Moltke 1985, 404–5.   [239] Skautrup 1969.
[240] Lundt Hansen 2001, 61–4.   [241] Gelting 2005, 87–93.
[242] On manuscripts *DGL*, vols. I–VIII + supplement to vol. IV.
[243] Gelting 2003; 2005, 92–3, 108–15. Cf. Fenger 1971, 433–4.
[244] Jørgensen 1947, 65.   [245] *SM*, vol. I, 23.

confirm them.[246] Customs concerning pious gifts to churches were basically similar to the *laudatio parentum* known from western Europe.[247]

None of the law books required written title deeds as proof of ownership to land, and this evidently reflects previous conditions too. Hence the issuing of charters was a comparatively late and rare phenomenon. The first Danish charter about which we have indirect but credible information was issued by the bishop of Roskilde in the early 1070s.[248] All the known Danish charters from the twelfth century were issued by the king, members of the clergy (mostly bishops), or members of the royal kindred. Charters by the lay aristocracy do not appear until the beginning of the thirteenth century,[249] and in some cases it is clear that important gifts by the lay aristocracy were given without any charter.[250] If charters were issued concerning pious gifts by laymen or settlements of disputes between laymen and ecclesiastical institutions, they were issued as confirmations or notifications by a bishop or by the king.[251]

The most important indigenous literature in Latin created in early Christian Denmark consisted of saints' *Lives* and historical writing. The earliest hagiographical text may be the life of St Thøger of Vestervig, now known only through excerpts in liturgical texts. The earliest parts of this *vita* may have been written in the late eleventh century.[252] Although previous shorter texts were composed,[253] the official life of the royal saint King Knud IV (d. 1086, canonized *c.* 1100) was written early in the reign of King Niels by the Benedictine monk Ailnoth, whose name shows that he must have been one of the English monks who had come from Evesham to staff the new Benedictine abbey at Odense.[254] It begins as a short chronicle of the reigns of Knud's father Sven Estridson and of his elder brother King Harald Hén before shifting into the hagiographical mode. Continuing influence from Anglo-Norman hagiography is evidenced by the official life of St Canute *dux* (d. 1131), written by a monk called Robert of Ely, probably shortly after 1135. This work is lost except for a few excerpts.[255] The lives of the later twelfth-century saints, Kjeld of Viborg and Niels of Århus, written as evidence for their canonization processes,[256] are only preserved in excerpts. The Danish transmission of the life of St William of Æbelholt is no better, but in this case the text also circulated in William's original monastic milieu in Paris, where it has survived in complete form.[257]

---

[246] *VSD*, III.   [247] Esmark 2004.   [248] *DD*, ser. 1, vol. II, 18–19, no. 9.
[249] The earliest certain case is *DD*, ser. 1, vol. V.3, no. 3 (1211).   [250] *SM*, vol. II, 169.
[251] E.g. *DD*, ser. 1, vol. III, 406–7, no. 257 (1199).   [252] *VSD*, 3–26.
[253] *VSD*, 28–42, 60–76.   [254] *VSD*, 42–54, 77–147.   [255] *VSD*, 183–6, 234–41.
[256] *VSD*, 251–83, 395–408.   [257] *VSD*, 287–369.

William of Æbelholt was also the author of the only letter-collection to have survived from twelfth-century Denmark, although in fragmentary form.[258]

Indigenous Danish historiography began with the writing of the short *Chronicle of Roskilde c.* 1138.[259] In relating the history of the Danish kingdom from the conversion of the exiled King Harald (Klak) in Mainz in 826 to 1138, it attempts to picture Denmark as having been ruled continuously by Christian kings since 826, although with occasional resurgences of paganism. From the mid-eleventh century it is as much a history of the bishops of Roskilde as a regnal history. The chronicle's depiction of Denmark as an old Christian kingdom is likely to have been made in conscious opposition to Hamburg-Bremen's claim to ecclesiastical supremacy over Denmark, which had met with temporary success at the time of the author's writing. Its purpose might have been to support arguments for resurrecting the Danish archiepiscopal see, but at Roskilde instead of Lund.[260] Nonetheless, the chronicler's main source of information was Adam of Bremen's chronicle of the archbishops of Hamburg-Bremen until its end in 1072. Besides that, he seems to have used an early version of Henry of Huntingdon's English chronicle and the life of St Edmund. The Roskilde chronicler does not seem to have been able to draw upon other Danish sources than his own cathedral's archives and traditions.[261]

Shortly after its composition, the Roskilde chronicle was used by the author of the first indigenous annalistic work, composed at the archiepiscopal see of Lund *c.* 1140, but known as the Colbaz Annals from the Pomeranian Cistercian abbey where it was continued later.[262] Lund became the main centre of the writing of Danish annals; for the period before the early twelfth century, its annals relied upon an as yet unidentified version of the Anglo-Norman annalistic tradition.[263] One or more further redactions of the Lund Annals were perhaps composed during the twelfth century, but the surviving text dates from the late thirteenth century.[264] This redaction incorporates a series of probably native tales of pagan kings, which modern editors have excised from the annals and published separately under the name 'Chronicle of Lejre'. The tales, which are stylistically dependent upon the *Continuation of the Chronicle of Roskilde*, are highly fantastic and devoid of factual substance.[265]

---

[258] *DD*, ser. 1, vol. III, pt 2, 'Epistolæ abbatis Willelmi', 413–576. Damsholt 1978.

[259] *SM*, vol. I, 3–33.

[260] Gelting 2004a, 181–202; cf. 2002, 78–88. The reactions to this hypothesis have so far been sceptical; Pajung 2003.

[261] Gelting 2002, 41–51.   [262] *DMA*, 1–11.   [263] Kristensen 1969, 27–30.

[264] *DMA*, 21–70; Kristensen 1969, 25–30, 37–116, 121–4.   [265] *SM*, vol. I, 34–53.

The two most important Danish chronicles were both written in the learned milieu around Archbishop Absalon at the turn of the twelfth century. Sven Aggeson wrote a history of Denmark from legendary antiquity to 1185, probably shortly after that year.[266] Saxo Grammaticus's *Gesta Danorum*, written over a period of several decades around 1200,[267] is one of the most accomplished examples of history in late classical Latin style in Europe, and it is one of the last great works of *prosimetrum*.[268] Like Sven Aggeson, Saxo begins with the earliest legendary kings and carries the story up to 1185, but with a profusion of detail and a rhetorical flourish that go far beyond his colleague's. His main focus was writing a national history that should demonstrate that Denmark had an ancient history no less dignified than that of the Romans, and with main epochs that paralleled the history of the world and of the Church.[269] For the legendary past, Saxo relied largely on skaldic poetry and other lore that he explicitly says were got from Icelanders.[270] While the reliability of Saxo's account of Danish history in the twelfth century is a matter for controversy, the legendary part of the *Gesta Danorum* has always been appreciated as an important but difficult source for pagan Scandinavian myths and legends.

Saxo's work is a remarkable testimony to Denmark's integration into European learned culture by 1200. The same integration is visible in church art. The early wooden stave churches were uniformly replaced by stone churches, the majority of which were built during the twelfth and thirteenth centuries. While the architecture of most of the rural churches is rather simple, the quality of the surviving wood sculpture, gilded altars and wall paintings from the Romanesque period is often impressive and witnesses to close contacts with the art of Germany and France; Anglo-Saxon and Anglo-Norman influence is mainly visible in the oldest stone churches.[271] The architecture of the great cathedrals mostly reflected the style of the German Empire; however, the first building phase of the cathedral of Lund (*c.* 1100–30) looked to the Flemish region for inspiration, while the Lombard inspiration in the second, mid-twelfth-century phase may have been direct rather than transmitted from the cathedrals in the Rhineland.[272] Archbishop Absalon's rebuilding of Roskilde cathedral may

[266] *SM*, vol. I, 94–141; for the date, cf. Friis-Jensen 1987, 12. On poor textual transmission Gertz 1916; Christensen 1978.
[267] Saxo; date, Friis-Jensen 1987, 11–12.   [268] Friis-Jensen 1987, esp. 52–63.
[269] Skovgaard-Petersen 1987, 65–94; 1969; 1975.
[270] Saxo, Præfatio chap. 1.4 (vol. I, 74–6). For his use of this material, cf. Friis-Jensen 1987, esp. 18–28.
[271] For this and the following paragraph Andersson 1970 remains fundamental; on early stone churches, 31–6.
[272] Cinthio 1957, 204–6, cf. 203–4 n. 25; Andersson 1970, 36–41; Rydén and Lovén 1995, 17–62.

have been inspired by northern French cathedrals, at first Tournai, later superseded by Arras and Noyon.[273] On the west coast of Jylland, the stones for a substantial number of churches were imported from the Rhineland,[274] and the dominant stylistic influences came from the same region, vehicled by the twelfth-century cathedral of Ribe.[275]

While churches were still being built of wood, the traditions of native craftsmen mingled with influences from abroad. A surviving plank from the stave church of Hørning in Jylland seems symptomatic: it carries a carved dragon-lace motif in the late Viking Age Urnes style on one side and a painted acanthus motif in pure Romanesque style on the other side.[276] The church has been dated to the 1060s.[277] In the decorative arts, some motifs lingered on from traditional art into the twelfth century. On the earliest of the Danish Romanesque golden altars, that of Lisbjerg close to Århus, late Urnes-style dragon-lace still coexists with acanthus and other typical Romanesque motifs on the altar's frames; the altar dates from the mid-twelfth century.[278] But by the end of the century Danish art was entirely in line with the dominant European Romanesque style.[279] Conversion brought new needs for art, new models and new ideals – not least that of building and sculpting in stone, a technique that had not been used by the pagan Scandinavians. The technical difficulties posed by the local stone, mainly granite boulders from the Scandinavian peninsula deposited during the last glaciation, conditioned the development of distinctive local styles, notably in Jylland; but the models were predominantly German.[280] Where such limitations did not apply, e.g. in mural painting, Danish art of the later twelfth century, although essentially derivative, maintained a quality that was hardly inferior to that of the major northern European centres.[281]

The Anglo-Saxon and Anglo-Norman stylistic influence that is visible in the early stone churches had some parallels in the liturgical traditions of the Danish church. In general, however, little is known of Danish liturgy in these early centuries, due to severe losses of documentation. Most of the surviving liturgical books date from the end of the Middle Ages and represent the result of centuries of modifications and reforms. But in some dioceses, it is possible to discern several strands of influence dating back to the first centuries of Danish Christianity. In the diocese of Odense, whose

---

[273] *DK*, vol. III.3, 1320.   [274] Helms 1894.   [275] Andersson 1970, 48–51.

[276] Krogh and Voss 1961, 7–9, 17–18.   [277] Roesdahl 2004, 202.

[278] Nørlund 1926, 79–90; cf. Christiansen 1968, 9*–10*, on the find of fragments of a similar altar in the nearby church of Råsted.

[279] Andersson 1970, esp. 241–5, 265–76, 330–43; cf. Liebgott 1985, 17–32.

[280] Norn and Larsen 1968; Mackeprang 1948; 1941; Andersson 1970, 53–62, 113–14.

[281] Andersson 1970, 241.

cathedral chapter was a daughter house of the English abbey of Evesham, certain affinities with the liturgy of the mother abbey were still traceable in the fourteenth century, while other elements that were related to liturgical practices of Anglo-Saxon Winchester are probably remnants of the liturgy of Knud the Great's church.[282] But despite its problematic relationship with Hamburg-Bremen, the traditions of the Danish church were mainly shaped by German influence. The pontifical liturgies of the dioceses of Lund and Roskilde have been studied in detail; they were based essentially on the early Ottonian *pontificale romano-germanicum*, which is likely to have been introduced in connection with Sven Estridson's realignment with Hamburg-Bremen and reorganization of the Danish church *c.* 1059. However, they contain a number of variants that point towards French influence, particularly from the diocese of Reims.[283] From the second half of the twelfth century the Danish higher clergy increasingly sought contacts and education in France.[284] Archbishop Absalon, educated in France,[285] introduced a major liturgical reform in 1187 or 1188, and it has been suggested that the influence from Reims was introduced at that time;[286] however, the problematical nature of the surviving evidence has hitherto discouraged detailed analysis.[287] This reform is the only extant evidence of synodal statutes from the twelfth century.

6. CONCLUSION

In Denmark, kings wielding considerable social and military power can be traced back to the very first years of the eighth century. Initially their power may have been based primarily on tribute and plunder, but it is likely that some forms of taxation had already been adopted before the conversion, inspired by Anglo-Saxon and Frankish models. German pressure brought about the conversion of King Harald Bluetooth *c.* 963, but it did not result in German overlordship. The dynastic union between Denmark and England 1014/16–1042 brought considerable English influence, but practically nothing is known of such administrative structures as may have been introduced during the reign of Knud the Great. Despite the breakdown of Knud's North Sea empire, English influences on Danish kingship continued to be strong throughout the twelfth century. Relations with the powerful German neighbour to the south were obviously important, but

---

[282] Ottosen 1970, 21–2; 2004, 18.   [283] Strömberg 1955, 32–54.
[284] *Exordium magnum*, excerpt in *SM*, vol. II, 430. Strömberg 1955, 36–9, 53–4.
[285] Munk Olsen 1996; 1985.   [286] Strömberg 1955, 54.
[287] Skyum-Nielsen 1992; Strömberg 1955 did not know this source.

only in the troubled years from 1131 to the mid-1160s did the Danish kings recognize direct German overlordship.[288]

Thus there is no reason to assume that Christianization resulted in any radical transformation of Danish kingship. On the other hand, it obviously facilitated the importation of professional know-how from other European kingdoms in order to bring royal administration up to date with recent innovations. It also enabled the Danish kings to pursue territorial expansion aggressively in the Baltic region by participating in the Baltic branch of the crusading movement. Legislation, documented from 1169–70 onwards, was strongly inspired by the Church, but its enactment was firmly in the hands of the king.

Under these circumstances, the Christianization of Denmark was dependent upon the kings from the outset. Before the conversion, missionaries could only work with royal permission, and the Christianization of the realm began from the top, the king and his court giving the lead. The bishops were closely dependent upon the king and essentially remained so even after the acquisition of vast estates and royal prerogatives had provided them with a substantial material basis. When after the papal schism of 1159 Archbishop Eskil challenged King Valdemar by adhering to Pope Alexander III, the result was a painful demonstration of the relative weakness of the archbishop's power.

The first century of Danish Christianity after Harald Bluetooth's conversion is obscure as to the inner life of the Danish church. Knud the Great's church obviously relied on his English kingdom for its staff and its liturgy, but after the middle of the eleventh century German influence became predominant, especially after the final reorganization of the diocesan structure c. 1059. This situation did not change fundamentally even after the creation of the archdiocese of Lund in 1103–4, although some French influence may be discerned in the second half of the twelfth century. With the introduction of the tithe c. 1100, parish churches multiplied, and the administrative structures of the Danish dioceses followed European patterns, although with some particularities. Monastic houses do not seem to have been founded before the second half of the eleventh century, and the great phase of growth of Danish monasticism belongs to the twelfth century.

While the organization of the Danish church thus remained rudimentary for most of the eleventh century, and the conversion phase may have extended until the mid-eleventh century, the integration of Denmark into

---

[288] Gelting 2004a, 184–92, 220–3.

Latin Christian culture appears to have been both fast and thorough. By the beginning of the thirteenth century, Denmark was in every respect a western, Christian and European kingdom. Ideologically and in the organization of their administration, the Danish kings had patterned themselves on western and central European models. The Danish church was headed by prelates with a thoroughly international education. Royal legislation was bringing Danish customs in accordance with both Roman and especially canon law. The parish network was being completed, and the architecture and art of the rural parish churches reflected European influences practically to the exclusion of any reminiscences of the artwork of the Viking Age.

REFERENCES

Adam of Bremen, *Gesta Hammaburgensis ecclesiae pontificum*, ed. B. Schmeidler, *MGH SRG*, Hanover and Leipzig, 1917.
Andersen, H. 1988, 'Gåden om Gorm', *Skalk* 1988/6, 18–28.
Andersen, H. 1995, 'Man tvinges til at overveje –', *Skalk* 1995/1, 20–31.
Andersen, H. H. 1998, *Danevirke og Kovirke: Arkæologiske undersøgelser 1861–1993*, Århus, 1998.
Andersson, A. 1970, *The Art of Scandinavia*, vol. II, London.
Anz, C. 1998, *Gilden im mittelalterlichen Skandinavien*, Göttingen.
Arhnung, J. O. 1937, *Roskilde Domkapitels Historie*, vol. I, *Tiden indtil 1416 med Altrenes og Kapellernes Historie*, Roskilde.
Banning, K. ed. 1976–82, *A Catalogue of Wall-Paintings in the Churches of Medieval Denmark 1100–1600: Scania Halland Blekinge*, vols. I–IV, Copenhagen.
Bartholdy, N. G. 1984, 'Valdemarernes løvevåben: Hovedtræk af en teori om de danske kongers politiske motivering for at antage løvefiguren i det 12. århundrede', in *Heraldik i Norden*, ed. A. Tønnesen *et al.*, Copenhagen (*Heraldisk Tidsskrift*, 5:2), 21–30.
Bekker-Nielsen, H. *et al.* 1974, 'Thomas Becket', in *KLNM*, vol. XVIII, cols. 244–9.
Beskow, P. and W. Swensen 1964, 'Kröning', in *KLNM*, vol. IX, cols. 497–502.
Blomqvist, R. 1951, *Lunds historia*, vol. I, *Medeltiden*, Lund.
Bolin, S. 1931a, 'Danmark och Tyskland under Harald Gormsson: Grundlinjer i dansk historia under 900-talet', *Scandia* 4, 184–209.
Bolin, S. 1931b, *Om Nordens äldsta historieforskning: Studier över dess metode och källvärde*, Lund.
Bonde, N. and Kj. Christensen 1982, 'Trelleborgs Alder. Dendrokronologisk Datering', *Aarbøger for Nordisk Oldkyndighed og Historie*, 111–52.
Breengaard, C. 1982, *Muren om Israels hus: Regnum og sacerdotium i Danmark 1050–1170*, Copenhagen.
Carelli, P. 2001, *En kapitalistisk anda: Kulturella förändringar i 1100-talets Danmark*, Stockholm.

Christensen, A. E. 1969, *Vikingetidens Danmark paa oldhistorisk baggrund*, Copenhagen.

Christensen, A. S. 1988, *Middelalderbyen Odense*, n.p.

Christensen, K. 1975, 'Forholdet mellem Saxo og Sven Aggesen', in *Saxostudier (Saxo-kollokvierne ved Københavns universitet)*, ed. I. Boserup, Copenhagen, 128–37.

Christensen, K. 1978, *Om overleveringen af Sven Aggesens værker*, Copenhagen.

Christensen, Kj. 1995, 'Kanhave-kanalen', in *Stavns Fjord: Et natur- og kulturhistorisk forskningsområde på Samsø*, ed. H. H. Hansen and B. Aaby, Copenhagen, 99–117.

Christensen, Kj. 2003, 'Ravning-broens alder: En af Danmarks sikreste dendrokronologiske dateringer?', *Kuml*, 213–26.

Christensen, T. 2004, 'Fra hedenskab til kristendom i Lejre og Roskilde', in Lund 2004a, 191–200.

Christiansen, E. 1997, *The Northern Crusades: The Baltic and the Catholic Frontier 1100–1525*, 2nd edn, London.

Christiansen, T. E. 1968, 'Tillæg: Fyrretyve Aar', in *Gyldne altre: Jysk metalkunst fra Valdemarstiden*, ed. P. Nørlund, 2nd edn, Århus, 1*–19*.

Christiansen, T. E. 1982, 'Trelleborgs Alder. Arkæologisk Datering', *Aarbøger for Nordisk Oldkyndighed og Historie*, 84–110.

Cinthio, E. 1957, *Lunds domkyrka under romansk tid*, Bonn and Lund.

Cinthio, E. 1966, 'Kungapalatset i Dalby', *Ale: Historisk Tidskrift för Skåneland* 1966/3, 16–19.

Cinthio, E. 1983, 'Dalby kungsgård: Medeltidsarkeologien som historisk vetenskap', *Kungl. Vitterhets, Historie och Antikvitets Akademiens Årsbok*, 89–100.

Cinthio, E. 1992, 'Dalby kyrkas stiftare och donatorer: en spekulativ bildtolkning', in *Från romanik till nygotik: Studier i kyrklig konst och arkitektur tillägnade Evald Gustafsson*, ed. M. Ullén, Stockholm, 1–10.

Cinthio, M. 2004, 'Trinitatiskyrkan, gravarna och de första lundaborna', in Lund 2004a, 159–73.

Dahlerup, T. 1968, *Det danske Sysselprovsti i Middelalderen*, Copenhagen.

Damsholt, N. 1970, 'Kingship in the Arengas of Danish Royal Diplomas 1140–1223', *Mediaeval Scandinavia* 3, 66–108.

Damsholt, N. 1978, 'Abbed Vilhelm af Æbelholts brevsamling', *Historisk Tidsskrift* 78, 1–22.

DD: *Diplomatarium Danicum*, ser. 1, vols. I–VII, Copenhagen, 1957–90.

'De sancto Willibrordo episcopo Traiectensi et Fresonum apostolo', in *Acta sanctorum novembris*, ed. C. de Smedt *et al.*, III, Brussels, 1910, 414–500.

Demidoff, L. 1973, 'The Poppo Legend', *Mediaeval Scandinavia* 6, 39–67.

DGKL: *Danmarks gamle købstadlovgivning*, vols. I–V, ed. E. Kroman and P. Jørgensen, Copenhagen, 1951–61.

DGL: *Danmarks gamle landskabslove med kirkelovene*, general ed. J. Brøndum-Nielsen and P. J. Jørgensen, vols. I–VIII + supplement to vol. IV, Copenhagen, 1933–61.

DK: *Danmarks Kirker*, Copenhagen and Herning, 1933–.

DMA: Danmarks middelalderlige annaler, ed. E. Kroman, Copenhagen, 1980.

Drescher, H. 1984, 'Glockenfunde aus Haithabu', in *Archäologische Fundmaterial der Ausgrabung Haithabu*, IV, Neumünster, 9–62.

Eisenschmidt, S. 2004, 'Kristendommens indtrængen i Syddanmark belyst ud fra gravfund i området mellem Kongeåen og Ejderen', in Lund 2004a, 123–41.

Esmark, K. 2004, 'Godsgaver, *calumniae* og retsantropologi: Esrum kloster og dets naboer, ca. 1150–1250', in *Ett annat 1100-tal: Individ, kollektiv och kulturella mönster i medeltidens Danmark*, ed. P. Carelli *et al.*, Göteborg and Stockholm, 143–80.

Fenger, O. 1971, *Fejde og mandebod: Studier over slægtsansvaret i germansk og gammeldansk ret*, Copenhagen.

Friis-Jensen, K. 1987, *Saxo Grammaticus as Latin Poet: Studies in the Verse Passages of the Gesta Danorum*, Rome.

Fuhrmann, H. 1955, 'Studien zur Geschichte mittelalterlicher Patriarchate, III. Teil (Schluss)', *Zeitschrift der Savigny-Stiftung für Rechtsgeschichte, Kanonistische Abteilung* 41, 120–70.

Fuhrmann, H. 1964, 'Die Synoden von Ingelheim', in *Ingelheim am Rhein. Forschungen und Studien zur Geschichte Ingelheims*, ed. J. Autenrieth, Stuttgart, 147–73.

Gad, T. 1961, *Legenden i dansk middelalder*, Copenhagen.

Gad, T. 1963a, 'Kjeld', in *KLNM*, vol. VIII, cols. 435–7.

Gad, T. 1963b, 'Knud den Hellige', in *KLNM*, vol. VIII, cols. 596–600.

Gad, T. 1963c, 'Knud Lavard', in *KLNM*, vol. VIII, cols. 600–3.

Gad, T. 1966, 'Margrethe', in *KLNM*, vol. XI, cols. 351–2.

Gad, T. 1967, 'Niels af Århus', in *KLNM*, vol. XII, cols. 306–7.

Gad, T. *et al.* 1966, 'Mikael', in *KLNM*, vol. XI, cols. 616–26.

Gaethke, H.-O. 1999, *Herzog Heinrich der Löwe und die Slawen nordöstlich der unteren Elbe*, Frankfurt a/M.

Gallén, J. and S. Iuul 1965, 'Kyrkorätt', in *KLNM*, vol. X, cols. 1–6.

Gelting, M. H. 1992a, 'Burglanensis eccl. (Børglum)', in *Ser. ep.*, 6:2, 46–53.

Gelting, M. H. 1992b, 'Ripa (Ribe)', in *Ser. ep.*, 6:2, 64–75.

Gelting, M. H. 1992c, 'Wiberg (Viborg)', in *Ser. ep.*, 6:2, 117–23.

Gelting, M. H. tr. and comm. 2002, *Roskildekrøniken*, 2nd edn, Højbjerg.

Gelting, M. H. 2003, 'Skånske Lov og Jyske Lov: Danmarks første kommissionsbetænkning og Danmarks første retsplejelov', in *Jura & Historie: Festskrift til Inger Dübeck som forsker*, ed. F. Taksøe-Jensen *et al.*, Copenhagen, 43–80.

Gelting, M. H. 2004a, 'Da Eskil ville være ærkebiskop af Roskilde: Roskildekrøniken, *Liber daticus Lundensis* og det danske ærkesædes ophævelse 1133–1138', in *Ett annat 1100-tal: Individ, kollektiv och kulturella mönster i medeltidens Danmark*, ed. P. Carelli *et al.*, Göteborg and Stockholm, 181–229.

Gelting, M. H. 2004b, 'Elusive Bishops: Remembering, Forgetting, and Remaking the History of the Early Danish Church', in *The Bishop: Power and Piety at the First Millennium*, ed. S. Gilsdorf, Münster, 169–200.

Gelting, M. H. 2005, 'Pope Alexander III and Danish Laws of Inheritance', in *How Nordic are the Nordic Medieval Laws?*, ed. D. Tamm and H. Vogt, Copenhagen, 86–115.

Gertz, M.Cl. 1916, *En ny Text af Sven Aggesøns Værker genvunden paa Grundlag af Codex Arnamagnæanus 33, 4to*, Copenhagen.

Green, D. H. 1998, *Language and History in the Early Germanic World*, Cambridge.

Green-Pedersen, S. E. 1981, 'De danske cistercienserklostres grundlæggelse og den politiske magtkamp i det 12. årh.', in *Middelalder, metode og medier: Festskrift til Niels Skyum-Nielsen på 60-årsdagen den 17. oktober 1981*, ed. K. Fledelius et al., Viborg, 41–65.

Grinder-Hansen, P. 2002, 'Historie, arkæologi og vendere – hvad kilderne ikke siger om Svantevits tempel i Arkona og om venderne i Danmark', in *Venner og Fjender: Dansk-vendiske forbindelser i vikingetid og tidlig middelalder*, ed. A.-E. Jensen, Næstved, 5–16.

Grund, O. 1871, 'Kaiser Otto des Großen angeblicher Zug gegen Dänemark', *Forschungen zur Deutschen Geschichte* 11, 561–92.

Hald, K. 1965, *Vore Stednavne*, 2nd edn, Copenhagen.

Halvorsen, E. F. et al. 1968, 'Personnavn', in *KLNM*, vol. XIII, cols. 198–234.

Hamre, L. et al. 1974, 'Tiend', in *KLNM*, vol. XVIII, cols. 280–300.

Hårdh, B. 2005, 'Uppåkra in the Viking Age', in *Viking and Norse in the North Atlantic: Select Papers from the Proceedings of the Fourteenth Viking Congress, Tórshavn, 19–30 July 2001*, ed. A. Mortensen and S. V. Arge, Tórshavn, 383–91.

Hauberg, P. 1900, *Myntforhold og Udmyntninger i Danmark indtil 1146*, Copenhagen (*Det Kgl. danske Videnskabernes Selskabs Skrifter, Historisk og filosofisk Afdeling*, ser. 6, vol. V:1).

Heinrich of Latvia, *Livländische Chronik*, ed. and tr. A. Bauer, Darmstadt, 1975 (*AQ XXIV*).

Helms, J. 1894, *Danske Tufstens-Kirker*, 2 vols., Copenhagen.

Henriksen, M. B. 2003, 'Før Nyborg', *Skalk* 2003/5, 11–17.

Hermanson, L. 2000, *Släkt, vänner och makt: En studie av elitens politiska kultur i 1100-talets Danmark*, Göteborg.

Hill, T. 1992, *Könige, Fürsten und Klöster. Studien zu den dänischen Klostergründungen des 12. Jahrhunderts*, Frankfurt a/M.

Housted, F. W. 1994, *Stednavne af slavisk oprindelse på Lolland, Falster og Møn*, Copenhagen.

Housted, F. W. 2002, 'Venderne på Lolland-Falster: . . . . hvor boede de?', in *Venner og Fjender: Dansk-vendiske forbindelser i vikingetid og tidlig middelalder*, ed. A.-E. Jensen, Næstved, 29–32.

Jacobsson, B. 1995, 'Den arkeologiska undersökningen', in *Trelleborgen: en av Harald Blåtands danska ringborgar*, ed. B. Jacobsson et al., Lund, 9–61.

Jankuhn, H. 1986, *Haithabu. Ein Handelsplatz der Wikingerzeit*, 8th edn, Neumünster.

Janson, H. 2004, 'Konfliktlinjer i tidig nordeuropeisk kyrkoorganisation', in Lund 2004a, 215–34.

Jensen, J. 2004, *Danmarks Oldtid: Yngre Jernalder og Vikingetid 400–1050 e.Kr.*, Copenhagen.

Jensen, J. S. 1995, *Tusindtallets Danske Mønter fra Den kongelige Mønt- og Medaillesamling / Danish Coins from the 11th Century in The Royal Collection of Coins and Medals*, n.p.

Jeppesen, J. and H. J. Madsen 1991, 'Storgård og kirke i Lisbjerg', in Mortensen and Rasmussen 1991, 269–75.

Jexlev, T. 1986, 'Om Knud den Hellige som dateringshelgen i Danmark', in Nyberg *et al.* 1986, 86–92.

Jón Viðar Sigurðsson 1999, *Chieftains and Power in the Icelandic Commonwealth*, Odense.

Jørgensen, E. 1908, 'Fremmed Indflydelse under den danske Kirkes tidligste Udvikling', in *Det Kgl. Danske Videnskabernes Selskabs Skrifter*, ser. 7, *Historisk og filosofisk Afd.*, vol. I:2, 123–243.

Jørgensen, E. 1909, *Helgendyrkelse i Danmark: Studier over Kirkekultur og kirkeligt Liv fra det 11te Aarhundredes Midte til Reformationen*, Copenhagen.

Jørgensen, L. 2002, 'Kongsgård – kultsted – marked: Overvejelser omkring Tissøkompleksets struktur og funktion', in *Plats och praxis: Studier av nordisk förkristen ritual*, ed. K. Jennbert *et al.*, 215–47.

Jørgensen, P. J. 1947, *Dansk Retshistorie: Retskildernes og Forfatningsrettens Historie indtil sidste Halvdel af det 17. Aarhundrede*, 2nd edn, Copenhagen.

KLNM: Kulturhistorisk leksikon for nordisk middelalder fra vikingetid til reformationstid, vols. I–XXII, Copenhagen, 1956–78.

Kofod-Hansen, E. 1986, 'Knud den Hellige i middelalderlige malerier og træskærerarbejder: Et bidrag til Knud Konges ikonografi', in Nyberg *et al.* 1986, 61–78.

Kong Valdemars Jordebog, ed. S. Aakjær, vols. I–III, Copenhagen, 1926–45.

Kousgård Sørensen, J. 1974, 'Odinkar og andre navne på – kar', in *Nordiska namn: Festskrift till Lennart Moberg 13 december 1974*, ed. H. Ståhl and T. Andersson, Lund and Uppsala (*Namn och bygd*, 62), 108–16.

Kristensen, A. K. G. 1969, *Danmarks ældste Annalistik: Studier over lundensisk Annalskrivning i 12. og 13. Århundrede*, Copenhagen.

Krogh, K. 1993, *Gåden om Kong Gorms Grav: Historien on Nordhøjen i Jelling*, Herning.

Krogh, K. J. and O. Voss 1961, 'Fra hedenskab til kristendom i Hørning: En vikingetids kammergrav og en trækirke fra 1000-tallet under Hørning kirke', *Nationalmuseets Arbejdsmark*, 5–34.

Kroman, E. 1936, *Kong Valdemars Jordebog: Et Haandskrifts Historie*, Copenhagen.

Krongaard Kristensen, H. 1998, 'Viborgs topografiske udvikling i middelalderen 1000–1300', in *Viborg Søndersø 1000–1300: Byarkæologiske undersøgelser 1981 og 1984–85*, ed. J. Hjermind *et al.*, Højbjerg, 349–58.

Kruse, A. 2004, 'Pillegravens gåde', *Skalk* 2004/4, 9–14.

Lerche Nielsen, M. 2004, 'Runesten og religionsskifte', in Lund 2004a, 95–102.

Liebgott, N.-K. 1985, *Elfenben – fra Danmarks Middelalder*, Copenhagen.

Lind, J. H. *et al.* 2004, *Danske korstog – krig og mission i Østersøen*, Copenhagen.

Lund, N. 1991, '"Denemearc", "tanmarkar but" and "tanmaurk ala"', in *People and Places in Northern Europe 500–1600: Essays in Honour of Peter Hayes Sawyer*, ed. I. Wood and N. Lund, Woodbridge, 161–9.

Lund, N. 1998, *Harald Blåtands Død og hans begravelse i Roskilde?*, Roskilde.

Lund, N. 2002, 'Horik den Førstes udenrigspolitik', *Historisk Tidsskrift* 102, 1–22.

Lund, N. ed., 2004a, *Kristendommen i Danmark før 1050: Et symposium i Roskilde den 5.–7. februar 2003*, Roskilde.

Lund, N. 2004b, 'Mission i Danmark før Harald Blåtands dåb', in Lund 2004a, 20–7.

Lundt Hansen, A. 2001, *I Begyndelsen var Ordet . . .: Overgangen fra runer til romerskrift i Danmark 800–1300*, www.net-bog-klubben.

McGuire, B. P. 1982, *The Cistercians in Denmark: Their Attitudes, Roles, and Functions in Medieval Society*, Kalamazoo.

Mackeprang, M. 1941, *Danmarks middelalderlige Døbefonte*, Copenhagen (2nd edn, with postscript by J. Vellev, Højbjerg, 2003).

Mackeprang, M. 1948, *Jydske Granitportaler*, Copenhagen.

Meldgaard, E. V. 2000, 'Navneskifte i Norden', in *Viking og Hvidekrist: Et internationalt symposium på Nationalmuseet om Norden og Europa i den sene vikingetid og tidligste middelalder*, ed. N. Lund, Haslev, 113–27.

Meulengracht Sørensen, P. 1991, 'Håkon den gode og guderne: Nogle bemærkninger om religion og centralmagt i det tiende århundrede – og om religionshistorie og kildekritik', in Mortensen and Rasmussen 1991, 235–44.

MGH DO I: *MGH, Diplomata regum et imperatorum Germaniae*, vol. I, *Conradi I., Heinrici I. et Ottonis I. diplomata*, ed. T. Sickel, 2nd edn, Berlin, 1956.

MGH DO III: *MGH, Diplomata regum et imperatorum Germaniae*, vol. II pt 2, *Ottonis III. diplomata*, ed. T. Sickel, 2nd edn, Berlin, 1957.

Møller, E. and O. Olsen 1961, 'Danske trækirker', *Nationalmuseets Arbejdsmark*, 35–58.

Møller Jensen, J. 2000, 'Danmark og den hellige krig: En undersøgelse af korstogsbevægelsens indflydelse på Danmark ca. 1070–1169', *Historisk Tidsskrift* 100, 285–328.

Moltke, E. 1985, *Runes and their Origin: Denmark and Elsewhere*, tr. P. G. Foote, Copenhagen.

Mortensen, P. and B. M. Rasmussen, eds. 1991, *Høvdingesamfund og kongemagt*, Århus (*Fra Stamme til Stat i Danmark*, 2).

Moseng, O. G. *et al.* 1999, *Norsk historie*, I, *750–1537*, Oslo.

Munk Olsen, B. 1985, 'Anders Sunesen og Paris', in *Anders Sunesen: Stormand, teolog, administrator, digter*, ed. S. Ebbesen, Copenhagen, 75–97.

Munk Olsen, B. 1996, 'Absalons studier i Paris', in *Absalon, fædrelandets fader*, ed. F. Birkebæk *et al.*, Roskilde, 57–72.

Nielsen, H. 1976, 'Vilhelm', in *KLNM*, vol. XX, cols. 69–71.

Nielsen, I. 1985a, 'Den hellige Liufdag af Ribe', in *Festskrift til Thelma Jexlev: Fromhed og verdslighed i middelalder og renaissance*, ed. E. Waaben *et al.*, Viborg, 1–8.

Nielsen, I. 1985b, *Middelalderbyen Ribe*, n.p.

Nielsen, J. N. 2004, 'Sebbersund – tidlige kirker ved Limfjorden', in Lund 2004a, 103–22.

Nielsen, L. C. 1991, 'Hedenskab og kristendom: Religionsskiftet afspejlet i vikinge-tidens grave', in Mortensen and Rasmussen 1991, 245–67.

Nilsson, B. 2004, 'Varför just Lund? Påvedömet och norra Europa under 1000-talet', in *Lund – medeltida kyrkometropol: Symposium i samband med ärkestiftet Lunds 900-årsjubileum, 27–28 april 2003*, ed. P.-O. Ahrén and A. Jarlert, Lund, 9–26.

Nilsson, B. 2005, 'Helgon i kyrkans propaganda under kristningsprocessen i Skan-dinavien', *Historie*, 1–26.

Nørlund, P. 1926, *Gyldne altre: Jysk metalkunst fra Valdemarstiden*, Copenhagen (2nd edn, Århus, 1968).

Nørlund, P. 1948, *Trelleborg*, Copenhagen.

Norn, O. and L. Larsen 1968, *Jydsk granit*, Copenhagen.

Nyberg, T. 1979, *Sankt Peters efterfølgere i brydningstider: Omkring pavedømmets historie, Rom og Nordeuropa 750–1200*, Odense.

Nyberg, T. 1986, *Die Kirche in Skandinavien. Mitteleuropäischer und englischer Einfluss im 11. und 12. Jahrhundert; Anfänge der Domkapitel Børglum und Odense in Dänemark*, Sigmaringen.

Nyberg, T. 2000, *Monasticism in North-Western Europe, 800–1200*, Aldershot.

Nyberg, T. *et al.* eds. 1986, *Knuds-bogen 1986: Studier over Knud den Hellige*, Odense.

Nyborg, E. 1979, 'Enkeltmænd og fællesskaber i organiseringen af det romanske sognekirkebyggeri', in *Strejflys over Danmarks bygningskultur: festskrift til Harald Langberg*, Herning, 37–64.

Nyborg, E. 1986, 'Kirke – sognedannelse – bebyggelse: Nogle overvejelser med udgangspunkt i et bebyggelsesprojekt for Ribeområdet', *Hikuin* 12, 17–44.

Nyborg, E. 1992, 'Arusiensis eccl. (Århus)', in *Ser. ep.*, 6:2, 38–45.

Nyborg, E. 2004, 'Kirke og sogn i højmiddelalderens by', in *Middelalderbyen*, ed. S. B. Christensen, Århus, 113–90.

Nyborg, E. forthcoming, 'Harald Hen', in *Danske Kongegrave*.

Ødegaard, V. 1994, 'Mellem sagnhistorie, videnskab og nationalpolitik', *Fortid og Nutid*, 3–23.

Odenius, O. 1957, 'Botulf', in *KLNM*, vol. II, cols. 190–2.

Øeby Nielsen, G. 2004, 'Runesten og religionsskifte', in Lund 2004a, 86–94.

Olsen, O. 1966, *Hørg, hov og kirke: Historiske og arkæologiske vikingetidsstudier*, Copenhagen.

Olsen, O. and H. Schmidt 1977, *Fyrkat: En jysk vikingeborg*, I, *Borgen og bebyggelsen*, Copenhagen.

Olsen, R. A. 1996, *Borge i Danmark*, 2nd edn, Copenhagen.

Ottosen, K. ed. 1970, *The Manual from Notmark: Gl. kgl. Saml. 3453,8°*, Copen-hagen.

Ottosen, K. 2004, 'Liturgi og ritualer i middelalderen', in Lund 2004a, 13–19.

Page, R. I. and M. L. Nielsen 2003, 'Runenmünzen', in *Reallexikon der Germanis-chen Altertumskunde*, vol. XXV, Berlin and New York, 546–56.

Pajung, S. 2003, review of *Roskildekrøniken*, tr. and comm. M. H. Gelting, 2nd edn, *Historie*, 479–82.

Paludan, H. 1988, 'Skt. Clemens og Hellig Niels: Fromhedsliv og politik i Århus stift omkring 1190', in *Kongemagt og samfund i middelalderen: Festskrift til Erik Ulsig på 60-årsdagen 13. februar 1988*, ed. P. Enemark *et al.*, Århus, 41–53.

Pedersen, A. 2004, 'Religiøse symboler i vikingetidens arkæologiske materiale', in Lund 2004a, 60–74.

Perron, A. 2003, 'Metropolitan Might and Papal Power on the Latin-Christian Frontier: Transforming the Danish Church around the Time of the Fourth Lateran Council', *The Catholic Historical Review* 89, 182–212.

Petersen, H. 1917, *Danske kongelige Sigiller samt sønderjydske Hertugers og andre til Danmark knyttede Fyrsters Sigiller 1085–1559*, ed. A. Thiset, Copenhagen.

Radtke, C. 1992, 'Sliaswig (Schleswig/Haithabu)', in *Ser. ep.*, 6:2, 96–116.

Radtke, C. 1995, 'Die Entwicklung der Stadt Schleswig. Funktionen, Strukturen und die Anfänge der Gemeindebildung', in *Die Stadt im westlichen Ostseeraum. Vorträge zur Stadtgründung und Stadterweiterung im Hohen Mittelalter*, ed. E. Hoffmann and F. Lubowitz, Frankfurt a/M, vol. I, 47–91.

Rahbek Schmidt, K. *et al.* 1975, 'Varjager', in *KLNM*, vol. XIX, cols. 534–8.

Rasmussen, P. 1975, 'Valdemars jordebog', in *KLNM*, vol. XIX, cols. 456–60.

Refskou, N. 1985, '"In marca vel regno Danorum": En diplomatarisk analyse af forholdet mellem Danmark og Tyskland under Harald Blåtand', *Kirkehistoriske Samlinger*, 19–33.

Ribe Bispekrønike, ed. E. Jørgensen, *Kirkehistoriske Samlinger*, ser. 6, vol. I, 1933–5, 23–33.

Riis, T. 1977, *Les Institutions politiques centrales du Danemark 1100–1332*, Odense.

Riis, T. 2003, *Studien zur Geschichte des Ostseeraums*, vol. IV, *Das mittelalterliche dänische Ostseeimperium*, Odense.

Roesdahl, E. 1977, *Fyrkat: En jysk vikingeborg*, II, *Oldsagerne og gravpladsen*, Copenhagen.

Roesdahl, E. 2004, 'Hvornår blev kirkerne bygget?', in Lund 2004a, 201–6.

Rydén, T. and B. Lovén 1995, *Domkyrkan i Lund*, Malmö.

Sawyer, B. 2000, *The Viking-Age Rune-Stones: Custom and Commemoration in Early Medieval Scandinavia*, Oxford.

Sawyer, P. 1988, *Da Danmark blev Danmark: Fra ca. år 700 til ca. 1050*, Copenhagen (*Gyldendal og Politikens Danmarkshistorie*, ed. O. Olsen, 3).

Sawyer, P. 1991a, 'Konger og kongemagt', in Mortensen and Rasmussen 1991, 277–88.

Sawyer, P. 1991b, *När Sverige blev Sverige*, tr. and rev. B. Sawyer, Alingsås.

Saxo Grammaticus, *Gesta Danorum – Danmarkshistorien*, ed. K. Friis-Jensen, Danish tr. P. Zeeberg, 2 vols., Copenhagen, 2005.

Seegrün, W. 1967, *Das Papsttum und Skandinavien bis zur Vollendung der nordischen Kirchenorganisation (1164)*, Neumünster.

Ser. ep., 6:2: *Series episcoporum ecclesiae catholicae occidentalis ab initio usque ad annum MCXCVIII*, ed. O. Engels and S. Weinfurter, ser. 6, *Britannia, Scotia et Hibernia, Scandinavia*, II, *Archiepiscopatus Lundensis*, cur. H. Kluger *et al.*, Stuttgart, 1992.

Skautrup, P. 1969, 'Runehåndskrifter', in *KLNM*, vol. XIV, cols. 460–2.

Skovgaard-Petersen, I. 1969, 'Saxo, Historian of the Patria', *Mediaeval Scandinavia* 2, 54–77.

Skovgaard-Petersen, I. 1975, 'Gesta Danorums genremæssige placering', in *Saxostudier (Saxo-kollokvierne ved Københavns universitet)*, ed. I. Boserup, Copenhagen, 20–7.

Skovgaard-Petersen, I. 1987, *Da Tidernes Herre var nær: Studier i Saxos historiesyn*, Copenhagen.

Skovgaard-Petersen, I. 1988, 'Lund og Roskilde', in *Gåvobrevet 1085: Föredrag och diskussioner vid Symposium kring Knut den heliges gåvobrev 1085 och den tidiga medeltidens nordiska samhälle*, ed. S. Skansjö and H. Sundström, Arlöv, 79–89.

Skovgaard-Petersen, K. 2001, *A Journey to the Promised Land: Crusading Theology in the Historia de profectione Danorum in Hierosolymam (c. 1200)*, Copenhagen.

Skyum-Nielsen, N. 1971, *Kvinde og Slave*, Copenhagen.

Skyum-Nielsen, N. (†) 1992, 'En nyfunden kilde til Absalons historie', ed. M. H. Gelting, *Historie*, n.s. 19, 244–64.

SM: Scriptores minores historiæ Danicæ medii ævi, ed. M. C. Gertz, vols. I–II, Copenhagen, 1917–22.

Staecker, J. 1999, *Rex regum et dominus dominorum. Die wikingerzeitlichen Kreuz- und Kruzifixanhänger als Ausdruck der Mission in Altdänemark und Schweden*, Stockholm.

Steenstrup, J. 1892–4, 'Dobbelte Navne. – Erik Lam-David', *Historisk Tidsskrift*, ser. 6 vol. 4, Copenhagen, 729–41.

Strömberg, B. 1955, *Den pontifikala liturgin i Lund och Roskilde under medeltiden: En liturgihistorisk studie jämte edition av pontificale lundense enligt handskriften C 441 i Uppsala universitetsbibliotek och pontificale roscildense enligt medeltidshandskrift nr 43 i Lunds universitetsbibliotek*, Lund.

Thaastrup-Leth, A. K. 2004, 'Trækirker i det middelalderlige Danmark indtil ca. 1100: Hvornår blev de bygget?', in Lund 2004a, 207–14.

Thietmar of Merseburg, *Chronicon*, ed. and tr. W. Trillmich, 7th edn with supplement by S. Patzold, Darmstadt, 1957 (*AQ* IX).

Ulsig, E. 1981, 'Landboer og bryder, skat og landgilde: De danske fæstebønder og deres afgifter i det 12. og 13. århundrede', in *Middelalder, metode og medier: Festskrift til Niels Skyum-Nielsen på 60-årsdagen den 17. oktober 1981*, ed. K. Fledelius *et al.*, Viborg, 137–65.

Ulsig, E. 1991, 'Valdemar Sejrs kongemagt', in *Jydske Lov 750 år*, ed. O. Fenger and C. R. Jansen, Viborg, 65–78.

Venge, M. 2002, *Danmarks skatter i middelalderen indtil 1340*, Viborg (*Dansk skattehistorie*, 1).

VSD: Vitae sanctorvm Danorvm, ed. M. C. Gertz, Copenhagen, 1908–12.

Wagnkilde, H. 2000, 'Gravudstyr og mønter fra 1000-tallets gravpladser på Bornholm', in *Middelalderens kirkegårde: Arkæologi og antropologi – indsigt og udsyn*.

Nordisk Seminar 2.-5. juni 1999 Ribe, Danmark, ed. H. D. Koch, Højbjerg (*Hikuin*, 27), 91–106.

Wagnkilde, H. and T. Pind 1996, 'Tæt på 1000-tallets indbyggere i Aaker sogn: Gravpladser fra tidlig kristen tid ved Ndr. Grødbygård', *Bornholmske Samlinger*, ser. 3 vol. 10, 167–86.

Wallin, C. 1986, 'Knudskulten i Lund', in Nyberg *et al.* 1986, 79–85.

Weeke, C. 1884–9, 'Indledning', in *Libri memoriales capituli Lundensis: Lunde Domkapitels Gavebøger ('Libri datici Lundenses')*, ed. C. Weeke, Copenhagen, I–XX.

Weibull, L. 1946, *Skånes kyrka från älsta tid till Jacob Erlandsens död 1274*, Copenhagen.

Widukind, *Die Sachsengeschichte des Widukind von Korvei*, ed. P. Hirsch and H.-E. Lohmann, Hanover, 1935 (*MGH SRG*).

Wood, I. 2001, *The Missionary Life: Saints and the Evangelisation of Europe, 400–1050*, Harlow.

Worsaae, J. J. A. 1856, *Minder fra Valdemar den Stores Tid, især i Ringsted- og Sorö-Egnen*, Copenhagen.

CHAPTER 4

The kingdom of Norway

Sverre Bagge and Sæbjørg Walaker Nordeide

I. BEFORE CHRISTIANITY: RELIGION AND POWER

The sources for the early history of Norway, including its Christianization, are relatively abundant, although most of them are late. It is therefore very often difficult to distinguish between reliable information and later inventions. This also applies to the information about pagan religion. Best known is the mythology, for which the most important source is the *Elder Edda*, a collection of twenty-nine pieces of pagan poems, ten of which deal with the gods, collected in written form around 1230 and preserved in an Icelandic manuscript from around 1270.[1] The best known of these poems is *Voluspá*, 'the Volve's prophecies', which deals with the creation of the world and its end.[2] Other well-known writings in the collection include *Hávamál*, 'the words of the High', i.e. Odin, on how to live, and *Skírnismál*, which some scholars believe refers to a fertility cult. Further, the skaldic poetry, poems composed in praise of kings and chieftains, contains frequent allusions to the mythology.

There has been a long discussion on the date of the Eddic poems, but the majority of scholars believe that they have been preserved orally since the pagan period, or at least that the mythology contained in them goes back to this period. There is also some evidence to support this view, such as a quotation from the poem *Hávamál* in a skaldic stanza from the tenth century and from a Viking Age runic inscription in the Eddic metre. Further, poetry is more likely to be preserved orally than prose; in particular, the very complicated metre of the skaldic poems gives some protection against change in oral transmission. However, examples of different versions in the medieval manuscripts show that some changes did take place, and we cannot exclude the possibility that some skaldic or Eddic poems were composed or were subject to considerable changes in the Christian period.

---

[1] Vries 1956–7; Lindow 1985; Harris 1985; Fidjestøl 1999; Clunies Ross 1987; 1994.
[2] A volve, ON *volva*, is a woman with divinatory powers.

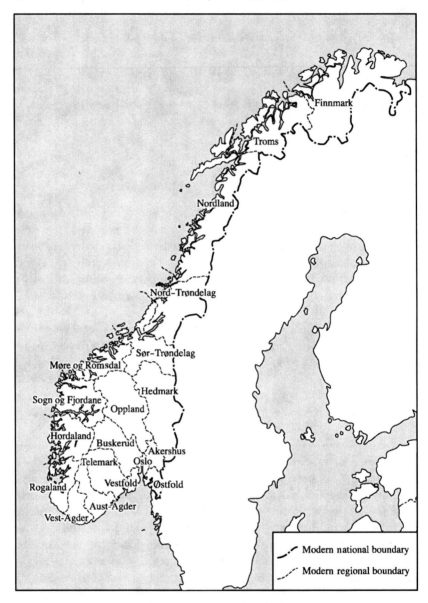

5. Norway: modern regions (*fylker*)

Skaldic poems were still being composed in the thirteenth century, which might give rise to suspicion about the authenticity of the oral transmission. On the other hand, this fact also serves to explain the continued familiarity during the Christian period with the ancient mythology. This use of pagan mythology was hardly more opposed to Christianity than the contemporary European use of the Greek and Roman mythology and literature.

The second main source for the ancient mythology is Snorri Sturluson's (1179–1241) *Edda*, usually referred to as the *Younger Edda*, composed between *c.* 1220 and Snorri's death. This work is allegedly intended as a book of instruction for skalds, who need to be familiar with the ancient mythology, above all in order to master the metaphorical language (*kenningar*) of skaldic poetry. The work contains myths about the gods and their genealogies, about the activities of the gods and about the history of the world from the time it was created until it ends. Snorri's sources for this were ancient skaldic poems, preserved orally, and poems from the *Elder Edda*, but Snorri must also to a considerable extent have used his own imagination, based on thirteenth-century Christian ideas.

The Eddic and skaldic poems contain allusions to and stories about a number of male and female gods and the relationship between them, but give no systematic account of the mythology. Snorri's *Edda* is more organized, but this may be the result of Snorri's familiarity with the far more systematic Christian theology. The mythological sources depict the gods as married, having families and living on individual farms, in a similar way to their human worshippers. Odin seems to have been regarded as the leader of the gods, or at least the most prominent of them, but he was no absolute monarch. He was a warrior god and in addition known for his wisdom and magical powers. His son Thor (Tor) was known for his strength but also appears as a somewhat comical figure in some of the poems. He seems to have been more connected to fertility, as were also the god Frøy and the goddess Frøya. The names of the gods occur in a number of place names, e.g. Onsøy or Onarheim (derived from Odin) and Tysnes (from the war god Tyr), which may be used to draw conclusions about their cult and popularity in various parts of the country. These do not necessarily correspond to their status in the poetry. Thus, a large number of the place names, e.g. Ullensaker, Ullevål, suggest that Ull, usually referred to as a sky god, must have been very important, although he does not occur in the extant mythological sources. In addition to the gods, there was another category of supernatural figures, the giants (*jotnar*), who were their enemies and inferior to them in rank, though resourceful and often dangerous. The relationship between these two 'tribes' does not correspond to that between good and evil in Christianity, nor were they always enemies.

In contrast to the mythology, very little is known about the cult, which was probably the most important part of the religion. The sagas contain some descriptions of it, the most famous of which is Snorri's account of the sacrifice (*blót*) at Mære, in which Håkon den gode is forced to take part. The reliability of this account has been subject to much discussion, but it is difficult to imagine that Snorri knew very much about religious practices that had been banned for more than 200 years. Most of his details seem to be derived from contemporary Christian practice or from accounts of sacrifices in the Old Testament.[3] It seems likely, however, that cult had the form of sacrificial meals – the introduction of common drinking-parties three times a year in the earliest Christian laws is clearly intended to replace such meals – and further that the eating of horsemeat formed an important part of these meals, as this was strictly forbidden in Christian times.

Cult and religion must have been an integrated part of life in pagan society, and there was a close connection between the cult and political, social and economic activities. There is no evidence of a professional priestly class; most probably chieftains and prominent men or women acted as cultic leaders. However, some places are believed to have been specialized for cult more than others. Pagan cult buildings are referred to as *hof* in the sagas. Farm names such as Hov, -hov, Hove etc., which are numerous in Norway, indicate the sites of pagan cult places. For instance at Hove in Trøndelag an irregular row of ten cylindrical, 0.4–0.6 metres wide, stone-packed holes are interpreted as bases for deity figures, associated with many pits containing the remains of charcoal and animal bones. The pits are interpreted as traces of cult, maybe offerings or sacred meals. Burial mounds are found as well, but no traces of houses. The activity is dated *c.* 100 BC–AD 1000.[4] Farms with names indicating cult are often centrally located and thus well suited for gatherings. Against the background of Danish and Swedish evidence, scholars today are of the opinion that the *hof*, the same word as German *Hof*, was a hall or large building on farms.[5] The excavations in the church at Mære in Trøndelag for instance indicate that the church was built on the site of a pagan cult building. This building was identified by small pictures made of goldleaf, 'gullgubber', engraved with pagan motifs which were found in postholes belonging to a building older than the medieval church. 'Gullgubber' depicted one or two persons in relief interpreted as deities, on

---

[3] Düwel 1985. For alternative points of view, Steinsland 2000, 111–12; Meulengracht Sørensen 2001.
[4] Farbregd 1986b. Also Narmo 1996.   [5] Olsen 1995.

a small golden sheet. Since these excavations in the 1960s, gullgubber have been found near posts in (often large) buildings where pagan cult activities are believed to have taken place, for instance in a chieftain's hall at Borg in Lofoten, at Klepp in Rogaland and at Hov at Hedmark. Farm names such as Horg or ending in -horg refer to outdoor cult sites. One skaldic poem refers to Olav Tryggvason as a 'horg breaker', that is, as the destroyer of these sites. The oldest Christian legislation prohibited the location of cults near hills and 'horgs'. A stone construction, found near Egersund, may be a pagan altar. Other place names like 'vang', 've', 'leik' and 'lund' may indicate cult as well, but we do not know the character of the cult. Although, due to the lack of systematic archaeological research, it is impossible to prove a strong correspondence between archaeological evidence of pagan cult and farm names, nevertheless burials have often been observed in places with names indicating cult.

Burials provide the most common archaeological evidence of the pagan religion. Both cremation and inhumation were practised. The two types appear side by side in some areas from the same period, and even sometimes in the same burial mound, while only one type dominates in others. There is no difference between the indications of wealth in the two kinds of burials. We do not know what determined the choice between them, whether it was the life of the buried person, the cause of death, practical reasons or simply a coincidence. The orientation of the body varies as well, between south–north, east–west and in between. In the cremation burials the burial gifts and the body are often neatly arranged and burnt at the same time, and the grave is sometimes covered by a mound. The amount of burial gifts increases during the Viking period, with many particularly rich cremation burials from the tenth century.[6] Visible monuments above the grave vary considerably, many graves having none. The burial mounds are generally quite visible; they are usually in groups from a few to about twenty, and located near farmyards or along farm paths. It is generally believed that only the members of the social elite were buried in monumental graves, and that the size of the burial monument as well as the amount of grave gifts depended on wealth and social status. The graves of the poor have no visible signs.

The characteristics above concern the Norse people in all parts of Norway. However, the belief system and cult of the Saami, who lived as nomads in the north of Norway as well as further south, were different. The sources on Saami religion are from the Christian era. Adam of Bremen around 1073–5

---

[6] Solberg 2000.

appears to be writing of the Saami religion, when he relates that those who live along the sea farthest to the north are not yet Christian. 'These people are still so skilled in sorcery and prayer that they claim to know what everyone in the world is doing.'[7] The *Historia Norvegiae* contains a section on the special characteristics of the Saami's religion: shamanism, cultic dance, trances and clairvoyance. The clerical author gives the impression that there was much contact and trade between the Christians and the Saami in the second half of the 1100s. *Heimskringla* links the Saami for the most part to 'wizardry'. The *Law of Eidsivating*, legislation concerning the east of Norway and brought to bear in early Christian times, implies that the Saami were known for their healing abilities and methods. The most important Saami good gods were female (for instance Sáráhkká, Juksáhkká), while the most important evil power was male (Stallo). The goddess Jábmeáhkká dominated the place for the dead. The sun, Beaivi, was also an important god. Throughout the period *c.* 800–post-1800 the dead were buried in rocky areas where loose stones stood in piles, often with a Saami sledge and birch bark. The importance of the naked stone is reflected in this burial custom; the Saami believed in Sieiddit, a god inhabiting rocks and stone. Animals and dress accessories are a common grave gift in both Norse and Saami cultures, but the standard weapons and rich household equipment and boats which we find in many of the Norse graves seem to be missing in the Saami graves. The lack of weapons is explained by the belief about conflict between the goddess of death and the god of hunting.[8]

There seem to be some similarities between Saami and Norse religions, such as the stratified cosmos and the idea of a free soul which can travel between the different levels. The bear is present in rituals in both cultures, and both Norwegian and Saami religion have a god of thunder with a hammer, Thor and Horagalles.

Principalities are likely to have existed before the unification of the kingdom, but little is known about them. Ottar of Hålogaland, who visited King Alfred's court around 870 and whose narrative is preserved in the preface to the Anglo-Saxon translation of Orosius, uses the term Norway (Norðveg) saying that he lives in the land of the Norwegians, but makes no mention of political units. He must have been a powerful chieftain, who drew income from taxation of the Saami in northern Norway, and from trade of traditional Saami merchandise in southern Norway and northern Europe. Ottar's power was to a much lesser extent based on ownership of land. This, however, must have been a main source of political power further

---

[7] Adam of Bremen IV.32.   [8] Schanche 2000.

south, particularly in south-eastern Norway, Trøndelag and some parts of western Norway. Various smaller principalities are mentioned in the later sources as existing here before the unification. Their existence seems likely but we do not know whether they were fairly permanent entities with some kind of administrative structure, or mainly based on personal lordship and thus short-lived and changing. In any case, grave finds indicate the presence of powerful chieftains during pagan times. The best known and best preserved are the Oseberg (*c.* 834) and Gokstad ship graves (*c.* 900–5) in Vestfold, but such burials have also been found in other parts of the country, for instance at the outlet of Glomma in Østfold and on Karmøy in Rogaland (tenth century). Some very well-furnished women's graves in Sogn indicate the existence of powerful chieftains in this region, as do also house and dock foundations, discovered in north Jæren in south-western Norway. Further, scholars believe that income from Viking activities and the military power possessed by the Vikings provided the basis for power at home. The Eddic and early skaldic poems particularly honour chieftains who distinguished themselves in battle.

There is some evidence that kings and magnates had a religious function in the pagan period as cultic leaders, and formed the link between people and the gods, whose 'luck' ensured 'good years and peace' as well as victory in war.[9] There are even examples of some of them claiming descent from the gods. The poem *Ynglingatal*, quoted in Snorri's *Heimskringla*, traces a dynasty in south-eastern Norway (Vestfold) back to the god Odin. This dynasty was later identified with that of Harald Hårfagre. The age of the poem has been the subject of much discussion, but the majority of scholars believe that it dates from the Viking Age.[10] The divine descent of the Ynglingar is further developed in the later prose sources *Historia Norvegiae* and *Heimskringla*, the latter probably dependent on Ari's lost work. Further, the skaldic poem *Håløygjatal*, composed by Øyvind Skaldespille in the tenth century and preserved in a fragmented form in four sagas, including *Heimskringla* and *Fagrskinna*, lists the ancestors of Håkon jarl back to Odin.

Harald Hårfagre (Fairhair) allegedly unified the whole country, but most of the evidence for this is very late. The oldest narrative source, Ari fróði's *Íslendingabók*, from the first half of the twelfth century, relates that he ruled for seventy years and died at the age of eighty, in 931–2. Details about his

[9] Bagge 1991, 218–24; Steinsland 2000, 53–9; 2001; Krag 2001.
[10] An exception is Claus Krag who claims that it was actually composed in the twelfth century in order to serve as legitimation for the Norwegian kings in their struggle with Denmark over the south-eastern part of the country (Krag 1991): this hypothesis has been rejected by most scholars; e.g. the reviews by Fidjestøl 1994 and Sandnes 1994.

conquest of Norway are only given in the sagas from the thirteenth century (they are most elaborate in *Heimskringla*), and are most probably later constructions. The only event for which there is contemporary evidence is the battle of Hafrsfjord, just south of present-day Stavanger, which is celebrated in a skaldic poem, quoted in the sagas. As far as can be gathered from this poem, Harald defeated a number of chieftains mentioned by name, most probably arriving at Hafrsfjord from the south. The battle has been dated to between around 870 and 900. Several chieftains contemporary with Harald are mentioned in the sources: Atle earl of Fjordane, Ragnvald earl of Møre and Håkon earl who belonged to the powerful chieftain families in northern Norway and Trøndelag. The current opinion is that Harald's kingdom was mainly confined to western Norway, as all early evidence links Harald to this part of the country.[11]

Sources described Norwegian rulers as king (Old Norse *konungr*, Latin *rex*), earl (Old Norse *jarl*, Latin *comes*) and chieftain (Old Norse *hofðingi*, Latin *princeps*). The titles have fairly exact meanings in the prose sources that probably reflect twelfth- and thirteenth-century conditions. According to *Heimskringla*, Harald Hårfagre even established a fixed hierarchy, with one *jarl* in each *fylki* (territorial division),[12] each with four *hersir* under him. *Hofðingi* is a more general term, in the kings' sagas mainly used to denote independent rulers. The title 'earl' in the sagas normally refers to men ranking just below the king, who ruled more or less independently over large areas, such as the Lade earls of Trøndelag. This resembles the use of the title in the thirteenth century, when there was normally only one earl at a time in the country, who was a kind of co-ruler, ranking next to the king. The title *hersir* – 'ruler' – has been the subject of much discussion. According to *Heimskringla*, St Olav replaced this title with that of *lendr maðr*, i.e. 'landed man', a man who held land from the king. Most probably, however, this neatly arranged hierarchy is a later construction, whereas in reality before the twelfth century the differences between the various titles were vague and depended on time and place. This is reflected in the early Eddic and skaldic poetry where for instance the title 'earl' refers to powerful men in general, as in the poem *Rígspula*, where mankind is divided into three categories: slave, commoner (*bóndi*) and *jarl*.[13]

[11] Krag 2003, 185–9.
[12] Trøndelag was divided into eight *fylki* and western Norway into six. The units probably date from well before the Viking Age, in Trøndelag possibly from 300–600. *Fylki* apparently did not exist in eastern Norway, until they were introduced after the western Norwegian model in the late thirteenth century.
[13] The date of *Rígspula* has been the subject of much discussion, the opinions varying from the ninth until the mid-thirteenth century: See 1981, 84–95, 96–8, 514–16; Bagge 2000, 20–38.

If the tradition about Harald Hårfagre's unification is correct, then unification came before Christianization. However, even if Harald did rule the whole country, which is doubtful, none of his successors did so until St Olav Haraldsson (1015–30), who was responsible for the final Christianization. The sagas depict the struggles in the intervening period as a conflict between two dynasties, the descendants of Harald Hårfagre and the earls of Lade. Modern historians have modified this on two points. They pay greater attention to the intervention of the Danish kings who apparently controlled the south-eastern part of the country and sometimes even more during most of the period, and they have questioned the existence of the Hårfagre dynasty. Most probably, Harald's grandsons, the Eirikssons, were the last of his descendants to rule the country, whereas the two missionary kings, Olav Tryggvason (995–1000) and St Olav Haraldsson, did not belong to the dynasty.[14] The competition over Norway thus seems to have been more open during the first century after Harald's death than the sagas admit. The later Norwegian dynasty cannot trace its line further back than to Harald Hardråde (1046–66), St Olav's half-brother.

2. CONTACTS

In contrast to Denmark and Sweden, which were the targets of Ansgar's mission in the ninth century, there is no evidence of individual missionaries in Norway, nor do we know of any *Lives* of missionaries. All the missionaries mentioned in the sources were apparently brought in by the missionary kings in the tenth and early eleventh centuries. By contrast, the Viking Age was a period of close connections between Scandinavia and Christian Europe, through travel, trade, plundering or conquering expeditions and Scandinavians serving as mercenaries abroad. Contemporary European sources mention that pagan Scandinavians were marked with the sign of the cross, although not baptized, before entering Christian countries, so that they could move freely among the Christian members of the population. There are also references to Scandinavians being baptized abroad, in the sagas as well as in non-Scandinavian sources. Thus, of the two missionary kings, Olav Tryggvason was baptized in England in connection with a peace settlement, whereas St Olav was baptized in Normandy, probably in connection with an alliance with the exiled English king. In both cases, a number of warriors must have been baptized together with their leader.

[14] Krag 1989; 2003, 185–96.

Moreover, as the sources are meagre, there must have been many other, similar examples that are not mentioned.

The evidence of Christian influence in Norway itself is mainly archaeological. An important category of sources in this context is the ninety-three stone crosses, mostly found along the western coast between Rogaland and Sogn og Fjordane. The crosses are interpreted by Birkeli as a sign of a gradual process of Christianization prior to the establishment of any organized church in Norway.[15] He points out that the location of the crosses corresponds to the core area of Håkon den gode's sphere of influence. Birkeli also shows that these crosses resemble the stone crosses found in England and Ireland, thus forming evidence of close contacts with the British Isles. Both the existence of the crosses themselves and their style seem to link southern Norway, especially its western parts, to the British Isles, although the style in Norway is very rough compared to the British crosses. Stone crosses in Britain with runic inscriptions form further evidence of contact across the North Sea. Recent research has dated most of the crosses to the period *c.* 950–*c.* 1030, but some of them may be younger. The dating is based on comparative studies of style, inscriptions, whether they are situated on an older grave and whether they are associated with a church.[16] However, the dating is very rough, as the crosses are not dated by their context. Birkeli's theories about the influence from the British Isles have received general support, but both his theory about the gradual process of conversion and whether or not the geographic and chronological framework of the stone crosses corresponds to Håkon den gode's reign are debated.

Trade was an important means of cultural and religious exchange and may in many cases have contributed to conversion. Archaeology reveals objects in Norway from the rest of north-western Europe from Roman times onwards. Numerous imported objects from the British Isles are found in pagan graves in Norway in the Viking period. Although not all of these are Christian cult objects, they indicate contact with Christian areas. How they arrived in Norway, by trade, plundering or gift exchange, may vary from case to case and often cannot be decided. Nevertheless, the exchange of objects with foreign countries facilitated a long period of religious influence in Norway prior to its 'official' Christianization. Ottar of Hålogaland recounts that extensive trade existed between commercial centres in Norway (Kaupang/Skiringssal), Rus' and Saami areas of the north, the continent (Hedeby) and England.

---

[15] Birkeli 1973.   [16] Gabrielsen 2002, 57–60.

Kaupang in Vestfold was a trade centre from *c.* 800 to *c.* 960, and a possible arena for various cultures to meet. Arabic, French and English coins, ceramics from the Rhine, the North Sea area of northern Holland and the Baltic have all been found in Kaupang, and there are traces of at least the Norse and Christian religions. Three Thor's hammers were found in the settlement area, one in the form of a pendant and two incised on Arabic dirhams.[17] The latter indicate that the Norse people recognized the dirhams as foreign, and maybe threatening, since they have found it necessary to add a familiar god's symbol. Lead brooches with a simple cross decoration may be produced by Christians, but not necessarily.[18] However, the burial customs seem not to have changed markedly even when grave gifts include Christian objects. Even a woman with a cross pendant, thought to be a Christian of non-Scandinavian origin, is buried in a non-Christian way. The only possible evidence of Christian influence on burial customs is the fact that Christian objects occur more often in inhumation than in cremation burials.[19] Inhumation and cremation burials appear side by side during the 900s, and boat graves as well as coffin graves have been discovered, some totally without burial goods, one with a reliquary. Although the burial traditions vary in Viking Age Norway in general, the different burial practices within the same burial place at Kaupang could be explained by the fact that Kaupang attracted a variety of travellers. The situation in Kaupang is very much a parallel to Birka in Sweden, where Christian objects are found as well.

Although there is a considerable amount of archaeological evidence of contacts with Christian Europe, it is more difficult to decide to what extent this evidence expresses adherence to Christianity. Graves with little or no burial gifts are not unequivocally Christian; neither is an east–west grave orientation or inhumation burial. Many people were already buried in a simple manner in Norway in the Viking period. As only landowners got a rich burial, a process of concentration of property owners would also lead to a reduction in rich burials.[20] Many Christian objects may have been plundered from churches or monasteries; they were used purely for decoration or were destroyed, as for instance book mountings torn off a book, in order to use the precious metal, which clearly shows that contact with Christians did not lead to Christian influence. Other instances are more ambiguous. Ann-Sofie Gräslund interprets Christian objects in the

---

[17] Skre and Stylegar 2004, personal communication from Christoph Kilger.
[18] Skre, Pilø and Pedersen 2001, 24; Lager 2002, 140.
[19] Blindheim, Heyerdahl-Larsen and Tollnes 1981, 119.   [20] Solberg 2000.

graves as an indication of the Christianity of the dead (often a woman).[21] However, the women were often buried with dress accessories and jewellery, and the Christian objects may be interpreted as such, particularly if they are found in an obviously pagan cultic context. An increase in richly furnished cremation burials appears in many districts during the 900s, e.g. in Innvik, Nordfjord and in Grytten, Romsdal. In the last, the dead woman was buried in a boat with rich gifts, like jewellery and a reliquary, most likely plundered from the British Isles.[22] The grave is dated to the first half of the tenth century, and the site is not far from the contemporary Christian graves at Veøy. The grave goods including Christian objects in a pagan context suggest opposition rather than adherence to Christianity.

It is unclear when Norwegians began to use Christian cult objects for cultic purposes. A possible example is a complex of Christian objects found at a chieftain's farm at Borg: a glass with gold decoration including a cross, a 'Tating' pitcher,[23] also decorated with a cross, and an insular bronze bowl, all possibly for liturgical hand washing. In addition, a gold pointer possibly for reading holy manuscripts was found, with insular parallels. The date range for the objects is *c.* 770–900.[24] The top of a bishop's crosier in bronze, dated by style to the eleventh–twelfth century has been found at Hunstad, by Bodø.[25] A mould for a cross found at Kaupang is probably the oldest evidence for local production of Christian objects. As pagan cult was still practised in Kaupang at the time, the mould is not necessarily evidence of a strong local Christian community, but may also have been used for production intended for foreigners or indicate syncretism or the peaceful coexistence of pagans and Christians.

Very early Christian burials are traced at Veøy in Romsdal: two tenth-century Christian churchyards surrounded by stone fences, and the remains of what is interpreted as a church in the centre of the churchyard. The first of these burial places is dated to about 950 or a bit earlier, and the other to the second half of the 900s. The dates and the area fit Håkon den gode's church-building activities as described in the sagas.[26] An early Christian churchyard is also found under the stone church of St Clement in Oslo, where some of the bodies are buried wrapped up in birch bark and in coffins made of tree trunks. The graves are probably from the early eleventh century. Of a similar date or slightly later are seven graves interpreted as Christian from Hernes in Frosta, Trøndelag. The farm was mentioned as a royal estate in 1135, but no church has been found at Hernes. Graves and

---

[21] Gräslund 2002.   [22] Farbregd 1986a.
[23] A type of pitcher from Westphalia, often used for liturgical purposes.
[24] Munch, Johansen and Roesdahl 2003.   [25] Cruickshank 2002.   [26] Solli 1996.

house remains excavated at Hadsel in Nordland are interpreted as Christian, but the remains are very fragmentary and the interpretation is not without problems. The oldest grave is dated *c.* 1030–1150 by Carbon 14 dating.[27]

Regional differences regarding Christian influence are considerable: no evidence of Christian burial practice is found before the eleventh century in the interior of eastern Norway and in Agder, Trøndelag and northern Norway, while Østfold, Rogaland and some parts of Møre appear to have been significantly influenced by Christianity after 950. Most pagan burials disappear between 950 and 1050 at different times in different areas, with the general exception of the Saami. By contrast, we find pagan burials in Agder in the second half of the eleventh century. In Hordaland there seems to be a rapid shift to Christianity around 1000–50, and pagan graves disappear almost completely some time in the eleventh century.[28] Such change is typical of most areas. However, the earlier, Migration Age inhumation burials were not the result of Christian influence; inhumation was part of pagan burial customs. Archaeological evidence from Østfold and Vestfold, on either side of the Oslofjord, is very different throughout the Iron Age. There is no evidence of Christian influence in Vestfold; on the contrary, Vestfold is characterized by an increase in rich burials (for example at Borre and Gokstad) during the tenth century, whereas the burials became simpler in Østfold, which was subject to influences from Sweden and from the Christian Danes.[29] The Danes may also have influenced Oslo.

Because Christian burials are less visible and more difficult to date, we have very few examples of Christian burials before 1100, but the pagan burial customs stop very suddenly in many places during the eleventh century. However, more research is needed to gain a more complete picture. It is difficult to know whether or not the two religions coexisted in the same locality. No examples are known of pagan and Christian burials in the same burial ground simultaneously, although Christian churches were often built on the ground of earlier pagan gravefields. But the fact that we never find Christian graves while excavating non-Christian graves indicates that churches and pagan cemeteries did not exist simultaneously. Within larger areas, however, such as Romsdal, pagan burials can be found from a later date than the first Christian churchyard. From the archaeological material it looks as if Christian and non-Christian communities mostly lived separately, although they overlapped chronologically.

Thus, although the archaeological evidence indicates a fairly complex picture, it clearly suggests the existence of Christian impulses in Norway

[27] Eide 1974; Farbregd 1986c; Sandmo 1990.   [28] Gellein 1997.   [29] Forseth 2003.

6. Medieval towns and central places in Norway and places mentioned in the chapter

well before the official conversion of the whole country in the early eleventh century. There must have been a number of conversions by individuals and family groups in the tenth century, and pagans and Christians must have coexisted within some larger areas.

3. CHRISTIANIZATION

Håkon den gode (ruled *c.* 934–61) was brought up by the English king Athelstan, and returned to Norway as a Christian. Why he was sent to England is not known – the explanation in the sagas is late and hardly trustworthy – but it was probably the result of some alliance between his father, Harald Hårfagre, and King Athelstan. Håkon's successors, the Eirikssons, were also baptized in England. As for Olav Tryggvason's baptism (ruled 995–1000), Adam of Bremen gives two alternative versions, one that he was baptized in England, another that he was baptized by Danish missionaries, most probably in Norway. The Norwegian–Icelandic sources all agree that he was baptized in England, although they give different accounts of the circumstances. Olav's baptism in England is confirmed by the *Anglo-Saxon Chronicle*, according to which the Viking chieftain Anlaf, usually identified with Olav Tryggvason, was baptized in Andover, at King Æthelred's court, in 991. This statement is likely to be correct and indicates that Olav's baptism should be understood as part of the peace settlement between the Vikings and the Anglo-Saxon king. As for Olav Haraldsson, the Norman chronicle of William of Jumièges from the end of the eleventh century relates that he was baptized at Rouen in 1013 or 1014, which is probably true. This piece of information is also referred to by Theodoricus Monachus, who has some doubts about the matter, referring to an alternative, Norwegian–Icelandic tradition that also occurs in the later sagas, that he was baptized as a child in Norway by Olav Tryggvason. This, however, is clearly an invention, possibly an expression of the analogy between the two Olavs and John the Baptist and Christ, the first Olav preparing the way for the second. The sagas agree for the most part that the missionary kings were baptized along with their followers.

According to the sagas, Håkon den gode was the first to bring missionaries to Norway. *Ágrip* (*c.* 1190) as well as the later sagas mention that Håkon built churches and installed priests, but the people of Møre in the north-western part of southern Norway burnt down the churches and killed the priests, and the people of Trøndelag further north forced the king to give up the mission and take part in the pagan cult. Håkon was succeeded by his nephews the Eirikssons, the sons of his brother Eirik, who were also

Christian, but according to the sagas did not act as missionaries. They were in turn succeeded by Håkon of the Lade dynasty, the last pagan ruler of Norway, who fought to restore the pagan religion. This is attested by the skaldic poem *Vellekla* which praises Håkon for protecting the pagan sanctuaries. Whereas the core area of the Hårfagre dynasty was western Norway, Håkon's stronghold was Trøndelag and northern Norway. His famous victory over a Danish force at Hjørungavåg in Sunnmøre may indicate that his power extended to western Norway or parts of it as well, but there is no evidence that he had any control over eastern Norway which was probably part of the Danish sphere of influence.

Håkon's death in a local rebellion paved the way for Olav Tryggvason (ruled 995–1000), who according to Adam was 'the first to bring Christianity to Norway'. Adam has otherwise little information about him and even hints that he may later have lapsed from the faith. By contrast, three Norwegian works from the late twelfth century depict him as a great missionary, but give very few details about how he carried out his missionary work. The *Saga of Olav Tryggvason*, written by the monk Odd Snorrason in Iceland around 1190, credits Olav with having Christianized five countries, and narrates in great detail Olav's missionary expeditions in the various parts of Norway. Olav Tryggvason was later the subject of several longer sagas, including *Heimskringla*. No attempt was apparently made to canonize him, but the accounts about him have strongly hagiographic features, notably Odd Monk's work, which contains a detailed story of Olav's conversion through divine intervention, as well as an account of his reign as a decisive phase in the spiritual battle between God and the devil over the souls of the Norwegians.[30]

After Olav's death in a battle against the neighbouring kings, Norway was ruled by the two earls of Lade, Eirik and Svein, under the suzerainty of the Danish and Swedish kings. The earls were both Christian, but according to the narrative sources did little to promote Christianity. They were succeeded by the second great missionary king, Olav Haraldsson, who also brought many bishops and priests from England, the most important of whom according to the sagas was Bishop Grimkjell. According to Adam of Bremen, Olav Haraldsson established contact with the archbishopric of Hamburg-Bremen and asked for missionaries to be sent to Norway. In addition to Grimkjell, Adam names Siegfried, Rudolf and Bernhard, whose names suggest German origin.

[30] Lönnroth 1963; Andersson 2003; Bagge 2006.

Olav had to leave the country in 1028–9 as the result of an alliance against him of Norwegian chieftains and Knud the Great. He went to Rus', returned in the summer of 1030 to regain his kingdom, but was defeated and killed in the battle of Stiklestad. Adam of Bremen claims that the internal opposition against Olav was caused by Olav's decision to have the wives of some chieftains executed for having practised magical arts, which would mean that the rebellion was a pagan reaction. However, there is no other evidence for such an interpretation, either in the contemporary skaldic poems, or in the later written sources. If Adam's information were true, it would probably be corroborated, given the strong hagiographic tradition. Most of Olav's leading enemies were also Christians, including of course Knud the Great, and nothing suggests that his death led to a return to paganism. Quite the contrary, Olav was almost immediately regarded as a saint.

The earliest primary sources on Olav's sainthood are the skaldic poems *Glælognskviða*, from approximately 1032, and the *Erfidrápa*, from about 1040.[31] According to *Glælognskviða*, Olav, after his death, began to mediate between humans and God: 'through God he procures prosperity and peace for all people'. Scholars have had different explanations of Olav's canonization. Some point to political reasons: his sainthood could be used as a weapon against the ruling Danish king. Another explanation points to influence from the cult of royal saints in Anglo-Saxon England. Attempts have also been made to link the canonization to pagan ideas about sacred kingship, a much debated concept: the king had a special relationship with the gods, and possessed supernatural abilities.[32] As the holy king is not a specifically Norwegian phenomenon, however, but occurs in most of the newly converted countries, the problem should be discussed against a more general religious, cultural, and political background.

The chronological distance between the lives of the two missionary kings and the narrative sources, as well as the strongly hagiographic character of the latter, makes it difficult to draw firm conclusions about the actual lives and characters of the two kings. As for Olav Tryggvason, Adam of Bremen's negative comments are hardly trustworthy, as Adam was strongly biased in favour of his own church, Hamburg-Bremen, whereas Olav brought his missionaries from England. Further, Adam derived most of his historical information from the Danish king Sven Estridson, a descendant of Olav's

[31] Mortensen and Mundal 2003, 354–7.
[32] Thus Steinsland 2000; 2001; cf. the criticism by Krag 2001.

enemy Sven Forkbeard (Tveskæg). Olav is therefore likely to have worked for the introduction of Christianity in Norway, but there is little evidence about the details of his work, and the narrative sources may well have exaggerated its importance. As for Olav Haraldsson, there can be no doubt about his Christianity, mentioned in contemporary skaldic poetry. There is also relatively good evidence of his work for the organization of the Norwegian church,[33] and laws refer to his introducing Christian regulation, notably at a meeting at Moster.

The existence of local saints is likely to have been an important factor in strengthening the position of Christianity in the population. Apart from St Olav, St Hallvard and St Sunniva also appear from early on; both are mentioned by Adam of Bremen. Hallvard was a young man, related to the royal house, from the region near Oslo, who was killed around 1050 in order to save a woman falsely accused of theft. The woman's pursuers threw him into the water with a millstone around his neck, but the body floated. Hallvard became the patron saint of the diocese of Oslo. Sunniva was supposedly an Irish princess who left her country by ship in order to escape a pagan suitor and was stranded on the coast of Norway. Being discovered by pagans, she and her followers prayed to God to be saved from them and were buried in the caves where they had been hiding. After their death, light began to pour out from the caves, and the bones found there gave a wonderful fragrance. King Olav Tryggvason ordered the holy relics to be venerated. The earliest legend only refers to the holy people of Selja; Sunniva is a later addition. Sunniva became the patron saint of the diocese of Bergen. Neither St Hallvard nor St Sunniva became as popular as St Olav.

All the missionary kings had met Christianity in England, and both the sagas and most modern historians have emphasized the English influence on the Christianization of Norway. There is also some firm evidence for this view. Both the Old Norse Christian terminology and the Norwegian Christian laws show Anglo-Saxon influence. Further, Adam of Bremen, who generally emphasizes the importance of his own diocese, Hamburg-Bremen, at the cost of other missionary centres, including England, has little to say about Norway. However, the connection with England has been studied more thoroughly than that with Germany, and future research may find more evidence of German influence.[34] An inscription on the Jelling stone in Denmark, erected by Harald Bluetooth in the middle of the

[33] Krag 2003, 194.
[34] Myking 2001. The standard work on the English influence is still Taranger 1890.

900s, declaring that Harald 'made the Danes Christian', may form indirect evidence of German influence, via Denmark. As the area around the Oslo fjord was at this time under Danish rule, Christianization probably took place here as well. There is some archaeological evidence for this: sixty-two Christian graves were found under the church of St Clement in Oslo, which was built *c.* 1100. The graves are traditionally dated by Carbon 14 dating to the period *c.* 980–1030, although this is now under review. According to some of the sagas, King Harald sent two earls to the Oslofjord area to convert the people there. This may possibly be the mission referred to by Adam of Bremen, who writes that many were converted when German missionaries came to Norway at the time of Archbishop Adaldag (d. 988). According to written sources Trondheim was also conquered by the Danish king Knud the Great (1017–35). The archaeological finds confirm that there was an urban settlement in Trondheim from the end of the tenth century, and there are no traces of pagan cult from this time. Nevertheless, there is little to suggest that political pressure from abroad played any part in the Christianization of Norway, in contrast to the situation in Germany's neighbours.

The Christian kings' background as Vikings and mercenaries abroad may also have formed a reason for them to act as missionaries, as this would strengthen their own position at the cost of the old kings and magnates who at least partly based their local power on religious leadership. However, the division between centralization and local power does not correspond completely to that between Christianity and paganism. Most of St Olav's opponents were also Christians, and some local chieftains may have played a similar part in the introduction of Christianity as the Christianizing kings.

The focus on the missionary kings in the sagas also means that the conversion is understood in political and cultural rather than strictly religious terms. People convert out of loyalty to the king or to win his friendship or because the king forces them to do so, and faith and dogma play a subordinate part. In light of what we know about Old Norse society in general, there are reasons to believe that this picture contains some truth. Dynastic alliances through marriage or the fostering of children were an important channel of cultural contacts. The sources give several examples of marriage alliances being used to promote Christianity, as both Olav Tryggvason and St Olav are said to have married off female relatives to important chieftains in return for their conversion to Christianity. Although the trustworthiness of each particular example may be open to doubt, marriage was clearly an important instrument in forming alliances and is likely to have been so in the religious as well as in the secular sphere. By contrast, there are no examples of Christian princesses converting their royal husbands. Furthermore, the kings' generosity and personalities may have been important factors in conversions. This applies to the two Olavs as well as to their predecessor Håkon den gode who according to *Ágrip* made 'many people' convert because of his personal popularity. The sagas give some drastic examples of the missionary kings' use of force to obtain conversion, some of which may well be true, but force can hardly have been a main factor in the conversion. Given the frequent rebellions against unpopular kings, it is difficult to imagine that it would have been possible to force the majority of the population to accept a religion they did not want.

The archaeological material presented above gives no definite answer to the question of gradual or sudden Christianization or of the relative importance of the kings in the process. There are some very early examples of Christian influence, but it is difficult to know how representative they are. As for regional differences, the archaeological material gives the same impression as the written sources, that the coast was Christianized before the inland, which is also what we would expect. However, only a limited part of the archaeological material has been studied so far, and more will probably be uncovered, so more exact conclusions might be drawn in the future. There is already reason to believe that Christianization was a more complex and gradual process than the one represented in the saga tradition, but that the kings probably did play an important part, particularly in organizing the Church and banning pagan cult. The most serious objection to the account in the sagas is that they focus too exclusively on the two Olavs, underestimating the importance of the rulers who were Christian but allegedly failed to promote Christianity. As for Håkon den gode, the early churches and churchyards at Veøy, together with a possible reference to an English missionary bishop during his reign,[35] may indicate that his efforts to introduce Christianity were more successful than the sagas admit. The fact that the sagas only refer to the outskirts of Håkon's field of influence, Trøndelag and north-western Norway, as opposing Christianity, may point in the same direction. As for his successors, the Eirikssons, a skaldic poem mentions that they destroyed pagan cult places, whereas another praises their successor Håkon Ladejarl for restoring them. Curiously enough, the later sagas give the Eirikssons no credit for this attack on the pagan cult,

---

[35] Birkeli 1960; Jørgensen 1996. The reference is to a list in William of Malmesbury of monks of Glastonbury who became bishops, one of whom was Sigfrid who became bishop in Norway. No date is mentioned but his position in the list is compatible with Håkon's reign.

regarding it as evidence of greed rather than Christianity. As the Eirikssons were actually Christian, the latter interpretation would seem equally plausible, or rather, it is hardly possible to distinguish between 'purely' religious and more secular motives for fighting paganism; the most important is that both motives contributed to the victory of Christianity.

The Saami people converted to Christianity in different ways and later than the rest of the people in the area. In Finmark people from Rus', Karelia and further south in Norway encountered the Saami. As a result, some Saami groups in north-eastern Finmark converted to Orthodox Christianity, while Catholicism and later Lutheranism dominated in other areas. The Saami in the coastal regions were under the influence of Norwegians from the thirteenth century on, and a church was consecrated in Vardø in 1307. But the most intensive missionary work was performed from the seventeenth century on.

4. ROYAL POWER

St Olav Haraldsson (1015–30) is considered by modern historians to have been the first king who ruled the whole country.[36] His stronghold seems to have been in the south-east. There is evidence of his interference in Trøndelag which appears as an occupied region and where he met with the greatest resistance. His conflicts and alliances with magnates in northern Norway form evidence of his attempts to control this region, as does also his conflict with the powerful magnate Erling Skjalgsson in western Norway. To judge from the extant sources, however, this was the region where he was weakest, apart from the inner part of eastern Norway. His successors seem to have been able to control most of the country, his half-brother Harald (1046–66) even conquering the area around the lake Mjøsa in the east. Throughout the Middle Ages, however, royal control was considerably stronger along the coast than in the inner regions. The main military power in early medieval Scandinavia was sea power, which largely explains how the area was divided between the three kingdoms of Norway, Denmark and Sweden.[37] The sheltered coastline was also ideal for trade and transport, and the export of commodities from northern Norway, furs and later fish, was of great economic importance, from Ottar's age to the period of the Hansa in the later Middle Ages and the early modern period.

The early royal administration was probably rudimentary: the king had to rule through personal friendship with the leading men and by travelling

---

[36] Bagge 2002b; Krag 2003, 193–6.   [37] Bagge 2002a.

around the country in order to make his presence felt. Landed estates as well as gold and silver were important means to achieve this aim. The king's generosity towards friends and allies is an important and often mentioned theme in sagas and the skaldic poems. Land in particular served to attach powerful men to the king's service on a more long-term basis. The Old Norse term for such men is *lendir menn* (singular *lendr maðr*), i.e. 'men with land'. The term has been understood as either a man holding land from the king or simply a man owning much land. These men were powerful local chieftains whom the king attached to himself as allies or clients. They pledged allegiance to the king, who in return gave them income in the form of crown land. However, the most important basis for their status was apparently their own land. By the early twelfth century, there were apparently between 80 and 100 *lendir menn* in the country. According to the laws, the *lendir menn* were supposed to take part in the local administration. In addition the laws as well as the sagas mention a royal representative of lower status, the *ármaðr* who acted as the king's local representative and resided on one of his estates.

The kings' generosity to the Church, which was considerable, served similar purposes as his alliances with lay magnates. The bishops belonged to the kings' supporters and travelled around with them until permanent bishoprics were established. Through his leadership of the Church, the king accumulated power and attached to his service competent counsellors who were familiar with affairs of state abroad. For its part, the Church was well served by supporting the monarchy, which gave it economic security and created stable conditions for the development of Christianity.

The king's economic basis was landed estates. The sagas mention various royal estates from the reign of Harald Hårfagre onwards. On some, such as Alrekstad near Bergen, significant remains of buildings have been excavated. Many of these estates were probably acquired through confiscations during the numerous struggles for the throne in the tenth and early eleventh centuries and in the period 1130–1240. Thus, sixteen farms located in Trøndelag are mentioned in the sagas whose owners were in opposition to the kings during the period from Håkon den gode to St Olav. Fifteen of these were owned by the king or by the Church during the high Middle Ages, which indicates that they had been confiscated. Olav's son, Magnus the Good, tried to confiscate the land of his father's opponents when he became king. One of the court poets gives his reaction to this in *Bersoglisvísur* ('outspoken verses', i.e. the skald presents the king with unpleasant truths instead of flattering him). Further, the many kings returning from careers abroad as Viking chieftains or mercenaries often brought with them considerable wealth in the form of precious metals.

Although traces of seasonal marketplaces have been found from the pagan period, at least one of which, Kaupang in Vestfold, may be considered a town, it seems that urbanization was to a considerable extent linked to Christianization: most of the towns were founded by Christian kings. Trondheim (Nidaros in the Middle Ages) was founded by King Olav Tryggvason at the end of the tenth century. The royal residence here appears, according to the sagas, to have been built in stages by several kings from the late tenth century and during the eleventh century. Oslo and Tønsberg are approximately contemporary or somewhat later. According to the sagas, Harald Hardråde founded Oslo. This is compatible with the archaeological evidence, or the town may be somewhat older. The largest town later in the Middle Ages, Bergen, was probably founded around 1070 by King Olav Kyrre. The original royal residence was located just outside Bergen during Olav Kyrre's reign, and was moved to the town at the beginning of the twelfth century by King Øystein Magnusson, who also built a palace of wood. Olav Haraldsson built a residence and a church in Borg (Sarpsborg) in the early eleventh century. No traces of pagan symbols or graves contemporary with the urban settlement have been found in these towns. A Christian king as founder would probably monopolize the religion, as part of his ideological basis of power. A separate town law (*Bjarkøyretten*), issued for Trondheim, must have existed from the twelfth century.

Royal castles were mainly located in or near the towns. According to written sources royal residences already existed in the Viking period. However, very few, and only medieval, castles have survived. Due to poor preservation, later alterations and the lack of excavations, very little is known about these strongholds which were probably built in wood, earth and stone. King Olav Haraldsson's castle in Borg and Sigurd Jorsalfar's castle in Konghelle are among the oldest in Norway. The most important royal castle in Bergen, Bergenhus, was built of wood starting in the early twelfth century, and by its location it controlled the access to the harbour. The next royal castles we know of are hilltop strongholds built by King Sverre in the late twelfth century, in Trondheim, Bergen and Tønsberg.

Marriage was also important in forming alliances within as well as outside the country. Olav Tryggvason was married to Tyra, the sister of the Danish king Sven Tveskæg. Olav married off his sister to one of the most powerful chieftains of western Norway. Two of the king's half-sisters were married to chieftains in eastern Norway. Olav Haraldsson built up a network of familial connections with chieftains in the interior of eastern Norway. One of the chieftains was married to the king's half-sister, another to his aunt. Olav was himself married to Astrid, daughter of the Swedish king Olof Skötkonung. The next generation of Norwegian kings was linked to the Swedish, Danish and Rus' royal houses through marriage. Marriage could occur as part of peacemaking or as part of cooperative agreements between countries. The kings moreover often had mistresses from prominent Norwegian families.

Generosity and personal ties formed the positive side to the king's government. The negative is well expressed by the advice the able and cynical Erling Skakke (d. 1179), the real ruler during most of his son Magnus's reign, allegedly gave to his son: 'You will not rule in peace for long, if you make only mild decisions.'[38] As in other countries at the time, fear was an important element in ruling. Normal practice during internal conflicts seems to have been to kill the chief opponents and pardon the rest, on the condition that they joined the victor.

There has been considerable discussion about the consequences of Christianization for the aristocracy. Early scholarship, represented above all by Ernst Sars (1835–1917), regarded the introduction of Christianity as an important step in undermining the authority of the aristocracy, whereas the Marxist historians of the early twentieth century, notably Halvdan Koht (1873–1965), maintained that the local aristocracy used Christianity as a basis of their power in a similar way to the old religion. More recent scholarship tends to take an intermediate position.[39] The introduction of Christianity probably led to some purges within the local aristocracy, pagan magnates being replaced by Christian ones. According to the sagas, the kings donated ground for the building of churches. However, the new religion certainly provided good opportunities for local magnates to continue in their position as leaders, by building churches and controlling the priests. While Christianity certainly led to political centralization, this did not necessarily run against the interests of the aristocracy but also provided new opportunities for this group.

The hundred years following the death of St Olav in the battle of Stiklestad in 1030 were a period of internal peace, which, however, was followed by another hundred years of frequent struggles over the succession to the throne (1134–1240). Some scholars have seen these struggles as the expression of regional or social conflicts, but the sources seem rather to indicate that the parties were based on personal connections between individual members of the elite. Social change, i.e. the change from an economy

[38] Snorri Sturluson, *Heimskringla, The Saga of Magnus Erlingsson*, chap. 35.   [39] Skre 1998.

of plunder to an economy of agrarian exploitation, or ideological factors, notably the rise of the ecclesiastical hierarchy and the struggle for *libertas ecclesiae*, may, however, have contributed to the length and bitterness of the struggles. The effect of the struggles was to strengthen the centralizing powers, the monarchy and the Church.[40]

Compared to modern conditions, government continued to be largely personal throughout the Middle Ages. Nevertheless, more impersonal structures developed from the twelfth and above all the thirteenth century in the royal as well as the ecclesiastical administration, a clearer idea of the distinction between person and office, more regular administrative districts and clearly defined functions for the officials, and a transition from oral to written administration which made control over longer distances easier. The Church served as an important model for the monarchy in this respect, although there were probably also parallel developments and influence in the other direction. A new royal official, the *syslumaðr* came into being, replacing the two older ones and combining the high status of the *lendr maðr* with the *ármaðr's* close connection to the king. From the late twelfth or early thirteenth century the whole country was divided into permanent administrative districts, *syslur*, around fifty altogether. Probably from the second half of the twelfth century, a regular tax was introduced, originating in the defence organization in the coastal regions, the *leiðangr*. A part of the provisions prescribed to be delivered in connection with an expedition had to be rendered annually whether an expedition was to take place or not. The growth of towns can also be regarded as an expression of the development of royal as well as ecclesiastical administration. From the late twelfth century onwards, the king normally spent the winter in a town. The country had no permanent capital, but Adam of Bremen refers to Trondheim as Norway's most important city around 1070. Later, in the twelfth and above all the thirteenth century, Bergen became the city most often visited by the king, and the cathedral there the main burial church for members of the dynasty.

Olav Haraldsson's shrine in Trondheim became the most important symbol of Norway's Christian kingdom. The Olav cult was religiously and politically significant. The skaldic poem *Glælognskviða* from the first half of the 1030s indicates that even Olav's political opponents recognized him as a saint. The poem directs the following advice to the reigning king: 'Ask Olav to bestow upon you his country – he is a friend of God; he gets prosperity and peace for all people from God himself.' The most likely addressee for

[40] Bagge 1986; 1999; Helle 2003b.

this advice is Olav's political opponent, the Danish king Sven, son of Knud the Great. The shrine of the dead king was, according to the sagas, first kept in St Clement's church, the town's main church, but as soon as the cathedral had been built, it was kept on the high altar there. Olav became *rex perpetuus Norvegiae*, Norway's eternal king. His presence as a saint was recognized in Trondheim, and the religious cult dedicated to him gained importance, both in Norway and abroad. Olav also became a political ideal for later kings.

Many sculptures and paintings of Olav Haraldsson have been preserved. The earliest paintings are from the 1200s. Olav appears with the royal crown. His attribute is the axe, which was later used in the royal seal and on the banner and coat of arms. Olav also often carries a globe marked with a cross, a symbol of royal power. All these symbols are clearly developed after Olav's lifetime; there is no contemporary evidence of them, except that a bust of a king holding a sceptre, based on English design, is depicted on some of the earliest coins, Olav Haraldsson's penning.

The king's power in the early Christian period was primarily expressed as military power. The skaldic poems praise the kings for military feats. As is usual in the Middle Ages, the main emphasis in the narrative sources is also on war and conflicts. Thus, Snorri's saga about Harald Hardråde (ruled 1046–66), who participated in many military actions, comprises seventy pages while the longer but entirely peaceful reign of his son Olav Kyrre (1066–93), is dealt with in just a few pages, despite its importance for urbanization, the development of ecclesiastical organization and possibly royal government and legislation.

The earliest Christian sources continue to celebrate warlike qualities, but also point to the king's military strength as a means of upholding justice. Thus, Olav Haraldsson is praised in *Erfidrápa* for executing thieves and Vikings. Olav was also known as a legislator, thus corresponding to the Christian ideal of the just king (*rex iustus*). Olav's successors could use their relationship to the Holy King as a supplement to military power. Apart from some skaldic poems, there is little evidence of royal ideology and ideas about politics and government before the mid-twelfth century. After that, but above all during the thirteenth century, the sources become fairly numerous and varied.

The coronation of King Magnus Erlingsson in 1163 or 1164, the first royal coronation in Scandinavia, marks a new epoch. The event took place in a situation where there were many pretenders to the throne and was intended to give Magnus a unique advantage in the competition, but the coronation was also an occasion for the Church to emphasize the Christian doctrine of the *rex iustus* and insist on the king's duties towards the Church and the people. The documents issued on this occasion or shortly afterwards – Magnus's coronation oath, the *Law of Succession*, and the privilege to the Church – present these ideas in a succinct form.

The *Law of Succession* expresses the Church's perception of the monarchy as an office established by God. It decrees that there should only be one king at a time, and that he should be elected by a central assembly in Trond-heim. By contrast, before this law, all male descendants of kings had the same right to claim the kingdom. They were accepted as kings by different assemblies all around the country. The heirs to the throne opposed each other with varying support, or they might agree to share power between them, thus ruling simultaneously with the same royal titles and status. The law has been subject to much scholarly discussion, especially concerning the relationship between elective and hereditary monarchy. The law states that the eldest legitimate son of the late king should succeed to the throne, unless he is disqualified by *illzca æða uvizca*, because he is evil or unwise. The interpretation of these words determines the importance of election in this case. It has been shown fairly convincingly that these terms refer to ecclesiastical ideas of the *rex iustus* and his antithesis, the *tyrannus*, and that consequently, there is at least in principle a relatively strong element of election in the law.[41] The following paragraphs regulate the right to succes-sion in accordance with the degree of kinship with the previous king but in such a way that there is free election between candidates within the same degree. Finally, a special committee, consisting of elected representatives, the archbishop and the bishops, is entrusted with the election. The law here conforms to the canonical rule about episcopal elections, in giving the 'better part' of the assembly, the bishops, a decisive voice. Although the exact relationship between inheritance and election may be subject to discussion, there is no doubt that both the elective element and the posi-tion of the Church are stronger in this law than in the later ones of 1260 and 1273. The substantial discussion about the law would seem to be in inverse proportion to its importance, as it was never actually practised and was later replaced by the law of 1260. However, its importance does not lie in its effects but in what it can tell us about the relationship between monarchy and Church in the mid-twelfth century and the introduction of ecclesiastical ideas about monarchy and government to Norway.

[41] Tobiassen 1964.

Magnus Erlingsson's coronation oath expresses similar ideas, containing fairly specific expressions about loyalty to Pope Alexander III and his successors – a clear reference to the schism at the time – and about respecting the privileges of the Church. The exact interpretation of the oath has been the subject of considerable scholarly discussion, as have also the passages in the *Law of Succession* and Magnus Erlingsson's charter about the king's crown being sacrificed to St Olav at the altar of the cathedral of Trondheim for the soul of the deceased king and of the king being St Olav's knight or vassal. There are two main interpretations of this latter provision. One, that the king acknowledged that he had received his office from the Church, formally at least agreeing to submit to the archbishop's control and guidance. The second, that the vassalage was a tactical move in a situation where the Danish king claimed control over the south-eastern part of the country, intended to create a legal foundation for refusing to submit to this claim. The recent tendency has been more in the direction of the second explanation. Comparative studies, e.g. of the French king's vassalage to St Denis or John Lackland's to Pope Innocent III, have supported this view. However, the consistent refusal by the new dynasty of King Sverre (1177–1202) and his successors to renew this provision, does suggest that it did contain some element of submission.[42]

A specifically royal ideology was developed in opposition to these ideas in the milieu around King Sverre and his successors who fought and eventually defeated the 'Magnus line'.[43] *A Speech against the Bishops* (*c*. 1200) is an apology for King Sverre in his struggle against the Church, but also presents a general monarchical doctrine, strongly emphasizing the king's relationship to God and the subjects' duty to obey him. These ideas are developed in great detail in *The King's Mirror* (*Konungs skuggsiá, Speculum regale*), most probably from the 1250s, as well as in the legislation from the 1270s, the National Law, the Town Law and the *Hirðskrá* (the law of the king's retainers). They are also expressed in charters and amendments to laws. The practice of royal coronation was taken over by the new dynasty founded by King Sverre who was himself crowned in 1194, as was his grandson Håkon Håkonsson in 1247. From then on, coronation became a permanent element in the accession to the throne, but considerable energy was spent in the milieu around King Håkon to reject the interpretation of the coronation as meaning that the king had received his office from the Church.

---

[42] As the privilege was never put into practice, we do not know what was to happen to the crown. No crown or other royal insignia have been preserved.

[43] Bagge 1987, 113–53.

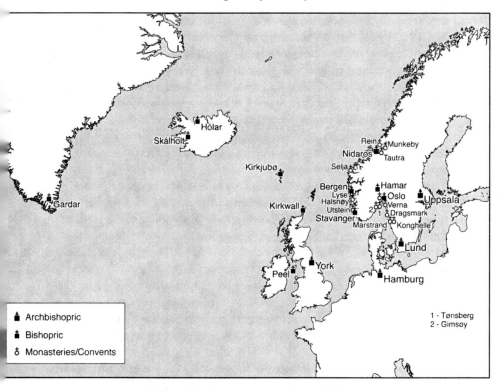

7. Nidaros church organization and its neighbours

5. THE EFFECTS OF CHRISTIANIZATION

According to Adam of Bremen, permanent bishoprics did not yet exist in Norway at the time of his writing, around 1073–5, but must have come into being shortly afterwards, probably during the reign of Olav Kyrre (1066–93).[44] The three oldest are Oslo, Bergen and Nidaros (Trondheim). Olav appointed Bjarnhard bishop of Selja in western Norway, but he later moved to Bergen. Further, Olav Kyrre was responsible for the establishment of the diocese of Trøndelag, with residence in Trondheim. During his reign or shortly thereafter, the diocese of eastern Norway was established, with residence in Oslo. The boundaries of the oldest dioceses were generally the same as those of legal jurisdictions. The diocese of Bergen comprised the entire Gulating law district, from Møre to Agder, from which Sunnmøre was transferred to Trondheim some time before 1223. The diocese of Trondheim

[44] On the growth of the church organization: Bagge 2003, 51–80; Orrman 2003, 421–62.

came to consist of the eight Trøndelag *fylki*, Møre og Romsdal and northern Norway. The diocese of Oslo comprised the areas around the Oslo fjord, the interior part of eastern Norway and Båhuslen (now in Sweden), which at that time belonged to Norway. The early dioceses were thus very large and difficult for the bishops to administer. This is probably the reason for the erection of two new dioceses, Stavanger and Hamar, through subdivisions of Bergen and Oslo respectively. Stavanger, founded around 1125 at the latest, comprised the south-western part of the country and the inland valleys of Valdres and Hallingdal, whereas Hamar, founded in 1152 or 1153, covered the inner parts of eastern Norway.

Prior to its establishment as an archbishopric in 1152–3, the Norwegian church belonged to the church province of Hamburg-Bremen, and from 1104 to that of Lund. The full development of the diocesan organization thus coincided with the foundation of the church province. According to *A Speech against the Bishops* from the end of the twelfth century, the cathedral chapters were also organized on this occasion. All Norwegian chapters were secular, each canon having his separate prebend, in addition to which there was a *mensa communis*. In Bergen, the cathedral chapter came to consist of twelve canons, which appears to have been the norm. Hamar cathedral probably had less than this number, whereas the chapter of the archdiocese was twice as large.

Given the king's importance in introducing Christianity to Norway, combined with his central role in the government of the Church in other parts of early medieval Europe, it would seem a likely deduction that he in practice functioned as the head of the Norwegian church in the early period, until the foundation of the church province. This is further confirmed by a papal letter to King Harald Hardråde, quoted by Adam of Bremen, which reveals a conflict between the king and the archbishop of Hamburg-Bremen between 1061 and 1066 over the appointment of bishops. According to Adam, the king replied to the archbishop's protests that he knew no other ruler of the Norwegian church than himself.[45] In his letter, the pope considered the Norwegian monarchy to be inexperienced in the ways of Christianity and the laws of the Church. A similar attitude is also reflected in the more accommodating letter of Pope Gregory VII to Olav Kyrre from 1078. After the establishment of the archbishopric, the leading prelates sought to implement the Gregorian ideas of *libertas ecclesiae*, and obtained some important privileges to this effect, concerning the appointment of priests and episcopal elections without royal interference. King

---

[45] Adam of Bremen III.17; the letter is also printed in Vandvik 1959, no 1.

Sverre (1177–1202) sought to revoke these privileges, which resulted in a major conflict between the Church and the monarchy. His successors recognized most of the privileges but some tension remained.

The Norwegian archbishop had jurisdiction over eleven bishoprics. In addition to the five Norwegian ones, these included Skálholt and Holar in Iceland, Greenland, the Faroes, the Orkneys and the Hebrides-Man. The Norwegian archbishop's jurisdiction over the other bishops was limited, but he seems to have retained a stronger position than was usual in the period after the Gregorian reform, when the archbishop's power was usually reduced in favour of the pope on the one hand and the suffragans on the other. The social status of the higher clergy is reflected in the secular rank accorded to its members in Norwegian law. The archbishop ranked next to the king, and had the same status as a duke. The bishops had the rank of earls, whereas the abbots and abbesses ranked above the *lendir menn*.

Church administration was centralized in the towns where the bishops resided, and these cities simultaneously became the kingdom's administrative centres from the time of Olav Kyrre onwards. As for the relationship between royal and ecclesiastical administrative districts in general, it seems that the earliest ecclesiastical divisions were to some extent based on earlier regional divisions, such as the law districts and the *fylki*, but that the monarchy as well as the Church developed new administrative units during the following period, which often did not correspond to one another.

The first monasteries in Norway were Benedictine. According to English accounts, monks with connections to Norway are mentioned from the first half of the eleventh century, including a monk named Sigurd who was bishop at the time of Olav Haraldsson. An English source also states that Knud the Great established a monastery near Trondheim in 1028, but this is rejected by most scholars. Norwegian–Icelandic sources attribute the foundation of this monastery (Munkholm) to a Norwegian magnate around 1100. Benedictine monasteries were also founded in Bergen (Munkeliv) and on the holy island of Selja at the beginning of the twelfth century, and a Benedictine nunnery was apparently founded in Trondheim at about the same time. The Nonneseter convent, located in Bergen, was probably established in the 1140s, and the nuns most likely belonged to the Cistercian order. The Gimsøy nunnery, located in eastern Norway, was founded by a Norwegian magnate in the first half of the twelfth century, whose daughter became its abbess. The Augustinian monastery of St John was built around the middle of the 1100s or a little later. Lyse monastery, located on the outskirts of Bergen, was founded by the bishop in 1146 as the first Cistercian monastery in Norway. The Cistercian monastery on Hovedøya

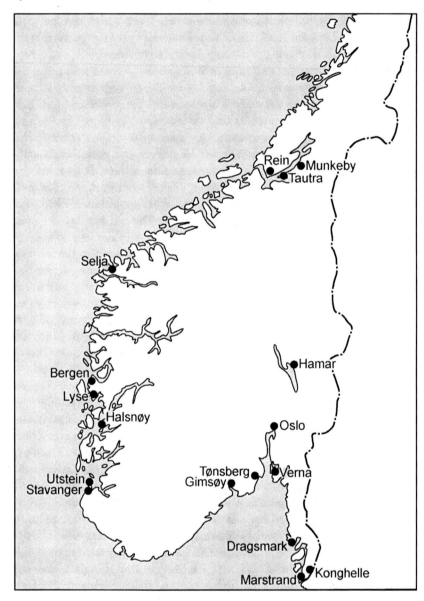

8. Norwegian monasteries
(Number of monasteries in Bergen: 5; Nidaros (Trondheim):
5; Oslo: 4; Tønsberg: 2; Hamar: 1; Stavanger: 1)

was established in 1147, also by the bishop, and a monastery of the same order, Tautra, was established somewhat later in Trøndelag. Some of the early Norwegian monasteries, including the two oldest Cistercian ones, recruited their monks from abroad, especially from the east of England to which some of them returned. Halsnøy monastery was Augustinian, and was founded by the earl Erling Skakke, King Magnus Erlingsson's father, around 1160. Several more Norwegian monasteries, nunneries and other religious houses were established later. There were altogether thirty-one such institutions in Norway during the Middle Ages. Most of them were small, and some existed for only short periods of time. The sources mention kings, bishops and lay magnates as founders of monasteries, but in most cases there is no evidence of the identity of the founder. It is therefore not possible to point to particular patterns or changes over time in the way monasteries were founded.

A permanent division of the church parishes was not complete before well into the 1200s. Terms like 'parish', 'vicar', 'parishioners' and the like do not become common in historical sources before the second half of the thirteenth century. However, the regional laws of the twelfth century contain detailed provisions about the local ecclesiastical organization. According to the *Law of Gulating*, there was to be one church in each *fylki*, which is referred to as the main church. Moreover, the *fylki* were to be divided into fourths and eighths, each with one church of minor rank. Maintenance of these was the common responsibility of the residents. These provisions may go back as far as the time of Olav Haraldsson. The law also refers to *heraðskirkjur* for smaller local communities, and *hægendiskirkjur*, 'convenience churches', built by wealthy people for private use, to avoid travelling long distances to get to church. According to the laws, the founder was responsible for the maintenance of such churches. In the towns, 'congregation churches' and royal chapels were erected. Bishops were responsible for appointing priests in the churches. There was clearly a difference of rank between these churches, and there is some evidence that the priests of the smaller units were subordinated to those of the larger. The complicated church organization of western Norway may be modelled on the older pattern of local church organization, the *ecclesiae baptismales*, which were centres for large areas and existed, for example, in Anglo-Saxon England.[46] It is, however, unlikely to have existed in practice in complete form. The parish organization then developed gradually from the *hægendiskirkjur*. Thus, 'private' as well as 'public' churches came to function in much the

---

[46] Skre 1998.

same way as the old main churches, and all became parish churches. According to Adam, Norwegians had great respect for priests and churches, but had to pay for all transactions with the church. The tithe was, according to a list from Trondheim bishopric, instituted during the reign of King Sigurd Jorsalfare (ruled 1103–30), but was hardly accepted generally until the second half of the twelfth century. According to twelfth-century laws, the tithe was to be divided evenly among the bishop, the church, the priest and the poor.

Church architecture is slightly different in different parts of Norway. In the earliest period the churches in the western and middle parts of Norway were influenced by England and Normandy (Anglo-Norman style), while those of eastern Norway were influenced by Denmark and Germany. The Romanesque style dominated the twelfth century and the early 1200s. Churches in eastern Norway usually had a simple ground plan where the nave was not divided by posts, but the cathedrals in Hamar and Oslo were basilicas, as were a handful of other churches. A more local style developed as well, for example in Trondheim which was the country's most important town in the eleventh century. A community of stonemasons developed here that became important for the style and construction of churches in the district as well. A similar tendency is true for the architecture of the bishops' palaces, which resemble the architecture of the local region as well as each other within the archbishopric.

The relationship between the architecture in wooden and stone churches has been discussed, and the construction of the stave churches is thought to be influenced by the stone churches. The early stone churches are decorated in the Romanesque style, whereas representations of pagan myths sometimes occur on the porches of stave churches. This has recently been interpreted as an aspect of the general interest people took in the past during the thirteenth century, but may also be understood as a parallel to the 'chaos' creatures among the decorations on the stone churches.

Generally, recent archaeological research has proved that most of the stone churches have had one or more wooden predecessors, stave churches. The majority – perhaps three-quarters – of the churches built during the Middle Ages were made of wood. The earliest were supported by poles; after around 1000 the poles or staves were put on cross-ties and eventually on foundations so that the construction became more permanent. Several remnants recognized by archaeologists as churches are dated around the middle of the eleventh century, for example at Høre in Valdres and Lom in Gudbrandsdalen. The oldest dendrochronological dating of a stave church is from Urnes in Sogn, dated 1129–30. According to the sagas, the earliest-known stone building in the country is a palace constructed in Trondheim by Magnus the Good, which was later turned into a church by his successor Harald Hardråde and finished around 1050. The sagas particularly attribute the building of churches to the kings Olav Tryggvason, Olav Haraldsson, Harald Hardråde, Olav Kyrre and Sigurd Jorsalfare (1103–30).

Several ecclesiastical stone buildings, and even more wooden ones, were erected during the twelfth century. A cathedral, three stone monasteries and seven or eight stone churches were built in Bergen before 1200. The building of Christ Church cathedral in Bergen was started by Olav Kyrre, but took about 100 years to complete. It had a basilica nave. The construction of St Mary's church and the Cross church in Bergen was begun sometime in the 1130s or 1140s and must have been finished in 1181, when the two churches are mentioned in *Sverris saga*. The closest parallel to St Mary's of a similar age is the cathedral in Lund. Hans-Emil Lidén finds similarities between the masonry, ornaments and style which may indicate that the masons came from the Lund region.[47] On the other hand, he points out that the monastery at Lyse was founded directly from Fountains Abbey in Yorkshire, and the monks brought their own craftsmen. The two-tower west front was also normal in England and Normandy, and the architecture of St Mary's church may have been influenced from there.

The cathedral in Trondheim was the largest construction in Norway during the Middle Ages, serving as the centre of the national cult of St Olav, as the cathedral for the bishopric and later the archbishopric, and until the first half of the twelfth century also as the royal burial church. Olav Kyrre built the Christ Church, the earliest phase of what would later be the Nidaros cathedral. After the establishment of the archbishopric and the cathedral chapter in the middle of the 1100s, the church was expanded in the Romanesque style. In the 1180s, after Archbishop Øystein's exile in England, the cathedral was expanded in the Gothic style. The first stage in this was the eight-sided extension, the octagon, built over St Olav's grave and finished between 1210 and 1220. A chancel in Early English Gothic style was then added. Gerhard Fischer called the oldest parts of the cathedral in Trondheim 'Anglo-Saxon' because of the similarity between its ground plan and that of Anglo-Saxon churches, but he also found some differences.[48] Very little was left of this church to give evidence of a particular style. He called the next building phase of the cathedral 'Norman' in style, based on the chevron-decoration and on other parts of the decoration with strong

---

[47] Lidén 2000.   [48] This and following: Fischer 1965, 23–340.

similarity to churches in Normandy, but particularly in England. There are for instance similar masks, and a capital in Nidaros cathedral which is almost identical with a capital in Lincoln cathedral. The craftsmen might even have been English. But this style does not characterize the whole church: after a short while, the chevron-decoration has been given up and replaced with water-leaf decoration, which probably represents purely English influence. Nidaros cathedral reached its present length by the mid-thirteenth century.

The archbishop's palace was built to the south of the cathedral in Trondheim, and consisted at all times of both stone and wooden constructions, from the foundation in 1153, with a strong stone curtain wall or stone buildings facing outwards. The cathedral was richly decorated, built of well-shaped stones with a smooth, grey surface; in contrast the palace was off-white, simple, with a rough surface which had to be covered in lime.

It is not clear when Norwegians began to enter the priesthood. The clerics who came over with the missionary kings were highly educated Englishmen whose status corresponded to their attachment to the royal household. The first bishops to be appointed in Norway were foreigners, but from around the middle of the twelfth century most of them seem to have been Norwegian, often belonging to prominent families. In a letter to Olav Kyrre, the pope offered to receive selected Norwegians in Rome to be educated for the service of the Church and the papacy, but the practical consequences of this initiative are unknown. The main evidence for Norwegians studying abroad comes from the mid-twelfth century and later. The laws from around the middle of the eleventh century demand that the bishop appoint priests 'who know how to perform their service', which indicates that inexperienced priests were not uncommon. Norwegian priests were educated under the tutelage of the bishop. When permanent bishoprics were established at the end of the eleventh century, the training of priests was relocated to these. This was the beginning of the cathedral schools. According to one of the earliest laws, the *Law of Borgarting*, which covered the area around the Oslofjord, the farmers had the right to appoint priests in the local churches, whereas the bishops had this right in the other laws. Priests attached to private churches were considered to be part of the church owner's household. They had low status, as did other servants. According to a passage in the *Law of the Gulating*, probably from the mid-twelfth century, this was eventually changed, and the priests became respected members of the community to whom respectable men could marry their daughters. The introduction of celibacy was late in Norway. Cardinal Nicholas Brekespear, who acted as papal representative by the establishment of the archdiocese, tried to limit clerical marriages but did not categorically ban them. A general prohibition was not issued until a papal letter in 1237. Almost nothing is known about rectories from the high Middle Ages.

Olav Tryggvason is said to have converted five countries, i.e. Shetland, the Orkney and Faroe Islands, Iceland and Greenland. Odd Monk's saga also states that Olav converted King Vladimir of Rus' and many of his circle to Christianity. Adam of Bremen relates that Olav Haraldsson sent bishops and priests to evangelize Sweden and the islands in the west. Olav is also credited with the Christianization of Gotland. Olav Tryggvason's contribution to the conversion of Iceland is attested by Ari fróði in the early twelfth century and must be considered trustworthy, despite the general tendency in the narrative sources to exaggerate the two Olavs' importance for Christianization.

King Sigurd Jorsalfare left on a crusade in 1108, lasting for three years. According to *Heimskringla*, he had sixty ships and many people with him and participated in eight battles against Muslims in the Mediterranean, as well as in the capture of a Muslim castle in Syria. The sagas emphasize the honour and the number of captives that this expedition brought to the king. While the crusade itself is well attested, its success and importance may well be exaggerated in the sagas. It is also difficult to say anything exact about its motives and background. The most likely interpretation seems to be a combination of religious zeal and the wish for booty, prestige and adventure, as in other parts of Europe, to which can be added the existence of a military apparatus and organization well suited to such purposes, notably a large fleet and skilled sailors. There were several large overseas expeditions in the post-Viking Age, such as Harald Sigurdsson Hardråde's expeditions against Denmark in the 1050s and 1060s and against England in 1066, and his grandson Magnus Olavsson's (1093–1103) expeditions against Ireland and other areas in the west. By contrast, there is little evidence of Norwegian participation in Baltic crusades, but it is likely that individual magnates took part in the Danish expeditions in this area. An expedition against the Kalmar area in Sweden, allegedly to fight the pagans, may also be mentioned in this context, but the religious aim is likely to be a pretext rather than the real reason, as the area in question was hardly pagan by that time (1123).

The introduction of Christianity brought about a number of important cultural, social and administrative changes, one of the most important of which is the introduction of writing. However, script was not unknown in pagan times. The old Nordic runic alphabet was in use, its earlier version consisting of twenty-four symbols, its later of sixteen.[49] The runes were in use from the sixth or seventh century until the end of the Middle Ages. There has been disagreement as to whether the runes were mainly used for the purpose of communication, or were magical symbols. The latter has been claimed in relation to the way in which the runes are sometimes referred to in the ancient poetry, e.g. as an instrument of divination in *Hávamál* strophe 80. Most runic inscriptions from the pagan and early Christian period are found on stone memorials of the dead, but there are also examples of inscriptions on wood, bone and metal. We do not know to what extent runes were used in everyday life, or if they were used to write poetry. Only one complete stanza of skaldic verse, written in runic script, has been found in all of the northern countries. This is inscribed on a stone pillar found in Öland, erected in memory of a Danish chieftain around the year 1000. Rune-stones, inscriptions on church walls and a quantity of wooden pegs with runic inscriptions have been found from the centuries following Christianization. Throughout the Middle Ages, the runic alphabet was used to write labels on goods, short messages, poems, prayers, including names of saints, and magical inscriptions. Although most of these inscriptions are in the vernacular, there are also examples of runic inscriptions in Latin.

It is an open question whether the use of runes for practical purposes was a novelty during the Christian period or whether they were used in a similar way in the pagan period as well. The evidence from the Christian period comes from excavations in medieval towns, to which there are few parallels in the pagan period. The impression of a fairly exclusive use of runes during this period may therefore be explained by the fact that inscriptions on stone are more likely to be preserved than brief notes on perishable material. Nevertheless, there is much to suggest that runes were not used for the composition of longer texts and that consequently, from a literary point of view, pagan Norwegian culture was predominantly oral. Important knowledge about religion, law and history was preserved orally, and the skalds who composed oral poetry had high status. Thus, what was introduced by Christianity was not primarily the technology of writing, but the need for writing.

The most pressing need for texts after the introduction of Christianity was that of the Latin liturgy. The early missionaries must have brought with them liturgical books, and from fairly early on such books must also have been copied in Norway. Fragments of liturgical texts of English origin dating

[49] Liestøl 1969; Moltke 1985; Odenstedt 1990.

from the eleventh century have been found as bindings of post-Reformation account books; some, from the end of the century, were probably written in Norway.[50] Further, the introduction of specifically Norwegian saints from the 1030s onwards resulted in the composition of liturgical texts for them. Some fragments from the office of St Olav are preserved from the mid-eleventh century, and the feast of this saint is mentioned in the skaldic poem *Erfidrápa* from around 1040. The main features of the legend of Olav may also have been composed fairly early, although the extant version dates from around 1160. It was originally written in Latin and later translated into Old Norse.

The earliest extant text and, with the possible exception of the laws, the first text written in Norway in the vernacular is the *Old Norse Book of Homilies* from the first half of the twelfth century, which consists of translations and adaptations of old Latin homilies. During the following period, the late twelfth and above all the thirteenth century, a rich literature developed, mainly in the form of narratives, historiography, saints' *Lives*, heroic tales, romance, but also didactic and ideological texts. Most of this literature is in Old Norse, partly in the form of original compositions, partly translations, mostly from Latin or French. A considerable part of this literature was written by Icelanders, and most extant manuscripts are also Icelandic, although many of the texts are likely to have existed in Norway as well. It is in practice often difficult to distinguish between Norwegian and Icelandic origins of manuscripts. Although the dialects of the two countries – as well as within Norway – are sufficiently different to identify the country or region of origin of manuscripts in the original where the dialect occurs in its pure form, there are many examples of mixtures of dialects and of originals in one dialect being transcribed in another.

The Icelander Sæmundr fróði (1056–1133) is usually believed to have laid the foundation for Norwegian–Icelandic historical studies with a work about the first Norwegian kings, probably written in Latin in the first half of the 1100s. This work has been lost, as has also the other earliest history, in Old Norse, by Ari fróði (1068–1148).[51] The earliest extant works date from the second half of the twelfth century: the *Historia Norvegiae*, Theodoricus Monachus's Latin history of the Norwegian kings (*Historia de antiquitate regum Norwagiensium, c.* 1180), and *Ágrip* (*c.* 1190) written in Old Norse. At this time, the archbishopric was established in Trondheim, and the town was the literary centre of Norway. In the following period, mainly the first half of the thirteenth century, a series of sagas of the Norwegian kings was

---

[50] Pettersen and Karlsen 2003.   [51] Ellehøj 1965; Andersson 1985; 2003; Lange 1989; Bagge 2006.

composed in Old Norse, most of them by Icelanders. The most famous of these works is Snorri Sturluson's *Heimskringla*, probably written around 1230. The relatively late development of historical writing means that the only contemporary information about the period before the end of the twelfth century is the skaldic poetry and some references in various foreign chronicles, both of which contain fairly meagre information.

Administrative literacy developed with the expansion of the ecclesiastical and royal bureaucracy. The first royal charter preserved in the original is from 1207 and is written in Old Norse, which was the usual administrative language in the following period. Latin was only used for correspondence with the Church or with other countries. Even the Church used Old Norse to a considerable extent for administrative purposes, although less than the royal chancery. There are references to various royal communications and decisions from the early twelfth century onwards, but we cannot be quite sure if they were in writing. A royal charter sealed by King Øystein is mentioned in connection with the establishment of the archdiocese in 1152–3 but its text has been lost. Some charters from King Magnus Erlingsson are preserved in transcript or through later renewals or summaries. Few Norwegian charters have been preserved before around 1250, after which they become more frequent, particularly from the last two decades of the thirteenth century. The style and formulas of the Old Norse charters were influenced by Latin charters from abroad, with some local variations. The oldest known papal letter to a Norwegian king is from around 1050. There are a few examples of correspondence with the pope and other ecclesiastical authorities in the following period until the 1160s, when the contacts with the Holy See became fairly regular.

With the increasing use of writing and correspondence with other countries, the skill of reading and writing became more important. The clergy must to some extent have been literate, although the education of ordinary priests was hardly very thorough. It is not known to what extent the laity acquired education in reading and writing. According to a report by an English abbot, King Olav Kyrre (1066–93) was probably able to read Latin. It is, however, unlikely that lay literacy was very widespread as early as the eleventh and twelfth centuries. Such skills probably became more common in the course of the thirteenth century. Evidence of this is that King Sverre (1177–1202) and his successors were well educated and had intellectual interests. Members of the secular aristocracy must also to some extent have been literate in the thirteenth century, some of them even having studied at universities abroad. During the relatively peaceful period after around

1240, the aristocracy seems to have developed into an administrative more than a military class.

The Norwegian system of representative assemblies was created in pagan times. The country consisted of four legal districts, each with its own law and representative assembly: the *Law of Gulating* for western Norway, the *Law of Frostating* for Trøndelag and northern Norway, the *Law of Borgarting* for the Oslofjord area and the *Law of Eidsivating* for the interior parts of eastern Norway. The two former laws are preserved in manuscripts from the mid-thirteenth century but must be considerably older. As for the two latter, only the parts concerning Christianity are extant. There is some evidence for Håkon den gode as the organizer of the *Gulating*. The district was most likely expanded during his time, and the system of representation introduced. The *Frostating* may be equally old, whereas the two eastern assemblies are probably somewhat younger. The legislation the missionary kings wanted to bring into effect had to be approved by the assembly (*þing*) of farmers and chieftains. The first Christian-era laws differed significantly in composition and content from one part of the country to another, but thorough studies are lacking. According to the narrative sources, the earliest Christian laws were issued by St Olav, and there are also references in the extant laws to provisions allegedly issued by him. To what extent these were preserved verbatim is more doubtful. The references in question may also be an expression of the widespread tendency to attribute legislation to some mythical legislator in the past.

By contrast, there is more to suggest that Olav Kyrre was the first legislator and thus that the passages in the *Law of Gulating* attributed to 'Olav' actually refer to him. Admittedly, the evidence for this is also fairly circumstantial, but his long reign might seem a likely period for putting the laws into writing.[52] The date of these laws, usually referred to as the regional laws (as opposed to the National Law, issued in the 1270s and common to the whole country), is uncertain but it is generally agreed that they are older than the mid-twelfth century. The laws deal in some detail with the Church and Christianity. Thus the *Law of Gulating* contains decisions attributed to Olav on the organization of the *þing* assembly and the number of representatives meeting there, on the liberation of a small number of slaves each year, on drinking parties in honour of Christ and the Virgin 'for prosperity and peace', on the building and maintenance of churches, on holidays, on Friday and Lenten fasting, on compulsory baptism, marriage and burials

---

[52] Helle 2001, 20–3.

in the churchyard, on prohibition against abandoning children and on prohibition of various kinds of magic and pagan cult. The paragraph on holidays defines all Sundays as holidays plus fourteen mass days allegedly introduced by St Olav and Bishop Grimkjell at the Moster *þing*. These include the feasts of the Virgin Mary, the apostles Peter, Paul, Bartholomew, Simon, Jude, Andrew and John the Evangelist, as well as John the Baptist, St Michael the Archangel, St Lawrence, All Saints, and finally three Norwegian saints, Olav, Hallvard and Sunniva.

The paragraph on abandoning children (severely handicapped newborns were to be baptized and brought to church to die) represents a compromise between the old rule, according to which the father decided whether a new-born child should be allowed to live, and the Church's general prohibition against child exposure. This concession was later abolished, probably during the reign of Magnus Erlingsson (1161–84). As for marriage, polygamy as well as marriage within seven degrees, according to the rules introduced in the western Church in the eleventh century, were prohibited (c. 24–5). However, divorce was still allowed in the early layers of the law. The law on drinking-parties was probably an attempt to Christianize the traditional gatherings in honour of the pagan gods. Finally, the prohibition of various kinds of magic and pagan cult specify animal sacrifice (*blót*), the eating of horsemeat and divination, magic chants (*galdr*) and witchcraft (*gerningar*) (c. 28). Late eleventh- or early twelfth-century regional laws also prohibited pagan burials.

The earliest Norwegian coins to have been found have the inscription *ONLAFREXNOR*, that is, 'Olav, king of Norway', who, corresponding to the date of the finds, is most probably Olav Tryggvason. The coins bear the symbol of the cross and a royal bust; they show the influence of English coinage. A few coins are also known from St Olav's reign, but none from those of his successors, Knud the Great and Magnus Olavsson. Norwegian coinage was taken into permanent usage in about 1047, during the reign of Harald Hardråde.

6. CONCLUSION

The fairly rich source material about the pagan period and its religion points to a certain cultural continuity between pagan and Christian times, as does also the continued existence until the thirteenth century of the skaldic poetry with its mythological allusions. This material forms an important but not unproblematic source of information about the pagan period and the transition to Christianity, which, however, has to be supplemented by archaeological evidence. Whereas the later narrative sources regard the Christianization as a brief process, mostly the result of the missionary activity of Olav Tryggvason and St Olav during the period 995–1030, the archaeological material suggests a longer period of Christian influence and considerable regional differences. In particular, the Saami population was relatively little influenced by Christianity during the Middle Ages. Nevertheless, it seems that the kings played a very important part in the conversion of the country, although most kings during the period from around 930 until 1030 were involved in this process and not only the two Olavs. By contrast, there is no evidence of individual missionaries coming from abroad, nor of political pressure from powerful Christian neighbours, with the possible exception of Danish influence in the south-east. This 'indigenous' Christianization process, combined with the impulses from Anglo-Saxon England, may possibly serve to explain the strong position of the vernacular and the continued existence of pagan traditions. However, the specificity of Norway should not be exaggerated; particularly after the mid-twelfth century the organization and position of the Church increasingly conformed to the rest of Europe, and the Church and Christianity played a crucial role in state formation and cultural development.

REFERENCES

Adam of Bremen, *Gesta Hammaburgensis ecclesiae pontificum*, ed. B. Schmeidler, Hanover, 1917 (*MGH SRG* II).

Andersson, T. 1985, 'Kings' Sagas', in Clover and Lindow, 197–238.

Andersson, T. 2003, 'Introduction', in *The Saga of Olaf Tryggvason*, tr. T. Anderson, Ithaca, 1–27.

Bagge, S. 1986, 'Borgerkrig og statsutvikling i Norge i middelalderen', *Historisk Tidsskrift* 65, 145–97.

Bagge, S. 1987, *The Political Thought of The King's Mirror*, Odense.

Bagge, S. 1991, *Society and Politics in Snorri Sturluson's Heimskringla*, Berkeley.

Bagge, S. 1999, 'The Structure of Political Factions in the Internal Struggles of the Scandinavian Countries During the High Middle Ages', *Scandinavian Journal of History* 24, 299–320.

Bagge, S. 2000, 'Old Norse Theories of Society, from *Rígspula* to *Konungs skuggsiá*', in *Speculum regale. Der altnorwegische Königsspiegel (Konungs skuggsiá) in der europäischen Tradition*, ed. J. E. Schnall and R. Simek, Vienna, 7–45.

Bagge, S. 2002a, 'Eleventh Century Norway: The Formation of a Kingdom', in *The Neighbours of Poland in the 11th Century*, ed. P. Urbańczyk, Warsaw, 29–47.

Bagge, S. 2002b, 'Mellom kildekritikk og historisk antropologi: Olav den hellige, aristokratiet og rikssamlingen', *Historisk Tidsskrift* 81, 173–212.

Bagge, S. 2003, 'Den heroiske tid – kirkereform og kirkekamp 1153–1214', in *Ecclesia Nidrosiensis 1153–1537: Søkelys på Nidaroskirkens og Nidarosprovinsens historie*, ed. S. Imsen, Trondheim (Senter for middelalderstudier, NTNU. Skrifter no. 5), 47–80.

Bagge, S. 2006, 'The Making of a Missionary King: The Medieval Accounts of Olaf Tryggvason and the Conversion of Norway', *Journal of English and Germanic Philology* 106, 473–513.

Birkeli, F. 1960, 'Hadde Håkon Adalsteinsfostre likevel en biskop Sigfrid hos seg?', *Historisk Tidsskrift* 40, 113–36.

Birkeli, F. 1973, *Norske steinkors i tidlig middelalder: et bidrag til belysning av overgangen fra norrøn religion til kristendom*, Oslo.

Blindheim, C., B. Heyerdahl-Larsen and R. Tollnes 1981, *Kaupang-funnene*, vol. I, *Norske oldfunn*, Oslo.

Clover, C. and J. Lindow, eds. 1985, *Old Norse-Icelandic Literature: A Critical Guide*, Ithaca (Islandica XLV).

Clunies Ross, M. 1987, *Skáldskaparmál: Snorri Sturluson's 'Ars Poetica' and Medieval Theories of Language*, Odense.

Clunies Ross, M. 1994, *Prolonged Echoes: Old Norse Myths in Medieval Northern Society*, I, Odense.

Cruickshank, M. 2002, 'Jern- og middelalderbosetning på Hunstad, Bodø kommune', *TROMURA, Kulturhistorie* 35, 27–33.

Düwel, K. 1985, *Das Opferfest von Lade*, Vienna (Wiener Arbeiten zur germanischen Altertumskunde und Philologie).

Eide, O. E. 1974, 'De toskipede kirker i Oslo: et forsøk på redatering og opphavsbestemmelse med utgangspunkt i de siste utgravinger i Clemenskriken' (Thesis for MA, Nordic Archaeology, University of Bergen, 1973), Stencil, author's edition.

Ellehøj, S. 1965, *Den ældste norrøne historieskrivning*, Copenhagen.

Farbregd, O. 1986a, 'Elveosar: Gamle sentra på vandring', *SPOR* 1986/2, 6–12.

Farbregd, O. 1986b, 'Hove i Åsen – kultstad og bygdesentrum', *SPOR* 1986/2, 42–6.

Farbregd, O. 1986c, 'Kongsmakt, kristning og Frostatinget: Gravfunn på Hernes, Frosta', *SPOR* 1986/2, 38–41.

Fidjestøl, B. 1994, 'Review of Claus Krag, *Ynglingatal og Ynglingesaga*', *Maal og Minne*, 191–9.

Fidjestøl, B. 1999, *The Dating of Eddic Poetry: A Historical Survey and Methodological Questions*, Copenhagen (Bibliotheca Arnamagnæana vol. XLI).

Fischer, G. 1965, *Domkirken i Trondheim: Kirkebygget i middelalderen. Nidaros erkebispestol og bispesete 1153–1953*, Oslo.

Forseth, L. 2003, 'Maktsentra og forskjeller mellom Østfold og Vestfold under jernalderen: en kildekritisk undersøkelse basert på de arkeologiske funnene og fornminnene', in *Over grenser, Østfold og Viken i yngre jernalder og middelalder*, ed. J. V. Sigurdsson and P. G. Norseng (Centre for Viking and Medieval Studies Occasional Papers 5), Oslo, 31–70.

Gabrielsen, K. H. 2002, 'Vestlandets steinkors: Monumentalisme i brytningen mellom hedendom og kristendom' (unpublished Master's thesis in archaeology, University of Bergen).

Gellein, K. 1997, 'Kristen innflytelse i hedensk tid? En analyse med utgangspunkt i graver fra yngre jernalder i Hordaland' (unpublished Master's thesis, University of Bergen).

Gräslund, A.-S. 2002, *Ideologi och Mentalitet: om religionsskiftet i Skandinavien från en arkeologisk horisont*, Uppsala (*OPIA* 29).

Harris, J. 1985, 'Eddic Poetry', in Clover and Lindow 1985, 68–156.

Helle, K. 2001, *Gulatinget og Gulatingslova*, Leikanger.

Helle, K. ed. 2003a, *The Cambridge History of Scandinavia* I, Cambridge.

Helle, K. 2003b, 'The Norwegian Kingdom: Succession Disputes and Consolidation', in Helle 2003a, 369–91.

Jørgensen, T. 1996, 'From Wessex to Western Norway: Some Perspectives on one Channel for the Christianization Process', in *Church and People in Britain and Scandinavia*, ed. I. Brohed, Lund, 29–44.

Krag, C. 1989, 'Norge som odel i Harald Hårfagres ætt', *Historisk Tidsskrift* 68, 288–301.

Krag, C. 1991, *Ynglingatal og Ynglingesaga: en studie i historiske kilder*, Oslo.

Krag, C. 2001, 'Trosskiftet og teorien om sakralkongedømmet', *Collegium Medievale* 14, 233–41.

Krag, C. 2003, 'The Early Unification of Norway', in Helle 2003a, 184–201.

Lager, L. 2002, *Den synliga tron: Runstenskors som en spegling av kristnandet i Sverige*, Uppsala (*OPIA* 31).

Lange, G. 1989, *Die Anfänge der isländisch-norwegischen Geschichtsschreibung*, Reykjavik (Studia Islandica XLVII).

Lidén, H.-E. 2000, *Mariakirken i Bergen*, Bergen.

Liestøl, A. 1969, 'The Literate Vikings', *Proceedings of the Sixth Viking Congress*, Uppsala, 69–78.

Lindow, J. 1985, 'Mythology and Mythography', in Clover and Lindow 1985, 21–67.

Lönnroth, L. 1963, 'Studier i Olav Tryggvasons saga', *Samlaren* 84, 54–94.

Meulengracht Sørensen, P. 2001, 'Den norrøne litteratur og virkeligheden', in *At fortælle historien: Telling History. Studier i den gamle nordiske litteratur: Studies in Norse Literature*, Trieste, 113–22.

Moltke, E. 1985, *Runes and their Origin: Denmark and Elsewhere*, Copenhagen.

Mortensen, L. B. and E. Mundal 2003, 'Erkebispesetet i Nidaros – arnestad og verkstad for olavslitteraturen', in *Ecclesia Nidrosiensis 1153–1537: Søkelys på Nidaroskirkens og Nidarosprovinsens historie*, ed. S. Imsen, Trondheim, 353–84.

Munch, G. S., O. S. Johansen and E. Roesdahl, eds. 2003, *Borg in Lofoten: A Chieftain's Farm in North Norway*, Bøstad and Trondheim.

Myking, M. 2001, *Vart Norge kristna frå England: ein gjennomgang av norsk forsking med utgangspunkt i Absalon Tarangers avhandling Den angelsaksiske kirkes inflydelse paa den norske (1890)*, Oslo.

Narmo, L. E. 1996, 'Kokekameratene på Leikvin', *Viking* 59, 79–100.

Odenstedt, B. 1990, *On the Origins and Early History of the Runic Script: Typology and Graphic Variation in the Older Futhark*, Uppsala.

Olsen, O. 1995, '"Hørg, hov og kirke" – 30 år etter', in *Møtet mellom hedendom og kristendom i Norge*, ed. H.-E. Lidén, Oslo, 121–8.

Orrman, E. 2003, 'Church and Society', in Helle 2003a, 421–62.

Pettersen, G. and E. Karlsen 2003, 'Katalogisering av latinske membranfragmenter som forskningsprosjekt', in *Arkivverkets forskningsseminar, Gardermoen 2003* (*Riksarkivaren. Rapporter og retningslinjer* 16), Oslo, 43–88.

Sandmo, A.-K. 1990, 'Haug i Hadsel – gårdshaug med graver og mulige kirkerester', *TROMURA Kulturhistorie* 17, 51–78.

Sandnes, J. 1994, 'Review of Claus Krag, *Ynglingatal og Ynglingesaga*', *Historisk Tidsskrift* 73, 229–31.

Schanche, A. 2000, *Graver i ur og berg: samisk gravskikk og religion fra forhistorisk til nyere tid*, Karasjok.

See, K. von 1981, *Edda, Saga, Skaldendichtung. Aufsätze zur skandinavischen Literatur des Mittelalters*, Heidelberg.

Skre, D. 1998, 'Missionary Activity in Early Medieval Norway: Strategy, Organization and the Course of Events', *Scandinavian Journal of History* 23, 25–43.

Skre, D., L. Pilø and U. Pedersen 2001, *The Kaupang Project: Annual Report 2001*, Oslo.

Skre, D. and F.-A. Stylegar 2004, *Kaupang: The Viking Town: The Kaupang Exhibition at UKM*, Oslo.

Snorri Sturluson, *Heimskringla*, I–IV, ed. F. Jónsson, Copenhagen, 1893–1901.

Solberg, B. 2000, *Jernalderen i Norge: 500 før Kristus til 1030 etter Kristus*, Oslo.

Solli, B. 1996, *Narratives of Veøy: An Investigation into Poetics and Scientifics of Archaeology*, Oslo (Universitetets Oldsaksamlings Skrifter. Ny rekke 19).

Steinsland, G. 2000, *Den hellige kongen: om religion og herskermakt fra vikingtid til middelalder*, Oslo.

Steinsland, G. 2001, 'Om Claus Krags syn på kilder og metoder', *Collegium Medievale* 14, 233–41.

Taranger, A. 1890, *Den angelsaksiske kirkes inflydelse paa den norske*, Kristiania.

Tobiassen, T. 1964, 'Tronfølgelov og privilegiebrev: en studie i kongemaktens ideologi under Magnus Erlingsson', *Historisk Tidsskrift* 43, 180–273.

Vandvik, E. ed. 1959, *Latinske dokument til norsk historie*, Oslo.

Vries, J. de 1956–7, *Altgermanische Religionsgeschichte* I–II, Berlin.

CHAPTER 5

The kingdom of Sweden

Nils Blomkvist, Stefan Brink and Thomas Lindkvist

I. BEFORE CHRISTIANITY: RELIGION AND POWER

The archaeological evidence for the Late Iron Age (*c.* 600–1100) is rich in Sweden,[1] particularly in central Sweden, around Lake Mälaren. A characteristic burial tradition evolved here in the Late Iron Age, with one or several burial grounds attached to every prehistoric settlement. These burial grounds have been preserved to a large extent because they were on barren land close to the settlements and not on arable land. The burials consist of both cremation graves and inhumations, and typically a low mound was placed over the burial. Some graves are exceptional, normally representing the upper stratum of society. For example, there are chamber graves with rich and plentiful grave goods; some, found at the Viking Age trading place Birka on Lake Mälaren are very famous.[2] Boat graves constitute another remarkable type of inhumation; the body was placed in a boat which was buried in the ground.[3] Many of the boat burials are exceptionally rich in grave goods. Famous sites are Valsgärde, Vendel, Alsike and Gamla (Old) Uppsala in the province of Uppland, and Tuna in Badelunda in Västmanland. As opposed to the low mounds, large mounds ('king's mounds') are very often found in the central places of settlement districts, for example in Gamla Uppsala or on royal farms (*husabyar*). Many of these seem to be connected to ancient *bona regalia*, what contemporary vernacular texts called *Uppsala öd* (literally 'the richness of Uppsala').[4] These burial grounds and mounds functioned as cult sites, attesting to the importance of the cult of ancestors.[5] In addition, some remains of what were probably cult houses have been excavated during the last few years, in Sanda in the province of Uppland, in Borg by Norrköping in Östergötland and at Järrestad in eastern Skåne. These cult houses were fairly small buildings

[1] Hyenstrand 1984.   [2] Gräslund 1980.   [3] Müller-Wille 1970.   [4] Hyenstrand 1974, 103–18.
[5] Birkeli 1938; Arrhenius 1970; Baudou 1989; Artelius 2000; Gräslund 2001; Vikstrand 2001; Andrén 2002; Brink 2004.

where archaeologists have found many animal bones and small pendants, especially so-called *Torshammarringar*, small pendants with miniatures of Thor's hammer.[6]

The two main written sources describing Sweden in the pre-Christian period are Rimbert's *Vita Anskarii* and Adam of Bremen's *Gesta Hammaburgensis ecclesiae pontificum* which both reflect the missionary efforts of the church of Hamburg-Bremen. The *Vita* was written soon after Ansgar's death by his former disciple Rimbert, who was elected the second archbishop of Hamburg-Bremen in 865; he finished it before 876. These circumstances make the *Vita Anskarii* an extremely valuable source, although Rimbert deals only briefly with Sweden in connection with Ansgar's two visits to Birka. Adam is obviously biased in his report on Sweden, emphasizing the role of the German church and suppressing the evidence of the English and other ecclesiastical initiatives which makes his account problematic as a historical source. Apart from these sources, several Old Norse sagas and poems written outside Sweden deal with Sweden during the pre-Christian period. Due to the lack of contemporary sources, we know least about the folklore and mythology that do not concern the 'higher' gods: everyday pagan traditions and less significant deities.

A number of later written sources, however, provide information on gods. The most important source on the pagan religion of Scandinavia is Snorri Sturluson's *Edda*.[7] Snorri was a Christian himself, writing in thirteenth-century Iceland, in a Christian society; this must give us pause in the way we use the information he provides. His work is complemented by some Eddic poems,[8] material that Snorri himself seems to have drawn on. Snorri's *Edda* and the *Poetic Edda* depict the pagan pantheon, with a wide range of gods and goddesses, Ódhinn (Wodan), Ullr, Thórr, Freyr, Heimdallr, Balder, Ægir, Ran, Freyja, Síf and others. However, the pagan religion of Scandinavia was clearly not homogeneous, as highlighted by the toponyms, an important contemporary source. They also have the advantage of being unbiased, not having apparently been produced with any political or religious purpose. The place names of Sweden, Norway and Denmark suggest that only some of the gods listed by the *Edda* were actually worshipped in each. Their cults were not found all over Scandinavia, but only in certain regions. Some gods, who have a prominent position in the mythological histories, like Heimdallr and Balder, do not seem to have had an actual cult, whereas the name of a god like Ullr, who plays a minor role in the mythology presented by Snorri, occurs in significant numbers in the

---

[6] Åquist 1996; Nielsen 1997; Kaliff 2001.   [7] Snorri Sturluson, *Edda*.   [8] Snorri Sturluson, *Edda*.

place names of Sweden (Ullr) and Norway (Ullr and Ullinn). Other gods obviously worshipped in Sweden were Freyr, Ódhinn, Thórr (Thor) and the goddesses Freyja and *Niærdher. The god tied to law seems to have been Tyr, found in place names in Denmark and southern Norway, but never in Sweden.

Rimbert describes the decision-making process of the people in Birka.[9] Before they could agree on a major matter, they consulted the gods by casting lots, a custom well known in pagan societies. Adam as well as the Old Norse sources focus on (Gamla) Uppsala, which is said to be the seat of the pagan kings. We get the impression that the king of the Svear, the people living in Svitjod (early Sweden), had an important function as a cult leader at Uppsala: Adam talks about the famous temple with three major gods as idols, and the sagas call the king of the Svear Yngvi-Freyr (in Old Ingi-Frø) and state that the male god Freyr was especially connected to Uppsala and the king of the Svear.[10]

The provincial law of the island of Gotland and the so-called *Guta saga*, preserved together with the law code, supply information on a different aspect of pagan customs. 'They sacrificed', the saga says, 'their sons and daughters and cattle together with food and drink.' The supreme sacrifice (*blót*) involving humans was held by the 'entire land', whereas each *treding* (third part) conducted its own sacrifice, and the lesser *þing* had lesser sacrifices with cattle, food and drink.[11] One may question the reliability of this description, whose author was of course a Christian.

The passage just quoted has a corresponding article in the actual text of the law, which forbids precisely these rituals. However, it particularly criminalizes 'haizl . . . miþ mati eþa miþ dryckiu', that is, 'invocations using food and drink', not according to Christian practices.[12] Torsten Blomkvist has shown the great extent to which these prohibitions refer to the cult of the ancestors: *haugr* denotes ancestral burial mounds, *staf garþr* the characteristic traces of Iron Age house-foundations usually known as *kämpagravar*, and there is the reference to invocation with food and drink. The enigmatic stone enclosures, *stensträngar*, that sometimes lead to burial mounds, and the famous Gotlandic picture stones are also drawn into this systematic interpretation.[13] The author found striking parallels in Orthodox Setomaa

---

[9] *RVA*, chap. 27. [10] Sundqvist 2002. [11] *GS*, chap. 1.
[12] 'No one may invoke groves or mounds or pagan gods, neither at the *vi* nor at stone foundations. If somebody is found guilty, and it is witnessed that he has such an invocation with his food and drink as follows not Christian customs, then he will be made to pay three marks to the parishioners' (*GL*, chap. 4).
[13] Blomkvist 2002, 135–55.

9. Sweden: provinces and places

in south-eastern Estonia (and generally in Rus'), where the custom of eating meals on the grave has been traced archaeologically from pre-Christian times to the present.[14]

A major source for Viking Age Sweden, the contemporary rune-stones, numbering over 3,000, also provides information on pre-Christian religion. The majority of these were raised during the very process of Christianization, and most of them are stereotypical, saying that someone has erected a rune-stone in memory of someone else (normally a relative), God bless his soul. The one for whom the stone was erected was nearly always a male, a husband, a father or a son, and the one who set up the stone was very often a female, a wife or a mother. Some of the rune-stones have longer inscriptions, sometimes giving us unique information regarding religion, society or events.[15] A few hundred inscriptions belong to pagan times (200–1000). The use of the runes, and especially the use of *lönnrunor* ('secret runes', a kind of cipher), shows that runes and the art of carving runes had obvious religious overtones, evidenced already by the word rune itself, meaning 'mystery, secret wisdom'.[16] The most famous and the longest – and unfortunately probably the most problematic – is the Rök rune-stone in the province of Östergötland, dated to around 800. Its text contains references and allusions to narratives; our insufficient knowledge of these prevents the full understanding of the rune-stone. One of the legends concerns the famous Gothic king Theodoric.[17] The text of the Ramsunds rune carving, describing the building of a bridge, is not very important. The iconography, however, that has been carved into the rock is unique. It depicts scenes from the well-known myth of Sigurd killing Favner the dragon.[18] On the Altuna rune-stone from Uppland the famous story of the god Thor fishing the mighty Midgardhs Serpent is represented; the serpent is so heavy that Thor's foot is forced through the bottom of the boat.[19]

The Old Swedish word *vi* that goes back to the Proto-Germanic adjective *wiha ('holy') is found in many place names in Scandinavia, often together with the name of a pagan god or goddess as a qualifier, as in Frösvi, Odense (< *Othinsvœ*), Torsvi and Frövi. These are normally understood as cult sites for these gods and goddesses. We possess a few contemporary references that help us explain the institution of the *vi*; the most remarkable of these is the Forsa runic ring from Hög, northern Sweden.[20] The text is in some parts obscure or a matter of discussion, but as of now a probable translation is:

[14] Valk 1999, 61–86. [15] Jansson 1987; Sawyer 2003. [16] Green 1998, 255.
[17] Jansson 1987, 31–7. [18] Jansson 1987, 144–5. [19] Jansson 1987, 150; Meulengracht Sørensen 1986.
[20] An iron ring with runes cut into it. Brink 1996a.

One ox and two *aura* [i.e. *ørar*, as a fine] [to the?] *staf* [the meaning of the word is unknown] for the restoration of a *vi* to a good state the first time; two oxen and four *aura* the second time; but for the third time four oxen and eight *aura*; and all property is confiscated, if he does not make amends.

All this, the people are entitled to demand, according to the law of the people that was decreed and ratified before.

But they themselves made this [probably the ring, or the law], Anund from Tåsta and Ofeg from Hjortsta.

But Vibjörn carved.

This is the earliest known legal text in Scandinavia, a rule from the early Viking Age, around 800. Most probably it regulates the maintenance of a *vi*, that is a cult and assembly site.[21] For failure in restoring the *vi* according to the law, one had to pay fines, one ox and two *aura* (*ørar*) the first time, two oxen and four *ørar* the second time and four oxen and eight *ørar* the third time. If this was not done, all one's property was to be confiscated. Perhaps the most important part of the inscription is the phrase *svadh liudhir œigu at liudhretti* 'all this, the people are entitled to demand, according to the people's right (the law of the land)'. This evidence points to the existence of a specific law of the people (the Hälsingar) or the land (most certainly Hälsingland), a *liudhrettr* or Old Norse *lyrettr*.[22] This contemporary statement is unique for Viking Age Scandinavia so far as we know, and it corresponds to a statement by Snorri Sturluson in his *Heimskringla*,[23] that different people had their own different laws in early Scandinavia. This rune ring was most probably used at the *þing* site for the whole province of Hälsingland at Hög with its *þing* mound, and it is tempting to think it is an example of a prehistoric oath ring.

Besides the Forsa rune ring, a ninth-century runic inscription on a flat rock in the hamlet of Oklunda in the province of Östergötland is one of the most important pieces of evidence we have of pre-Christian legal customs in Sweden. The somewhat obscure runic text may be translated as: 'Gunnar cut this, cut these runes. And he fled guilty [of homicide], sought this pagan cult site (*vi*), and got a safe-conduct [to the assembly] then, and he tied Vi-Finn [meaning unknown].' As this inscription shows, a malefactor was allowed protection at a *vi* after committing homicide and officially announcing his crime, that is, if he managed to get there before his adversaries killed him, as they had a right to do. We also know a similar custom from Christian laws, where churches were regarded as places where people had a right of asylum.[24] There are many problems

[21] Ruthström 1990.   [22] Cf. See 1964, 57–63.
[23] Snorri Sturluson, *Heimskringla. Nóregs Konunga Sôgur*, 260.   [24] Nilsson 1991, 486–8.

of interpretation with this important inscription, but it is safe to say that it is a legal document from the early ninth century whose purpose was to announce that a man called Gunnar followed the law correctly after committing a crime of homicide. He escaped to a *vi*, a cult and assembly site, and there received asylum and perhaps drew up a protected space (*fridskrets*) where he was safe.

We may thus conclude that it is still possible to a great extent to reconstruct the focal societal arena of a settlement district, which would most probably be the assembly place for legal, cultic and trading matters as well as for feasting and playing games in general.[25] The indicators are particularly the place-name elements *vi, hov, hög, ljung, vall* and *lund*.[26]

Probably no comprehensive laws, complete prototypes of the later provincial laws, existed in Viking Age Scandinavia.[27] In all likelihood legal customs and legal traditions differed between provinces. We get an insight, thanks to the runic evidence, into some of these legal customs: in the province of Hälsingland we have evidence of *liudhrettr* 'the law of the people (the *land*)', which is probably to be understood as the law of the *hælsing(i)ar*, the people living in the province of Hälsingland. This implies that, in the ninth century, the people of Hälsingland thought of themselves as having a corpus of legal rules and customs, that were seen as a *liudhrettr*, 'laws of the people', hence not a royal law. This fact is important when comparing the Swedish case with the early continental laws. As the Forsa Ring mentions, the maintenance of the *vi*, the pagan cult site, was part of these rules, but in our opinion the *vi* was also the assembly place for many communal matters. And in a society where it was practically impossible to distinguish between legal and cultic matters, the *vi* obviously had both legal and cultic prerogatives, something that is so remarkably illustrated in the Oklunda runic inscription. In other words it becomes clear that it is impossible to separate 'religion' from law in pre-Christian and pre-Roman-law Scandinavia.

In the Middle Ages the idea became established that Sweden was formed through the amalgamation of two great pagan nations, the Svear and the Götar. The Svear (*Suiones*) are mentioned in Tacitus's *Germania*, composed in the first century AD, and in a handful of other continental and British sources from the first millennium.[28] It is obvious from ninth-century sources such as Rimbert's *Vita Anskarii* and the translation of Orosius produced at the court of King Alfred that the Svear formed some kind of multi-regional polity, stretching from their core area around Lake Mälaren

---

[25] Brink 1997b.   [26] Cf. Andersson 1992; Brink 1996b.
[27] Cf. Brink 2002.   [28] Tacitus, *Germania*, chap. 44.

(which was then a gulf open to the Baltic) towards Denmark in the south, and towards the east Baltic territory in the east. Götar are mentioned by Jordanes in the sixth century. His *Getica* contains a history of the genesis of the Ostrogoths, then living in Byzantium and Italy, in which he claims for them an origin in the Scandinavian peninsula (*Scandza*). Jordanes presents a long list of Scandinavian *gentes* among which no less than three 'Gothic' tribes, the *Uagoth*, *Gautigoth* and *Ostrogotha*, appear alongside – among others – the Suehans.[29] Other regional groups, however, also carry related names, notably the island of Gotland and the peninsula of Jutland (in what was to become Denmark), and similar expressions occur in even more diffuse early medieval contexts, for example the Anglo-Saxon *Beowulf*. It hardly seems possible to interpret these observations as evidence of a multi-regional Swedish or Gothic polity; rather, we should see them as an indication of a patchwork of local communities, some larger, others smaller.

Adam of Bremen, writing in the 1070s, is the first author to discuss the relationship between the Svear and Götar. To him the two regions Östergötland and Västergötland are parts of the Swedish kingdom. However, he also connects them with the Visigoths who ransacked Rome in 410, and – taking a further bold step – with Ezekiel's prophecy of Gog and Magog, which for him may have been applicable to the Götar. Perhaps inspired by this, Pope Gregory VII a few years later addressed the Swedish kings 'I and A' as *reges visigothorum*, using the Gothic terminology of Late Antiquity. From then on the idea that some of the Swedish population were the heirs of the conquerors of Rome took root in Sweden, and the myth was gradually improved over the centuries.[30]

In fact, several chiefdoms and petty kingdoms existed in the area that later became Sweden, though our knowledge of most of them is tenuous and purely based on archaeological evidence. The (main) power centres of both a superior king and petty kings and chieftains of the Late Iron Age have been found especially in eastern Sweden. These individuals were probably never geographically static. The finds probably signal the sites of the hall buildings of these leaders. Place names and rune-stones indicate the existence of military escorts (*karlar*, *thegnar*, *rinkar*, *sveinar*) and other military leaders (for example, *visi*, *stýrir*, *hersi(r)*). The same few sources attest cult leaders, or perhaps secular and cultic leaders, such as the *goði*, the *thulr*, the *lytir*, or the *vífill*, who also belonged to these upper social strata.[31]

[29] Jordanes, chap. 9, 16–24. Cf. Svennung 1972.
[30] For all this Blomkvist 2005, 572–623; cf. Johannesson 1982.   [31] Brink 1999.

Place names provide significant source material from Sweden for the Late Iron Age not only for cultic-religious matters, for which they are vital, but also, although the majority of them deal with agrarian aspects of life and the usage of land, for an analysis of power in society. Many may be dated to this period. In many Swedish districts, especially in central-eastern Sweden, around Lake Mälaren, we find the toponym Hus(e)by in central locations. These names go back to the Old Swedish word *husaby* and represent a king's farm or hamlet. The *husabyar* made up the major part of the *bona regalia* during the Swedish early Middle Ages (*c.* 1050–1300).

In many districts other place names with *tuna(r)*, *salr* and *husa(r)* occur in the most central or strategic locations in the landscape. All are probably to be seen as a prehistoric king's or chieftain's farm or 'manor'. Notably, many of the names containing *tuna* are of a theophoric type, which include a pagan god's or goddess's name as the first element, such as Torstuna 'the *tuna* dedicated to the god Thórr', Frötuna 'the *tuna* dedicated to the goddess Freyja', Ultuna 'the *tuna* dedicated to the god Ullr'. Most interesting are some settlements with a name including *tuna* (Ultuna and Torstuna) in the province of Uppland. In that particular administrative hundred district the hundred takes its name from the same god (*Ulleråkers hundare* and *Torsåkers hundare*), and the name of the district is originally the name of the *þing* and assembly site of the district (Ulleråker and Torsåker).[32] These assembly sites with names incorporating the names of gods have been interpreted as places in the middle of arable lands, where pagan cultic rituals were performed probably in conjunction with judicial matters.

Scandinavian Late Iron Age central places were *complexes* of different functional sites in close proximity to each other, consisting of elements like a prominent farm of a king, sub-king or chieftain probably with a special hall building for official purposes, farms for craftsmen, such as smiths, farms for cult leaders and military leaders, farms allocated to a retinue, cult sites and cultic groves, marketplaces and assembly places all spread out in the landscape, normally in a small settlement district. Late Iron Age central-place complexes must have followed a 'model', a mentally fixed structure. This is most easily visible in the middle Swedish landscape, especially around the lake Mälaren, but such complexes are also found in Östergötland, Småland, Västergötland and Bohuslän. The model seems to have been pan-Scandinavian, since there are traces of it in Denmark and more clearly in Norway as well.

[32] E.g. Brink 1996b, 263–4.

Most of the places that relate to social order in the Swedish landscape were probably interrelated in some way. From archaeological finds, written evidence from *Beowulf*, Icelandic sagas and rune-stones and the place-name evidence, an image of Late Iron Age community in Sweden emerges: different types of alliances existed between leaders in society, bonds that resulted from strategic marriages or gift exchanges. Certain families controlled certain settlement-districts over long periods of time. In each district, a hall building for official secular or ritual meetings and banquets was probably built on an elevated, prestigious site. Craftsmen and most of the retinue lived on their own farms and hamlets as farmers most of the time, while some retainers in the *hirdh* dwelt in the hall. Farms or strongholds in strategic sites controlled trade and probably facilitated the charging of tolls on goods. Farms may also have been allocated to cult leaders. Certain assembly sites, that most probably had a metaphysical status in local tradition, connecting people to their ancestors as well as to the gods, were very often situated on a large grave mound. Several pagan cult sites and cultic groves were dedicated to different gods and goddesses of the pre-Christian Scandinavian pantheon.

2. CONTACTS

In Rimbert's *Vita Anskarii* we hear of an embassy from the 'Svear' to the Emperor Louis the Pious. As part of the mandate of their legation, they told the emperor that many of their nation (*gens*) wished to become Christians, and their king (*rex*) was so favourable to this idea that he would permit priests to go there. Ansgar, a Benedictine monk, was chosen to go and see 'if this people was prepared for the faith'. This occurred in the late 820s.[33] After a dramatic journey to Birka in Sweden, where he met the then ruling king Björn (*Bern*), Ansgar was appointed as the first archbishop of Hamburg, the see which later was transferred to Bremen.

The establishment of contacts between the king and the emperor clearly had a political aspect. Moreover, Ansgar's mission need not have been the only one of its kind.[34] The Carolingian missionary offensive towards Scandinavia is also attested by a problematic collection of copied charters, some of which show signs of 'improvements' and manipulations in the interest of the church of Hamburg-Bremen. Even according to a letter of 31 May 864 from Pope Nicholas I, preserved at Rome and thus not one of the Hamburg falsifications, however, the bishop of Bremen was to

---

[33] *RVA*, chap. 9, 10.   [34] Staecker 1999.

carry archiepiscopal dignity *super Danos et Svevos*.[35] One of the central aims of such contact was presumably to establish peace for imperial subjects, especially traders, on the sea routes of the Baltic and in emporia controlled by Swedish wealth. (Possibly the Svear also wished for such peace.) It seems that Ansgar's mission was in fact confined to the chief trading place of Birka on Lake Mälaren. Within sight across the water was the important royal estate of Alsnö. The text provides valuable glimpses of life at that multinational site, and of the constitution of the realm, according to which the kings had to negotiate their propositions at *þing* assemblies.[36]

Ansgar's closest contact among the Swedes was Herigarius or Hergeir, King Bern's *praefectus* in Birka. He was among the first who asked to be baptized, and soon built a church on his own land, which was later to function as a refuge for Christians when pagan repercussions began. Rimbert presents him as a man capable of working miracles, in order to demonstrate the power of Christ compared to the futility of the pagan gods.[37] Another of Rimbert's stories tells of a pious woman called Frideburg who endured the scorn of pagans all her life, and kept a bottle of wine for three years in order to get Holy Communion before her death. She was rich and had always given alms. Since, however, few people in Birka were poor, her last wish was that her daughter Catla should go to Dorestad (in the Carolingian Empire) 'where there are many churches, priests and spiritual people, as well as many that need help' and give all her money in alms for the salvation of her soul. This was done and rewarded by another miracle.[38] These narratives clearly show the close connection of the Carolingian mission to trade, and the social implications of trade. As the political leader of Birka, Hergeir was defending the rights of Christians to practise their religion openly. Most Christians may have been traders from western Europe. The pious women of the latter story clearly had close connections to Dorestad; their names may well be Frisian.

After two decades a pagan reaction occurred. The missionary bishop Gautbert was forced to leave Birka, and his follower and kinsman, Nithard, became the first known Christian martyr in the country.[39] These events prompted Ansgar to make a second journey to Birka in 852, when he met the new king Oleph (Olof), whom he persuaded to make arrangements

---

[35] *Regesta Pontificum Romanorum*, 30–2. Cf. Reincke 1960, 57–78. Seegrün 1976, 5–13, 101–10. *DD* no. 117.

[36] Further Blomkvist 2005, 270–1   [37] *RVA*, chap. 11, 19.

[38] 'quia hic [in Birka] minus pauperes inveniuntur . . . Ibi [in Dorestad] sunt ecclesiae plurimae et sacerdotes ac clerici; ibi indigentium multitudo': *RVA*, chap. 20.

[39] *RVA*, chap. 14, 17.

to secure the right to conduct Christian cult activities within the realm. The decision process took place at assemblies on local and higher levels, where the king saw to the acceptance of Christian cult activities. It has been assumed that a missionary bishop remained in Birka, at least until the death of Ansgar in 865,[40] but Christian practices seem to have disappeared quite soon afterwards. Birka itself continued to flourish until around 975. Adam of Bremen mentions Ansgar's visits to Birka, as well as a journey to Birka some hundred years later by Archbishop Unni, who was said to have died there in September 936.[41] By then Swedish culture was more influenced from the east than from the west, and all organized forms of Christian cult had obviously lapsed.

The failure of the ninth-century mission can be partly – perhaps largely – explained by patterns of trade. An extraordinary number of Viking Age (c. 800–1150) silver hoards have been retrieved around the Baltic. By the ninth century the flow of silver had assumed a constancy and richness which suggest that considerable economic interaction was already at work between the caliphate, Byzantium, the Baltic rim and the Carolingian Empire in the ninth and tenth centuries. Shortly before 800 a flood of Abbasid coins started to reach the Baltic, and from the second half of the ninth century Arabic currency began to dominate. From around 890 (Arabic coins contain the exact year of minting) the key source of the incoming silver was the Samanid dynasty, which ruled over a territory in and around Turkestan (Transoxania) close by the silk road.

The more than century-long close eastern links had cultural consequences as well. Archaeological objects in a general way demonstrate an Islamic influence. The centres with which northerners interacted were however too distant, in miles as well as in culture, to be able to dominate the Baltic rim. Instead, its inhabitants developed indigenous cultural forms more freely, incorporating what they found suitable from the eastern civilizations. A good example is provided by the frequent finds of Viking Age scales and weights around the Baltic. As Heiko Steuer has shown, they represent Arabic trading techniques that were used on the vast north-east borders of the caliphate. They were kept very accurate during the period of Islamic dominance, but gradually lost their exactness afterwards.[42] In many aspects of life, independent phenomena developed, in which traits borrowed from almost all directions matured into Nordic originality: examples include the abstract representation of animal forms, probably connoting aspects of the

---

[40] *RVA*, chaps. 26–8; Hallencreutz 1986, 163–7; 1993.
[41] Adam of Bremen I.15; 21, schol. 127; I.61; 62, III.72, schol. 127, 142.   [42] Steuer 1987.

cult. The rune-stones, which have already been mentioned, often also carry a pictorial content of that kind.

For almost a century, hardly any western European coins reached the Baltic rim. This order of things however changed dramatically around 975, when the eastern silver-flood suddenly disappeared, immediately to be replaced by incoming German and Anglo-Saxon coins. Many causes for this change have been suggested, but one conclusion is indisputable: the mutual exclusion and quick replacement of silver currencies clearly mark the shift of conjunctures. The shift in the 970s 'mirrors a change of position for the Nordic countries, that could only be called enormous', Sture Bolin wrote in 1945: the north thereby began to become a part of western Europe.[43] There is an obvious connection between this change in the economic conditions affecting the rather populous social strata that were involved in wide-ranging travel and the quick breakthrough of Christianity that was to follow around the Baltic.

The first Christian mission to Sweden in the ninth century was closely connected to the contemporary expansion of Carolingian long-distance trade. It failed at the time when the Baltic rim began to receive large quantities of Arabic dirhams, which we may see as markers of a dominant eastern connection. For reasons that remain disputed, this eastern influence collapsed in the 970s, which by and large coincided with Sweden's lasting conversion to Christianity.

3. CHRISTIANIZATION

Sweden's definite conversion to Christianity occurred in the decades around 1000. Even so it took more than a century-long and partly violent struggle before the whole population was fully converted and the worship of the pagan gods was abolished. The struggle is mirrored in the sudden popularity of raising rune-stones. The majority of the younger rune-stones show signs of the acceptance of Christianity, although combined with sophisticated snake or dragon motifs, which have non-Christian connotations. It is often argued that these monuments signal a general crisis in attitudes and outlook. Some may have been raised by free commoners on the border of their 'odal' property, facing a road or a stream, sometimes in connection with the regional infrastructure (building bridges, organizing assembly places), or in connection with the homestead's pagan burial grounds, and usually as a monument over a dead father, husband, brother,

---

[43] Bolin 1945; 1953b.

wife or son. Some inscriptions give details about individual cases of conversion, such as an Uppland inscription on a rune-stone that a wife had erected over her husband, saying: 'He died in Denmark in white clothes' (*Hann varð dauðr a Danmarku i hvitavaðum*). We know of seven inscriptions in Uppland that mention someone dying in their baptismal robes, white clothes that the neophyte had to wear for a week after baptism. Such inscriptions indicate that the people commemorated had accepted Christianity on their deathbed; two of the inscriptions claim that such conversion had occurred in Denmark.[44] Several Scandinavian sources mention prime-signing, a preliminary acceptance of the sign of the cross, by which people became catechumens; this was a means for pagans to be able to communicate with Christians in a Christian environment as equals.[45]

The expressions of religious conviction in runic inscriptions are fairly conventional, at least by later standards. It is easy to see that they follow fashion, particularly if one merely reads the texts.[46] Many inscriptions contain prayers, like 'God help his soul' (*Guð hialpi salu hans*) or more developed such as 'God and God's mother help his spirit and soul, grant him light and paradise' (*Guð hialpi hans and ok salu ok Guðs moðir, le hanum lius ok paradis*). There is, however, also a harsher variety, asking God to save a person's soul 'better than he deserved' (*bœtr þæn hann gœrði til*). Interpreting the rune-stones as works combining different arts makes them more complex: text, cross and dragon motifs were composed together, and the stones were erected as value-loaded components in the landscape. The impression they give is of an enormous effort by many at almost the same time to experiment with a new form of expressing existential basics. Furthermore their dating allows us to follow this sensitive process as a moving frontier, gradually unfolding from the south-west towards the north-east. In Götaland the practice flourished chiefly in the first half of the eleventh century; to the north of Lake Mälaren it ended in a crescendo that stopped only around 1125, the youngest monuments being gathered around the pagan centre of worship in (Old) Uppsala. Gotland deviates from the pattern, by continuing the habit several centuries longer.[47]

In Uppland some rune-stones close to the new royal town of Sigtuna belong to the first decades of the eleventh century, when coins were produced showing crosses and Christian inscriptions such as *SITUNE DEI* under the kings Olof Skötkonung (d. 1022) and Anund Jakob (d. 1035). They mark an early endeavour to introduce Christianity from above that

---

[44] Jansson 1987, 112–20; Sawyer 2003.   [45] Molland 1968.
[46] Chiefly after Jansson 1987; cf. Zachrisson 1998. The Swedish inscriptions are edited in *SR*.
[47] Blomkvist 2005, 149–52, with fig. 5.

failed. After this period no coins were produced for more than a century.[48] The interpretation of some of the evidence on the introduction of Christianity is debated. The northernmost rune-stone, erected on the island of Frösön (close by present-day Östersund) about 1020–30 by a certain Östman Gudfastsson, commemorates that 'he had Jämtland made Christian' (*that han lit kristną eątaląnt*). The stone was erected at the traditional meeting place of the regional assemblies. The place name connects it to the pagan god Freyr. The province of Jämtland probably turned to the Christian religion mainly during the eleventh century. According to one interpretation, there was no external political or royal power involved in the process; rather, the people under the leadership of chieftains or law-speakers (Östman may have been the law-speaker of the region), took a formal decision to Christianize themselves.[49] Östman, however, may have been a royal reeve, sent there from Sigtuna with a commission to initiate the new creed.[50]

In spite of richness in artefacts, the political dimension of the Christianization of the Swedish realm is little known. The scholar is by and large dependent on a single narrative, that of Adam of Bremen. His *Gesta* of the archbishops of Hamburg, written around 1075, is not only a valuable source, but also a forceful pamphlet for the rights of these bishops (presented as the rightful heirs of Ansgar, though having their see in Bremen) to evangelize in the north. Their offensive started in the 1050s with Archbishop Adalbert as an energetic organizer. By then however the Swedish kings had been baptized and appearing as Christian monarchs already for half a century.

King Erik Segersäll (the Victorious), who also held lordship in Denmark in the 990s, came into close contact with Christian practices. He is said to have witnessed an ordeal performed by Poppo, designated bishop of Schleswig, and married a Christian princess called Gunhild, possibly daughter to Prince Mieszko I of Poland. Erik, according to Adam of Bremen, was baptized in Denmark, but reverted to paganism when he returned to Uppsala. However, he allowed Christian missionaries in his kingdom according to Adam. The first Christian king was his son Olof Skötkonung. He is said to have founded the bishopric of Skara in Västergötland. Adam claims that he was compelled to settle there after having attempted to eliminate the temple at Uppsala.[51] According to the list of kings preserved

---

[48] E.g. Malmer 1989.   [49] Brink 1997a.   [50] Ahnlund 1948, 110–36.

[51] Adam of Bremen II.35; 38; 58. Poppo's ordeal in front of Erik the Victorious is evidently a copy of the ordeal of another (or the same) Poppo in front of King Harald Bluetooth in 966; Adam of Bremen II.25, schol. 20. Adam got all his information about Erik the Victorious from the Danish king Sven Estridson.

alongside the Old Västgöta code, the king was baptized by a certain Sigfrid. Adam of Bremen tells of a Swedish bishop called Sigfrid, and in another context he mentions a Sigfrid who had come from England to Norway and preached both to Swedes and Norwegians, adding that he lived until 'our own times' together with 'other priests not unknown in these parts'. Hence it seems that an Englishman baptized the first Christian king of Sweden, which may explain why Adam does not mention the event.[52]

As to who actually baptized King Olof there is a much discussed alternative, claiming that the Polish archbishop Bruno of Querfurt had sent a monk called Robert to the *Suigi*, and he succeeded in baptizing *ipsum seniorem Suigiorum*, whose wife was already a Christian. The dating of the event to 1008 fits the Swedish context and the name *Suigi* may be a mutilated version of *Suioni* not beyond possible understanding, whereas the rest of the information is quite vague. Many scholars have taken this hypothetical claim for granted. Recently, however, Bertil Nilsson has rejected it, claiming that the *Suigi* were to be found 'on the shores of the Black Sea'.[53]

The church of Bremen was a late starter in the Swedish mission-field. Its representatives met missionaries who had been there far before them. If we are to judge from the rune-stone material almost all of the Götalands and a large part of Svealand were devoted to the cross already by the mid-eleventh century, and many claimed to be Christians, although perhaps not entirely rejecting the pagan cult; in Adam's words the Swedes by a general decision (*communi sententia*) had declared the Christian God to be the strongest one. But only in Västergötland do we hear of a fully established bishopric in the eleventh century. By 1075 Adam knew of four early bishops,[54] none of whom was appointed in Bremen, as well as four sent out by Adalbert.[55]

Adalbert's mission was not only late, it was also based on ignorance. Some of his projects were founded on written claims that were in fact illusions. Thus he saw a great potential in Birka, the bishopric founded by Ansgar, and visited by Unni.[56] Not knowing that the place had by then lost its importance, he appointed a bishop for 'Birka and the islands of the sea', who spent a couple of years in Sweden, apparently without achieving any results. Then, however, in the 1060s, the bishop appointed for Sigtuna took the opportunity to visit Birka, where he had found the place 'so devastated that there are hardly any traces of the town left'. He was unable to find

[52] Adam of Bremen II.64, IV.34 with schol. 148; *SSGL*, vol. I, 298; Schmid 1949, 60–2; 1931a, 54–67; Hellström 1996, 13–41; Lundberg 2000, 115–23.
[53] Nilsson 2003, 207–13.   [54] Adam of Bremen II.58; 64, IV.22–3.
[55] Adam of Bremen III.76–7, IV.24.   [56] Adam of Bremen I.15; 26; 62; Blomkvist 2005, 581–6.

St Unni's grave.[57] The idea of sending a bishop to the *Scridephinni* or Saami people in the north was another shot in the dark. Living a nomadic life, by and large not under the control of the authorities of the kingdom (who were satisfied by getting a valuable fur-tribute), their conversion was seriously undertaken only in the seventeenth century.

Even the effort to establish a suffragan in Sigtuna, the successor of Birka, failed, since there was already another bishop there, an Englishman (possibly of Scandinavian descent) called Osmund.[58] Another Englishman, Eskil, functioned as a missionary bishop in Tuna in Södermanland, and was martyred during a pagan reaction, possibly around 1080. This is related by Ailnoth, an Englishman in Denmark, writing at the beginning of the twelfth century. Eskil was soon considered a saint, and the place where he had worked was to carry the name of Eskilstuna. As such it became a monastery of the Order of St John not later than 1185.

There is no claim that either of the English ecclesiastical provinces was launching a missionary operation: rather, the background to the English missionaries in Sweden may be found in the Danish North Sea empire in the first half of the eleventh century. Svend Aggesen, writing in the late twelfth century, says that Knud (Canute) the Great, while visiting his native country 'brought with him many priests and bishops; some he kept by him and others he sent out to preach. Scattered abroad throughout Sweden, Götaland and Norway, and sent over to Iceland as well, they sowed the seed of God's word and gained many souls for Christ.'[59] This type of ecclesiastical immigration continued in the twelfth century. The first bishop of Uppsala, Siward, had an Anglo-Scandinavian background, though he received his title when, as one of the entourage of Archbishop Adalbero of Bremen, he went to Rome in 1123. There he was appointed by Pope Calixtus II at an audience in a spontaneous gesture of reconciliation after the Concordat of Worms. The national saint of Finland, Henry, said to have been killed by a pagan after the so-called First Swedish Crusade to Finland, is also claimed to have been of English origin, and so was the first archbishop of Uppsala, the Cistercian Stephen.

It is, however, possible that the first successful mission arrived neither from Bremen nor from England, but from Lotharingia and Cologne. Henrik Janson has shown that some of the early bishops of Skara had intensive contacts with the Lotharingian reformers; one of them, Ancelinus, had in fact been the dean of Cologne. Even Osmund, who had been appointed in Poland, represented according to Janson a missionary tradition emanating

---

[57] Adam of Bremen, schol. 142.   [58] Adam of Bremen III.15; 77.   [59] Svend Aggesen 64, chap. 9.

from the church of Gaul. Gregory VII, writing for the first time to King Inge of Sweden in 1080, particularly mentioned that he had heard that the church of Gaul (*Gallicana ecclesia*) was already represented in Sweden. The reformer pope commended it for preaching the true creed.[60]

A considerable Orthodox influence persisted particularly on Gotland until around 1150. According to the *Guta saga*, the Gutar (Gotlanders) took an interest in Christianity when visiting foreign countries on trading journeys and some of them brought priests to Gotland. Botair of Akebeck who – as the saga claims – built the first church, must have been one of these merchants, but his interest in Christianity was not shared by the broader population, so we are told that he had to build another church in the *vi*, a holy place according to pagan custom, later to become Visby. It was precisely the sacred status of the pagan *vi* that allowed Botair to build a Christian church there: a remarkable example of a legalism that was to characterize the Gotlandic attitude to foreigners and their customs.[61] Another part of the saga relates the visit of St Olav,[62] the sainted Norwegian king who was to become the most revered saint in Scandinavia and on the routes towards Rus'.[63] The passage contains a reference to the pilgrimage site of Akergarn, which was a station on the sea route towards the east. The cult of St Olav here was linked to trade; large amounts of wax, chiefly a Rus' export commodity, were given as offerings.

All in all, when in the middle of the eleventh century Hamburg-Bremen launched its second missionary wave, Sweden was already a flourishing mission-field, with Christianity arriving from all of its more or less Christian neighbours. There seems to have existed two dioceses in the making, which we may identify as Gothia (Skara) and Sueonia (Sigtuna), neither, however, under full archiepiscopal control.

The oldest preserved piece of direct communication between the Roman curia and a Swedish king is a letter issued by Gregory VII in 1080. According to the heading it had been dispatched *ad regem Sueciae* and addressed to *I. glorioso Sueonum regi*.[64] Because of a pagan rebellion it probably reached King Inge I in Västergötland. Having asked for a representative of the Swedish church to go to Rome, Gregory in a second letter mentioned conversations with the Swedish Bishop R. The pope addressed this letter of 1081, however, to *Visigothorum regibus I. et A.*[65] This is not only a recognition of the probable temporary address of King Inge and possibly some

---

[60] Janson 1998, 105–75.   [61] *GS*, chap. 4.
[62] The name is normally spelt Olof in a Swedish context, but Olav in a Norwegian one.
[63] *GS*, chap. 3.   [64] *DS*, no. 24; Seegrün 1967, 93–4; cf. Janson 1998, 106–7 and for further literature.
[65] *DS*, no. 25; Seegrün 1967, 95.

co-regent – either (H)alsten or (H)åkan[66] – but furthermore a clear reference to the Gothic myth, since Gregory chose to write the name of the people (*Visigothi, Visigothae*) the way it was written in classical times with reference to the host that sacked Rome in 410. Only a few years earlier Adam of Bremen had suggested that the Götar, whom missionaries had encountered in the southern parts of the Swedish realm, were not only to be identified with the *Gothi* of Late Antiquity, but also with the biblical people of Gog and Magog.[67]

This idea was to have a great impact upon the continued process of the Catholic integration of the Swedish realm. The tradition and reputation of the Visigoths were also upheld in those days in the Iberian peninsula, where they 'became an emblematic concept of the Reconquest'.[68] By this time, then, the barbarian connotations had given way to visions of a noble stock of militant Christians. Gregory's letters of 1080–1 to the Swedish kings also belong to the writings through which he launched his most radical ideas of *regimen universale*, suggesting papal dominance over secular kings.[69] They express satisfaction over the fact that the Gallican church was invited to preach in Sweden. They teach that *sacerdotium* was to advise *regnum*, and that the latter, that is secular government, should take care of peace and justice. In the second of his two letters, the pope shows knowledge of the ongoing pagan reaction in Sweden, and he stresses that secular government should guarantee the material survival of the *sacerdotium*, furthering diocesan organization, the collection of tithes and support of the poor. The tenor of the letter to the *reges visigothorum* hence reflects ideas on the formation of proper Christian states. This resulted – as the following events make clear – in the proclamation of a Christian Göta kingdom as opposed to the still half-pagan Svea kingdom. This conflict was to haunt the realm until the latter part of the twelfth century, when the ecclesiastical province of Uppsala was established over the territory of a double monarchy of Götar and Svear.[70]

In 1103 Lund was declared an archbishopric over all Scandinavia, which must be seen as part of the ongoing struggle between reformer popes and the western emperors. It seems that the establishment of the archbishopric was a signal to promote the erection of dioceses; a source from around 1120

---

[66] Hallencreutz 1992, 167, however argues that the title might refer to *all future* kings of the realm.
[67] Blomkvist 2005, 586–9; cf. Hallencreutz 1992, 167 n. 58. Whether Gregory was familiar with Adam's text cannot be established, but he had met Archbishop Liemar of Bremen who commissioned it, e.g. at Canossa in 1077; Janson 1998, 49–104.
[68] Söhrman 1998, 939.   [69] *DS*, nos. 24, 25; Blomkvist 2005, 572–608 with further references.
[70] Blomkvist 2005, 617–23.

186 NILS BLOMKVIST, STEFAN BRINK AND THOMAS LINDKVIST

mentions six Swedish episcopal sees: Skara, Linköping, Strängnäs, (Eskils-) Tuna, Sigtuna, Västerås. As already mentioned, the reconciliation between Archbishop Adalbero of Hamburg-Bremen and Pope Calixtus II in 1123 led to the formation of yet another Swedish diocese, that of Uppsala. Its bishop, Siward, however, is known to have spent the years 1134–57 in Germany.[71] We also hear that Henry, the last bishop of Sigtuna who was a suffragan of Lund, died on the battlefield at Fotevik in Skåne in 1134, as 'expelled from Sweden' (*expulsus de Swethia*).[72] These circumstances suggest that the last struggle for the values of paganism was raging in Sweden at that time.

Apart from the narrative of Olof Skötkonung's forced relocation to Västergötland, traditions exist of movements rejecting Christianity around 1080 and 1120. The Icelandic *Hervararsaga* (from the thirteenth century) relates that King Inge I (1070s–1110) refused to perform the pagan rituals (*blót*), and like his predecessor had to go into exile in Västergötland. His pagan brother-in-law Blót-Sven (literally, 'servant at a sacrifice') is said to have ruled for three years. King Inge, however, returned with an armed force and killed Sven. The story may well be a literary construct, but a pagan rebellion around 1080 is confirmed by other sources.[73] A few decades later Ailnoth criticized the Svear and Götar alike for being barbaric, rough and merely keeping their Christian faith as long as their fortune was good, but if the gales of misfortune blew against them – 'either the earth doesn't bring harvest or heaven its rain, or enemies attack them or fire strikes' – turning against the Christians, and trying to expel them from the country.[74]

As to a last, decisive pagan revolt in the 1120s, the remarkable *vita* of St Botvid offers a description of the period of unrest together with a precise dating. The *vita* is preserved in a manuscript from the second part of the thirteenth century, a text that is thought to be a slightly revised version of a twelfth-century original.[75] Botvid, a prosperous inhabitant of Södermanland, had been baptized during a trading voyage to England, and was later slain by an ungrateful Wendic slave, whom he had baptized and intended to send back to his native country. Botvid was buried in a proprietary church, where his corpse was to rest 'for about nine years', during which the Lord performed innumerable miracles due to the merits of

---

[71] Kumlien 1962; Seegrün 1967, 137; Smedberg 1983, 63; Johnsen 1981, 29–38; Christensen 1976, 40–5; *Confirmatio Calixti pontificis ad Henricum caesarem de episcopatu Sueciae, Gotlandiae, Norvegiae, ST* I.30.

[72] *Chronicon Roskildense*, chap. 15; cf. Saxo XIII.11.11 who mentions *Henricus Sueticarum partium pontifex*.

[73] *DS*, no. 25; *Vitae sanctorum Danorum*, 83; *SRS* II, 389–404.   [74] *Vitae sanctorum Danorum*, 83.

[75] Schmid 1931a, 102–14. Cf. Lundén 1944; Odenius 1957.

Botvid. During the years when Botvid's body rested in this grave, such a great fear spread among the infidels in the realm of the Svear, and particularly in the buildings where they gathered, that they leapt about, tearing at their own bodies; they could not be cured unless they were baptized, calling on St Botvid for help. This was done, all sacrificial groves were cut down and temples destroyed. During these years churches were built at those places where the superstitious worship of demons had been carried out. In the meantime, Botvid's brother built a wooden church on their inherited land, and when it was ready, two bishops, 'Henry of Uppsala and Gerder of Strängnäs *bonae memoriae* consecrated it to the honour of God and St Botvid . . . This happened in 1129.'[76]

With all its deficiencies as a historical source, Botvid's story is the only narrative of these events that we possess: the 1120s are an epoch of which we know next to nothing from Swedish sources. Foreign sources indicate that a civil war took place, one of the issues of which was the eradication of paganism in the area around Uppsala. In these years the tradition of erecting rune-stones with ambivalent Christian/pagan connotations definitely came to an end in that area. In the early 1130s a new king, Sverker, who founded his own dynasty, gained power over the Götar as well as the Svear. He favoured ecclesiastical reform and during his reign the first Cistercian monasteries were founded in Sweden as direct daughters of Clairvaux.[77]

With the Christianization of Sweden, a change in burial practice also took place. During the Viking Age various pagan burial customs coexisted, with differences concerning both the internal construction of the actual burial and the mound or other construction above the ground. Different regions had different customs, and differences also occurred within one and the same area. Whether these local differences were linked to social strata or to family traditions has been debated. During the pagan period cremation burials as well as inhumations existed, both with grave goods. Among the latter were ship graves and chamber graves, very often with a luxurious set of grave goods. The external construction over the grave in eastern-central Sweden was very often a flat mound, and the graves often made up a large burial ground linked to a Viking Age farm or hamlet. However, we also find flat stone settings and both extremes of huge mounds, often called king's mounds, and burials with no constructions at all above the ground.[78] In the early phase of Christianization (the eleventh century and perhaps also the tenth) burials became stereotyped as inhumations with no or very

---

[76] 'Vita sancti Botvidi', 378, 381–2. [77] Blomkvist 2005, 603–8.
[78] E.g. Gräslund 1980; 1992; 2001.

few grave goods, and with no visible constructions above the ground. The pagan burial grounds continued to be used for these early Christian burials; there is an ongoing debate concerning ecclesiastical views on the matter of Christian graves in pagan cemeteries rather than in consecrated graveyards around a church. With the erection of the earliest churches, we find typical Christian burials around them.[79]

The reception of traditional Christian saints was widespread and early; many, such as Sts Lawrence, Peter, John, Nicholas and Mary quickly became popular. It is, however, difficult to see any deliberate and obvious importation of saints.[80] Imported saints, furthermore, were complemented by traditions of many local saints, most of them martyrs from the virtually undocumented period of religious struggles. This period produced many indigenous saints, such as St Nicholas of Edsleskog, St Torgils of Kumla, St Sven of Arboga and the two early female martyrs Ragnhild of Tälje and Helena (Elin) of Skövde.[81] Most of them were worshipped locally or regionally. St Erik the king also remained a local saint for a long time; his rise to greater prominence from the fourteenth century will be discussed below. Most of these indigenous cults are known from late, liturgical sources, and they have a more than coincidental connection with late medieval marketplaces, which may indicate the rediscovery of some of the cults for functional purposes.

Some of the most notable saints were English missionaries, such as Sigfrid and Eskil, who have already been mentioned. Sigfrid's cult was appropriated by the diocese of Växjö, which was a controversial addition to the Swedish episcopate initiated from Lund in the 1160s, when the independent Swedish ecclesiastical province was declared. The oldest version of the legend is from the 1160s and it is connected with the foundation and legitimization of the bishopric.[82] Later the tradition developed considerably,[83] and in the late Middle Ages Sigfrid was considered to be one of the patrons of Sweden.[84] Eskil's legend was composed in the 1280s, containing references to the time of Inge I and the pagan uprising of Blót-Sven. His see at Tuna was mentioned as a bishopric in the 1120s, later to be abolished in favour of Strängnäs nearby. The legend solves the problem of legitimization by localizing his martyrdom at the assembly in Strängnäs.[85]

---

[79] E.g. Grundberg 2005.   [80] Fröjmark and Krötzl 1997, 121–44.
[81] Lundén 1972, 52–4, 78–82, 96–7, 98; 1983, 279–89.   [82] Önnerfors 1968.
[83] Schmid 1931a; Larsson 1982; Hellström 1996, 13–41.
[84] DS, no. X.1. Berglund 2003, 64–9. The patron saints of the kingdom varied, but Sigfrid, Erik, Henry, Eskil are almost always included.
[85] Lindqvist 1915; Schmid 1931b. The legend is edited in Lundén 1946.

St Henry (or Henrik) was also a missionary bishop from England, who accompanied St Erik the king on the 'first crusade' to Finland proper, where he was martyred in the 1150s on Lake Kjulo in Satakunta. He is mentioned in the legend of St Erik from the 1280s, and his own legend was written in the 1290s. He was buried in the church of Nousiainen (Swedish Nousis), but was moved to the cathedral of Turku (Swedish Åbo) in 1296.[86] The late medieval cult of St David of Munktorp,[87] like that of Botvid, also testifies to an English impact.[88] One reason for the popularity of English missionaries may have been that they did not seem to represent an external power group that was later active in the country, so that they could be evoked by Swedish churchmen in later centuries without the risk of giving any prerogatives to competitors in Lund and Bremen. The legends were usually produced considerably after the death of the saints: the late thirteenth century was a vital and productive period.

4. ROYAL POWER

There is no tradition in medieval Sweden of an apostolic ruler converting the country, unlike, for example, those concerning St István of Hungary. King Olof (d. 1022) was the first baptized king in Sweden, but no narrative tradition exists of him as an active converter. The only example of a holy ruler in Sweden is St Erik. Although St Erik was half-heartedly and reluctantly accepted as a national patron he was never associated with converting and Christianizing the country. A stereotyped *vita* from c. 1280 claims that he led a crusade to Finland and that he was murdered at Uppsala; in any case he was buried in the patron's position in the middle of the stone cathedral that was being built at Old Uppsala, despite the fact that his opponent and assumed murderer, Magnus Henriksen, actually carried the blood of the ancient dynasty of Stenkil in his veins. The cult of St Erik was promoted by his son Knut, who won the royal title from Karl Sverkersson in 1167. Knut Eriksson was probably inspired by King Valdemar I of Denmark, who succeeded in having his father canonized in 1170. The question of papal consent in the case of St Erik is more doubtful. In a papal letter from 1171 or 1172 Alexander III mentioned that the Swedes venerated as a saint a man who had died in a state of drunkenness.[89] He did not state whose cult he referred to, but it is possible that St Erik was in his mind. In any case, the papal letter indicates that there were Swedish saints who were considered suspect.

---

[86] Maliniemi 1961.   [87] Fröjmark 1996, 398–400.
[88] 'Vita sancti Botvidi', 377–88. Schmid 1931b.   [89] *DS*, no. 41; Krötzl 1994, 76–7.

What remains a certainty is that the cult of St Erik was meant to exploit a remembrance of Uppsala as an ancient, pre-Christian royal and cultic centre.[90] In the late eleventh century and the twelfth almost all kings were associated with the Götaland provinces. Thus during the early Christian monarchy Uppsala was a rather atypical royal centre. The cult is first explicitly recorded in the calendar of Vallentuna from 1198. The mural painting of a royal saint from *c*. 1170 in the church of Eriksberg in Västergötland, although poorly preserved, possibly points to an early cult of St Erik.[91] A coin type with the inscription *REX UPSALIE* was issued around 1250, during a period of civil unrest. It has been suggested that the idea was to claim St Erik as the perpetual king of Sweden (like St Olav of Norway and St Knud *rex* of Denmark). In due course, and very clearly in the fifteenth century, St Erik was generally accepted as a patron of Sweden.[92]

Expressions of royal power through Christian symbols were rather weak in Sweden. The first Christian kings started to mint coins with Christian symbols. The earliest coinage in Sweden was minted at Sigtuna *c*. 995–1030 during the reign of Olof Skötkonung. The coins, after English models, often bear Christian symbols, most often a cross. Some coins have ambiguous inscriptions such as *SIDEI*, which has been understood as *SITUNE DEI*. This earliest coinage has been interpreted as King Olof's way of promoting Christianity. The intention behind this first monetarization was also presumably to adopt foreign models of representation of power. This minting collapsed after 1030. It only recommenced at Sigtuna and Lödöse during the second half of the twelfth century.[93] Early churches were normally built on land belonging to a *husaby*, which reveals that kings must have been important in the erection of the first churches.[94] Some churches were connected more strongly with royal power: the most notable example is Husaby in Västergötland, the place that tradition connects with the baptism of the first Christian king of Sweden. The church has a massive western tower, with galleries for ceremonial purposes. Its prototype is Westphalian and it has been interpreted as a royal church. It has a minor counterpart, Örberga, in Östergötland, which has a similar tower with a gallery. Both towers are dated to the beginning of the twelfth century: according to dendrochronology to the late 1110s.[95] The dating of the church of Husaby, apart from the tower, is more uncertain. Both churches are from a politically chaotic period, when kingship was very much

---

[90] Sundqvist 2002.   [91] Sjöberg 1989, 369–79; Hernfjäll 1993, 40–2.
[92] E.g. Stjerna 1898; Bolin 1953a; Westman 1954; Ahnlund 1954; Lindkvist 1999.
[93] Malmer 1996, 85–113, summarizes previous research.
[94] Brink 2000.   [95] Lindgren 1995, 98–9.

disputed. They have been assumed to be royal churches, built for ceremonial representations.

Urbanization was also linked to royal power. It was weak in Sweden before the middle of the thirteenth century. Birka on the island of Björkö in Lake Mälaren, an emporium or port of trade, was the goal of the first mission of Ansgar in the ninth century where he met a King Bern and his *praefectus*. Sigtuna, founded in the 970s, was a planned town, intended to be a royal and Christian centre. In some respects it was a successor of Birka, but the royal presence was much more visible. Lödöse on Göta Älv emerged as a town of trade in the eleventh century. Three churches and a mint indicate that Lödöse was of substantial importance in the mid-twelfth century. In the fourteenth it also became an important royal administrative centre. Skara in Västergötland emerged around the bishop's see as a minor town in the eleventh century. With the exception of the deliberate royal presence at Sigtuna in Uppland, the kings during the early Christian period (before the mid-thirteenth century) mainly resided in Östergötland and Västergötland. The small castle on the island of Visingsö in Lake Vättern was a frequent royal seat.

Symbols of power were to a certain extent connected to the inauguration of a new king. The election and inauguration of a king is prescribed and described in the law codes, although not in a uniform way. For example, the law code of the realm from the middle of the fourteenth century clearly separates the secular or profane election from the subsequent coronation in the cathedral. The former consisted of homage by representatives of the communities and the *eriksgata*, that is, the prescribed journey a new king had to make on horseback to the main provinces of Svealand and Götaland in order to be elected or rather to have the election confirmed. This journey, described first in Upplandslagen from 1296, went clockwise through the provinces, from Uppsala in Uppland to Södermanland, Östergötland, Västergötland, Närke, Västmanland and back to Uppland. Exchanges of hostages would be made at the borders, which must have been considered as a formality in the late thirteenth century. The journey evidently reflects a ritual that might appear ancient and archaic, and was possibly a reflection of an older tradition of the secular election of kings. According to the provincial law of Uppland and the law code of the realm, the election had to take place outdoors at *Mora sten* some kilometres to the east of Uppsala.[96] A separate ecclesiastical ceremony, the coronation, was added to the secular election in 1210, the date of the first coronation of a king

[96] Sundqvist 2002, 311–33; Lindkvist 2002.

(Erik Knutsson) in Sweden known from the sources. The division between a secular and a sacral ceremony was clear-cut. Although the law code of the realm recommended that the coronation take place in Uppsala, other places of coronation are known: Linköping, Söderköping, Stockholm and Kalmar, only the first being a bishop's see.[97] There was thus no established tradition that bound the coronation to a definite place or church. No medieval coronation *ordines* are preserved from Sweden.

Sweden remained an electoral monarchy throughout the Middle Ages. Although we have no information on individual elections before the mid-thirteenth century, Christian monarchy was based on the dynastic principle: the king was always elected from the same two families. In the first half of the fourteenth century a Swedish *King's Mirror*, an adapted translation of Giles of Rome's work, *Om styrilse konunga ok höfdinga*, advocated an hereditary monarchy.[98]

5. THE EFFECTS OF CHRISTIANIZATION

Ecclesiastical organization and institutions developed over several centuries. According to Adam of Bremen, Birka was a bishopric in the tenth century; it was considered as a missionary see and a foothold for his archbishopric.[99] The nature of the bishop's power is in fact unclear, as highlighted by Adam of Bremen's claim that the province of Hälsingland was also a bishopric, although it probably was not.[100] The information is rather vague and possibly reflects missionary intentions rather than reality. A listing of the Swedish dioceses survives from the 1120s, often called the Florence list, since it is preserved in the *Biblioteca Medicea Laurenziana*. It lists the following sees: Skara, Linköping, Tuna (Eskilstuna), Strängnäs, Aros (possibly Västra Aros, i.e. Västerås) and Sigtuna.[101]

Sigtuna became a bishop's see in the 1060s. It was, however, vacant for certain periods; according to Adam of Bremen this was due to pagan resistance. Adam juxtaposes a Christian Sigtuna to a pagan Uppsala (Gamla Uppsala). This is probably an oversimplification, but Sigtuna represented an ecclesiastical organization favoured by the archbishopric of Hamburg and Bremen.[102] What is possibly the oldest church of Sigtuna has recently

---

[97] Beskow 1964; MEL, *Konungabalken*, chap. 7. [98] Moberg 1984; *Konunga styrilse och höfdinga*.
[99] On the earliest bishoprics in Sweden: Hellström 1971, esp. 16–86; Adam of Bremen IV.20, schol. 127, 146.
[100] Adam of Bremen IV.24; Hellström 1971, 63–73.
[101] Edited in Fabre and Duchesne 1910. Concerning the Florence list, Tunberg 1912. Concerning the names, Schück 1952; Gallén 1958; Envall 1961; Nilsson 1998, 79–84.
[102] Adam of Bremen III.76, IV.23, schol. 136, IV.26, IV.29.

been found, including the burial of a bishop, close to the supposed royal residence.[103] There were at least five stone churches in Sigtuna in the twelfth century, marking the town as Christian and as a royal residence.[104] It remained a bishop's see until the beginning of the twelfth century. A bishop of Sigtuna is mentioned for the last time in 1134, and evidently the see was definitely abandoned in the 1140s when Uppsala became a bishopric. The cathedral at (Gamla) Uppsala was a Romanesque church, built as a cathedral from the twelfth century on, but never completed. The awkward architectural technique indicates that the building was not the work of foreign specialists.[105]

Skara has the longest continuity as a bishop's see. A late tradition attributes its foundation to King Olof Skötkonung, and Turgot is mentioned as its first bishop.[106] The bishopric there was established during the first half of the eleventh century. The first cathedral in the eleventh century was probably built of wood. A limestone cathedral was inaugurated in 1150, and rebuilt and extended in the thirteenth and fourteenth centuries.[107] The bishopric of Skara initially also included the province of Östergötland, which became an autonomous bishopric, with Linköping as its see, in the early twelfth century.[108]

The first bishop of Linköping to be known by name is Gisle from 1139; the name is Swedish (or Scandinavian) and he was thus of domestic origin.[109] The first stone cathedral in Linköping was probably built in the 1120s and 1130s,[110] during the ascendancy and early period of Sverker I's reign. It was later replaced by a larger stone cathedral, commenced *c.* 1230. Gamla Uppsala became a bishopric in the 1140s, succeeding Sigtuna. It became the archbishopric of Sweden in 1164 and in the 1270s the see was transferred to the then emerging town of Östra Aros further south. The name Uppsala followed the see: the earliest evidence for the renaming of Östra Aros as Uppsala is from 1286.[111] The choice for the location of the archbishopric was far from self-evident. Different explanations have been proposed: one is that Uppsala was already a Christian centre.[112] Another is that Uppsala was chosen because of its association with ancient kingship and its role as cult centre.[113]

In the provinces of Svealand the establishment of bishoprics came later, and their location was looser and more fluid than in Götaland. The bishopric of Tuna (now Eskilstuna) is only mentioned in the Florence list from

---

[103] Tesch and Edberg 2001.   [104] Bonnier 1989, 9–12; Redelius 1975.
[105] Bonnier 1991, 94–108.   [106] Adam of Bremen II.58.   [107] Sigsjö 1999, 51–69.
[108] Hellström 1971, 45–53.   [109] Schück 1959, 47–50.   [110] Cnattingius 1987, 306–8.
[111] Ferm 1986, 42–77.   [112] Janson 1998, esp. 304–20.   [113] Sundqvist 2002, 302.

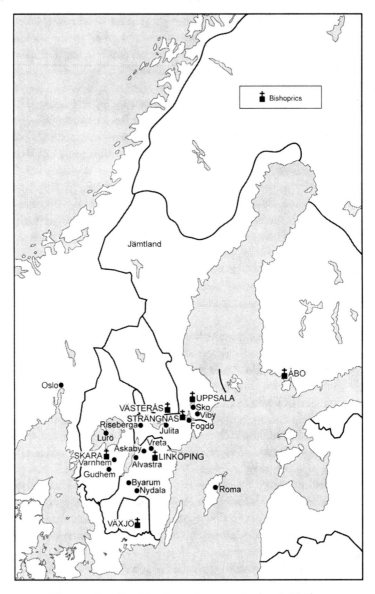

10. Dioceses of medieval Sweden and monasteries founded before 1230

the early twelfth century. The place is associated with the legend of St Eskil. Strängnäs however replaced Tuna, became the permanent bishopric in the province of Södermanland and is mentioned in the Florence list and in 1164.[114] Västerås (*Arusia* in the Florence list) is recorded otherwise for the first time in 1164, when its bishop is mentioned as one of the suffragans of the archbishop of Uppsala.[115] Växjö is not mentioned as one of the bishoprics in 1164, and it has been demonstrated that the diocese was founded in the late 1160s. This part of Småland had until then been a part of the diocese of Linköping. The first known bishop of Växjö was Baldvin in 1170. Although the legend of St Sigfrid from the thirteenth century claims that Växjö was founded as a bishopric as early as the beginning of the eleventh century, that tradition is a late construction.[116] The last of the dioceses was Turku (Åbo) in Finland. Finland gradually became a part of the kingdom of Sweden and of the ecclesiastical province of Uppsala. The emerging Finnish diocese at Nousiainen (Nousis), north of Turku, is considered to be the earliest see of a missionary bishop. From *c.* 1220 Korois on the river Aura probably became the see of the bishopric.[117] At the end of the thirteenth century the see was moved again, some kilometres south to Unikankare, close to the emerging town of Åbo. The construction of the cathedral began in the late thirteenth century, and at that time the diocese was more firmly organized.[118]

Apart from cathedrals, the first churches in Sweden were built by kings, chieftains and farmers on their farms and estates. In Götaland many were built in the late tenth century and during the eleventh, on both royal and other estates. Several examples of these have been found by archaeological excavations. The earliest are dated to the tenth century. Although the *Vita Anskarii* mentions a church in Birka, which thus would have been there in the first half of the ninth century, there is no trace of it. In a next phase kings erected fortified stone churches on the royal estates (*husabyar*), controlled market towns and brought other vital and central sites under royal control. This enterprise seems to have taken place especially in the twelfth century. Around 1,150 stone churches were built in medieval Sweden, with great regional variations. The Romanesque churches in the provinces of Götaland which date from the twelfth and early thirteenth centuries have been interpreted as private churches. In Västergötland almost all the stone churches are from the Romanesque period, that is, the twelfth century. Many early Romanesque churches are found in Östergötland, especially in the western parts, as well as on Öland and around Kalmar.[119]

---

[114] *DS*, no. 49.   [115] Hellström 1971, 59–63.   [116] Larsson 1982, 49–64.
[117] In 1229 Pope Gregory IX gave permission to move the bishop's see to a better place. *REA*, no. 1.
[118] Gardberg 1973, 55–87, 110–21.   [119] Claesson 1989; Dahlberg 1998; Lindgren 1995; Redelius 1972.

After the establishment of the bishoprics, especially in the twelfth century, and after the introduction of the tithe (*c.* 1100–50), the foundation was laid for the formation of parishes. The Church together with the central power initiated the vast enterprise of building hundreds of stone churches during the late twelfth century and the thirteenth, to be the centres of the parishes that were formed. In Götaland the existing private churches on farms, in hamlets and towns were turned into parish churches, but for large parts of northern Sweden, churches had to be constructed for parishes which were normally formed of the older settlement districts (*bygd*). In these districts the church was built either on the most central site from the point of view of communication or on the older assembly and cult site, probably common land in the centre of the district. In these cases we obviously have a continuity of cult activity.[120] In some provincial laws, such as the law code of Uppland, there is some information on an early church hierarchy: clergy in *hundares* churches and *tolft* churches. This hierarchy must have been interlinked with the administrative districts of *hundare* and *tolft*.[121] It seems that the organization of the ecclesiastical hierarchy proceeded in two stages, which may also suggest the existence of an organizational structure with 'mother churches' predating the establishment of the parishes (*socknar*). Recent research has indeed suggested that an older parish structure can be traced, a system of large parishes, equivalent to the minster parishes found in Anglo-Saxon England. Around an early church (equivalent to a minster) was a territorially undefined area where the clerical duties were fulfilled by a mobile *presbyterium*. This early structure seems to have been entirely wiped out by the later parish formation.[122] During the second half of the twelfth century and in the early thirteenth in southern Sweden, and during the thirteenth in the rest of the country, parishes were established with churches, and a priest was attached to each parish.[123] In the past, prevalent opinion held that ecclesiastical organization copied or built on an earlier administrative system, based on the *ledung*, the naval defence organization in early Sweden that is mentioned in the provincial laws.[124] Scholars today, however, think that the Church was organized independently on the parish level, and did not use an earlier administrative division.[125]

Monasticism entered Sweden late, not in immediate connection with the conversion but rather at the time of ecclesiastical and secular institutionalization. The first monastery in Sweden was probably the nunnery of Vreta in Östergötland, founded by King Inge I and Queen Helena around

---

[120] Brink 1990; 1996c; 2000.   [121] E.g. Andersson and Göransson 1982.   [122] E.g. Brink 1998.
[123] Brink 1990.   [124] Hafström 1949.   [125] Rahmqvist 1982.

1100. The widowed Helena may have entered it.[126] The great advent of monasticism came with the Cistercians in the 1140s after the restoration of Christian monarchy during Sverker I's reign. Alvastra, on the slopes of Mount Omberg in Östergötland, and Nydala, near Lake Rusken in Småland, were founded in 1143. According to the early thirteenth-century *Exordium Magnum Cisterciense* of Conrad of Eberbach, monks were sent by Bernard of Clairvaux at the request of the Swedish queen. King Sverker and his queen Ulfhild evidently played an active role in the foundation of Alvastra on royal dynastic land. Archaeological excavations uncovered an earlier crypt church near the monastery, which has been interpreted as a royal church, planned before the foundation of the monastery. Alvastra became the burial church of the kings of the Sverker dynasty.[127] Alvastra, like most Swedish Cistercian monasteries, was placed in an ancient cultivated area, and the *conversi* played a less significant role in its estate economy than they did in other countries. Nydala, founded under the auspices of Bishop Gisle of Linköping, was, however, an exception, since it was in a more or less uninhabited area and played a major role in the colonization and reclamation of land in central Småland.[128]

Several monasteries were founded from Alvastra and Nydala within a relatively short period, such as Roma from Nydala and Varnhem from Alvastra. The monastery of Roma on Gotland had several estates on the eastern side of the Baltic.[129] Varnhem in Västergötland was founded *c.* 1150, and a woman named Sigrid donated land for its foundation. Varnhem had probably had a predecessor on Lurö, a tiny island in the middle of Lake Vänern. Varnhem became the burial monastery of the kings of the Erik dynasty. Viby, north of Sigtuna, was founded in the 1160s. It possibly had connections with the foundation of a regular chapter at the archbishopric of Uppsala. King Knut Eriksson, however, transferred this monastery *c.* 1185 to Julita in Södermanland.[130]

A remarkably high proportion of the Cistercian foundations in Sweden were nunneries and many women of aristocratic and royal families entered them. There were greater difficulties in recruiting aristocratic men to a monastic life; monasticism was introduced late in Sweden and there was no previous monastic tradition.[131] Vreta was transformed into a Cistercian house by King Karl Sverkersson, whose sister, Ingegerd, probably entered it. Askaby in Östergötland was founded in the 1160s. One of the more important nunneries was Gudhem in Västergötland, founded on royal

---

[126] Ahnlund 1945, 301–45. [127] Holmström and Tollin 1994, 34–7; Tollin 2002, 216–34.
[128] Tollin 1999, 143–9. [129] Markus 1999, 22–57, 146–52.
[130] Stensland 1945. [131] Concerning the gender perspective, Andersson 2003.

land in the twelfth century and later supported by King Erik Eriksson and his queen Katarina, who was buried there. The nunnery on the isle of Fogdö in Mälaren in Södermanland was founded in the twelfth century; a more precise dating is not possible. According to a cadastre from the middle of the thirteenth century it was founded by the otherwise completely unknown *jarl* Sivard (or Sigvard) and his daughter Ingeborg.[132] The nunnery at Byarum in Småland is known from the late twelfth century, but was later transferred to Sko in Uppland. It was probably founded on estates belonging to the dynastic fraction of the *folkungar*.[133] Riseberga nunnery in Närke founded in the late twelfth century was promoted by the mighty *jarl* Birger Brosa, and his widow entered it.[134]

The Cistercians were closely connected to the royal dynasties and to other mighty families. Their political importance was great in Sweden: they provided the emerging Christian monarchy with both administrative skill and a legitimizing ideology. A house of the Order of St John was founded at Eskilstuna and confirmed by the archbishop, the king and *jarl* Birger Brosa before 1185, but the Cistercians completely dominated monasticism in Sweden until the advent of the friars during the thirteenth century.[135]

The cathedrals seem at first to have been served by monastic, rather than secular, chapters. The first chapter at Uppsala, which dates from the foundation of the archbishopric in 1164, was monastic, though whether it belonged to the Augustinian, the Benedictine or the Cistercian order has been discussed.[136] Convincing arguments have recently been put forward claiming that it was Cistercian. The Cistercians, otherwise averse to the secular church, played an important role in the early Uppsalian archbishopric. The first archbishop, Stephen, was one of the pioneer monks at the monastery of Alvastra in 1143. The monastery at Viby, north of Sigtuna, may possibly have served as the residence of the chapter. The early regular chapter lapsed and there was no chapter at Uppsala in 1224.[137] Bishop Bengt founded, or at least intended to found, a chapter at Skara in 1220.[138] The earliest evidence for the existence of a chapter there is from 1257.[139] Linköping had the earliest known secular collegiate church among the Swedish dioceses, founded in 1232 during the bishopric of Bengt, one of the *jarl* Birger's brothers.[140] The cathedral of Linköping had close connections with the

---

[132] Ossiannilsson 1945, 84.   [133] Sjödén 1942, 1–24.
[134] *DS*, no. 185; Mattsson 1998.   [135] Collijn 1929, 2.
[136] Gallén 1938, 139–43; 1976 advocated on vague grounds, that Benedictine monks of English origin held the earliest functions in Uppsala.
[137] *DS*, no. 225. Letter by Pope Honorius III concerning the election of Archbishop Olof Basatömer by the *populus*.
[138] *DS*, no. 194.   [139] *DS*, no. 440.   [140] Schück 1959, 399–414.

Sverkerian royal dynasty and political power; and in many respects the cathedral and church of Linköping were the earliest organized according to the norms and demands of Rome. At Åbo, a chapter with the right to elect the bishop is known from 1276. The general establishment of collegiate churches was a result of the mission of the papal legate, William of Sabina, and the meeting at Skänninge in 1248.[141]

The first liturgical books intended for Sweden never arrived. Ansgar lost almost forty books in an assault by pirates on his way to Sweden. The earliest liturgical works used in Sweden came from various parts of northern Europe. It has been assumed that manuscripts of English origin dominated over French and German ones.[142] The examples are few, but England, northern Germany and the Rhineland are all well represented. Imports from Flanders and northern France have also been identified. English and French influence was stronger in western Sweden (Västergötland and Värmland) and German in eastern Sweden (Småland and Östergötland). During the thirteenth century influence from the Danish province of Lund was equally important. What we can reconstruct of the earliest liturgy in Sweden shows that dioceses had separate traditions. The cult of diocesan or regional saints was often promoted. The calendar of the parish church of Vallentuna from 1198 is the oldest preserved liturgical book from Sweden. According to Toni Schmid it was composed in the region and reflects German, English and Anglo-Norman influences. Some of these influences could possibly have been mediated through the see of Lund.[143] Five Nordic saints were celebrated: Erik the king (18 May), Sunniva of Selja (8 July), Knud (Canute) the king (10 July), Botvid (28 July) and Olav (29 July). Only two of them were connected with Sweden.

At the archiepiscopal see of Uppsala there was probably an early Cistercian influence on the liturgy: the first archbishop, Stephen, was a Cistercian.[144] The liturgy of the cathedral had, however, no influence on the liturgy of the secular churches of the diocese. Initially a very fragmented and mixed liturgical tradition existed in the diocese, due to varied influences, although early liturgical books were mainly English. From the late thirteenth century onwards a substantial domestic production of liturgical works started. The secular chapters of the cathedrals were mainly initiated in the late 1240s and this promoted a liturgical coherence within the respective dioceses. Regional saints were favoured; they were mainly connected with mission and conversion. This partly served to legitimize the diocese

---

[141] Rosén 1940, 60–81.   [142] Helander 1993, 101–17.
[143] *Liber ecclesiae Vallentunensis*. English influence: Gallén 1976. Helander 2001, 90–1.
[144] Helander 2001, 64–8.

and the cathedral historically. Thus this liturgy presented the medieval image of Christianization.[145]

The period from 1164 to 1248 was one of normalization and consolidation. In 1152 the papal legate Nicholas Brekespear approved the emancipation of the Norwegian church from the Danish archbishopric.[146] He had corresponding authority in the Swedish case as well, but Saxo tells us that since the Svear and the Götar were unable to agree upon which city and which person were suitable for such a favour, and Nicholas found the conflict undignified, he thought this coarse and, in religious matters, still barbarian people unworthy of the highest ecclesiastical honour.[147] Later, in the dispute between the Emperor Frederick Barbarossa and Pope Alexander III, when Cistercians remaining loyal to Alexander had to leave Germany, the Danish king Valdemar I sided with the emperor and, as an extension of the struggle, Archbishop Eskil of Lund went into exile in 1159.[148] Himself an enthusiast of the Cistercians, Eskil launched the church province of Sweden by consecrating the former Alvastra monk Stephen as the first archbishop of Uppsala. This happened on 5 August 1164 in the cathedral of Sens in France, in the presence of Pope Alexander. At the same time, the controversy between Svear and Götar (who fought a series of civil wars in the twelfth century over the independence of the Götar) was apparently to some extent pacified, since the pope addressed the then king as 'our son Karl [Sverkersson] the illustrious king of Svear *and* Götar' (*filii nostri caroli illustris regis sweorum et gothorum*), while the bishops and *jarl* Ulf are ascribed to his kingdom (*regni illius*). Hence the Swedish kingdom was considered to be a double monarchy. This Salomonic balance is likely to have been worked out by Pope Alexander III, Archbishop Eskil of Lund and the first Swedish archbishop, Stephen, in an understanding with King Karl Sverkersson, who immediately adopted the title in royal documents.[149]

From this time on, the ecclesiastical organization gradually began to conform to canonical norms. The borders of parishes were determined and the bishops began to establish some control over the aristocratic owners of private churches. Each ecclesiastical region (*prepositura*) was led by a *prepositus* or provost, who normally resided in urban centres. The bishops possessed their own estates at the same regional level, to a large extent donated by the kings and the aristocracy. By the end of the twelfth century

---

[145] Schmid 1934.   [146] Cf. Kaufhold 2001, 115–17.
[147] Saxo XIV.11.1; cf. *DS*, nos. 38, 820; *ST* I.38–9; Palme 1959, 128–32; Seegrün 1967, 166–75.
[148] Ehlers 1996, 502–18 with further references.
[149] *DS*, nos. 49, 50; cf. *DS*, no. 51 and many subsequent charters.

not only the parish priests, but also the bishops, began to enjoy a portion of the tithes, which in the latter case opened up entirely new dimensions in their mercantile potentials.

The regulation of Christianity in a canonical sense did not occur in Sweden until 1248. One may see this as a result of the rise of the lineage of *jarl* Birger Magnusson to kingship. Belonging to one of the most influential families in the realm, Birger married a sister of King Erik Eriksson. Achieving jarlship around 1247–8, he set up his own son Valdemar as king after his brother-in-law's death. He also staged a full conquest of the Mälar valley in 1247–51, decapitating its leading aristocrats, imposing taxation, starting to erect castles, probably founding Stockholm and certainly inviting Lübeck merchants to live there. Birger also hosted the epochal synod at Skänninge in 1248, at which Cardinal William of Sabina issued statutes that implemented the essence of the reformed *ecclesia*, including the celibacy of the clergy.[150] Sweden accepted the norms of the Roman church and the introduction of canon law regulations.

The Christian monarchy in Sweden also spread the new religion eastwards. Through warfare and through the emergence of a bishopric, present-day Finland became gradually integrated within the Swedish realm from the middle of the twelfth century on. No Swedish king or prince is known to have participated in crusades to the Holy Land and the Levant but St Erik allegedly went on crusade to Finland, accompanied by St Henry, probably in the middle of the 1150s. This crusade is, however, first mentioned in the legends of the two saints from the late thirteenth century. The historicity of this crusade has therefore been called into question. There is no contemporary written evidence and the Christianization of Finland was a prolonged and complex process rather than the result of a conquest and mission by the sword.[151] According to the archaeological evidence a shift to Christian burial practice took place in southern and south-western Finland as early as the eleventh and twelfth centuries.[152]

Christianization did not immediately affect literacy: the runic script continued to be used and the Latin script was introduced only when both the monarchy and ecclesiastical institutions were more established. There was widespread literacy long before Christianity, using the runic script in its simplified form of sixteen phonemes for many daily purposes, on wood or birchbark. Ansgar brought Louis the Pious a letter written by the king's own hand in the manner of the Svear as a result of his first visit to Birka;

[150] Carlsson 1953; Lönnroth 1959, 23–47. Biography of *jarl* Birger Magnusson: Harrison 2002, 175–235.
[151] E.g. Lindkvist 2001.   [152] Edgren 1993, 249–51.

and on the second visit brought a letter of introduction to the new Swedish king from his Danish counterpart.[153] People of the lower social strata used runes for communicating in the vernacular throughout the Middle Ages, at least in peripheral regions.

The literacy assumed by the emerging Christian monarchy and church of Sweden was in Latin. The oldest preserved charter known to have been written in Sweden is datable to the period 1164–7. It was issued by the first archbishop, Stephen, who is thought to have been of English descent, in the presence of King Karl Sverkersson, *jarl* Ulf, a handful of other lay dignitaries and the three *prepositi* (regional deans), who had the quite un-Swedish names of Johannes, Walterus and Ricardus. The charter concerned a donation of property by a woman for the purpose of founding a Cistercian monastery, which had been contested by her son. The archbishop negotiated a reconciliation between the two, and added a personal donation in order to help the foundation. Altogether the document provides a convincing snapshot of the cultural climate of Christianization in a region that had been definitely converted perhaps only some four decades before.[154] During the reign of Knut Eriksson (1167–95/6) the first royal literate administration emerged. The incipient royal chancery was entirely handled by clerics,[155] who used Latin in administration and adapted the administrative practices of the Church. Vernacular literacy using the Latin rather than the runic alphabet developed in the thirteenth century and its great achievement was the law codes, one for each of the major provinces. These were written in the vernacular Swedish language in the thirteenth and fourteenth centuries. The vernacular became accepted as suitable for writing charters only in the fourteenth century; the first charters written in Swedish are from the 1330s. The first major rhymed chronicle in Swedish, *Erikskrönikan* (The Chronicle of Erik), probably written in the 1320s, tells at length the dramatic events of a civil war between the three sons of King Magnus Birgersson Ladulås in the period 1302–19. Unlike its Scandinavian neighbours, Sweden produced neither saga literature by commissioning Icelanders, nor Latin *Gestae* or *Historiae* by its clergy. The exceptions come from two rebellious or fairly independent regions: for Gotland a short *Guta saga* exists in a manuscript from the first half of the fourteenth century, and for Västergötland there is a series of lists of kings, bishops and law-speakers akin to a chronicle, found in a late thirteenth-century manuscript. The *Guta saga* includes an account of the Christianization of the island, as described above.

---

[153] *RVA*, chap. 12, 24.   [154] *DS*, no. 51.   [155] Larsson 2001, 26–35.

The pre-Christian legal system was transformed through the law codes.[156] Legislation was a consequence of Christianization and the establishment of the Christian monarchy. The first, or at least the first preserved, law code from Sweden is the first version of the *Västgöta* law, probably from the 1220s. It has been assumed that the law was written down on the initiative of the law-speaker Eskil Magnusson of Västergötland, because Eskil is mentioned as the great legislator of Västergötland in the list (or rudimentary chronicle) of the law-speakers of Västergötland probably written shortly before the middle of the thirteenth century.[157] The bulk of the Swedish provincial laws are, however, from the late thirteenth and early fourteenth centuries. The influence of canon law on them is nowadays considered to be significant, although the thesis by Elsa Sjöholm that the laws in toto were the result of foreign influences is hardly accepted.[158] The law code of Uppland (*Upplandslagen*) was promulgated in the name of the minor king in 1296. It was the result of deliberate political legislation, notably by representatives of the aristocracy and the cathedral of Uppsala. The law code of Uppland served as the model for later provincial law codes of Södermanland, Västmanland and Hälsingland, and probably to some extent the law of Dalarna (Dalecarlia). All the Swedish law codes are thus rather late, especially in comparison with Norway. They are all from the period when the Church was well established. Its rights are often prescribed in detail, with regulations, for example, concerning the tithe, the building of churches, and the rights and duties of the church in relation to the parish and local society. Exemptions from royal duties on land for the maintenance of the priest and the church were prescribed in *Upplandslagen* and other provincial law codes.[159] Some references are however made to the age of conversion. The law code of Uppland states that sacrifices to idols were forbidden.[160] There is a similar reference in the law code of Gotland against pre-Christian cult practice.[161] Relations between ecclesiastics and kings were set out in charters of privileges. Royal privileges were first mentioned in a charter from 1185.[162] The rights to royal fines and duties were granted to the Church in general by kings in 1200 and 1219; to institutions like Riseberga monastery in 1224 and to the cathedral of Linköping in the middle of the thirteenth century.[163] In 1281 King Magnus Birgersson issued a charter granting extensive privileges to the Church. The bishops were given the right to the fines from all land belonging to the secular clergy.[164]

---

[156] All edited in *SSGL*.   [157] Holmbäck and Wessén 1933–46, vol. V, xviii–xxiii.
[158] Sjöholm 1988; 1990, 65–87; Lindkvist 1997, 211–28.   [159] *UL*, Kyrkobalken, chap. 2.
[160] *UL*, Kyrkobalken, chap. 1.   [161] *GL*, chap. 4.   [162] *DS*, no. 85.
[163] *DS*, nos. 115, 184, 690, 144, 863.   [164] Andræ 1960, 111–71.

The relations between the church and the monarchy in Sweden were thus largely settled during the thirteenth century.

6. CONCLUSION

There is no explicit tradition of an apostolic ruler converting Sweden, nor is any tradition connected with an individual event. The first known Christian king in Sweden was Olof Skötkonung (c. 995–1022). The tradition of his baptism at Husaby by the missionary bishop Sigfrid is late. His father, Erik, was a Viking king who participated in plundering and pillage in the Baltic Sea area and elsewhere. He was baptized while in Denmark, but no tradition of him as a king promoting Christianity in Sweden exists. On the contrary, he returned to paganism when back in Svealand. A pre-Christian kingship is mainly connected with the Svealand provinces. Gamla Uppsala is known as a royal centre especially in the Norse literary tradition, but also, and foremost, as a religious, cultic centre. Very little is known about the structure and functions of pre-Christian kingship. There is no evidence of a similar kingship in the Götaland provinces; the Christian monarchy of the eleventh and twelfth centuries, however, is almost exclusively associated with them and it was there that the first bishoprics and earliest ecclesiastical organization emerged.

Olof is closely associated with Christianization. Sigtuna, founded as a royal residence and town by his father, was the site of the first mint in Sweden, and the early coinage is witness to a deliberate policy of Christianization. It is evident that the provinces of Västergötland and Östergötland were connected with a Christian monarchy during the eleventh century. A permanent diocese at Skara evolved, and later one at Linköping. Olof is credited with the foundation of Skara as a bishop's see. Christianization was earlier in the Götaland provinces, which is indicated not least by the early church buildings. No evidence exists as to how Götaland was Christianized, but Christian graves existed there from at least the mid-tenth century. The Christian kingdom was often contested, but Götaland seems to have been the basis of Christian kingship. King Inge and his queen Helena promoted the first monastery. During the reign of Inge papal connections became established.

At the beginning of the twelfth century the Christian monarchy fell into a crisis. Pagan uprisings, mostly located in the Svealand provinces, probably indicate an opposition against the monarchy, at least a monarchy with more extensive objectives of political control. The coming of the Sverker dynasty meant a change. Even if kingship continued to be

contested by rival dynasties and aristocratic factions, the kingdom gradually became more settled and recognized, and ecclesiastical organization
more established and formal. The interdependence of king and Church also
became more evident. During the reign of Sverker I the Cistercians became
established in Sweden and this order was closely connected to secular and
royal power. Even the rival Erik dynasty supported and was supported by
the Cistercians. The order's legitimizing function was apparent in the two
Cistercian monasteries that served as sepulchral churches to the respective
dynasties. Other monasteries were connected with other mighty aristocratic
groups, for example Sko in Uppland with the *folkungar*. An incipient royal
chancery in the late twelfth century was possibly staffed by Cistercians in
the service of King Knut Eriksson.

The collaboration between kings and the bishopric of Linköping in
particular was profound in the twelfth and early thirteenth centuries. It has
been assumed that the Sverker dynasty followed the ideals of the Gregorian
reform and the papacy, while the rival dynastic faction, the descendants
of St Erik, maintained a more 'conservative' and 'national' ideal. Because
of internal political conflicts the promotion of St Erik as patron of the
kingdom was far less successful than that of notably St Olav of Norway.
The initial lack of success may also have been due to papal doubt about
Erik's sanctity. The martyrdom and subsequent cult of St Erik was closely
connected with (old) Uppsala and could thus be considered as an association
between an ancient pre-Christian and the new Christian kingships. Both
political structures and culture took on a fixed form in the middle of the
thirteenth century during the reign of Birger Magnusson the *jarl* and his
sons, especially King Magnus Birgersson Ladulås. Extensive legislation and
the introduction of regulations in accordance with canon law were the
products of this period.

REFERENCES

Adam of Bremen, *Gesta Hammaburgensis ecclesiae pontificum*, ed. B. Schmeidler,
    MGH SRG, Hanover and Leipzig, 1917.
Ahnlund, N. 1945, 'Vreta klosters äldsta donatorer', *Historisk Tidskrift* 65, 301–51.
Ahnlund, N. 1948, *Jämtlands och Härjedalens historia*, I, Stockholm.
Ahnlund, N. 1954, 'Den nationella och folkliga Erikskulten', in *Erik, den helige.
    Historia, kult, reliker*, ed. B. Thordeman, Stockholm, 109–54.
Andersson, C. 2003, 'Varför satte Svantepolk Knutsson sina döttrar i kloster? Om
    egendom, kloster och aristokrati i 1200- och 1300-talets Sverige', in *Hans och
    hennes. Genus och egendom i Sverige från vikingatid till nutid*, ed. M. Ågren,
    Uppsala, 61–79.

Andersson, T. 1992, 'Kultplatsbeteckningar i nordiska ortnamn', in *Sakrale navne. Rapport fra NORNASs sekstende symposium i Gilleleje 30.11 – 2.12 1990*, ed. G. Fellows Jensen and B. Holmberg, Uppsala (NORNA-rapporter 48), 78–105.

Andersson, T. and S. Göransson, eds. 1982, *Äldre territoriell indelning i Sverige*, Stockholm (Bebyggelsehistorisk tidskrift, 4).

Andræ, C. G. 1960, *Kyrka och frälse i Sverige under äldre medeltid*, Uppsala.

Andrén, A. 2002, 'Platsernas betydelse. Norrön ritual och kultplatskontinuitet', in *Plats och praxis. Studier av nordisk förkristen ritual*, ed. K. Jennbert, A. Andrén and C. Raudvere, Lund, 299–342.

Åquist, C. 1996, 'Hall och harg – det rituella rummet', in *Arkeologi från stenålder till medeltid*, ed. L. Engdahl and A. Kaliff, Linköping.

Arrhenius, B. 1970, 'Tür der Toten. Sach- und Wortzeugnisse zu einer frühmittelalterlichen Gräbersitte in Schweden', *Frühmittelalterliche Studien* 4, 384–94.

Artelius, T. 2000, *Bortglömda föreställningar. Begravningsritual och begravningsplats i halländsk yngre järnålder*, Göteborg.

Baudou, E. 1989, 'Hög – gård – helgedom i Mellannorrland under den äldre järnåldern', *Arkeologi i Norr* 2, 9–43.

Berglund, L. 2003, *Guds stat och maktens villkor. Politiska ideal i Vadstena kloster ca. 1370–1470*, Uppsala.

Beskow, P. 1964, 'Kröning', *Kulturhistoriskt lexikon för nordisk medeltid*, vol. IX, 497–502.

Birkeli, E. 1938, *Fedrekult i Norge. Ett forsøk på en systematisk-deskriptiv fremstilling*, Oslo.

Blomkvist, N. 2005, *The Discovery of the Baltic: The Reception of a Catholic World-System in the European North (AD 1075–1225)*, Leiden (The Northern World 15).

Blomkvist, T. 2002, *Från ritualiserad tradition till institutionaliserad religion. Strategier för maktlegitimering på Gotland under järnålder och medeltid*, Uppsala.

Bolin, S. 1945, 'Gotlands vikingatidsskatter och världshandeln', in *Boken om Gotland*, I, ed. M. Stenberger, Visby, 125–37.

Bolin, S. 1953a, 'Erik den helige', *Svenskt biografiskt lexikon*, vol. XIV, 248–57.

Bolin, S. 1953b, 'Mohammed, Charlemagne and Ruric', *Scandinavian Economic History Review* 1, 5–39.

Bonnier, A. C. 1989, 'Sigtuna och kyrkorna', in *Avstamp för en ny Sigtunaforskning*, ed. S. Tesch, Sigtuna, 9–15.

Bonnier, A. C. 1991, 'Gamla Uppsala – från hednatempel till sockenkyrka', in *Kyrka och socken i medeltidens Sverige*, ed. O. Ferm, Stockholm, 81–111.

Brink, S. 1990, *Sockenbildning och sockennamn. Studier i äldre territoriell indelning i Norden*, Uppsala.

Brink, S. 1996a, 'Forsaringen – Nordens äldsta lagbud', in *Femtende tværfaglige Vikingesymposium, Aarhus Universitet 1996*, ed. E. Roedahl and P. Meulengracht Sørensen, Århus, 27–55.

Brink, S, 1996b, 'Political and Social Structures in Early Scandinavia: A Settlement-Historical Pre-Study of the Central Place', *Tor: Journal of Archaeology* 28, 235–81.

Brink, S. 1996c, 'Tidig kyrklig organisation i Norden – aktörerna i sockenbildningen', in *Kristnandet i Sverige. Gamla källor och nya perspektiv*, ed. B. Nilsson, Uppsala, 269–90.

Brink, S. 1997a, 'Kristnande och kyrklig organisation i Jämtland', in *Jämtlands kristnande*, ed. S. Brink, Uppsala, 155–88.

Brink, S. 1997b, 'Political and Social Structures in Early Scandinavia II: Aspects of Space and Territoriality – the Settlement District', *Tor: Journal of Archaeology* 29, 389–437.

Brink, S. 1998, 'The Formation of the Scandinavian Parish, with Some Remarks Regarding the English Impact on the Process', in *The Community, the Family and the Saint*, ed. J. Hill and M. Swan, Turnhout, 19–44.

Brink, S. 1999, 'Social Order in the Early Scandinavian Landscape', in *Settlement and Landscape*, ed. Ch. Fabech and J. Ringtved, Århus, 423–39.

Brink, S. 2000, 'Husaby', *Reallexikon der germanischen Altertumskunde*, vol. XV, 274–8.

Brink, S. 2002, 'Law and Legal Customs in Viking Age Scandinavia', in *The Scandinavians from Vendel Period to the Tenth Century: An Ethnographic Perspective*, ed. J. Jesch, Woodbridge, 87–117.

Brink, S. 2004, 'Some New Perspectives on the Christianization of Scandinavia and the Organization of the Early Church', in *Scandinavia and Europe*, ed. K. Holman and E. Adams, Turnhout (Texts and Cultures in Northern Europe 4), 163–75.

Carlsson, S. 1953, 'Folkungarna – en släktkonfederation', *Personhistorisk Tidskrift* 51, 73–105.

Christensen, A. E. 1976, *Danmark, Norden og Østersoen. Udvalgte afhandlinger*, Copenhagen.

Chronicon Roskildense. Scriptores Minores Historiae Danicae Medii Aevi, I., ed. M. Cl. Gertz, Copenhagen, 1917–18.

Claesson, E. 1989, *Cuius ecclesiam fecit. Romanska kyrkor i Västergötland*, Lund.

Cnattingius, B. 1987, *Linköpings domkyrka, 1, Kyrkobyggnaden*, Stockholm (Sveriges kyrkor, 200).

Collijn, I. 1929, 'Ett nekrologium från johanniterklostret i Eskilstuna', *Nordisk Tidskrift för Bok- och Biblioteksväsen*, 1–21.

Dahlberg, M. 1998, *Skaratraktens kyrkor under äldre medeltid*, Skara.

DD: Diplomatarium Danicum, 1–4:7, ed. F. Blatt *et al.*, Copenhagen, 1938–2000.

DS: Diplomatarium Suecanum, 1–9, ed. J. G. Liljegren *et al.*, Stockholm, 1829–2000.

Edda. Die Lieder des Codex Regius nebst verwandten Denkmälern, ed. G. Neckel and H. Kuhn, Heidelberg, 1962.

Edgren, T. 1993, 'Den förhistoriska tiden', in *Finlands historia*, I, ed. T. Edgren and L. Törnblom, Helsingfors, 9–270.

Ehlers, J. 1996, *Ausgewählte Aufsätze*, Berlin (Berliner historischer Studien, 21).

Envall, P. 1961, 'Florenslängden', *Historisk Tidskrift* 81, 35–55.

Fabre, P. and L. Duchesne, eds. 1910, *Liber censuum de l'église romaine*, 2.6, Paris.

Ferm, O. 1986, 'Från Östra Aros till Uppsala. Uppsala under tidig medeltid', in *Från Östra Aros till Uppsala. En samling uppsatser kring det medeltida Uppsala*, ed. T. Nevéus, Uppsala, 42–77.

Fröjmark, A. 1996, 'Från Erik pilgrim till Erik konung. Om helgonkulten och Sveriges kristnande', in *Kristnandet i Sverige. Gamla källor och nya perspektiv*, ed. B. Nilsson, Uppsala, 387–418.

Fröjmark, A. and C. Krötzl 1997, 'Den tidiga helgonkulten', in *Kyrka – samhälle – stat. Från kristnande till etablerad kyrka*, ed. G. Dahlbäck, Helsinki, 121–44.

Gallén, J. 1938, 'Reguljära domkapitel i Sverige och Finland', *Historisk Tidskrift för Finland* 23, 137–50.

Gallén, J. 1958, 'Kring det s. k. Florensdokumentet', *Historisk Tidskrift för Finland* 43, 1–26.

Gallén, J. 1976, 'De engelska munkarna i Uppsala – ett katedralkloster på 1100-talet', *Historisk Tidskrift för Finland* 61, 1–21.

Gardberg, C. J. 1973, *Åbo stads historia från mitten av 1100-talet till år 1366*, Åbo.

GL: *Gutalagen*, SSGL, vol. VII, 1–93, 104–234.

Gräslund, A.-S. 1980, *Birka IV: The Burial Customs: A Study of Graves on Björkö*, Stockholm.

Gräslund, A.-S. 1992, 'Kultkontinuitet – myt eller verklighet? Om arkeologins möjligheter att belysa problemet', in *Kontinuitet i kult och tro från vikingatid till medeltid*, ed. B. Nilsson, Uppsala, 129–50.

Gräslund, A.-S. 2001, 'Living with the Dead: Reflections on Food Offerings on Graves', in *Kontinuitäten und Brüche in der Religionsgeschichte*, ed. M. Satusberg, Berlin and New York (Ergänzungsbände zum RGA 31), 222–35.

Green, D. H. 1998, *Language and History in the Early Germanic World*, Cambridge.

Grundberg, L. 2005, 'Torsåker, Björned och kyrkorna. Möten mellan hednisk och kristen kult', in *Stora Ådalen. Kulturmiljön och dess glömda förflutna*, ed. G. Boström, L. Grundberg and T. Puktörne, Härnösand, 254–349.

GS: *Guta saga*, SSGL, vol. VII, 93–104.

Hafström, G. 1949, 'Sockenindelningens ursprung', in *Historiska studier tillägnade Nils Ahnlund*, ed. S. Grauers and Å. Stille, Stockholm, 51–67.

Hallencreutz, C. F. 1986, 'Rimbert, Sverige och religionsmötet', in *Boken om Ansgar. Rimbert: Ansgars liv*, ed. C. F. Hallencreutz and T. Hållander, Stockholm, 163–80.

Hallencreutz, C. F. 1992, 'När Sverige blev europeiskt', *Kyrkohistorisk Årsskrift* 92, 163–73.

Hallencreutz, C. F. 1993, *När Sverige blev europeiskt. Till frågan om Sveriges kristnande*, Stockholm.

Harrison, D. 2002, *Jarlens sekel. En berättelse om 1200-talets Sverige*, Stockholm.

Helander, S. 1993, 'Böcker och liturgi i medeltidens katolska kyrka', in *Helgerånet. Från mässböcker till munkepärmar*, ed. K. Abukhanfusa et al., Stockholm, 101–17.

Helander, S. 2001, *Den medeltida Uppsalaliturgin. Studier i helgonlängd, tidegärd och mässa*, Lund.

Hellström, J. A. 1971, *Biskop and landskapssamhälle i tidig svensk medeltid*, Stockholm.

Hellström, J. A. 1996, *Vägar till Sveriges kristnande*, Stockholm.

Hernfjäll, V. 1993, *Medeltida kyrkmålningar i gamla Skara stift*, Skara.

Hervararsaga saga ok Heiðreks, ed. G. Turville-Petre and C. Tolkien, London, 1956.

'Historia sancti Davidis abbatis et confessoris', in *SRS* II, 404–12.

'Historia sancti Sigfridi episcopi et confessoris', in *SRS* II, 344–76.

Holmbäck, Å. and E. Wessén, eds. *Svenska landskapslagar tolkade och förklarade för nutidens svenskar*, I–V, 1933–46.

Holmström, M. and C. Tollin 1994, *Det medeltida Alvastra*, Stockholm.

Hyenstrand, Å. 1974, *Centralbygd-Randbygd. Strukturella, ekonomiska och administrativa huvudlinjer i mellansvensk yngre järnålder*, Stockholm (Studies in North-European Archaeology 5).

Hyenstrand, Å. 1984, *Fasta fornlämningar och arkeologiska regioner*, Stockholm (RAÄ Rapport 1984:7).

Janson, H. 1998, *Templum Nobilissimum. Adam av Bremen, Uppsalatemplet och konfliktlinjerna i Europa kring år 1075*, Göteborg.

Jansson, S. B. F. 1987, *Runes in Sweden*, Stockholm.

Johannesson, K. 1982, *Gotisk renässans. Johannes och Olaus Magnus som politiker och historiker*, Uppsala.

Johnsen, A. O. 1981, 'Siwardus episcopus ubsallensis', *Kyrkohistorisk Årsskrift* 81, 29–38.

Kaliff, A. 2001, 'Ritual and Everyday Life: The Archaeologist's Interpretation', in *Kontinuitäten und Brüche in der Religionsgeschichte*, ed. M. Satusberg, Berlin and New York (Ergänzungsbände zum RGA 31), 442–63.

Kaufhold, M. 2001, *Europas Norden im Mittelalter. Die Integration Skandinaviens in das christliche Europa (9.-13. Jahrhundert)*, Darmstadt.

King Alfred's Orosius, ed. H. Sweet, Oxford, 1883.

Konunga styrilse och höfdinga, ed. L. Moberg, Uppsala, 1964.

Krötzl, C. 1994, *Pilger, Mirakel und Alltag. Formen des Verhaltens im skandinavischen Mittelalter*, Helsinki.

Kumlien, K. 1962, 'Sveriges kristnande i slutskedet – spörsmål om vittnesbörd och verklighet', *Historisk Tidskrift* 82, 279–88.

Larsson, I. 2001, *Svenska medeltidsbrev. Om framväxten av ett offentligt skriftbruk inom administration, förvaltning och rättsutövning*, Stockholm.

Larsson, L.-O. 1982, 'Den helige Sigfrid och Växjöstiftets äldsta historia. Metod- och materialfrågor kring problem i tidigmedeltida kyrkohistoria', *Kyrkohistorisk Årsskrift* 82, 68–94.

'Legenda sancti Eskilli episcopi et martyris', in *SRS* II, 389–404.

Liber ecclesiae Vallentunensis, ed. T. Schmid, Uppsala, 1945.

Lindgren, M. 1995, 'Stenarkitekturen', in *Den romanska konsten*, ed. E. Lindqvist Sandgren, Lund (Signums svenska konsthistoria, 3), 119–34.

Lindkvist, T. 1997, 'Law and the Making of the State in Medieval Sweden: Kingship and Communities', in *Legislation and Justice*, ed. A. Padoa-Schioppa, Oxford, 211–28.

Lindkvist, T. 1999, 'Erik den helige och det svenska kungadömets framväxt', in *Kongemøte på Stiklestad*, ed. O. Skevik, Verdal, 119–34.

Lindkvist, T. 2001, 'Crusades and Crusading Ideology in the Political History of Sweden, 1140–1500', in *Crusade and Conversion on the Baltic Frontier 1150–1500*, ed. A. V. Murray, Aldershot, 119–30.

Lindkvist, T. 2002, 'Mora stenar', *Reallexikon der germanischen Altertumskunde*, vol. XX, 236–8.

Lindqvist, S. 1915, *Den helige Eskils biskopsdöme*, Stockholm.

Lönnroth, E. 1959, *Från svensk medeltid*, Stockholm.

Lundberg, S. 2000, 'Olof Skötkonung och Husaby', in *En bok om husabyar*, ed. M. Olausson, Stockholm (Riksantikvarieämbetet: Avdelningen för arkeologiska undersökningar. Skrifter, 33), 115–23.

Lundén, T. 1944, 'S:t Eskil och S:t Botvid. Södermanlands skyddshelgon', *Bidrag till Södermanlands Äldre Kulturhistoria* 37, 3–24.

Lundén, T. ed. 1946, *Brynolf Algotssons samlade diktverk*, in *Credo. Katolsk Tidskrift* 27, 73–124.

Lundén, T. 1972, *Svenska helgon*, Stockholm.

Lundén, T. 1983, *Sveriges missionärer, helgon och kyrkogrundare. En bok om Sveriges kristnande*, Storuman.

Maliniemi, A. 1961, 'Henrik, S:t', *Kulturhistoriskt lexikon för nordisk medeltid*, vol. VI, 452–60.

Malmer, B. 1989, *The Sigtuna Coinage c. 995–1005*, Stockholm.

Malmer, B. 1996, 'Sigtunamyntningen som källa till Sveriges kristnande', in *Kristnandet i Sverige. Gamla källor och nya perspektiv*, ed. B. Nilsson, Uppsala, 85–113.

Markus, K. 1999, *Från Gotland till Estland. Kyrkokonst och politik under 1200-talet*, Tallinn.

Mattsson, A. C. 1998, *Riseberga kloster – förutsättningar och framväxt*, Örebro.

MEL: Magnus Erikssons landslag, SSGL, vol. X.

Meulengracht Sørensen, P. 1986, 'Thor's Fishing Expedition: Words and Objects: Towards a Dialogue between Archaeology and History of Religion', in *Words and Objects*, ed. G. Steinsland, Oslo, 257–78.

Moberg, L. 1984, *Konungastyrelsen. En filologisk undersökning*, Uppsala.

Molland, E. 1968, 'Primsigning', *Kulturhistoriskt lexikon för nordisk medeltid*, vol. XIII, 439–44.

Müller-Wille, M. 1970, 'Bestattung im Boot. Studien zu einer nordeuropäischen Grabsitte', *Offa* 25–6, 7–149.

Nielsen, A.-L. 1997, 'Pagan Cultic and Votive Acts at Borg: An Expression of the Central Significance of the Farmstead in the Late Iron Age', in *Visions of the Past*, ed. H. Andersson, P. Carelli and L. Ersgård, Lund (Lund Studies in Medieval Archaeology 19), 373–92.

Nilsson, B. 1991, 'Frids- och asylföreskrifter rörande den medeltida sockenkyrkan', in *Kyrka och socken i medeltidens Sverige*, ed. O. Ferm, Stockholm (Studier till Det medeltida Sverige 5), 473–504.

Nilsson, B. 1998, *Sveriges kyrkohistoria, 1, Missionstid och tidig medeltid*, Stockholm.

Nilsson, B. 2003, 'Kring några bortglömda tankar om Suigi och Olof Skötkonungs dop', *Fornvännen* 98, 207–13.

Odenius, O. 1957, 'Botvid', *Kulturhistoriskt lexikon för nordisk medeltid*, vol. II, 192–4.

Önnerfors, A. 1968, *Die Hauptfassungen des Sigfridsofficiums*, Lund.

Ossiannilsson, F. 1945, 'Fogdö (Vårfruberga) klosters jordebok. En obeaktad källa från tidig medeltd. Med kommentar utgiven', *Vetenskapssocieteten i Lund, Årsbok*, 81–104.

Palme, S. U. 1959, *Kristendomens genombrott i Sverige*, Stockholm.

Rahmqvist, S. 1982, 'Härad och socken – världslig och kyrklig indelning i Uppland', *Bebyggelsehistorisk Tidskrift* 4, 89–96.

REA: Registrum ecclesie Aboensis eller Åbo domkyrkas svartbok, ed. R. Hausen, Helsingfors, 1890.

Redelius, G. 1972, *Kyrkobygge och kungamakt i Östergötland*, Stockholm.

Redelius, G. 1975, *Sigtunastudier. Historia och byggnadskonst under äldre medeltid*, Stockholm.

Regesta Pontificum Romanorum, Germania Pontifica VI (Provincia Hammaburgo-Bremensis), ed. W. Seegrün and T. Schieffer, Göttingen, 1981.

Reincke, H. 1960, 'Zur Geschichte des Hamburger Domarchivs und der "Hamburger Fälschungen"', *Veröffentlichungen an dem Staatsarchiv der Freien und Hansestadt Hamburg* 5, 57–78.

Rosén, J. 1940, 'De sekulära domkapitlens tillkomst', *Svensk Teologisk Kvartaltidskrift* 16, 60–81.

Ruthström, B. 1990, 'Forsa-ringen – vikingatida vi-rätt?', *Arkiv för Nordisk Filologi* 195, 41–56.

RVA: Rimbert, Vita Anskarii, in *Quellen des 9. und 11. Jahrhunderts zur Geschichte der hamburgischen Kirche und des Reiches (AQ XI)*, ed. and tr. W. Trillmich, Berlin, 1961, 1–133.

Sankt Erik konung, ed. J. Gallén and T. Lundén, Stockholm, 1960.

Saxonis Gesta Danorum, ed. J. Olrik, H. Raeder and F. Blatt, Copenhagen, 1931–57.

Sawyer, B. 2003, *The Viking-Age Runestones: Custom and Commemoration in Early Medieval Scandinavia*, Oxford.

Schmid, T. 1931a, *Den helige Sigfrid*, Lund.

Schmid, T. 1931b, 'Eskil, Botvid och David. Tre svenska helgon', *Scandia* 4, 102–14.

Schmid, T. 1934, *Sveriges kristnande från verklighet till dikt*, Stockholm.

Schmid, T. 1949, 'Sankt Sigfrid och missionen', in *Skara stift i ord och bild*, ed. Y. Rudberg, Stockholm, 51–64.

Schück, A. 1952, 'Den äldsta urkunden om Svearikets omfattning', *Fornvännen* 47, 178–87.

Schück, H. 1959, *Ecclesia Lincopensis. Studier om Linköpingskyrkan under medeltiden och Gustav Vasa*, Stockholm.

See, K. von 1964, *Altnordische Rechtswörter. Philologische Studien zur Rechtsauffassung und Rechtsgesinnung der Germanen*, Tübingen (Hermaea. Germanistische Forschungen 16).

Seegrün, W. 1967, *Das Papsttum und Skandinavien bis zur Vollendung der nordischen Kirchenorganisation (1164)*, Neumünster.

Seegrün, W. 1976, *Das Erzbistum Hamburg in seinen älteren Papsturkunden*, Cologne.

Sigsjö, R. 1999, 'Skara domkyrkor', in *Skarastudier*, Skara, 51–69.

Sjöberg, R. 1989, 'Erik den helige – Sveriges rex iustus', in *LLt. Festskrift till Lars O. Lagerqvist*, ed. U. Ehrensvärd, Stockholm, 369–79.

Sjödén, C. C. 1942, 'Studier i Sko klosters godspolitik', *Rig* 25, 1–25.

Sjöholm, E. 1988, *Sveriges medeltidslagar. Europeisk rättstradition i politisk omvandling*, Lund.

Sjöholm, E. 1990, 'Sweden's Medieval Laws: European Legal Tradition – Political Change', *Scandinavian Journal of History* 15, 65–87.

Smedberg, G. 1983, 'Uppsala stifts äldsta historia', *Kyrkohistorisk Årsskrift* 83, 58–77.

Snorri Sturluson, *Edda*, ed. F. Jónsson, Copenhagen, 1900.

Snorri Sturluson, *Heimskringla. Nóregs Konunga Sôgur*, ed. F. Jónsson, Copenhagen, 1911.

Söhrman, I. 1998, 'The Gothic Tradition: Its Presence in the Baroque Period', in *Spain and Sweden in the Baroque Era (1600–1660)*, ed. E. Martínez Ruiz and M. de Pazzis Pi Corrales, Madrid, 937–48.

SR: Sveriges runinskrifter, ed. S. B. F. Jansson *et al.*, 15 vols., Stockholm, 1900–81.

SRS: Scriptores rerum Suecicarum medii aevi, 2 vols., ed. E. M. Fant, Uppsala, 1818–28.

SSGL: Samling af Sveriges gamla lagar, 13 vols., ed. H. S. Collin (I–II) and C. J. Schlyter, Stockholm and Lund, 1827–69.

ST: Sveriges traktater med främmande magter, ed. O. S. Rydberg, Stockholm, 1877.

Staecker, J. 1999, *Rex regum et dominus dominorum. Die wikingerzeitlichen Kreuz- und Kruzifxanhänger als Ausdruck der Mission in Altdänemark und Schweden*, Stockholm.

Stensland, P. G. 1945, *Julita klosters godspolitik*, Stockholm (Nordiska museets handlingar, 22).

Steuer, H. 1987, 'Gewichtgeldwirtschaften im frühgeschichtlichen Europa. Feinwaagen und Gewichte als Quellen zur Währungsgeschichte', in *Untersuchungen zu Handel und Verkehr der vor- und frühgeschichtlichen Zeit in Mittel- und Nordeuropa*, ed. K. J. Düwel, H. Siems and D. Timpe, Göttingen, 405–527.

Stjerna, K. 1898, *Erik den helige. En sagohistorisk studie*, Lund.

Sundqvist, O. 2002, *Freyr's Offspring: Rulers and Religion in Ancient Svea Society*, Uppsala.

Svend Aggesen, *The Works of Sven Aggesen, Twelfth-Century Danish Historian*, tr., intr. and notes E. Christiansen, London, 1992.

Svennung, J. 1972, *Jordanes und die gotische Stammsage*, Stockholm.

Tesch, S. and R. Edberg, eds. 2001, *Biskopen i museets trädgård. En arkeologisk gåta*, Sigtuna.

Tollin, C. 1999, *Rågångar, gränshallar och ägoområden. Rekonstruktion av fastighetsstruktur och bebyggelseutveckling i mellersta Småland under äldre medeltid*, Stockholm.

Tollin, C. 2002, 'Alvastra kloster och Sverkerätten. En rumslig studie av det tidigmedeltida ägoinnehavet', in *Ny väg till medeltidsbreven. Från ett medeltidssymposium i Svenska Riksarkivet 26–28 november 1999*, ed. C. Gejrot, Stockholm, 216–44.

Tunberg, S. 1912, 'En romersk källa om Norden vid 1100-talets början', *Språkvetenskapliga sällskapets förhandlingar 1910–1912*, Uppsala, 14–34.

UL: Upplandslagen, SSGL, vol. III.

Valk, H. 1999, *Rural Cemeteries of Southern Estonia 1225–1800 AD*, Visby and Tartu.

Västgötalagen, SSGL, vol. I.

Vikstrand, P. 2001, *Gudarnas platser. Förkristna sakrala ortnamn i Mälarlandskapen*, Uppsala.

'Vita et miracula sancti Henrici episcopi et martyris', in *SRS* II, 331–43.

'Vita sancti Botvidi martyris', in *SRS* II, 377–88.

'Vita sancti Erici regis et martyris', in *SRS* II, 270–330.

Vitae sanctorum Danorum, ed. M. C. Gertz, Copenhagen, 1908–12.

Westman, K. B. 1954, 'Erik den helige och hans tid', in *Erik, den helige. Historia, kult, reliker*, ed. B. Thordeman, Stockholm, 1–108.

Zachrisson, T. 1998, *Gård, gräns, gravfält. Sammanhang kring ädelmetalldepåer och runstenar från vikingatid och tidig medeltid i Uppland och Gästrikland*, Stockholm.

CHAPTER 6

Bohemia and Moravia

Petr Sommer, Dušan Třeštík and Josef Žemlička
with additional material on art by Zoë Opačić

I. BEFORE CHRISTIANITY: RELIGION AND POWER

In the ninth century two independent and separate units existed, the Great Moravian Christian polity and the pagan *gens* of the Czechs. Moravia emerged as a political unit sometime after 830. It is traditionally referred to by the name Emperor Constantine Porphyrogenitus gave it: Great Moravia. Great Moravia collapsed under Magyar assault in 906. From the tenth century a Christian state developed consisting of two lands, Bohemia and Moravia. While nothing at all is known from the written record about the society of Great Moravia prior to the turn of the ninth century, there are numerous reports dealing with Bohemia in ninth-century Frankish annals and chronicles. The inhabitants of Bohemia appear in these sources under the name *Bohemani* and variations thereon, taken from the name of the country, either the Latin *Bohemia* or the Germanic *Baiahaim*. Their own name for themselves, Czechs (of unknown etymology), is first documented in the tenth century.

From the point of view of the Empire these *Bohemani* formed a single political unit on the territory of Bohemia; numerous princes (*duces Bohemanorum*), however, would often treat on their behalf. This apparently contradictory situation – with a unified 'tribe' on the one hand and a number of chiefs on the other – is resolved in the earlier literature by a preference for one of two alternatives. The founder of modern Czech history, František Palacký (1798–1876), presumed a single 'tribe' under a single government, but from the end of the century onwards his opponents sought a multiplicity (perhaps eleven to fifteen) of smaller tribes in the Bohemian Basin, assuming that the princes were tribal chiefs. They saw the appearance of a unified state in the tenth century as a gradual coalescence of the land under the rule of the princes of the central Bohemian tribe of the Czechs, with the Přemyslid family at their head. The last act of this unification process was seen in the liquidation of the powerful Slavník family (supposedly descended from one of the tribal princes of east Bohemia) in 995.

Modern historiography sees this problem with far more differentiation,[1] relying on the concept of the *gens*, as developed by R. Wenskus, H. Wolfram and others.[2] The early medieval, pre-state *gentes* were loose political units, in which forms of power in particular were highly variable. Some had at their head a single ruler, a 'king'; in others power was wielded by the tribal assembly itself (the Germanic *thing* or the Slavonic *věče* or *sobor*). The situation in Bohemia (and perhaps among the Western Slavs as a whole) indicates a certain division of powers between the *gens Bohemanorum* and its *duces*, the princes, whose domestic title was *knędz*.[3]

The princes always (for the last time in 911) treated only in the name of the *Bohemani*, of whom they were the representatives, and not in their own names. From at least the turn of the ninth century they had their strongholds, inherited within families, and their small military retinues. The princes were elected (and could be deposed), albeit each probably from the ranks of just one family.[4] In the mid-ninth century there were perhaps fifteen such princely families in Bohemia. During the ninth century their territorial power apparently became firmer, so that by the tenth century Bohemia was rather like an association of principalities. Nothing is known of this process in detail, beyond the career of the central Bohemian Přemyslid family, which gained dominant status among the other princes from the end of the ninth century, and which after 935 ruled the whole country.

The basis of the existence of the *gens* was its own life order, its *pravda* ('truth, the true order of things') serving to regulate the relationship between people, the *mír*. This order, in Latin sources called *lex*, encompassed not just the law, but the cult of the gods and a broad range of associated beliefs. Very little is known of Czech paganism, thanks to rapid and effective Christianization. From the echoes in later sources it may be adjudged that the Czechs had the same pantheon as other Slavs, at the head of which stood the thunder god Perun and his chthonic antagonist, Veles.[5] The multifunctional female goddess was Mokoš, of whose specific cult, however, no traces remain.

---

[1] Třeštík 1997; Sláma 1995.   [2] Overview: Pohl 1994.

[3] Other titles included *vladyka* (from 'vládnouti', i.e. 'ruling, reigning'), *gospod* ('lord of guests' or 'lord guest') and *lech* (of unknown etymology), attested, unlike the other Old Slavic terms, only in Bohemia (*Nejstarší . . . kronika Dalimila*, chap. 2, at 20).

[4] Cf. the tale of Bořivoj's overthrow and the election of Strojmír (Christian, chap. 2, at 16–24).

[5] Evidence: Niederle 1924.

Archaeological remains of cult include, in particular, sites of pagan sacrifice; these are known mainly from Moravia; the alleged sites in Bohemia are in most cases highly dubious.[6] Two indisputable sites of this nature have been found at Mikulčice, which was apparently the primary stronghold of the Moravians. The first was a rectangular post enclosure with ritual horse burial and a cemetery in the vicinity where various anomalies were found, such as the burial of human limbs. The enclosure was extant from the end of the eighth until at least the mid-ninth century, that is, in the period of the official Christianization of Moravia.[7] The second cult feature at Mikulčice is close to the buildings of the first and second churches, defined by a ring ditch in which fire originally burned.[8] In the ninth century another cultic enclosure (built close to a wooden structure open to the west and with a wooden casket within) stood at the Great Moravian settlement at Chotěbuz-Podbora.[9] Another type of cult site is represented by the two sanctuaries discovered at Pohansko near Břeclav; these are round, and comprise eight pits (evidently for idols) grouped around a central idol. The second of these sanctuaries was established in the tenth century on the site of a demolished church.[10] The sacred pool in its own sacred precinct by the family cemetery of the princes at Stará Kouřim is another example of a cult site in Bohemia. The multiple fire sites in this area bear witness to cult activities.[11] Prague is a special case, where the most recent research has (with a certain degree of likelihood) identified the existence of a sacred precinct enclosed by a ditch on the 'acropolis' of the later castle.[12] The mount here is called *Žiži* or *Siži*, which may be related to *žár* ('heat'), and thus to burnt offerings; of greater substance, however, is that it was here, *in medio civitatis*, that the stone throne stood, on which, until the end of the twelfth century, the Czech princes were enthroned. In the ninth century the sacred precinct thus seems to have delimited the place of enthronement. Cult activity within the castle area is also shown by the finds of the skeletons of whole young boar close to the earliest church in the stronghold, dedicated to the Virgin.[13] Pagan cult features undeniably existed in association with cemeteries and funerary rites, too. Archaeological evidence comes for example from excavations at the Stará Kouřim cemetery, where traces of fires and food consumption indicate cultic practice, and at Lahovice u Prahy where a wooden sanctuary was found over a tomb.[14] In general, it can be said that these finds are difficult to interpret. The written sources, too, are silent on the subject of pagan

---

[6] Overview: Profantová and Profant 2000 (under the relevant headings).

[7] Klanica 1985; 1986, 150–2 .   [8] Klanica 1986, 149.

[9] Kouřil 1994, 71–167; Měřínský 2002, 531–64.   [10] Macháček 2000.   [11] Šolle 1966, 136–46.

[12] Frolík 2000, 101–20.   [13] Borkovský 1953, 168.   [14] Šolle 1966; Krumphanzlová 1997, 394–401.

cults in Bohemia and Moravia, not least because even the earliest come from as late as the second half of the tenth and the eleventh centuries. In these, references to a pagan *fana* are vague, with no further details.[15] References also appear to reverence for natural features and sacred groves, which still existed at the end of the eleventh century.[16] From Bohemia there are also traces of a mountain cult at Mount Říp, regarded as the centre from which the land was occupied by the first settlers, the retinue of the eponymous Čech. In the tenth century a church was built on the summit to Christianize the place.[17]

Traditional Slavic cremation burial is attested in the territories of Bohemia and Moravia in the sixth to eighth centuries. The first inhumation graves are known from the eighth century in Moravia, but coexisted until the ninth century with cremation burials. The latter are essentially graves in the form of pits, into which the ashes of the deceased were placed either with no container (or in a container made of some organic material), or in a ceramic vessel. Contemporary notions of life after death are implied by the apertures in some urns, the purpose of which was presumably to enable the movement of the spirit of the deceased, and by the remnants of grave goods damaged by fire (such as combs, beads, knives, steel). While in Bohemia there are finds of individual graves, Moravian cemeteries contained dozens, and exceptionally hundreds, of graves. From the eighth century onwards tumuli appear in such cemeteries in Bohemia, and there were also cemeteries which consisted solely of tumulus burials (barrow fields).

The main remnants of Czech paganism are the myths written down and refashioned in the tenth and subsequent centuries, and especially by a dean of Prague, Cosmas, around 1120.[18] All of these, however, relate to the origins of the dynasty and state, and not to the beginning of the world or to the deeds of gods, like much mythology. It is known that in tenth-century Bohemia a myth was told of the beginnings of mankind, of the Slavs and of their kingdom, which was the Slavic variant of the Indo-European creation myth, with the Slavonic 'first king' *Muž* (man) or *Mužik* (son of man) taking the place of the Indo-European Manus.[19] Nothing of this, however, is reflected in the later tradition.

The myth of the origin of the Czechs was important, with the tale of seven brothers led by Čech from Dalmatian Croatia to Bohemia and the

---

[15] Christian, chap. 6 (at 58).   [16] Cosmas II.1 (at 161).   [17] Třeštík 2003b, 76.
[18] Třeštík 2003b with bibliography; Banaszkiewicz, 1982; 1993.
[19] *Geographus Bavarus*, 289; al-Masúdi, 405.

brotherly (and thus equal and non-distributive) occupation of the land with the sacred Mount Říp at its centre.[20] This was certainly originally the ethnogenetic myth of the Czech tribe, which was formed in the Bohemian Basin sometime at the beginning of the seventh century in resistance to the Avars. A separate myth concerns 'how women came under the rule of men', that is, the origins of well-arranged human society on the basis of marriage. It tells of the war of the girls and men, in which the former were defeated.[21] This reflected the annual meeting of girls and boys in which marriages were closed by simulated abduction.

The most important myth concerned the calling of the first prince, the divine Přemysl the ploughman, from his plough by the seeress and undoubtedly goddess Libuše, culminating in their sacred marriage.[22] The originally Indo-European myth of a queen who selected her husband was appropriated in the tenth century by the dynasty of the Prague princes claiming descent from Přemysl, also attaching great importance to Libuše's foundation of Prague as the main stronghold (*metropolis*) of Bohemia.

One inheritance from the pagan period was the ritual of the princes' inauguration on the stone throne, which stood until the twelfth century in the middle of Prague Castle.[23] Such Indo-European heritage is well known from Carinthia, where the practice was followed until the late Middle Ages, but also from Ireland, Scotland, Denmark and Sweden, while traces of it can also be found in Poland and among the Rus'. Its meaning probably lay in the sealing of a holy wedding between the prince and the land, embodied in the stone throne. It is thus a ritual accompanying the myth of the marriage of Libuše as a personification of government (and the land) with the blessed ploughman.[24]

Cosmas also recorded a list of the names of the pagan Czech princes.[25] It is not clear, however, whether these are the ancestors of the first Christian prince, Bořivoj, a Přemyslid, as the chronicler suggests, or a catalogue (rather than a genealogy) of other Czech princes. At the beginning stand the divine (or semi-divine) twins Přemysl and Nezamysl ('thinking' and 'unthinking', literally corresponding to the Greek pair Prometheus and Epimetheus). This suggests the notion of a sacred kingdom among the pagan Czechs.

---

[20] Cosmas I.1–3 (at 4–8); *Nejstarší . . . kronika Dalimila*, chaps. 1–2 (at 19–21); *Chronicon imperatorum*, 223.
[21] Cosmas I.9 (at 19–20).   [22] Christian, chap. 2 (at 16–18); Cosmas I.4–9 (at 9–22).
[23] Letopis Vincentia, a. 1142 (at 412); Schmidt 1978.   [24] Třeštík 2003b, 156–67.
[25] Cosmas I.9 (at 21–2).

2. CONTACTS

In the sixth to eighth centuries the Slavic princes of the Carpathian Basin lived under the cultural influence of the Avar Empire, which set the tone of life for the aristocracy. The Slavs were in contact with Christianity, in particular from Byzantium, but it did not apparently awaken their interest. The situation fundamentally, and very quickly, changed after the destruction of the Avar Empire by the forces of Charlemagne. Although Charlemagne gained the great treasure of the Avar *khagan*, the true fruits of his victory were plucked by the Slavic princes who carried off great plunder from the Avars. The result was a significant growth in the wealth and power of the Slavic princes in the areas around the Carpathian Basin.[26] These rich and powerful princes began to live in permanent contact with the even more powerful Frankish aristocracy, in particular the strong border counts. The high standard of living of Charlemagne's paladins and counts and their deputies, with which they would have met for negotiations, whose daughters they took – or at least tried to take – as wives, and among whom many spent their youths as hostages or later as exiles, made a truly deep impression on the Slavic aristocracy: it was a real culture shock. This phenomenon resulted in the building of new strongholds by the princely families, and in princely graves and family cemeteries, with jewellery in the completely new 'Blatnice/Mikulčice' style.[27] In addition there was a general transition to inhumation burial, which also affected the free population.

In their relations with the Franks, the princes' paganism was disadvantageous but did not pose an absolute obstacle. The Franks maintained a modus vivendi with the Slavs across their eastern frontier, although it included continual antagonism. On the western frontier the same relationship existed with the Bretons, who were Christians – which concerned the Franks as little as the paganism of the Slavs.[28] The only exception was the Avars, berated – for a short period – in a great propagandistic campaign by Charlemagne as pagans, the enemies of Christianity. This is in important contrast to the tenth century, when the paganism of the Polabian Slavs in particular became the ideological pretext for the expansion of the Ottonian Empire, and is thus heavily reflected in the sources of the period. The pagan Slavs were not under pressure in the ninth century, and therefore did not necessarily see in the Christian God a German god who was in

[26] Klanica 1987, 74–82; Daim 1996, 479–97.   [27] Wachowski 1992; Profantová 1997.
[28] Třeštík 2001b, 157–60.

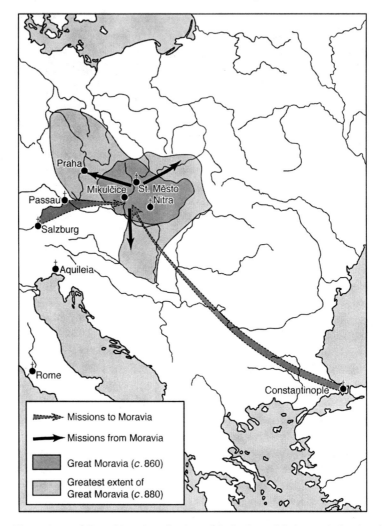

11. The territory of Great Moravia at the time of Duke Svatopluk (870–94) showing the
routes of the missions to and from Moravia

principle unfriendly. They understood Christianity as the way of life of the
gens christianorum. This consisted not only of religion but of all aspects of
life, the overall organization of society, its *ordo vivendi*. For the rich and
power-hungry Slavic aristocracy this was an acute attraction. Their *gens*
however could not voluntarily or lightly give up its order of life (as well as
its religion), as to do so would be to threaten its very existence; the result

would be that 'the earth will not grant crops, the trees will not bear fruit, new animals will not be born and the old will perish'.[29] If the princes had a significant role in the public cult of the *gens*, they were bound by it, like Scandinavian kings, to sacrifice for the *gens*. At the most they might accept Christianity as a personal religion. Several churches in Moravia (particularly that at Modrá[30]) seem to date to the period preceding the official Christianization, thus confirming the existence of such individual conversions of princes. This is illustrated by the case of the Moravian prince Pribina with his seat in the newly conquered Nitra, who took as his wife a member of the powerful Bavarian Wilhelm family. He vowed to receive baptism, and even had a church built at Nitra, but he remained a catechumen and was only baptized in exile in Bavaria. In order to guarantee themselves a position matching that with which they had met in the Empire, the princes had to impose the new order by force. This meant the destruction of the old political institutions and the establishment of a state: Christianization was therefore inseparably bound to the appearance of the state.

The Moravian princes led by Mojmír (?–846) received baptism from the Eastern Frankish Empire in 831, at the hands of Reginhar, bishop of Passau.[31] Nothing more is known of the circumstances of the baptism, but it seems certain that a decision to this effect must have been made by the assembly 'of the princes and the Moravians'.[32] The decision to accept baptism was perhaps accompanied by stipulations to allow continued pagan practices, as was the case in Iceland. In the main stronghold of the Moravians, at Mikulčice, the pagan sanctuary continued in uninterrupted use until the middle of the ninth century, if not longer; in the 860s Constantine reproached the priests of Passau active in Moravia for 'not preventing the holding of sacrifices according to earlier custom',[33] and as late as the last third of the ninth century Methodius was credited with returning many pagan Moravians to the faith.[34] Emperors normally insisted that baptism also meant subjection and attachment to the *imperium*.[35] The Empire at this time, however, was engaged in internal struggle regarding the succession to Louis the Pious. Nonetheless, Mojmír's actions were seen

[29] As expressed by the Prussians according to Bruno chap. 25 (at 32), and Canaparius, chap. 28 (at 42–3).
[30] Klanica 1986, 138–9.
[31] *Notae de episcopis Pataviensibus*, a. 831, at 623; *Historia episcoporum Pataviensium*, a. 838 (at 620); Bernardi Cremifarensis, a. 813–38 (at 655). Třeštík 2001b, 117–21.
[32] *Žitije Konstantina*, chap. 14 (at 98): Rostislav, before sending the Emperor Michael his request for 'teachers', held an assembly with 'his princes and the Moravians'.
[33] *Žitije Konstantina*, chap. 15 (at 103). [34] *Žitije Mefodija*, chap. 10 (at 154).
[35] Stated by Theotmar, archbishop of Salzburg in 900: *Conversio*, 140.

as a rebellion, and Louis the German, as soon as he was able to devote himself to consolidating cross-border relations with the Slavs, attacked the new monarch in 846, deposing Mojmír and setting Rostislav (846–70) in his place.

At the beginning of the 850s Moravian Christianity was still regarded as 'coarse',[36] not only because baptism did not put an end to paganism, but also because its institutional framework was unstable. While an archpresbytery of the bishop of Passau was active in Moravia, this could hardly have had real control over all. Priests from the area of northern Italy around Venice and from 'Greece', that is the Dalmatian towns subject to Byzantium, were also active in Moravia. All of these priests 'taught differently', according to their customs, set differing penances, observed the feast days and fasts differently, and adjudged marital affairs variously.[37] After Bishop Hartwig of Passau (840–66) suffered a stroke in 860 he was unable to fulfil his duties and the bishopric quickly fell apart.

The Moravian ruler therefore in around 862 turned first to Rome and, having met with no success, then asked for 'teachers' in Constantinople, in order to educate local Moravians as priests. Such measures were meant to unify the 'teachings' in order to enable the consecration of churches and priests and eventually the establishment of an archbishopric. In 863 or 864[38] Michael III sent him the brothers Constantine and Methodius, who undertook the task assigned to them by using the Slavonic language for teaching and for divine mass.[39] Through this, Constantine acknowledged the cultural legitimacy of the barbarian languages, creating a script for the Slavs, contrary to Byzantine definitions of barbarians by a lack of culture.[40] He also had practical reasons: using the local language to educate future priests for the Moravian church in the shortest possible time.

Archaeological evidence of Christianization from the ninth century comes in particular from jewellery bearing Christian symbols (e.g. belt-ends in the shape of ecclesiastical codices from Mikulčice and Pohansko), items with Christian imagery (e.g. a belt-end depicting a bishop), items directly related to Christian cult (e.g. the silver cross from the cemetery around the basilica at Mikulčice) and sacred buildings. Some of these artefacts may have appeared in Moravia and Slovakia as early as the first third of the ninth

---

[36] *Concilium Maguntinum*, a. 852, chap. 11 (at 184).
[37] Rostislav's letter to Nicholas III: *Žitije Mefodija*, chap. 5 (at 144).
[38] Cibulka 1965; Tkadlčík 1969.
[39] Vavřínek 2000; 1986; Dittrich 1962; Dvornik 1970; Marsina 1985. Bibliographies: Možajeva 1980; Dujčev, Kirmasova and Paunova 1983.
[40] Vavřínek 1978; 1986; Thomson 1992.

century.[41] The arrival of Christianity in the lands of the Great Moravian Empire was associated with direct missionary influences from the Salzburg archbishopric and its suffragan bishoprics in Passau and Regensburg, as shown by references in the written record and from such archaeological finds as a necklace with lead missionary crosses of Passau provenance in the cemetery at Dolní Věstonice. Another wave of missionary activity came from the patriarchate of Aquileia, and this contact with northern Italy may have had some influence on the popularity of churches with a centralized ground plan in Great Moravia in this period.

The churches erected in the Great Moravian Empire and contemporaneously in Bohemia during the ninth century are generally simple rotundas or rectangular structures. They were built at sites that played an important role in administration. Excavations have unearthed a series at Mikulčice, Staré Město, Pohansko and Modrá u Velehradu. It is likely that their origin lies with the missions of the Salzburg archbishopric and its suffragan dioceses. The church complex at Sady u Uherského Hradiště, and the rotunda and church no. 10 at Mikulčice, demonstrate striking similarities to contemporary Dalmatian/Istrian architecture. It is probable that wooden buildings were also erected, for example at Mikulčice. At the central stronghold there, there is also a basilica.[42]

In 871, Svatopluk, the ruler of Moravia, immediately after coming to power, expelled East Frankish priests from his lands, and turned to Rome. In 873 Methodius, who had previously been archbishop of Pannonia and had been imprisoned by Frankish bishops, was freed and installed by the pope in Moravia, which thus became the seat of the archbishopric of Pannonia – a territory which Svatopluk did not hold, and a title which the Franks, who did hold most of the territory, did not recognize. It is not clear whether Moravia itself was actually a formal part of Methodius's Pannonian archbishopric. In 880 Svatopluk received from Pope John VIII a Moravian archbishopric with Methodius at its head. As part of this process Svatopluk 'gave' his land to St Peter, placing it under the aegis of the pope, legitimizing a Moravian Christian polity and thus rejecting, under the protection of the other supreme authority in Christendom, the hegemonial aspirations of the Empire.[43] The new archbishop faced opposition, however, in the person of Wiching, bishop of Nitra, who used Methodius's stubborn insistence on a Slavonic liturgy in particular to frame endless complaints to the pope.[44] After Methodius's death in 885, Svatopluk expelled all his adherents

---

[41] Wieczorek and Hinz 2000, 228–35.   [42] Galuška and Poláček forthcoming.

[43] John VIII, 18–21. Havlík 1965; 1969.   [44] Marsina 1972; 1970; 1985; Ratkoš 1974.

while the pope forbade the use of the Slavonic liturgy. Methodius's students fled to Bulgaria in particular, where they founded a new centre of Slavic education.

The fate of the Moravian church after 885 is obscure. It had only one other bishop, Wiching, who departed before 891, leaving Moravia without a bishop. It seems that perhaps soon after 885 an attempt was made to renew the activity of the archpresbyterate of Passau in Moravia; in this period lead crosses are found in relative abundance only in the graves of Slavs in the Passau diocese, including Moravia.[45] Mojmír II attempted to restore the Moravian archbishopric in 898. Permission was obtained from Pope John IX, and a papal delegation comprising an archbishop and two bishops named a new archbishop and ordained the requisite four suffragans.[46] The Moravian archbishopric was thus formally renewed, but it is not clear whether the new archbishop (whose name is unknown) ever took up his office. In 906 Great Moravia collapsed under the assault of the Magyars, and ecclesiastical life came to an end.[47] It seems that there was a pagan backlash, but its scale and nature cannot be ascertained. The only direct evidence comes from a pagan place of sacrifice at Pohansko, which was created on the ruins of the church on the site.

The Moravian example had affected the Bohemian princes, who in 845 decided on a similar, common course. At the beginning of 845, 'fourteen of the Bohemian princes', together with their retinues, appeared unexpectedly before Louis the German at Regensburg and requested baptism. The astonished king could do nothing but rapidly accede.[48] This act on the part of the Bohemian princes is unique in the history of the Christianization of the transalpine barbarians. It could not have been the result of some mission about which we now know nothing: missionaries might have convinced one or a small number of the Bohemian princes, but not all of them at once. Virtually all of the princes in Bohemia participated (fourteen princes from the fifteen Bohemian *civitates*).[49] The request for baptism arose from the initiative of the princes themselves; it must have been agreed as a common undertaking not only by the princes, but by the whole *gens Bohemanorum*, in which the princes – as always – represented the *gens*, and accepted baptism in their name. The reason was political. Louis the German, in order to strengthen his power, began to consolidate relations along his eastern frontier in 845. The Czechs evidently judged that they could head off this

[45] Třeštík 1998a.   [46] Theotmar, in *Conversio*, 140.
[47] Třeštík 1991.   [48] *Annales Fuldenses*, a. 845 (at 35). Třeštík 1995.
[49] The *Geographus Bavarus*, a geographical tract written at the court of Louis the German in these years, mentions fifteen *civitates* in Bohemia (at 287).

threat if, like the Moravians, they received baptism. Louis the German, however, attacked Christian Moravia the very next year, removing Mojmír and setting Rostislav in his place. The disappointed Czechs reacted immediately and in force, attacking Louis's army as it returned from Moravia through Bohemia. This was the end to the first Czech experiment with Christianity.

In Bohemia among the first evidence for local contact with Christianity from this period is a princely grave from Kolín,[50] which among other things includes a Carolingian liturgical chalice which may have been a baptismal gift, but was probably used as a drinking vessel. The jewellery discovered bearing the symbol of the cross in the cemetery at Prague Castle comes from the very end of the period; it consists of *gombík* buttons made in Bohemian domestic workshops influenced by Great Moravian production.[51] During the course of the ninth century cremation burial was gradually abandoned, to be replaced by inhumation. This process is sometimes seen as evidence of the spread of Christian burial, but it is necessary to allow for the possibility of acculturation: inhumation was slowly beginning to dominate the whole of central Europe. The latter explanation is linked in particular to the fact that ninth-century society was still only lightly touched by Christianity, thus a deliberate and massive switch to the Christian burial rite seems unlikely.[52] No development reflecting attempts at Christianization can be observed in the orientation of the dead or in grave fittings, beyond the general trend in the change of grave goods from collections of items intended for use in the afterlife to collections of protective objects and status symbols.

3. CHRISTIANIZATION

The first Czech attempt at receiving Christianity in 845 ended as quickly as it began, leaving no traces in either the domestic or the Regensburg traditions. The central Bohemian Přemyslids accepted baptism with a lasting impact from Great Moravia, perhaps in 884. When Svatopluk of Great Moravia governed Bohemia between 883–94, one of the Czech princelings, Bořivoj of central Bohemia, was baptized. With his sons Spytihněv and Vratislav he then refashioned his principality after the model of Great Moravia as a kind of statelet with a territorial administration, tax-collection, and Christianity as the state religion. The tale of the baptism of Bořivoj I (r. 872–89) is told in the Legend of Václav (Wenceslas) and Ludmila by Christian. Bořivoj came to his lord Svatopluk in Moravia. During a banquet, however, he was

---

[50] Lutovský 1994.   [51] Sklenář and Sláma 1976, 659–65, 720.   [52] Lutovský 2001.

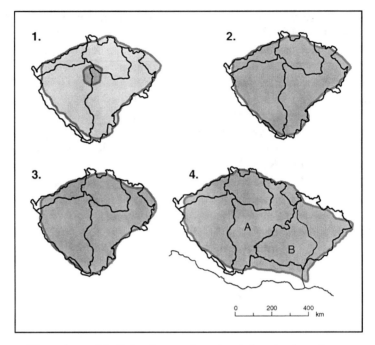

12. The territory of the Bohemian state from the ninth to the eleventh century
  1. The central-Bohemian Přemyslid principality at the end of the ninth and beginning of the tenth century
  2. Boleslav I's state *c.* 940
  3. The Bohemian state after the crisis of the year 1000
  4. The Bohemian state after the annexation of Moravia
    (A) Bohemia
    (B) Moravia

seated as a pagan on the floor next to the table. Methodius suggested that he receive baptism to avoid such insult. Bořivoj agreed, and was baptized along with his retinue. On returning home, Bořivoj built a church at Levý Hradec near Prague, dedicated to St Clement. The people of his principality, however, could not accept the 'new and unheard-of law of Christian sanctity', and rose up, forcing him to flee.[53] In his place they set up one Strojmír, who was called back from exile in Bavaria. Bořivoj went to Svatopluk's court in Moravia, and promised to build a new church in honour of the Virgin if he could return. In the Přemyslid principality meanwhile, there was dissatisfaction with Strojmír. It was agreed with his supporters that

[53] Christian, chap. 2 (at 20).

the issue would be decided by an assembly. Strojmír's supporters planned to kill Bořivoj's men at the cry 'Let us change!' Coming to the meeting at the parliament field (*campus*) before Prague Castle, however, Bořivoj's supporters were faster and slaughtered their enemies. Bořivoj returned, and fulfilled his promise by building the church of the Virgin at Prague Castle.[54]

Although including a number of fabulous motifs, the story seems as a whole to reflect actual events. Bořivoj's had been a political baptism. After his conquest of Bohemia (perhaps in 883), Svatopluk chose Bořivoj from among the many Bohemian princes, and by means of becoming his god-father at baptism established a bond of spiritual relationship with him, accepting him into the royal family,[55] and then installed him as his representative in Bohemia. Svatopluk would certainly have sent aid against the pagan uprising, enabling Bořivoj's return to Bohemia (perhaps in 885). The only inconsistency in the tale is that Prague Castle did not yet exist at that time: its site was occupied by the parliament field (*campus*) mentioned by Christian, and within this (in the middle of the modern castle) was a sacral precinct delimited by ditches, with the stone throne on which the princes were enthroned in the middle. Bořivoj established the church of the Virgin immediately in front of this precinct, thus 'Christianizing' the most holy place in his principality. His son and heir Spytihněv brought this process to conclusion, building his stronghold over the place of enthronement.

The incorporation of Bohemia and Bořivoj's central Bohemian domains into Methodius's archdiocese in 884–95 did not entail the ecclesiastical organization of the Přemyslid lands. Between 885 and 895 the Moravian church could hardly have had any influence in Bohemia. After his baptism Bořivoj received the priest Kaich,[56] who was to care for the spiritual needs of the newly baptized, and in all likelihood a priest or priests would have been sent from Moravia to St Clement's church at Levý Hradec and the church of the Virgin in Prague. An ecclesiastical organization was formed under Spytihněv I. He established a rudimentary territorial government in central Bohemia, resting on strongholds,[57] probably along the Moravian model, although the Bohemian system of strongholds, distributed more or less evenly across the territory, which is known from the eleventh and twelfth centuries, was undoubtedly a domestic product. In the Přemyslid

---

[54] Christian, chap. 2 (at 16–24). Třeštík 1986; 1997, 312–47. According to the legend *Crescente fide* (Bavarian recension), 183, the first Christian prince in Bohemia was Spytihněv, Bořivoj's son, who subjugated the Přemyslid domains to the bishopric in Regensburg, but this is a polemic of the Bavarian clergy against the domestic tradition of Bořivoj's baptism by Methodius, which the Bavarian church did not recognize.
[55] Angenendt 1973; 1984. [56] Christian, chap. 2 (at 20). [57] Sláma 1987; 1988b, III, 71–81.

principality these strongholds became local centres of administration, and of all aspects of the public, legal, military, economic and cultural life of the region. It was here that courts and markets were held, and on the messengers' summons (*viti*) the army took to the field from these strongholds; taxes and contributions were paid here, and it was from here that the building of bridges and the repair of ramparts and roads was arranged.[58]

The same organizational scheme applied to the so-called ecclesiastical administration. In fact it was not the Church that created such a territorial system, but the ruler, who used priests in his secular administration. In the eleventh and twelfth centuries a church, with its own archpriest and group of priests, probably stood at every stronghold. Each had full parochial rights, but the archpriest also had extensive authority in relation to the faithful within the stronghold's bounds: he punished their sins, such as breaking the obligation not to work on holy days. He was not subject to a bishop, but rather to the local stronghold steward.[59] This organizational principle of closely linking the stronghold and the church (otherwise evident in the etymology of the word *kostel* – 'church' – from *castellum*[60]) was taken from Moravia, where the *Life of Methodius* reports that in 874 Svatopluk gave into the care of the newly ordained bishop of his 'provincial' Church 'all the churches and all the clergy in all the strongholds'.[61] The same principle applied already in the stewardship system of Spytihněv I's Přemyslid principality.

When in 895 Spytihněv submitted to King Arnulf in Regensburg, his principality must ecclesiastically have become part of the diocese of Regensburg.[62] According to the Václav legend, a 'greater priest' (*maior presbyter*) named Paul appeared as the head of a staff of priests.[63] *Maior presbyter* is simply another term for archpriest, that is, a representative of a bishop entrusted with the performance of some of the bishop's duties, in particular baptism and other sacraments. Such archpresbyterates of the bishop of Passau are known from contemporary Moravia.[64] The Prague archpresbyterate was probably established by Tuto, bishop of Regensburg; its priests certainly came mainly from the monastery of St Emmeram in Regensburg, where Tuto was abbot.

It was however the prince who founded the churches in the strongholds, allotted priests to them, ensured that they had a means of support and took on the tasks that would otherwise have been the responsibility of the bishop: obtaining liturgical items, relics necessary for altars and liturgical

---

[58] Žemlička 1997, 149–63 with bibliography.   [59] Žemlička 1997, 180.
[60] Němec 1992, 61–5.   [61] *Žitije Mefodija*, chap. 10 (at 154).   [62] Cf. Graus 1969, 17.
[63] *Crescente fide* (Bavarian recension), 184.   [64] *Žitije Konstantina*, chap. 15 (at 102).

books. The legend *Crescente fide* says that priests came to the Přemyslid ruler Václav (Wenceslas, 921–35) from Bavaria, Swabia and elsewhere 'with the relics of saints and books',[65] which is a reflection of Václav's concern about equipping his churches. To obtain a sufficient number of priests was extremely difficult. The collapse of Great Moravia in 906 was, however, advantageous to the Přemyslids in Prague: among the refugees to Bohemia were priests. The *Crescente* may refer to Bavarian and Swabian priests in the Přemyslid principality, but with the exception of the aforementioned Paul the names that have come down to us are Slavic: Bořivoj's priest Kaich; the priest at the Stará Boleslav stronghold, Krastěj, and one at Budeč, Učen, i.e. 'the learned'. They must have been priests from Moravia because no school for educating priests from among the local population is known: it is a misunderstanding to think that a 'school' existed at Budeč where St Václav supposedly 'studied'.[66] These priests brought the Slavonic script to Bohemia, and some of the customs of the Moravian church, which Adalbert would later try unsuccessfully to purge.[67] In this way a separate Bohemian church developed at the turn of the century, without major influence from Regensburg.

It was, however, only a central-Bohemian church, restricted to the Přemyslid principality. The other Bohemian princes, and the people of their principalities, were not yet Christians. Bohemia was regarded as a Christian land, because during Spytihněv's reign the princes acknowledged the supreme government of the Christian Přemyslids.[68] In reality, however, they were neither dependent on the Přemyslids nor Christians. This is reflected in Christian's tale of the Kouřim prince who, having rebelled against Václav and been defeated militarily, was nevertheless left in possession of his stronghold.[69] It is surely no coincidence that thus far, despite extensive excavations, it has been impossible to find even one church at those strongholds that can be ascribed to non-Přemyslid princes, while a church stood – and in most cases still stands – at virtually all of the Přemyslid strongholds.

Everything changed after the murder of Václav at Stará Boleslav in 935 and the coming to power of Boleslav I. The latter's first act was the liquidation of the Bohemian princes: their strongholds were either razed to the ground like that of the underking (*subregulus*) whom he attacked

---

[65] *Crescente fide* (Bavarian recension), 185.   [66] Sláma 1988a; Třeštík 1997, 365–7.
[67] Bruno, chap. 11 (at 12).
[68] Widukind I.35 (at 50–1) regarded Václav as the lord of all Bohemia as early as 929.
[69] Christian, chap. 10 (at 100–2).

first[70] or abandoned, and it seems that Boleslav created his own, new stronghold nearby (although further research is needed on this topic),[71] which he garrisoned and to which he named a steward from among his retinue. Only in east Bohemia did he choose a somewhat different approach, naming as steward his relative Slavník and granting him authority over a far larger area than was the case with the other strongholds.[72] In essence this was an extension of the stewardship system – including its ecclesiastical elements – of the Prague principality across the whole of Bohemia.

According to the 'privilege of St George' cited by Cosmas, Boleslav I established twenty churches,[73] undoubtedly at his new administrative centres. If he wished to establish priests at each, then he would have required around a hundred clerics and a large number of liturgical items, books and relics. This was an almost insuperable problem: Boleslav could expect virtually no help from Michael, bishop of Regensburg. Initially at least, many of these stronghold churches must have remained vacant. When in 976 the first bishop of Prague, Dietmar, took office, he consecrated numerous churches that were evidently already standing but had remained unconsecrated.[74]

Christianization in one sense was not a gradual process, but rather a single act organized by the prince himself. This is attested by the holding of Boleslav's markets at the strongholds on Sundays, in order that the people from the area around the stronghold be obliged to attend at least Sunday mass.[75] Several decades later, this pragmatic measure, running counter to directives on the sanctity of Sundays, so enraged Adalbert that he found it sufficient reason to leave Bohemia.[76] The quality of the priests secured by Boleslav must also have of necessity been variable, and their undoubtedly diverse origins brought problems similar to those encountered a century earlier in Moravia by Rostislav, who had complained that the priests of different origins 'taught differently'.[77] If, sometime around 974, Wolfgang, bishop of Regensburg really wrote in a document allegedly in his own hand that the Czechs, who had only recently abandoned paganism, 'do not know well enough how an orthodox religion is conducted', he was quite right, just as he was also correct in identifying the cause: they did not have their own bishop.[78] Without a bishop, Christianization could not advance any further.

---

[70] Widukind II.3 (at 67–80). Cf. Třeštík 1997, 435–7 with bibliography.
[71] Sláma 1988b, III, 80–5; 1987, 182–4.   [72] Sláma 1995, 197.   [73] Cosmas I.22 (at 42).
[74] Cosmas I.24 (at 46).   [75] Lalik 1977, 25.   [76] Bruno, chap. 15 (at 18).
[77] *Žitije Konstantina*, chap. 14 (at 98–9); *Žitije Meťodija*, chap. 5 (at 144).
[78] *Othloni Vita*, chap. 29 (at 538).

A bishopric was an absolute necessity for Bohemia. The history of its establishment, however, is obscure.[79] Boleslav and his successors organized the Church under their control. As Bohemia lay within the orbit of the archbishop of Salzburg, the bishop of Regensburg's approval was necessary for the establishment of a Bohemian bishopric. The restoration of the bishopric of Moravia was also proposed: the northern part of Moravia, at least, had fallen to Boleslav shortly after 935. Although a devastated region,[80] de jure it still had an archbishopric. Thus Boleslav requested bishoprics for Moravia and Prague from Pope John XIII. In 967 Mlada, Boleslav's sister, went to Rome; she returned with John's agreement to establish bishoprics in Prague and at the main stronghold of Přemyslid Moravia, Olomouc. The latter was until the twelfth century not called the diocese of Olomouc, but 'of Moravia',[81] bearing the title of Methodius's old see. It was also necessary to obtain the agreement of Michael, bishop of Regensburg, and of the emperor, Otto I. Michael, however, withheld his approval, and so the matter rested until his death in 972, when he was succeeded by the reformist bishop Wolfgang. Boleslav II, heir to Boleslav I, won over Otto, and the matter was decided at the great assembly of the court at Quedlinburg in 973. Wolfgang received estates from the emperor as compensation for the lost income from Bohemia, and gave his agreement to the foundation of a bishopric at Prague. Both dioceses were made subject to Mainz and not Salzburg, as might have been expected; Willigis, archbishop of Mainz, was probably being compensated for losses suffered by the establishment of an archbishopric at Magdeburg. Otto died soon afterwards, and Boleslav II participated in a revolt led by the Bavarian duke, Henry II the Quarreller. Reconciliation came only in 975, and the two bishops, Dietmar (a monk from the Saxon monastery at Corvey) in Prague and an unidentified bishop in Moravia, were ordained in January 976.[82]

The Moravian diocese seems not to have survived the death of its first bishop. Sometime after 983 the second bishop of Prague, Adalbert (Vojtěch), took it under his administration.[83] Extensive missionary activity, also in surrounding lands, especially Hungary, thus fell to him. In 982 Adalbert was elected bishop of Prague, not in Prague but at Levý Hradec, because it was here that 'Christianity began in Bohemia', with the foundation of

[79] Holtzmann 1918, 177–93; Fiala 1962, 53–8; Büttner 1965, 1–22; Labuda 1994, 94–6; Třeštík 2003a; 2000b; Kalhous 2004, 195–208.

[80] Christian, chap. 1 (at 16). Archaeology: Měřínský 1986; Kouřil 2003.   [81] Charouz 1987.

[82] Letter of John XIII to Boleslav I, cited by Cosmas I.22 (at 43–4). Cosmas stylistically amended the letter, but clearly had the original text at his disposal. Fiala 1962, 56–63; Třeštík 2004.

[83] Třeštík 1998b; 2000c.

the first church.[84] Boleslav II had claimed the Moravian legacy probably in order to establish an archbishopric. This idea became the central motif in the work of Christian,[85] a close collaborator of Adalbert. Another 'Great Moravian' motif was the granting of the land to St Peter, following the precedent set by Svatopluk in 880. This was imitated again – perhaps not without Adalbert's participation – by the Polish Mieszko I in 990[86] and perhaps by István of Hungary.[87] In this way the new central-European states came under the protection of the pope, giving them a Christian legitimacy. The Bohemian domains however fell apart at the beginning of the 990s, and, in contrast to Poland and Hungary, no archbishopric was created until 1344.

Christianization is also attested by the evidence of burials. For a long time (perhaps until the eleventh century) the enduring pre-Christian burial rite and the slowly spreading Christian ritual existed alongside one another. For example, even in the context of tumuli burials, the burial of cremated bodies gradually ceased and was replaced by inhumation beneath the tumuli, which continued until the tenth century.[88] Every settlement was accompanied at a certain distance by a 'cluster cemetery'. With the advancing Christianization of society at the end of the ninth century 'row cemeteries' appeared, which in both central and western Europe are taken to be evidence for the Christian regulation of burial practices.[89] In these, the dead were laid out in rows (hence the name), although the cemetery was not spatially delimited. Grave goods changed from collections of items of everyday use into collections of jewellery, insignia and apotropaic items. It is nevertheless likely that pre-Christian burial customs continued at all levels of society.[90] This is attested by the remains of grave gifts in the form of foodstuffs, eggshells and coffins hewn from tree trunks found during the investigation of the graves of the tenth- and eleventh-century Přemyslids in St George's basilica at Prague Castle,[91] and the traces of pre-Christian practices at the cemetery of the princes' retainers in the Lumbe Gardens in the northern bailey of Prague Castle.[92]

During the eleventh century row cemeteries were replaced by regular Christian graveyards, which appeared in delimited and consecrated areas, generally around sacred buildings. In these, the later graves were set over

---

[84] Cosmas I.25 (at 47).
[85] On the disputed question of the identity of the author of Christian's legend Třeštík 1999; 2000a.
[86] On Adalbert's involvement Warnke 1980.   [87] *Das Register Gregors VII* II.13 (at 145).
[88] Lutovský and Tomková 1993; Lutovský 1997; 1999.   [89] Krumphanzlová 1990; Sommer 2000a.
[90] Sommer 2001, 39–47.   [91] Borkovský 1975, 22–4.
[92] Smetánka, Hrdlička and Bajerová 1973; 1974.

the earlier in layers. The advance of the Christian burial rite was accompanied by the appearance of a simple manner of burying the dead, head to the west and without any grave goods. Even in the fully Christian cemeteries administered by the Church, however, archaeologists have encountered traces of apparently pagan practices such as the obol for the dead or protective measures against vampirism: the secondary opening of graves accompanied by interference with the decaying body to prevent the undead from rising.[93] The edicts of princes Břetislav I (1035–55) and Břetislav II (1092–1100) are a reminder that country-dwellers (whom the chronicler Cosmas, d. 1125, refers to as half-pagan) were still burying their dead outside Christian cemeteries, and that they still maintained such pagan burial rituals as wild night-time wakes for the dead. Some archaeologists claim to have identified traces of memorial banquets above graves, in the form of wood charcoal, which, found in grave fills, is supposed to attest to funerary feasts. There is however no unambiguous evidence of this kind.[94]

Little is known of Christian lawmaking. Methodius had translations made of several Byzantine legal codes, but it is unclear whether these had any practical significance.[95] The earliest known domestic collection of laws is the statutes promulgated by Břetislav I in 1039, on the occasion of the translation of St Adalbert's body to Prague.[96] They served to 'reconcile' Bohemia and St Adalbert, and follow the complaints of St Adalbert against the sins of people in Bohemia, as related in the Adalbert legends.[97] The statutes are preserved only by Cosmas in a literary rewriting; their original is unknown. Their content focuses on Christian regulations. Every man is to have only one wife, and marriage is to be indissoluble. Disturbers of marriage and women who had had abortions are to be sold into slavery in Hungary. A woman's complaint of abuse by her husband may be decided by ordeal, as may accusations of murder. Ale-houses are forbidden as 'the root of all evil'. Markets are forbidden on Sundays, as is work on Sundays and holy days. Burials in the fields and woods and outside 'the cemeteries of the faithful' are forbidden.

A peculiarity of Moravian and partially of Bohemian Christianization may be seen in the double Latin and Slavonic liturgy. The nature of Methodius's Slavonic liturgy remains open to debate. According to one hypothesis it was a translation of the Roman 'Liturgy of St Peter', but this is most likely erroneous.[98] Another debatable question is the extent to which Methodius's

---

[93] Krumphanzlová 1961; 1966.   [94] Sommer 2000b, 162–3, 172–3.   [95] Vavřínek 1986, 266–7.
[96] Cosmas II.4 (at 86–8). Hrubý 1916, 29–36; Novotný 1928, I.3, 359–61.
[97] Canaparius, chap. 12; Bruno, chap. 11.
[98] Mareš 2000 shows that the translation first appeared in the fourteenth–fifteenth centuries.

Slavonic liturgy was used in Bohemia. With the exception of the monastery at Sázava, there is no direct evidence: only the use of the Slavonic script is attested.[99] The question of the Slavonic liturgy was considered in detail at a meeting in Rome in 968. The pope expressly forbade its use,[100] repeating the decision previously made by Pope Stephen V.[101] We do not know the impact this had in Prague and in the former archbishopric of Methodius. Slavonic liturgy was definitely nurtured at Sázava, a Benedictine monastery founded in 1032 near Prague by a Czech hermit, Procopius, and persisted there until 1096/7.[102] The monastery had close ties to the newly crowned king; in 1080 Vratislav II applied unsuccessfully to the curia for permission to use the Slavonic liturgy.[103]

The favourite patrons of the earliest churches in Bohemia were St George[104] and St Clement, but not St Emmeram, patron of the diocese of Regensburg, under which Bohemia fell until 973–6.[105] The cult of St Clement, whose relics were brought by Constantine and Methodius to Rome, appears in tenth- and eleventh-century Bohemia: the first Bohemian church, founded at Levý Hradec, was dedicated to St Clement.[106] The favour in which St George was held relates perhaps to his association with the hills on which strongholds with churches stood. The dedication of the oldest church in Prague to the Virgin was no mere reflection of the dedication of Methodius's cathedral church in Moravia; the Virgin had a special position in central Europe during the period of Christianization. The oldest parts of the church at Budeč were dedicated to St Peter, and date from the time of Prince Spytihněv I (d. 915). The dedication of the rotunda built at Prague Castle by Prince Václav (d. 935) to St Vitus is undeniably linked to Saxon influence, again mediated through Bavaria.

Bohemia was, however, very soon to have its own saints. The first attempt at a domestic saint was to create a cult for Ludmila, grandmother of Václav, murdered in 921 and supposedly canonized through the translation arranged by Václav around 925. The cult did not take hold, and Ludmila was revered mainly at St George's nunnery in Prague Castle, where her grave was located.[107] Prince Václav, murdered in 935, became the second Slavic saint. His translation was arranged according to some of the legends

---

[99] Hauptová 1998; Konzal 1998. Cf. Clifton-Everest 1996; Třeštík forthcoming.
[100] Cosmas I.22 (at 43). The reference to Russia is a later amplification.
[101] Letter of Pope Stephen V to Svatopluk in 885, 26.
[102] Reichertová *et al.* 1988; Kadlec 1968; Sommer forthcoming; Merhautová and Sommer 2000, 411–17.
[103] *CDB* I, 88, no. 81; Novotný 1912.   [104] Sláma 1977.   [105] Graus 1969.
[106] Christian, chap. 2 (at 20). This was a relatively common dedication for churches in the old Přemyslid strongholds.
[107] Třeštík 1997, 179–81.

three years after his death, and according to D. Třeštík at the end of the 960s, by his brother and murderer, Boleslav I. The reasons for this were presumably political: a saint from the Přemyslid dynasty would serve as an argument in the attempts to obtain a bishopric for Prague. Václav became patron of the dynasty and the land, and at the turn of the tenth century became the 'eternal prince' ruling from heaven over his *familia* – all free Czechs. He was one of the first 'eternal sovereigns' in the Europe of the time.

The fate of another domestic saint, Bishop Adalbert of Prague, was different. He was canonized at the instigation of the emperor, and was at first not accepted as a saint in his own country. Only when Břetislav I brought his remains from Gniezno to Prague in 1039 did the Czechs begin to revere him. At the beginning of the twelfth century Adalbert became patron of the diocese of Prague and was styled its founder, and for a period he was also co-patron of the land with St Václav.[108] The third domestic saint was the founder and first abbot of the monastery at Sázava, Procopius, canonized in 1203.

Essential preconditions for the foundation of churches were relics. The presumption on the part of church historians that there were at first few official relics in the land is undoubtedly correct. It is thought that secondary relics (*brandea, paliola*) or pieces of the consecrated host were used instead.[109] The presence of relics is, however, attested both by archaeology, for example the rare find of a tenth-century reliquary frame at Libice (birthplace of St Adalbert),[110] and by written sources. In the 920s, for example, explicit reference is made to a saint's relics at St Michael's church at Přemyslid Tetín.[111] The first specifically mentioned relic is the shoulder of St Vitus, given by Henry I to Václav in 929 for the latter's newly erected church.[112] There is also a series of mid-twelfth-century altar authentications that contain lists of relics.[113] A cult of relics is attested by Christian's story about Václav's sister Přibyslava who, together with a priest and a recluse walled up in Prague, stole the jaw from her brother's grave sometime in the 980s, and distributed pieces of it to her friends.[114]

4. ROYAL POWER

The appearance of the Přemyslid polity, first as a central-Bohemian principality (*c.* 884–935) and after 935 encompassing the whole of Bohemia, and

[108] Graus 1980; Radoměrský and Ryneš 1958.   [109] Cibulka 1934, 312.
[110] Turek 1981, 44, 62.   [111] Sommer 2001, 102–25.   [112] Třeštík 1997, 411–15.
[113] Pavlíková 1951.   [114] Christian, chap. 10 (at 98).

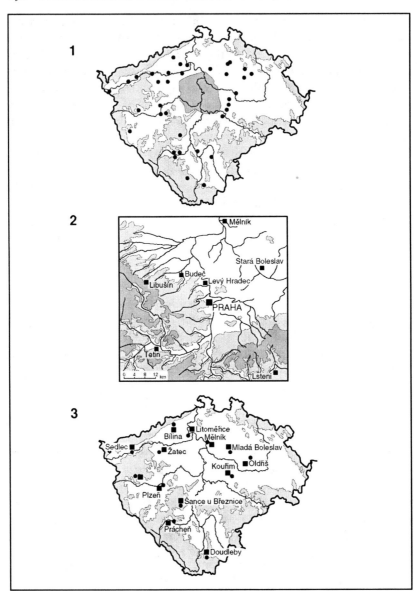

13. Přemyslid dominions
1. Castles of the Bohemian dukes in the ninth century, with the territory of the central-Bohemian Přemyslid principality (after J. Sláma)
2. Central-Bohemian Přemyslid domain in the ninth to tenth centuries
3. The process of unification of Bohemia during Boleslav I's reign, when the old ducal castles (dots) were supplanted by the new Přemyslid castles (squares)

then also Moravia, was a revolutionary event.[115] The effective authority of the Přemyslid ruler was established over all free Czechs. In terms of social qualification they were free, but they had to provide taxes, contributions and services to the prince and to what was for the time quite a large administrative apparatus.[116] Although they held property, the prince became the owner of virtually all the land in the country.[117] Cosmas calls this servitude (*servitus*), the reverse of freedom (*libertas*).[118] Nothing remained of the older institutions.

The celebration and underpinning of sovereign power were also played out through the medium of monumental architecture. The link is demonstrated from the outset with the earliest church buildings erected in the Přemyslid central-Bohemian strongholds of Levý Hradec and Prague during Bořivoj's reign.[119] These were significant but modest structures; soon, however, Prague would take the lead as the architectural capital of the Přemyslids. The written sources speak of the palaces and courts of the monarchs, and in particular of the Přemyslid palace that stood in close proximity to the bishop's residence at Prague Castle during the reign of Václav (921–35). In the course of the tenth century several prestigious religious and secular buildings were erected in the castle. Sometime in the late 920s or early 930s the modest ninth-century church of the Virgin was joined by a far more spectacular structure, the rotunda of St Vitus, which became the seat of the bishop of Prague in 973. According to a recent hypothesis, the church was originally planned as a rotunda with an eastern apse, only to have additional apses added on the north and the south side in order to accommodate the shrines of St Václav and St Adalbert.[120] In its multifunctional purpose (royal chapel, bishopric, Přemyslid mausoleum, national sanctuary), and its choice of architecture, the St Vitus rotunda finds its precedents in the most illustrious religious institutions of the Empire (e.g. Aachen) and of Late Antiquity (of both Christian and pagan use). Perhaps following the example of Moravia, rotundas have since the late ninth century become a recognizably Bohemian building type which continued well into the twelfth century. The importance of St Vitus's as a nexus of royal and sacred symbolism is demonstrated by its continuously evolving structure: in the eleventh century the rotunda was replaced by a large cruciform basilica with an east and west choir, only to be rebuilt again in the fourteenth

[115] Moravia was perhaps appended to the domains of the Bohemian Přemyslids shortly after 935, and definitively after 1020.
[116] Třeštík and Krzemieńska 1979.   [117] Třeštík 1971.   [118] Cosmas I.5 (at 14).
[119] Merhautová and Třeštík 1984; Merhautová 1971; Merhautová and Sommer 2000, 411–17.
[120] Frolík *et al.* 2000; Benešovska *et al.* 2001.

century, each phase inaugurating the most up-to-date architectural forms in Bohemia.[121]

Another important royal foundation in Prague Castle has a longer and more chequered history. The convent of St George was first founded by Vratislav I (912–21) who was also the first to be buried there,[122] although the church was consecrated only in 925 when the body of St Ludmila was translated from Tetín (the place of her murder) by her grandson Václav. The church was one of the very few stone buildings in the castle and was originally erected to serve the ceremonial needs of the Přemyslid dukes and to provide a suitable base for the group of priests at Prague Castle who represented the bishop of Regensburg in Bohemia. It was also used for a while as a burial church and Vratislav may have hoped that the bishopric would be established there in the future. St George's found its true purpose in 976 with the foundation of a Benedictine nunnery at the church, almost simultaneously with the erection of the bishopric of Prague at St Vitus. The two institutions remained closely connected: a covered passageway (via longa) ran between the south wing of the chapter's cloister and St George's. In the following centuries the nunnery was governed by some of the most capable female members of the Přemyslid dynasty, who acted as abbesses. The structure underwent several important architectural changes, the most substantial after a fire in 1142, when a German architect, Wernerus, was employed to rebuild the church. Devotional and expiatory gestures could also be expressed through architecture: the basilica at Stará Boleslav was built after 1039 as part of both Břetislav I's atonement for his assault on Poland, and the declaration of his devotion to St Václav.[123]

Although no noble class holding large estates and enjoying a privileged status existed, the prince nevertheless had his rivals in power and politics. They were referred to as all the Czechs (omnes Bohemi)[124] and were an aristocratic group consisting almost exclusively of the prince's senior officials, 'on whom the Czech lands stand, stood and will always stand'.[125] They were bound to the prince by their almost complete dependence on the income from their offices and by ties of loyalty (fidelitas). At the same time the prince himself had to remain 'faithful' to his Czechs.

The election and enthronement of the prince exclusively from the Přemyslid line was the cornerstone of the power structure. The prince came to power through a ritual enthronement on the stone throne in the

---

[121] Merhautová 1994.   [122] Merhautová-Livorová 1972.

[123] Špaček and Boháčová 2000, 307–22; Boháčová and Špaček 2001, 259–78.

[124] Žemlička 1992; 1993a; Wolverton 2001.   [125] Cosmas I.42 (at 79).

middle of Prague Castle. No one could become a prince without being seated there.[126] There is only a single reference to its appearance, which indicates that it was a plain, unworked or only crudely hewn boulder. Břetislav I, who had five living sons at the end of his life, regulated the succession. The principle of seniority was established, whereby rule passed to the eldest living member of the family, who was to be formally elected by 'all the Czechs' (and Moravians), and enthroned. In reality, however, the electors chose and installed the prince. Agreements and pledges by the magnates, securing all important, long-term decisions, became the guarantee of continuity and stability.[127] The state stood and fell with the balance of power created between the prince and 'all the Czechs'.

The central ordering category of society was peace (*mír*). All the free paid a tax, the *tributum pacis*, to the Přemyslid prince 'for peace'.[128] In Old Slavonic the word meant both what is now called 'peace' and 'the world' (as it still does in Russian), but also 'all people, the human race, the assembled'. Peace was thus not the absence of war, but tranquillity, the balance of different opinions and efforts, tied to the inner state of society.[129] This peace also appears from the twelfth century onwards on the seals of the Bohemian princes, depicting St Václav on one side and the ruling prince on the other. The inscription explained that the peace of St Václav is in the hands of the ruling prince: *pax sancti Vencezlai in manus duci N. N.*[130] The prince is the representative of the eternal sovereign, St Václav, and the saint merely lends him government to hold 'in his hands'. This government was called 'peace', the Old Slavonic pagan peace, for which the 'Czech men' paid their prince the tax.[131]

While *mír* was thoroughly interwoven with the old paganism, St Václav conspicuously represented new Christian concepts, that were as strongly bound up with the domestic situation as the traditional pagan ideas had been. As early as the end of the tenth century Václav became not only patron of the Prague church, but also of the whole of Bohemia and of the ruling dynasty.[132] He was seen as a saint, a powerful intercessor for the dynasty and the land. His patronage of the dynasty appears in book illuminations: an outstanding example is a miniature in the Wolfenbüttel manuscript (made outside Bohemia) of Gumpold's St Václav legend, showing Princess Emma (d. 1006, widow of Boleslav II) in an attitude of adoration before St Václav, to whom Christ is giving a martyr's crown. Such an open association of the ruling dynasty with the protection of the saint is exceptional.[133] Similar

---

[126] Schmidt 1978, 439–63.   [127] Žemlička 1993b.   [128] Žemlička 1997, 165–6.
[129] Gasparini 1962, 3–21.   [130] Čarek 1934.   [131] Třeštík 1988, 23–41.
[132] Gieysztor 1994.   [133] Milde 1972, 64–6; Kostílková 2000, 280–1.

significance may be attached to the depiction of Prince Václav and other saints on Czech coins. An exceptional declaration of the protection of the sovereign appears in a miniature in the 'Vyšehrad Codex', which was completed in the mid-1080s in conjunction with the coronation of the first king of Bohemia, Vratislav II (1085–6). A picture of St Václav between the texts of the gospels manifested a link between the sacred world and the ruling family and their polity.[134] Such representation occurs on wall painting as well. In 1134 the minor, appanaged prince of Znojmo had his castle chapel decorated with a magnificent pictorial catalogue of the Přemyslid rulers, beginning with the calling of Přemysl Oráč from the plough, based on the newly completed chronicle of Cosmas.

In the second half of the eleventh century Václav started to be depicted in armour as a prince and a warrior.[135] His feast day, 28 September, was transformed into a holiday,[136] during which the prince would hold a great assembly and banquet for 'all the Czechs'. Václav was thought to intervene in important affairs of state, and to provide aid in battle. The imperial lance given by Henry IV to Vratislav II in 1080 became the lance of St Václav and, fitted with the banner of St Adalbert, served as the battle standard of the Bohemian forces.[137] St Václav is shown as a prince with lance and banner before 1006 on the miniature in the Wolfenbüttel manuscript of the Gumpold legend.[138] From the eleventh century the prince is also regularly shown on coins with a lance and banner in his hand; all the princes are shown in the same way in the sequence of princes that appears in the frescoes decorating the castle chapel at Znojmo.[139] The so-called helmet of St Václav from the tenth century may or may not have been one of the insignia of the Bohemian princes; but it was definitely revered.[140] Václav's image, common on coins since the beginning of the eleventh century, also appeared on the seals of Vladislav II and his successors, which served as a *sigillum citationis*, shown by the chamberlain issuing summons to court. It was therefore Václav who had justice or law, embodied in the court, in his hands.[141] From the beginning of the twelfth century St Adalbert, the co-patron of the leading church in the land, began to appear next to Václav as a patron of the land itself. They were regularly shown together on coins and elsewhere.

All this led, in the first half of the twelfth century, to the notion that the real ruler of Bohemia was not the ruling prince, but the eternal, undying,

---

[134] Merhautová and Spunar 2006.   [135] Třeštík 1968, 192–201; Wolverton 1998.
[136] Žemlička 1991.   [137] Třeštík 1968, 201–6.   [138] Merhautová and Třeštík 1984, 65.
[139] Merhautová and Třeštík 1984, 155–6; 1983, 120–2; Merhautová-Livorová 1983; Krzemieńska 1987.
[140] Merhautová 1992.   [141] Třeštík 1968, 208–12; Nový 1976.

Prince Václav. He was also the owner and possessor of the princely estates and the supreme lord of all the soil and people in the land. The prince was merely his representative or *vicarius*, the representative of a saint from the domestic dynasty. This concept of an eternal sovereign was an expression of the abstract idea of the state. It implied something that existed independently of the current ruler, going beyond his mortal body and lasting eternally, providing continuity for the political community. A similar symbol was the crown of the kingdom, which appeared in Bohemia in the mid-twelfth century.[142]

The political community in Bohemia was designated as the *familia sancti Wencezlai*.[143] Symbolically, they were held together by loyalty to their lord, by the contract established with the Přemyslid family in the distant past, when Přemysl Oráč was called to the stone throne, and by their common aim, peace. This political community was depicted around the year 1170 in a miniature of a manuscript of St Augustine's *De civitate Dei*.[144] The title page bears a full-page illustration of the City of God, filled with figures of the chosen people of God, angels, prophets, apostles, martyrs, proselytes, holy virgins and the Czechs, represented by four half figures of a bishop, a monk, a bearded layman and a married woman in the extreme right corner. The Czechs were thus understood as a chosen nation.[145] The miniature is the first known pictorial representation of a nation in medieval Europe.

The Bohemian princes sought to free themselves from dependence on the magnates during the investiture struggle, when both pope and emperor sought allies. In 1085–6 Vratislav II (1061–92) received a royal title from Henry IV (1056–1105) and in 1158 Frederick Barbarossa bestowed the crown on Vladislav II (1140–72). In each case there was opposition from the magnates. It was not until 1198 that Přemysl Otakar I (1197–1230) obtained a crown and royal title not just for himself but for all his heirs. As king, he stood far above the struggles of his cousins, the princes (*duces*). This new dignity redefined the relationship between the prince and 'all the Czechs', from among whom rose the 'barons'.[146] It is not known which Bohemian prince was the last to ascend the stone throne in Prague Castle. The last traditional election was held in 1216, but Václav did not, perhaps, physically ascend the throne. Later only the coronation was recognized; the first of these was performed on 6 February 1228 by the archbishop of Mainz. This and all the subsequent coronations took place in Prague Cathedral, which stood just a few dozen metres from the old stone throne;

---

[142] *CDB* I, 215, no. 245, a. 1165. Třeštík 1968, 214.   [143] *Kanovník vyšehradský*, a. 1126 (at 203).
[144] Prague, Library of the Prague Chapter. Cf. Merhautová and Třeštík 1984, 214, with illustration.
[145] Merhautová and Třeštík 1983, 106–15.   [146] Schramm 1968; Fritze 1982.

the latter quickly fell into oblivion. Nothing else expressed the opening of a new era so well.[147] With a royal title, the Přemyslids broke away from the role of deputy to St Václav. From princes, whose dark pagan roots and enthronement were purified by reverence for St Václav and by the Christian ecclesiastical elements of the enthronement ritual, they became kings by the grace of God.[148] In the thirteenth century the most important Bohemian royal insignia became the crown, with other motifs including the throne (the enthroned monarch), the sceptre and the sword.

5. THE EFFECTS OF CHRISTIANIZATION

The establishment of bishoprics in the two regions was determined by the interests of Boleslav I (935–72); both dioceses were then subordinated to the metropolitan of Mainz. At the turn of the eleventh century, the Moravian bishopric became vacant and its administration fell to the bishops of Prague. In 1063 Prince Vratislav II (1061–92) 'restored' the Moravian bishopric with its seat at Olomouc, and despite the ill will of the Prague bishops this endured.[149] As early as under Břetislav I (1035–55) there were attempts to raise Prague to an archbishopric, bringing the remains of St Adalbert from Gniezno to Prague, but this attempt failed.[150]

Until the twelfth century the vast majority of ecclesiastical institutions (bishoprics, monasteries, chapters and stronghold churches) were founded by ruling Přemyslids, who involved them in state administration, and regarded them as their property. The clergy, far more dependent on their princely (and in general secular) lords than on the authority of the bishop, lived initially on a part of the prince's income.[151] The prince's officials also ensured the collection of ecclesiastical tithes which, according to Cosmas's report, were initially paid in grain. Only later did their collection fall within the purview of the Church itself. Even so the form and extent of tithe receipts were complicated until as late as the thirteenth century by the proprietary demands of the sovereign and the nobility on ecclesiastical property.[152] While the Church soon began to receive gifts of land, it was not until the beginning of the thirteenth century that it could dispose of it as its owner. Judicial and administrative control was for a long time claimed

---

[147] Novotný 1928, 580–2; Žemlička 2002, 570–80.   [148] Žemlička 1990, 248–54.
[149] Medek 1971.   [150] Cosmas II.2–7 (at 82–93). Krzemieńska 1999, 188–229; Žemlička 1997, 55–63.
[151] Žemlička 2001, 125–33.
[152] On the first tithes, Cosmas I.40 (at 75–6); Schmid 1938, 99–147; Žemlička 1997, 170–1.

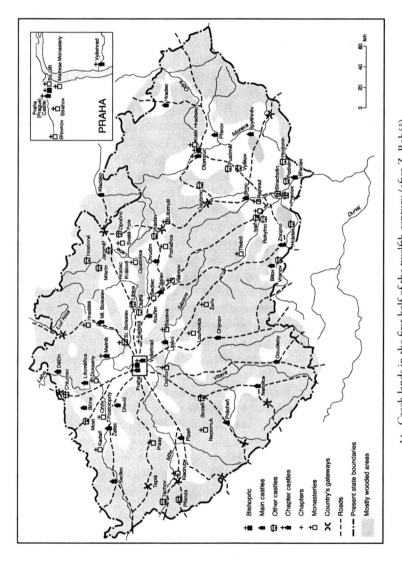

14. Czech lands in the first half of the twelfth century (after Z. Boháč)

Legend:
- ✝ Bishopric
- ■ Main castles
- ⌂ Other castles
- ✝ Chapter castles
- ✝ Chapters
- ⌂ Monasteries
- ✕ Country's gateways
- – – – Roads
- –··– Present state boundaries
- ▨ Mostly wooded areas

PRAHA (inset):
- ✝ Praha (Prague) Castle
- ✝ Břevnov
- ⌂ Strahov
- ■ Sv. Jiří
- ✝ Maltese Monastery
- ✝ Vyšehrad

Place names:
Klatisko, Hostinné, Jaroměř, Svatě Pole, Opočno, Miletín, Hradec Králové, Opatovice, Václav, Litomyšl, ÚŠgoproz, Litomyšl, Hradec, Kláší Hradisko, Přerov, Olomouc, Morava, Spytihněv, Pustiměř, Vyškov, Hodonín, Strachotín, Podivín, Břeclav, Pravlov, Brno, Rajhrad, Oslavany, Rokytno, Znojmo, Hrádek, Ivaň, Třebíč, Vranov, Bítov, Vilémov, Podlažice, Chrudim, Čáslav, Kouřim, Sázava, Sezemice, Oldříš, Sedlec, Úhce, Libice, St. Boleslav, Mělník, Mt. Boleslav, Hradiště, Litoměřice, Dolánky, Děčín, Chlumec, Labe, Luž. Niša, Most, Bílina, Postoloprty, Ohře, Žatec, Kadaň, Sedlec, Teplá, Tachov, Přimda, Klášruby, Mže, Plasy, Nepomuk, Plzeň, Bozeň, Přácheň, Netolice, Vltava, Doudleby, Dunaj, Zeliv, Lštění, Čhýnov, Loučovice, Ostrov, Praha, Vyšehrad, Osřrov

0 20 40 60 km

by the organs of princely and provincial administration, so that the Church received only the economic benefits of the people and properties donated to it.[153]

The ties of the domestic Church to the sovereign were also expressed in the status of the bishops. The Bohemian prince acted as lord, protector and patron of what was seen as his Church. Laws concerning the enforcement of ecclesiastical precepts and determining the punishments and fines for failure to adhere to them were issued under his authority: in 1039 the statutes of Břetislav I from Gniezno, in 1092 the measures of Břetislav II against non-Christian practices.[154] The bishop of Prague above all was closely dependent on the Přemyslids. His tithes initially came not from the faithful but from the prince's chamber, and even at the end of the twelfth century he was regarded as a 'chaplain' to the princes.[155] The wishes of the princes were decisive in the filling of the bishop's throne; they favoured foreigners, as they would be fully dependent on the prince.[156] On the other hand, the election of a Přemyslid bishop (Jaromír/Gebhard 1068–90, Jindřich 1182–97) could cause the prince discomfiture, as such a bishop might attempt to achieve his secular ambitions through his ecclesiastical office. By contrast, the bishop of Olomouc was more independent; as a representative of the Bohemian princes in Moravia, he came into conflict with the Moravian appanaged princes.[157] Relations with the metropolitan in Mainz and the Roman curia remained spasmodic for a long time, and were maintained more by the Bohemian sovereign than by the bishops.[158] The canonical election of bishops and other church dignitaries was introduced only gradually, while the monarch for long retained influence over it.[159]

A description of the boundaries of the diocese of Prague appears in connection with the attempts of Bishop Jaromír/Gebhard of Prague to prevent the restoration of the bishopric of Olomouc. Supposedly this description gives the extent of the diocese at the time of Bishop Adalbert (982–97); it is contained in a 1086 privilege of Emperor Henry IV, a version that also appears in Cosmas's chronicle. It is not clear to what extent it reflects late tenth-century reality. According to the description, the diocese

[153] Nový 1972, 115–36. On the holdings of the Prague bishopric Boháč 1979. On immunity Vaněček 1933–9; Žemlička 2003b, 33–46; 2003a, 509–41.
[154] Cosmas II.4 (at 85–90), III.1 (at 161).   [155] *Letopis Jarlocha*, 480.
[156] Cosmas III.7 (at 168).   [157] Matzke 1969; Huber 1973a.
[158] The fundamental reference remains Hrubý 1916; 1917. Fiala 1967; Hilsch 1969; 1972; Nový 1972, 71–85, 153–60; Huber 1973b; Kejř 1994.
[159] Breitenbach 1904; Fiala 1967.

encompassed not only Bohemia and Moravia, but also large parts of Silesia, western Slovakia and Lesser Poland.[160] From the end of the eleventh century and during the twelfth, the boundaries of the Prague and Moravian (i.e. Olomouc) bishoprics essentially coincided with those of the polity. At first the whole diocese was one great parish, with the bishop as its administrator and shepherd. With the development of the system of stewardship strongholds the princes built churches at their strongholds, and established a congregation of priests for each, whose superior was called an archpriest (*archipresbyter*). The so-called great parish system, modelled on the stronghold administration, remained functional until the beginning of the thirteenth century. The centre of the great parish was the main stronghold church, situated in the area of its castle. The priests were more dependent on the ruler and his officials than on the bishop, and within the framework of their 'great parishes' were incorporated into the state administration, especially the judicial system.[161] The priests of the castle church were also sustained from the income and receipts of the administrative stronghold. The archdeaconries of the twelfth and thirteenth centuries coincided with the older stronghold districts from which they took their names (e.g. the archdeaconries of Kouřim, Žatec, Litoměřice, etc.) only to a certain extent. The medieval parish system thus grew out of both the great parishes and the churches and chapels that were later added in large numbers on the initiative of the sovereign, the bishops, the monasteries and the nobility, and then gained rights as parishes.[162]

A systematic parish organization began sometime in the course of the twelfth century, but its development was uneven. The key question concerned parish rights (the rights to baptize and to bury), which were transferred to the new parish churches, thus reducing the income of the older churches. The drawing of parish boundaries (*limitatio*) underwent a complicated development. The papal legate, Cardinal Guido, who visited Bohemia and Moravia in 1143, exhorted the local bishops to define their parishes more precisely (*ut in parrochiis suis plebales ecclesias distinguant*). The relationship between the parish church and the actual organization of the parish was brought to some order only at the beginning of the thirteenth century; documentation of the definition of parish boundaries – which might include one, two or more than ten neighbouring villages – rapidly accumulated at this time. The parish network was fully established

---

[160] *CDB* I, 92–5, no. 86. [161] Cf. the decrees of Břetislav I, 1039, Cosmas II.4 (at 86–7).
[162] Novotný 1928, 354–73; Schmid 1938.

only in the fourteenth century, as is described for the Prague archdeaconry (central Bohemia) in the visitation protocol for the years 1379–82.[163]

The concurrence of ecclesiastical and secular administration lasted from the end of the tenth century to the beginning of the thirteenth, throughout the period in which the stewardship system functioned. From the mid-twelfth, but mainly from the thirteenth century, however, the ecclesiastical system began to establish its own administrative supports, based on the division of the land into archdeaconries and deaconries.[164]

German priests – mainly from Bavaria and Saxony – occupied influential positions from the start, often arriving in the retinues of the German wives of the Přemyslids. Many rose to the rank of bishop, including the first bishop of Prague, Dietmar, called 'the Saxon' (973–82), who 'had perfect command of the Slavonic language'.[165] Other princes too gave preference to foreign priests within their orbits, particularly to 'Germans', seeing them as more reliable because dependent on the good will of the prince. Such practices aroused opposition from among the domestic clergy. This is expressed bluntly by Cosmas in a fictitious speech directed against the election of the Saxon, Lank, whose installation was sought in 1068 by Vratislav II.[166] The monasteries also boasted a strong, at times decisive, contribution from Germans: the monks and priests from German districts both far and near who formed the earliest cores of Benedictine, Cistercian and Premonstratensian communities, as they did in chapters of all kinds. Only in the thirteenth century did the balance tip in favour of the domestic clergy and monks; diocesan and other high offices began at this time to be occupied mainly by individuals who came from high-born noble families.[167]

The first monastic foundations were Benedictine, and initially their founders and donors came exclusively from among the ruling Přemyslids. In perhaps the 960s Benedictine nuns were installed beside St George's church at Prague Castle, founded on the model of imperial nunneries, as are known from Gernrode, for example, and the daughters and sisters of the rulers became abbesses there. The monastery at Břevnov (now part of Prague) was established jointly by Prince Boleslav II and Bishop Adalbert in 993, and populated from the Greco-Latin monastery of St Boniface and St Alexius in Rome. After the massacre of the Slavník family, from which Adalbert came, this monastery was abandoned. It was restored in the first quarter of the eleventh century by Benedictines oriented towards

[163] CDB I, 138, no. 135; CDB II, 30–1, no. 33; Protocollum visitationis. Žemlička 2002, 450–2.
[164] For the fourteenth century, Horák and Mucha 1976; for central Bohemia, Boháč 2001.
[165] Cosmas I.23 (at 44).   [166] Cosmas II.23–4 (at 115–17).   [167] Žemlička 1997, 210–11.

the reforms of Gorze, coming from Altaich in Bavaria. Other monastic houses soon followed (Ostrov *c.* 1000, Sázava *c.* 1032), all situated in central Bohemia within the domains of the Přemyslids. It was here that conditions allowed their material support, as the first monastic communities lived mainly from grants made from the prince's revenues. Only later did property ownership play an important role. From the mid-eleventh century monasteries also began to be established in Moravia (Hradiště u Olomouce, 1078). From the beginning of the twelfth century noble foundations appeared as well. The first wave of Benedictine activity came to a close around the middle of the twelfth century, by which time there were ten houses of monks and two nunneries.[168]

The end of the first wave of Benedictine foundations coincided with the arrival of the Cistercians and Premonstratensians. While the first Premonstratensians settled at Strahov (*Mons Sion*) in the immediate vicinity of Prague Castle in 1143–4, at the initiative of Prince Vladislav II (1140–72), his wife Gertrude and Jindřich Zdík, bishop of Olomouc (1126–50), the establishment of the first Cistercian monastery at Sedlec, founded in 1142–3, was mainly due to the nobleman Miroslav. The proportion of noble foundations grew and began to outnumber those of the Přemyslids, and to match them in the wealth of property donated. In west Bohemia the magnate Hroznata founded the Premonstratensian houses at Teplá (1193) and Chotěšov (1202–10), while in the north-west of Bohemia the nobleman Slavek, of the powerful Hrabišice family, established a Cistercian house at Osek (1197–9). Among the most senior ecclesiastical dignitaries, who also occupied a leading position in the political community of the Czechs, were the abbots and provosts of influential monastic institutions. Until the beginning of the thirteenth century their appointment was entirely at the discretion of the ruler, who generally chose them from among the court clergy (the so-called court chapel).

The beginnings of Bohemian sacral buildings were linked to wooden architecture. The first church at Levý Hradec was wooden, as was the church over the grave of St Ludmila (d. 921) at Tetín. At the same time, the first stone structures appeared, in the form of the single-aisled church with an apse (the church of the Virgin at Prague Castle) and the characteristic Bohemian (originally Moravian) rotunda (as for example at Budeč, Prague Castle). The first cathedral was St Vitus's rotunda at the castle, dating from the time of Prince Václav (d. 935), which was replaced between 1060 and the 1090s by a monumental, twin-chancel basilica with a western transept. The

---

[168] Sommer 1991; 1996.

first monasteries were equipped primarily with wooden buildings, as has been shown by archaeological excavations at the Benedictine sites of Ostrov u Davle and Sázava, where wooden complexes served for over a century, and were not therefore merely temporary structures. The monastery at Břevnov was from the outset given stone buildings (possibly with wooden provisional structures). As early as 1045 the east end of the convent's basilica was extant, and the whole masonry complex was complete by perhaps 1089.[169] Soon after the establishment of the bishopric, a diocesan residence with a single-aisled chapel with an apse existed at Prague Castle. A special princely chapel next to the palace at the castle is known in the twelfth century.[170]

With the establishment of cathedrals, cathedral chapters started as probably loose associations of priests without firm rules rather than true capitular societies. They depended on the ruler, and non-canonical behaviour continued well into the twelfth century, including the marriage of priests, so that in 1143 the legate Cardinal Guido removed from office and punished capitular dignitaries from both Prague and Olomouc during his visitation.[171]

A reform of the Prague chapter was undertaken in 1068 by Provost Marek. The number of members in the chapter was limited to twenty-five, priestly clothing was prescribed, and the reformed congregation was made financially secure.[172] Olomouc had to wait for changes until the time of Bishop Jindřich Zdík (1126–50), who moved the cathedral from the church of St Peter to that of St Václav, which lay within the confines of the Olomouc castle and was consecrated in 1131. Zdík added the archpriest of all six Moravian stronghold churches to the newly established chapter of twelve members, giving him the title of archdeacon. Since he brought to the chapter the property of the stronghold churches he had held, the chapter could become a functional element in the bishop's administration. These reforms, documented in two extensive (but undated) documents, were probably undertaken in the latter half of the 1130s.[173]

In addition to the cathedral chapters, the Přemyslids also founded several collegiate chapters of priests and canons in Bohemia. After Stará Boleslav (founded by Břetislav I, 1035–55), where the still-extant basilica has recently been dated by excavation to the time of its founder,[174] and Litoměřice (founded by Spytihněv II, 1055–61), the collegiate chapter at Vyšehrad

---

[169] Sommer 1994, 206–11.   [170] Cf. Frolík *et al.* 2000.
[171] *CDB* I, 136–8, no. 135. Novotný 1928, 139–45.
[172] Cosmas II.26 (at 118–20); Hledíková 1972, 5–48.
[173] *CDB* I, 116–23, no. 115, 124–5, no. 116. Medek 1971, 53–4; Žemlička 1997, 245–8; Zemek 1988–9.
[174] Boháčová and Špaček 2001, 259–78.

(now part of Prague) was founded around 1070 by Vratislav II (1061–92) and subjected directly to the pope. This benefit was augmented by the decision to allow capitular dignitaries to wear the mitre and sandals (indicating their connection to the papacy), and was tied to an ordinance requiring the delivery of twelve talents of silver to Rome.[175] The structural elements of its eleventh- to twelfth-century twin-choir basilica have been found during archaeological research.[176]

One of the major results of Christianization was the introduction of literacy, even if it was partial and at first limited to the Church. Thus far there is no evidence whatsoever that writing was used by lay people in the early Middle Ages. The Latin (Bavarian) missions in Moravia left few traces: prayers, the Lord's Prayer, the Creed. It is nevertheless symptomatic that the text of the Lord's Prayer that is still used today in the Czech lands is a translation of the Old High German text used in the Eastern Frankish Empire at the beginning of the ninth century, and is thus the translation that would have been arranged for the Moravian mission from the Passau diocese.[177] Most of the literary works originating in Moravia were the result of the missions of Constantine-Cyril and Methodius in 863–7 and 873–86 and are written in Old Church Slavonic. Most are translations from the Greek, but there are also original works of a very high standard; these are translations of biblical texts from both the New and Old Testaments needed for mass. Constantine's prologue in verse to the translation of the gospels, the *Proglas*, an enthusiastic celebration of the new, Slavonic literary language, is of considerable literary and intellectual value.[178] A range of ecclesiastical legal texts, the Nomocanon and the *Zakon sudnyj ljudem* (a civil legal code based on the Byzantine Ecloga) were also translated.[179] A penitential, the *Zapoved sventych otcov* was translated from the Latin.

In Bohemia the first domestic literary works are the numerous legends of St Václav and St Ludmila, in both Latin[180] and Old Church Slavonic.[181] The earliest surviving Latin Legend of St Václav apparently originated in the 960s, in conjunction with the translation of the saint's remains; the first Old Church Slavonic Legend of St Václav is a reworking of this. Soon after 973–6 a new Legend of St Václav appeared, along with the first Legend of St Ludmila; they were the work of a Regensburg monk active in Prague (the *Crescente fide christiana* and *Fuit in provincia Bohemorum*). The legend

---

[175] *Kanovník vyšehradský*, 206; *CDB* I, 365–7, no. 384, 371–91, no. 387. On Vyšehrad, Pleszczyński 2002. On the chapter, Hledíková 1997.
[176] Nechvátal 1992, 112–41.   [177] Cibulka 1956.
[178] Overview: Bláhová 1988a.   [179] *MMFH* IV, 147–98.
[180] Overview: Ludvíkovský 1973–4.   [181] Vajs 1929; overview: Konzal 1976.

of both saints was written in 992–4 by a member of the ruling dynasty, the monk Christian.[182] Domestic hagiography continued to flourish long afterwards, continuing at a similar intensity until the late Middle Ages.

The first annalistic work appeared as early as the end of the tenth century, perhaps at the Břevnov monastery,[183] while the first chronicle was written by Cosmas, dean of Prague, in 1110–25.[184] The latter was the foundation for a rich historiography that lasted continuously into the twelfth century. The monastery at Sázava was a special case, where considerable literary activity was conducted in Old Church Slavonic; the literary contacts that the monastery maintained with Kievan Rus' were also important.[185] From the twelfth century wills written at ecclesiastical initiative also appear among Czech documents.[186]

Virtually no law codes appear in this rich collection of literary works. The so-called law of the land, the customary law which from ancient times governed free Czechs, was recorded in private handbooks for the first time in the thirteenth century; it had very little in common with the law of the Church and Christianity. The statutes of Břetislav I, dating to 1039, are the only collection of laws concerning Christianity.[187] In their structure they resemble synodal resolutions. They are not founded on any earlier tradition of lawgiving, and relate to Christian discipline. The land is understood to be fully Christian, and the task set is merely to make its religion more perfect.

The Přemyslids began to mint coins relatively early, probably at the beginning of the 960s,[188] and these replaced the previously used medium of exchange in the form of woven kerchiefs.[189] Coins were not primarily a manifestation of princely power, but played an important economic role. In the tenth century Bohemia was an important staging point in international trade, a leading market for slaves,[190] and coins made it easier for the princes to take advantage of this. The first Bohemian coin is a Bavarian-type penny (*denarius*) of Boleslav I, with a cross on the obverse and a chapel on the reverse, probably minted about 960–2.[191] Minting on a small scale was later carried out by Bishop Adalbert in 983–9,[192] Princess ('queen') Emma (d. 1006) and Adalbert's brother Soběslav (981–95) at Libice. These coins

---

[182] Třeštík 1997.   [183] Třeštík 1978.   [184] On the chronicle: Třeštík 1968.
[185] Overview: Bláhová 1988b.   [186] Fiala 1960; Šebánek and Dušková 1956.
[187] The Statutes of Konrád Ota (*CDB* II, 222–5, no. 234, 329–32, no. 325, *CDB* III, 202–5, no. 164) are purely secular.
[188] Hahn 1977; 1978–9; 2002; 1981–2; Suchodolski 1973–4; debate over dating: Petráň 1998b; 2003. Overview of Bohemian coinage: Cach 1970–2.
[189] Ibrahim ibn Yaqub, 49. 'Kinshar' here is the penny (denarius), cf. Štěpková 1957.
[190] Třeštík 2001a.   [191] Cach 1970–2, I, no. 2.   [192] Petráň 1998a.

were predominantly modelled on the Bavarian penny, but from the end of the tenth century (and for unclear reasons) the Anglo-Saxon coins of Æthelred II had a significant influence. At the beginning of the eleventh century the influence of the Byzantine *solidus* was apparent. On the coins from the beginning of the reign of Prince Oldřich (*c.* 1014)[193] the obverse shows a bust of the ruler and his name, *Odalricus dux*, while on the reverse is a cross with the inscription *regnet* [sic] *in Praga sancta*. The use of the phrase *in Praga sancta* emphasizes the role of Prague in ruling the whole land. Prague is *sancta* – and thus something like a holy metropolis – through the presence of St Václav's body, the latter's name appearing on the coins of Oldřich's predecessor Jaromír from around 1008. Bohemian coins reached an apex in terms of ideological content and artistic merit in the twelfth century.[194]

6. CONCLUSION

Christianization started from ninth-century Bavarian missionary centres and through influences from the south (Dalmatia, northern Italy). Great Moravia, especially the mission of Cyril and Methodius and the foundation of the basic ecclesiastical organization, played a key role. Similar processes began in perhaps 883 or 884 in Bohemia, which was first attached to Great Moravia, but was then an independent polity. At the beginning of the tenth century, the Christianization of Bohemia continued slowly. After the foundation of the Prague and Moravian bishoprics in the 970s, the establishment of an ecclesiastical organization of large parishes linked the Bohemian church to the system of the prince's administrative strongholds. After the definitive annexation of Moravia to Bohemia *c.* 1020, this structure was also implemented on Moravian territory. Only in the thirteenth century, however, was a parish network created.

Christianization was inseparably linked to the process of the creation and building of the polity. This is not because the Church was a 'state' Church, but because in many respects it was identical with the polity. Christianity, understood as a new life order, offered the intellectual justification for the radical changes in society that accompanied the creation of a newly united and organized state. Just as the creation of the new political order was probably accomplished by force (even though there is no direct evidence of this), so too the installation of Christianity was made essentially from above.

---

[193] Hásková 1974.   [194] Nohejlová-Prátová 1955; Hásková 1975.

Christianity – at the time understood to consist of practices, for example the observance of holy days, or the regulation of marriage – was imposed by the prince and not by the independent action of the clergy. Christianity was nevertheless accepted and reshaped by society, as social relations became governed by Christian rituals, rules and symbols, although little is known of the faith of Bohemian Christians. In the process, as a new focus of Christian social identity, the Czechs created the 'eternal king' St Václav, who, as a never-dying, heavenly monarch, symbolized the polity. This role of Václav also meant the self-identification of the Czechs as the *familia* of St Václav, and not of the temporary sovereign, leading to the birth of the 'political nation'. In the early Middle Ages the Church played no central role, but was as much a servant of the state as the bishop of Prague was chaplain of the Přemyslid princes until the twelfth century. Christianization was thus almost exclusively the work of the rulers, and Christianity reinforced the power of the state.

REFERENCES

al-Masúdi, 'Rýžoviště zlata a doly drahokam ů', ed. I. Hrbek, *MMFH*, vol. III, 404–8.

Angenendt, A. 1973, 'Taufe und Politik im frühem Mittelalter', *Frühmittelalterliche Studien* 7, 143–68.

Angenendt, A. 1984, *Kaiserherrschaft und Königstaufe. Kaiser, Könige und Päpste als geistliche Patrone in der abendländischen Missionsgeschichte*, Berlin and New York.

Annales Bertiniani, ed. G. Waitz, *MGH SRG*, Hanover, 1883.

Annales Fuldenses, ed. F. Kurze, *MGH SRG*, Hanover, 1891.

Annales Hildesheimenses, ed. G. Waitz, *MGH SRG*, Hanover, 1878.

Banaszkiewicz, J. 1982, 'Königliche Karrieren von Hirten, Gärtner und Pflüger. Zu einem mittelalterlichen Erzählschema vom Erwerb der Königsherrschaft (die Sagen von Johannes Agnus, Přemysl, Ina, Wamba und Dagobert)', *Saeculum* 3–4, 265–86.

Banaszkiewicz, J. 1993, 'Slawische Sagen "de origine gentis". (al-Masudi, Nestor, Kadlubek, Kosmas) – Dioskurische Matrizen der Überlieferungen', *Mediaevalia Historica Bohemica* 3, 29–58.

Benešovska, K. *et al.* 2001, *Ten Centuries of Architecture*, vol. I, *Architecture of the Romanesque*, Prague.

Bernardi Cremifarensis Historiae, *MGH SS* XXV, 651–78.

Bláhová, E. 1988a, 'Počátky slovanské knižní vzdělanosti, slovanské písmo a spisovný jazyk', in Reichertová, Bláhová, Dvořáčková and Huňáček 1988, 28–45.

Bláhová, E. 1988b, 'Staroslověnská literární činnost Sázavského kláštera', in Reichertová, Bláhová, Dvořáčková and Huňáček 1988, 104–51.

Boháč, Z. 1979, 'Pozemková držba pražského arcibiskupství v době předhusitské', *Historická Geografie* 18, 165–203.

Boháč, Z. 2001, *Topografický slovník k církevním dějinám předhusitských Čech. Pražský archidiakonát*, Prague.

Boháčová, I. and J. Špaček 2001, 'Raně středověké kostely sv. Václava a sv. Klimenta ve Staré Boleslavi', *Archaeologia Historica* 26, 259–78.

Borkovský, I. 1953, 'Kostel Panny Marie na Pražském hradě', *Památky Archeologické* 44, 129–200.

Borkovský, I. 1975, *Svatojiřská basilika a klášter na Pražském hradě*, Prague.

Breitenbach, A. 1904, 'Die Besetzung der Bistümer Prag und Olmütz bis zur Anerkennung des ausschlüßlichen Wahlrechtes der beiden Domkapitel', *Zeitschrift des deutschen Vereines für Geschichte Mährens und Schlesiens* 8, 1–46.

Bruno of Querfurt, 'Vita S. Adalberti', ed. J. Karwasińska, *MPH* n.s. IV/2, Warsaw, 1969.

Büttner, H. 1965, 'Erzbischof Willigis von Mainz und das Papsttum bei der Bistumserrichtung in Böhmen und Mähren im 10. Jh.', *Rheinische Vierteljahrsblätter* 30, 1–22.

Cach, F. 1970–2, *Nejstarší české mince*, 2 vols., Prague.

Canaparius, 'Vita S. Adalberti', ed. J. Karwasińska, *MPH* n.s. IV/1, Warsaw, 1962.

Čarek, J. 1934, *O pečetech českých knížat z rodu Přemyslova* (repr. in Sborník příspěvků k dějinám hlavního města Prahy 8, 1938), Prague.

CDB: Codex diplomaticus et epistolaris regni Bohemiae, ed. G. Friedrich, I (805–1197), Prague, 1904–7; II (1198–1230), Prague, 1912.

Charouz, Z. 1987, 'Několik poznámek k významu slov Morava, moravský v pramenech 9.–13. století', *Slavia* 56, 71–4.

Christian, *Vita et passio S. Wencezlai et S. Ludmilae, ave eius*, ed. J. Ludvíkovský, *Kristiánova legenda – Legenda Christiani*, Prague, 1978.

Chronicon imperatorum et pontificum bavaricum, *MGH SS* XXIV, 220–5.

Cibulka, J. 1934, 'Václavova rotunda sv. Víta', *Svatováclavský Sborník* 1, 230–685.

Cibulka, J. 1956, 'Επιούσιος – nasoštъ nyi – quotidianus – vezdejší', *Slavia* 25, 406–15.

Cibulka, J. 1965, 'Der Zeitpunkt der Ankunft der Brüder Konstantin-Cyrillus und Methodius in Mähren', *Byzantinoslavica* 26, 318–64.

Clifton-Everest, J. M. 1996, 'Slavisches Schrifttum im 10. und 11. Jahrhundert in Böhmen', *Bohemia* 37, 257–70.

Concilium Maguntinum a. 852, MGH Capitularia regum Francorum II, Hannover, 1890, 184–90.

Die Conversio Bagoariorum et Carantanorum und der Brief des Erzbischofs Theotmar von Salzburg, ed. F. Lošek, *MGH, Studien und Texte*, vol. XV, Hanover, 1997.

Cosmae Pragensis Chronica Boemorum, ed. B. Bretholz, *MGH SRG* n.s. II, Berlin, 1923.

Crescente fide (Bavarian recension), ed. J. Emler, *FRB*, vol. I, 183–90.

Daim, F. 1996, 'Archäologie und Ethnizität. Awaren, Karantanen, Mährer im 8. Jahrhundert', *Österreichische Zeitschrift f. Geschichtswissenschaft* 7, 479–97.

Dittrich, Z. R. 1962, *Christianity in Great Moravia*, Groningen.
Dujčev I., A. Kirmasova, and A. Paunova 1983, *Kirilometodievska bibliografia 1940–1980*, Sofia.
Dvornik, F. 1970, *Byzantine Missions Among the Slavs*, New Brunswick, NJ.
Fiala, Z. 1960, 'K otázce funkce našich listin do konce 12. století', *Sborník Prací Brněnské University* C 7, 5–34.
Fiala, Z. 1962, 'Dva kritické příspěvky ke starým dějinám českým', *Sborník Historický* 9, 5–65.
Fiala, Z. 1967, 'Die Organisation der Kirche in Přemyslidenstaat des 10.–13. Jahrhunderts', in *Siedlung und Verfassung Böhmens in der Frühzeit*, ed. F. Graus and H. Ludat, Wiesbaden, 133–43.
FRB: Fontes rerum Bohemicarum, ed. J. Emler, I, Prague, 1873; II, Prague, 1874.
Fritze, W. H. 1982, 'Corona regni Bohemiae. Die Entstehung des böhmischen Königtums im 12. Jahrhundert im Widerspiel von Kaiser, Fürst und Adel', in W. H. Fritze, *Frühzeit zwischen Ostsee und Donau. Ausgewählte Beiträge zum geschichtlichen Werden im östlichen Mitteleuropa vom 6. bis zum 13. Jahrhundert*, ed. L. Kuchenbuch and W. Schich, Berlin (Germania Slavica, 3), 209–96.
Frolík, J. 2000, 'Pražský hrad v raném středověku', in *Přemyslovský stát kolem roku 1000. Na pamět knížete Boleslava II.*, ed. L. Polanský, J. Sláma and D. Třeštík, Prague, 101–20.
Frolík, J. *et al.* 2000, *Nejstarší sakrální architektura Pražského hradu*, Prague.
Fuit in provincia Bohemorum (Vita S. Ludmilae), ed. V. Chaloupecký, in *Prameny X. století legendy Kristiánovy o svatém Václavu a svaté Ludmile (Svatováclavský sborník* II/2), Prague, 1939, 459–75.
Galuška, L. and L. Poláček, forthcoming, 'Církevní architektura v centrální oblasti velkomoravského státu', in *České země v raném středověku*.
Gasparini, E. 1962, 'L'orizonte culturale del "mir"', *Ricerche Slavistiche* 10, 3–21.
Geographus Bavarus, Descriptio civitatum et regionum ad septentrionalem plagam Danubii, ed. L. E. Havlík, *MMFH*, vol. III, 285–91.
Gieysztor, A. 1994, 'Politische Heilige im hochmittelalterlichen Polen und Böhmen', in *Politik und Heiligenverehrung im Hochmittelalter*, ed. J. Peterson, Sigmaringen (Vorträge und Forschungen 42), 324–41.
Graus, F. 1969, 'Böhmen zwischen Bayern und Sachsen. Zur böhmischen Kirchengeschichte des 10. Jahrhunderts', *Historica* 17, 5–42.
Graus, F. 1980, 'St. Adalbert und St. Wenzel. Zur Funktion der mittelalterlichen Heiligenverehrung in Böhmen', in *Europa Slavica-Europa Orientalis. Festschrift für Herbert Ludat*, Berlin (Giessener Abhandlungen zur Agrar- und Wirtschaftsforschung des europäischen Ostens, 100), 205–31.
Gumpold, *Vita Venceslai, FRB*, vol. I, 146–66.
Hahn, W. 1977, 'Herzog Heinrich II. von Bayern und die Anfänge der böhmischen Münzprägung', *Wiadomości Numizmatyczne* 21, 162–7.
Hahn, W. 1978–9, 'Blagota coniunx und Emma Regina – einige Randbemerkun zu den ältesten böhmischen Herzogsmünzen', *Jahrbuch für Numismatik und Geldgeschichte* 28–9, 65–80.

Hahn, W. 1981–2, 'Die administrativen Grundlagen der Typenvariation in der älteren bayerichen Münzprägung und ihre Signifikanz für die Datierung der ersten böhmischen Herzogsmünzen', *Jahrbuch für Numismatik und Geldgeschichte* 31–2, 103–15.

Hahn, W. 2002, 'Die älteste böhmische Münzprägung Boleslaus II. – eine Materialzusammentsellung', in *Moneta Medievalis. Studia numizmatyczne i historyczne ofiarowane Profesorowi Stanislawowi Suchodolskiemu w 65. rocznicę urodzin*, Warsaw, 379–92.

Hásková, J. 1974, 'K státní ideologii raně feudálních Čech', *Numismatické Listy* 29, 71–7.

Hásková, J. 1975, *Česká mince doby románské*, Cheb.

Hauptová, Z. 1998, 'Církevněslovanské písemnictví v přemyslovských Čechách', in *Jazyk a literatura v historické perspektivě*, Ústí n. Labem, 5–42.

Havlík, L. E. 1965, 'The Relationship between the Great Moravian Empire and the Papal Court in the Years 880–885 AD', *Byzantinoslavica* 26, 100–22.

Havlík, L. E. 1969, 'Der päpstliche Schutz und die slawischen Völker. Zur Problematik der den Herrschern in den Ländern Südost- und Osteuropa gewährten päpstlichen patronatus-protectio', *Annales Instituti Slavici* II/1, 10–32.

Hilsch, P. 1969, *Die Bischöfe von Prag in der frühen Stauferzeit. Ihre Stellung zwischen reichs- und Landesgewalt von Daniel I. (1148–1167) bis Heinrich (1182–1197)*, Munich.

Hilsch, P. 1972, 'Der Bischof von Prag und das Reich in sächsischer Zeit', *Deutsches Archiv für Erforschung des Mittelalters* 28, 1–41.

Historia episcoporum Pataviensium et ducum Bavarie, MGH SS XXV, 617–19.

Hledíková, Z. 1972, 'Pražská metropolitní kapitula, její samospráva a postavení do doby husitské', *Sborník Historický* 19, 5–48.

Hledíková, Z. 1997, 'Das Studium von mittelalterlichen kirchlichen Korporationen in Böhmen und Mähren', *Quaestiones Medii Aevi Novae* 2, 61–9.

Holtzmann, R. 1918, 'Die Urkunde Heinrichs IV. für Prag vom Jahre 1086', *Archiv für Urkundenforschung* 6, 177–93.

Horák, J. V. and L. Mucha, eds. 1976, *Regni Bohemiae mappa historica*, Prague (repr. of F. Palacký and J. Kalousek, *Historická mapa Čech rozdělených na archidiakonaty a dekanaty 14ho století*, Prague, 1874).

Hrubý, F. 1916, 'Církevní zřízení v Čechách a na Moravě od X. do konce XII. století a jeho poměr ke státu', *Český Časopis Historický* 22, 17–53, 257–87, 385–421.

Hrubý, F. 1917, 'Církevní zřízení v Čechách a na Moravě od X. do konce XII. století a jeho poměr ke státu', *Český Časopis Historický* 23, 38–73.

Huber, A. K. 1973a, 'Das Verhältnis der Bischöfe von Prag und Olmütz zueinander', *Archiv für Kirchengeschichte von Böhmen-Mähren-Schlesien* 3, 58–75.

Huber, A. K. 1973b, 'Die Metropole Mainz und die böhmischen Länder', *Archiv für Kirchengeschichte von Böhmen-Mähren-Schlesien* 3, 24–57.

Ibrahim ibn Yaqub, *Relacja Ibrahima ibn Ja'kuba z podróży do krajów slowiańskich w przekazie al-Bekriego*, ed. T. Kowalski, *MPH* n.s. I, Cracow, 1946.

John VIII, *Industriae tuae, CDB*, vol. I, 18–21, no. 24.

Kadlec, J. 1968, *Svatý Prokop*, Řím.

Kalhous, D. 2004, 'Záhadné počátky pražského biskupství', in *Evropa a Čechy na konci středověku*, ed. E. Doležalová, Prague, 195–208.

Kanovník vyšehradský, ed. J. Emler, *FRB*, vol. II, 201–37.

Kejř, J. 1994, 'Böhmen zur Zeit Friedrich Barbarossa', in *Kaiser Friedrich Barbarossa. Landesausbau – Aspekte seiner Politik – Wirkung*, ed. E. Engel and B. Töpfer, Weimar, 101–13.

Klanica, Z. 1985, 'Mikulčice-Kláštěřisko', *Památky Archeologické* 86, 474–539.

Klanica, Z. 1986, 'Religion und Kult, ihr Reflex in archäologischen Quellen', in *Grossmähren und die Anfänge der tschechoslowakischen Staatlichkeit*, ed. J. Poulík and B. Chropový, Prague, 120–58.

Klanica, Z. 1987, 'Padenie avarskoj deržavy v Podunavje', in *Etnosocial'naja i političeskaja struktura rannefeodal'nych slavjanskich gosudarstv i narodnostej*, ed. G. G. Litavrin, Moscow, 74–82.

Konzal, V. ed. 1976, *Staroslověnské legendy českého původu*, Prague.

Konzal, V. 1998, 'Církevněslovanská literatura slepá ulička na prahu české kultury?', in *Speculum medii aevi. Zrcadlo středověku*, Prague, 150–8.

Kostílková, M. 2000, 'Gumpold von Mantua. Vita des heiligen Wenzel', in Wieczorek and Hinz 2000, vol. I, 280–1.

Kouřil, P. 1994, *Slovanské osídlení českého Slezska*, Brno and Český Těšín, 71–167.

Kouřil, P. 2003, 'Staří Madaři a Morava z pohledu archeologie', in *Dějiny ve věku nejistot*, ed. J. Klápště, E. Plešková and J. Žemlička, Prague, 110–46.

Krumphanzlová, Z. 1961, 'K otázce vampyrismu na slovanských pohřebištích', *Památky Archeologické* 52, 544–9.

Krumphanzlová, Z. 1966, 'Der Ritus der slawischen Skelettfriedhöfe der mittleren und jüngeren Burgwallzeit in Böhmen', *Památky Archeologické* 57, 277–327.

Krumphanzlová, Z. 1990, 'Svědectví náboženského synkretismu na pohřebištích doby hradištní v Čechách', *Archeologické Rozhledy* 42, 362–8.

Krumphanzlová, Z. 1997, 'Kultovní místo na pohřebišti v Lahovicích', in *Život v archeologii středověku*, ed. J. Kubková, J. Klápště, M. Ježek, P. Meduna *et al.*, Prague, 394–401.

Krzemieńska, B. 1987, 'Die Rotunde in Znojmo und die Stellung Mährens in böhmischen Přemyslidenstaat', *Historica* 27, 5–59.

Krzemieńska, B. 1999, *Břetislav I. Čechy a střední Evropa v prvé polovině XI. století*, 2nd edn, Prague.

Labuda, G. 1994, 'Czeskie chrześcianstwo na Śląsku i w Małopolsce w X i XI wieku', in *Chrystianizacja Polski poludniowej*, Cracow, 94–6.

Lalik, T. 1977, 'Targ', *Slownik Starożytności Slowiańskich* 6, 25.

Letopis Jarlocha, opata kláštera milevského, ed. J. Emler, *FRB*, vol. II, 461–516.

Letopis Vincentia, kanovníka pražského, ed. J. Emler, *FRB*, vol. II, 407–60.

Letter of Pope Stephen V to Svatopluk in 885, *CDB* I, 22–6, no. 26.

Ludvíkovský, J. 1973–4, 'Latinské legendy českého středověku', *Sborník Prací Filosofické Fakulty Brněnské University* E 18/19, 267–87.

Lutovský, M. 1994, 'Kolínský knížecí hrob: ad fontes', *Sborník Národního Muzea v Praze, Řada A – Historie* 48, 37–76.

Lutovský, M. 1997, 'Brandbestattungsritus im frühmittelalterlichen Böhmen: drei Überlegungen', in *Život v archeologii středověku*, ed. J. Kubková, J. Klápště, M. Ježek, P. Meduna *et al.*, Prague, 433–8.

Lutovský, M. 1999, 'Frühmittelalterliche Hügelgräber in Südböhmen', *Archäologische Arbeitsgemeinschaft Ostbayern/West- und Südböhmen* 8, Treffen, Rahden/Westf., 173–82.

Lutovský, M. 2001, *Encyklopedie slovanské archeologie v Čechách, na Moravě a ve Slezsku*, Prague.

Lutovský, M. and K. Tomková 1993, 'K problematice nejmladších raně středověkých mohyl v Čechách – pohřebiště u Hlohoviček', *Mediaevalia Archaeologica Bohemica, Památky Archeologické – Supplementum* 2, 86–106.

Macháček, J. 2000, 'Die heiligen Bezirke in Pohansko bei Břeclav – ein Beitrag zur Kenntniss des Heidentums und des Christentums der mitteleuropäischen Slawen im frühen Mittelalter', in Wieczorek and Hinz 2000, vol. I, 405–6.

Mareš, F. V. 2000, 'Slovanská liturgie sv. Petra', in F. V. Mareš, *Cyrilometodějská tradice a slavistika*, Prague, 166–87.

Marsina, R. 1970, 'Povolenie slovanskej liturgie na Velkej Morave', *Historický Časopis* 18, 4–16.

Marsina, R. 1972, 'La Lutte pour la liturgie slave en Grande Moravie', *Studia Historica Slovaca* 6, 47–68.

Marsina, R. 1985, *Metodov boj*, Bratislava.

Matzke, J. 1969, *Das Bistum Olmütz im Hochmittelalter von Heinrich Zdik bis Bruno von Schaumburg, 1126–1281*, Königstein-Taunus.

Medek, V. 1971, *Osudy moravské církve do konce 14. století, I díl dějin olomoucké arcidiecéze*, Prague.

Merhautová, A. 1971, *Raně středověká architektura v Čechách*, Prague.

Merhautová, A. 1992, 'Der St. Wenzelshelm', *Umění* 30, 169–79.

Merhautová, A. ed. 1994, *Katedrála sv. Víta v Praze*, Prague.

Merhautová, A. and P. Sommer 2000, 'Christliche Architektur und Kunst im böhmischen Staat um das Jahr 1000', in Wieczorek and Hinz 2000, vol. I, 411–17.

Merhautová, A. and P. Spunar 2006, *Kodex vyšehradský*, Prague.

Merhautová, A. and D. Třeštík 1983, 'Spezifische Züge der böhmischen Kunst im 12. Jahrhundert', in *Architektur des Mittelalters. Funktion und Gestalt*, ed. F. Möbius and E. Schubert, Weimar, 105–40.

Merhautová, A. and D. Třeštík 1984, *Románské umění v Čechách a na Moravě*, Prague.

Merhautová-Livorová, A. 1972, *Bazilika sv. Jiří na pražském hradě*, Prague.

Merhautová-Livorová, A. 1983, 'Ikonografie znojemského přemyslovského cyklu', *Umění* 31, 18–27.

Měřínský, Z. 1986, 'Morava v 10. století ve světle archeologických nálezů', *Památky Archeologické* 77, 18–80.

Měřínský, Z. 2002, *České země od příchodu Slovanů po Velkou Moravu* I, Prague.

Milde, W. 1972, *Mittelalterliche Handschriften der Herzog-August-Bibliothek*, Sonderband I, Frankfurt a/M.

MMFH: Magnae Moraviae Fontes Historici, ed. L. E. Havlík *et al.*, vols. I–V. Prague and Brno, 1966–77.

Možajeva, Je. 1980, *Bibliografija po kirilo-mefodievskoj problematike 1945–1974 gg*, Moscow.

Nechvátal, B. 1992, 'Vyšehrad a archeologie', in *Královský Vyšehrad. Sborník příspěvků k 900. výročí úmrtí prvního českého krále Vratislava II. (1061–1092)*, ed. B. Nechvátal, Prague, 112–41.

Nejstarší česká rýmovaná kronika t. ř. Dalimila, ed. B. Havránek and J. Daňhelka, Prague, 1957.

Němec, I. 1992, 'Nejstarší české názvy kostela', *Slavia* 61, 61–5.

Niederle, L. 1924, *Život starých Slovanů. Víra a náboženství*, 2nd edn, Prague (Slovanské starožitnosti, II.1).

Nohejlová-Prátová, E. 1955, *Krása české mince*, Prague.

Notae de episcopis Pataviensibus, MGH SS XXV, 623–4.

Nově zjištěný rukopis legendy Crescente fide a jeho význam pro datování Kristiána, ed. J. Ludvíkovský, *Listy Filologické* 81, 1958, 58–63.

Novotný, V. 1912, 'Vratislav II. a slovanská liturgie', *Časopis pro Moderní Filologii* 2, 289–390.

Novotný, V. 1928, *České dějiny* I, 3, Prague.

Nový, R. 1972, *Přemyslovský stát 11. a 12. století*, Prague.

Nový, R. 1976, 'K počátkům feudální monarchie v Čechách I. (Sigillum commune regni)', *Časopis Národního Muzea* 145, 144–64.

Othloni Vita s. Wolfkangi, ed. G. Waitz, *MGH SS* IV, 377–428.

Pavlíková, M. 1951, *O oltářních autentikách biskupa Daniela I*, Věstník.

Petráň, Z. 1998a, 'Mince biskupa Vojtěcha', in Třeštík and Žemlička 1998, 55–78.

Petráň, Z. 1998b, *První české mince*, Prague.

Petráň, Z. 2003, 'Jaké mince vlastně viděl na pražském trhu Ibrahím ibn Jákúb? Několik poznámek k počátkům českého mincovnictví', in *Dějiny ve věku nejistot*, ed. J. Klápště, E. Plešková and J. Žemlička, Prague, 209–19.

Pleszczyński, A. 2002, *Vyšehrad. Rezidence českých panovníků. Studie o rezidenci panovníka raného středověku na příkladu českého Vyšehradu*, Prague.

Pohl, W. 1994, 'Tradition, Ethnogenese und literarische Gestaltung. Eine Zwischenbilanz', in *Ethnogenese und Überlieferung*, ed. K. Brunner and B. Merta, Vienna and Munich (Veröffentlichungen des Instituts für Österreichische Geschichtsforschung 31), 9–26.

Profantová, N. 1997, 'Blatnicko-mikulčický horizont v Čechách. Současný stav a problémy', in *Ślask i Czechy a kultura wielkomorawska*, ed. K. Wachowski, Wrocław, 85–94.

Profantová, N. and M. Profant 2000, *Encyklopedie slovanských bohů a mýtů*, Prague.

Protocollum visitationis archidiaconatus Pragensis annis 1379–1382 per Paulum de Janowicz archidiaconum Pragensem factae, ed. I. Hlaváček and Z. Hledíková, Prague, 1973.

'První staroslověnská legenda o sv. Václlavu', ed. J. Vajs, *Sborník staroslověnských literárních památek o sv. Václavu a sv. Lidmile*, Prague, 1929, 29–43.

Radoměrský, P. and V. Ryneš 1958, 'Společná úcta sv. Václava a sv. Vojtěcha, zvláště na českých mincích a její historický význam', *Numismatické Listy* 13, 35–48.

Ratkoš, P. 1974, 'Die slawische liturgische Sprache im Lichte der päpstlichen Politik in den Jahren 869–880', *Studia Historica Slovaca* 7, 185–204.

Das Register Gregors VII, ed. E. Caspar, *MGH Epistolae selectae*, vol. II, 2nd edn, Hanover, 1955.

Reichertová, K., E. Bláhová, V. Dvořáčková and V. Huňáček, eds. 1988, *Sázava*, Prague.

Schmid, H. F. 1938, *Die rechtlichen Grundlagen der Pfarrorganisation auf westslavischem Boden und ihre Entwicklung während des Mittelalters*, Weimar.

Schmidt, R. 1978, 'Die Einsetzung der böhmischen Herzöge auf den Thron in Prag', in *Nationes*, vol. I, *Aspekte der Nationenbildung im Mittelalter*, ed. H. Beumann and W. Schröder, Sigmaringen, 439–63.

Schramm, P. E. 1968, 'Böhmen und das Regnum. Die Verleihungen der Königswürde an die Herzöge von Böhmen (1085/86, 1158, 1198/1203)', in *Adel und Kirche. G. Tellenbach zum 65. Geburtstag*, ed. J. Fleckenstein and K. Schmid, Freiburg, Basel and Vienna, 346–64.

Šebánek, J. and S. Dušková 1956, 'Česká listina doby přemyslovské', *Sborník Archivních Prací* 6, seš. 1, 136–211, seš. 2, 99–160.

Sklenář, K. and J. Sláma 1976, 'Nález slovanských kostrových hrobů v bývalé Královské zahradě Pražského hradu v roce 1837', *Archeologické Rozhledy* 28, 659–65.

Sláma, J. 1977, 'Svatojiřské kostely na raně středověkých hradištích v Čechách', *Archeologické Rozhledy* 29, 269–80.

Sláma, J. 1987, 'K počátkům hradské organizace v Čechách', in *Typologie raně feudálních slovanských států*, Prague, 175–90.

Sláma, J. 1988a, 'Příspěvek ke kulturním dějinám raně středověkých Čech', *Sborník Kruhu Přátel Muzea Hlavního Města Prahy* 1, 65–75.

Sláma, J. 1988b, *Střední Čechy v raném středověku III: Archeologie o počátcích přemyslovského státu*, Prague.

Sláma, J. 1995, 'Slavníkovci – významná či okrajová záležitost českých dějin 10. století?' *Archeologické Rozhledy* 47, 182–224.

Smetánka, Z., L. Hrdlička and M. Bajerová 1973, 'Výzkum slovanského pohřebiště za Jízdárnou na Pražském hradě', *Archeologické Rozhledy* 25, 265–70.

Smetánka, Z., L. Hrdlička and M. Bajerová 1974, 'Výzkum slovanského pohřebiště za Jízdárnou Pražského hradu v roce 1973', *Archeologické Rozhledy* 26, 386–405, 433–8.

Šolle, M. 1966, *Stará Kouřim a projevy velkomoravské hmotné kultury v Čechách*, Prague.

Sommer, P. 1991, 'První dvě století benediktinských klášterů v Čechách', *Studia Mediaevalia Pragensia* 2, 75–100.

Sommer, P. 1994, 'Early Mediaeval Monasteries in Bohemia', in *25 Years of Archaeological Research in Bohemia, Památky Archeologické – Supplémentum* 1, Prague, 206–11.

Sommer, P. 1996, 'Zum Stand der monastischen Archäologie in Böhmen', *Beiträge zur Mittelalterarchäologie in Österreich* 12, 169–77.

Sommer, P. 2000a, 'Die Christianisierung Böhmens aufgrund archäologischer, kunsthistorischer und schriftlicher Quellen', in Wieczorek and Hinz 2000, vol. I, 401–5.

Sommer, P. 2000b, 'Heidnische und christliche Normen im Konflikt-Die Vorstellungswelt der böhmischen Gesellschaft im frühen Mittelalter', in *Prozesse der Normbildung und Normveränderung im mittelalterlichen Europa*, ed. D. Ruhe and K.-H. Spieß, Stuttgart, 161–86.

Sommer, P. 2001, *Začátky křesťanství v Čechách (kapitoly z dějin raně středověké duchovní kultury)*, Prague.

Sommer, P. forthcoming, *Svatý Prokop*.

Špaček, J. and I. Boháčová 2000, 'Výsledky záchranného archeologického výzkumu v okolí baziliky sv. Václava ve Staré Boleslavi', *Archaeologia Historica* 25, 307–22.

Štěpková, J. 1957, 'Das Wort Kinšár im Reisebericht des Ibrahim b. Ja'kub', *Archiv Orientální* 25, 38–56.

Suchodolski, S. 1973–4, 'Zur Frage der Anfänge der böhmischen Münzprägung', *Numismatický Sborník* 13, 75–84.

Thomson, F. J. 1992, 'SS. Cyril and Methodius and a Mythical Western Heresy: Trilinguism', *Annalecta Bollandiana* 110, 67–122.

Tkadlčík, V. 1969, 'Datum příchodu slovanských apoštolů na Moravu', *Slavia* 38, 542–51.

Třeštík, D. 1968, *Kosmova kronika. Studie k počátkům českého dějepisectví a politického myšlení*, Prague.

Třeštík, D. 1971, 'K sociální struktuře přemyslovských Čech. Kosmas o knížecím vlastnictví půdy a lidí', *Československý Časopis Historický* 19, 537–67.

Třeštík, D. 1978, 'Die ältesten Prager Annalen', *Studia Źródłoznawcze* 23, 1–37.

Třeštík, D. 1986, 'Bořivoj und Svatopluk. Die Entstehung des böhmischen Staates und Grossmähren', in *Grossmähren und die Anfänge der tschechoslowakischen Staatlichkeit*, ed. J. Poulík and B. Chropový, Prague, 311–44.

Třeštík, D. 1988, 'Mír a dobrý rok. Státní ideologie raného přemyslovského státu mezi křest anstvím a "pohanstvím"', *Folia Historica Bohemica* 12, 23–41.

Třeštík, D. 1991, 'Kdy zanikla Velká Morava?', *Studia Medievalia Pragensia* 2, 7–27.

Třeštík, D. 1995, 'The Baptism of the Czech Princes in 845 and the Christianization of the Slavs', *Historica* 2, n.s., 7–59.

Třeštík, D. 1997, *Počátky Přemyslovců. Vstup Čechů do dějin (530–935)*, Prague.

Třeštík, D. 1998a, 'Großmähren, Pasau und die Ungarn um das Jahr 900', *Byzantinoslavica* 59, 137–60.

Třeštík, D. 1998b, 'Svatý Vojtěch a formování střední Evropy', in Třeštík and Žemlička 1998, 81–108.

Třeštík, D. 1999, 'Přemyslovec Kristián', *Archeologické Rozhledy* 51, 602–13.

Třeštík, D. 2000a, 'Der Mönch Chritian, Bruder Boleslavs II', in Wieczorek and Hinz 2000, vol. I, 424–5.

Třeštík, D. 2000b, 'Die Gründung des Prager und des mährischen Bistums', in Wieczorek and Hinz 2000, vol. I, 407–10.

Třeštík, D. 2000c, 'Von Svatopluk zu Bolesław Chrobry. Die Entstehung Mitteleuropas aus der Kraft des Tatsächlichen und aus einer Idee', in *The Neighbours of Poland in the 10th Century*, ed. P. Urbańczyk, Warsaw, 111–45.

Třeštík, D. 2001a, '"Eine große Stadt der Slawen namens Prag". Staaten und Sklaven in Mitteleuropa im 10. Jahrhundert', in Sommer 2001, 93–138.

Třeštík, D. 2001b, *Vznik Velké Moravy. Moravané, Čechové a střední Evropa v letech 781–871*, Prague.

Třeštík, D. 2003a, 'Moravský biskup roku 976', in *Ad vitam et honorem. Prof. J. Mezníkovi k pětasedmdesátým narozeninám*, Brno, 211–20.

Třeštík, D. 2003b, *Mýty kmene Čechů. Tři studie ke 'starým pověstem českým'*, Prague.

Třeštík, D. 2004, 'K založení pražského biskupství v letech 968–976: pražská a řezenská tradice', in *Vlast a rodný kraj v díle historika*, ed. J. Pánek, Prague, 179–96.

Třeštík, D. forthcoming, *Slawische Liturgie und Schrifttum im Böhmen des 10. Jahrhunderts. Vorstellungen und Wirklichkeit*.

Třeštík, D. and B. Krzemieńska 1979, 'Wirtschaftiche Grundlagen des frühmittelalterlichen Staates in Mitteleuropa (Böhmen, Polen, Ungarn im 10.-11. Jahrhundert)', *Acta Poloniae Historica* 40, 5–31.

Třeštík, D. and J. Žemlička eds. 1998, *Svatý Vojtěch: Čechové a Evropa*, Prague.

Turek, R. 1981, *Libice nad Cidlinou. Monumentální stavby vnitřního hradiska (Sborník Národního muzea v Praze, řada A-Historie, XXXV)*.

Vajs, J. ed. 1929, *Sborník staroslovanských literárních památek o sv. Václavu a sv. Lidmile*, Prague.

Vaněček, V. 1933–9, *Základy právního postavení klášterů a klášterního velkostatku ve starém českém státě (12.–15. stol.)*, Prague.

Vavřínek, V. 1978, 'The Introduction of the Slavonic Liturgy and the Byzantine Missionary Policy', in *Beiträge zur byzantinischen Geschichte im 9.-11. Jahrhundert*, ed. V. Vavřínek, Prague, 255–81.

Vavřínek, V. 1986, 'Die historische Bedeutung der byzantinischen Mission in Grossmähren', in *Grossmähren und die Anfänge der tschechoslowakischen Staatlichkeit*, ed. J. Poulík and B. Chropový, Prague, 245–79.

Vavřínek, V. 2000, 'Mission in Mähren – zwischen dem lateinischen Westen und Byzanz', in Wieczorek and Hinz 2000, vol. I, 304–10.

Wachowski, K. 1992, *Kultura karolińska i Słowiańszczyzna Zachodnia*, Wrocław.

Warnke, C. 1980, 'Ursachen und Voraussetzungen der Schenkung Polens an den heiligen Petrus', in *Europa Slavica – Europa Orientalis. Festschrift f. H. Ludat z. 70. Geburtstag*, ed. K.-D. Grothusen and K. Zernack, Berlin, 127–77.

Widukind, *Res gestae Saxonicae*, ed. P. Hirsch and H. F. Lohmann, *MGH SRG*, Hanover, 1935.

Wieczorek, A. and H.-M. Hinz, eds. 2000, *Europas Mitte um 1000. Beiträge zur Geschichte, Kunst und Archäologie*, 3 vols., Stuttgart.

Wolverton, L. 1998, 'From Duke to King: Transforming the Iconography of Ruler-ship in the Medieval Czech Lands', *Majestas* 6, 51–77.

Wolverton, L. 2001, *Hastening Toward Prague: Power and Society in the Medieval Czech Lands*, Philadelphia.

Zemek, M. 1988–9, 'Das Olmützer Domkapitel. Seine Entstehung und Entwick-lung bis 1600', *Archiv für Kirchengeschichte von Böhmen-Mähren-Schlesien* 9, 66–86; 10, 58–88.

Žemlička, J. 1990, *Přemysl Otakar I. Panovník, stát a česká společnost na prahu vrcholného feudalismu*, Prague.

Žemlička, J. 1991, '"Politický kalendář" přemyslovských Čech', *Český Časopis Historický* 89, 31–47.

Žemlička, J. 1992, '"Moravané" v časném středověku', *Český Časopis Historický* 90, 17–32.

Žemlička, J. 1993a, '"Omnes Bohemi". Od svatováclavské čeledi ke středověké šlechtě', *Medievalia Historica Bohemica* 3, 111–33.

Žemlička, J. 1993b 'Te ducem, te iudicem, te rectorem. Sněmovní shromáždění v časně středověkých Čechách – kontinuita či diskontinuita?', *Český Časopis Historický* 91, 369–84.

Žemlička, J. 1997, *Čechy v době knížecí (1034–1198)*, Prague.

Žemlička, J. 2001, '"Decimae trium provinciarum" pro klášter v Břevnově (K hmotnému zajištění nejstarších klášterních fundací v Čechách)', in *Ludzie, Kosciól, Wierzenia. Studia z dziejów kultury i spoleczenstwa Europy Środkowej*, Warsaw, 125–33.

Žemlička, J. 2002, *Počátky Čech královských 1198–1253. Proměna státu a společnosti*, Prague.

Žemlička, J. 2003a, 'České 13. století: "privatizace státu"', *Český Časopis Historický* 101, 509–41.

Žemlička, J. 2003b, 'Němci, německé právo a transformační změny 13. století', *Archaeologia Historica* 28, 33–46.

Žitije Konstantina, ed. R. Večerka, *MMFH*, vol. II, 57–115.

Žitije Mefodija, ed. R. Večerka, *MMFH*, vol. II, 134–63.

CHAPTER 7

Poland

Przemysław Urbańczyk and Stanisław Rosik

1. BEFORE CHRISTIANITY: RELIGION AND POWER

A Polish polity appears in the narrative records in the seventh decade of the tenth century, ruled by Prince Mieszko I (before 965–92). He decided to convert in 966 and with this act entered the geopolitical stage of central Europe. The names 'Poles' (*Polani, Poleni, Poloni*) and 'Poland' (*terra Polanorum, Polenia, Polonia*) appear in the written sources about ten years after his death.[1] For the tenth century, therefore, it is better to use the description 'Piast state' rather than 'Poland', although even this conventional term is merely a matter of convenience since Piast as the founder of the dynasty is mentioned for the first time in the second decade of the twelfth century.

The oldest reference to Mieszko's state may be found in the report of the Jewish merchant Ibrahim ibn Yaqub of Tortosa who in about 965 travelled from Spain to Magdeburg and Prague where he collected information. He called Mieszko the 'king of the north' and claimed that his state was the largest in the Slavic area. Ibrahim focused on the military power of Mieszko and on the wealth of natural resources in his country. About 973 Widukind of Corvey also called Mieszko *rex Misica/Misaca*.[2] Later, however, Thietmar and the Gallus Anonymus treated Mieszko only as *dux*. Apparently, for Widukind the title 'king' indicated sovereign rulers elected by their own people according to the early local tradition. Half a century after Widukind, Thietmar clearly distinguished 'princes' from anointed 'kings' whose coronation was confirmed by the emperor and the pope.[3]

Widukind's interpretation was based on the *saxonica interpraetatio* of Slavic reality: his use of the title *rex* suggested that Mieszko had authority

---

[1] Canaparius, chap. 25; Bruno of Querfurt, *S. Adalberti . . . vita altera*, chaps. 10, 30; Thietmar of Merseburg V.23, 34; VI.10, 19; VIII.31.

[2] Widukind III.69.

[3] Thus Widukind treated Henry I's decision to refuse anointing and coronation as the testimony of humility, but Thietmar condemned it (Erdmann 1938; Beumann 1950, 261; Ott 2001).

15. Medieval Poland

over all the peoples. It is therefore important to discuss how the Polish state emerged: did it develop as a result of the evolution of earlier institutions or did it appear in contradiction to earlier power structures? Currently the second hypothesis is increasingly popular. Some authors even question the existence of the 'Polanie' whose territory was formerly treated as the cradle of Poland.[4] Such an interpretation overcomes the difficulties of explaining the absence of this allegedly pre-Polish 'tribe' in contemporary written sources.[5]

The origins of the main centres of the Piast domain in Greater Poland, such as Giecz, Gniezno, Ostrów Lednicki and Poznań have been dated to the mid-tenth century, that is, to the reign of the first historical monarch,

---

[4] E.g. Urbańczyk 2000.

[5] Other accounts of territorial organizations include *Ditzike* on *Wisla* mentioned by Constantine Porphyrogenitus (*De administrando imperio*, 33) and *Wisle lond* in King Alfred's version of Orosius.

Mieszko I. However, recent excavations and the re-evaluation of earlier studies have shown that Giecz and Ostrów Lednicki have roots going back to the ninth century.[6] This may suggest the continuity of the process of building the dynasty's political domination in its homeland where it had started its career before Mieszko and from which it steadily expanded its power over an ever larger territory. Revolutionary changes imposed by a centralizing power may be indicated by the discontinuity of many local power centres in Greater Poland, where almost all earth-and-wood strongholds were destroyed during the Piasts' expansion in the tenth century.[7] The oldest and extensively discussed account of a monarchical structure is contained in the hagiography of St Methodius where 'the mighty prince of Wisle' is said to have been forcibly baptized by the Moravians sometime in the late ninth century. This minute piece of information gave rise to theories whose aim was to reconstruct an alleged state of the *Vislane* who are mentioned in the *Geographus Bavarus* in the mid-ninth century. In fact, we cannot say what real power the mysterious 'prince of Wisle' exercised and whether any principality existed so early in the south-west part of Lesser Poland.

The proximity of the region of Lesser Poland to Moravia may have resulted in an early development of local power centres,[8] which is indicated by the strongholds that were already built there by local rulers in the late eighth century.[9] The fact that the subsequent expansion of the Piast state into Lesser Poland was not followed by the destruction of these local political–military centres, the strongholds, may indicate that the incorporation of the region was more a matter of alliance than of conquest. This may have been the reason for calling this part of the Piast state 'Lesser Poland'. Its importance is further attested by the location of the royal seat in Kraków when the Polish state was restored after the crisis of the 1030s. At the beginning of the twelfth century Gallus Anonymus listed three *sedes regni principales* (Kraków, Wrocław and Sandomierz) in south Poland.[10] Some of these centres eventually developed their own local traditions connected to the alleged eponymous founders: *Krak* for Kraków, and *Sudomir* for Sandomierz.

The oldest tradition of the *origines* of Poland, however, is connected to Gniezno and Greater Poland. Gallus Anonymus located the predecessors of Mieszko there: Popiel, Piast (as the son of Chościsko), Siemowit, Lestek and Siemomysł. In his chronicle written in the second decade of the twelfth century he tells the story of a simple farmer, Piast, starting the dynasty by

[6] Kurnatowska 2004a; 2004b.   [7] E.g. Kurnatowska 1998; Kurnatowscy 2003, 174.
[8] Kurnatowscy 2003, 169.   [9] E.g. Gancarski 2003, 174.   [10] Gallus II.8.

taking over political power from the former 'prince' Popiel.[11] The reliability of this story has been discussed for almost 200 years. Some historians have treated the list of the five ancestors of Mieszko I as historical fact, whereas others have accepted only Siemowit, Lestek and Siemomysł as real persons, while seeing Piast, his father Chościsko and Popiel as legendary constructs. In the first half of the twentieth century the tendency was to treat the entire list as an invention, since there is no independent confirmation of any of the names in earlier or contemporary sources. According to an interpretation using structural and functional analysis, the story is a literary realization of the universal Indo-European scheme of mythical origins, though probably based on a vernacular tradition.[12]

Whatever the truth was, these ancestors of Mieszko I functioned as popular founders of the state and society. Despite their paganism they were accepted as positive heroes by the medieval chroniclers who attempted to include the legendary progenitors of the Piast dynasty in the story of the Polish *praeparatio evangelica*.[13] About ninety years later Master Vincent introduced biblical or ancient Roman and Greek motifs and more 'historical' figures in order to deepen the time perspective of the dynasty's origins. Thus, he listed Krakus/Grakhus, Wanda, Lestek I, Lestek II and Lestek III before Popiel's reign. This fabulous story combined elements of the local Lesser Poland tradition with Gallus's account in order to stress the capital role of Kraków, and of Lesser Poland as the cradle of all Poland.

Master Vincent influenced the later medieval tradition of Polish origins much more than did Gallus Anonymus. In subsequent variants of the story further new motifs were added, which were often inspired by geopolitical circumstances. According to Banaszkiewicz, a comparative study of Slavic and Indo-European parallels indicates the presence in Master Vincent's story of basic elements of the myths of the foundation of society *cum lege et rege*.[14] The universal framework of these narratives contains symbolic structures of interpretation, while princely or royal power was linked to a sacred mountain or hill as the mythical centre of the world. Thus, the tradition following Master Vincent's story located the early princely power centre of Kraków at the Wawel Hill. This eminent rock strategically placed over the bank of the Vistula looks like an ideal place for the location of a stronghold that would overlook the adjacent plains. The mythical importance of Wawel has also been emphasized.[15] Generations of historians

[11] Gallus I.3   [12] Banaszkiewicz 1986b.   [13] Deptuła 1990; Wiszewski 2004.
[14] Banaszkiewicz 1986b; 1998.   [15] E.g. Słupecki 1994, 185.

accepted that Wawel must have housed the seat of some pre-Piast dynasty or, at least, of a representative of the Moravian and/or Bohemian princes. However, careful analysis of all available archaeological evidence gave an obviously negative answer. Despite finds of single older items,[16] there is no material evidence for a stronghold built before the late tenth century.[17]

Another tradition developed as well, claiming that monumental mounds still visible today in Kraków contained burials of the members of the early princely dynasty of Lesser Poland, namely of Krakus and Wanda. Various explanations have been advanced concerning the function of these mounds.[18] Raising the mounds could be evidence of the emergence of elites that used traditional but radically expanded topographic symbols to signal their dominant position. It was perhaps the first evidence of processes of hierarchization that started among the Slavs living north of the Carpathians after their Avar lords were defeated by Charlemagne.[19] Promoters of the idea that the state-formation process started in Lesser Poland take these monumental mounds for an 'indication of the functioning of a dynastic clan connected to Kraków'.[20] During the nineteenth century other similar monuments were steadily incorporated into local legends and into the more or less scientific literature. The series of great mounds, thought to be burials, concentrated in the south-eastern part of Poland were treated as a characteristic regional phenomenon.[21]

The end of the twentieth century brought some corrections to the map of these monumental mounds. The alleged grave mound Salve Regina near Sandomierz turned out to be of natural post-glacial origin; the Kopiec Tatarski/Przemysla near Przemyśl is also a natural formation. In Gniezno, however, the stronghold on the Lech Hill (Góra Lecha) was built in the tenth century upon an earlier stone mound surrounded by 'ritual' hearths that are interpreted as elements of a regional pagan cult centre. By analogy to the sacred mountain Řip that marked the symbolic centre of Bohemia, Zofia Kurnatowska attached a similar function to the Lech Hill.[22] The ancient symbolic power of that allegedly old pagan centre was to explain why Gniezno gained such an importance in the early Piast state when it housed the seat of the archbishopric and the coronation site.

Written sources provide meagre data on pagan cults. Few pagan motifs are present in the early chronicles. This may indicate that local pre-Christian traditions were either quickly and effectively suppressed by the Church

---

[16] E.g. Zoll-Adamikowa 1998.   [17] Kukliński 2003.   [18] E.g. Słupecki 1998.
[19] Urbańczyk 2000, 91–3.   [20] Kurnatowscy 2003, 171; also Radwański 2000.
[21] E.g. Buko 2003.   [22] Kurnatowska 2000, 115.

or were extensively 'filtered' by the priest-chroniclers. Attempts at using toponyms to identify the otherwise unknown cult sites brought more disappointments than successes.[23] The earliest account of the pagan deities was included in the fifteenth-century chronicle of Jan Długosz, who constructed a pre-Christian Polish pantheon probably by identifying folk tradition with classical gods, for example Iessa with Jove, or Nyia with Pluto. Many later authors also tried to produce pre-Polish Slavic pantheons using the *interpraetatio Romana*. These attempts were built on the premise that the ancestors of the Poles had been one people having a uniform system of beliefs and cult. The debate on the traditional spiritual culture of the Slavs still includes arguments referring to a 'Polish mythology' or, more often, to the 'religion of the Slavs'. In fact, by analogy to the situation in the Polabian area which is well described by the written sources, we should expect many pagan cults and beliefs to have been observed locally in pre-Christian times.[24] It is, however, possible to construct an organizing framework for the structure of all Slavic beliefs and rituals by comparative studies using sources from different Slavic areas.[25] It is also important to remember that contacts existed between some parts of contemporary Polish lands and non-Slavic cultures such as those of Scandinavia and Prussia.

The question of the development of Slavic spiritual and symbolic culture remains controversial. The thesis that the absence of the later Slavic terms referring to 'god' (*bog*) and 'goddess' (*bogyni*) in the proto-Slavic vocabulary proves the lack of the idea of such beings[26] is not convincing. The first account of Slavic beliefs and cult written by Procopius of Caesarea in the sixth century explicitly refers to the chief god (της αστραπης δημιουργος) and other deities (αλλα αττα δαιμονια).[27] Thus, the thesis that a revolution took place in the belief system of the Slavs compared to proto-Slavic times cannot be sustained. According to linguists the oldest Slavic vocabulary did not contain notions of temples, statues or priests and this indicates that proto-Slavs had not known such forms of religious expressions.[28] Nevertheless, this is not the final word on the issue because Slavs did have some common notions for objects of cult (*modła, balvan, słup*) and for places of veneration (*contina, kącina*).[29] Some of these terms, however, also had everyday meanings: for example *kącina* also meant a 'household'. Therefore the lack of an exclusive sacral terminology cannot

[23] E.g. Kowalczyk 2000.   [24] See the appendix on Polabia and Pomerania, below.
[25] Urbańczyk 1991; Gieysztor 1982; Rybakov 1981; Słupecki 1994; Szyjewski 2003.
[26] E.g. Moszyński 1990, 39.   [27] *De bellis* III.14, 1.
[28] Moszyński 1992, 115–17; cf. Popowska-Taborska 1991, 115.
[29] Gieysztor 1982, 186; Słupecki 1994, 12–13, 200–1.

be used to deny the existence of objects and buildings of cult among the early Slavs. They were just not clearly separated from daily life. Thus, we should discern 'pagan sanctuaries in the world of "nature" and sanctuaries in the world of "culture". The former were connected (really or symbolically) with the zone of the *anaecumene.*'[30] The latter belonged integrally to the space controlled by men, for example to towns. Temple buildings appeared there, while in the world of nature there existed sacred groves, sacred waters, mountains and stones, that is, sites where cult was concentrated around some natural feature. Such places are hardly traceable archaeologically, but there are parallels known from the Polabian area.

Faced with these problems, the attention of both historians and archaeologists has for a long time concentrated on several mountains that boast elaborate dry-stone ramparts that are very unusual for Poland.[31] The best known is Ślęża (German Zobtenberg) in Silesia, which occupies an eminent position in the landscape. According to Thietmar, in pagan times *cum execranda gentilitas ibi* [in Silesia] *veneraretur*, the veneration was addressed directly to the mountain Ślęża because of its qualities and size.[32] Therefore, Ślęża seemed to be the symbolic centre of the *pagus Silensis* (the territory of the Silensi/Slensane tribe), which took its name from the mountain long ago. Thietmar's account was used to construct a hypothesis concerning an alleged Slavic sanctuary on the top of Ślęża,[33] although the chronicler had said nothing about it. Archaeological investigation[34] did not furnish any final answer because the whole surface of the summit had been frequently levelled and all finds (from the late Bronze Age to the Middle Ages) had been mixed up.[35] The chronology of the famous stone sculptures known as 'the Bear', 'St Peter/Girl with a fish' and 'the Mushroom' has still not been decisively established either. They are sometimes considered to be of Celtic origin. The hopes of identifying a cult place were sustained by the discovery in 1993 of a very small 'stronghold' built in the ninth century on the eastern slope of the mountain. Constructed on an artificially cut plateau and with an artificially made pond, this site, devoid of any traces of stable settlement, may be interpreted as a pagan cult site.[36]

By analogy to Ślęża, Łysiec (or Łysa Góra) in the Holy Cross Mountains, with its top plateau partly surrounded by massive stone ramparts, has also

[30] Słupecki 1994, 229–38.
[31] Leciejewicz 1987; Gieysztor 1982, 176–85; Gąssowski 1992a, 142–6; Słupecki 1994, 176–81.
[32] Thietmar of Merseburg VII.59.   [33] Domański 2002.   [34] Domański 2000b.
[35] Domański 2000a, 102.   [36] Domański 2002.

been considered the central cult place of a region.[37] Analogy to Ślęża is further reinforced by two stone sculptures placed at the eastern foot of the mountain. Adherents of this idea[38] supported their argument by reference to a sixteenth-century account,[39] which however has been shown to be completely unreliable.[40] Neither did archaeological investigations show any traces that might be connected to pagan cultic activities. However, the lack of houses and a very small quantity of pottery indicate the atypical function of this 'stronghold',[41] which was used until the eleventh or twelfth century.

Recently there has been a tendency to view the oldest Slavic strongholds as sites that, rather than having military and/or settlement functions, served as symbolic and/or religious centres for the local societies around them.[42] Three early examples (Szeligi, Haćki and Zimne) in eastern Poland are dated to the seventh century by close parallels in Belarus. They are all small hill-forts with courtyards surrounded by rather weak ramparts and with no evidence of permanent settlement. When we add to these the presence of foreign imports and haphazardly spread human bones, an argument may be developed to interpret the sites as local centres of power that sought reinforcement in religious rituals.[43] A similar but much later example has been recently identified in Gostyń in Silesia. The verification of the results of old excavations at the Kowalowa Góra (German Schmiedeberg) also revealed a small 'hill-fort' with a rather weak defence system (a shallow ditch) and no definite settlement layers but incorporating a series of large pits that contained partly burned, incomplete or partly destroyed human skeletons; such finds may indicate a local cult site that functioned in the late ninth or early tenth century.[44]

At the very beginning of the eleventh century Thietmar[45] mentioned sanctuaries with idols (*fana idolorum*) in Pomerania, which was then under the rule of Bolesław Chrobry. The next information refers to the early twelfth century, when Bishop Otto of Bamberg encountered temples in Szczecin, one of them containing a statue of the pagan deity Triglav,[46] and an open-air sanctuary in Wolin.[47] However, taking into consideration the possibility of the dynamic evolution of Slavic religion in the eleventh and twelfth centuries and contacts between Polabians and Pomeranians, it seems reasonable to discuss this information in the context of the paganism of the

---

[37] Gąssowska and Gąssowski 1970; Gąssowski 1992b, 22.   [38] Recently Buko 2000, 65–7.
[39] E.g. Słupecki 1991.   [40] Derwich 1992, 33–8; 1996.
[41] Gąssowska and Gąssowski 1970, 24–43.   [42] Urbańczyk 2002, 39.
[43] Discussion, drawings and literature in Dulinicz 2000.   [44] Moździoch 2000a, 156–75.
[45] Thietmar of Merseburg VII.72.   [46] *Vita Prieflingensis* II.11–12; Herbord II.31–2.
[47] Ebo II.1, III.1; according to *Vita Prieflingensis* II.16 (at 102) there was a temple (*contina*) in Wolin.

Polabians. The most reliably identified pagan cult building, the remains of a wooden 'shrine' closely resembling those known from the Polabian area (for example Arkona and Gross Raden), was discovered in Wrocław.[48] The rectangular structure (9 by 4–4.5 metres) was built on a surface formed by dismantling the ramparts of the royal stronghold that was probably destroyed during the pagan uprising in 1032. A possible local cult centre of an earlier date has been recently discovered at the stronghold of Kałdus in north-central Poland. There under the eleventh-century foundations of an unfinished basilica, a heap of stones containing many animal bones was piled near the water source.[49] Another similar cult centre may have functioned at the top of the Góra Lecha in Gniezno in Greater Poland before the stronghold was built there in the late tenth century.

Although few finds may be accepted as material evidence for everyday pagan practices, some discoveries made at the settlements are convincing. A miniature wooden sculpture of a four-faced male figure dated to the ninth or tenth century was discovered in Wolin on the Baltic coast. It may be identified with the Slavic deity Svantevit, known from written sources as the chief god of the island of Rügen (Rugia) in the twelfth century.[50] This small *światowid*[51] is not the only known 'pocket-size' idol. The multi-faced or multi-headed presentation seems typical in the Baltic and North Sea area. In twelfth-century Polabia and Pomerania polycephalism was the typical attribute of the chief gods, which seems to have resulted from the evolution of the late Slavic religion.[52] Specific animal bones found in unusual contexts have also been understood as indications of pagan practices. These are usually skulls and jaws of large domestic animals (horses, cattle, pigs) buried under houses as foundation deposits. Recently evidence of apotropaic magical practice was unearthed at the early tenth-century stronghold in Spławie in Greater Poland. A collection of jaws and a horse skull seemed to have been hung there on the outer face of the defensive rampart.[53]

Studies of pagan burial practices are more advanced. Thietmar confirms that cremation was practised before Mieszko's baptism.[54] According to the same chronicler widows were beheaded after the burial ceremony of their husbands. This information, however, is a topos connected to the opinion

---

[48] Moździoch 2000a, 176–87.   [49] Chudziak 2003.   [50] Saxo XIV.39.

[51] The Latin name *Svantevit* is equated by linguists to the Slavic *Świętowit*, 'holy, mighty, Lord'. However, in the nineteenth century it was read as *Światowid* or *Światowit*, 'seeing the world'; therefore, all four-headed or four-faced Slavic idols are conventionally called *światowid/światowit*, including the stone sculpture that was found in the Ukrainian river Zbruch (Szymański 1996). However, the four-headed god of the Rans is identified as *Świętowit*.

[52] Lamm 1987; Słupecki 1994; Rosik 1995.   [53] Brzostowicz 2003, 23.

[54] Thietmar of Merseburg VIII.2.

concerning the unusual fidelity of Slavic women. Such an opinion had also been expressed by Winfryth-Boniface in the context of the suicide of Slavic widows.[55] In the twelfth century Otto of Bamberg forbade the Pomeranians to bury people in fields and woods or to place sticks on the graves.[56]

Despite this scarcity of written sources archaeologists have no trouble discerning pre-Christian burial practices in the lands that belong to contemporary Poland, since until the late tenth century, even if regional differences existed, there was a fairly uniform burial ritual. This is manifested by small grave mounds in which burned bones were buried in various ways.[57] There are also some mounds with no bones inside or with just a few burned bones spread in the uppermost layer. These are so-called 'over-the-mound' burials, which are also confirmed by medieval written sources referring to other areas.[58] The southern border of the zone of the small mounds with cremation burials runs along the Carpathian and Sudeten mountains and this boundary seems to have been fairly stable during the ninth and tenth centuries.[59] A different type of grave characteristic of West Slavs was identified in Germany.[60] These burials of the so-called Alt Käbelich type were made in large rectangular pits that are reminiscent of typical Slavic sunken houses. Similar features were excavated in south-western Poland.[61]

2. CONTACTS

History does not furnish much reliable information on Christian influences before the baptism of Mieszko I in 966. The short account contained in the life of St Methodius concerning the 'prince of Wisle' allegedly converted in the late ninth century gave rise to suppositions that the Slavic liturgy could have already been introduced to southern Poland in the ninth century.[62] In its extreme version this line of thought has even led to the suggestion that a diocese of the Cyrilo-Methodian church may have been installed in Kraków. There were attempts to interpret Gallus Anonymus's information that Poland had two archbishops in the time of Bolesław Chrobry as evidence for the existence of a Latin archbishopric in Gniezno and a Slavic one in Kraków. This duality was even taken to explain the conflict between King Bolesław II the Bold and Bishop Stanisław of Kraków in 1079. In fact there is no written basis for such speculations just as there is no evidence

[55] Bonifatius 342; cf. Tyszkiewicz 1993.   [56] *Vita Prieflingensis* II.21.
[57] Overview: Zoll-Adamikowa 1979.   [58] Zoll-Adamikowa 1997, 68.
[59] Cf. Zoll-Adamikowa 1998, fig. 1– zone C_2; and 2000b, fig. 1.   [60] Schmidt 1983.
[61] Moździoch 2000a, 175, n. 40.
[62] *Żywoty . . . Metodego*, 114–15; cf. Paszkiewicz 1954; Lanckorońska 1961.

that the area of Lesser Poland belonged to the Great Moravian state.[63] There have also been speculations about an Irish mission to Poland, based mostly on Gallus Anonymus's story of two pilgrims who visited Piast's house.[64] Other arguments referred to the etymological interpretation of priests' names known from tenth- and eleventh-century sources. Today only the name of Aaron, bishop of Kraków during the reign of Prince Kazimierz, and the first abbot of the Benedictine abbey in Tyniec suggests Irish connections.[65]

Archaeologists have so far failed to find unquestionable material evidence of the penetration of Christian ideology before Mieszko I. Following historians' interpretations of the account concerning the 'prince of Wisle', they have tried in vain to find material evidence of the early Christianization of Lesser Poland: no Christian cult object may be safely dated to the pre-966 period.[66] Only a very indirect effect of trade can be pointed out, which brought to the Polish lands some west European coins bearing Christian symbols. The debate was reanimated by the discovery of two extensively discussed fragments of ceramic 'tablets' with unclear inscriptions, found in the ninth-century stronghold of Podebłocie in Masovia, in north-central Poland. Some scholars, for example Tadeusz Wasilewski, have read the inscriptions as the Greek abbreviation of *Iesos Chrestos Nika*, while others, such as Edward Tryjarski, have seen in them a runic alphabet used by the nomadic Pechenegs. Despite numerous objections,[67] the discoverer claims that the tablets were made by Christians who lived in the area during the time of the supposed Great Moravian mission.[68]

Burial practices offer another field of study for possible Christian influences. In particular, the interpretation of the introduction of inhumation has been debated. Traditionally, the appearance of skeleton burials has been explained as the result of Christianization,[69] which led to the conclusion that all inhumation burials in Poland must be dated *ex definitione* to the time after the official conversion in 966. Jerzy Gąssowski proposed an alternative interpretation of looking at early inhumations as results of the cultural influence of the Carolingian world.[70] He suggested that the transition to the burial of unburnt bodies might have taken place within the general trend observed in large areas of Europe. So far, however, there are no inhumation burials in Poland that may be safely dated earlier than the mid-tenth century. One of the rare exceptions is the cemetery

[63] Labuda 1988, vol. II, 83–166; Polek 1997.   [64] Gallus I.1–2.   [65] Strzelczyk 1987, 419–22.
[66] Żaki 1981, 36; 1994, 56.   [67] E.g. Suchodolski 1990.   [68] Gąssowski 1992a.
[69] Esp. Zoll-Adamikowa 1998, 227; 2000a, 103.   [70] Gąssowski 1971.

in Przemyśl where some Magyar (Hungarian) nomads identified by their grave goods were buried in the first half of the tenth century.[71] There is no such direct evidence for the inhumation cemetery discovered in Niemcza, but historical evidence has led to its interpretation as possibly Bohemian.[72] Thus no missionary activity has been reliably recorded in Polish lands prior to Mieszko's decision to marry the Bohemian princess Dobrava in 965.

Irregular early contacts existed with non-Christian monotheistic religions. In the tenth century a transcontinental trade route led from Iberian Al-Andalus, through France, Germany and Prague to Kraków, and further to Kiev and to the Caspian Sea. One of the Jewish merchants who travelled this route, Ibrahim ibn Yaqub of Tortosa mentioned Kraków (*Cracoa*) in 965 as one of the largest of the Bohemian towns.[73] His story, which is contained in Al Bekri's 'al-Masalik wa-al-Mamalik' (written before 1074), may be taken as indirect evidence that Kraków and south-eastern Poland were early on visited by Jewish slave traders. However, suggestions that Jewish groups had settled permanently in Poland before the eleventh century[74] cannot be supported by any reliable evidence. One should also mention indirect contacts with Muslim civilization, through the influx of dirhams into Polish lands during the ninth and tenth centuries. It is, however, impossible to estimate the extent to which the entirely different symbolism on these coins could have been understood by the inhabitants of central Europe. We do not know whether Muslim merchants visited Poland.

3. CHRISTIANIZATION

The Christianization of the lands between the Baltic Sea in the north and the mountain belt in the south is usually presented as a rather unproblematic transformation that was effectively implemented by Mieszko I after his decision to convert in 966. This picture was reinforced by the political successes of his son Bolesław Chrobry (992–1025) who thirty-four years later received an independent archbishopric and in 1025 was anointed as king. Despite the pagan reaction in the 1030s and the crisis of the centralized monarchy that followed, Christianity was seen by scholars as uncontested. Despite periodic tensions, the cooperation between political and ecclesiastical powers looked fairly unproblematic. The unchallenged Latin-Roman orientation of Polish Christianity was also seen as obvious.

[71] Koperski 1985.   [72] Żydok 2004, 61.
[73] Ibrahim ibn Yaqub 49.   [74] Werbart 2000, 44 and fig. 2.

This rather uniform view, however, took shape not because of the clear evidence of rich and versatile sources but, rather, as a result of the scarcity of written material. The almost total lack of reliable information on the pre-966 situation and concentration of the later sources on the deeds of the ruling dynasty implied a picture of the sudden success of Christianity and its subsequent stable continuation. This perspective changed with the flood of archaeological discoveries that furnished information on periods and areas not covered by the documents. As often happens, however, more data have not necessarily clarified the picture. Some aspects are still difficult to understand and some questions are still difficult to answer.

Mieszko I, the first historical ruler, was baptized most probably in 966. This commonly accepted date, however, may be questioned since Thietmar was not sure whether the Bohemian princess Dobrava spent one or three years with Mieszko before he converted.[75] In the oldest written sources this act is treated as the turning point that led to the Christianization of the whole country, and its importance is emphasized by the literary convention of the descriptions. Bishop Thietmar of Merseburg, using the metaphor of a people as one body with the ruler as their head, conveys an idealistic vision of the conversion of Mieszko I and his people.[76] Almost a century later Gallus Anonymus presented a legend about how Mieszko's miraculously healed childhood blindness was a prophetic sign of his enlightenment of Poland, which had been blind in its paganism.[77]

To achieve his goal of building his power to equal that of his neighbours, Mieszko sealed a dynastic alliance with the Bohemian prince Boleslav I and married Princess Dobrava. According to Thietmar, she came to a pagan country and only subsequently did she induce her husband to convert, using 'sweet promises'. The chronicler mentioned some people who condemned her controversial behaviour, which included eating meat during periods of fast, but he himself emphasized Dobrava's pious motivation and the positive outcome. Almost a century later Gallus Anonymus paints an idealized picture of Dobrava, assuring readers that she did not share Mieszko's bed until he became a Christian. At the same time the Bohemian chronicler Cosmas pictured Dobrava as a stupid woman, who despite being quite old, wore the maiden wreath during her wedding. Dobrava's arrival in Mieszko's household and his baptism are also recorded by the Polish annals, for example the *Rocznik dawny* ('The Old Annals') and the *Rocznik kapituły*

---

[75] Thietmar of Merseburg IV.56.   [76] Thietmar of Merseburg IV.56.   [77] Gallus I.4.

krakowskiej ('The Annals of the Kraków Capitulary').[78] Although they were written in the twelfth and thirteenth centuries, historians have attempted to locate their sources in the period of the early Piast state.[79] No new reliable data are contained in the later sources from the fourteenth and fifteenth centuries, such as the *Kronika Wielkopolska*.[80] The site of Mieszko's baptism has never been identified and various possibilities have been proposed, for example Gniezno, Poznań, Ostrów Lednicki and Ratisbon (Regensburg).

The last area of contemporary Poland to be Christianized was Pomerania. Although the first attempts to convert the people of the region were undertaken by Bishop Reinbern of Kołobrzeg in 1000,[81] the *gens Pomeranorum* did not receive Christianity until later. In contrast to Poland, literary tradition connected the beginning of Pomerania's Christianization not to the baptism of the ruler (Prince Wartislav I converted before 1124) but to the two missions in 1124–5 and 1128 of Bishop Otto of Bamberg, whom the ecclesiastical tradition called *Apostolus Pomeranorum*.[82] His three hagiographies, written before his canonization in 1189, offer a mass of reliable information, analysed in the appendix below.

In contrast, the beginning of Polish Christianity is much less clear. The most important testimony, written by Thietmar, mentions only the hard work of the first Polish bishop Jordan.[83] Surprisingly enough, the chronicler described in more detail the later activity of the above-mentioned Bishop Reinbern, who apparently faced pagan resistance in 1000, although Pomerania had already been annexed by Mieszko I in the 970s. There were two phases of Christianization: first the *abrenuntiatio diaboli*, that is, the destruction of pagan sanctuaries and idols, and then the *confessio fidei*, that is, teaching people and baptizing them.[84] Despite his open hostility towards Bolesław Chrobry, the German chronicler considered his state a truly Christian country. He especially stressed the zeal of the defenders of the Silesian stronghold Niemcza who in 1017 fought against the pagan Liutizi allied with Emperor Henry II.[85] This is the only account that suggests a broader spread of Christianity: other early sources (such as the letter of Bruno of Querfurt to Henry II and the letter of Princess Mathilde of Lotharingia to Mieszko II) refer to the Christian attitude of the monarchs alone.

[78] *Rocznik dawny*, a. 966 and 967; *Rocznik kapituły krakowskiej*, a. 965 and 966.
[79] Jasiński 2000; Dobosz 2002, 25; Drelicharz 2003.   [80] Dobosz 2002, 37.
[81] The bishopric of Kołobrzeg fell probably around 1007.   [82] Cf. Petersohn 1966.
[83] Thietmar of Merseburg IV.56.
[84] Górski 1960; Rosik 2000a, 89. Thietmar II.37; VI.37 described the Christianization of some parts of Germany in a similar way, including his own diocese which was inhabited by Slavs.
[85] Thietmar VII.60.

This scarcity of available written sources made archaeologists look for material evidence of Christianization. Round shallow depressions made of mortar discovered in Poznań, Kraków, Wiślica and Kalisz, medieval centres of Poland, were interpreted as 'baptismal basins' (*piscinae*) allegedly used for the mass baptism rituals. Today, after a critical re-evaluation of this long-accepted interpretation,[86] all such features are considered to be traces of large mechanical mortar mixers that are known from Switzerland, France and England. Although one archaeologist reinterpreted the records of old excavations to maintain that at least one rectangular building of an early *baptisterium* contained a round *piscina*,[87] this attempt to save the national 'relic' of Christianization has not found broader acceptance.

Another attempt to identify vague archaeological data with a historical event was the reinterpretation of the ruins of the stone *palatium* still visible at the island of Ostrów Lednicki in Greater Poland.[88] In the round chapel adjacent to this residential building two shallow symmetrical depressions interred in the gypsum floor were interpreted as 'baptismal basins'. These served as the basis for the conclusion that the whole architectural complex (residence, chapel and church) was built just before 966 as an *episcopium* for the first missionary bishop Jordan, and that Mieszko I was baptized there. This opinion did not find broader support either. The oldest and only reliably identified Polish baptistery was discovered at the Wawel Hill in Kraków. It is a rotunda with one apse, and a rectangular basin made of sandstone slabs is located in the middle of the floor.[89] Unfortunately, the structure, dated to the first quarter of the eleventh century, cannot be connected to any concrete royal baptismal celebration.

The earliest Polish chronicles by Gallus Anonymus and Master Vincent contain a reliable tradition on the pagan uprising that is also confirmed by the Rus' chronicler Nestor and by Cosmas of Prague. The chronology of these events, however, is still disputed. The earliest date, 1022, given by Cosmas is generally rejected due to the ten-year mistake that seems typical for parts of his chronicle.[90] According to several sources[91] King Mieszko II, defeated by a coordinated attack of the German and Rus' armies, escaped in 1031 to Bohemia. Here he was castrated, according to Gallus Anonymus as revenge for the blinding of the Bohemian prince Boleslav III by Mieszko II's father, when he took the Bohemian throne in 1003.[92] His half-brother Bezprim took supreme power but his despotism quickly led to his murder

[86] Urbańczyk 1995; 1996.   [87] Kurnatowska 1997.   [88] Żurowska 1993.
[89] Pianowski 1994, 111; Rodzińska-Chorąży 1994, 146.
[90] E.g. Labuda 1992, 93. Different opinion: Borawska 1964, 62, 154.
[91] *Annales Hildesheimenses*, a. 1031; *PVL*, a. 6539 (1031); Wipo, chap. 29.   [92] Gallus I.17.

in 1032 and to the return of Mieszko II (1025–34) to Poland.[93] Probably in 1031–2 the first wave of the pagan reaction took place.

Material evidence of the return to paganism has been recently identified in Wrocław where an alleged pagan temple was found. The walls were made in a particular 'frame construction', which has a close parallel in Wolin, where another pagan temple dated to the tenth century has been excavated.[94] The northern part of the building in Wrocław, or at least its corner, was panelled on the inside with vertical planks. Only one complete plank was found. Its upper end is sculpted in a way characteristic of the plank 'idols' found at other sacral sites of the Polabians, for example in Gross Raden in Mecklenburg.[95] The Wrocław plank was dendrochronologically dated to the period from the late autumn of the year 1032 to the early spring of the year 1033,[96] which probably indicates the age of the whole building. This date is quite near to the one provided by Nestor as the year of the rebellion (1030)[97] and of the persecution of clergy in Poland. The temple probably functioned for a short time before 1050, when Kazimierz the Restorer re-established his rule over Silesia. It must have been then that the temple was deliberately destroyed by cutting all the decorated planks near the ground. The entire area was levelled and covered with soil to make space for a new stronghold built sometime before 1051 when Bishop Hieronimus consecrated the new cathedral in Wrocław.[98]

The next wave of the pagan reaction supposedly took place during the first years of the reign of Kazimierz I the Restorer, who inherited the throne after Mieszko's II death in 1034, but was soon expelled. Until his return in 1038–9, Poland was divided among local princes and according to Polish chroniclers was devastated by an uprising. The destruction was compounded in 1038 by the Bohemian prince Břetislav I's invasion, which ruined the cathedral churches of Gniezno and Poznań. This crisis shook the Polish monarchy and temporarily destroyed the ecclesiastical organization. So far, however, historians have been unable to offer a clear picture of the pagan uprising. It may have been an element of a broader counter-reaction to the Piasts' centralizing policy supported by the clergy who were reportedly persecuted. The restoration of the monarchy and ecclesiastical institutions by Kazimierz I, supported by the military force of the emperor, curbed the disorder and prevented the decentralization of the power structure.

---

[93] *Annales Hildesheimenses*, a. 1031 and 1032; Labuda 1992, 89.
[94] Filipowiak 1982.   [95] Moździoch 2000b, 47, fig. 9.   [96] Krąpiec 1998.
[97] *PVL*, a. 6538 (1030).   [98] *Katalogi biskupów wrocławskich*, 560, 567, 576.

Despite its strong promotion by the monarchy, Christianity was diffused rather slowly among the masses of agricultural inhabitants of the formally converted kingdom. The Christianization of the hard-to-reach areas and peripheries was an especially slow process. In such areas especially syncretism occurred and is well documented by archaeological finds. However, there is also evidence of sustained pagan traditions even in the centres of the Christian state. Clearly visible and ostensibly pagan elements of the landscape must have posed a serious challenge to the Church's efforts to uproot the old beliefs. Some of the surviving pagan hierophanies (elements of nature treated as manifestations of the sacred) that were a part of local identity were Christianized in order to retain control over their symbolic power, which could not simply be discounted. Monasteries built on the top or at the foot of the pagan sacred mountains Łysiec and Ślęża are expressive evidence of this practice.

While the written sources concentrate on the ruling elites, the Christianization of the subject population may be studied by reference only to the archaeological data. At the individual level, conversion may possibly be indicated by small private items of daily use, such as small crosses made of silver, bronze, amber, wood and stone, found in graves but also at the settlements. Most of the general observations, typologies and chronology of the early Christian burial rites resulted from the so far unchallenged studies of the late Helena Zoll-Adamikowa.[99] It is generally accepted that the introduction of Christian eschatology is indicated by the halting of the cremation of dead bodies and the disappearance of grave mounds, with the exception of a narrow zone in the east that was under the influence of the Orthodox church. Subsequently new rules were introduced, concerning the east–west orientation of bodies, a reduction of grave goods, the location of cemeteries near churches and a sequence of changes in the arrangement of the arms (from straight at the side, through crossed on the pelvis to crossed on the chest). In any case, there are no cemeteries or even single graves in Poland that would indicate an acceptance of Christian eschatology before the late tenth century.

Using information provided by the written sources, Zoll-Adamikowa proposed five basic forms for the penetration and establishment of Christianity in Poland: nominal Christianization (the nominal inclusion of new areas in a diocese without the conversion of their inhabitants); individual conversions (by single persons who did not undertake the conversion of others); temporary formal Christianization (areas where after

---

[99] Zoll-Adamikowa 1979; 1988; 1998; 2000a.

rapid conversion regular evangelization was halted due to the negligence of the clergy or to massive resistance); durable formal Christianization; which then led to 'real' Christianization (when the canons of the new faith were commonly understood and accepted). According to this model, one should also distinguish between two different types of relevant ecclesiastical activity: missionary and established, carried out by the Church but organized by the political power and supported by administrative and coercive measures. It is not easy to observe these various stages because regional differences exclude a common chronology for the whole country and every area must be studied separately. Some correlations may be suggested only through archaeology.[100]

Nominal or temporary formal Christianization as well as missionary activity may be indicated by the parallel occurrence of cremation and inhumation, grave mounds and flat graves, as well as east–west orientation of the skeletons. Formal Christianization by the state-supported Church resulted in the introduction of cemeteries containing exclusively inhumation burials (so-called 'village or row cemeteries') that may still show some pagan elements, such as grave mounds, non-east–west orientation and rich grave goods (jewellery, tools, arms, pottery). These cemeteries were by preference located at elevated sites but never in the same place as an earlier pagan necropolis.[101] After 150 to 200 years Christianization was achieved, signalled by the concentration of all burials (without grave goods) around churches, which demonstrates that the Church had gained full control over the burial rites of the local populations. These stages were never very distinct and they did not occur at the same time everywhere. Thus, the process was faster around the ecclesiastic/political centres and slower in marginal areas. In general, 'real Christianization' in Poland began sometime before the mid-twelfth century with the development of the network of parish churches and monasteries.[102]

An interesting example of religious syncretism can be found in the *vitae* of Bishop Otto of Bamberg, where the coexistence of pagan and Christian altars is mentioned. Otto undertook his second missionary expedition to the Baltic region in 1128 because of the Pomeranians' reported return to paganism. As a result of this, a new syncretic current emerged, characterized by the hagiographers as the 'sin of the Samaritans'. The Pomeranians, inspired by their still-active pagan priests and frightened by climatic catastrophes and an epidemic, returned to their old gods, especially Triglav.

---

[100] Zoll-Adamikowa 1998; 2000a, 104.   [101] Zoll-Adamikowa 2000b, 217.
[102] Zoll-Adamikowa 1998, 233; Wrzesiński 1999, 261, 267.

However, they did not abandon the cult of the Christian God (regarded also as the 'Teutonic God'). In Szczecin, this dual faith held the position of the official religion until the second mission of Otto.

Syncretism in some form seems to have survived even during the Christian period. In the eleventh- to twelfth-century cemetery in Daniłowo near the north-eastern town of Łapy, a child and a young woman were buried with rich grave goods.[103] Necklaces in the grave were made up of pendant crosses, a so-called lunula (a reversed half-moon, well known as a pagan amulet) combined with a cross, circular pendants with in-built crosses and other elements (glass beads and lunulas), which indicate that they were used not as manifestations of Christianity but, rather, as magic amulets.[104] So-called 'foundation offerings', usually animal skulls but also clay or wooden pots, placed under the wall of a newly built house, are commonly accepted as the remnants of pagan religious or magic traditions.[105] Egg-shaped colour-glazed clay rattles and jewellery that combine signs identified with the two contrasting ideologies (like the lunulas mentioned above combined with crosses), may also be safely connected to the survival of pagan traditions. The survival of pagan rituals is, however, best observed in burials: different orientation of the skeletons; partially burned skeletons; bi-ritual cemeteries containing both cremation and inhumation burials, or even bi-ritual graves; special objects put into the graves (for example amulets made of animal teeth, rattles of various shapes, animal bones from the best edible parts, eggs, whole pots, bells, coins, half-moon pendants); and the so-called 'anti-vampire burials' which show practices that may be connected to those known from ethnographic studies, such as mutilations of the dead bodies aimed at preventing the dead from rising. In eastern Poland the openly pagan cremation ritual survived locally until the thirteenth century.

The status of the early Church in the Piast state is still debated. Although Thietmar[106] claimed that the first bishop, Jordan, was a suffragan of the archbishop of Magdeburg, this statement may be interpreted as a reflection of the attempts of the Magdeburg archbishopric to subordinate the Polish church (or at least the diocese of Poznań) during the war between Bolesław Chrobry and Henry II.[107] The prevalent opinion in Polish historiography has been that Jordan and his successor Unger were missionary bishops directly subordinate to Rome. This old idea is still upheld, and has been supported by arguments from canon law. Nevertheless, the idea of

---

[103] Krasnodębski 1998, 96, figs. 134 and 135.   [104] Wołoszyn 2000, 247; Koperkiewicz 2004.
[105] For Silesia: Gediga 1996, 160–3 and figs. 1–6.   [106] Thietmar of Merseburg II.22.
[107] Kehr 1920, 13–29; Labuda 1988, 429–41.

an *episcopus immediate subiectus sedis apostolicae*[108] is unacceptable to some historians.[109]

Yet at the same time, there is abundant evidence of direct contacts between Mieszko I, as well as his son, and Rome, that suggests the independence of their ecclesiastical policy. A good example is the letter called *Dagome iudex* written in the early 990s, in which Mieszko I subordinated his family and his state to the pope.[110] Close ties to Rome lasted until the early eleventh century as indicated by several events. In 997 the missionary bishop Vojtěch-Adalbert was sent from Rome to Poland with the aim of converting its pagan neighbours.[111] The first Polish archbishop, Radim-Gaudentius, was ordained in Rome in 999 and was brought from there to Gniezno by the Emperor Otto III in 1000.[112] In perhaps 1001 the emperor sent two Benedictine monks, John and Benedict, with an evangelizing mission to Poland from the monastery in Pereum near Ravenna.[113] During his wars with Henry II, Bolesław Chrobry reproached the German king for hindering his attempts to send the tribute due 'to St Peter'.[114] At the same time Bolesław sent several envoys asking the pope for missionaries.[115] As a result of these requests, the missionary archbishop Bruno of Querfurt, ordained in Rome, went to Poland *c.* 1007.[116] He called Bolesław a *tributarius* of St Peter.[117]

An independent ecclesiastical province was installed in Gniezno in 1000 by the Emperor Otto III in person, who surely acted in coordination with Pope Sylvester II. At the same time three bishops were subordinated to Archbishop Radim-Gaudentius: Poppo of Kraków, John of Wrocław, and Reinbern of Kołobrzeg.[118] Only the old Bishop Unger of Poznań maintained his independent position. From 1004 onwards he probably accepted subordination to the archbishopric of Magdeburg, but after his death in 1013(?), the archbishopric of Gniezno gained full control over the diocese of Poznań. The boundaries of these bishoprics may only be inferred from later documents, for example the bull of protection issued for Wrocław in 1155. Generally it is thought that the earliest dioceses of Kołobrzeg, Kraków and Wrocław covered the so-called *pertinentia* of the Piast state, that is, Pomerania, Lesser Poland and Silesia respectively,[119] and they may not have had precise boundaries until the late eleventh century.

---

[108] Weiss 1992; cf. Labuda 1988, 472.   [109] E.g. Sikorski 2003.   [110] Kürbis 1962, 394–6.
[111] Canaparius, chap. 27; Bruno of Querfurt, *S. Adalberti . . . vita altera*, chap. 24.
[112] Thietmar of Merseburg IV.45.
[113] Bruno of Querfurt, *Vita quinque fratrum*, chap. 2; Petrus Damian, chap. 28.
[114] Thietmar of Merseburg VI.92.   [115] Bruno of Querfurt, *Vita quinque fratrum*, chaps. 12–13, 21.
[116] Thietmar of Merseburg VI.94–5.   [117] Bruno of Querfurt, *Epistola*, 103.
[118] Thietmar of Merseburg IV.45.   [119] Labuda 1988, 474–510.

The crisis of the monarchy in the 1030s also disrupted the ecclesiastical structure. The reported killing of the clergy and burning of churches by the rebels and the invading Bohemian army in 1038 deeply shook the still fragile church organization. Its rebuilding took a long time due to the unstable political situation. The Gniezno archbishopric ceased to function in the 1030s;[120] in 1075 Pope Gregory VII wrote to Bolesław II the Bold that there were not enough bishoprics in Poland, and that the archbishopric was still not functioning.[121] It must, however, have been restored very soon after that because in the next year Bolesław's coronation, which must have been performed by the archbishop of Gniezno, took place. Other dioceses also recovered slowly. The bishopric of Kraków was active again in 1046 or even earlier since Aaron, the Benedictine abbot of the Tyniec monastery, is mentioned in the Polish annals as the bishop of Kraków in that year.[122] After the pagan uprising the bishopric of Wrocław may have been moved to Ryczyn or Smogorzewo to be reinstalled in Wrocław *c*. 1050.[123] The bishopric of Poznań ceased to function and was restored probably only in 1075–6. *Circa* 1075 a new bishopric in Płock was consecrated by Prince Władysław Herman who chose this Masovian town as his capital seat. Pomerania received its own diocese fifteen years after it was officially Christianized in 1124–5 by Otto of Bamberg. The first cathedral chapters in Poland were organized in the late eleventh and early twelfth centuries.

In 1131 Archbishop Norbert of Xanten returned to the idea of the subordination of the Poznań diocese to Magdeburg. He succeeded in engineering a papal decision that deprived Gniezno of the rank of archbishopric.[124] Three years later the counter-action of the Polish church and the diplomacy of Prince Bolesław III the Wrymouth led to the recovery of Polish ecclesiastical independence, which was confirmed in 1136 by the bull of Gniezno.[125] The real reason for the outbreak of this conflict was rivalry for the subordination of Pomerania. The crisis in the relations between Poland and the papacy, however, also resulted from the earlier decision of the Polish bishops to support the anti-pope during the schism of 1130.

The Polish church developed under various influences. Besides the connections to Rome, those to the neighbouring countries also need to be discussed. Linguists claim that the earliest Polish Christian vocabulary shows that Christianity was mediated by the Orthodox Slavic rite that was introduced during the Great Moravian period by Cyril and Methodius. This is not surprising if one remembers that Christianity came to Poland from

[120] 'Kraków Calendar', 918. [121] 'List Grzegorza VII', 367–8.
[122] E.g. *Rocznik Traski*, a. 1046; cf. Dobosz 2002, 113–16. [123] Jurek 1994; Dola 1996, 25–6.
[124] *Kodeks dyplomatyczny Wielkopolski*, no. 6. [125] *Kodeks dyplomatyczny Wielkopolski*, no. 7.

Bohemia, which may have inherited elements of the Great Moravian experiment with adjusting the Slavic language to the needs of the new religion.[126] This influence may be explained by the presence of the Bohemian clergy who surely arrived in Poland in 965 together with Princess Dobrava, establishing the first mission, which resulted in the conversion of Mieszko I. These contacts were renewed around the turn of the millennium when a number of Bohemians took part in the formation of the Polish church. The first was the bishop of Prague in exile, Adalbert, who arrived as a missionary with his half-brother Radim-Gaudentius at Bolesław Chrobry's court in 997. After Adalbert's martyrdom and the establishment of his shrine in Gniezno the same year, Radim-Gaudentius returned to Poland in 1000 as its first archbishop. The third influential person of that period was Adalbert's former servant Radla who, after some time spent in Poland, probably became the archbishop of Esztergom in Hungary.

Other obvious sources of influence must be sought in connections with the German church that tried to control the situation along the Empire's eastern marches. Unger, the second bishop attached to the Piast court, and maybe his predecessor Jordan as well, originated from Germany or, at least, were trained there. We have direct evidence only in the case of Unger, who came to Poland from Memleben where he served as the abbot of the monastery founded by the Emperor Otto II and his wife Theophano. Until the establishment of the independent ecclesiastical province in 1000, several of the German archbishoprics aspired for control over the Polish church. One of them was Mainz, to which Bohemia was already subject. In the late tenth century Archbishop Willigis of Mainz, who was also the imperial chancellor, was a mighty player on the geopolitical stage of central Europe.[127] Other German bishops also looked towards the east, eager to promote their own interests. On 6 December 995 Otto III enlarged the Meissen bishopric by including in it Silesia up to the Oder river.[128] This decision, probably aimed at the separation of Bohemia and Poland, which were then in open conflict over the control of Silesia, was annulled in 1000 when the emperor subordinated the bishop of Wrocław to the Polish metropolitan. After the crisis caused by the pagan uprising in the 1030s there were some connections to the archbishopric of Cologne because Kazimierz the Restorer had family connections there and it was from this town that Bishop Aaron of Kraków arrived.[129] In the second half of the eleventh century, Polish bishops and monasteries were in contact with

---

[126] Cybulski 2002.   [127] Urbańczyk 1997.   [128] *MGH DO* III, no. 186, 595–6.
[129] E.g. *Rocznik Traski*, a. 1046; *Vita s. Stanislai (vita maior)*, II.14; cf. Derwich 1998, 181; Dobosz 2002, 113–19.

Liège (*Leodium*). The first chronicler of Poland most probably arrived from France (via Hungary), which later gave birth to his designation as the Gallus Anonymus.

One should not forget the influence of the Orthodox church along the south-eastern periphery of contemporary Poland. This area was conquered by Prince Vladimir the Great in 981 and was under Rus' control (except for a short period in the eleventh century) until its Polish reconquest in the second half of the fourteenth century. At the beginning of the twelfth century the Rus' prince Volodar founded an Orthodox church of unknown dedication on the Castle Hill in Przemyśl. A high stone tower in Stołp near Chelm, dated to the late twelfth century, is reminiscent of monasteries on high points that are known from the Balkans.[130] From the eleventh century onwards the area dominated by the Orthodox church may be identified archaeologically by mapping the extent to which the tradition of burials under mounds survived. This ritual lasted in the zone along the Bug river until the beginning of the thirteenth century because it was tolerated by the eastern Church. Eastern influences are also indicated by finds of small crosses, often made of two folding halves and with rounded extremities, of the type called *encolpion*. Their spread and characteristic shape leave no doubts that they were used by the adherents of the Orthodox church or, at least, that they were imported from the east during the eleventh to thirteenth centuries, although some of them were made in south-eastern Poland.[131] Influences from the same religious–cultural zone are also indicated by other characteristic finds: the so-called 'Scandinavian-type' small crosses made in pseudo-filigree technique, circular pendants with in-built crosses, crosses decorated with enamel and small rectangular icons made of soft stones. They are all distinctively concentrated along the eastern border of contemporary Poland.[132]

No early Christian laws have survived in Poland. The earliest information on legislation can be found in Thietmar's chronicle where Bolesław Chrobry's cruel actions against sinners are described.[133] According to this source the first Polish king had the teeth of those who did not observe obligatory fasts knocked out and the testicles of men guilty of adultery nailed to a bridge. No other source confirms practices like these. In Pomerania, Otto of Bamberg prohibited pagan cults and traditional burial practices during his mission in the early twelfth century. The list recorded by his hagiographers includes prohibitions of female infanticide, idolatry and visiting

[130] Andrzej Buko provided this information.   [131] Wołoszyn 2000, 243.
[132] Map at fig. 7 in Wołoszyn 2000.   [133] Thietmar of Merseburg VIII.2.

fortune-tellers. At the same time, he ordered fasting, participation in holy mass on Sundays and feast days, participation in the sacraments and blessings, and penitence and marriage according to canon law.[134]

We do not know much about the furnishing of the earliest churches. Some early manuscripts survived in libraries, for example the Irish *Praedicatione p. Tractatus Evangeliorum* from the eighth century. In addition, objects used during the Christian liturgy were found during excavations. These include several utensils (patens and chalices) buried in the bishops' and/or abbots' graves discovered in Tyniec, Kraków, Poznań and Łęczyca.[135] Several of these items were made in the eleventh century. The golden set found in grave no. 8 in Tyniec, where an unknown abbot was buried in the mid-twelfth century, is outstanding. Apart from the metal parts of a crosier, a small golden chalice (8.8 cm high) and a paten (8.7 cm in diameter) decorated with a large cross and a *manus Dei* were also found. Besides these personal belongings that were buried with their owners there were also official items kept in the churches. The oldest surviving description of the Kraków cathedral treasury from 1101 lists six golden and twelve silver chalices. Nine years later the latter are described as gilded.[136]

The earliest monasteries were founded by Bolesław Chrobry. About 1001 a monastery was built in Greater Poland (probably in Międzyrzecz) for two Benedictines sent from Italy by Otto III and joined locally by two Polish brothers.[137] The wooden building was burned and the monks and their servant were murdered during an attempted robbery in 1003. The same source mentioned nuns present at the princely court *c.* 1001.[138] Their nunnery was probably located somewhere in Greater Poland. So far, there is no archaeological evidence for these two monasteries, which has led to debates on their location. Another early Benedictine monastery was sought in Trzemeszno. However, archaeological excavations have proved that the supposedly tenth-century building was a much later construction.[139] Thus the alleged account of the visit there by St Adalbert in 997 has turned out to be the product of later propaganda by the ambitious monks. The oldest monasteries of known location were built for the Benedictines in Tyniec (*c.* 1044), Mogilno (*c.* 1050) and Lubiń (*c.* 1076). The next wave of monastic foundations came with the expansion of the Cistercians, who in the mid-twelfth century expanded to Poland where they received monasteries in Jędrzejów (1149), Lekno (1153), Sulejów (1177), Wąchock (1179), Koprzywnica (1185), Mogiła (1222) and Szczyrzyc (1239).

[134] Ekkehard, a. 1125; *Vita Prieflingensis* II.21; Ebo II.12; Herbord II.18.
[135] E.g. Kalinowski 1971, 186–97.   [136] Vetulani 1953.
[137] Bruno of Querfurt, *Vita quinque fratrum*, chap. 6.
[138] Bruno of Querfurt, *Vita quinque fratrum*, chap. 13.   [139] Chudziakowa 2001.

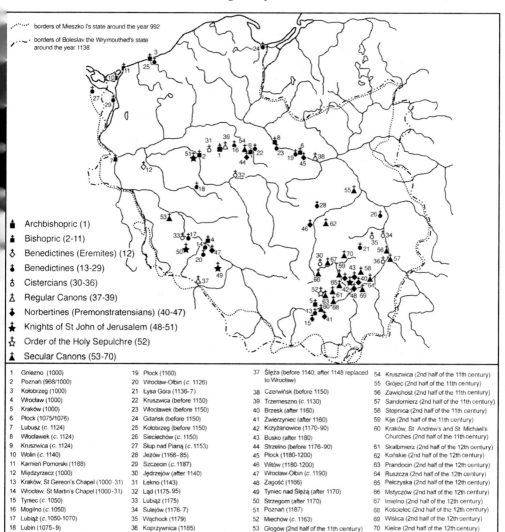

Archbishopric (1)

Bishopric (2-11)

Benedictines (Eremites) (12)

Benedictines (13-29)

Cistercians (30-36)

Regular Canons (37-39)

Norbertines (Premonstratensians) (40-47)

Knights of St John of Jerusalem (48-51)

Order of the Holy Sepulchre (52)

Secular Canons (53-70)

- borders of Mieszko I's state around the year 992
- borders of Boleslav the Wrymouthed's state around the year 1138

1 Gniezno (1000)	19 Płock (1160)	37 Ślęża (before 1140; after 1148 replaced to Wrocław)	54 Kruszwica (2nd half of the 11th century)
2 Poznań (968/1000)	20 Wrocław-Ołbin (*c.* 1126)		55 Grójec (2nd half of the 11th century)
3 Kołobrzeg (1000)	21 Łysa Góra (1136-7)	38 Czerwińsk (before 1150)	56 Zawichost (2nd half of the 11th century)
4 Wrocław (1000)	22 Kruszwica (before 1150)	39 Trzemeszno (*c.* 1130)	57 Sandomierz (2nd half of the 11th century)
5 Kraków (1000)	23 Włocławek (before 1150)	40 Brzesk (after 1160)	58 Stopnica (2nd half of the 11th century)
6 Płock (1075/1076)	24 Gdańsk (before 1150)	41 Zwierzyniec (after 1160)	59 Kije (2nd half of the 11th century)
7 Lubusz (*c.* 1124)	25 Kołobrzeg (before 1150)	42 Krzyżanowice (1170-90)	60 Kraków, St Andrew's and St Michael's
8 Włocławek (*c.* 1124)	26 Sieciechów (*c.* 1150)	43 Busko (after 1180)	Churches (2nd half of the 11th century)
9 Kruszwica (*c.* 1124)	27 Słup nad Pianą (*c.* 1153)	44 Płock (1180-1200)	61 Skalbmierz (2nd half of the 12th century)
10 Wolin (*c.* 1140)	28 Jeżów (1166-85)	45 Płock (1180-1200)	62 Końskie (2nd half of the 12th century)
11 Kamień Pomorski (1188)	29 Szczecin (*c.* 1187)	46 Witów (1180-1200)	63 Prandocin (2nd half of the 12th century)
12 Międzyrzecz (1000)	30 Jędrzejów (after 1140)	47 Wrocław-Ołbin (*c.* 1190)	64 Ruszcza (2nd half of the 12th century)
13 Kraków, St Gereon's Chapel (1000-31)	31 Łekno (1143)	48 Zagość (1166)	65 Pełczyska (2nd half of the 12th century)
14 Wrocław, St Martin's Chapel (1000-31)	32 Ląd (1175-95)	49 Tyniec nad Ślężą (after 1170)	66 Mstyczów (2nd half of the 12th century)
15 Tyniec (*c.* 1050)	33 Lubiąż (1175)	50 Strzegom (after 1170)	67 Imielno (2nd half of the 12th century)
16 Mogilno (*c.* 1050)	34 Sulejów (1176-7)	51 Poznań (1187)	68 Kościelec (2nd half of the 12th century)
17 Lubiąż (*c.* 1050-1070)	35 Wąchock (1179)	52 Miechów (*c.* 1163)	69 Wiślica (2nd half of the 12th century)
18 Lubin (1075-9)	36 Koprzywnica (1185)	53 Głogów (2nd half of the 11th century)	70 Kielce (2nd half of the 12th century)

16. Ecclesiastical institutions in medieval Poland

The existence of a parochial organization is indicated by documents from the mid-thirteenth century but its origins may be traced to the eleventh and twelfth centuries when the private churches of lords were probably opened to local communities.[140]

[140] E.g. Wiśniowski 1966.

4. ROYAL POWER

Conversion allowed the early Piasts to enter the geopolitical stage of Latin Christendom officially and to develop interpersonal relations with their Christian neighbours. Such ties were typically reinforced by opportunistic marriages between ruling dynasties and aristocratic clans. Both Mieszko I and his son Bolesław Chrobry were very active on the political and matrimonial stage. After Dobrava's death in 977, Mieszko turned to the Empire, from which he took his second wife Oda. He sent his daughter Sventoslava-Gunhilda to Sweden where she married Erik Segersäll. After his death she married Sven Forkbeard of Denmark in 996, and became the mother of Knud (Canute) the Great. Bolesław Chrobry was first married in 985–6 to an anonymous daughter of the margrave of Meissen, Rikdag, but left her a year later to marry a Hungarian princess. She was also abandoned in favour of the West Slavic princess Emnilda. After her death in 1013, Bolesław married Oda, the daughter of the mighty Margrave Ekkehard. Bolesław's daughter Regelinda went to Meissen to marry Margrave Herman in 1002. After 1005, his second daughter, whose name is unknown, went to Kiev to marry Prince Sviatopolk. The third daughter, Matilda, was sent to Swabia as the wife of Prince Otto of Schweinfurt.

Close ties to the imperial court are evidenced differently by the chronicles that belong to different historiographical traditions. Thus, Widukind[141] called Mieszko I *amicus imperatoris*, Thietmar described him as *tributum solvens usque ad vurta fluvium*, while Gallus Anonymus referred to Bolesław Chrobry as *frater et cooperator imperii* or *populi Romani amicus et socius*.[142] Although these descriptions are quite similar, in fact they had different meanings. Mieszko's relations to the Empire[143] have been widely discussed,[144] but it is still rather difficult to reconcile Widukind's title with Thietmar's account. In the light of studies on *amicitia*,[145] Widukind's account should be interpreted in terms of a rather free subordination (less than a vassal or a tribute payer) to the emperor since other early sources present the cases of *amicitia* as *spontanea deditio*. Widukind apparently used *amicus* in the sense of an ally[146] because the emperor is also called the *amicus* of Mieszko.[147] Thietmar, on the contrary, describes the Polish prince as the emperor's humble servant and tries to pass over in silence

---

[141] Widukind III.69.   [142] Gallus I.6.
[143] Thietmar mentioned, without exact dating, the subjection of Mieszko to Otto I as coinciding with the conquest of Lusatia (II.14). According to *Adalberti Continuatio Reginonis* that happened in 963. Cf. Strzelczyk 1992, 81.
[144] E.g. Labuda 1988, vol. I, 130–94, 475–500; Strzelczyk 1992, 142–67.   [145] Althoff 1992; Epp 1999.
[146] Labuda 2003, 82–6.   [147] Widukind III.69; cf. Rosik 2004.

Mieszko's attempts to maintain a certain extent of independence.[148] The attitude of Gallus Anonymus was different again; he wrote his chronicle in the early twelfth century, when Polish tradition saw Bolesław Chrobry as an ally equal to other magnates of the Empire.

The aspirations of the early Piasts to independence were partly fulfilled in 1000, which made Thietmar[149] complain that Otto III raised Bolesław from the position of *tributarius* to the level of a *dominus*. This elevation of the Polish ruler finds support in the descriptions used by Gallus Anonymus, which suggest an idea of a federation of Christian kingdoms allied with the Empire.[150] This political concept, however, fell with the death of Otto III in 1002. His successor, Henry II, had a Saxon rather than an imperial geopolitical vision and started a series of wars trying to curb Bolesław Chrobry's expansionary strategy. After the emperor's death, the Polish prince managed in 1025 to achieve official coronations both for himself and for his son Mieszko II. These coronations were treated as usurpations by the next German king and emperor, Conrad II.[151] In 1032 Mieszko II, pressed by the emperor, resigned the royal title;[152] already a year earlier the royal regalia had been taken to Germany by his wife Richeza. The next Polish coronation took place in 1076 during the conflict between Pope Gregory VII and the German king Henry IV, in which Bolesław II the Bold supported the papacy.

Despite successes in Christianizing their country and outside missionary activity, none of the early Polish rulers was later acknowledged as the holy patron of the state. This lack of a holy monarch may be explained by the rapid posthumous success of St Adalbert, bishop of Prague until 992, monk at the Roman monastery of St Boniface and St Alexius until 996, and the missionary who tried to convert the eastern Prussians and was killed by them on 23 April 997. By burying his body in Gniezno, Bolesław Chrobry created a widely venerated shrine that was visited in March 1000 by Otto III, who came there *orationis gratia*. The emperor installed an archbishopric there with the saint's half-brother Radim-Gaudentius bearing the title of *archepiscopus sancti Adalberti martyris*. Numerous churches were later dedicated to St Adalbert.[153] He was also the main patron of the kingdom until the competing cult of St Stanisław was initiated in Kraków in the thirteenth century. A reinterpretation of old excavations has shown

---

[148] Thietmar of Merseburg VII.12. The *Annales Altahenses maiores* (a. 973) mentioned that Mieszko's obedience to the emperor was guaranteed by giving his son as a hostage.
[149] Thietmar of Merseburg V.10.   [150] Strzelczyk 1999; 2000; Fried 2000.
[151] E.g. *Annales Magdeburgenses*, a. 1025 and 1030; *Annales Hildesheimenses*, a. 1028 and 1030.
[152] *Annales Hildesheimenses*, a. 1032.   [153] Młynarska-Kaletynowa 2000.

a simple, probably temporary, building erected in Gniezno before the large Romanesque cathedral was built in the early eleventh century. This structure is interpreted as a shrine where the body of St Adalbert was kept until the visit of the emperor in 1000.[154] Otto brought with him specially made golden plates to decorate the tomb and took away with him one arm of the saint. This relic was later subdivided to consecrate imperial memorial foundations in Aachen, Pereum (near Ravenna) and Rome; possibly also in Reichenau and Esztergom.[155]

The political success of the cult of St Adalbert prompted Bolesław Chrobry to acquire Bruno of Querfurt's body after the martyrdom of the archbishop in 1009. According to Thietmar,[156] Bruno's death occurred on the border of the Prussians and the Rus', which indicates that it took place among Iatvingians. This time, however, the political situation was different because of the long-lasting open conflict between Poland and the Empire under Henry II. There is thus no evidence that Bruno was ever officially canonized and no political gains were achieved.

Other early saints were the Five Martyr Brothers: two Italians (John and Benedict) and three Poles (Isaac, Matthew and Christinus) who were killed in Greater Poland in an attempted robbery in November 1003. Immediately acknowledged as martyrs, they were also buried in Gniezno. A fragment of a tombstone with a partially readable inscription that may be read as an invocation to three of the Five Martyr Brothers was found under the cathedral there.[157] The relics of St Adalbert and of the Five Martyr Brothers as well as the body of the first archbishop, Radim-Gaudentius, were all stolen by the invading Bohemian army in 1038 and reburied in Prague by Prince Břetislav.[158] The action proves the attractiveness of the symbolic power of the holy relics that reinforced the position of the Piasts, who received an independent ecclesiastical province and the royal crown, which Bohemian rulers were refused.

The Christian monarchy had recourse to various signs and symbols. The most numerous and the easiest to conceive were iconographic programmes promoted by coins circulating throughout its territory. It has long been believed that Mieszko I issued his own coin, a silver denarius with the inscription *MISICO*. Stanisław Suchodolski, however, proved that this coin must be connected to the grandson of the first Polish ruler, Mieszko II.[159] Thus, the earliest local coinage was started by Bolesław Chrobry shortly

---

[154] Janiak 1998.   [155] Dunin-Wąsowicz 2000.
[156] Thietmar of Merseburg VI.95.   [157] Kürbis 1998.
[158] The tomb of St Adalbert is still in the middle of the nave in the cathedral in Prague.
[159] Suchodolski 2000, 354–6.

before the turn of the millennium. The inscriptions that he used include *PRINCE[P]S POLONIE, GNEZDUN CIVITAS* and *BOLIZLAUS REX*.[160] Of these, the first denarius that was minted bore the inscription *GNEZ-DUN CIVITAS* (Gniezno city), which is interpreted as the identifier of Bolesław's state, which was not yet called Poland. This was a tradition continued from the times of Bolesław's father, who about 991 in the text known as *Dagome iudex* identified his domain as *Civitas Schignesne* or *Schinesghe*, which most probably also meant 'Gniezno city'.

Coins that introduced the title *PRINCES POLONIE* were issued shortly after Otto III's visit to Gniezno in 1000. The third denarius presenting the profile of a crowned man identified as *BOLIZLAUS REX* was produced about a decade before the official coronation of the Polish monarch in 1025. It was probably an element of the propaganda campaign aimed at the attainment of the royal crown. Bolesław's coins bear various iconographic motifs: the face of the ruler in profile, the *manus Dei*, a bird and various types of crosses. The bird depicted on the denarius bearing on both sides the same inscription *PRINCES POLONIE* until recently was believed to be the oldest example of the Polish national symbol, the White Eagle. Stanisław Suchodolski,[161] however, convincingly argued that it is a peacock that symbolized resurrection, eternal life and Christ. St Adalbert is pictured on a series of coins issued by several members of the Piast dynasty, who referred to the holy patron of the state. Especially after the subdivision of Poland in 1138 among the sons of the late Prince Bolesław III the Wrymouth, the saint was venerated as the symbol of the once united kingdom.

The alleged royal tombs of Mieszko I and Bolesław Chrobry, both once displayed in the middle of the nave of the cathedral at Poznań, probably fulfilled an important role in promoting the Christian vision of the monarchy as closely connected to the Church. Of the next rulers only the graves of Władysław Herman and his son Bolesław III the Wrymouth were discovered in Płock where the princes had their capital and founded the cathedral church. None of the remains of earlier monarchs have been discovered, which has resulted in long debates about the location of their original tombs.

Only two items survived of the regalia of the early Polish rulers. The most important is the copy of the imperial *Lancea Regis* (also called the Lance of St Mauritius[162]) that was brought by Otto III to Gniezno in 1000 as a gift for Bolesław Chrobry.[163] Kept in the archiepiscopal treasury in Kraków, this

---

[160] E.g. Kiersnowski 1959; Suchodolski 1967. [161] Suchodolski 2001.
[162] The original is in the Schatzkammer of the Hofburg in Vienna. [163] Gallus I.6.

is the only original element of the earliest regalia, because the first crowns of the Polish king and queen were taken to Germany by Queen Richeza, the wife of Mieszko II.[164] There is also a doubtful tradition recorded by Adémar of Chabannes of Otto III presenting Bolesław with the throne of Charlemagne that Otto had found in Aachen the same year.[165]

The second oldest surviving item of regalia is the coronation sword called *Szczerbiec*. According to a late legend, it was used by Bolesław Chrobry during his victorious campaign against Rus' in 1018 when he was to announce his control over Kiev symbolically by striking the famous Golden Gate with this very sword. The sword on view in the Wawel treasury, however, is a combination of different parts put together sometime in the thirteenth century. Other items associated with rulers and shedding light on their power and aspirations include ecclesiastical objects. Until the late eleventh century the foundation and endowment of churches and monasteries were the duty of the ruling dynasty. Luxurious gifts like the so-called golden codices donated by Bolesław II the Bold and Władysław Herman may even suggest ambitions of *imitatio imperii*.[166]

The close cooperation between the ruler and the Church offered prestige and the ideological and political reinforcement of paramount royal power. The Christianization of the people was also one of the methods employed to unify the population. The earliest stone residential buildings clearly exhibit the symbiotic relationship between lay and ecclesiastical powers. These so-called *palatia*, built in the late tenth and/or early eleventh century, were designed according to a single rather strict model, and comprised a long rectangular house connected to a round chapel. The most famous example is the still visible ruin of the *palatium* erected in the late tenth century on the island of Ostrów Lednicki in Greater Poland. The main building has the inner dimension of 30.6 by 13.4 m and the chapel with one apse has a diameter of 7.75 m. Another *palatium* discovered in Giecz was planned to be smaller, with the main building 20 m long and 10.6 m wide, and the rotunda 10 m in diameter. It has been suggested that the building process which started in the early eleventh century was never finished.[167] The *palatium* found on the Castle Hill in Przemyśl (south-east Poland) consisted of a residential part (29.7 by 11.5 m) and a round chapel (diameter of 7.6 m) with one apse. It was built in the early eleventh century.[168] The fourth, and probably the oldest, *palatium* in Poland has been recently identified in Poznań under the foundations of St Mary's. It was, probably, the residence

---

[164] 'Brunwilarensis monasterii fundatio'; *Annales Hildesheimenses*, a. 1032.   [165] Adémar, chap. 31.
[166] Michałowski 1989.   [167] Krysztofiak 1998.   [168] Sosnowska 1992; Pianowski 2002.

of Mieszko I and built in the third quarter of the tenth century. Attached to the thick stone wall was a goldsmith's workshop, but no royal chapel has yet been found.[169] The ruins of three supposed *palatia* in Wiślica (in Małopolska, Lesser Poland) that were once considered pre-Romanesque are today dated to the twelfth century.[170]

The clergy were indispensable in the administration of the polity and in diplomacy. A good example is provided by the activity of Bishop Reinbern who probably went with Bolesław Chrobry to Prague in 1003[171] and was later sent to Kiev as a chaplain of Bolesław's daughter.[172] Yet the symbiosis between the Piast monarchy and the Church was by no means ideal. Thietmar emphasized the protest of Bishop Unger against the foundation of the archbishopric of Gniezno. Gallus Anonymus mentioned an anathema of Archbishop Radim-Gaudentius on Poland.[173] The most famous conflict broke out in 1079, when King Bolesław II the Bold had Bishop Stanisław of Kraków punished and probably killed. According to Gallus Anonymus the king was expelled from the country after the bishop's cruel mutilation. The chronicler did not, however, explain the reason for the conflict and did not name the bishop. It was only Master Vincent in the early thirteenth century who furnished a precise story, which served in the promotion of the cult of St Stanisław. The hagiographical tradition initiated by Master Vincent presented the bishop as a martyr who defended his diocese against the cruel monarch.[174] As a result of long efforts led by Bishop Prandota, Stanisław was canonized in 1253 by Pope Innocent IV in Assisi. Three years later Pope Alexander IV issued the bull that gave the bishop of Kraków the second position in the Polish church after the archbishop of Gniezno. Almost immediately after the canonization of St Stanisław, his cult was promoted by the bishops of Kraków: a series of pilgrim badges were already produced in the thirteenth century. In fact we cannot definitely explain the reason for the conflict that probably ended with Bishop Stanisław's murder in 1079. Master Vincent's account is a rather late tradition recorded in the atmosphere of the late twelfth and early thirteenth centuries when the ideology of the Gregorian movement for the Church's independence from political powers was dominant among the clergy. It was the period when the long subdivision of Poland among the competing representatives of the Piast dynasty made any central political control illusory. At the same time

[169] Kočka-Krenz 2000.   [170] Gliński 1997.
[171] Reinbern's chaplain was mentioned by Thietmar (VI.10) in the company of Bolesław Chrobry in Bohemia in 1004.
[172] Thietmar of Merseburg VIII.72–3; cf. Rosik 2000b.   [173] E.g. Urbańczyk 2001.
[174] *Vita s. Stanislai (vita minor)*, chaps. 31–2; *Vita s. Stanislai (vita maior)*, II.18–19.

the Polish church gained effective control over the largely Christianized masses who were now served by a network of parish churches. The series of *privilegia* that the clergy received in 1180, 1210 and 1215 reinforced their position. By the end of the century it was the Church that played a leading role in the restoration of the monarchy.

5. THE EFFECTS OF CHRISTIANIZATION

The dynasty, converted in 966, quickly undertook missionary activity outside its domain and sent missions to its still-pagan neighbours. In 997 Adalbert went from Bolesław I Chrobry's court to the Prussians.[175] The mission undertaken in or after 1000 in Pomerania by Bishop Reinbern was unsuccessful.[176] At the very beginning of the eleventh century Archbishop Bruno of Querfurt organized a mission sent from Poland to Sweden.[177] Bruno himself tried to convert the Prussians in 1009 but was martyred despite his initial success in converting one of the local rulers.[178] In 1124–5 Bishop Otto of Bamberg went to Pomerania, enjoying the strong support of the Polish prince Bolesław III the Wrymouth. Otto organized mass baptisms there and had churches built, for example in Szczecin. This was the only missionary success of the early Piast monarchy.[179]

No pre-Christian literacy has been identified in the Polish lands despite the eager search for it that even led to the faking of 'Slavic runes' in the late nineteenth century. For many people the first, though unconscious, contact with Latin started with the more significant influx of imported coins in the second half of the tenth century and the minting of local coins after *c.* 995. It was Christianity that introduced literacy at least among the personnel of the Church. Liturgical needs led to the import of manuscripts, of which only a handful have survived.[180] We do not know whether Bolesław Chrobry knew Latin but we can be sure of the literacy of his son Mieszko II whose education, which included Latin and Greek, was praised in the dedicatory letter attached to the liturgical book *Ordo Romanus* (the so-called *Kodeks Matyldy*) sent to him as a gift by the German princess Mathilde *c.* 1028. Subsequent monarchs financed the importation of manuscripts as well as the writing of new texts, which included the earliest Polish chronicle by Gallus Anonymus, completed *c.* 1117. Later in the twelfth century the

---

[175] Canaparius, chap. 30.   [176] Thietmar of Merseburg VIII.72–3.
[177] Bruno of Querfurt, *Epistola*, 105.
[178] Wibert; and accounts in: Petrus Damian, chap. 27; Thietmar of Merseburg VI.94–5.
[179] Ekkehard, a. 1124–5; *Vita Prieflingensis* II; Ebo II; Herbord II.
[180] Potkowski 1984; Mews 2002.

aristocracy also showed interest in commissioning texts that recorded their deeds, for example the Silesian magnate Piotr Włast (*Carmen Mauri, Gesta Piotrkonis*, although the dating of these texts is controversial and they were perhaps composed much later). The main centres of literacy were, however, cathedrals and monasteries.

There are few finds that demonstrate knowledge of writing among the lay inhabitants of early medieval Poland. The largest collection of items bearing inscriptions or single characters was excavated at the eastern border that was an important centre for the expanding Rus' principalities. It is, therefore, not surprising that the items (a bone knife handle, and hundreds of lead seals used for marking imported textiles) are inscribed in the Cyrillic alphabet, which could have been used by the inhabitants of the frontier zone.[181]

The active use of script is witnessed by finds of *stili* that were commonly used for writing on wax tablets or for scratching letters on pieces of birch bark like those known from several Rus' towns. Such tools, usually made of iron, were found in several political–economic centres of the Polish–Rus' border zone, for example in Drohiczyn, Gródek, Przemyśl and Trepcza near Sanok. They are all dated to the twelfth or thirteenth century by numerous parallels known from Belarus and the Ukraine.[182] Similar finds have been unearthed in the centre of Piast Poland: Gniezno, Biskupin, Łęczyca, Poznań, Trzemeszno and Giecz. Some knowledge of yet another script may be inferred from the handful of items bearing runic inscriptions found along the Baltic coast: Koszalin, Świelubie-Bardy, Kamień Pomorski and Wolin. This alphabet, however, would have been used only by Scandinavian settlers and/or visitors.

One of the most striking results of joining Christian civilization was the appearance of stone architecture. There was no earlier tradition of masonry in Poland, which made the new type of buildings outstanding symbols of the new era. Despite the high cost of importing foreign specialists, the early Piasts invested extensively in stone architecture. Today, 201 remnants of pre-Romanesque and Romanesque buildings are known in Poland. Most of these were parish churches erected in the thirteenth century which are still in use today. Only eighty stone constructions may be dated to the tenth to twelfth centuries and most of these survive only as ruins discovered by archaeological excavations. In a letter sent in 1028 to the Polish king Mieszko II, his German cousin, Princess Mathilde of Lotharingia, congratulated him for building more churches than anybody else. However, it took well over

---

[181] Hanc-Maikowa 1988, 60–2.   [182] Ginalski 2003.

one and a half centuries before stone churches appeared in smaller centres of the Piast state.

In the first building phase, the rulers expressed their power at their main seats through stone structures. Stone churches first appeared, therefore, in the central strongholds of Greater Poland: Giecz, Gniezno, Poznań and Ostrów Lednicki. In the second half of the tenth century a series of both residential and ecclesiastic buildings were already being erected there. Elsewhere building in stone started later. The main architectural tasks connected with the introduction of Christianity included, first of all, the building of the royal and diocesan churches, all known thanks to extensive excavations.[183] Despite these discoveries, we do not know where the first royal church was built. Three royal chapels were discovered in Ostrów Lednicki, Giecz (both in Greater Poland) and in Przemyśl (south-eastern Poland). They were all small round annexes attached directly to the residential buildings (*palatia*) built in the late tenth or early eleventh century.

Not many traces of early wooden ecclesiastical architecture exist in Poland, although such constructions are likely to have accompanied the first phase of Christianization. The reason for the lack of archaeological remains may be that they were overlooked by the early excavators who were eager to uncover the stone constructions. Nonetheless, some wooden buildings have been identified. At the Benedictine monastery in Tyniec the early Romanesque church was preceded by a wooden one.[184] At the royal complex on the Wawel Hill in Kraków evidence of a possible tenth-century wooden church was uncovered under the pre-Romanesque cathedral.[185] Two wooden churches, dated to the turn of the tenth century and to the mid-eleventh, were discovered under the Romanesque church of St Adalbert that still stands in the main marketplace of Kraków.[186] In Kalisz-Zawodzie the princely stone church erected *c.* 1146 was preceded by a smaller wooden structure built in the early eleventh century. Finally, stone-and-mortar foundations of a small church at Ostrów Lednicki are now interpreted as the base of a wooden construction dated to the second half of the tenth century.

The three earliest cathedrals were erected in the sees of the most stable dioceses. The cathedral church in Gniezno mentioned by Thietmar in 1018 replaced a small church and the shrine of St Adalbert. The building

---

[183] Urbańczyk 2004.   [184] Kalinowski 1971.
[185] Pianowski 2000a, 67; 2000b, 237.   [186] Radwański 1975, 169.

with a nave and two aisles built for the archbishop at the beginning of
the eleventh century was soon destroyed during the pagan uprising of 1032
and looted by the Bohemian army in 1038. It was reconsecrated in 1064
and, for an unknown reason, again in 1097.[187] The cathedral was later
furnished with the monumental bronze door depicting the main stages
of St Adalbert's life.[188] This rare example of Romanesque art in central
Europe is still extant. In Poznań the cathedral was built in the late tenth
or early eleventh century by Bolesław Chrobry who placed the tomb of
his father Mieszko I there; he himself was subsequently buried there by
his son Mieszko II. Archaeologists identified these tombs located *in medio
ecclesia*; both seem to have been destroyed during the Bohemian invasion of 1038. Despite an intensive search there is no material evidence for
any church at the Wawel Hill in Kraków prior to the late tenth century;
St Václav's cathedral was built there in the eleventh century. Already in
the eleventh century Wawel attracted rich Christian 'investors' who established there about ten churches and other stone buildings of various shapes,
sizes and functions. 'It was undoubtedly the largest concentration of the
monumental sacral architecture . . . in the whole contemporary east-central
Europe.'[189] Numerous early churches in Greater Poland are spread over a
large area.

Besides the political centres in Greater and Lesser Poland, there are
also some early churches in relatively remote places. The foundations of a
large church were discovered at the stronghold of Kałdus near Chełmno.
The ambitious project, launched sometime in the first half of the eleventh
century, was never completed. The basilica, planned to be over 30 metres
long and divided into a nave with two aisles, each ending in an apse, may
be compared only with the cathedrals built in Gniezno and Poznań.[190]

When discussing influences that shaped the oldest Polish stone architecture, we should distinguish two trends. The overwhelming tendency was
to build round churches or, rather, chapels with one or more apses. Their
simple form and small scale meant that they could be erected relatively fast
and cheaply in order to establish focal points of the new religion.[191] Only
more important centres enjoyed more elaborate investment.

An ongoing debate concerning the origin of early architectural influences has not resulted in any agreement among art historians and archaeologists. Initially the hypothesis that the main inspirations came from

[187] Gallus II.5; *Rocznik Traski*, a. 1064; Długosz I.427.   [188] E.g. Gieysztor 1959.
[189] Żaki 1994, 64.   [190] Chudziak 2000, 130.   [191] Rodzińska-Chorąży 1994, 148.

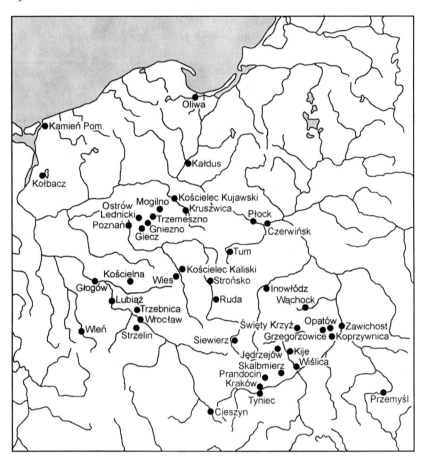

17. Pre-Romanesque and Romanesque buildings in Poland

the Carolingian–Ottonian zone and from neighbouring Bohemia found general approval. Later, Byzantine and/or South Slavic elements were discovered.[192] Italian connections have also been suggested.[193] Looking for 'southern inspirations'[194] soon became the main tendency in studies of Polish pre-Romanesque architecture. Today, early Polish architecture is viewed as the result of a combination of various influences, even if imperial Italo-German traditions were dominant.[195]

[192] E.g. Hawrot 1959; Żurowska 1983, 164.   [193] E.g. Nogieć-Czepielowa 1974.
[194] Rodzińska-Chorąży 1994, 149.   [195] Świechowski 2000, 33.

6. CONCLUSION

Scholars studying the Christianization of the Polish lands face the crucial difficulty posed by the extreme scarcity of sources depicting the situation before the official conversion of the dynasty in 966. The total lack of locally written sources, combined with the vagueness of reports composed outside Poland and the questionable reliability of the accounts recorded by the twelfth- and thirteenth-century chroniclers prompted scholars to develop speculative arguments that are largely based on parallels adapted from neighbouring countries. Thus, despite long debates, it has been impossible to reach a common point of view. The situation is better for the study of the post-966 period, but even for that era we do not have more than a handful of reliable written sources. Moreover, they offer interpretations of the geopolitical circumstances important for the royal house, rather than descriptions of internal developments. Only Gallus Anonymus's chronicle, finished *c.* 1117, offers a rich panorama of events that may be used to reconstruct the processes relevant to our study. His knowledge of the earlier periods, however, is rather vague and often biased by the needs of dynastic propaganda. These problems led to reliance on archaeologists, who were to furnish tangible facts that could be used to support the hypotheses constructed by historians. Yet the obvious need for interdisciplinary cooperation has rarely turned into real cooperation and both parties have tended to pillage data from the other discipline that would fit their own ready-made interpretations, rather than trying to apply common studies to the basic data.

The extensive collection of material gathered in response to the questionnaire agreed by the participants of the current project has made it possible to build a coherent, even if disputable, picture of the complex process of Christianization of the lands between the Baltic Sea and the Carpathian Mountains. It shows the political centre organized by and around the Piast dynasty, which entered the geopolitical stage of Latin Christendom by attaining an equal status as Christian monarchs. Its members played a complex game of changeable alliances with all their neighbours (including trans-Baltic contacts) who faced similar problems. Early Polish rulers used Christian signs and symbols extensively in order to reinforce their power both internally and at the level of inter-dynastic relations. Today it is obvious that the process of conversion, contrary to the reports of the chroniclers, was not a simple implementation of royal will. Accounts concerning the open pagan opposition of the 1030s as well as archaeological discoveries show a process that was both long and difficult, especially in the peripheral areas. However, Christianization was undoubtedly a very important part of the process that led to the organization of a stable Polish state and, much more slowly, to the formation of a common national consciousness among the populations within it.

APPENDIX

POLABIA AND POMERANIA BETWEEN PAGANISM
AND CHRISTIANITY

Stanisław Rosik and Przemysław Urbańczyk

The scarcity of written sources pertaining to the early Christianization of Poland prompted scholars to look for comparative material in the well-documented history of Polabia and Pomerania (including the south Baltic isles) between the tenth and twelfth centuries. Such an approach, however, may be controversial because these areas functioned in different geopolitical circumstances. In Polabia, the ideological, political and military pressure exercised by Christian neighbours resulted in a return to pagan beliefs. In Pomerania, the first attempt at Christianization about 1000 failed. Both cases, therefore, must be carefully discussed to avoid superficial parallels.

In the late eighth century Carolingian expeditions reached the territories of Polabian Slavs and conquered some of them. At that time, the common opinion expressed at a council held on the banks of the river Danube in 796 was that Slavs were not able to understand the new faith.[196] Some knowledge of Polabia is soon witnessed by the description of the so-called *Geographus Bavarus*, a text commissioned by Louis the German and written in the monastery at Fulda *c.* 848. The interpretation of this text suggests that the Polabians were divided between three zones: the north-west federation was dominated by the Abodrites; further east was the federation of Veletians and some other tribes including the Rans on the island of Rügen; and the southern part was settled by Sorbs and Lusatians.[197] An apocryphal Legend of Corvey[198] refers to the first mission sent from Corvey to Rügen in the mid-ninth century.[199] Effective evangelization, however, started in the southern Polabian area following its conquest by the East Frankish king Henry I.

---

[196] 'Conventus episcoporum', 172–6.   [197] Cf. Strzelczyk 2002, 13–19.

[198] The reliability of this source is questionable because the legend was recorded at the beginning of the twelfth century and had developed not earlier than the eleventh (Soszyński 1984).

[199] Cf. *Annales Corbeienses*, a. 1114; Helmold I.6 and II.108; Saxo XIV.39.

Polabian territories were subordinated to the archbishopric of Mainz, and two new bishoprics, those of Havelberg and Brenna/Brandenburg, were founded in 948. After the conquest of the northern Polabians in 955, Otto I decided to install a new archbishopric in Magdeburg that subordinated the old bishoprics of Havelberg and Brenna in 968 while new ones were founded in Merseburg, Meissen and Zittau.

In 967, the Saxon outlaw Wichmann Billung the younger found refuge in Starigard, the main centre of Wagria in north-eastern Polabia. As a consequence the stronghold was attacked by Prince Hermann Billung who, according to Widukind of Corvey, found there an idol of *Saturn ex aere fuso*.[200] A new bishopric was installed in Starigard itself[201] in 968, and was subordinated to the archbishopric of Hamburg-Bremen.

In the south Polabian area, where conversion followed conquest, the process was slow but successful. Christianization was initiated by the German clergy. Thietmar of Merseburg mentioned bishops of Merseburg who personally engaged in the missionary work. Thus, Bishop Boso *slavonica scripserat verba* and tried to teach the converts to sing 'Kyrie eleison'. Bishop Wigbert cut down the *Zutibure* (sacred grove) and built a church there. Nevertheless, at the beginning of the eleventh century the inhabitants of the area still combined the practices of two belief systems. This was noted with sorrow by Thietmar of Merseburg[202] who wrote that the Daleminzi (*Glomače*) venerated their eponymic holy source *Glomač* more than churches. This syncretism of a formally Christianized people who, although they went to church, did not abandon pagan sanctuaries that used elements of nature (e.g. groves or waters) to define sacred space, seems to be typical for the area. Another reported aspect of this syncretism was the cult of *domestici dei*. Complaining that *rustici* were not interested in being visited by their priests, seldom came to churches and revered 'household deities', Thietmar recalled an idol named *Hennil* which was represented as a hand holding a ring.[203] According to the same chronicler, Slavs did not accept Christian eschatology. He interpreted this as proof of the simple stupidity of *inliterati*.[204] Altogether, these conflicts should be viewed in terms of controversies between locals and clerics rather than as direct contradiction between paganism and Christianity.

---

[200] Widukind III.68.
[201] The Slavic name *Starigard* was translated to *Oldenburg*; both names are used in the historiography.
[202] Thietmar of Merseburg I.3.
[203] Thietmar of Merseburg VII.69. *Hennil* perhaps did not belong to Slavic folk culture because there were also German settlers in the area (Łowmiański 1979, 201). However, the cult of household deities was typical of the Slavs, attested by Helmold I.47.
[204] Thietmar of Merseburg I.14.

In 983 the great uprising removed both German rule and the ecclesiastical network in the lands controlled by the Veletians or Liutizi.[205] We do not know about the progress of their conversion between 955 and 983, but at the beginning of the eleventh century they were treated as an *apostatica gens* because they had rebelled after their reception of Christianity.[206] Bruno of Querfurt in his letter to King Henry II postulated their forcible reconversion according to the principle *compellere intrare* that was applied only to cases of apostasy.[207] Around 1047 the chronicler Wipo still remembered their alleged apostasy of 983 saying that despite being *semichristiani* they had returned to paganism.[208] These attitudes clearly attest the ecclesiastical tradition that equated the official end of paganism to the inclusion of whole peoples (*gentes*) into the Church.[209]

The Liutizi defended their independence against the German and Polish expedition of 985, and became an important player on the geopolitical stage. This was apparently accepted by Henry II who, despite their open paganism, allied with them in his prolonged wars against Bolesław Chrobry. In 1018 the invasion of the Liutizi initiated the pagan uprising in the lands of the Abodrites. As a result, German rule there was overthrown. At the very beginning of the eleventh century the Pomeranians freed themselves from Piast control, expelled Bishop Reinbern of Kołobrzeg, and joined the large pagan Slavic zone that stretched along the Baltic.

The most powerful among these Slavs was undoubtedly the Liutizi union. According to the chroniclers its capital in the eleventh century was a stronghold located by a lake and housing the main temple. Thietmar named it Radogošč (*Riedegost*) and stressed that the stronghold only contained a sanctuary where Svarožic (*Zuarasici*) was venerated. The name of this deity (confirmed also by Bruno of Querfurt) is interpreted as the diminutive or patronymic of Svarog, the god known from Kievan Rus' who is etymologically connected with heavenly fire[210] and, according to the myths, was considered to be the founder of social order.[211] Svarožic is described by Thietmar as the head of the Liutizi pantheon. The idols of other gods and goddesses stood around his statue. In his *interpraetatio Christiana* Thietmar treated all these statues as *dii manu facti* and sometimes directly as *simulacra demonum*. He also mentions some deities pictured on banners that he

---

[205] At the end of the tenth century the new tribal name Liutizi appeared in the sources. Sometimes used synonymously with 'Veletians', in fact the Liutizi were the main part of the Veletians.

[206] Thietmar of Merseburg III.17: *suscepta christianitate*.

[207] Kahl 1955.   [208] Wipo, chap. 33.   [209] E.g. Wavra 1991, 15.

[210] Gieysztor 1982, 131; Urbańczyk 1991, 29.   [211] Banaszkiewicz 1998, 132–40.

called *deae*. Bruno of Querfurt in his letter to King Henry II called these banners *diabolica vexilla*.

Thietmar also mentioned some local shrines housing idols but emphasized that the temple in Radogošč was honoured by all Liutizi.[212] An oracle was located there, that was used to make decisions about war and peace by the drawing of lots or by observing the behaviour of the holy horse as it crossed a spear that was placed on the ground. The reliability of this information is debated. Although the *interpraetatio Christiana* and a literary atmosphere of horror pervades the text, Thietmar seems to be well informed. He attended the court of Henry II and had the opportunity to observe the king's pagan allies directly. Parallels between his text and other accounts (the letter of Bruno of Querfurt to King Henry II and later sources) also support his reliability. Sometimes he even displayed a critical attitude towards his sources of information. For example, when he reported a story about a boar from the lake of Radogošč that appeared to prophesy war, he stressed that the information came from antiquity and might be wrong. The priests of the Radogošč temple had a decisive voice at the assemblies that according to Thietmar were the main source of political power in the Liutizi union. The existence of this theocratic system was confirmed half a century later by Adam of Bremen.[213] He, however, identified the main centre of the Liutizi (*civitas vulgatissima*) as *Rethre*, which was located on an island in a lake. According to his report, the name of the main deity was *Redigast* (which may stand for Radogost or the former temple's name Radogošč) and there was only one idol, made of gold and lying in a purple bed inside the temple. These discrepancies may indicate a change in the function of the stronghold housing the temple over time. However it is also possible that Adam created a fantastic and allegorical vision of a *civitas* ruled by the *princeps daemonum*. Both chroniclers, as well as the *Annales Augustani*, under the year 1068, highlighted the political role of the sanctuary in the federation of Liutizi.

In 1057 a civil war divided the Liutizi union, sparked by a rebellion against the primacy of the Redars who controlled the central temple.[214] The federation divided into several separate political organizations, with the Redars and Tolezans among them. They were still able to launch successful expeditions, for example killing Prince Godescalc of the Abodrites in 1066, but they were defeated by the Saxons in 1068 when, according to the

---

[212] Thietmar of Merseburg VI.25.   [213] Adam of Bremen II.21.
[214] Adam of Bremen III.22; Helmold I.21.

Annales Augustani, the expedition of Bishop Burchard of Halberstadt plundered the temple of Rethra (Rheda).[215] This undermined the supremacy of the Liutizi, and the Rans of Rügen gained a dominant position, with their famous sanctuary located on the cliff of Arkona becoming the main cult centre among all the Slavs who still practised paganism in the region. This is directly confirmed by Helmold, and indirectly by Ebo, who mentioned that after the destruction of the temple in Gützkow by Otto of Bamberg in 1128, the swarm of flies that symbolized evil powers flew towards Rügen.[216] Liutizian theocracy did not continue, because the veneration of the temple at Arkona did not lead to the formation of a regional political organization. The *vitae* of St Otto of Bamberg also mention pagan temples in the Liutizi centres of Wołogoszcz (Wolgast), dedicated to a god named Iarovit,[217] and Chocków (Gützkow). The bishop visited these places during his second mission in Pomerania, because they belonged to the west Pomeranian principality.

The beginning of this polity is unclear. The Pomeranians threw off Piast supremacy no later than during the crisis of the Polish monarchy in the 1030s. The first signal of the political integration of Pomerania is reported by the *Annales Altahenses maiores* that mention Prince *Zemuzil* who in 1046 ruled in the eastern part of Pomerania. According to the late and controversial tradition of the fourteenth-century *Kronika Wielkopolska* ('The Chronicle of Greater Poland'), a bishopric was installed in Kruszwica in the eleventh century which later moved to Włocławek in order to spread Christianity there. The west Pomeranian principality still existed in the early twelfth century, when one of Prince Wartislav I's centres was Wolin,[218] which since the tenth century had been a centre for artisanal production.[219] In 1043 Wolin (*Iumne*) was plundered by the Danish–Norwegian king Magnus and lost its dominant position,[220] but at the beginning of the twelfth century its religious position was still relatively significant among the pagans because it boasted a lance which the hagiographer of St Otto connected to Julius Caesar.

In the twelfth century, however, the main position in the lower Oder region was taken by Szczecin where the three-headed statue of Triglav

---

[215] *Annales Augustani*, a. 1068.   [216] Helmold II.108; Ebo III.11.
[217] The meaning of the name, 'mighty lord', is almost exactly the same as that of Svantevit (cf. Urbańczyk 1991, 181, 188, 193).
[218] *Iumne* according to Adam of Bremen III.22; *Iulin* in *Vita Prieflingensis* II.5–7, 15–19; III.12–14; Ebo II.1, 7, 11, 15, 18; III.1, 21; Herbord II.24, 26, 37, 38, 40; III.24, 25, 30. About the princely court in Wolin: Ebo II.7; Herbord II.24.
[219] Cf. Ibrahim ibn Yaqub, 50; Thietmar of Merseburg VI.33.
[220] Adam of Bremen, schol. 56 (57); Arnórr jarlaskáld.

was venerated in the main temple (*contina*). The existence of this cult is confirmed by Henry of Antwerp, who described the destruction of the three-headed idol near Brandenburg in 1127.[221] Divination involving a horse, as in Liutizi practices, is mentioned in Szczecin as well as the important role of priests in assemblies. According to Ebo, pagan priests claimed that the three heads of the idol represented pan-cosmic rule over heaven, earth and underground, while the golden band on his eyes symbolized Triglav's blindness to human sins.[222] Thus, the phenomenon of polycephalic deities, widespread in the Baltic and North Sea area,[223] in this case symbolically expressed the idea of the supremacy of one god in all zones of the cosmic order. Some scholars have suggested that this deity (the only god venerated locally) should be connected to the old Slavic idea of a cosmic mountain with three peaks that was made anthropomorphous in the three-headed idol and adopted as a universally competent deity.[224]

The situation was similar in Rügen, where the famous shrine of Arkona contained an idol of the main god Svantevit who had four heads looking at all parts of the world. There was no other idol in the shrine and no place for other gods in the Arkona theology. Svantevit, therefore, had a wide competence that included guiding military expeditions and supervising the agrarian sphere;[225] this seems to be the answer of Slavic theology to the Christian idea of the almighty God.[226] This interpretation is supported by the etymology of *Svantevit*, which means 'mighty/holy Lord'.[227]

The cases of Svantevit and Triglav seem to indicate that a tendency to promote the idea of one supernatural patron for the local community was a late development in the pagan Slavic religion. It was, probably, the ideological answer of the theocratic priests to the challenges of expanding Christianity. The multi-headed statues had an important function as symbolic expressions of the overarching competence of those deities. Our knowledge of this process is especially clear for the eleventh and twelfth centuries when Slavonic tribes developed the cults of their own god-patrons. Helmold listed a number of such deities: Prove in the Starigard area; Siva the goddess of

[221] Henricus de Antverpis, 482.   [222] Ebo III.11.
[223] Lamm 1987; Rosik 1995, 34–49, 52–8.
[224] Słupecki 1994, 238. Polycephalism used to be interpreted as the result of the Slavs' reception of the Holy Trinity (e.g. Łowmiański 1979, 190–5). This has recently been questioned (Rosik 1995, 66–110).
[225] Each year a priest filled the horn held by the idol with wine, and an oracle about future crop yields was made (Saxo XIV.39). On this ceremony for the West Slavic area (probably in Arkona or in Radogošč): William of Malmesbury II.189; cf. analysis by Pettazzoni 1967, 507; also Słupecki and Zaroff 1999) and R. Bartlett in this volume, Chap. 2.
[226] Rosik 1995, 74–104.   [227] Urbańczyk 1991, 188, 193.

the Polabians; Radogost the god-patron of the Abodrites; and Svantevit venerated by the Rugians.[228] In addition he mentioned both a mysterious father of all deities referred to by the biblical title of *deus deorum* (cf. Psalm 50: 1),[229] and the perpetrator of misery called *Zcerneboh* (Black God).[230] He also referred to local cults of idols like Podaga in Plön[231] and deities guarding houses and fields.[232] Helmold described the wood where the holy grove of the god Prove was located. Assemblies took place and princely judgements were announced there.[233] There was also a cult centre located in the princely stronghold of Starigard (Oldenburg) where another sanctuary containing an idol was located.[234] This shows the differentiation of political power: assemblies were connected to the 'open-air' sanctuary and princely centre controlling a temple that housed an idol. This dual aspect of the power structure is also confirmed for other West Slavic communities.[235] The Christianization of these territories did not, therefore, simply mean the destruction of pagan institutions, but also involved, as twelfth-century sources show, a certain level of acceptance of the new religion by local assemblies. Even if these usually acted under the pressure of military power, they offered political sanctions to the changes imposed by the new religion.

A good example is provided by the events that took place in 1124 in Pyrzyce, the centre of the Pomeranian tribe Prissani known from the account in the *Geographus Bavarus*. At the very beginning of St Otto's first mission the council of elderly men there tried to postpone the start of evangelization by using the excuse of a necessary consultation with their superiors. Finally, they decided to open the town gate for the missionaries, but this decision had to be accepted by the assembly of all the inhabitants.[236] One should remember that a military escort was given to St Otto by the Polish prince Bolesław III the Wrymouth, who had conquered west Pomerania two years earlier. Although the west Pomeranian prince Wartislav I had been converted some years earlier in Magdeburg,[237] it was only at the time of the conquest that he started actively to support a more widespread Christianization.

The situation in the last enclave of Slavic paganism on Rügen was similar: official paganism survived there until 1168. In the twelfth century the kingdoms of Denmark, Germany and Poland competed for the island. It was the Danish king Valdemar who besieged the stronghold of Arkona where

---

[228] Helmold I.52.   [229] Helmold I.84.   [230] Helmold I.52.   [231] Helmold I.84.
[232] Helmold I.52.   [233] Helmold I.84.   [234] Gabriel 1984; Słupecki 1994.
[235] Banaszkiewicz 1986a.   [236] Herbord II.14; cf. Boroń 1999, 82, 98.   [237] Ebo III.6.

the four-headed statue of Svantevit stood. Facing such changed circumstances, Jaromir, the prince of the Rans who inhabited the island, engaged so actively in spreading Christianity that Helmold called him 'a second Paul'.[238] This decision also allowed him to suppress the rival to his rule, the theocratic power that had its centre in Arkona.[239]

Similarly, the final Christianization of the Abodrites took place as the result of conquest by Duke Henry the Lion of Saxony in 1156. The situation there was, however, more complex. The Abodrite prince Henry (d. 1127) had been a Christian and had a church in his capital, Lübeck, but he had apparently decided not to spread Christianity in all of his domains. Such a modus vivendi between Christian princes and their pagan subjects was a specific Polabian phenomenon that probably resulted from a fear of pagan resistance. Henry's father Godescalc, active in the Christianization of his country, was killed during one such rebellion in 1066, when the invasion of Liutizi inspired a pagan uprising that demolished the local ecclesiastical organization.[240]

There were some cases of non-violent missions, for example the expedition of the Iberian bishop, Bernard, to Pomerania in 1122,[241] or a visit to the Liutizi by two Czech monks who were allowed to preach the Gospel in Rethra c. 1060 but were later murdered.[242] Helmold also described the cooperation between secular power and clergy in the missions. A good example is the story of Bishop Vicelinus of Starigard, called the apostle of Wagria, who, despite his unusual character and sanctity evidenced by miracles and exorcist practices, could do nothing without the support of princely power. However, the conquest of Polabians and Pomeranians was triggered by the crusade ideology. As early as around 1108 the archbishop of Magdeburg and other German bishops asked the Saxon lords to fight pagans who venerated a deity named *Pripegala*.[243] Nonetheless, the most radical position, promoted by St Bernard of Clairvaux who in 1147 offered only the alternative between 'baptism or death', faced opposition both in

---

[238] Helmold II.108.

[239] The princes of the Rans had already earlier attempted to challenge the power of Arkona's priests: they built at their seat in Karentia a complex of three temples that housed idols of Rugievit (the Lord of Rügen with seven faces and his military attributes) and his two satellites, Porevit and Porenut, each with five faces (Saxo XIV.39). This information is to some extent confirmed by the *Knytlingasaga* although the names of the deities are different. Helmold, however, did not mention them at all (cf. Miś 1997).

[240] Adam of Bremen III.51. Pagan uprisings among the Abodrites also took place earlier, e.g. in the 990s and in 1018 (Adam of Bremen II.43; Thietmar of Merseburg VIII.5).

[241] Ebo II.1. [242] Adam of Bremen III.21, schol. 71.

[243] *Epistola Adelgoti archiepiscopi Magdeburgensis*, in Labuda 2002, 804–6.

the Church (for example by St Norbert of Xanten) and among the land-holding lords.

All this shows the complexity of the process of Christianization in the Polabian and Pomeranian areas. It may be explained by the geopolitical situation of the Polabians, which was different from that of Poland since they were under strong military pressure from the German, Danish and Polish states.[244] They also had a different political structure without a paramount centre that was able to execute effective administrative control over larger areas. Christianization, therefore, was introduced step by step and often halted by temporary setbacks. The pagan uprising in 983 was the start of a long period of search for a religious system that could compete with Christianity and give ideological support to political power. The traditionally strong position of local assemblies, however, prevented the building of stable regional organizational structures that would stop the expansion of neighbouring Christian states.

REFERENCES

Adam of Bremen, *Gesta Hammaburgensis ecclesiae pontificum*, ed. B. Schmeidler, *MGH SRG*, Hanover and Leipzig, 1917.
Adémar de Chabannes, *Chronique*, ed. Y. Chauvin and G. Pon, Turnhout, 2003.
Althoff, G. 1992, *Amicitia und Pacta. Bündnis, Einigung, Politik und Gebetsgedanken im beginnenden 10. Jahrhundert*, Hanover (*MGH Schriften* XXXVII).
Annales Altahenses maiores, ed. E. von Oefele, *MGH SRG*, Hanover, 1891.
Annales Augustani, ed. G. Pertz, *MGH SS* III, Hanover, 1839, 123–36.
Annales Corbeienses, ed. G. Pertz, *MGH SS* III, Hanover, 1839, 1–18.
Annales Hildesheimenses, ed. G. Waitz, *MGH SRG*, Hanover, 1878.
Annales Magdeburgenses, ed. G. Pertz, *MGH SS* XVI, Hanover, 1859, 105–96.
Arnórr jarlaskáld, *O walce króla norweskiego Magnusa ze słowiańskimi korsarzami w Jómie–Wolinie w r. 1043*, in G. Labuda, *Słowiańszczyzna pierwotna. Wybór tekstów*, Warsaw, 1954, 305–6.
Banaszkiewicz, J. 1986a, 'Jedność porządku przestrzennego, społecznego i tradycji początków ludu (Uwagi o urządzeniu wspólnoty plemienno-państwowej u Słowian)', *Przegląd Historyczny* 77/3, 445–66.
Banaszkiewicz, J. 1986b, *Podanie o Piaście i Popielu. Studium porównawcze nad wczesnosredniowiecznymi tradycjami dynastycznymi*, Warsaw.
Banaszkiewicz, J. 1998, *Polskie dzieje bajeczne Mistrza Wincentego Kadłubka*, Wrocław.
Beumann, H. 1950, *Widukind von Korvei. Unterschungen zur Geschichtschreibung und Ideengeschichte des 10. Jahrhunderts*, Weimar.

[244] Cf. Petersohn 1979.

Bonifatius una cum aliis episcopis Aethelbaldum regem Mercionum ad virtutem revocat, in *MGH Epistolae* III, *Merovingici et Karolini aevi* I, Berlin 1892, no. 73.

Borawska, D. 1964, *Kryzys monarchii wczesnopiastowskiej w latach trzydziestych XI w.*, Warsaw.

Boroń, P. 1999, *Słowiańskie wiece plemienne*, Katowice.

Bruno of Querfurt, *Epistola Brunonis ad Henricum regem*, ed. J. Karwasińska, *MPH* n.s. IV/3, Warsaw, 1973, 85–106.

Bruno of Querfurt, *S. Adalberti Pragensis episcopi et martyris vita altera*, ed. J. Karwasińska, *MPH* n.s. IV/2, Warsaw, 1969.

Bruno of Querfurt, *Vita quinque fratrum eremitarum*, ed. J. Karwasińska, *MPH* n.s. IV/3, Warsaw, 1973, 9–84.

'Brunwilarensis monasterii fundatio', ed. R. Koepke, *MGH SS* XI, ed. G. H. Pertz, Hanover, 1854, 394–408.

Brzostowicz, M. 2003, 'Bruszczewo i Spławie – dwa przykłady grodów plemiennych z południowej Wielkopolski', *Wielkopolskie Sprawozdania Archeologiczne* 6, 15–31.

Buko, A. 2000, 'Pogańskie miejsca święte w krajobrazie osadnictwa Wyżyny Sandomierskiej', in Moździoch 2000c, 61–83.

Buko, A. 2003, 'Wielkie kopce małopolskie z okresu wczesnego średniowiecza', in Woźniak and Gancarski 2003, 287–310.

Canaparius, J., *S. Adalberti, Pragensis episcopi et martyris vita prior*, ed. J. Karwasińska, *MPH* n.s. IV/1, Warsaw, 1962.

Chudziak, W. 2000, 'Problem chrystianizacji Ziemi Chełmińskiej w świetle źródeł archeologicznych', in Moździoch 2000c, 127–35.

Chudziak, W. 2003, *Wczesnośredniowieczna przestrzeń sakralna in Culmine na Pomorzu Nadwiślańskim*, Toruń.

Chudziakowa, J. 2001, *The Romanesque Churches of Mogilno, Trzemeszno and Strzelno*, Toruń.

Constantinos Porphyrogenitus, *De administrando imperio*, ed. G. Moravcsik, Eng. tr. R. J. H. Jenkins, Budapest, 1949.

'Conventus episcoporum ad ripas Danubii 796 aestate', *MGH Legum sectio. Concilia* II/1, Hanover and Leipzig, 1906, 172–6.

Cosmae Pragensis Chronica Boemorum, ed. B. Bretholz, *MGH SRG* n.s. II, Berlin, 1923.

Cronica Petri comitis Poloniae wraz z tzw. Carmen Mauri, ed. M. Plezia, *MPH* n.s. III, Cracow, 1951.

Cybulski, M. 2002, 'Język staropolski a chrześcijaństwo. W związku z tysiącleciem Zjazdu Gnieźnieńskiego', in *Pokłosie Zjazdu Gnieźnieńskiego. O początkach kościoła w Łęczycy*, ed. B. Solarski and M. Stęczkowska, Łęczyca, 29–39.

Deptuła, Cz. 1990, *Galla Anonima mit genezy Polski. Studium z historiozofii i hermeneutyki symboli dziejopisarstwa średniowiecznego*, Lublin.

Derwich, M. 1992, *Benedyktyński klasztor św. Krzyża na Łysej Górze w średniowieczu*, Warsaw and Wrocław.

Derwich, M. 1996, 'Wiarygodność przekazów pisemnych na temat kultu pogańskiego na Łyścu. Archeolog a źródła pisane', in *Słowiańszczyzna w Europie średniowiecznej*, ed. Z. Kurnatowska, Wrocław, 97–104.

Derwich, M. 1998, *Monastycyzm benedyktyński w średniowiecznej Europie i Polsce. Wybrane problemy*, Wrocław.

Długosz, Jan, *Annales seu cronicae incliti Regni Poloniae*, lib. 1–6, ed. V. Semkowicz-Zarembina, D. Turkowska, C. Pieradzka and B. Modelska-Strzelecka, 3 vols., Warsaw, 1964–73.

Dobosz, J. 2002, *Monarcha i możni wobec Kościoła w Polsce do początku XIII w.*, Poznań.

Dola, K. 1996, *Dzieje Kościoła na Śląsku. Część I: średniowiecze*, Opole.

Domański, G. 2000a, 'Rola góry Ślęży w życiu plemiennego i wczesnopiastowskiego Śląska', in *Śląsk około roku 1000*, ed. M. Młynarska-Kaletynowa and E. Małachowicz, Wrocław, 101–13.

Domański, G. 2000b, 'Ślężański zespół osadniczy i kultowy we wczesnym średniowieczu', in Moździoch 2000c, 99–109.

Domański, G. 2002, *Ślęża w pradziejach i średniowieczu*, Wrocław.

Drelicharz, W. 2003, *Annalistyka małopolska XIII–XV wieku. Kierunki rozwoju wielkich roczników kompilowanych* (Rozprawy Wydziału Historyczno-Filozoficznego PAU, t. 99), Cracow.

Dulinicz, M. 2000, 'Miejsca, które rodzą władzę (najstarsze grody słowiańskie na wschód od Wisły)', in Moździoch 2000c, 85–98.

Dunin-Wąsowicz, T. 2000, 'Najstarsi polscy święci: Izaak, Mateusz i Krystyn', in *Kościół, kultura, społeczeństwo. Studia z dziejów średniowiecza i czasów nowożytnych*, ed. S. Bylina *et al.*, Warsaw, 35–47.

Ebo, *Vita S. Ottonis episcopi Babenbergensis, MPH* n.s. VII/2, Warsaw, 1974.

Ekkehard, 'Chronica', in *Frutolfi et Ekkehardi Chronica necnon Anonymi Chronica Imperatorum*, ed. F.-J. Schmale and I. Schmale-Ott, Darmstadt, 1972 (*AQ* XV).

Epp, V. 1999, *Amicitia. Zur Geschichte personaler, sozialer, politischer und geistlicher Beziehungen im frühen Mittelater*, Stuttgart.

Erdmann, C. 1938, 'Der ungesalbte König', *Deutsches Archiv für Geschichte des Mittelalters* 2, 311–40.

Filipowiak, W. 1982, 'Der Götzentempel von Wolin. Kult und Magie', *Beiträge zur Ur- und Frühgeschichte* 2, 109–23.

Fried, J. 2000, *Otton III i Bolesław Chrobry. Miniatura dedykacyjna z Ewangeliarza z Akwizgranu, zjazd gnieźnieński a królestwa polskie i węgierskie. Analiza ikonograficzna i wnioski historyczne*, tr. E. Kaźmierczak and W. Leder, Warsaw.

Gabriel, I. 1984, 'Strukturwandel in Starigard/Oldenburg während der zweiten Hälfte des 10. Jahrhunderts auf Grund archäologischer Befunde. Slawische Fürstenherrschaft, Ottonischer Bischoffssitz, heidnische Gegenbewegung', *Zeitschrift für Archäologie* 18/1, 63–80.

Gallus Anonymus, *Cronicae et gesta ducum sive principum Polonorum*, ed. C. Maleczyński, *MPH* n.s. II, Cracow, 1952.

Gancarski, J. 2003, 'The Early Medieval Stronghold at Trzcinica in the District of Jasło: Preliminary Research Results', in Woźniak and Gancarski 2003, 165–80.

Gąssowska, E. and J. Gąssowski 1970, *Łysa Góra we wczesnym średniowieczu*, Warsaw.

Gąssowski, J. 1971, 'Religia pogańskich Słowian i jej przeżytki we wczesnym chrześcijaństwie', *Archeologia Polski* 16, 557–74.

Gąssowski, J. 1992a, 'Archeologia o schyłkowym pogaństwie', *Archeologia Polski* 37, 135–57.

Gąssowski, J. 1992b, 'Problematyka wczesnej państwowości w świetle danych archeologicznych', in *Geneza i funkcjonowanie wczesnych form państwowości na tle porównawczym*, ed. M. Tymowski and M. Ziółkowski, Warsaw, 9–24.

Gediga, B. 1996, 'Chrystianizacja i utrzymywanie się przedchrześcijańskich praktyk kultowych na Śląsku', in *Słowiańszczyzna w Europie średniowiecznej*, ed. Z. Kurnatowska, vol. I, Wrocław, 159–67.

Geographus Bavarus, Descriptio civitatum ad septentrionalem plagam Danubii, Rozpravy Československé Akademie Věd 66, 1956/2, 2–3.

Gieysztor, A. 1959, *La Porte de bronze á Gniezno: document de l'histoire de Pologne au XIIe siècle*, Rome.

Gieysztor, A. 1982, *Mitologia Słowian*, Warsaw.

Ginalski, J. 2003, 'Fragmenty dwóch stilusów z grodziska "Horodyszcze" w Trepczy Kolo Sanoka', in Woźniak and Gancarski 2003, 369–80.

Gliński, W. 1997, 'Zespół palatialny w Wiślicy w świetle badań archeologicznych', in *Wiślica. Nowe badania i interpretacje*, ed. A. Grzybkowski, Warsaw, 257–67.

Górski, K. 1960, 'Niemieckie misje wśród Słowian i Prusaków', *Zapiski Historyczne* 25/2, 59–70.

Hanc-Maikowa, E. 1988, 'Plomby drohiczyńskie ze zbiorów Muzeum Archeologicznego i Etnograficznego w Łodzi', *Prace i Materiały Muzeum Archeologicznego i Etnograficznego. Seria numizmatyczna i konserwatorska* 8, 49–66.

Hawrot, J. 1959, 'Kraków wczesnośredniowieczny', *Kwartalnik Architektury i Urbanistyki* 4, 125–69.

Helmoldi presbyteri bozoviensis Chronica Slavorum, ed. B. Schmeidler, *SRG*, Hanover, 1937.

Henricus de Antverpis, 'Tractatus de captione urbis Brandenburgensis', ed. O. Holder-Egger, *MGH SS* XXV, Hanover, 1880, 482–4.

Herbordi Dialogus de vita s. Ottonis episcopi babenbergensis, ed. J. Wikarjak, *MPH* n.s. VII/3, Warsaw, 1974.

Ibrahim ibn Yaqub, *Relacja Ibrahima ibn Jakuba z podróży do krajów słowiańskich w przekazie al-Bekriego*, ed. T. Kowalski, *MPH* n.s. I, Cracow, 1946, 48–54.

Janiak, T. 1998, 'Gniezno – stołeczny ośrodek monarchii wczesnośredniowiecznej', in *Civitates principales. Wybrane ośrodki władzy w Polsce wczesnośredniowiecznej*, ed. T. Janiak and D. Stryniak, Gniezno, 17–21.

Jasiński, T. 2000, 'Początki polskiej annalistyki', in *Nihil superfluum esse. Prace z dziejów średniowiecza ofiarowane Profesor Jadwidze Krzyżaniakowej*, ed. J. Dobosz and J. Strzelczyk, Poznań, 129–46.

Jurek, T. 1994, 'Ryczyn biskupi. Studium z dziejów Kościoła polskiego w XI w.', *Roczniki Historyczne* 60, 21–66.

Kahl, H.-D. 1955, '*Compellere intrare*. Die Wendenpolitik Bruns von Querfurt im Lichte hochmittelalterlichen Missions- und Völkerrechts', *Zeitschrift für Ostforschung* 4, 161–93, 360–401.

Kalinowski, W. 1971, 'Przedmioty liturgiczne znalezione w grobach pierwszych opatów tynieckich', *Folia Historiae Artium* 6–7, 175–207.

Katalogi biskupów wrocławskich, ed. W. Kętrzyński, *MPH* VI, Cracow, 1893, 534–85.

Kehr, P. 1920, *Das Erzbistum Magdeburg und die erste Organisation der christlichen Kirche in Polen*, Berlin.

Kiersnowski, R. 1959, 'Teksty pisane na polskich monetach wczesnośrednio-wiecznych', *Wiadomości Numizmatyczne* 3, 4–22.

Knytlingasaga, Danakonunga Sögur, Islenzk Fórnrit, vol. XXXV, Reykjavik, 1982.

Kočka-Krenz, H. 2000, 'Badania zespołu pałacowo-sakralnego na Ostrowiu Tumskim w Poznaniu', in *Osadnictwo i architektura ziem polskich w dobie Zjazdu Gnieźnieńskiego*, ed. A. Buko and Z. Świechowski, Warsaw, 69–74.

Kodeks dyplomatyczny Wielkopolski, vol. I, ed. I. Zakrzewski, Poznań, 1877.

Kodeks Matyldy. Księga obrzędów z kartami dedykacyjnymi, ed. B. Kürbis, *Monumenta Sacra Polonorum*, vol. I, Cracow, 2000.

Koperkiewicz, A. 2004, 'Dusze maluczkie z Daniłowa', in *Dusza maluczka a strata ogromna*, ed. W. Dzieduszycki and J. Wrzesiński, Poznań, 119–29.

Koperski, A. 1985, 'Cmentarzysko staromadziarskie w Przemyślu', *Prace i Materiały Muzeum Archeologicznego i Etnograficznego w Łodzi. Seria Archeologiczna* 29, 261–6.

Kowalczyk, E. 2000, 'Sacrum. Z dziejów mitów toponomastycznych w archeologii', in Moździoch 2000c, 27–37.

'Kraków Calendar', ed. A. Bielowski, *MPH* II, Lwów, 1872, 905–40.

Krąpiec, M. 1998, 'Zestawienie dendrochronologicznie analizowanych prób drewna gatunków liściastych z Wrocławia /sezon badawczy 1956–1959/', unpublished manuscript in the archive of the Wrocław branch of the Institute of Archaeology and Ethnology, Polish Academy of Sciences.

Krasnodębski, D. 1998, 'Średniowieczni mieszkańcy pogranicza', in *Gazociąg pełen skarbów archeologicznych*, ed. M. Chłodnicki and L. Krzyżaniak, Poznań, 95–109.

Kronika Wielkopolska, ed. B. Kürbis, *MPH* n.s. VIII, Warsaw, 1970.

Krysztofiak, T. 1998, 'Giecz-Grodziszczko, stan. 1, gm. Dominowo', in *Civitas principales. Wybrane ośrodki władzy w Polsce wczesnośredniowiecznej*, ed. T. Janiak, Gniezno, 45–7.

Kukliński, A. 2003 'Spór wokół datowania wczesnośredniowiecznego wału obronnego na Wawelu w Krakowie', in Woźniak and Gancarski 2003, 419–41.

Kürbis, B. 1962, '*Dagome iudex* – studium krytyczne', in *Początki państwa polskiego. Księga tysiąclecia*, vol. I, Poznań, 363–424.

Kürbis, B. 1998, 'Inskrypcja nagrobna w katedrze gnieźnieńskiej z początku XI wieku', in *Christianitas et cultura Europae*, ed. H. Gapski, vol. I, Lublin, 551–66.

Kurnatowscy, Z. and S. 2003, 'Parę uwag o odmiennościach kulturowych Małopolski (widzianych od północy)', in Woźniak and Gancarski 2003, 165–80.

Kurnatowska, Z. 1997, 'Poznańskie Baptysterium', *Slavia Antiqua* 38, 52–69.

Kurnatowska, Z. 1998, 'Początki państwa I chrześcijaństwa w Polsce w świetle źródeł archeologicznych', in *Archeologia wielkopolska. Osiągnięcia i problemy ochrony zabytków*, ed. H. Kočka-Krenz, Poznań, 91–101.

Kurnatowska, Z. 2000, 'Elementy sacrum w topografii tworzonej przez pierwszych Piastów domeny i jej głównych ośrodków', in Moździoch 2000c, 111–26.

Kurnatowska, Z. 2004a, 'Ostrów Lednicki in the Early Middle Ages', in Urbańczyk 2004, 167–84.

Kurnatowska, Z. 2004b, 'The Stronghold in Gniezno in the Light of Older and More Recent Studies', in Urbańczyk 2004, 185–206.

Labuda, G. 1988, *Studia nad początkami państwa polskiego*, 2 vols., Poznań.

Labuda, G. 1992, *Mieszko II król Polski (1025–1034). Czasy przełomu w dziejach państwa polskiego*, Cracow.

Labuda, G. 2002, *Fragmenty dziejów Słowiańszczyzny Zachodniej*, Poznań.

Labuda, G. 2003, *Mieszko I*, Wrocław.

Lamm, J. P. 1987, 'On the Cult of Multiple-Headed Gods in England and in the Baltic Area', *Przegląd Archeologiczny* 34, 218–31.

Lanckorońska, K. 1961, 'Studies on the Roman-Slavic Rite in Poland', *Orientalia Christiana Analecta* 16, 19–113.

Leciejewicz, L. 1987, 'In pago Silensi vocabulo hos a quodam monte . . . sibi indito. O funkcji miejsc kultu pogańskiego w systemie politycznym Słowian Zachodnich doby plemiennej', *Sobótka* 42/2, 125–35.

'List Grzegorza VII papieża do Bolesława Śmiałego roku 1075', ed. A. Bielowski, *MPH* I, Lwów, 1864, 367–8.

Łowmiański, H. 1979, *Religia Słowian i jej upadek (VI–XII wiek)*, Warsaw.

Magistri Vincentii dicti Kadłubek Chronica Polonorum, ed. M. Plezia, *MPH* n.s. XI, Cracow, 1994.

Małecki, J. M. ed. 1994, *Chrystianizacja Polski Południowej*, Cracow.

Mews, C. 2002, 'Manuscripts in Polish Libraries Copied Before 1200 and the Expansion of Latin Christendom in the Eleventh and Twelfth Centuries', *Scriptorium* 56/1, 80–118.

MGH DO III: *MGH, Diplomata regum et imperatorum Germariae*, vol. II pt 2, *Ottonis III. diplomata*, ed. T. Sickel, Hanover, 1893.

Michałowski, R. 1989, *Princeps fundator. Studium z dziejów kultury politycznej w Polsce X–XII wieku*, Warsaw.

Miś, A. L. 'Przedchrześcijańska religia Rugian', *Slavia Antiqua* 38, 105–49.

Młynarska-Kaletynowa, M. 2000, 'Z dziejów kultu św. Wojciecha w Polsce na przełomie XI/XII i w XII wieku', in Moździoch 2000c, 137–54.

Moszyński, L. 1990, 'Staropołabski teonim Tjarnaglofi. Próba nowej etymologii', in *Tgolí chole Mestró. Gedenkschrift für R. Olesch*, ed. R. Lachmann, Cologne and Vienna, 33–9.

Moszyński, L. 1992, *Die vorchristliche Religion der Slaven im Lichte der slawischen Sprachwissenschaft*, Cologne, Weimar, Vienna and Böhlau.

Moździoch, S. 2000a, 'Archeologiczne ślady kultu pogańskiego na Śląsku wczesnośredniowiecznym', in Moździoch 2000c, 155–93.

Moździoch, S. 2000b, 'Społeczność plemienna Śląska w IX–X wieku', in *Śląsk około roku 1000*, ed. M. Młynarska-Kaletynowa and E. Małachowicz, Wrocław, 25–71.

Moździoch, S. ed. 2000c, *Człowiek, sacrum, środowisko. Miejsca kultu we wczesnym średniowieczu*, Wrocław.

Nogieć-Czepielowa, E. 1974, 'Pozostałości dekoracji rzeźbiarskiej katedry wawelskiej', *Folia Historiae Artium* 10, 5–36.

Ott, J. 2001, 'Kronen und Krönungen in frühottonischer Zeit', in *Ottonische Neuanfänge. Symposion zur Ausstellung 'Otto der Grosse, Magdeburg und Europa'*, ed. B. Schneidmüller and S. Weinfurter, Mainz.

Paszkiewicz, H. 1954, *The Origin of Russia*, New York.

Petersohn, J. 1966, '*Apostolus Pomeranorum*. Studien zur Geschichte und Bedeutung des Apostelepithetons Bischof Otto I von Bamberg', *Historisches Jahrbuch* 86/2, 257–94.

Petersohn, J. 1979, *Der südliche Ostseeraum im kirchlich-politischen Kräftespiel des Reichs, Polens und Dänemarks vom 10. bis 13. Jahrhundert. Mission – Kirchenorganisation – Kultpolitik*, Cologne and Vienna.

Petrus Damian, 'Vita beati Romualdi', ed. G. Tabacco, *Fonti per la storia d'Italia*, vol. XCIV, Rome, 1957.

Pettazzoni, R. 1967, *Wszechwiedza bogów*, Warsaw.

Pianowski, Z. 1994, 'Najstarsze kościoły na Wawelu', in Małecki 1994, 99–119.

Pianowski, Z. 2000a, 'Początki zespołu architektury sakralnej na Wawelu. Stan badań i interpretacji do roku 2000', in *Dzieje Podkarpacia*, vol. V, *Początki chrześcijaństwa w Małopolsce*, ed. J. Gancarski, Krosno, 63–79.

Pianowski, Z. 2000b, 'Relikty neistarši svatyně pod katedralnim kostelem na krakovskem Wawelu', in *Přemyslovský stat kolem roku 1000: Colloquia mediaevalia Pragensia*, vol. II, *Boleslav II. Der tschechische Staat um das Jahr 1000*, ed. L. Polanský, J. Sláma and D. Třeštík, Prague, 236–8.

Pianowski, Z. 2002, 'Królewska kaplica pałacowa na grodzie przemyskim w świetle najnowszych badań', *Rocznik Przemyski* 38/2, 91–9.

Polek, K. 1997, 'Północna i zachodnia granica państwa wielkomorawskiego w świetle badań historycznych', in *Śląsk i Czechy a kultura wielkomorawska*, ed. K. Wachowski, Wrocław.

Popowska-Taborska, H. 1991, *Wczesne dzieje Słowian w świetle ich języka*, Wrocław.

Potkowski, E. 1984, *Książka rękopiśmienna w kulturze Polski średniowiecznej*, Warsaw.

Procopius of Caesarea, *De bellis lib. I–VIII*, ed. J. Haury, Leipzig, 1963.

PVL: Powiest' wriemiennych let, part 1, text and tr., D. P. Lichaczew and B. A. Romanowa, ed. W. P. Adrjanowa-Peretc, Moscow and Leningrad, 1950.

Radwański, K. 1975, *Kraków przedlokacyjny. Rozwój przestrzenny*, Cracow.

Radwański, K. 2000, 'Raz jeszcze o wielkich kopcach krakowskich', *Acta Archaeologica Carpathica* 35, 174–89.

Rocznik dawny, in *Najdawniejsze roczniki krakowskie i kalendarz*, ed. Z. Kozłowska Budkowa, *MPH* n.s. V, Warsaw, 1978, 3–17.

Rocznik kapituły krakowskiej, in *Najdawniejsze roczniki krakowskie i kalendarz*, ed. Z. Kozłowska-Budkowa, *MPH* n.s. V, Warsaw, 1978, 21–105.

Rocznik Traski, ed. A. Bielowski, *MPH* II, Lwów, 1982, 826–61.

Rodzińska-Chorąży, T. 1994, 'Architektura kamienna jako źródło do najwcześniejszych dziejów Polski', in *Małecki* 1994, 145–51.

Rosik, S. 1995, *Udział chrześcijaństwa w powstaniu policefalnych posągów kultowych Słowian zachodnich*, Wrocław.

Rosik, S. 2000a, *Interpretacja chrześcijańska religii pogańskich Słowian w świetle kronik niemieckich XI–XII wieku (Thietmar, Adam z Bremy, Helmold)*, *Acta Universitatis Wratislaviensis*, *Historia* CXLIV, Wrocław.

Rosik, S. 2000b, 'Reinbern – "Salsae Cholbergensis aecclesiae episcopus"', in *Salsa Cholbergiensis. Kołobrzeg w średniowieczu*, ed. L. Leciejewicz and M. Rębkowski, Kołobrzeg, 85–93.

Rosik, S. 2004, 'Początki Polski w kronikach niemieckich XI–XII w. (w kręgu wiadomości Widukinda z Korwei)', in *Kolory i struktury średniowiecza*, ed. W. Fałkowski, Warsaw, 235–52.

Rybakov, B. 1981, *Jazyčestvo drievnih slavian*, Moscow.

Saxo Grammaticus, *Gesta Danorum*, ed. J. Orlik and H. Raeder, vol. I, Copenhagen, 1931.

Schmidt, V. 1983, 'Slawische urnenlose Brandbestattungen in Flachgräbern aus dem Bezirk Neubrandenburg', *Zeitschrift für Archäologie* 15, 333–54.

Sikorski, D. A. 2003, 'O rzekomej instytucji biskupstwa bezpośrednio zależnego od Stolicy Apostolskiej. Przyczynek do problemu statusu prawnego biskupów polskich przed rokiem 1000', *Czasopismo Prawno-Historyczne* 55/2, 157–85.

Słupecki, L. 1991, 'Powieść rzeczy istey jako źródło do dziejów pogaństwa na Łyścu', in *Kultura średniowieczna i staropolska. Studia ofiarowane Aleksandrowi Gieysztorowi w pięćdziesięciolecie pracy naukowej*, ed. D. Gawinowa, Warsaw, 377–86.

Słupecki, L. 1994, *Slavonic Pagan Sanctuaries*, Warsaw.

Słupecki, L. 1998, 'Monumentalne kopce Krakusa i Wandy pod Krakowem', in *Studia z dziejów cywilizacji*, ed. A. Buko, Warsaw, 57–72.

Słupecki, L. P. and R. Zaroff 1999, 'William of Malmesbury on Pagan Slavic Oracles: New Sources for Slavic Paganism and its Two Interpretations', *Studia Mythologica Slavica* 2, 9–20.

Sosnowska, E. 1992, 'Rotunda i palatium na Wzgórzu Zamkowym w Przemyślu w świetle badań z lat 1982–1985', *Kwartalnik Architektury i Urbanistyki* 37/1, 55–61.

Soszyński, J. 1984, 'Święty Wit a Świętowit Rugijski. Z dziejów legendy', *Przegląd Humanistyczny* 9–10, 133–9.

Strzelczyk, J. 1987, *Iroszkoci w kulturze europejskiej*, Warsaw.

Strzelczyk, J. 1992, *Mieszko Pierwszy*, Poznań.

Strzelczyk, J. 1999, *Bolesław Chrobry*, Poznań.
Strzelczyk, J. 2000, *Otto III*, Wrocław.
Strzelczyk, J. 2002, *Słowianie połabscy*, Poznań.
Suchodolski, S. 1967, *Moneta polska w X/XI wieku*, Warsaw.
Suchodolski, S. 1990, [Discussion], in *Stan i Potrzeby Badań nad wczesnym średniowieczem w Polsce. Materiały z konferencji Poznaniu 14–16 grudnia 1987 r.*, ed. Z. Kurnatowska, Poznań, Wrocław and Warsaw, 309–10.
Suchodolski, S. 2000, 'Początki rodzimego mennictwa', in *Ziemie polskie w X wieku i ich znaczenie w kształtowaniu się nowej mapy Europy*, ed. H. Samsonowicz, Cracow, 351–60.
Suchodolski, S. 2001, 'Czy orzeł polski ma już tysiąc lat? (Uwagi o zwierzyńcu numizmatycznym Tomasza Panfila)', *Biuletyn Numizmatyczny* 1 (321), 1–12.
Świechowski, Z. 2000, *Architektura romańska w Polsce*, Warsaw.
Szyjewski, A. 2003, *Religia Słowian*, Cracow.
Szymański, W. 1996, 'Posąg ze Zbrucza i jego otoczenie. Lata badań, lata wątpliwości', *Przegląd Archeologiczny* 44, 75–116.
Thietmar of Merseburg, *Kronika Thietmara*, text, Polish tr., intr. and comm. M. Z. Jedlicki, Poznań, 1953.
Tyszkiewicz, L. A. 1993, 'Slavi genus hominum durum', in *Wokół stereotypów Niemców i Polaków*, ed. W. Wrzesiński, *Acta Universitatis Wratislaviensis 1554, Historia* CXIV, Wrocław, 3–14.
Urbańczyk, P. 1995, 'Czy istnieją archeologiczne ślady masowych chrztów ludności wczesnopolskiej', *Kwartalnik Historyczny* 52/1, 3–11.
Urbańczyk, P. 1996, 'Jeszcze o funkcji wczesnośredniowiecznych "mis" wapiennych', *Kwartalnik Historyczny* 53/1, 63–6.
Urbańczyk, P. 1997, 'St. Adalbert-Voitech – Missionary and Politician', in *Early Christianity in Central and East Europe*, ed. P. Urbańczyk, Warsaw, 155–62.
Urbańczyk, P. 2000, *Władza i polityka we wczesnym średniowieczu*, Wrocław.
Urbańczyk, P. 2001, 'Paliusz Gaudentego', in *Viae historicae. Księga jubileuszowa dedykowana Profesorowi Lechowi A. Tyszkiewiczow*, ed. M. Goliński and S. Rosik, Wrocław, 242–60.
Urbańczyk, P. 2002, 'Wczesna urbanizacja ziem polskich', in *Civitas et villa. Miasto i wieś w średniowiecznej Europie środkowej*, ed. C. Buśko *et al.*, Wrocław and Prague, 37–47.
Urbańczyk, P. ed. 2004, *Polish Lands at the Turn of the First and the Second Millennia*, Warsaw.
Urbańczyk, S. 1991, *Dawni Słowianie. Wiara i kult*, Wrocław and Cracow.
Vetulani, A. 1953, 'Krakowska biblioteka katedralna w świetle swego inwentarza z roku 1110', *Slavia Antiqua* 4, 163–92.
Vita Prieflingensis (Sancti Ottonis episcopi Babenbergensis vita Prieflingensis), ed. J. Wikarjak and K. Liman, *MPH* n.s. VII/1, Warsaw, 1966.
Vita sancti Stanislai episcopi Cracoviensis. (Vita maior). Auctore fratre Vincentio de ordine fratrum predicatorum, ed. W. Kętrzyński, *MPH* VI, Lwów, 1884, 319–438.

Vita sancti Stanislai episcopi Cracoviensis. (Vita minor), ed. W. Kętrzyński, *MPH* VI, Lwów, 1884, 238–85.

Wavra, B. 1991, *Salzburg und Hamburg Erzbistumsgründung und Missionspolitik in karolinischer Zeit*, Berlin.

Weiss, A. 1992, *Biskupstwa bezpośrednio zależne od Rzymu w średniowiecznej Europie*, Lublin.

Wibert, *Hystoria de predicacione episcopi Brunonis cum suis capellanis in Pruscia et martirio eorum*, ed. G. H. Pertz, *MGH SS* VI, Hanover, 1841, 579–80.

Werbart, B. 2000, 'Judar under 1000-talet', *Meta. Medeltidsarkeologisk Tidskrift* 2, 39–54.

Widukind, *Res gestae Saxonicae*, ed. R. Buchner (*AQ* VIII), Darmstadt, 1971, 1–183.

William of Malmesbury, *De gestis regum Anglorum libri quinque*, ed. W. Stubbs (The Chronicles and Memorials of Great Britain and Ireland during the Middle Ages, vol. XC, 1), London, 1904.

Wipo, *Gesta Chuonradi II*, ed. H. Bresslau, in *Wiponis Opera, MGH SRG*, Hanover and Leipzig, 1915, 1–62.

Wiśniowski, E. 1966, 'Rozwój organizacji parafialnej w Polsce do czasów reformacji', in *Kościół w Polsce. Średniowiecze*, ed. J. Kłoczowski, Cracow, 237–372.

Wiszewski, P. 'At the Beginnings of the Piast Dynastic Tradition: The Ancestors of Mieszko in the *Chronicle* by Gallus Anonymous', *Quaestiones Medii Aevi Novae* 9, 153–82.

Wołoszyn, M. 2000, 'Bizantyńskie i ruskie zabytki o charakterze sakralnym z Polski – wybrane przykłady', in Moździoch 2000c, 243–55.

Woźniak, Z. and J. Gancarski, eds. 2003, *Polonia Minor medii aevi. Studia ofiarowane Panu Profesorowi Andrzejowi Żakiemu w osiemdziesiątą rocznicę urodzin*, Cracow and Krosno.

Wrzesiński, J. 1999, 'Cmentarzysko wczesnośredniowieczne jako centralne miejsce praktyk religijnych i odbicie lokalnej struktury społecznej: przykład dziekanowicki', in *Centrum i zaplecze we wczesnośredniowiecznej Europie Środkowej*, ed. S. Moździoch, Wrocław, 257–71.

Żaki, A. 1981, 'Początki chrześcijaństwa w Polsce południowej w świetle źródeł archeologicznych i pisanych', *Symposiones* 1, London, 9–108.

Żaki, A. 1994, 'Kraków wiślański, czeski i wczesnopiastowski', in Małecki 1994, 41–71.

Zoll-Adamikowa, H. 1979, *Wczesnośredniowieczne cmentarzyska ciałopalne Słowian na terenie Polski*, vol. II, Wrocław.

Zoll-Adamikowa, H. 1988, 'Przyczyny i formy recepcji rytuału szkieletowego u Słowian Nadbałtyckich we wczesnym średniowieczu', *Przegląd Archeologiczny* 35, 183–229.

Zoll-Adamikowa, H. 1997, 'Stan badań nad obrzędowością pogrzebowa Słowian', *Slavia Antiqua* 38, 65–80.

Zoll-Adamikowa, H. 1998, 'Zum Beginn der Köperbestattung bei den Westslawen', in *Rom und Byzanz im Norden. Mission und Glaubenswechsel im Ostseeraum während des 8.-14. Jahrhunderts'*, ed. M. Müller-Wille, vol. II, Mainz and Stuttgart, 227–38.

Zoll-Adamikowa, H. 2000a, 'Postępy chrystianizacji Słowian przed rokiem 1000 (na podstawie źródeł nekropolicznych', in *Święty Wojciech i jego czasy*, ed. A. Żaki, Cracow, 103–9.

Zoll-Adamikowa, H. 2000b, 'Usytuowanie cmentarzy Słowian w środowisku (doba pogańska i pierwsze wieki po przyjęciu chrześcijaństwa)', in Moździoch 2000c, 207–19.

Żurowska, K. 1983, *Studia nad architekturą wczesnopiastowską, Zeszyty Naukowe Uniwersytetu Jagiellońskiego. Prace z Historii Sztuki*, no. 17, Cracow.

Żurowska, K. ed. 1993, *Ostrów Lednicki. U progu chrześcijaństwa w Polsce*, vol. I, Cracow.

Żydok, P. 2004, 'Wczesnośredniowieczne pochówki antywampiryczne', in *Hereditatem cognoscere. Studia i szkice dedykowane Profesor Marii Miśkiewicz*, ed. Z. Kobyliński, Warsaw, 38–66.

Żywoty Konstantyna i Metodego (obszerne), ed. T. Lehr-Spławiński, Poznań, 1959.

CHAPTER 8

The kingdom of Hungary

Nora Berend, József Laszlovszky and Béla Zsolt Szakács

I. BEFORE CHRISTIANITY: RELIGION AND POWER

A Hungarian-speaking population, probably together with Turkic speakers, gradually conquered and settled the Carpathian Basin from the end of the ninth century onwards, after being attacked by Pechenegs. Scholars have speculated about the route and chronology of their migrations, about the ethnogenesis of the Hungarians and their social and political structure, with widely varied results.[1] No firm evidence exists before the ninth century. Even the sources for the period between the ninth and eleventh centuries are extremely fragmentary and controversial, therefore most interpretations remain open to debate.

Pre-Christian religious beliefs have been reconstructed as animistic-shamanistic by scholars, based on analogies, linguistic evidence (the dating of which is problematic), the analysis of modern folklore and archaeological data.[2] The worship of forces of nature characterized beliefs. Muslim sources describe the Hungarians as star-worshippers and sometimes as fire-worshippers.[3] Several sources mention oaths taken on dogs, where the dog was cut in half, to symbolize the fate of the oath-breaker.[4] Based on the prohibitions in Christian regulation, cult at holy groves and springs, where sacrifices were made, seems to have been an important part of traditional beliefs, but no archaeological evidence of cult sites is known. Folklorists point to the existence of helping spirits. Whereas traditionally scholars claimed that shamanism was a key element of pre-Christian beliefs, recently the existence of shamanism among the Hungarians has been disputed. According to this view the *táltos*, born with teeth and fighting in the shape of an animal for good weather, was not a shaman; there was a lack of

---

[1] Róna-Tas 1999, chaps. 6–7 with bibliography; Szűcs 1992; Vékony 2002, 91–3.
[2] Dienes 1972, 47–56; Fodor 1980, 196–201, 247–80; 1996, 31–5; 2003; Szegfű 1999; Vékony 2002; Pócs 1997 with bibliography.
[3] Zimonyi 1996, 55; Nyitrai 1996, 72.   [4] Göckenjan 1997.

shamanistic rituals.[5] Moreover, clear evidence for these specialists in contact with the other world does not appear before the early modern period. The most significant tenth-century source is art, but its interpretation – whether a system of beliefs had direct connections to art or not and, if it had, what the motifs meant – is debated. The bone stick handles carved in the shape of owls from Szeghalom and Hajdúdorog were interpreted as symbols of shamans, but no corroborating evidence exists.[6] In the case of the goldsmith-works, archaeologists argue for a shamanistic interpretation (the palmette motifs would then represent the 'Tree of Life'), whereas art historians do not accept such a view.[7] Some scholars suppose that a chief deity (the sky or the weather) or even monotheism existed.[8] The basis for such a hypothesis is only the word *isten* that came to mean the Christian God in Hungarian; according to one view the word was derived from Istemi, the ancestor of the Khazars who lived in heaven. There is however no conclusive proof about the period when the word was borrowed, the language it was borrowed from or about its original meaning.[9]

The most important source material for the belief system of the Conquest Period Hungarians is the archaeological finds from the excavation of thousands of contemporary burials.[10] Richly decorated dress, weapons, tools, and vessels that held food and drink demonstrate the belief in a life after death. According to the interpretation of some of the burial customs as well as the linguistic evidence, one soul was supposed to be in the body, and ceased to exist at the moment of death, while the other was in the head, and left during dreams or illnesses, but remained alive for a while even after death. This 'soul' could perturb living people, who needed protection. At Tiszafüred, one elderly woman was buried tied up outside the cemetery, while in another grave the skull of the deceased was separated from the body and reburied face down.[11] Decapitation or mutilation of the hands or of the feet of corpses, inspired by a fear of returning ghosts, was observed in other tenth- and eleventh-century cemeteries as well.[12] Similarly, small silver plates covering the eyes and the mouth in some burials were interpreted as obstacles that did not allow the soul to leave the head. Another

[5] Diószegi 1967; Szegfű 1999; Pócs 1997, 315–21.   [6] Fodor 1996, 226–7.
[7] Fodor 1980, 196–201, 247–80; 1996, 31–6; 2003; Marosi 1996, 1026–34.
[8] Mesterházy 1992; Vékony 2002, 120.
[9] Widely differing views: Györffy 1977, 29, 364 (Istemi); Pócs 1997, 311; Róna-Tas 1999, 191; Harmatta 1997, 73.
[10] Németh 1996; Mesterházy 2003; Mende 2005, 175–340. Interpretation of graves and grave goods: Tettamanti 1975; Révész and Nepper 1996; Révész 2003; Fodor 1996, 37–43; important regional studies: Bálint 1991; Kiss 1983; Révész 1996; Kiss 2000; Istvánovits 2003.
[11] Fodor 1996, 289–90.   [12] Rózsa and Vörös 1996, 70.

type of silver plate on shrouds symbolizing an open mouth and eyes, how-ever, may indicate the opposite, showing the way for the soul to the upper levels of the world. These beliefs may serve as explanation for the symbolic trepanations identified on the skulls from several burials of this period.[13]

One of the most characteristic features of burial customs, typical only for the most affluent families, is horse burial in this period.[14] The horses killed during the burial ceremony and deposited in the graves were valuable animals.[15] In most cases, the hide, which still contained the skull and the leg bones, was placed on the left side of the deceased, with a harness on top of it. It has been argued that other parts of the horse were eaten by members of the community during the feast following the burial. Later, eating horsemeat was understood as a sign of paganism, but it might have been the Christian observers rather than pagans who attributed special significance to the eating of horsemeat, which was probably eaten simply as food, without religious connotations, even during the eleventh century.[16] In symbolic horse burials only the harness was buried with the deceased. There was no link between the wealth of the deceased and the type of horse burial. Some symbolic horse burials contained rich grave goods made of precious metal. Variations of these burial types are often found in the same cemetery or even within individual grave groups. The burial of the whole body of the horse, typical of other nomadic groups, was not practised by Hungarians.

Several origin myths were incorporated into the medieval Hungarian chronicles, albeit in more or less rewritten versions: the tale of descent from Scythia, the story of the brothers Hunor and Magor led by a miraculous stag to new lands, and a tale about the conquerors exchanging a white horse for water, earth and grass, thereby buying the country.[17] Metal discs depicting an eagle or a *turul* (a mythological bird, perhaps a falcon) and objects decorated with stags and eagles also appear, and they have been interpreted as representations of animal ancestors.[18] The dynasty's own origin-myth was conserved in a distorted and fragmentary fashion: the birth of Álmos, the ancestor of the Árpád dynasty, from the union of a woman (Emese) and a *turul*, was reported by the Christian chronicler as a dream rather than an actual union.[19] Chronicles written from the twelfth century on refer to earlier forms of oral traditions, such as epic poems about the military

---

[13] Vékony 2002, 196. [14] Bálint 1970; 1971; Paládi-Kovács 1997.
[15] Vörös 1996. [16] Paládi-Kovács 1997, 106.
[17] Anonymous, 34–7; Simon of Kéza, 144–6; *Chronici Hungarici*, 288–9; Györffy 1993; Katona 1997; Kristó 2002c, chap. 1.
[18] Fodor 1996, 32–3. [19] Anonymous, 38.

deeds of heroes, and laments. Apart from a few instances when chroniclers quote or paraphrase a few lines from such oral works, none survives. The Hungarian Anonymous explicitly belittles such traditions.[20] For a long time the pagan past was more or less eradicated from the accounts provided by Hungarian sources, and on the few occasions when it was mentioned, the authors wrote about it with hostility. In the late thirteenth century, the pagan past was reclaimed to provide the dynasty and the people with a glorious past, equivalent to Roman origins.[21]

The accuracy of the information on paganism found in medieval Hungarian Christian sources is thus questionable, because of either the negative bias of the authors or their tendentious and learned use of the past, shaped according to literary models. Nor are contemporary accounts by authors outside Hungary more reliable: their point of view is determined by the fear of the raiding armies and a Christian condemnation of the unconverted.[22] Christian sources use topoi: the pagan Hungarians practise the foul rites of paganism, are uncouth and wander in darkness. They are cruel and even drink blood.[23] The evidence concerning certain social customs, notably hairstyle, is more reliable as it is confirmed by many sources in relation to both the Hungarians and other nomadic steppe people.[24]

The political organization of the Hungarians is subject to debate. From Arabic and Persian sources that reflect the conditions in the late ninth century, and from the mid-tenth-century narrative of Constantine Porphyrogenitus, it seems that power structures were changing already before Christianization. The Muslim sources mention two chiefs or kings: *k.nd.h* (*kündü* or *kende*), a nominal ruler or king, and *ǧ.l.h.* (*gyula*), who exercises power and/or is the military leader.[25] Traditionally this is interpreted as a dual kingship of one sacral and one military leader.[26] The sacrality of the leader has been questioned recently, and instead a political organization consisting of a ruler, a military commander and a governor of the tribes that joined the Hungarians has been suggested.[27] Western sources write about Hungarian military tactics but very little on their political structure; they mention Kusan or Kusal as *rex* or *dux*.[28] According to one

[20] Anonymous, 33–4; Benkő 1996, 225–9.   [21] Berend 2001, 203–6.   [22] Di Cave 1995, 275–340.
[23] *Rodvlfi Glabri* I.22 (at 38); Piligrim, 42; *Legenda S. Stephani maior*, 378; *Legenda S. Stephani minor*, 394; *Legenda S. Stephani ab Hartvico*, 402; Regino, 282, 284, 286 (drinking blood); Liudprand, *Liber Antapodoseos*, I.13 (at 266) and II.2 (at 300; drinking blood); cf. Kovács and Veszprémy 1996.
[24] E.g. Liudprand, *Legatio*, chap. 19 (at 540); Theotmar, 34.
[25] Zimonyi 1996; Nyitrai 1996 with Hungarian tr. of texts.
[26] Kristó 2001b, 8–10; and 2002a, 65–9.   [27] Róna-Tas 1999, 342–7; Vékony 2002, 185.
[28] *Annales Alamannici*, 53, 54, 56, on Chussal, a. 904 (at 54); *Annales Heremi*, 140–2, Chussal, a. 904 (at 140); *Annales Sangallenses Maiores*, 76–7, Chussol, a. 902 (at 77).

view, he was the military leader (*gyula*) at the time of the conquest of the Carpathian Basin until his death in 904.[29] At the end of the ninth century the Byzantine emperor Leo VI (who copied the earlier work of Maurikios) mentioned one leader. Constantine Porphyrogenitus about half a century later described an overall military leader from the Árpád dynasty who did not have supreme power in every respect over the confederation, two other chiefs, the *jila* (*gyula*) and *karcha* who exercised judicial functions (their role is not explained in detail), and the chieftain of each tribe. Constantine related that originally there was no 'prince' but only *voivodes*, of whom the first was Levedias. At the instigation of the Khazar *khagan*, a prince (*archon*) was appointed, the choice of the people falling on Árpád.[30] In medieval texts produced in Hungary, the genealogy of the Hungarian ruling dynasty was seen as continuous from pagan through Christian times. According to most scholars, before and during the conquest period Hungarians formed a tribal confederation, but one scholar argues that Constantine Porphyrogenitus wrote of clans, meaning either descent-groups or military units.[31] A large group of place names from the eleventh century and later refer to the same tribal names mentioned by Constantine Porphyrogenitus. Attempts to reconstruct the settlement of the conquering Hungarians on the basis of these failed.[32] It is impossible to determine when tribal organization disintegrated. Debates also continue about whether the Hungarians were nomads at the time of their entry into the Carpathian Basin.[33]

Centres of tenth-century leaders of the Hungarians were identified on the basis of later place-name evidence. Based on the same source material and influenced by ethnographic and historical parallels, one interpretation posits that local or regional leaders moved between summer and winter residential areas along rivers. Recent studies formulated serious doubts about the existence of such a system, and so far no archaeological traces of such residences were identified from the tenth century. Earlier attempts to date the building of some of the earthwork fortifications to this period were also criticized, although settlements excavated in the area of later fortified power centres indicate that non-fortified settlements had emerged at those sites in the course of the tenth century. The later county centres with their earthwork or stone castles perhaps emerged on the sites of the seats of high-ranking clan leaders, but no architectural remains of such seats exist.[34]

[29] Kristó 1996.
[30] Moravcsik 1988, 18, chap. 46, and 42–5, Greek text and Hungarian tr. Cf. Shepard 2004.
[31] Kristó 2001b, 10–15 traditional view; Vékony 2002, 193–4, 205–9.
[32] Berta 1999. Summary and bibliography: Györffy 1997; S. L. Tóth 1996.
[33] Summaries: Szabadfalvi 1997; Paládi-Kovács 1997.   [34] Wolf 1996; 2003; 2005.

Hungarian armies both raided and sold their services.[35] Muslim sources relate that the people followed the orders of the military leader, who had 20,000 horsemen. They attacked the Slavs and sold them as slaves.[36] Hungarian armies raided towards the west from the late ninth century onwards in order to plunder and to take captives. The Hungarians were military allies of the Byzantines at the end of the ninth century, but in the tenth century they started raiding against Byzantium as well. During the tenth century, the aim of Hungarian attacks increasingly became the extortion of protection payments. In addition, Bavarian, Italian, Frankish and Byzantine requests for military assistance were met in return for payment. Plundered precious objects from church treasuries and elsewhere, and captives, sold into slavery or in the tenth century increasingly ransomed immediately, contributed to the economic base of the elite, not of the entire population, and thus to the building of power by the elite.

Burial grounds of tenth-century wealthy people of middle rank provide additional information on the military character of the population. Grave goods contain bone parts of bows and iron arrowheads and many silver and some gold objects. In most of these cemeteries, female graves are richer. Yet in some areas the number and wealth of the male burials exceed those of the female graves, although female jewellery was made from precious metals. The most striking examples were excavated in the Upper Tisza region.[37] The men were buried, with few exceptions, with weapons – sabres decorated with silver and gold plates, bows and arrows, and strung bows kept in mounted leather bow cases (*gorytus*) – and richly decorated dress and horse harness. The highest number of sabretache plates were also found in the cemeteries of this region, indicating the high rank of the deceased. A recent interpretation suggested that these groups were artificially organized, and represent communities formed by rich nuclear families with servants and warriors in their retinue. Based on the archaeological material, these burials cannot be dated later than the middle of the tenth century. This corresponds to the idea that these communities were reorganized during the restructuring of power in the late tenth and early eleventh centuries.[38]

2. CONTACTS

Before settling in the Carpathian Basin, Hungarians were part of the Khazar Empire for a time, and there they came into contact with Muslims and

[35] Kristó 1995, 277–97; 2002a, 250–2.   [36] Nyitrai 1996.
[37] Fodor 1996, 125–208.   [38] Révész 1996, 193–206, 505–6.

probably Jews as well. We have, however, no evidence about the influence of these two groups on the process of religious change. According to Ibn Hayyān, captured Hungarian raiders in Iberia converted to Islam and became members of the caliph's guard.[39] As they did not return to Hungary, such conversions had no effect. Dirhams found in Hungary are probably signs of commercial activity, but no evidence exists of religious influences through such trade.[40] In the eleventh and twelfth centuries both groups appeared in Hungarian legislation, but the key issues then were already the regulation of contacts between them and Christians.[41]

Hypotheses abound concerning contacts between Hungarians and Christians before the 950s, some scholars even claiming that these led to conversions and a good knowledge of Christianity.[42] However, the evidence is very tenuous and seems to indicate that contacts, if they occurred, consisted of brief and often inimical encounters. Whether the Hungarians were affected by Byzantine Christianity in the Crimea in the eighth century remains an open question for lack of data. Linguistic evidence is controversial, in terms of both dating the incorporation of certain words into Hungarian and determining the area transmitting particular words. Slavic, including Bulgar-Slav, linguistic influence in the terminology of Christianity is generally accepted but whether these influences were absorbed into Hungarian before or after the settlement in the Carpathian Basin cannot be determined. If this terminology was adopted before the settlement, that might indicate contacts with and adoption of Christianity already prior to *c.* 900.[43] One scholar read a Muslim source as referring to the Hungarians being Christians but most disagree with his reading of a problematic word as 'Christian'.[44] The *Life* of Constantine mentions an encounter between Constantine and pagan Hungarians who wished to kill him but were tamed at the prayers of the saint and let him go; and Constantine referred to Toursïi or Tourci among those people who in 867 were Christians and had liturgical books and a liturgy in their own language. This is understood by some as a reference to Hungarians but there is no supporting data. The *Life* of Methodius recounts the favourable reception of Methodius by a Hungarian 'king' who asked the saint to remember him in his prayers.[45] None of these sources offers clear proof of Hungarian Christianity in the eighth–ninth centuries. At the end of the ninth century the Byzantine emperor Leo VI described the Hungarians as pagans.[46]

---

[39] Elter 1996, 179, Hung. tr. [40] Bálint 1981. [41] Berend 2001, 60–1, 64–5, 74–6, 84–5.
[42] All references in paragraph: Moravcsik 1938a; Pirigyi 1990, chap. 1; Mesterházy 1992; Vékony 2002, 196.
[43] Györffy 1977, 47–8. [44] Nyitrai 1996, 72. [45] Constantine and Methodius data: Király 1996.
[46] Moravcsik 1988, 18, chaps. 44–5, 20, chap. 61.

The only object with clear references to religious beliefs is the sabretache plate of Tiszabezdéd: it may have been made in the Etelköz habitation area prior to the conquest of the Carpathian Basin. It is decorated by a Greek cross in the middle and fantastic animals between palmette leaves. The left one resembles the *Senmurv* of Iranian Zoroastrianism, copied after a Persian or Byzantine textile. The leafy branch is often interpreted as a 'Tree of Life'. The plate may be evidence of pre-conquest Christian influences or may even express religious syncretism, but the uncertainty of its dating precludes firm conclusions. The male in the grave was certainly not a Christian: he was buried with his horse according to the pagan burial rite.[47]

Christianity existed in the Carpathian Basin before the Hungarian conquest, but the question of continuity is unresolved.[48] The western half of the country, Transdanubia, was a province of the Roman Empire as Pannonia. Then the western part of former Pannonia was under Carolingian rule in the middle of the ninth century. Some of the Christian buildings erected during the Roman period in the third and fourth centuries and during Carolingian times were rebuilt, used or redecorated in the eleventh century.[49] The ruins of large Roman cities were reused by the Hungarians. At Sopianae-Pécs, the new episcopal centre was situated in the cemetery of the Roman town. Some of the burial chapels were still in use in the early Middle Ages. Frescoes in one building prove that it was renewed in the eleventh century.[50] In the region of Keszthely on Lake Balaton, a late Roman Christian population survived perhaps until the Carolingian period. In the former city of Valcum (today Fenékpuszta) an early Christian basilica was enlarged during the sixth and seventh centuries. It was also used as a burial place.[51]

The *Conversio Bagoariorum et Carantanorum c.* 871–3 attests to the success of the Frankish mission in Pannonia and its subjection to the archbishopric of Salzburg, and Theotmar's letter in 900 relates that Hungarian raids destroyed churches in Pannonia.[52] In the most important centre, Mosaburg (Zalavár),[53] archaeologists excavated the foundations of a large (50 m long) church, with ambulatory, radiating chapels and a western complex. The building was probably not in use in the time of István I (Stephen, 997–1038): burials around the church came to an end in the tenth century. Its stone carvings were reused in the eleventh century for the Benedictine monastery founded there by István. A smaller church in the neighbourhood,

[47] Photo and analysis Fodor 1996, 180–4; Wieczorek and Hinz 2000, *Katalog*, no. 07.06.15.
[48] Vida 2003.   [49] Szőke 1998; 2003.   [50] Fülep, Bachmann and Pintér 1988.
[51] Szőke 1990–1; Vida 2003, 305–6.   [52] *Conversio*, 50–9; Theotmar, 34; Wolfram 1995.
[53] Tóth 1999; Szőke 2001; Wieczorek and Hinz 2000, vol. I, 217–20; Szőke 2003, 313–16.

the basilica of Zalavár-Récéskút, was also rebuilt at the same time. The church of St Martin in Szombathely goes back to the Carolingian period or earlier: this perhaps meant the continuity of cult, but perhaps only the continuity of the ruins that were later used again.[54]

The question surrounding the heritage of Great Moravia in the Carpathian Basin is also problematic. Slovak scholars usually suppose some continuity between the Christianity of Great Moravia and the Christianization of the eleventh century, while their Hungarian colleagues frequently reject it.[55] Although the Christian people of this polity may have played a role in the Christianization of Hungary, no direct influence is detectable. Architectural remains were found at Dévény (Devin), Pozsony (Bratislava) and elsewhere,[56] but the ruins did not influence later Christian architecture which followed contemporary fashions and reused pieces only as building material.

Some of the local Christian population probably survived the Hungarian conquest: toponyms entered Hungarian from Slavic, some forms of pottery are continuous before and after the conquest, and the anthropological analysis of burials shows the continuity – the chronology of which varied according to regions – of parts of the population.[57] Such local population perhaps transmitted Christian influence.[58] Many slaves, taken by raiders from Christian areas, perhaps also had a role in familiarizing Hungarians with Christianity. In addition, after their settlement in the Carpathian Basin at the end of the ninth century, the Hungarians developed trading connections with various areas. Trade entailed contacts with both east and west during the tenth and eleventh centuries. Trade with Polish and German lands, and especially with the Balkans and Byzantium, is shown by finds of objects such as jewellery and weapons. Trade also meant dealings with Christians, but there is no direct evidence of Christianization through trade: the relative number of imported Christian objects compared to all imported objects is small.[59]

Byzantine Christianity was the first to have a significant influence, attested by the sources, on the Hungarians. As military allies, several chieftains travelled to the imperial court and encountered Byzantine Christianity. Ioannes Skylitzes in the second half of the eleventh century recounted

---

[54] Kiss and Tóth 1993.
[55] These debates are not independent from the actual political situation. Cf. Wieczorek and Hinz 2000, vol. I, 297–338.
[56] Štefanovičová 1975; Wieczorek and Hinz 2000, vol. I, 296–338.
[57] Takács 1997, 208; Pálfi, Farkas and Molnár 1996.   [58] Váczy 1938.
[59] Mesterházy 1993, with further bibliography.

(using earlier written sources) the baptism of the Hungarian chieftains Bulcsú and Gyula in Constantinople in the mid-tenth century.[60] Emperor Constantine Porphyrogenitus lifted them from the baptismal font: conversion was also a means of buttressing alliances. According to Ioannes, Bulcsú only pretended to convert whereas Gyula stayed true to his new faith and took a missionary bishop, Hierotheos, with him who became the bishop of Turkia and converted many. Historians also infer the possible conversion of Termachu, Árpád's descendant, from his friendly relations with Emperor Constantine. By the early eleventh century Turkia was mentioned as a metropolitanate and probably continued to exist throughout the eleventh century, signalled by the surviving seals of subsequent bishops.[61] A territorial lord in eastern Hungary, Ajtony, also converted to Byzantine Christianity at the beginning of the eleventh century.[62] Perhaps he cultivated Byzantine connections for political reasons, in the hope of military aid: Ajtony was one of those who resisted the expansion of István's power. Byzantine influence is also mirrored by material finds: around thirty Byzantine reliquary crosses dating from the tenth to the twelfth century have been found in Hungary, and other objects of Byzantine origin.[63] The tombs in which such pectoral crosses were found in some cases (e.g. Tiszafüred-Nagykenderföldek where the cemetery fell out of use c. 970) predated the time of official Christianization, while at other places (e.g. Püspökladány-Eperjesvölgy) pectoral crosses were found together with coins of István I.[64] The presence of Christian objects, however, did not necessarily signify the religious beliefs of the dead; such objects were also used as jewellery.

Latin missions started in the second half of the tenth century, probably linked to the ruler Géza's (d. 997) initiative.[65] According to German sources, Hungarian envoys were among those who attended the imperial court at Quedlinburg at Easter 973. They do not specify the nature of the embassy, but Hungarian historiography has linked this embassy to Géza's decision to convert and ask for missionaries after defeats suffered by Hungarian raiding armies (933, 955). According to one interpretation, Géza, realizing that the German–Byzantine rapprochement put him in a dangerous position, sent envoys to Otto I in order to accept Christianity, and the emperor sent him Prunwart, inviting him to Quedlinburg; according to others Géza did not

---

[60] Moravcsik 1988, 85–6; on Gyula as title vs personal name: Benkő 2002, 18–35.
[61] Oikonomidès 1971; Shepard 1996; Baán 1996; 1997.   [62] *Legenda S. Gerhardi*, 489–90.
[63] Pirigyi 1990, 21, 39.   [64] Fodor 1996, 290–2, 245–56.   [65] Sólymos 2001; Kristó 2001b, 19–28.

wish to be second in Byzantium behind Gyula.[66] One scholar speculated that the Hungarian envoys in 973 heard the discussion about the creation of the bishopric of Prague and that Géza was influenced by this, although there is no evidence for direct copying.[67] Western European sources mention several missions, but most are known from one reference alone, so their authenticity is an open question. Liudprand cites Bishop Zacheus sent by the pope before 972; the *Annales Heremi* writes of a monk from Einsiedeln called Wolfgang, later bishop of Regensburg, who went to the Hungarians in 972, but never entered Hungary because Bishop Piligrim of Passau demanded his presence – this might be a reference to missionary rivalry. Letters attest to the activity of Bruno, sent by Emperor Otto I probably in 972 (according to others by Otto II), who might have been a missionary or a diplomatic envoy; and of Piligrim, bishop of Passau, who sent missionaries in 973–4. The necrology of the monastery of Sankt-Gallen included the name of Bishop Prunwart (according to Györffy identical with Bruno) who according to the entry baptized many Hungarians together with the king of Hungary.[68] The *Life* of Adalbert, bishop of Prague, and later sources relate that he visited Hungary and sent his envoys there probably between 983–94. Many hypotheses were built on the scanty evidence. Speculations that either the ruler Géza or his predecessor Taksony (the date when the former started to rule is not known) sent to the pope asking for a mission were based on Liudprand's account which claimed that a Bulgarian who had been brought up in Hungary was caught together with Zacheus as conspiring against the emperor.[69] Some historians think that Adalbert of Prague had some role in baptizing or teaching István,[70] whereas others see a later exaggeration of his role due to the prominence of Adalbert's disciples in Hungary and to the desire to suppress the memory of German missionaries.[71] The basis of the first opinion is later hagiography which attributed the conversion of Géza and/or István to Bishop Adalbert (including István's *Legenda maior*, in which Adalbert is also his *susceptor*), and Adalbert's cult in Hungary. His contemporary *Life*, however, only talked about some, not

---

[66] *Annales Hildesheimenses*, a. 973 (at 62); *Annales Altahenses maiores*, a. 973 (at 11); Thietmar of Merseburg II.31 (at 68); Györffy 1977, 68; Kristó 2001b, 24; Bóna 2000.

[67] Koszta 2001, 68.

[68] Liudprand, *Liber de Ottone*, chap. 6 (at 502); *Annales Heremi*, 143; Otto I, 101; Piligrim, 41–3; Bruno of Querfurt, *Adalberti vita redactio longior*, chap. 16 (at 19), and *redactio brevior*, chap. 23 (at 61); *Libri Anniversariorum*, 466. Györffy 1977, 68–71.

[69] Györffy 1977, 51; Kristó 2001b, 19–24; Török 2002a, 14–16. The assertion that Taksony converted has no foundation: Gerics and Ladányi 2000.

[70] Kristó 2001b, 33–4; 2002a, 231–2; Bogyay 1988, 28–34; Török 2002a, 23.   [71] Györffy 1977, 78–80.

very successful contacts between Adalbert and the Hungarians, and it is possible that the spread of Adalbert's cult was due to its promotion by Emperor Otto III.[72]

The outcome of tenth-century missions, as related by the narrative sources, was mixed. Many ended in failure. Some medieval sources questioned the 'sincerity' of the early converts. Bulcsú was depicted as insincere in his conversion to Greek Christianity. Ajtony after his conversion to the Greek rite is represented in a later source, the *Legenda maior* of St Gerard, as not perfect in the Christian faith because he had seven wives even after his conversion. Whether the *Legenda* was written in the thirteenth or fourteenth century, or in the twelfth century, containing information from eleventh-century sources or local traditions, and was then rewritten in the fourteenth century is debated: it may or may not be a reliable source of information on Ajtony.[73] Thietmar of Merseburg claimed that even after his conversion, Géza sacrificed to various gods, and when a prelate reprimanded him he responded that he was rich and powerful enough to do so.[74] Bruno of Querfurt in the shorter version of his *Life* of Adalbert described Sarolt, Géza's wife, as responsible for the mixing of Christianity with paganism.[75] It is possible that these references reflect syncretism and/or the political motivations for conversion. Others reported success. Piligrim claimed that about 5,000 converted from the elite and that Christian slaves were now allowed to practise their religion. Piligrim modelled his account on the work of the Venerable Bede, and he also had an agenda, which makes him an unreliable witness to the conversion process: he claimed that his see was an heir to Lauriacum (Lorch) and wished to 're-establish' his bishopric's seven suffragans, including Pannonia (western Hungary), over which the archbishop of Salzburg also demanded ecclesiastical rights.[76] Adémar de Chabannes in version C of his *Chronicon* (which according to some scholars is a twelfth-century interpolated text rather than an authentic eleventh-century one[77]) recounts that Bishop Bruno of Augsburg converted 'White Hungary'.[78] By the beginning of the eleventh century no memory of the tenth-century missionaries (except Adalbert) remained: they are not mentioned in any of the texts written at that time.

---

[72] *Legenda S. Stephani maior*, 380; Bruno of Querfurt, *Adalberti vita redactio longior*, chap. 16 (at 19), and *redactio brevior*, chap. 23 (at 61).
[73] *Legenda S. Gerhardi*, 489; Klaniczay and Madas 1996, 113–14, 138–40; Kristó 2002c, 22–3.
[74] Thietmar of Merseburg VIII.4 (at 444).
[75] Bruno of Querfurt, *Adalberti vita redactio brevior*, chap. 23 (at 61). According to Kristó 2001b, 36, Sarolt propagated Byzantine Christianity.
[76] Piligrim, 42–3.   [77] Veszprémy 2003 argues for the authenticity of remarks on Hungarian history.
[78] Ademar III.31 (at 152).

3. CHRISTIANIZATION

Historians have debated whether Géza was the last 'nomad' ruler or the first 'Christian' one.[79] The initiative for conversion certainly came from him; he began promoting Christianity in Hungary among the chief military leaders, subjugating the recalcitrant ones by military force.[80] Yet it was only during the reign of his son István (997–1038) that Christianity was systematically established for the population, its reception enforced by laws. From then on, the inhabitants of the kingdom were expected to be Christians unless they belonged to a recognized religious minority. Both Géza and István were baptized (according to one source, Géza also received the baptismal name István[81]) but there is speculation about the dating of the baptisms, whether they happened at the same time, and whether István was baptized as a child or later on.[82] Different sources name different people as responsible for the baptisms: Bishop Prunwart of Sankt-Gallen, Bishop Bruno of Augsburg and Adalbert of Prague, as discussed above. An eleventh- and twelfth-century German tradition attributes the conversion of István and of the Hungarians to Gisela, István's wife.[83] This was not the case, although marriage and conversion were linked in Géza's policy. István was canonized by a Hungarian synod in 1083 for political reasons linked to dynastic legitimacy; his *Lives* turned him into the apostle of the Hungarians, who organized the Hungarian church, converted the Hungarians and was recognized by the pope in that capacity.

Missionary work continued under the auspices of King István. Missionaries came from several areas: among them were Slavs, Germans and a Venetian. The written evidence of Slav missionaries is confined to the disciples of Adalbert, who filled some important ecclesiastical positions in Hungary, but there is linguistic evidence of substantial borrowing of ecclesiastical terminology from Slavic (words such as Christian, bishop, priest); this may indicate the presence of many Slavic priests or interpreters, although an alternative explanation suggests the transmission of Christianity to the Hungarian conquerors by the local Slavic population (see above).[84] Bruno of Querfurt recounts his unsuccessful attempts in the early

---

[79] Kristó 1995, 299–316; Györffy 1977, 67–81; Veszprémy 2000. Summary of views on Géza's role: Kristó 2002b.
[80] Thietmar of Merseburg VIII.4 (at 442, 444); *Legenda S. Stephani minor*, 394.
[81] Ademar III.31 (at 152) also erroneously stating that Otto III elevated him from the baptismal font.
[82] Kristó 2002a, 225–32; and above under tenth-century missions, pp. 328–30.
[83] Wipo, chap. 24 (at 582); Sigebertus Gemblacensis, a. 1010 (at 354); Gerics 1995, 71–6; Veszprémy 2000, 141–2.
[84] Moravcsik 1953, 52.

18. The first bishoprics in the kingdom of Hungary

years of the eleventh century at evangelizing the 'black Hungarians' whose identification is debated among historians.[85] He mentions (in 1008–9) how they were forced to accept baptism after many were blinded by Christian armies sent to subjugate them. Bishop Gerard, a monk from Venice, was also active in Hungary in the first half of the eleventh century. His *Deliberatio* refers to his teaching pagans and their subsequent conversion.[86] His *Legenda maior* gives details (whose reliability is an open question) about Gerard's activities: seven monks acted as his interpreters while he preached and baptized many, with royal officials bringing people to be baptized. He also consecrated cemeteries.[87] István's *Life* mentions Boniface (according to some scholars identical with Bruno of Querfurt), who was wounded

[85] Bruno of Querfurt, *Vita quinque fratrum*, chap. 10 (at 52) and *Epistola*, 98; e.g. Kristó 2001b, 63–5; Benkő 2002, 101–3; Györffy 1977, 166.
[86] *Gerardi Deliberatio*, bk VII (at 123); on this work Nemerkényi 2004, chap. 3.
[87] *Legenda S. Gerhardi*, 493–4.

while evangelizing in the southern parts of Hungary.[88] Christianization after the official turning point was not unhampered, and coercion played a part in the process. The *Lives* of István emphasize that he had to break the resistance of pagans, defeat them in battle and force them to accept Christianity.[89] Bishop Gerard in his *Deliberatio* commented on how adulterers, idol-worshippers and drunkards were respected, while the holy rituals, the Church, priests and Jesus were blasphemed; people wanted to reclaim the alms given for the souls of the dead; the teaching of new converts was in vain.[90]

There was a flurry of royal legislative activity connected to Christianization and many of the early laws survived.[91] This is in striking contrast to most of the other areas under consideration in this book. The earliest legislation is linked to István I; his laws as well as those of his successors survive in later manuscripts. It has been proven that legislation was produced piecemeal, and compiled into collections later. According to some scholars, the third book of the laws of László I (Ladislas, 1077–95) contains the laws of Solomon from 1064 or of Géza I (1074–7). The 'synod of Esztergom' contains a collection of various synodal decrees, seventy-two canons by one synod (of Esztergom) and the rest by others. The dating of the Esztergom synod itself is debated; the oldest manuscript (Codex Prayanus) is from the late twelfth century. Based on the nature of the regulations, some scholars believe that some of these decrees predate the synod of Szabolcs (1092) and were issued during the reign of László, but more commonly they are thought to have been issued during the reign of Kálmán (1095–1116).

This legislation contains detailed information on Christianization, showing that at least in part it proceeded through compulsion. Christianity, its personnel and the new ecclesiastical property were elevated to a sacred sphere and were protected by the king. Christian regulations were laid down for the population, attesting to Christianization from above, requiring major behavioural changes. Traditional rituals were prohibited, although penalties changed over time. The synod of Szabolcs punished those who made sacrifices next to wells or made offerings to trees, springs or stones according to pagan custom by exacting an ox from them. According to the synod of Esztergom, high-ranking people (*maiores*) observing pagan rites

[88] *Legenda S. Stephani maior*, 382; Kristó 2001b, 64.
[89] *Legenda S. Stephani maior*, 381–2; *Legenda S. Stephani minor*, 395; *Legenda S. Stephani ab Hartvico*, 408–9.
[90] *Gerardi Deliberatio*, bk III (at 37), bk IV (at 51) and bk VI (at 85–6).
[91] On the history of the laws and synods Jánosi 1996; edition Bak *et al.* 1989, 1–33, 55–67. Cf. Bak 2000.

had to do penance for forty days; lesser people (*minores*), for seven days but also received a flogging. Changes in the treatment of *strigae* (witches) and *malefici* (practitioners of black magic) between the reigns of István and Kálmán attest to the penetration of canon law both in defining practitioners of magic and in transferring judgement to ecclesiastics. Some social customs, especially those concerning marriage and sexual conduct, were also targeted by the new legislation: the abduction and rape of women, fornication, adultery and the repudiation of one's wife. As elsewhere, this ecclesiastically inspired legislation was meant to redraw the rules of sexuality and marriage. Many of the regulations were redefined over time; for example, while the killing of adulterous wives and the husband's remarriage were accepted in some early laws, eventually penance was prescribed for the woman and remarriage was forbidden: ecclesiastical norms were substituted for the traditional rights of the husband. All this represented a forced transformation of key social institutions and customs.

To be Christian in eleventh- and early twelfth-century Hungary meant satisfying some basic demands. These included contributing to the construction of churches, paying the tithe, observing feast days and fasts, making a deathbed confession and attending church on Sundays, except by those guarding the fire. The synod of Szabolcs added that villages that were too far away could satisfy this requirement by sending one representative per village to the church. This was, however, not meant to offer the possibility of escape by simply moving away from the church building: the synod of Szabolcs also decreed that the villagers were to be compelled to return if they abandoned their church, and another synod imposed a fine on villages that tried to move. The synod of Esztergom prescribed punishments for relatives and village elders if deathbed confession was omitted. The late eleventh-century synod of Szabolcs and the laws of Kálmán insisted on the burial of Christians in churchyards. Christian burial was denied to those who died excommunicated.

Retribution for infringing the new Christian regulations was central in legislation. A multitude of sanctions protected holy days, especially Sundays. For example, the tools and animals of those working on Sunday were to be confiscated, as were the dogs and horses of those out hunting and visiting markets. Those who disturbed the divine service by murmuring and not paying attention were to be expelled in disgrace if they were high-ranking people (*maiores*); if commoners (*minores et vulgares*) they were to be bound in the narthex of the church, beaten and shorn. Those eating meat during fasts were to be imprisoned for a week. The synod of Szabolcs punished the non-observance of Sundays, feast days or fasts by fasting at the pillory. Another canon incorporated into the textual tradition of the synod of Esztergom prescribed penance for freemen, and lashes for the unfree, for not celebrating compulsory feast days. Those negligent in Christian observance were to be judged first by the bishop, and if that was not sufficient, by the royal court. At the same time, the ecclesiastical spirit left its mark on the penal code more generally: for example, fasting according to the canons and penance were incorporated into legislation for many different crimes, including murder. Eleventh-century laws prescribed the shaving off of hair as punishment, in István's laws especially for the violation of Christian regulations: for non-attendance at church on Sunday, for disturbing the divine services by murmuring in the case of commoners, and for fornication. Such retribution struck at the core of pre-Christian identity, of which hairstyle was an important expression. Pagan Hungarians shaved off their hair on top of their head, braiding the rest in one or three tresses.[92] The new regulations turned the shaven head into a degradation.

Compared to the voluminous legislation concerning obligatory adherence, there is very little on the content of the Christian faith that the recent converts were to adhere to. The synod of Esztergom was the first to introduce more detailed regulations concerning the content of the religion that was imposed: it defined the material to be explained to the people on Sundays (the Gospel, Epistle and Creed, but in lesser churches only the Creed and the Lord's Prayer); and prescribed confession and communion at Easter, Pentecost and Christmas. Legislation emphasized behaviour and outward conformity. The *Legenda maior* of Gerard confirms that baptism often came first, and the teaching of Christian precepts afterwards.[93]

Key influences on the Christianization of Hungary can be reconstructed based on a variety of sources. Papal involvement is attested by the earliest *Life* of St István (late eleventh century) and the foundation charter of the bishopric of Pécs (1009) that survives in an interpolated version in a fifteenth-century copy: according to these, the pope agreed to or conveyed his blessing for the establishment of the ecclesiastical organization.[94] One author also speculated on the possible Roman influence on the dedication of the cathedrals of Pécs (St Peter) and Kalocsa (St Paul).[95] The early Hungarian liturgy was influenced by the neighbouring ecclesiastical centres, such as Salzburg, Passau, Magdeburg, Mainz and Aquileia.[96] Liturgical manuscripts demonstrate ties to southern German areas, the Rhineland, northern Italy and Lotharingia. These may reflect where missionaries came from, bringing with them their local liturgical practices,

---

[92] Berend 2001, 258.   [93] *Legenda S. Gerhardi*, 494.
[94] *Legenda S. Stephani maior*, 383; Györffy 1992 no. 9/I–II, at 58.
[95] Koszta 2001, 68.   [96] Török 1986.

but ecclesiastical manuscripts were also imported and donated to churches by the king. A fragment of a sacramentary, dated to the first half of the eleventh century, and thus the earliest known liturgical manuscript,[97] follows south German traditions, as do other early manuscripts donated to the newly founded bishopric of Zagreb at the end of the eleventh century,[98] which seems to be typical in central Europe. Written sources also refer to the spread of liturgy from Regensburg and Passau to Hungary. Arnold of Regensburg travelled to Esztergom in 1028 where he taught the office of St Emmeram to the canons of the cathedral.[99] It is supposed that Radla and other associates of St Adalbert might have been quite influential, as well as the priests who arrived with Gisela from Bavaria. Certain features of some of the early liturgical manuscripts can be explained by Lotharingian influences.[100] For example, the Szelepchényi or Nitra Evangelistary[101] follows a system known only from ninth- and tenth-century Lotharingian manuscripts, and the codices at Zagreb also contain Lotharingian elements. Still-extant manuscripts also show eleventh-century northern French styles; a northern French manuscript originally produced for the monastery of St Vaast was imported into Hungary.[102] Gyula Moravcsik saw Byzantine influence in some liturgical formulas, the dates of feast days for certain saints and the late eleventh-century rule on fasting, although the Hungarian custom mirrored outdated western custom as well as the outdated Byzantine one.[103]

As the artistic heritage of the Christianization period in Hungary is small and its interpretation is debated, the hypotheses regarding influences are also controversial. Traditionally, the role of Italy has been seen as the most important.[104] Italian precedents can be supposed in the case of longitudinal basilicas such as Székesfehérvár (e.g. Rome, SS Nereo e Achilleo), the 'Benedictine ground plan', crypts (the hall crypts from Lombardy and the transversal crypts from central Italy) and stone carvings (capitals decorated with *Acanthus spinosa* from the region of Venice, Padua and Istria). Even the centralized ground plans of Szekszárd (cf. Paderna) and Feldebrő (cf. S. Vittore alle Chiuse near Genga) are Italian rather than Byzantine.

[97] Takács 2001, no. IV.10.
[98] The earliest manuscripts are the St Marguerite (or Hahót) Sacramentary, decorated in the style of late eleventh-century south German manuscripts; Agenda pontificalis of Harwick, bishop of Győr, end of eleventh century; Evangelistary (or Gospels?) of Zagreb, late eleventh century, following earlier north French prototypes. Zagreb, Metropolitanska knjižnica, MR 126, 165, 153 respectively.
[99] Arnold of Regensburg, 547.   [100] Török 1991.
[101] Nitra, Archív nitrianskej kapituly, no. 118; facsimile edition: Sopko and Valoch 1987.
[102] Benedictionale, Zagreb, Metropolitanska Knjižnica MR 89, c. 1100.
[103] Moravcsik 1953, 63–4; also Pirigyi 1990, 46–7.
[104] Traditional view: Gerevich 1938; new arguments: Tóth and Buzás 2001.

In the research of the 1960–80s south German influence became mostly accepted.[105] The basilical type is connected to these territories, as well as the western apse and westworks. Recent research cannot find direct connections between Bavaria and Hungary: Swabia seems to have been more influential. The influence of Byzantium is supposed from time to time (especially in the 1950s and 60s).[106] However, although the centralized buildings and the palmette decoration are Byzantine in character, the Hungarian examples are closer to the Italian than to the Balkan or Caucasian parallels.

Saints' cults are known from various sources. The dedication of churches shows the popularity of both eastern and western saints, notably the Virgin Mary, Sts George, Martin, Nicholas, Michael and Peter. There are also dedications to St Adalbert (the martyred bishop of Prague), Adrian (fourth-century martyr from Nikomedia), Benedict (of Nursia), Demetrius (a fourth-century local martyr whose cult was important in the Carpathian Basin), Giles (linked to the monastery of Saint-Gilles in France) and Clement in the early period.[107] The saints represented on the chasuble donated by István and Gisela show German and Byzantine influence in the first half of the eleventh century. In addition, narrative sources mention the Virgin Mary and St Martin as important for István.[108] The cult of local saints grew after the canonizations of István, Imre, Gerard, Zoerard and Benedict in 1083. A late eleventh-century synod prescribed the list of saints whose feasts were to be celebrated, including Hungarian saints, the apostles, feasts of the Virgin and of the Cross; that the legislation was effective can be seen in the choice of subsequent church titles.[109] The extent to which the cults show eastern influences and/or are linked to an Orthodox population in Hungary are debated: one view sees cults such as those of Nicholas, George, Cosmas and Damian as a sign of such influences, while another points to the cults of the same saints in the Ottonian Empire (for example the St George chapel in Regensburg), which may have transmitted them to Hungary.[110] It was also important for new churches to acquire relics; there are no data on the possible acquisition of relics prior to István's reign. References exist on István himself gathering relics, perhaps from Cluny, from Emperor Otto III, and from Ochrid when he was on a military campaign there. István's successors continued to collect relics: King Peter received the relics of a martyred pilgrim from Trier, László I in 1091 asked for part of the

---

[105] Tóth 1988. [106] Zádor 1972. [107] Mező 1996; Kovács 1989–90.
[108] Bardoly 2002; *Legenda S. Stephani maior*, 381; *Legenda S. Stephani minor*, 395–6; *Legenda S. Stephani ab Hartvico*, 408, 424, 431.
[109] Klaniczay 2002; Bak *et al.* 1989, 60, c. 38; Mező 1996, 38; Kovács 1989–90.
[110] Mező 1996, 85; Mesterházy 1968–70.

relics of St Benedict from the abbot of Montecassino. Relics started to be produced locally already in the eleventh century: István's right hand and a chain St Zoerard wore are mentioned in contemporary sources. Kálmán decreed that the relics of saints were to be carried by honourable ecclesiastics during processions.[111]

Ecclesiastics who filled high positions were invited from abroad in the early stage of Christianization. Sources mention that during István's reign, many ecclesiastics, monks, canons and hermits flocked to the kingdom. We know of a few individuals by name: the Frankish or Lombard bishop Bonipert of Pécs (1009–36) and his cleric Hilduin from Chartres or Reims, Liedvin (Leodvin) from Lotharingia, bishop of Bihar in the mid-eleventh century, the hermits Zoerard and Benedict, perhaps from Poland or Istria, the hermit Gunther from Altaich, who visited István's court many times, and Bishop Gerard from Venice. We already know of a native cleric who rose to a high ecclesiastical position from the mid-eleventh century, Mór bishop of Pécs.[112]

Archaeology and art attest to changes due to Christianization as well as to resistance. The largest cemeteries of the period often contain more than a hundred, sometimes even over a thousand, graves in rows, interpreted as the burial places of the commoners. Many contain no grave goods, but some of the graves are rich in dress decorations, belts, weapons and jewellery. Some of these large cemeteries of commoners were used between the early tenth century and the end of the eleventh century or the early twelfth century, based on numismatic evidence from graves containing *obulus* coins, showing a growing stability of the local communities. This is confirmed by village excavations revealing buildings of rural settlements in a growing number. The transition from pagan graveyards to Christian cemeteries is one of the most debated issues in the archaeology of this period. According to the traditional view, tenth- and eleventh-century cemeteries organized in rows were pagan cemeteries; now archaeologists argue that they were Christian or at least at one stage were converted to Christian cemeteries. Some churches were built on top of graves in existing cemeteries. Pre-Christian cemeteries could also be Christianized by the ecclesiastical ceremony of consecration, but only one late source describes this, the *Legend* of St Gerard. Graveyards around churches appeared earliest during the eleventh century and by the

---

[111] Györffy 1992, no. 24; Ademar III.31 (at 153) (relics sent to Géza according to him); *Fundatio ecclesiae S. Albani*, 964 (Cesaries interpreted as Ochrid: Györffy 1977, 288); Györffy 1977, 294; Györffy 1992, no. 91; *Legenda S. Stephani ab Hartvico*, 438–40; *Legenda S. Zoerardi*, 360; Bak et al. 1989, 31, c. 69.

[112] Györffy 1992, nos. 9, 18; *Fundatio ecclesiae S. Albani*, 963–4; *Legenda S. Zoerardi*, 357–8; *Legenda S. Stephani maior*, 388.

turn of the eleventh century at the latest.[113] Grave goods from the tenth to the end of the eleventh century declined especially in the graves of men, as weapons ceased to be put in the graves. Archaeological evidence shows that pagan cemeteries end with coins of László I and Kálmán.[114] Human sacrifice built into the foundations of a house still existed in the eleventh century.[115] Pre-Christian aesthetic style does not seem to have been continued in the eleventh century, and speculations concerning the influence of conquest-age art on late eleventh-century stone carving are generally rejected by modern scholarship.[116]

There was resistance to István's Christianizing efforts, and also pagan rebellions after his death.[117] Some texts written outside Hungary mention the blinding of King Peter by pagans who killed almost all prelates, many priests, monks and foreigners.[118] A detailed account, the interpretation of which is debated, comes from the fourteenth-century chronicle composition.[119] It is based on earlier versions of the chronicle, as the text refers to written information from the old books on the deeds of the Hungarians, but there is no certainty about the date of composition of these particular passages. According to these, in 1046, opposition to King Peter took on a religious component, and people returned to 'the custom of the pagans'. These customs included eating horsemeat, idolatry, recourse to 'magicians' and fortune-tellers, the killing of ecclesiastics and the destruction of churches, as well as abolishing tithes. Hair became one of the key symbols of resistance to Christianity. The leader, Vata (a chieftain probably in eastern Hungary), was the first who offered himself to the 'demons', shaved his head and separated his hair in three tresses in the pagan manner. The rebels recalled András (Andrew; a Christian, baptized according to Moravcsik in Kiev[120]) and Levente (a pagan), pretenders to the throne from another branch of the dynasty. Although initially they permitted the return to paganism (the *Annales Altahenses maiores* claim that András prior to his coronation behaved cruelly towards the Church[121]), after the rebellion András was crowned king and put an end to pagan practices, making paganism punishable by death. According to the chronicle, Levente would have favoured the continuity of paganism but he died and was buried according to pagan custom. The chronicle describes another rebellion in 1060–1, triggered by a meeting that King Béla called, where the people demanded the right to live according to

[113] Laszlovszky 1991, 40–3; Ritoók 1997; Bálint *et al.* 2003, 386; Mende 2005, 341–50.
[114] Bakay 1978, 218; Kovács 1997.   [115] Vályi 1992.
[116] Gerevich 1938, 12; Marosi and Tóth 1978.   [117] Kristó 1965.
[118] *Annales Altahenses maiores*, a. 1046 (at 42–3).   [119] *Chronici Hungarici*, 337–44.
[120] Moravcsik 1953, 60.   [121] A. 1046 (at 43).

the pagan rite of their fathers, kill ecclesiastics and destroy churches. The king brought the 'sedition' to an end with his army. This rebellion has been interpreted as the rising of impoverished freemen.[122]

Evidence of opposition to István's Christianizing efforts by those who did not wish to relinquish old customs, a conspiracy to assassinate the elderly István, and the so-called pagan rebellions of 1046 and 1060–1 show that those opposed to the changes defined their own identity as consisting of traditions and religious beliefs that István and his successors were trying to eradicate. These groups expressed their discontent through a return to 'the ways of their fathers'. Political motivations were intertwined with resistance to Christianity: territorial lords wished to safeguard their separate power, and members of the dynasty who were involved in the pagan resistance during István's reign and the rebellion of 1046 tried to maintain or gain power. There are no archaeological signs of the rebellion and reconstruction; no buildings survive from before the mid-eleventh century, and the construction of new buildings at the end of the eleventh century is not necessarily linked to these events.

The question of heresy in early eleventh-century Hungary has not been explored. Independent sources (Gerard's *Deliberatio*, the *Admonitions* and the fourteenth-century chronicle composition) mention anti-Trinitarian heretics.[123] Historians assume these were Bulgarian refugees but since these sources portray the problem of heresy as crucial in the early eleventh century, even more important than the problem of paganism, these heretics might have been converts who were evangelized by a non-Catholic mission. Gerard wrote that they denied the resurrection of the body and aimed to weaken the Church with the help of the followers of Methodius.

Contemporary sources described the process of conversion in different ways. Some use the topos of a fast transformation, as God led a pagan people to Christianity.[124] Several refer to István converting with his whole people.[125] Many focus on István alone, like Fulbert, bishop of Chartres, who mentioned István as a newly adopted son of the King of Kings.[126] István's piety is often mentioned, most notably by pilgrims who passed through Hungary on their way to Jerusalem and thanked István for his

---

[122] *Chronici Hungarici*, 359–60; Kristó 1965.
[123] *Libellus*, 621; *Gerardi Deliberatio*, bk I (at 10) and bk IV (at 51); *Chronici Hungarici*, 341. Cf. Nemerkényi 2004, 85.
[124] Piligrim, 42.
[125] *Rodulfi Glabri* I.22 (at 38) and III.2 (at 96); Hermann of Reichenau, *Chronicon* a. 1038 (at 672); Bonizo, 583.
[126] Györffy 1992, 104, no. 18.

generosity.[127] István's links to Bavarian ecclesiastical reform circles is reflected in his friendship with the hermit Gunther from Altaich and the fact that István and his wife Gisela appear among the beneficiaries of the monks' prayers at the Benedictine monasteries in Salzburg and Tegernsee.[128] All the sources that mention István recognize him as a Christian king. Even Wipo, while describing Emperor Conrad's attack against István, depicts István as a pious Christian turning to God against an unjust attack.[129] It is, however, rare for Géza to be recognized in such a way, although Hungarian narratives, especially the various *Lives* of István, stress the role of Géza in deciding to convert together with his household. They also emphasize that István had to force the people under the yoke of the law.[130] The *Admonitions* stated that Christian faith was a novelty in the kingdom and had to be protected.[131] During Kálmán's reign, Christianity at the time of István's death is described as being in a precarious position in Hungary. Hartvic depicts István worrying on his deathbed about safeguarding the new Christianity, and the preface of Kálmán's laws contrasts the situation during István's reign – when coerced converts to Christianity were nominal believers who had to be forced by stringent laws to keep the new religion – with that during Kálmán's reign when the population was already willing to die for their Christian faith.[132]

4. ROYAL POWER

As described in section 1, the power structure before the introduction of Christianity was changing. This process of change was radically speeded up by Géza and István, using violence as well as conversion to facilitate the building of monarchical power. While ninth- and tenth-century Muslim and Byzantine sources had described a variety of Hungarian leaders designated by numerous different terms (e.g. *kündü; gyula; voivode; archon*), contemporary sources describe Géza as *senior magnus* (Bruno of Querfurt) and even *rex* (*Legenda minor* of István, Otto I). This signals a fundamental shift in the balance of power towards rulership. Géza is portrayed by several independent sources as strong-handed, strict and cruel, which probably reflects

---

[127] Azecho bishop of Worms (Györffy 1992, 108, no. 21); Berno, abbot of Reichenau (Györffy 1992, 112, no. 25); Wipo, chap. 22 (at 578); *Rodvlfi Glabri* III.2 (at 96). Supposed letter of Odilo of Cluny (Györffy 1992, 110–11, no. 24). Ademar III.65 (at 184).
[128] Bogyay 1988, 115.   [129] Wipo, chap. 26 (at 582, 584).
[130] *Legenda S. Stephani maior*, 378–82; *Legenda S. Stephani minor*, 394–5; *Legenda S. Stephani ab Hartvico*, 403–5, 408–9.
[131] *Libellus*, 622.   [132] *Legenda S. Stephani ab Hartvico*, 431; Bak *et al.* 1989, 24–5.

Key to Royal Strongholds

1	Sopron	24	Kolozsvár
2	Moson	25	Zaránd
3	Trencsén	26	Torda
4	Bars	27	Varasd
5	Selmecbánya	28	Kemlék
6	Zólyom	29	Körös
7	Hont	30	Marócsa
8	Nógrád	31	Roviscsa
9	Pest	32	Oklics
10	Gömör	33	Gorica
11	Borsod	34	Garics
12	Abaújvár	35	Verőce
13	Zemplén	36	Gerzence
14	Ungvár	37	Gora
15	Borsova	38	Dubica
16	Heves	39	Pozsegavár
17	Szatmár	40	Orbászvár
18	Kraszna	41	Valkóvár
19	Beszterce	42	Temesvár
20	Tolna	43	Hunyadvár
21	Csongrád	44	Küküllővár
22	Békés	45	Keve
23	Doboka	46	Haram

19. The kingdom of Hungary in the twelfth century

his activity in building his power.[133] The break with the traditional pattern where power was shared by many chiefs was based on the efforts of Géza, and was completed by István. Historians hold differing views about the possibilities of a structural continuity between a 'nomadic' and a Christian Hungarian state; however, attempts to describe the 'nomadic Hungarian state' are based on analogies and hypotheses alone.[134] Although Géza may have done more than the existing sources suggest (because the chronicles do not describe his reign), from the sources that we do have, the establishment of a Christian kingdom under King István meant discontinuity through the introduction of a territorial organization, royal administration, written legislation, minting and taxation, none of which existed under Géza.

[133] Bruno of Querfurt, *Adalberti vita redactio brevior*, 61; *Legenda S. Stephani minor*, 394; Otto I, 101; Thietmar of Merseburg VIII.4 (at 442, 444); *Legenda S. Stephani ab Hartvico*, 403. On legends of István: Klaniczay and Madas 1996, 106–12.
[134] Kristó 1995.

István was crowned king probably in 1001. The persistent tradition that István received a crown from the pope, however, is based on the early twelfth-century *Life* by Hartvic. There, the story was created with the specific political aim of proving Hungary's independence from the Empire, by drawing a parallel to imperial coronations.[135] Thietmar of Merseburg described the coronation as a result of the emperor's favour and encouragement; some maintain without any basis that this is a reference to the emperor encouraging the pope to send a crown.[136] István's *Legenda maior*, Hartvic's main source, mentions only a papal blessing prior to the coronation. Even Pope Gregory VII who wished to claim lordship over Hungary said nothing of a papal crown sent to István, although it would have strengthened his argument.[137] Györffy speculated that the emperor conceded to István's wishes (in contrast to the wishes of the Polish ruler) because he feared the possibility of István's turning to Byzantium instead.[138] The coronation secured recognition and independence for István within Latin Christendom, although his power was not dependent on the coronation itself. No clear distinction was made in contemporary sources between king and (uncrowned) ruler: already Géza was called *rex* by some of them.[139] István's royal title in the charters varied: *Ungrorum rex, Pannoniorum rex, Hungarie rex*.[140]

The *Admonitions* clearly linked Christianity and royal power. This text, attributed to István, was composed by an unknown author, most probably an immigrant cleric, and survives in late medieval codices. Its authenticity has generally been accepted. Its content matches that described in the *Legenda maior* of István. Its exact dating is debated, but most scholars agree that it was written in the early eleventh century.[141] The text emphasizes that only a Catholic can be king, highlights the importance of defending the faith and the Church, and maintains that the king has to give to the Church and take counsel from prelates but can chastise them if they sin. The *Lives* of István portray the king as installing bishops and priests in churches, giving estates and servants as well as liturgical objects to them, and overseeing monastic life.[142] He also opened the pilgrimage route to Jerusalem

[135] *Legenda S. Stephani ab Hartvico*, 412–14; Gerics 1981; Váczy 1994, 77–93.
[136] Thietmar of Merseburg IV.59 (at 174); detailed argument representative of this view: Kristó 2001b, 52–8.
[137] *Legenda S. Stephani maior*, 384; *Gregorii papae VII Epistolae*, 110, no. 33; Gerics 1981; Váczy 1994, 77–93; Székely 1984.
[138] Györffy 1977, 139.   [139] Otto I, 101; *Legenda S. Stephani minor*, 394.
[140] Györffy 1992, 39, no. 5/II, 52, no. 8, 58, no. 9/I.
[141] *Libellus*; *Legenda S. Stephani maior*, 391; Nemerkényi 2004, 31–4.
[142] *Legenda S. Stephani maior*, 383–5; *Legenda S. Stephani minor*, 396; *Legenda S. Stephani ab Hartvico*, 411–12.

through Hungary. Hartvic's *Life* aimed to offer proof against papal claims to displace rulers as the head of the Church; he claimed that the pope called István apostle and granted him the right to rule by both laws.[143] The king throughout the period retained control over the Church, as is evident from royal involvement in legislation, and in the choice of prelates (even in the thirteenth century). Kings presided over the synods of the period (the first synodal decrees survive from the late eleventh century), where prelates and nobles participated and legislated on lay as well as ecclesiastical matters. Christianity and royal power were connected on many levels. István's coronation is described by Thietmar of Merseburg as linked to his creation of bishoprics in his own country. At least some bishoprics were established in centres with a royal castle. Some ecclesiastical and royal administrative territorial units corresponded to each other. To some extent all of the effects of Christianization outlined below were associated to royal power. Most of all, Christianity, through bringing literacy and enabling the promulgation of written laws, also made a new expression of royal power possible: legislation in the name of the king.

Christianity also offered new means of legitimation. From the later eleventh century the cult of Hungarian royal saints developed, prompted by canonizations initiated by László I for political aims. Two of the new saints were buried at Székesfehérvár: the tomb of St István stood in the middle of the basilica, while his son, St Imre, was buried between the two eastern piers of the south aisle. This unusual position can be explained by the fact that the church was not ready in 1031 when Imre suddenly died. The tomb of St István in the middle of the nave was found in a small crypt, with stairs leading to it, and probably a pulpit with an altar built above it. This structure can be connected to the canonization of the king in 1083. The original burial of István is archaeologically not known. A sarcophagus, recarved from a Roman original, is also connected to Székesfehérvár, most probably to St István. According to recent scholarship, it was carved not for his burial (1038) but for his canonization. Its front side represents a soul in the form of a baby carried to heaven by an angel, a reference to the saintly character of the buried person.[144] The number of dynastic saints continued to grow in the twelfth and thirteenth centuries, and royal sanctity conferred legitimacy on royal power.[145]

Christianization did not automatically entail the creation of a unified kingdom. István built his power through wars as well. He subjugated several

---

[143] Gerics 1981; *Legenda S. Stephani ab Hartvico*, 414.
[144] Entz and Szakál 1964; Marosi 2000.   [145] Klaniczay 2002.

territorial lords including his own relatives. In his war against his relative Koppány, who sought to take power after Géza's death in 997, he used the help of German warriors.[146] István also defeated Gyula, his maternal uncle, in 1003. The *Annales Hildesheimenses* called the latter *rex* and his territory *regnum*, suggesting that his area was autonomous.[147] Historians usually see Koppány as pagan and Gyula as Byzantine Orthodox; however the only information about the Christianity of Gyula's family is from the mid-tenth century. The *Annales Hildesheimenses* state that Gyula's *regnum* was converted by István; the Hungarian Anonymous and the fourteenth-century chronicle composition describe Gyula as pagan, resisting conversion to Christianity.[148] Some historians interpret this to mean that although Gyula and his family were converts to the Greek rite, the majority of the population was pagan.[149] István also waged war against Ajtony, who was definitely a convert to Byzantine Christianity, and defeated him, incorporating his territory into the kingdom: according to some scholars in 1008, according to others just before 1030.[150] The chronicle tradition also mentions István defeating Keán: who he was is debated.[151] The subjugation of territorial lords was a means of increasing royal power; it was not necessarily linked to their resistance to Christianity. At the same time, István did insist on spreading Christianity as well: Bruno of Querfurt and Adémar de Chabannes recounted István's forced Christianization of the 'black Hungarians' after he defeated them.[152]

Most probably, at the time of Géza and István's succession the ruler from the Árpád family was one among several chieftains, even if holding nominal overall leadership. Local rulers (chieftains) were de facto autonomous. Western Hungary was under the power of the Árpád rulers, and from here they expanded their control towards the east, subjugating local potentates.[153] István eliminated those who opposed him within the dynasty: Koppány was quartered, Vazul was blinded and his sons exiled. Those who conspired against István were mutilated.[154] István incorporated the territories of his

---

[146] *Chronici Hungarici*, 296, 313; Simon of Kéza, 189.
[147] *Annales Hildesheimenses*, a. 1003 (at 92). Benkő 2002, 35–41; Curta 2001.
[148] *Annales Hildesheimenses*, a. 1003 (at 92); Anonymous, 65; *Chronici Hungarici*, 314–15.
[149] Kristó 2001b, 60–1.
[150] Ajtony: Anonymous, 50, 89–90; *Legenda S. Gerhardi*, 487, 489–92. Kristó 2001b, 66–7 (just before 1030); cf. criticism by Curta 2001.
[151] *Chronici Hungarici*, 315; Kristó 2001b, 62–3; Benkő 2002, 91–9.
[152] Bruno of Querfurt, *Epistola*, 100; Ademar III.33 (at 155).
[153] Northern Transdanubia and southern Felvidék originally; István took the territory of Somogy from Koppány in 997: Kristó 2001b, 49–51.
[154] *Legenda S. Stephani minor*, 399; *Chronici Hungarici*, 313–14, 320 (attributing the deed to Queen Gisela's order).

defeated enemies into the realm, thus creating the kingdom of Hungary. István's use of violence was emphasized by his *Legenda minor*, written at the end of the eleventh century, although according to some historians it reflects not István's but Kálmán's character, who used the *Legenda* as self-justification for his deeds.[155] Alliances with neighbouring and other realms were also important for the king. As elsewhere, dynastic marriages played a role in the consolidation of power. In the eleventh and twelfth centuries marriages of Hungarian princes and princesses created ties to German, Polish, Czech, Rus', Byzantine, Serbian, Italian and French territories.

The economic and administrative base of royal power was established by István. He created royal seats as local power centres, providing royal income and a county system. Counties (*vármegye*) were districts around strongholds (*vár*, *castrum*; usually called castles in scholarship) governed through royal representatives (*ispán*; *comes*) which fulfilled military and judicial functions.[156] Castle warriors (*várjobbágy*) provided military service. Recent consensus holds that about thirty counties were in existence by the end of István's reign. Many were subdivided and new ones were created afterwards: by the second half of the twelfth century there were seventy-two counties. István also organized a system of strongholds to oversee royal lands; these did not have a castle-district. The counties and the royal lands however often had the same centre and the same *ispán*.[157] The chronology of castle-building has been controversial. According to some views, they predated the formation of the kingdom by István. Archaeologists, however, date the earliest strongholds (made of wood, earth and some of them of stone) to the beginning of the eleventh century, with alterations made during that century.[158] The only exception is ninth-century Zalavár. Thirty-one strongholds of *ispán*s have been found so far. Based on the uniformity of construction technique, the pattern of distribution, the building of a network of strongholds within a short period, as well as the manpower needed to build a stronghold, historians have assumed that they were constructed on the orders of the king. Exceptionally, Roman town walls made of stone were used to stabilize the outer side of the earthwork rampart, while the Late Roman stone fortification was reused with some modifications and additions also built in stone at Visegrád-Sibrik domb. There are debates about possible German, Lombard, Khazar, Bulgar or Moravian models. Similarities between strongholds in Hungary and those in Bohemia, Poland and Kievan Rus' have been noted. Cemeteries started around these strongholds

[155] Györffy 1977, 128–9.   [156] Kristó 1988; 2001b, 68–74.
[157] Kristó 1988; 2001b, 74–5.   [158] Bóna 1998; 2002; Wolf 1996; 2003; 2005.

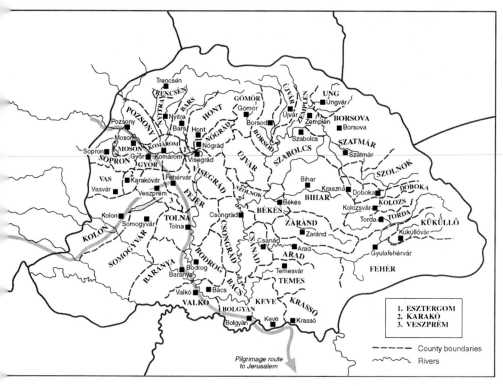

20. Counties in the kingdom of Hungary in the early Árpád age

in the first decades of the eleventh century. None can be dated to the tenth century or earlier; most are dated by coins of István I found in the graves. They are interpreted as the cemeteries of castle servants. If this is correct, there was rapid and dramatic change. Seventeen cemeteries of castle warriors and servants have been excavated to date.[159] Esztergom (also the seat of the archbishop) and Fehérvár emerged during the reign of István as key centres.[160] On dynastic lands, serving people provided for the needs of the court. István created a system of royal revenues from customs duties, the sale of salt, mining, coinage and penalties that had to be paid to the royal treasury. The system of taxation was reformed by King Kálmán in the early twelfth century.[161]

[159] Wolf 2003.   [160] Altmann *et al.* 1999; Buzás, Laszlovszky and Magyar 2003, 348–53.
[161] Bak *et al.* 1989, 29, c. 45.

Legislation also included passages on royal power: kingship and Christianity were inextricably tied together. A probably late eleventh-century interpolation in the laws of István asserts that the king governs his *monarchia* by the grace of God, and that the work of royal dignity is linked to the Catholic faith. The laws also state that the king protects ecclesiastical lands, provides vestments and altar clothes to the churches and is the final judge of those negligent in Christian observance. Goods, warriors and servants belonging to the king are protected. Conspiracy against the king and the kingdom is punished by anathema, although this passage might be a twelfth-century interpolation. László I legislated on litigation and the right of sanctuary at the royal court, and royal licences concerning trade in the borderlands of the kingdom. A system of royal messengers and the royal court as a place of judgement demonstrated that the court took over functions from local society. László also ordered the punishment of those violating royal decrees. Kálmán's laws emphasized the importance of the honour and riches of the royal court. The king ensured the growth of these riches by laying claim to the land of people who died without heirs and to taxes and services from freemen and warriors from the villages. His legislation also describes the king moving around the kingdom giving judgement and prescribes punishment for holding fugitives without royal permission. Canons in the collection known as the synod of Esztergom introduced daily prayers for the king and the kingdom and the excommunication of those who conspired against the king or knew of such conspiracy. Legislation therefore shows the growing sphere of royal power in the period.[162]

Art and archaeology attest to royal self-representation linked to Christianity. Not much remains of royal burials of the period. The original entombment of István and Imre is overshadowed by their later cult. Other kings of the period were buried in their own monasteries, but only the tomb of András I is known.[163] He was buried in the abbey church of Tihany in 1060. In the middle of the crypt a privileged burial was found, which was protected during the centuries. Nearby, a tomb slab was preserved, representing a cross (similar to the tomb of Queen Gisela in Passau). Although no written source or inscription exists, the identification of this tomb with that of the founder king is probable. Large-scale churches were financed by the king for representative purposes. According to narrative sources, Hungarian rulers followed the Ottonian model of donations of luxurious

[162] Bak *et al.* 1989, I, preface; 2, c. 1; 9, c. 1; 4, c. 13; 3, c. 7; II, c. 19; 61, c. 41–2; 12–13, c. 1–2; 15–16, c. 16–18; 18, c. 1–2; 19, c. 2; 14, c. 8 and 21, c. 15; 19, c. 3; 21, c. 15; 27, c. 15; 27, c. 20; 29, c. 45 and 32, c. 78–9; 28, c. 36–7; 29, c. 39; 66, c. 73; 66, c. 74–5 respectively.
[163] Uzsoki 1984; Tóth 2001.

codices to monasteries and of precious objects to churches. Among the secular centres, the early phase of the fort of Esztergom is known. This was the first royal residence of wood-earth construction which may have been built already during the reign of Géza or perhaps that of István, and was replaced by a stone construction during the eleventh or early twelfth century.[164] The site of the stone castle of Székesfehérvár was also excavated. Almost nothing remained of the castle itself; the centrally planned church in the middle of it can be dated to the twelfth century.[165]

The Hungarian coronation regalia are some of the earliest of this type preserved in Europe.[166] Later tradition connected them to St István, but this identification is only partially correct. The coronation mantle was commissioned by István as a chasuble, and was transformed into a mantle in the early thirteenth century. The portrait of István on the chasuble depicts the ruler with his insignia: a diadem-type crown, a lance and a globe. This is generally regarded as an authentic representation of the once-existing insignia. This view, however, is questionable, as all the saints are represented in the same way on the chasuble. According to this portrait and a coin of István bearing the inscription *LANCEA REGIS*,[167] originally a copy of the Imperial Lance belonged to the Hungarian regalia; it was probably similar to the example preserved in Kraków.[168] The donation of the lance to the Hungarian ruler is recorded by Adémar de Chabannes.[169] It was sent to Rome together with the crown by Emperor Henry III after defeating the Hungarian king Samuel Aba in 1044,[170] where it was seen by late eleventh-century eyewitnesses.[171] The lance never appeared again in the Hungarian insignia. Although a globe is already depicted on the mantle, the existing object is much later: a coat of arms of the Angevin dynasty dates it to the fourteenth century.

The sceptre in the insignia, not represented on the mantle, is first mentioned in the foundation charter of the Benedictine abbey of Tihany (1055).[172] It consists of a crystal ball representing three lions, carved in Egypt in the tenth century, and golden and silver filigree work, which is the basis of dating the sceptre to the end of the twelfth century. Recent scholarship, however, challenges the dating of the filigree work, and points out the rarity of the club form, known from the seals of Rudolf III (996), king

---

[164] Torma 1979; Horváth 2002.   [165] Buzás, Laszlovszky and Magyar 2003, 350–1.
[166] Overall: Kovács and Lovag 1980.   [167] Huszár 1979, H2.
[168] Wieczorek and Hinz 2000, *Katalog*, no. 27.01.05.
[169] Ademar III.31 (at 153); Gerics 1995, 43–50; Veszprémy 2003.
[170] *Gregorii papae VII Epistolae*, 110, no. 33.
[171] E.g. Bonizo (d. 1091), 583–4.   [172] Györffy 1992, 149, no. 43/I.

of Burgundy, and Emperor Henry II (1004). No later parallels are known, therefore the form seems to be contemporary with István.[173] Henry II was famous for his interest in such objects: the crystal may have been his gift to István, or the Hungarian king might have imitated the custom of the German emperor. The present-day sword of the regalia is from the late Middle Ages. Two swords connected to the early Árpádians were not part of the regalia.[174]

The most remarkable piece of the regalia is the Holy Crown of Hungary. It consists of two parts. The lower part, *Corona graeca*, is a Byzantine queen's crown, dated on the basis of the represented rulers (Géza I of Hungary, 1074–7, and Emperor Michael VII, 1071–8) to around the 1070s.[175] Most probably it arrived in Hungary together with the Byzantine wife of Géza I. The upper part, the cruciform *Corona latina*, is decorated with enamels, usually dated to the end of the twelfth or early thirteenth century but redated on the basis of epigraphic arguments by Endre Tóth to the first half of the eleventh century.[176] The unification of the two objects is traditionally connected to Béla III (1172–96) or the thirteenth century; however, the best parallels to the filigree work of the upper part, probably produced for the unification, are known from late eleventh-century Germany.[177] It is possible that during the reign of Kálmán (1095–1116) or later, the Byzantine piece, kept at Székesfehérvár, and the Latin enamels were unified because they were regarded as venerable objects due to their age. Thus, the original unit of the regalia of István, as far as we can know, is comparable to the contemporary imperial and Polish examples.

5. THE EFFECTS OF CHRISTIANIZATION

The establishment of a Christian kingdom can be traced through the development of ecclesiastical structures and the introduction of key practices. Ecclesiastical organization and institutions were erected after the ruler's conversion. Not all levels of this organization were put in place at once: bishoprics and monasteries were the first to appear. Györffy hypothesized the existence of a mobile missionary bishopric at the end of the tenth century on Géza's territory, based on Thietmar of Merseburg's mention of a prelate at the ruler's court.[178] The establishment of a permanent ecclesiastical structure was perhaps begun by Géza, who according to some

[173] Tóth 2000.   [174] Fodor 2000; Wieczorek and Hinz 2000, *Katalog*, nos. 15.04.01 and 27.01.09.
[175] Kiss 2002.   [176] E. Tóth 1996.   [177] Szakács 2002.
[178] Györffy 1977, 76, 177; Thietmar of Merseburg VIII.4 (at 444).

historians founded the bishopric of Veszprém.[179] Traditional historiography erroneously attributed the foundation of ten bishoprics to István. In fact, by the first years of the eleventh century, the bishoprics of Veszprém and Győr and the archbishopric of Esztergom were organized in the territories under the rule of the Árpáds. As István subjugated and attached new areas, he also founded more bishoprics: those of Transylvania, Pécs, Kalocsa, Eger and Csanád.[180] Whether Kalocsa (from the thirteenth century Bács-Kalocsa) was an archbishopric without an ecclesiastical province from the beginning or a bishopric is debated.[181] When it was first mentioned in the mid-eleventh century it was already an archbishopric. István's successors founded several other bishoprics: in the mid- to late eleventh century Bihar (modern Biharea, later moved to Várad, modern Oradea), Vác, Zagreb and, *c.* 1100, Nyitra (Nitra). Further bishoprics continued to be added parallel to the kingdom's expansion. Hartvic's *Legenda* depicts István marking out the borders of the bishoprics in the eleventh century, while two early charters provide inconclusive evidence. The originally early eleventh-century but interpolated foundation charter of the bishopric of Pécs describes precise boundaries (which according to Györffy were part of the original text), while the charter of privileges for the bishopric of Veszprém only lists possessions.[182] Bishops received the tithe,[183] which was probably introduced by István, although the decree on tithes in the laws of István might be a later addition.[184] The bishop's tithe definitely existed by the second half of the eleventh century, as it is mentioned several times in the synods and laws of both László and Kálmán. The interpolated charter of privileges to Pannonhalma also mentions a tithe (*decimatio*) granted to the monastery, and according to Györffy this was part of the original charter from 1002.[185] In 1175 a papal letter referred to the tithe of the Somogy territory given to the monastery of Pannonhalma by István. The late eleventh-century *Legenda maior* also described the tithe.[186]

The dissemination of Christianity needed buildings and objects.[187] The most important task was to build cathedrals and baptismal churches: their

[179] Summary and criticism: Kristó 2002b, 373, 378.
[180] Koszta 2001; Thorockay 2002a; Kristó 2001b, 88–93.
[181] Baán 1997; Koszta 2001, 70; Török 2002a, 37, 131–8.
[182] *Legenda S. Stephani ab Hartvico*, 415; Györffy 1992, 54–8, no. 9/I, 49–53, no. 8.
[183] Mályusz 1971, 16–18.   [184] Bak *et al.* 1989, 11, c. 20; Jánosi 1996, 77–8.
[185] Bak *et al.* 1989, 59, c. 27, c. 30; 60, c. 33; 61, c. 40; 21, c. 13; 27, c. 25; 31, c. 66; 66, c. 64; 67, c. 90; Györffy 1992, 26–41, no. 5/II; on the controversy about which parts are later interpolations: Thorockay 2002b.
[186] Erdélyi and Sörös 1902–16, vol. I, 606–7; *Legenda S. Stephani maior*, 384.
[187] Tóth 1988; Szakács 2000.

location shows that ecclesiastical structures were first put in place in western Hungary, the heartland of the ruling Árpád dynasty. No eleventh-century cathedral remains in intact form, and only a few are known partially. One of the most important buildings connected to István was the royal basilica of Székesfehérvár, which served as a 'chapel' of the king, although it was one of the largest buildings of the kingdom. The three-aisled basilica had a rounded apse at the east together with two separate chambers and a complex western part, a westwork or western towers. This was the church where István and his son Imre were buried, together with many of the later Hungarian kings; where the regalia were preserved in the first centuries; and where the Hungarian kings were crowned. The archaeological excavations of the church are only partially published, therefore the dating of the different parts is problematic.[188] The first phase of the cathedral of Kalocsa is usually dated to the time of István; however, the archaeological evidence itself cannot be dated securely.[189] The cathedral of Veszprém may still preserve some original parts, especially the western towers, the galleries over the aisles and fragments of a crypt, but the related stone carvings are not earlier than the middle of the eleventh century.[190] At Pécs some sections of the crypt and the western part date to the eleventh century, but the majority of the church is from the following centuries.[191] Collegiate churches developed gradually from the royal chapels that were established from the early eleventh century on and cathedral chapters appeared beginning in the late eleventh century.[192] A canon in the collection known as the synod of Esztergom legislated on the life of the canons.[193]

Monasteries appeared from the very beginning, founded by rulers, and monks played an active role in Christianization. The majority were Benedictine houses.[194] The letter of privileges to Pannonhalma mentions the founder as Géza, with the foundation completed by István. Pannonhalma still preserves fragments of a western apse and a crypt, and possibly a transept and tower(s).[195] István founded other Benedictine monasteries at Pécsvárad, Zalavár, Bakonybél, Somlóvásárhely and Zobor. The St Hadrianus monastery, founded by the king at Zalavár (Mosaburg), is known only after a sixteenth-century drawing.[196] A two-storey chapel of the monastery of Pécsvárad preserved its early structure on the ground floor. It is debated whether it was built before, during or after the time of István. The fresco in the apse is probably from the twelfth century and a fragment of a carving

[188] Biczó 2001.   [189] Szakács 1997.   [190] Tóth 1963; 1993–4.   [191] Tóth 1983.
[192] Koszta 1996; Török 2002a, 87–8, 148.   [193] Bak et al. 1989, 63, c. 26; 66, c. 58.
[194] Kristó 2004; Takács 2001; Sólymos 2001.   [195] László 1996.   [196] Takács 2001, 322–7, 673–6.

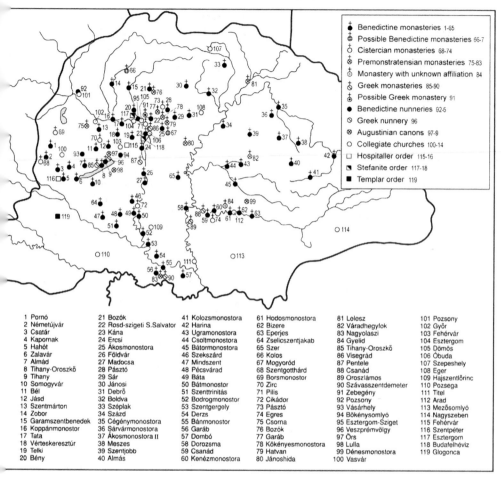

Legend:
- ● Benedictine monasteries 1-65
- Possible Benedictine monasteries 66-7
- Ô Cistercian monasteries 68-74
- ⊗ Premonstratensian monasteries 75-83
- Monastery with unknown affiliation 84
- Greek monasteries 85-90
- Possible Greek monastery 91
- ● Benedictine nunneries 92-5
- ◎ Greek nunnery 96
- ⊗ Augustinian canons 97-9
- ○ Collegiate churches 100-14
- ◻ Hospitaller order 115-16
- ◼ Stefanite order 117-18
- ■ Templar order 119

1 Pornó	21 Bozók	41 Kolozsmonostora	61 Hodosmonostora	81 Lelesz	101 Pozsony
2 Németújvár	22 Rosd-szigeti S.Salvator	42 Harina	62 Bizere	82 Váradhegyfok	102 Győr
3 Csatár	23 Kána	43 Ugramonostora	63 Eperjes	83 Nagyolaszi	103 Fehérvár
4 Kapornak	24 Ercsi	44 Csoltmonostora	64 Zselicszentjakab	84 Gyelid	104 Esztergom
5 Hahót	25 Ákosmonostora	45 Bátormonostora	65 Szer	85 Tihany-Oroszkő	105 Dömös
6 Zalavár	26 Földvár	46 Szekszárd	66 Kolos	86 Visegrád	106 Óbuda
7 Almád	27 Madocsa	47 Mindszent	67 Mogyoród	87 Pentele	107 Szepeshely
8 Tihany-Oroszkő	28 Pásztó	48 Pécsvárad	68 Szentgotthárd	88 Csanád	108 Eger
9 Tihany	29 Sár	49 Báta	69 Borsmonostor	89 Oroszlámos	109 Hajszentlőrinc
10 Somogyvár	30 Jánosi	50 Bátmonostor	70 Zirc	90 Szávasszentdemeter	110 Pozsega
11 Bél	31 Debrő	51 Szenttrinitás	71 Pilis	91 Zebegény	111 Titel
12 Jásd	32 Boldva	52 Bodrogmonostor	72 Cikádor	92 Pozsony	112 Arad
13 Szentmárton	33 Széplak	53 Szentgergely	73 Pásztó	93 Vásárhely	113 Mezősomlyó
14 Zobor	34 Százd	54 Derzs	74 Csorna	94 Bökénysomlyó	114 Nagyszeben
15 Garamszentbenedek	35 Cégénymonostora	55 Bánmonostor	75 Bozók	95 Esztergom-Sziget	115 Fehérvár
16 Koppánmonostor	36 Sárvármonostora	56 Garáb	76 Bozók	96 Veszprémvölgy	116 Szentpéter
17 Tata	37 Ákosmonostora II	57 Dombó	77 Garáb	97 Örs	117 Esztergom
18 Vérteskeresztúr	38 Meszes	58 Dorozsma	78 Kökényesmonostora	98 Lulla	118 Budafelhéviz
19 Telki	39 Szentjobb	59 Csanád	79 Hatvan	99 Dénesmonostora	119 Glogonca
20 Bény	40 Almás	60 Kenézmonostora	80 Jánoshida	100 Vasvár	

21. Religious orders in the kingdom of Hungary during the eleventh and twelfth centuries

representing a Byzantine Madonna was found there from around 1100.[197] Greek monastic foundations were also linked to István. The foundation charter of the convent of nuns in Veszprémvölgy issued by 'Stephanos kralés', which survives in a bilingual (Greek and Latin) royal transcript from 1109 was originally a Greek charter, suggesting that the convent was one of Greek rite. Some historians attribute the foundation of the convent to Géza, who according to Adémar de Chabannes (whose text is erroneous

---

[197] Takács 2001, 328–34; Bodó 2004.

in many details) also received the name István in baptism.[198] It is much more likely that the founder was King István. The dating of the recently discovered remains of the monastery is controversial.[199] Ajtony, one of István's opponents, also founded a Greek monastery at Csanád. Other communities of Greek monks (at Szávaszentdemeter and Pentele) were perhaps established by or received donations from István, although clear evidence is lacking. Oroszlámos was founded by one of István's military leaders, in order to rehouse the monks he expelled from Csanád when he conquered Ajtony's lands.[200]

István's successors on the throne continued to found monasteries, in the eleventh century Benedictine monasteries and nunneries, in the twelfth century also Cistercian and Premonstratensian ones.[201] In the eleventh century Greek monasteries were also founded by King András I (whose wife was from Kiev) and members of the elite. Greek monasteries flourished in the kingdom throughout the period, but were abandoned and turned over to other monastic orders during the thirteenth century.[202] Already in the eleventh and increasingly in the twelfth century monasteries were established by nobles as well, especially to serve as burial places, as they did for early rulers.[203] The crypt of the Benedictine abbey of Tihany, founded in 1055 by King András I, is well preserved. In other cases, the ground plan can be reconstructed, as that of Szekszárd (1061, Béla I), Feldebrő (a member of the Aba family, possibly King Samuel Aba before 1044) and Zselicszentjakab (*comes* Otto, 1061).[204] Many of these churches had a centralized ground plan and were decorated with stone carvings representing palmette leaves. In the last quarter of the eleventh century the new so-called 'Benedictine plan' was introduced.[205] The first dated examples are the royal monasteries of Garamszentbenedek (Hronský Beňadik) (1075) and Somogyvár (1091). The same plan was applied during the rebuilding of the cathedrals of Eger, Győr and (with only one apse) at Gyulafehérvár (Alba Julia), probably from the late eleventh and early twelfth centuries. The complete rebuilding of almost all the eleventh-century churches may be partially the result of the pagan uprisings, but even more probably the consequence of the building

[198] Györffy 1992, 81–5, no. 13; Kristó 2001b, 36; Ademar III.31 (at 152); Pirigyi 1990, 48–9.
[199] Fülöp and Koppány 2002.
[200] Moravcsik 1938b; Török 2002a, 195; *Legenda S. Gerhardi*, 492; Pirigyi 1990, 49–50.
[201] Seven Cistercian monasteries in the twelfth century: Hervay 1984; Koszta 1993; Török 2002b, 47–53, 87.
[202] Moravcsik 1953, 61; Pirigyi 1990, 50–1.
[203] Fügedi 1991; Takács 2001: in 1142–1241 between forty and eighty Benedictine monasteries were founded by families.
[204] Takács 2001, 335–46, 677–9.   [205] Szakács 2004.

technique of the early period and the spread of the new Romanesque style which replaced the old-fashioned Ottonian buildings.

The churches of the early eleventh century may have looked somewhat rigid, without rich ornamental or figurative decoration. In contrast, the liturgical equipment was splendid. Although no complete series of Christian cult objects survived from the eleventh or twelfth century, some existing objects may be representative. According to its inscription, the so-called coronation mantle, originally a chasuble, was donated by István and Queen Gisela to the Holy Virgin church of Székesfehérvár in 1031.[206] Another chasuble, donated to Pope John XVIII *c.* 1004, is known from a description and representation. While these closely resemble the Bamberg paraments of Henry II, and are usually discussed together, Éva Kovács argued on the basis of technical and iconographic observations that they might have been produced in Hungary.[207] Similarly, whether the cross ordered by Queen Gisela for the tomb of her mother at Regensburg (Munich, Schatzkammer der Residenz) was made in Regensburg or in Hungary is debated.[208] Such splendid objects did not survive from Hungary, but a stylistically related small (7 cm) gold corpus was found in Újszász. A golden pectoral cross found at Feldebrő is dated to the second half of the eleventh century. The top of a crosier, carved at the end of the eleventh century in the Rhineland or Westphalia, comes from the same monastery.[209]

Parishes, as elsewhere, developed gradually over several centuries. Little information exists on small churches serving the population. In many places wooden or wattle-and-daub churches predated stone constructions.[210] Archaeological excavations unearthed archdeaconal as well as parish churches in or near the strongholds of the county centres.[211] István decreed that every ten villages should build a church together and stipulated the provision of churches with vestments and liturgical objects; to what extent such regulation was carried out cannot be known.[212] Despite this regulation and the prescription that the population had to participate at mass, many scholars do not talk of parishes in the early period, although no unanimity exists on the question. The *ecclesia parochiana* of late eleventh-century legislation and the synod of Esztergom's *parochianus presbyter* were not yet representative of a fully developed parish system. In this period monks also participated in preaching and the cure of souls. The synod of Esztergom started to prohibit monastic involvement in preaching, baptism and the

---

[206] Bardoly 2002. [207] Wieczorek and Hinz 2000, vol. II, 640–51. [208] Kovács 1994.
[209] Wieczorek and Hinz 2000, *Katalog*, nos. 16.04.01–03.
[210] Bakay 1978, 157; Bálint *et al.* 2003, 386.
[211] Laszlovszky and Romhányi 2003, 372; Wolf 2005. [212] Bak *et al.* 1989, 9, c. 1.

giving of absolution, and similar prohibitions recurred.[213] The main period
of parish development was probably from the end of the twelfth to the middle of the thirteenth century, although little is known about the process of
parish formation. Especially from the thirteenth century on, many small
churches existed, and the fourteenth-century papal tithe lists are the best
sources for the parish organization. Private churches founded by lay patrons
played an important role throughout the period; such churches were sold
as part of the property and the owner had the right to appoint the priest. A
papal legate in the late thirteenth century legislated against private churches
and demanded their transformation into patronal churches. These became
the centres of parishes. The parish organization was completed in the fourteenth and fifteenth centuries.[214]

Whereas during the reign of István the clergy almost exclusively consisted of foreigners, by the late eleventh and twelfth centuries legislation
demanded that nobody be accepted as a cleric into the kingdom without verifying their background.[215] The kingdom itself became the base for
attempts to convert others to Christianity. In the late eleventh and twelfth
centuries, legislation aimed at the conversion of Muslims living within the
kingdom. In the early thirteenth century, Dominicans from Hungary went
to the Cumans, the eastern neighbours of the kingdom, to convert them.
Béla III took a crusading vow and his son King András II participated in
crusade to the Latin East in 1217.[216]

Liturgy was first imported from abroad but it was composed in Hungary already in the late eleventh century: the Sacramentary of St Margaret
includes liturgy for St István.[217] A charter from the end of the eleventh
century lists around forty liturgical manuscripts in the possession of the
Benedictine monastery of Pannonhalma.[218] The earliest antiphonal with
musical notations is the Codex Albensis (c. 1120, probably from south
Hungary[219]), which proves that the common elements of the liturgical
usage of the dioceses of Esztergom, Kalocsa and Transylvania go back at
least to the early twelfth century. This suggests that the basic structure of
the Hungarian liturgy is datable either to the time of the organization of
the church under István, although there is no direct evidence for that, or
to the ecclesiastical reorganization under László and Kálmán. This basic
structure is common in the entire Hungarian kingdom, but not known in

[213] Bak et al. 1989, 64, c. 34; Kłoczowski 1977; Cevins 1999.
[214] Kłoczowski 1977; Cevins 1999; Fügedi 1991; Hube 1856, 88–90, 107–12; Mályusz 1966.
[215] Györffy 1977, 190; Bak et al. 1989, 26, c. 3; 63, c. 21.   [216] Berend 2001, 211–23.
[217] Takács 2001, no. IV.13.   [218] Török 2002a, 181; Györffy 1992, 295–301, no. 100.
[219] Facsimile edition: Falvy and Mezey 1963.

other places.[220] It was later enriched with other elements, for example a reform in Esztergom at the end of the twelfth century was connected to the newly invented type of Hungarian musical notation.[221]

Literacy was chiefly introduced in Hungary as a result of Christianization. Some of the population in the conquest period used runic script.[222] Objects such as needle-holders, belt-ends, horse-accoutrements and purse-lids with runic inscriptions were found during excavations. These objects contain short inscriptions, sometimes only one word. Had extensive texts been produced on the Scandinavian scale we should have some evidence of it; there was no widespread use of runes. Although some scholars claim that a runic Hungarian script existed, there is no inscription that is undoubtedly in Hungarian. Some of the inscriptions are Turkic; some are in an unknown runic script. The reading of the runic inscriptions on many objects is controversial. The Székely runic script is sometimes used as proof of ancient Hungarian runic literacy. The extant texts that are dated securely, however, only come from the fifteenth century and later. L. Benkő sees Turkic cultural influence in the adoption of runic script, suggesting that it was used by a small part of the population only.[223] The function of writing changed after the introduction of Christianity. Latin literacy started with charters; the first known one is dated 1002. At least one Greek charter was also issued by István (see above). A charter of donation and two charters of foundation, although they contain later interpolations, probably date from István's reign; several later forgeries claimed to be István's charters as well. István's charters reflect the usage of the German imperial chancery and were produced by former imperial scribes.[224] Beginning in the second half of the eleventh century, charters were also issued in the name of members of the lay elite, and several wills survive from the twelfth century.[225] Charters were first issued to the benefit of ecclesiastical institutions; lay people became their recipients in the mid-twelfth century. Charter production continued during the reign of István's successors, although from the period between István's reign and 1055 only a seal of King Peter survives.

During the eleventh century, other Latin genres appeared as well: in the first half of the century the *Admonitions*, advice to a young prince on Christian kingship, and legislation; in the second half saints' *Lives*, and by *c.* 1100 a chronicle (although it only survives in a fourteenth-century

---

[220] Dobszay 1988.   [221] Rajeczky 1988, 191–9 and 418–20.
[222] Györffy and Harmatta 1997.   [223] Benkő 1997, 175.
[224] Györffy 1992, nos. 4, 5, 8, 9, 10, 12, 13, 14, 16, 17, 26, 28; Szentpétery 1938; Kristó 2001b, 77.
[225] Kristó 2002c, 20.

form which incorporates later additions and changes).[226] The first extant
surviving chronicle is from *c.* 1200, and several chronicles were written in
the thirteenth century. Between the 1060s and the early thirteenth century,
Lives were written in the kingdom of probably all the saints canonized in
Hungary (István, Imre, Zoerard, Benedict, László and Gerard, whose *Life*
might be later). Vernacular Hungarian words were incorporated into Latin
charters in the mid-eleventh century; the first extant vernacular texts survive
from the end of the twelfth century. These are religious texts: a burial speech
and a prayer to the Virgin Mary. Vernacular lay literacy only appeared in the
later Middle Ages.[227] Literacy in its administrative, religious and historical
narrative uses thus all developed after Christianization. Although all these
forms of Latin literacy were introduced in the eleventh century, charter
production as well as the writing of narrative texts started to flourish only
in the thirteenth century. It was not simply the introduction of Christianity
itself but social conditions as well that influenced literacy. The intimate link
between literacy, social status and Christianity is expressed in an interesting
canon of the collection known as the synod of Esztergom: those who taught
a slave or a man of the castle to read were to be punished.[228]

Legislation similarly started with István and was continued by his successors.[229] Much of the legislation dealt with Christianization itself as described
above. In addition, the laws set out the status of ecclesiastics and regulated
society, covering issues such as murder, fornication, adultery, marriage,
property and theft (the last was particularly important in the laws of László
I). Influences and verbatim borrowing from German synods and canon law
(e.g. Pseudo-Isidore) characterized some of the early legislation. From the
time of László I there is increasingly regulation for the Church itself, for
example on clerical marriage, bishops' duties and ordeal, and detailed regulation on tithes. Under Kálmán, legislation radically increased on internal
ecclesiastical matters such as how bishops can dispose of their property, the
regulation of the life of canons and monks, the need to approve liturgy by
the synod and compulsory attendance of clerics at episcopal synods.[230]

Coinage was also introduced by István; his silver deniers were found in
graves in Hungary, and some (including imitations) circulated in northern
and eastern Europe as well.[231] Both known types – the first issued before
1006, the other before 1025 (the exact dating is debated) – contain Christian
symbolism. One includes the inscription *LANCEA REGIS* with an image

---

[226] Klaniczay and Madas 1996; Kristó 2002c, chaps. 2, 3, 4; Veszprémy 2004. On influences:
Nemerkényi 2004.
[227] Korompay 1999.   [228] Bak *et al.* 1989, 66, c. 69.   [229] Bak *et al.* 1989.
[230] Bak *et al.* 1989, 12–33, 55–67.   [231] Huszár 1979.

of an arm holding a lance with a flag attached, and *REGIA CIVITAS* with a church building (or crown) on the reverse; the current consensus is that this was the first coin. The other is inscribed *STEPHANUS REX* and *REGIA CIVITAS* with the images of crosses. The coins show similarities to Bavarian coinage in their weight and design and it has been supposed that minters came from Bavaria. There are inconclusive debates concerning the provenance and date of other coins (some found only outside Hungary that may be imitations), notably a gold coin with the inscription *STEPHANUS REX* and *PANNONIA*, bearing a royal portrait and a female head (perhaps the Virgin Mary).[232] After István all subsequent rulers continued to issue coinage regularly.[233]

It is clear that not all the effects of Christianization emerged at once in the early eleventh century.

6. CONCLUSION

In Hungary, Christianity and royal power were established in parallel. Both the belief system and the power structure changed radically. Art and archaeology both show rupture around the end of the tenth and early eleventh centuries. Although changes started in the early eleventh century, many processes continued for centuries. Influences penetrated Hungary from many areas, and were quickly absorbed and transformed by local adaptations. The establishment of a new compulsory religion together with a new form of rule, sole monarchical power, led to resistance, even expressed in several revolts. Warfare, violence and compulsion cannot be divorced from this dual process of change, but, although Christianity was doubtless mainly imposed from above, there was also variety. Byzantine as well as Latin influences, particularly in monasticism, continued to play a role. Nobles claimed an increasing part in the foundation of monasteries and used new forms, such as wills. Of the meaning of Christianity for the population at large, however, we have almost no information.

REFERENCES

Ademari Cabannensis Chronicon, ed. P. Bourgain, R. Landes and G. Pon, Turnhout, 1999 (Corpus Christianorum Continuatio Mediaeualis 129).
Altmann, J. *et al.* 1999, *Medium Regni: Medieval Hungarian Royal Seats*, Budapest.
Annales Alamannici, ed. G. H. Pertz, *MGH SS* I, Hanover, 1826, 22–60.
Annales Altahenses maiores, ed. E. von Oefele, *MGH SRG*, Hanover, 1891.

[232] Kovács 1997; 2001.   [233] Kovács 1997.

Annales Heremi, ed. G. H. Pertz, *MGH SS* III, Hanover, 1839, 138–45.

Annales Hildesheimenses, ed. G. H. Pertz, *MGH SS* III, Hanover, 1839, 22–116.

Annales Sangallenses Maiores, ed. I. Von Arx, *MGH SS* I, Hanover, 1826, 73–85.

Anonymi (P. Magistri) Gesta Hungarorum, ed. E. Jakubovich, *SRH*, vol. I, 13–117.

Armstrong, G. and I. N. Wood, eds. 2000, *Christianizing Peoples and Converting Individuals*, Turnhout.

Arnold of Regensburg, 'Ex Arnoldi libris de S. Emmerammo', ed. G. Waitz, *MGH SS* IV, Hanover, 1891, 543–74.

Baán, I. 1996, 'The Metropolitanate of Tourkia: The Organization of the Byzantine Church in Hungary in the Middle Ages', in Prinzing and Salamon 1996, 45–53.

Baán, I. 1997, 'The Foundation of the Archbishopric of Kalocsa: The Byzantine Origin of the Second Archdiocese in Hungary', in *Early Christianity in Central and East Europe*, ed. P. Urbańczyk, Warsaw, 67–73.

Bak, J. M. 2000, 'Signs of Conversion in Central European Laws', in Armstrong and Wood 2000, 115–24.

Bak, J. M. *et al*. eds. and trs. 1989, *The Laws of the Medieval Kingdom of Hungary 1000–1301*, Bakersfield, CA.

Bakay, K. 1978, *A magyar államalapítás*, Budapest.

Bálint, Cs. 1970, 'Ló a magyar hitvilágban', *Móra Ferenc Múzeum Évkönyve* 1970/1, 31–43.

Bálint, Cs. 1971, 'A honfoglaláskori lovastemetkezések', *Móra Ferenc Múzeum Évkönyve* 1971/2, 85–108.

Bálint, Cs. 1981, 'Einige Fragen des Dirhem-Verkers in Europa', *Acta Archaeologica Academiae Scientiarum Hungaricae* 33, 105–31.

Bálint, Cs. 1991, *Südungarn im 10. Jahrhundert*, Budapest.

Bálint, M., J. Laszlovszky, B. Romhányi and M. Takács 2003, 'Medieval Villages and their Fields', in Visy 2003, 383–8.

Bardoly, I. ed. 2002, *A magyar királyok koronázó palástja*, Budapest and Veszprém.

Benkő, L. 1996, 'Anonymus élő nyelvi forrásai', in Kovács and Veszprémy 1996, 221–47.

Benkő, L. 1997, 'A honfoglaló magyarság nyelvi viszonyai és ami ezekből következik', in Kovács and Veszprémy 1997, 163–76; French tr. in Csernus and Korompay 1999, 121–36.

Benkő, L. 2002, *Az ómagyar nyelv tanúságtétele. Perújítás Dél-Erdély korai Árpád-kori történetéről*, Budapest.

Berend, N. 2001, *At the Gate of Christendom: Jews, Muslims and 'Pagans' in Medieval Hungary, c. 1000–c. 1300*, Cambridge.

Berta, Á. 1999, 'Le Système des noms de tribus Hongroises d'origine turke', in Csernus and Korompay 1999, 45–59.

Biczó, P. 2001, 'Archäologische Beobachtungen zur Baugeschichte der Stiftskirche Unserer Lieben Frau zu Székesfehérvár', *Acta Historiae Artium* 42, 283–95.

Bodó, B. 2004, 'A pécsváradi kolostor I. István korában', in *Etűdök*, ed. I. Bardoly, Budapest, 21–33.

Bogyay, T. von 1988, *Stephanus Rex*, Budapest.

Bóna, I. 1998, *Az Árpádok korai várai*, 2nd edn, Debrecen.

Bóna, I. 2000, 'Quedlinburg és következményei (973)', in *A magyarok és Európa a 9–10. században*, Budapest, 72–5.

Bóna, I. 2002, 'Várak Szent István korában', in Veszprémy 2002, 296–301.

Bonizo of Sutri, *Liber ad amicum*, ed. E. Dümmler, *MGH Libelli de lite imperatorum et pontificum saeculis XI et XII conscripti*, vol. I, Hanover, 1891, 568–620.

Bruno of Querfurt, *Epistola Brunonis ad Henricum regem*, ed. J. Karwasińska, *MPH* n.s. IV/3, Warsaw, 1973, 97–106.

Bruno of Querfurt, *S. Adalberti Pragensis episcopi et martyris vita altera*, ed. J. Karwasińska, *MPH* n.s. IV/2, Warsaw, 1969, *redactio longior* 1–41; *redactio brevior* 43–69.

Bruno of Querfurt, *Vita quinque fratrum eremitarum*, ed. J. Karwasińska, *MPH* n.s. IV/3, Warsaw, 1973, 27–84.

Buzás, G., J. Laszlovszky and K. Magyar 2003, 'Medieval Royal Centres', in Visy 2003, 348–63.

Cevins, M. M. de 1999, 'Les Paroisses hongroises au Moyen Âge', in Csernus and Korompay 1999, 341–57.

Chronici Hungarici compositio saeculi XIV, ed. A. Domanovszky, *SRH*, vol. I, 217–505.

Conversio Bagoariorum et Carantanorum, Das Weißbuch der Salzburger Kirche über die erfolgreiche Mission in Karantanien und Pannonien, ed. H. Wolfram, Vienna, Cologne and Graz, 1979.

Csernus, S. and K. Korompay, eds. 1999, *Les Hongrois et l'Europe: conquête et intégration*, Paris and Szeged.

Curta, F. 2001, 'Transylvania around AD 1000', in *Europe around the Year 1000*, ed. P. Urbańczyk, Warsaw, 141–65.

Di Cave, C. 1995, *L'arrivo degli ungheresi in Europa e la conquista della patria. Fonti e letteratura critica*, Spoleto.

Dienes, I. 1972, *A honfoglaló magyarok* (Eng. tr. *Hungarians Cross the Carpathians*), Budapest.

Diószegi, V. 1967, *A pogány magyarok hitvilága*, Budapest.

Dobszay, L. 1988, 'A középkori magyar liturgia István-kori elemei?', in *Szent István és kora*, ed. F. Glatz and J. Kardos, Budapest, 151–5.

Elter, I. 1996, 'A magyar kalandozáskor arab forrásai', in Kovács and Veszprémy 1996, 173–80.

Entz, G. and E. Szakál 1964, 'La Reconstitution du sarcophage du roi Etienne', *Acta Historiae Artium* 10, 215–28.

Erdélyi, L. and P. Sörös, eds. 1902–16, *A Pannonhalmi Szent-Benedek-rend története*, 12 vols., Budapest.

Falvy, Z. and L. Mezey, eds. 1963, *Codex Albensis. Ein Antiphonar aus dem 12. Jahrhundert*, Budapest and Graz.

Fodor, I. 1980, *Verecke híres útján* (Eng. tr. *In Search of a New Homeland: The Prehistory of the Hungarian People and the Conquest* 1982), Budapest.

Fodor, I. ed. 1996, *The Ancient Hungarians: Exhibition Catalogue*, Budapest.

Fodor, I. 2000, *A bécsi szablya és a prágai kard*, Szeged.

Fodor, I. 2003, 'The Art and Religion of the Ancient Hungarians', in Visy 2003, 333–7.

Fügedi, E. 1991, 'Sepelierunt corpus eius in proprio monasterio. A nemzetségi monostor', *Századok* 125/1–2, 35–67.

Fülep, F., Z. Bachmann and A. Pintér 1988, *Sopianae-Pécs ókeresztény emlékei*, Budapest.

Fülöp, A. and A. Koppány 2002, 'A veszprémvölgyi apácakolostor régészeti kutatása (1998–2002)', *Műemlékvédelmi Szemle* 12/1 [2004], 5–40.

Fundatio ecclesiae S. Albani Namucensis, ed. O. Holder-Egger, *MGH SS* XV/2, Hanover, 1888, 962–4.

Gerardi Moresenae Aecclesiae seu Csanadiensis Episcopi Deliberatio supra hymnum trium puerorum, ed. G. Silagi, Turnhout, 1978 (Corpus Christianorum Continuatio Mediaeualis 49).

Gerevich, T. 1938, *Magyarország románkori emlékei*, Budapest.

Gerics, J. 1981, 'A Hartvik-legenda mintáiról és forrásairól', *Magyar Könyvszemle* 97, 175–88.

Gerics, J. 1995, *Egyház, állam és gondolkodás Magyarországon a középkorban*, Budapest.

Gerics, J. and E. Ladányi 2000, 'A magyarországi keresztény egyházszervezés forráskritikájához', in *Magyaroknak eleiről. Ünnepi tanulmányok a hatvan esztendős Makk Ferenc tiszteletére*, ed. F. Piti, Szeged, 187–96.

Göckenjan, H. 1997, 'Eskü és szerződés az altaji népeknél', in Kovács and Paládi-Kovács 1997, 333–45.

Gregorii papae VII Epistolae Selectae, ed. F.-J. Schmale, *Fontes litem de Investitura Illustrantes*, Darmstadt, 1978 (*AQ* XIIa).

Györffy, Gy. 1977, *István király és műve*, Budapest.

Györffy, Gy. 1992, *Diplomata Hungariae Antiquissima*, vol. I, *1000–1131*, Budapest.

Györffy, Gy. 1993, *Krónikáink és a magyar őstörténet. Régi kérdések – új válaszok*, Budapest.

Györffy, Gy. 1997, 'A magyar törzsnevek és törzsi helynevek', in Kovács and Veszprémy 1997, 221–34.

Györffy, Gy. and J. Harmatta 1997, 'Rovásírásunk az eurázsiai írásfejlődés tükrében', in Kovács and Veszprémy 1997, 145–62.

Harmatta, J. 1997, 'Iráni nyelvek hatása az ősmagyar nyelvre', in Kovács and Veszprémy 1997, 71–83.

Hermann of Reichenau, *Chronicon*, ed. R. Buchner, *Fontes Saeculorum noni et undecimi historiam ecclesiae Hammaburgensis necnon Imperii illustrantes*, Darmstadt, 1961 (*AQ* XI), 628–707.

Hervay, F. L. 1984, *Repertorium Historicum Ordinis Cisterciensis in Hungaria*, Rome.

Horváth, I. 2002, 'Az Árpád-kori Esztergom', in *Központok és falvak a honfoglalás és kora Árpád-kori Magyarországon*, ed. J. Kisné Cseh, Tatabánya (Tudományos Füzetek 6), 233–54.

Hube, R. 1856, *Antiquissimae Constitutiones Synodales Provinciae Gneznensis*, St Petersburg.

Huszár, L. 1979, *Münzkatalog Ungarn von 1000 bis heute*, Budapest.

Istvánovits, E. 2003, *A Rétköz honfoglalás és Árpád-kori emlékanyaga*, Nyíregyháza.

Jánosi, M. 1996, *Törvényalkotás a korai Árpád-korban*, Szeged.

Katona, I. 1997, 'A magyar honfoglalás mondaköre', in Kovács and Paládi-Kovács 1997, 267–73.

Király, P. 1996, 'A Konstantín- és Metód-legenda magyar részletei', in Kovács and Veszprémy 1996, 113–18.

Kiss, A. 1983, *Baranya megye X–XI. századi sírleletei*, Budapest.

Kiss, E. 2002, 'La Couronne greque dans son contexte', *Acta Historiae Artium* 43, 39–51.

Kiss, G. 2000, *Vas megye 10–12. századi sír- és kincsleletei*, Szombathely.

Kiss, G. and E. Tóth 1993, 'A szombathelyi Szent Márton-templom régészeti kutatása 1984–1992', *Communicationes Archaeologicae Hungariae*, 175–99.

Klaniczay, G. 2002, *Holy Rulers and Blessed Princesses: Dynastic Cults in Medieval Central Europe*, Cambridge.

Klaniczay, G. and E. Madas 1996, 'La Hongrie', in *Hagiographies*, ed. G. Philippart, Turnhout, vol. II, 103–60.

Kłoczowski, J. 1977, 'Les Paroisses en Bohême, en Hongrie et en Pologne (XI–XIII siècles)', in *Le istituzioni ecclesiastiche della 'Societas Christiana' dei secoli XI–XII: diocesi, pievi e parocchie. Atti della sesta settimana internazionale di studio Milano, 1–7 settembre 1974. Miscellanea del Centro di Studi Medioevali* 8, Milan, 187–98.

Korompay, K. 1999, 'Naissance des premiers textes Hongrois', in Csernus and Korompay 1999, 359–73.

Koszta, L. 1993, 'Ciszterci rend története Magyarországon a kolostorok alapítása idején 1142–1270', *Magyar Egyháztörténeti Vázlatok* 1993/1–2, 115–28.

Koszta, L. 1996, 'Székeskáptalanok és kanonokjaik Magyarországon a 12. század elejéig', *Acta Universitatis Szegediensis de Attila József Nominatae. Acta Historica* 103, 67–81.

Koszta, L. 2001, 'Egyház- és államszervezés', in Kristó 2001a, 65–74.

Kovács, B. 1989–90, 'Magyarország középkori patrocíniumai', *Agria* 25–6.

Kovács, É. 1994, 'Gizella királyné keresztjének feliratai és ikonográfiája', in *Veszprém kora középkori emlékei*, ed. Zs. Fodor, Veszprém, 22–33.

Kovács, É. and Zs. Lovag 1980, *The Hungarian Crown and Other Regalia*, Budapest.

Kovács, L. 1997, *A kora Árpád-kori magyar pénzverésről*, Budapest.

Kovács, L. 2001, 'Szent István pénzverése', in Kristó 2001a, 93–100.

Kovács, L. and A. Paládi-Kovács, eds. 1997, *Honfoglalás és néprajz*, Budapest.

Kovács, L. and L. Veszprémy, eds. 1996, *A honfoglaláskor írott forrásai*, Budapest.

Kovács, L. and L. Veszprémy, eds. 1997, *Honfoglalás és nyelvészet*, Budapest.

Kristó, Gy. 1965, 'Megjegyzések az ún. "pogánylázadások" kora történetéhez', *Acta Universitatis Szegediensis de Attila József Nominatae. Acta Historica* 18, 1–57.

Kristó, Gy. 1988, *A vármegyék kialakulása Magyarországon*, Budapest.

Kristó, Gy. 1995, *A magyar állam megszületése*, Szeged.

Kristó, Gy. 1996, 'Honfoglaló fejedelmek. Árpád és Kurszán', in *Honfoglalás és társadalom*, Budapest, 65–109.

Kristó, Gy., ed, 2001a, *Államalapítás, társadalom, művelődés*, Budapest.

Kristó, Gy. 2001b, *Szent István király*, Budapest.

Kristó, Gy. 2002a, *Árpád fejedelemtől Géza fejedelemig. 20 tanulmány a 10. századi magyar történelemről*, Budapest.

Kristó, Gy. 2002b, 'Géza fejedelem megítélése', in Veszprémy 2002, 369–80.

Kristó, Gy. 2002c, *Magyar Historiográfia I. Történetírás a középkori Magyarországon*, Budapest.

Kristó, Gy. 2004, 'Tatárjárás előtti bencés monostorainkról', *Századok* 138/2, 403–11.

László, Cs. 1996, 'Archäologische Beobachtungen zur mittelalterlichen Baugeschichte der Abtei von Pannonhalma', *Acta Historiae Artium* 38, 5–13.

Laszlovszky, J. 1991, 'Social Stratification and Material Culture in 10th–14th Century Hungary', in *Alltag und materielle Kultur im mittelalterlichen Ungarn*, ed. A. Kubinyi and J. Laszlovszky, Krems (Medium Aevum Quotidianum 22), 32–67.

Laszlovszky, J. and B. Romhányi 2003, 'Cathedrals, Monasteries and Churches: The Archaeology of Ecclesiastic Monuments', in Visy 2003, 372–6.

Legenda S. Gerhardi episcopi, ed. I. Madzsar, *SRH*, vol. II, 461–506.

Legenda S. Stephani regis maior et minor, atque legenda ab Hartvico episcopo conscripta, ed. E. Bartoniek, *SRH*, vol. II, 363–440.

Legenda SS. Zoerardi et Benedicti, ed. I. Madzsar, *SRH*, vol. II, 347–61.

Libellus de institutione morum, ed. I. Balogh, *SRH*, vol. II, 611–27.

Libri Anniversariorum et Necrologium monasterii Sancti Galli, ed. F. L. Baumann, *MGH Necrologia Germaniae*, vol. I, Berlin, 1888, 462–87.

Liudprand, *Legatio ad imperatorem Constantinopolitanum Nicephorum Phocam*, ed. A. Bauer and R. Rau, *Fontes ad Historiam Aevi Saxonici Illustrandam*, Darmstadt, 1971 (*AQ* VIII), 524–89.

Liudprand, *Liber Antapodoseos*, ed. A. Bauer and R. Rau, *Fontes ad Historiam Aevi Saxonici Illustrandam*, Darmstadt, 1971 (*AQ* VIII), 244–495.

Liudprand, *Liber de Ottone rege*, ed. A. Bauer and R. Rau, *Fontes ad Historiam Aevi Saxonici Illustrandam*, Darmstadt, 1971 (*AQ* VIII), 496–523.

Mályusz, E. 1966, 'Die Eigenkirche in Ungarn', *Studien zur Geschichte Osteuropas* 3, 76–95.

Mályusz, E. 1971, *Egyházi társadalom a középkori Magyarországon*, Budapest.

Marosi, E. 1996, 'A honfoglalás a művészetben', *Magyar Tudomány* 103, 1026–34.

Marosi, E. 2000, 'Das Grab des heiligen Stephan in Stuhlweißenburg (Székesfehérvár)', in Wieczorek and Hinz 2000, vol. II, 625–7.

Marosi, E. and M. Tóth, eds. 1978, *Árpád-kori kőfaragványok*, Budapest and Székesfehérvár.

Mende, B.G. ed. 2005, *Research on the Prehistory of the Hungarians: Papers Presented at the Meetings of the Institute of Archaeology of the HAS, 2003–2004*, Budapest.

Mesterházy, K. 1968–70, 'Adatok a Bizánci kereszténység elterjedéséhez az Árpád-kori Magyarországon', *Debreceni Múzeum Évkönyve*, 145–77.

Mesterházy, K. 1992, 'A honfoglaló magyarok hitvilága és a monoteizmus', in *Hiedelmek, szokások az Alföldön I*, ed. L. Novák, *Acta Musei de János Arany Nominati* VII, 89–120.

Mesterházy, K. 1993, 'Régészeti adatok Magyarország 10–11. századi kereskedelméhez', *Századok* 127/3–4, 450–68.

Mesterházy, K. 2003, 'The Archaeological Research of the Conquest Period', in Visy 2003, 321–5.

Mező, A. 1996, *A templomcím a magyar helységnevekben (11–15. század)*, Budapest.

Moravcsik, Gy. 1938a, 'A honfoglalás előtti magyarság és a kereszténység', in Serédi 1938, 171–212.

Moravcsik, Gy. 1938b, 'Görögnyelvű monostorok Szent István korában', in Serédi 1938, 387–422.

Moravcsik, Gy. 1953, *Bizánc és a magyarság*, Budapest, repr. 2003.

Moravcsik, Gy. 1988, *Az Árpád-kori magyar történet bizánci forrásai*, Budapest.

Nemerkényi, E. 2004, *Latin Classics in Medieval Hungary: Eleventh Century*, Debrecen and Budapest.

Németh, P. 1996, 'The Archaeology of the Conquest Period: A History of Research', in Fodor 1996, 19–26.

Nyitrai, I. 1996, 'A magyar őstörténet perzsa nyelvű forrásai', in Kovács and Veszprémy 1996, 61–76.

Oikonomidès, N. 1971, 'À propos des relations ecclésiastiques entre Byzance et la Hongrie au XIe siècle: le métropolite de Turquie', *Revue des Études Sud-Est Européennes* 9/3, 527–33.

Otto I, Letter to Bishop Piligrim of Passau, *MGH Epistolae selectae*, ed. K. Strecker, vol. III, Berlin 1925, 100–1, no. 96.

Paládi-Kovács, A. 1997, 'A magyar lótartás jellege a honfoglalás korában', in Kovács and Paládi-Kovács 1997, 95–107.

Pálfi, Gy., Gy. L. Farkas, E. Molnár 1996, *Honfoglaló magyarság Árpád kori magyarság. Antropológia – régészet – történelem*, Szeged.

Piligrim, Letter to Pope Benedict VI, *c.* 973–4, *Codex diplomaticus et epistolaris Slovaciae*, ed. R. Marsina, vol. I, Bratislava, 1971, 41–3, no. 44.

Pirigyi, I. 1990, *A magyarországi görögkatolikusok története*, vol. I, Nyíregyháza.

Pócs, É. 1997, 'A magyar mitológia és Európa' in Kovács and Paládi-Kovács 1997, 309–22.

Prinzing, G. and M. Salamon eds. 1996, *Byzanz und Ostmitteleuropa 950–1453*, Copenhagen.

Rajeczky, B. 1988, *Magyarország Zenetörténete I. Középkor*, Budapest.

Regino of Prüm, *Chronica*, ed. R. Rau, *Fontes ad Historiam Regni Francorum Aevi Karolini Illustrandam*, Berlin, 1960 (*AQ* VII), 179–319.

Révész, L. 1996, *A karosi honfoglalás kori temetők. Régészeti adatok a Felső-Tisza-vidék X. századi történetéhez*, Miskolc.

Révész, L. 2003, 'The Cemeteries of the Conquest Period', in Visy 2003, 338–43.

Révész, L. and I. Nepper 1996, 'The Archaeological Heritage of the Ancient Hungarians', in Fodor 1996, 37–56.

Ritoók, Á. 1997, 'A magyarországi falusi templom körüli temetők feltárásának újabb eredményei', *Folia Archaeologica* 46, 165–77.

Ritoók, Á. and E. Simonyi, eds. 2005, '. . . a halál árnyékának völgyében járok'. A középkori templom körüli temetők kutatása, Budapest.

Rodvlfi Glabri historiarvm libri qvinqve, ed. and tr. J. France, in *Rodulfus Glaber Opera*, Oxford, 1989 (Oxford Medieval Texts XXIV), 1–253.

Róna-Tas, A. 1999, *Hungarians and Europe in the Early Middle Ages: An Introduction to Early Hungarian History*, Budapest.

Rózsa, G. and G. Vörös 1996, 'Legenda és valóság (Árpád-kori temető emlékei Szentesen)', in Pálfi, Farkas and Molnár 1996, 65–78.

Serédi, J. ed. 1938, *Emlékkönyv Szent István király halálának kilencszázadik évfordulóján*, Budapest, abridged repr. 1988.

Shepard, J. 1996, 'Byzantium and the Steppe-nomads: The Hungarian Dimension', in Prinzing and Salamon 1996, 55–83.

Shepard, J. 2004, 'Byzantine Writers on the Hungarians in the Ninth and Tenth Centuries', *Annual of Medieval Studies at CEU* 10, 97–123.

Sigebertus Gemblacensis, *Chronica a. 381–1111*, ed. D. L. C. Bethmann, *MGH SS* VI, Hanover, 1894, 300–74.

Simon of Kéza, *Gesta Hungarorum*, ed. A. Domanovszky, *SRH*, vol. I, 129–94.

Sólymos, Sz. 2001, 'Az első bencés szerzetesek hazánkban', in Takács 2001, 48–60.

Sopko, J. and J. Valoch 1987, *Codex Nitriensis – Nitriansky Kódex*, Martin.

SRH: Scriptores Rerum Hungaricarum, ed. I. Szentpétery, 2 vols., Budapest, 1937–8, repr. 1999.

Štefanovičová, T. 1975, *Bratislavsk hrad v 9.–12. storičí*, Bratislava.

Szabadfalvi, J. 1997, 'A honfoglalás kori magyarság állattenyésztő technikája', in Kovács and Paládi-Kovács 1997, 69–83.

Szakács, B. Zs. 1997, 'Western Complexes of Hungarian Churches of the Early Eleventh Century', *Hortus Artium Mediaevalium* 3, 149–63.

Szakács, B. Zs. 2000, 'Az államalapítás korának építészete Magyarországon', *Műemlékvédelem* 44, 67–74.

Szakács, B. Zs. 2002, 'Remarks on the Filigree of the Holy Crown of Hungary', *Acta Historiae Artium* 43, 52–61.

Szakács, B. Zs. 2004, 'Állandó alaprajzok – változó vélemények? Megjegyzések a "bencés templomtípus" magyarországi pályafutásához', in *Maradandóság és változás*, ed. Sz. Bodnár *et al.*, Budapest, 25–37.

Szegfű, L. 1999, 'Le Monde spirituel des Hongrois païens', in Csernus and Korompay 1999, 103–20.

Székely, Gy. 1984, 'Koronaküldések és királykreálások a 10–11. századi Európában', *Századok* 118/5, 905–49.

Szentpétery, I. 1938, 'Szent István király oklevelei', in Serédi 1938, vol. II, 133–202.

Szőke, B. M. 1990–1, 'The Question of Continuity in the Carpathian Basin of the 9th century AD', *Antaeus* 19–20, 145–57.

Szőke, B. M. 1998, 'A korai középkor hagyatéka a Dunántúlon', *Ars Hungarica* 26, 257–319.

Szőke, B. M. 2001, 'Mosaburg/Zalavár a karoling korban', in Takács 2001, 21–34, 573–80.

Szőke, B. M. 2003, 'The Carolingian Period', in Visy 2003, 312–17.

Szűcs, J. 1992, *A magyar nemzeti tudat kialakulása*, Szeged.

Takács, I. ed. 2001, *Paradisum plantavit. Bencés monostorok a középkori Magyarországon. Benedictine Monasteries of Medieval Hungary*, Pannonhalma.

Takács, M. 1997, 'A honfoglaláskori edényművesség', in Kovács and Paládi-Kovács 1997, 205–23.

Tettamanti, S. 1975, 'Temetkezési szokások a X–XI. században a Kárpát medencében', *Studia Comitatensia* 3, 79–122.

Theotmar, Letter to Pope John IX, 900, in *Codex Diplomaticus et epistolaris Slovaciae*, ed. R. Marsina, I, Bratislava, 1971, 32–5, no. 39.

Thietmar of Merseburg, *Chronicon*, ed. W. Trillmich, Berlin, 1957 (*AQ* IX).

Thorockay, G. 2002a, 'Szent István egyházmegyéi – Szent István püspökei', in Veszprémy 2002, 482–94.

Thorockay, G. 2002b, 'Szent István pannonhalmi oklevelének kutatástörténete', in Veszprémy 2002, 237–63.

Torma, I. ed. 1979, *Magyarország Régészeti Topográfiája*, vol. V, *Esztergom és a dorogi járás*, Budapest.

Török, J. 1986, 'A középkori magyarországi liturgia története', in *Kódexek a középkori Magyarországon*, ed. Cs. Csapodi *et al.*, Catalogue, Budapest, 49–63.

Török, J. 1991, 'A hazai és a lotharingiai liturgia kapcsolata a XI. században', in *Boldogasszony ága*, ed. Zs. Erdélyi, Budapest, 223–8.

Török, J. 2002a, *A tizenegyedik század magyar egyháztörténete*, Budapest.

Török, J. 2002b, *A tizenkettedik század magyar egyháztörténete*, Budapest.

Tóth, E. 1996, 'A Szent Korona apostollemezeinek keletkezéséhez', *Communicationes Archaeologicae Hungariae*, 181–210.

Tóth, E. 1999, 'Szent Adorján és Zalavár', *Századok* 133/1, 3–40.

Tóth, E. 2000, 'Das ungarische Krönungszepter', *Folia Archaeologica* 48, 111–53.

Tóth, E. and G. Buzás 2001, *Magyar építészet I. A rómaiaktól a román korig*, Budapest.

Tóth, M. 1983, 'A pécsi székesegyház nyugati karzata', *Építés-Építészettudomány* 15, 429–55.

Tóth, M. 1988, 'A művészet Szent István korában', in *Szent István és kora*, ed. F. Glatz and J. Kardos, Budapest, 113–32.

Tóth, S. 1963, and 1993–4, 'A veszprémi székesegyház középkori kőfaragványai I–II', *A Veszprém Megyei Múzeumok Közleményei* 1, 115–42; 19–20, 327–45.

Tóth, S. 2001, 'Tihany', in Takács 2001, 335–8 and 677–8.

Tóth, S. L. 1996, 'A honfoglaló magyar törzsek szállásterületei', in Pálfi, Farkas and Molnár 1996, 17–22.

Uzsoki, A. 1984, 'I. András király sírja Tihanyban és a sírlap ikonográfiai vonatkozásai', *A Veszprém Megyei Múzeumok Közleményei* 17, 145–88.

Váczy, P. 1938, 'Magyarország kereszténysége a honfoglalás korában', in Serédi 1938, 213–65.

Váczy, P. 1994, *A magyar történelem korai századaiból*, Budapest.

Vályi, K. 1992, 'Építőáldozat az Árpád-kori Szeren', *Hiedelmek, szokások az Alföldön I*, ed. L. Novák, *Acta Musei de János Arany Nominati* VII, 121–35.

Vékony, G. 2002, *Magyar őstörténet – magyar honfoglalás*, Budapest.

Veszprémy, L. 2000, 'Conversion in Chronicles: The Hungarian Case', in Armstrong and Wood 2000, 133–45.

Veszprémy, L. ed. 2002, *Szent István és az államalapítás*, Budapest.

Veszprémy, L. 2003, 'Adémar de Chabannes krónikájának magyar vonatkozásai. Textus és kontextus', *Századok* 137/2, 459–67.

Veszprémy, L. 2004, 'Megjegyzések korai elbeszélő forrásaink történetéhez', *Századok* 138/2, 325–47.

Vida, T. 2003, 'The Early and Middle Avar Period', in Visy 2003, 302–7.

Visy, Zs. ed. 2003, *Hungarian Archaeology at the Turn of the Millennium*, Budapest.

Vörös, I. 1996, 'A honfoglaló magyarok lovai', in *A magyar honfoglalás korának régészeti emlékei*, ed. L. Révész and M. Wolf, Miskolc, 335–45.

Wieczorek, A. and H.-M. Hinz, eds. 2000, *Europas Mitte um 1000*, 2 vols. and *Katalog*, Stuttgart.

Wipo, *Gesta Chuonradi II imperatoris*, ed. W. Trillmich, *Fontes Saeculorum noni et undecimi historiam ecclesiae Hammaburgensis necnon Imperii illustrantes*, Darmstadt, 1961 (*AQ* XI), 522–613.

Wolf, M. 1996, 'Earthen Forts and Ispán's Castles', in Fodor 1996, 57–61.

Wolf, M. 2003, 'Earthen Forts', in Visy 2003, 328–31.

Wolf, M. 2005, '"Ecclesia baptismalis, ecclesia parochialis" – A borsodi ispánsági vár templomai', in Ritoók and Simonyi 2005, 131–9.

Wolfram, H. 1995, *Salzburg, Bayern, Österreich. Die Conversio Bagoariorum et Carantanorum und die Quellen ihrer Zeit*, Munich.

Zádor, M. 1972, 'Byzantine Influences in Early Medieval Hungarian Architecture', in *Évolution générale et développements régionaux en histoire de l'art. Actes du XXIIe Congrès International d'Histoire de l'Art, Budapest 1969*, ed. Gy. Rózsa, Budapest, 185–90.

Zimonyi, I. 1996, 'A 9. századi magyarokra vonatkozó arab források. A Dzsajháni hagyomány', in Kovács and Veszprémy 1996, 49–59.

CHAPTER 9

Rus'

Jonathan Shepard

1. BEFORE CHRISTIANITY: RELIGION AND POWER

It is difficult to reconstruct from extant sources the concatenation of peoples, routes and hazards which gave rise to the earliest political formations in the land of Rus'. Yet some consideration – however speculative – is important in understanding the processes of 'state formation' and the significance of the adoption of Christianity by a leader who, having fought his way to paramountcy, felt the need to dignify, legitimize and define his regime. Two centuries before Vladimir's reign (*c.* 978–1015), the region appears to have lacked an overarching political authority or any associations with a former occupying power, such as Rome. Nor is there any indication that the indigenous peoples had generated intricate or finely meshed forms of governance for themselves.

The 'aboriginal inhabitants' of the ninth century were described in the *Rus' Primary Chronicle*[1] over 200 years later, but lack of written or physical evidence makes working out where these groupings were based, and to what extent they were organized into clear-cut tribes or clans, problematic. In the northern region lived a scattering of Finnic-speaking peoples, with intermingled groupings of Balts and Slavs further south, stretching westwards to the Baltic, eastwards beyond the Upper Dnieper region and north as far as Lake Ilmen. Lakes such as Ilmen, Pskov, Ladoga and Beloe Ozero acted as communication hubs, since their fertile soil and surrounding resources could sustain sizable numbers of hunters, fishermen and farmers, and these population concentrations could trade along the riverways leading from the lakes.[2]

---

[1] Our principal literary source is a composite work which reached its present-day form towards 1113; there are indications that a Rus' chronicle was composed *c.* 1090, which had drawn on narrative sources probably dating from the mid-eleventh century. Although reference is made to the English translation of the *Russian Primary Chronicle* by Cross and Sherbowitz-Wetzor, all quotations given here are translated from the Slavonic by the author.

[2] Dolukhanov 1996, 167–9.

Determining a sequence of events leading towards the establishment of a power structure in the huge area between the Gulf of Finland and the Black Sea steppes is equally difficult. The *Primary Chronicle* offers a variant of the brotherly foundation myths encountered in diverse European cultures.[3] It recounts the local peoples calling in a ruler from overseas, appealing to 'the Varangians, to the Rus'', saying 'our land is vast and abundant, but there is no order in it. Come and reign as princes and have authority over us!'[4] Three brothers, princes of Scandinavian stock, reportedly responded around 862; two soon died, but the surviving eldest brother, Riurik, consolidated their lands with his own, and by 882 princely rule had been extended southwards from Novgorod as far as Kiev on the Middle Dnieper.[5] The *Primary Chronicle*'s tale, while mythical, could well contain a grain of truth. Although it is most unlikely there was one such single event, by the mid-ninth century a political order and overarching leadership, albeit of a very rudimentary kind, do seem to have been introduced from outside. The indigenous inhabitants were largely made up of scattered kin groups, but many now lived under an umbrella of essentially Scandinavian overlordship, held together partly by force, but partly by consent. What the *Primary Chronicle* version leaves out is the reason for this development.

The earliest Scandinavians were motivated by prospects of the fur trade, rather than dominance. By the mid-ninth century considerable numbers of persons were involved in the complex yet mutable chains of hunting and trapping, then curing, storing and transporting pelts. Seasonal and highly variable fur stocks meant new sources were constantly sought, leading to a corresponding flexibility of routes and means of transport. Initially, the trade was mainly voluntary, with traders both sourcing and teaming up to transport furs. However, once Scandinavian overlords demanded furs as tribute, this gave rise to a nexus of authority and potential coercion extending over an enormous area. The fur trade was fuelled by luxury and semi-luxury objects and trinkets from the wealthy markets of the south (the Khazar- and Muslim-dominated regions of the Caspian and Middle East for silver; Byzantium for silks and gold brocade; and the Carolingian markets, above all the Frankish Rhineland, for glass beads and swords), encouraging indigenous peoples to trap, or themselves trade in, furs and involving even longer-range travelling. Thus any political authority attaching itself to the fur trails that were coterminous with the land of the Rus' had to cover vast distances from the start, and faced the problem of how to legitimize such an

[3] Petrukhin 1995, 108–17; Franklin and Shepard 1996, 38–9.
[4] *PVL*, 13; *RPC*, 59: in this context, 'Varangians' can only mean Scandinavians.
[5] *PVL*, 14; *RPC*, 61.

unusual, ad hoc regime, based primarily on a common interest in fur and treasure. This problem of political legitimization was resolved in part by the sword: armed groups of Scandinavians roamed the riverways, imposing their demands for tribute and services from the indigenous population in return for providing a minimum of order in which to trade. The Rus' were also directly engaged in the fur trade, presiding over its markets and in some cases themselves hunting.

Seen in isolation, the earliest known unit of Rus' political authority – the khaganate – might appear something of a paradox. The first mention that we have of the existence of a ruler of the *Rhōs* (Rus' in its Byzantine Greek form, transmitted to the Franks) comes from around 838, when a Rus' mission accompanied a Byzantine embassy to the court of Louis the Pious, who was requested to assist them back to their 'homeland'. The contemporary Frankish court annal shows that the Rus' were well enough organized under a 'king' (*rex*) to send a mission to the Byzantine emperor, implying sufficient resources for long-range embassies. These Rus' described their ruler as a *chaganus*, although when Louis investigated he discovered that they 'belonged to the people of the Swedes'.[6]

By 838 it would therefore appear that there existed a *gens* bearing the name of *Rhōs*, seemingly fronted by Scandinavians, yet with a ruler bearing a Turkic rather than a Scandinavian title. The title of *chaganus* – khagan – was almost certainly borrowed from the Khazars, and the Rus' appear to have adopted it to underpin and legitimize their own regime. Given the diversity of peoples needed to service the fur trade, it is understandable that the Rus' should have selected the title and rituals most likely to resonate with a large number of the indigenous population. Khazaria was the only prestigious polity that lay within the ken of most of them. Its capital, Itil, was located on the Lower Volga and the Khazars were already involved to some extent in the fur trade, and had sporadically imposed tribute on the local indigenous populations. It was only on the fringes of Khazar dominion that the Rus' would presume initially to establish an alternative polity.

Details of the terminology of early Rus' rulership are virtually impossible to recover, given the lack of contemporary native evidence. But there was probably little gradation between the types of prince or notable other than the term *khagan*, which was reserved for the paramount ruler. The most common term in later Slavic texts for a legitimate ruler is *kniaz'*; this may well be the counterpart of Old Norse *konungr*. The '*khagan* of the

---

[6] *Annales Bertiniani*, 30–1.

Northmen',[7] as he was sometimes known in the later ninth century, may well have been based near Lake Ilmen, south of what later developed into Novgorod. Acting as a communications hub between Lake Ladoga in the north, the Volga to the east and the Western Dvina and Upper Dnieper to the south, this large, fortified emporium with outlying settlements probably dates from the early ninth century, if not earlier, and could well have inspired Arabic descriptions of a huge boggy 'island', three days' journey wide, where 'the *khāqān* of the Rūs' resided.[8] However, we know next to nothing about the political structure of the khaganate. Presumably it was based on variegated elements of military force and legitimizing mystique, with some sort of religion or supernatural rites presided over by the semi-sacred figure of the *khagan*.[9]

There is little literary or archaeological evidence of pagan cult sites in Rus', or of the rites practised in them. The most detailed description we have is that of the 'pantheon' of idols set up by Prince Vladimir outside his hall in Kiev around 978.[10] Most of the excavated East Slav pagan sanctuaries lie well to the west of the Dnieper, along the Pripet or its tributaries, or towards the Carpathians and the Dniester in the south-west.[11] There were also sanctuaries in the towns along the main north–south riverways, reportedly destroyed at the time of Vladimir's conversion.[12] The most extensive coverage of pagan practices in Rus' literary sources, emphasizing the savagery, impurity and above all ignorance of the pre-Christian peoples of Rus', comes from the *Rus' Primary Chronicle*.[13] Brief references to the past ways and sheer ignorance of the pagans are made in Ilarion's *Sermon on Law and Grace*, composed c. 1050 in Kiev,[14] and from the later literary evidence it would seem that the pre-Christian Rus' venerated both their ancestors and spirits of place. However, it would appear that worship was not confined to one or two gods or types of god, nor did it involve a high degree of organization or specialist priests.

Some of the most promising evidence about pagan activities comes from excavations of pagan burial grounds, although inventories are mostly very meagre. Unsurprisingly, ways of life and burial practices varied greatly between the southern wooded steppes and the far north. In general,

---

[7] The term was used in a Byzantine imperial letter of 871 (*chaganum . . . Northmannorum*): Louis II, 'Epistola', 388.
[8] Ibn Rusta, *Kitāb al-A'lāk*, 38–41; tr. Wiet, 163. The site is probably Riurikovo Gorodishche.
[9] Franklin and Shepard 1996, 45–6.   [10] *PVL*, 37; *RPC*, 93.
[11] Rusanova 1992, 50–67; Franklin and Shepard 1996, 159; Rusanova and Timoshchuk 1998, 147–9, 151–61.
[12] Petrukhin 2000, 273–4.   [13] *PVL*, 10–11; *RPC*, 56–7.
[14] Ilarion, *Sermon*, 38–41; Franklin 1991, 14–15.

cremation prevailed among the populations of the forest zones, whereas inhumations were more common among the peoples in the vicinity of the wooded steppes,[15] and traditionally cremations have been associated with the Slavs.[16] However, judging by some burial grounds at Kiev and elsewhere in the Middle Dnieper region, inhumation was making headway among better-off sections of the population on the main north–south riverways during the tenth century, well before the baptism of the ruler, Vladimir, *c.* 988.[17] A number of funerary rites are almost certainly of Scandinavian type, notably boat-burnings at places such as Staraia Ladoga and Gnezdovo, and chamber graves.[18]

The contents of chamber graves and also much humbler graves suggest that talismans were linked to the fur trade. A considerable number of burial grounds suggestive of the cult of the beaver have been excavated on the Upper Volga. Clay paws, often together with small clay rings, were placed in graves, and one may infer that veneration of the beaver tended to accompany the fur trade: clearly connected with material prosperity, the beaver was deemed sacred, bringing blessings, even as it was hunted.[19] Pendant Thor's hammerlets are another very likely indicator of a Scandinavian presence.[20] These lucky charms have been found attached to the rings or necklaces of the dead, although the majority have recently been shown to be quite a late development of around the mid-tenth century. Found in Rus' along the north–south riverway in such locations as Gnezdovo (near modern Smolensk), on the 'Way from the Varangians to the Greeks' and also on the Upper Volga, this relatively late type of amulet has a comparable distribution-pattern to that of Christian symbols. The hammerlets could indicate something of a 'crisis of paganism': the increased production of such charms could signal a reaction to the perceived potency of their Christian counterparts, symbols that the god-fearing pagan could attach to his or her person.[21]

The vastness of the Rus' territories and our lack of literary sources help explain the patchiness of the evidence about paganism. But there is reason to suppose a broad spectrum of beliefs, fears and collective rituals, varying

---

[15] Dolukhanov 1996, 63, 67–8.

[16] On the East Slav funerary practices: Sedov 1982, e.g. 96–8, 104–8, 116–20, 136–66; Sedov 2002; Rybakov 1987.

[17] Motsia 1990, 70–1, 75, 85, 96; Petrukhin 1995, 195–215; Musin 2002, 146–7.

[18] Franklin and Shepard 1996, 127–8; for important caveats: Stalsberg 2001, 380.

[19] Franklin and Shepard 1996, 66–7, 125, 132.

[20] Jansson 1987, 776–7, 781–2; Novikova 1992, 76, 84–7; Golubeva 1997, 153–65. Cf. Staecker 2003, 467–70, 478–9.

[21] Divergent views in Wamers 1997, 89–101; Staecker 2003, 467–70.

somewhat according to means of subsistence. It may be no coincidence that the little we do know about organized paganism dates from the eve of its collapse. But it would appear that by the earlier tenth century the Rus' had incorporated leading Slavic gods such as Perun (god of lightning and power) and Volos (god of cattle) into their own rites and rituals. This was the time when the locus of political power was shifting southwards to the Middle Dnieper region.

2. CONTACTS

Little is said in the *Primary Chronicle* about other, non-Christian religions in Rus' before *c.* 988, but a letter found in the Cairo Geniza attests the presence of Judaist traders in Kiev in the tenth century. It is written in Hebrew but some of its eleven signatories have non-Semitic – apparently Turkic – names and they refer to themselves as the 'community of Kiev'.[22] There were most probably also Muslims living in Kiev by the tenth century, drawn to the town by long-distance trade. A stone mould bearing an Arabic inscription variously interpreted as the personal name 'Yazid' or the ethnic name 'Turk'/'Tork' has been excavated in the Podol and presumably belonged to a Muslim craftsman working there.[23] Indeed, Rus' might well have developed into a 'multicultural' society in the tenth century, along the lines of Khazaria.

Pre-Christian Rus' was an essentially itinerant society, as is suggested by archaeological evidence from the tenth-century graves found on the north–south axis, the 'Way from the Varangians to the Greeks'. The ruling elite travelled more or less continuously, collecting tribute and trading, which gave them an urgent desire for talismans offering personal survival and protection that more static, rooted pagan rites and spirits might not have satisfied. Dealings with the wealthy southern Christian and Muslim traders may also have influenced the Rus', engendering a desire to emulate some of their ritual in order to tap into their successful divine power and, through it, material well-being.

The Rus' traders whom Ibn Fadlan encountered on the Middle Volga seem to have been anxious about profits rather than personal survival, at the time when he observed them in 922. The gods were held responsible for particular transactions, and each trader would make offerings to an idol, listing his goods for sale and praying to meet a rich trader 'who does not haggle with me'. If business did not match up to expectations, the trader

---

[22] Golb and Pritsak 1982, 13.   [23] Tolochko 1981, 307–8.

would return to his idol repeatedly and make further offerings, a kind of commission paid in return for the god's intervention in the market.[24] But the hazards of voyaging also fostered exchanges with gods. Constantine VII's *De administrando imperio* treats as routine the sacrifices offered by Rus' traders bound for Constantinople after negotiating the dreaded Dnieper Rapids successfully: 'they sacrifice live cocks', having thrown lots as to whether 'to slaughter them, or to eat them as well, or to leave them alive'.[25] Ibn Fadlan himself was not a trader, but many other Muslims did business on the Middle Volga. From the beginning of the tenth century, the Volga Bulgars were themselves Muslims, replete with mosques and muezzin, and the Rus' traders in the Middle Volga were thus in regular contact with the organized worship of Islam. Equally, Rus' traders going to Byzantium would have had frequent contact with Christians.

Already at the time of negotiation of the first full treaty between the Byzantines and the Rus', the Rus' envoys were reportedly taken on a tour of the churches and shown relics such as the instruments of Christ's passion.[26] While the historicity of this episode in 911 is open to question, it gives a general idea of the Byzantines' method of hosting Rus' visitors in the tenth century. Not that the Rus' gained experience of Christianity only from the Greek-speaking south. From the ninth century there were Christian households at Birka in central Sweden, which was in close commercial contact with the Rus'. And one of the very first mentions of the Rus' as traders in the eastern lands has them pretending to be Christians so as to lessen their tax obligations. Rus' traders in the Abbasid caliphate could, in claiming to be Christians, get away with paying only the poll tax, rather than the full customs dues.[27]

The clearest hints of the connection between trading and the adoption of one's trading partner's religion come from the story of Rus' dealings with Byzantium. Princess Olga, who sailed to Byzantium for baptism, was accompanied by more than forty traders at each of the receptions held for her in the Great Palace.[28] Some years earlier, the Russo-Byzantine treaty of 944, many of whose clauses concern items of commerce such as slaves, mentions the Rus' negotiators who had sworn to uphold its terms 'by the Holy Cross set before us'. It further stipulates: 'if any of the princes or any Rus', whether Christian or non-Christian, violates the terms . . . , he

---

[24] Ibn Fadlan, *Risala*, 69; tr. Montgomery, 10. [25] Constantine VII, *De administrando*, 60–1.
[26] *PVL*, 20; *RPC*, 68–9.
[27] Ibn Khurradadhbih, *Kitab al-Masalik*; translation of 'reconstructed' text by Pritsak 1970, 256; see also Franklin and Shepard 1996, 42–3.
[28] Constantine VII, *De cerimoniis*, I, 597, 598.

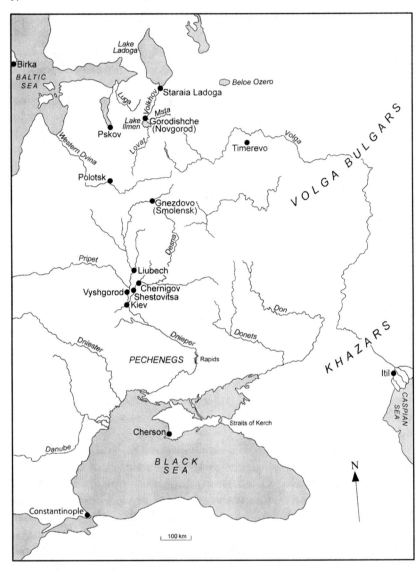

22. Rus' settlements in the tenth century and the 'Way from the Varangians to the Greeks'

shall deserve death by his own weapons and be accursed of God and of Perun'.[29] Clearly there were enough Christian Rus' for the treaty to make special provision for their Christian oaths. A significant number of them were, at the very least, passing themselves off as Christians and they had probably been baptized. The 'church of St Elijah' in Constantinople, where the Rus' negotiators swore their oaths in 944, was located in the imperial Great Palace.[30] The *Book of Ceremonies* singles out the Christian Rus' for display: 'the baptized *Rhōs*' were allocated a specific station at the palace reception for Muslim envoys in May 946, being positioned among the guards of honour.[31] Viewed together, these scraps of evidence suggest that encouragement was given by the imperial authorities to Rus' who became Christian, and also that it was not uncommon for visiting Rus' to be baptized in Constantinople itself, quite possibly in a palace church; they would then have been rewarded with gifts.

There is evidence that individual high-status Rus' – several of them female – were buried with Christian symbols such as crosses in the mid-tenth-century Middle Dnieper region. Finds of valuable pendant crosses of sheet silver have been made in graves there and at Gnezdovo.[32] A number of pit graves, some originally containing coffins, have been excavated at Kiev, Gnezdovo and at Timerevo in the Upper Volga region, and their association with Christianization seems plausible, particularly at Kiev, where some of the coffins have an east–west orientation. Grave goods such as axes, knives and necklaces made up of glass beads and pierced coins have been found in these pit graves. Further, a number of chamber graves, sometimes very rich ones, contained crosses or cross-shaped pendants.[33] Occasionally candles are found in or on the chamber graves and these have been taken to be elements of Christian ritual. However, it is still unclear whether the occupants of these chamber graves were baptized and whether they were practising exclusively Christian rites.[34] What is likely is that the general idea of a well-stocked chamber for the next world was stimulated by Christian worship, perhaps an attempt to outdo it. Chamber graves first appeared in the Scandinavian world at peripheral points of Christendom, for example Hedeby, spreading

---

[29] *PVL*, 26; *RPC*, 77. The treaty, originally drafted in Greek, survives in a Slavic translation in the *Primary Chronicle*. The authenticity of the text as a whole is not in serious doubt: Franklin and Shepard 1996, 135–8.

[30] Malingoudis 1994, 46–7 and n. 100. Magdalino 1987, 61; 1988, 193–6; Janin 1969, 136–7, 232–6.

[31] Constantine VII, *De cerimoniis*, I, 579. See Mango 1959, 21–2, 97–8.

[32] Petrukhin 1995, 216–33; Shepard forthcoming; Petrukhin and Pushkina 1998, 249–50.

[33] Mikhailov 2001.   [34] Petrukhin and Pushkina 1998, 249–52; Musin 2002, 124, 126–7, 146–52.

to Staraia Ladoga by the end of the ninth century.[35] Chamber-grave finds at Kiev and Shestovitsa indicate that while Rus' may have evoked aspects of Christian burial practices, many still expected a material, even sensual, afterlife. Men were equipped for the next world with arms and riding gear – often with horses and slave girls, too – while their continual personal dealings in trade are signalled by the weights and balances accompanying them. Most were probably the retainers of the princes and other leading notables.

Crosses and cross-shaped pendants were the most unambiguous symbols of Christian affiliation, especially when forming part of the necklaces of tenth-century Rus'. Where such pendants were manufactured is controversial: the 'Scandinavian type' of pendant cross is so called because examples have been found in Scandinavia, Finland and in regions just east of the Baltic, but more than seventy examples have been discovered in the land of Rus', and it has been argued that the model for this sort of cross was Byzantine.[36] Rare finds of Christ represented on humdrum items such as a Byzantine cone-seal are suggestive: seemingly they were treated by the Rus' as cult objects.[37]

The ritual significance of crosses as amulets devoted to Christian religion is not diminished by the fact that they are accompanied by amulets with plainly non-Christian connotations in some graves, notably those of children: the young were probably being given every possible chance in the afterlife by grieving kin. Indeed, assortments of amulets placed in graves do not necessarily denote rejection of Christianity, and similar combinations of Christian and non-Christian symbols occur in burials long after the formal conversion of Rus'. They represent a kind of 'pick-and-mix' form of Christian devotion, rather than what has been termed 'dual belief' (*dvoever'e*).[38] Syncretism and eclecticism may also be found in the choice of amulets worn by the more-or-less Christian inhabitants of the eastern Mediterranean region in Late Antiquity and the early Byzantine period.[39] At any rate, the literary sources offer clear evidence that the Rus' warriors and traders on the Middle Dnieper were in regular and intensive trading contact with Byzantium by the mid-tenth century, making it difficult to dismiss outright the cultic significance of the above-mentioned finds. They

---

[35] Mikhailov 2001.
[36] Petrukhin and Pushkina 1998, 249–50, 255; line drawings of crosses, 248, fig. 1, and map of finds of Christian symbols in early Rus', 254, fig. 2.
[37] Shepard 1986, 252–74.
[38] Ryan 1999, 14, 219; Senyk 1993, 191–201; Rusanova and Timoshchuk 1998, 156–61.
[39] Gager 1992, 219–22, 224–5, 232–4; Russell 1995.

also suggest that some of the first Rus' to embrace the new religion were women, the impression given by the archaeological evidence.

The most important of all the individual conversions is that of Princess Olga, whom both Byzantine and Rus' sources represent as journeying to Constantinople and being baptized there in the mid-tenth century. The precise date of her journey is immensely controversial, ranging from 946 to *c.* 960.[40] Less controversial are the simple facts that she did journey to Constantinople – with a priest named Gregory, and a large number of princely emissaries and traders[41] – and that she was baptized there under the auspices of Emperor Constantine VII, his wife Helena and the patriarch. Olga became Constantine's goddaughter and took the Christian name of Helena. That Olga did not take a bishop or other missionaries back with her to Kiev suggests this was a 'private' conversion; however, this was presumably because Olga was unable to persuade the Byzantines to send a mission, rather than because she did not ask.[42]

There are indications of resentment at, if not resistance to, attempts by Olga to foster Christianity among the notables of Rus'. The *Primary Chronicle* recounts Sviatoslav's response to Olga, upon being urged to adopt her faith; he apparently refused, saying 'my retainers will laugh at this!'[43] The German religious mission to Rus', sent in response to Olga's request for 'a bishop and priests for [. . . her] people', was led and subsequently recounted by Adalbert of Trier. The failure of this enterprise suggests that the full-scale conversion presumably hoped for by Adalbert and his lord, Otto I of Germany, was not practicable.[44] Adalbert and his companions left Rus' about a year after their arrival, around 961, complaining that Olga's invitation had been fraudulent and that he was 'wearing himself out to no purpose'. Adalbert himself barely escaped to Germany alive, and members of his party were killed on the journey back.

Adalbert's was not the first mission to be sent to the Rus', or to fail. A Byzantine religious mission, headed by a 'bishop and pastor', had been dispatched to the Rus' soon after their first attack on Byzantium in 860, apparently at their request. Attributed in one Byzantine version to the reign – and credit – of Basil I (867–86), the mission is there represented as being successful.[45] But it does not seem to have made lasting converts or even to have left discernible literary or archaeological traces among the Rus'.

---

[40] Featherstone 2003, 241–51.   [41] Constantine VII, *De cerimoniis*, I, 596–8.

[42] Franklin and Shepard 1996, 134–6; Shepard forthcoming.

[43] *PVL*, 46; *RPC*, 84; Franklin and Shepard 1996, 142–3; Shepard forthcoming.

[44] Adalbert, *Continuatio Reginonis*, 214–15.   [45] Theophanes Continuatus, *Chronographia*, 343–4.

The precise destination is uncertain,[46] as is the mission's actual date: the acceptance of a prelate by the Rus' features in a circular letter of Patriarch Photius of 867, and this points to a mission occurring in the reign of Michael III, and thus *before* the accession of Basil I.[47] This Byzantine mission seems to have petered out, but the attack on Adalbert's party perhaps bears out the *Primary Chronicle*'s tale of Sviatoslav's and his retainers' hostility to conversion: the attackers may have been motivated by hostility specifically to Christian missionaries, rather than just by material greed or general antipathy towards strangers.[48]

As well as these formal, state-sponsored endeavours, it is worth taking into account the likelihood of ad hoc or unintentional evangelizing on the part of monks and churchmen from the Black Sea towns, especially the most sizable emporium, Cherson. It may well be that individual Orthodox monks spread the word – or simply wandered – among settlements to the north of the Black Sea steppes. Moreover, clergymen in the Crimean town of Cherson were active in assisting with Byzantine mission work, and the archbishop was from time to time given the task of arranging ecclesiastical affairs in Khazaria.[49] Cherson is known to have been a frequent port of call of Rus' traders in the ninth and tenth centuries. It may be no coincidence that parallels to the earliest type of sheet-metal crosses found in Rus' have been observed in the ornamentation of churches at Cherson, although Anglo-Saxon parallels have also been noted.[50] Orthodox monks were active at Cherson and in monasteries along the south-east Crimea and on the Straits of Kerch, coasts which Rus' traders were passing in the tenth century.[51] Yet none of these outflows of Christian example or deliberate evangelization could make up for a certain hesitance to sponsor 'state conversions' on the part of the Byzantine imperial establishment.

3. CHRISTIANIZATION

Christian and pagan cults might have continued to coexist – and to inter-act – in Rus' indefinitely, had Sviatoslav's son, Vladimir, not taken the lead and introduced Christianity as the official religion. One key factor was Vladimir's position of political and military supremacy over Rus', without

[46] Theophanes Continuatus, *Chronographia*, 196, 342–4; Franklin and Shepard 1996, 54–5.
[47] Photius, *Epistulae*, I, 50.   [48] Adalbert, *Continuatio Reginonis*, 218–19.
[49] Nicholas I, *Letters*, 314–15, 388–91.
[50] Musin 1998, 279; Musin 2002, 138, 140–1; Staecker 1999, 91–6. Obolensky 1993, 108–10; Shepard 2002, 241–3.
[51] Shepard 2006.

serious rivals from within his own family, from other powerful magnates or from outsiders. This gave him a freer hand than his predecessors in determining which form public worship should take and the extent to which his subjects should participate. At the same time Vladimir suffered from 'legitimacy-deficit'. He had usurped the throne of Kiev around 978 from his half-brother, Iaropolk, having fought his way back from exile in Scandinavia, overpowering such magnates as Rogvolod of Polotsk, whom he put to death. Vladimir had raised a war band of 'Varangians' – Scandinavian warriors – while in exile, and greatly augmented his forces with large numbers of Novgorodians once he had regained his former throne-town. But he still faced potentially formidable opposition in Kiev, far to the south. The *Primary Chronicle* does not fight shy of describing Vladimir's treacherous treatment of his half-brother there: having persuaded him to negotiate, he had Iaropolk assassinated as he entered the hall outside town for their meeting.[52]

As both violent usurper and 'a slave's son', Vladimir had good reason to seek ways of dignifying and legitimizing his regime, and this most probably accounts for his attempts to revitalize pagan worship soon after seizing power. The *Primary Chronicle* describes how six wooden idols were set up outside the princely hall in Kiev, and there was a comparable display in Novgorod. Besides appealing to the heterogeneous population of the Middle Dnieper, the 'pantheon' of wooden idols – headed by Perun, the Slavic god of lightning and power – is the first recorded example of a Rus' prince's attempt to institute regular public worship. The medley of gods appears to have been closely bound up with expectations of military victory for the ruler: the gods were expected to deliver success in war in return for human sacrifices, and Vladimir's subjects were to join in the devotions.[53] The only opposition from Christian, Muslim or Jewish communities in Kiev reported by the *Primary Chronicle* came from a wealthy Christian of Scandinavian origin, Tury, whose son was selected for sacrifice to the pagan gods: both father and son were slain for protesting.[54] This incident highlights the potential embarrassment to Vladimir of promoting a cult offensive to the monotheistic powers with which Rus' traded, although it also demonstrates his control over communal worship.

It was only when Vladimir's run of victories came to an end with his failure to subjugate the Volga Bulgars in the mid-980s, and the 'pantheon'

[52] *PVL*, 55; *RPC*, 92–3.
[53] *PVL*, 56; *RPC*, 93; Franklin and Shepard 1996, 155. According to Ibn Rusta, human sacrifices occurred in ninth-century Rus', but generally on the orders of shamans: *Kitāb al-A'lāk*, 40–3; tr. Wiet, 164.
[54] *PVL*, 38–9; *RPC*, 95–6.

of gods was seen publicly to be failing to deliver, that Vladimir began his quest for a better guarantor of victory, sometimes termed his 'Investigation of the Faiths'. There is reason to think that Vladimir carried out some sort of enquiry into the monotheist religions – the Byzantine and western variants of Christianity, Islam and Judaism – even though the account given by the *Primary Chronicle* is thin on substance and stylized. The dynamics of the situation seem to have been similar to those of the early 860s when, upon failing to gain much valuable loot from their raid on Constantinople, the Rus' showed their respect for the powerful God of the Christians and sent to Byzantium for a religious mission. Likewise, Vladimir's setback at the hands of the Muslim Volga Bulgars may have prompted him to make further enquiries about their seemingly more potent God. He appears to have cast far beyond the Volga Bulgars for instruction in Islam. According to an eleventh-century Persian source, a certain *V-ladmir*, 'king' of the Rus', wanted to become Muslim together with his people, and four of his kinsmen announced his desire to the ruler of Khorezm in central Asia. Reportedly, the latter sent back 'someone to teach them the religious laws of Islam'.[55] This wholly independent evidence of Vladimir's investigation of Islam gives credibility to the *Primary Chronicle*'s account that a public enquiry took place.

In the event, Vladimir effectively struck a deal with Basil II and adopted Byzantine Christianity. In return for sending some 6,000 warriors to counter a massive military revolt threatening Basil's throne, Vladimir was baptized in preparation for taking the emperor's sister Anna as his bride, and a full-scale religious mission, headed by metropolitans, was sent to Rus'. Both marriage alliance and mission were in contrast to previous Byzantine policy, and give an indication of the altered balance of power between Kiev and Constantinople at this point. Vladimir's specific requests were probably not so very different from those of his grandmother, Olga, but now, at a moment of grave internal political crisis for the Byzantine emperor, it was the Rus' who had leverage.

Vladimir also captured the city of Cherson, on the Crimea, around this time, although the interconnections between these events and their chronological sequence cannot be determined with certainty. A strong case for supposing that Vladimir attacked Cherson in his capacity as an ally of Basil was presented by A. Poppe.[56] Poppe also argues for Kiev as the location of Vladimir's baptism. There is, however, still merit in the traditional hypothesis that Vladimir's capture and partial sack of Cherson were in

---

[55] Minorsky, *Marvazi*, 36; Shepard 1992, 76–7.   [56] Poppe 1976, 197–244.

retaliation for Basil's delay in implementing his part in the deal whereby Rus' troops were to be sent in exchange for the marriage of Anna to Vladimir. Such a hypothesis is consistent with the very full description of events in Cherson, including topographical details about the baptism and wedding of Vladimir given by the *Primary Chronicle*. And one cannot rule out the possibility that Vladimir launched a 'first strike', seizing Cherson and using it as a bargaining counter to negotiate an agreement with Basil.[57]

Technical aid soon followed Anna and the metropolitans to Kiev: 'Greek' (i.e. Byzantine) craftsmen are said to have been summoned by Vladimir and they built splendid brick-and-stone churches – notably the palace church, known as the 'Tithe-Church' and constructed in the 990s on Starokievskaia Hill – and monumental princely halls, decorated with mosaics and wall paintings.[58] Christianity brought to Rus' a better organized cult, more sharply focused on the ruler's authority than previous ones had been.

The imagery of later churchmen, painting Vladimir as an 'apostle among rulers' who had saved Rus' from the devil's wiles,[59] was fostered by the spectacular way in which he had replaced the old cult with the new in the land of Rus'. Backed up by unchallengeable military power, Vladimir ordered the mass baptism of Kiev's citizens in the Dnieper: 'idols were smashed and icons of saints . . . installed', and 'wood was cut and churches put up on the sites where idols had stood'.[60] The idol of Perun was reportedly dragged down to the Dnieper and flung in the river. We must treat these set-pieces of transformation with caution. Many members of the Rus' elite had to some degree already been Christianized long before the 980s, whereas the extent to which the non-elite became Christian, even after baptism, is uncertain. What emerges from the *Primary Chronicle* and, still more emphatically, from Ilarion's account in the mid-eleventh century, is that the focal points of pagan worship – idols, sanctuaries and communal rituals – were swept away. There is no literary record of resistance to Vladimir or his agents and neither is opposition likely, in view of Vladimir's ruthlessness and record of success in reimposing tribute on recalcitrant Slav tribes earlier in his reign. Ilarion praises Vladimir's readiness to use his 'strength and . . . might': no one resisted Vladimir's 'command' to be baptized, 'for if some were baptized not for love, then in fear of Vladimir's command, since his piety was coupled with power'.[61]

---

[57] Shepard 1992, 59–95. See also Obolensky 1989, 244–56; Obolensky 1993, 110–14; Senyk 1993, 49–71.
[58] Franklin and Shepard 1996, 164–5.
[59] Ilarion, *Sermon*, 52–3; Franklin 1991, 25; *PVL*, 58; *RPC*, 125.
[60] *PVL*, 53; *RPC*, 117; Ilarion, *Sermon*, 44–5; Franklin 1991, 19.
[61] Ilarion, *Sermon*, 44–5; Franklin 1991, 19.

The subject of Ilarion's *Sermon on Law and Grace*, our earliest complete extant Slavic Rus' text, is the coming of divine Grace to the Rus', albeit belatedly. Ilarion attempts to fit the conversion of the Rus' into the general framework of biblical and world history: a people that had long stayed idolatrous and deaf to the Word finally entered the Christian fold.[62] From early on, the Rus' elite treated the conversion as an event of world-historical significance, and a major step in the formation of Rus' as a polity. The *Primary Chronicle* also attempts some appreciation of the wider significance of the supposed transformation of the Rus' into 'a new Christian people', putting Vladimir at the centre of the process.[63] It has been suggested that these, and other *Chronicle* passages describing the arrival of Christianity in Rus', originally formed part of a text focused on the conversion, and composed during the reign of Prince Iaroslav in the later 1030s or 1040s.[64] Ilarion's overall presentation of Vladimir as a pivotal figure who underwent a personal conversion – a new Constantine[65] – contains at least a grain of substance: 'How shall we marvel at your goodness . . . you, through whom we were delivered from idolatrous delusion . . .?'[66]

Both Ilarion and the *Primary Chronicle* portray the mass baptism in terms of Vladimir's power and his violence against false gods, and by the early twelfth century his achievement in leading his people to salvation was being cited as grounds for sanctification. The *Primary Chronicle* describes him as 'the new Constantine of mighty Rome, who baptized himself and also his subjects'.[67] The preoccupation of our extant texts with the roles of Vladimir and, to some extent, of his son Iaroslav playing 'Solomon' to his father's 'David', helps explain the dearth of *Lives* or other texts covering later missionary saints' activities. Admission of the extent of the mission work still to be done in the later eleventh century – after Ilarion had delivered his *Sermon* – would have detracted from the magnitude of Vladimir's achievement. The few accounts of later missionary work tend to focus on the failures; for example, the martyrdom of Kuksha, a monk of the Cave Monastery, by the still pagan Viatichi tribe, or the killing of Bishop Leontius of Rostov in the later eleventh century by pagans.[68]

---

[62] Franklin's introduction to his translation of the *Sermon* (1991, xxvii–xliv); Franklin and Shepard 1996, 209–17; Shepard forthcoming; Franklin 1991, 19–20.

[63] Particularly *PVL*, 50–4, 56, 58; *RPC*, 113–19, 121, 124–6.   [64] Likhachev 1981, 81–96.

[65] Ilarion, *Sermon*, 48–9; Franklin 1991, 22–3.   [66] Ilarion, *Sermon*, 46–7; Franklin 1991, 20.

[67] *PVL*, 58; *RPC*, 124–6. Controversy as to when he was recognized as a saint: Vodoff 2003, 119–33; Uspensky 2002a, 274–8.

[68] *Paterik*, ed. Likhachev *et al.*, 372–3; Heppell, tr. *Paterik*, 128. On Leontius: Lenhoff 1992, 359–80; Podskal'sky 1996, 225–30.

Some regions where princely clout was restricted became rallying-points for pagan practices. For example, several shrines on the river Zbruch (a tributary of the Dniester) seem actually to have been instituted around the time of Vladimir's conversion, and sacrifices were offered there until the thirteenth century.[69] The north-eastern forest regions were also touched fairly lightly by the evangelizing efforts of Vladimir and Iaroslav, and the *Primary Chronicle*'s account of Ian, a prince's tribute collector, shows that severe material hardship, such as famine, could drive the population to *volkhvy* (wizards). In around 1071, 300 people are said to have become followers of two *volkhvy*, who produced food out of the bodies of 'the best women' as they travelled along the Volga Basin. These *volkhvy* seem to have been invoking dualist beliefs rather than simply reviving pre-Christian concepts and rites.[70] The *Primary Chronicle* also mentions the activities of *volkhvy* at a time of famine on the Upper Volga around the year 1024–5.[71]

Princes are not recorded as having been involved in any pagan reaction. Indeed, in Novgorod *c.* 1071, Prince Gleb was decisive in putting a stop to the activities of a *volkhv*, who had won most of the citizens to his side and incited them to kill the bishop. Gleb narrowly saved the bishop's life, supported only by his retinue. He made a mockery of the *volkhv*'s claim to be able to predict the future and slew him with an axe.[72] What is striking is the *lack* of princely engagement with pagan manifestations after Vladimir's conversion: princely authority and the Rurikid dynasty appear to have become virtually interchangeable with sponsorship of the Christian religion and shepherding of the Christian flock.

The importance of the princely family in binding together the 'land of Rus'', and gaining respect through incomparable sponsorship of the true religion, can hardly be overestimated. Rus' operated effectively as a vast family concern, with all the ties and tensions that term implies.[73] One way of expressing princely piety and near sanctity was the foundation of family churches and the practice of burying the founder of a church and his offspring there.[74] Thus, for example, in 1115 Oleg was buried at the church of St Saviour, Chernigov, 'in the tomb of his father' Sviatoslav.[75] Monasteries founded by princes and princesses could likewise become the burial place for them and subsequently for their descendants. For example, Mstislav Vladimirovich was buried in the monastery of St Theodore, Kiev, in 1132, as later were his children and grandchildren. This also reflects the continuing strong sense of kinship between descendants of a common ancestor; at the

---

[69] Rusanova and Timoshchuk 1998, 150–61.   [70] *PVL*, 75–8; *RPC*, 150–4.
[71] *PVL*, 65; *RPC*, 134–5.   [72] *PVL*, 154; *RPC*, 78.   [73] Tolochko 2002, 155–68.
[74] See below, pp. 396–8.   [75] *PVL*, 128.

level of princes, as well as lower down the social scale, the clusters of family burials were important constituents of Rus' political culture.[76] A couple of pagan princes were even baptized posthumously and reburied in Kiev's Tithe-Church, a mark of kin solidarity and special status.[77]

A proliferation of spectacular marriage ties shows that the Rus' princely family also sought kinship with other Christian ruling families, many from western Europe or Scandinavia. Tensions between the eastern and western Church hierarchies in the eleventh and twelfth centuries did not put paid to such marriages, and a certain sense of community persisted among elite Christians, irrespective of confessional differences. In the mid-eleventh century, Iaroslav's daughters were married to King Henry I of France, Harald Hardråde of Norway and András of the Hungarians, and one of Iaroslav's sons, Vsevolod, was married to a Byzantine princess, while other sons wedded western wives.[78]

Although there is no firm evidence of direct exchanges between the Roman papacy and Rus' in the late tenth or earlier eleventh century,[79] it is overwhelmingly probable that individual Latin churchmen frequented Rus', particularly western towns such as Peremyshl (present-day Przemyśl in Poland) where, before Vladimir's formal conversion, communities had had links with the Christian west.[80] And clearly by the beginning of the eleventh century, the Rus' were regarded as forming part of Christendom. The *Primary Chronicle*'s picture of rivalry between the Byzantine and Latin churches around 988 could be a later overlay, and is anyway not sharply drawn.[81] Moreover, competition did not preclude coexistence between missionaries once they were in Rus'. Bruno of Querfurt's letter of 1008 to Emperor Henry II recounts his missionary experiences in Rus' and his meeting with Vladimir, showing no sense of hostility or hint that the Rus' were now other than a fully Christian people.[82] Tracts denouncing

---

[76] Artamonov 2001, 11–20; Dimnik 2003b, 170–2, 182–5, 202–4, 209.

[77] *PVL*, 67; *RPC*, 139; Petrukhin 2002, 126. According to Uspensky 2002b, 141–55, this may reflect a *prima signatio* bestowed on the princes in their lifetime; cf. Nazarenko 2001, 368–80; and Korpela 2001, 77–8 and n. 356. There is no positive evidence that these two late tenth-century princes were other than pagan. By the 1040s this could have appeared anomalous, and Iaroslav, who instigated the translation of Iaropolk and Oleg, may simply have been seeking to venerate kinsmen and pay respects to victims of dynastic strife: Petrukhin 2002, 126.

[78] Nazarenko 2001, e.g. 339–90, 505–58, attempted to place much greater emphasis on the ties between Rus' and the Latin west, to some extent downgrading the ties with Byzantium; cf. Korpela 2001, 102–12.

[79] *Contra* Korpela 2001, 89. Statements in much later Russian chronicles, such as the *Chronicle of Nikon*, concerning contacts between Rus' and Rome in this early period should be treated very cautiously (*Nikonovskaia Letopis'*, IX, 64–5, 68; *Nikonian Chronicle*, I, 111, 118).

[80] Franklin and Shepard 1996, 174–5.   [81] *PVL*, 40; *RPC*, 98.

[82] Bruno of Querfurt, *Epistola*, 98–100.

the practices of the 'Latins' were translated from Greek into Slavonic as relations between the Byzantine hierarchy and Rome deteriorated, and by the twelfth century at latest, Rus'-born churchmen were issuing their own denunciations of Latin errors. However, western priests continued to frequent important emporia and to mix freely with their inhabitants: one of the questions upon which the Novgorodian monk Kirik provided a ruling in the mid-twelfth century was the penance appropriate for a woman who had borne a child to 'a Varangian priest'![83]

One indication of the kind of cult propounded by the Church to the laity is the range of saints venerated in Rus'. The dedication of Rus' churches and chapels corresponds closely with the pattern in contemporary Byzantium. Mirroring Constantinople, the cathedral churches of Kiev, Novgorod and Polotsk were dedicated to St Sophia, 'the Holy Wisdom', while the Tithe-Church was dedicated to the Mother of God, as was the main palace church in Constantinople, the Pharos. The Mother of God remained in demand as a dedicatee of churches through the eleventh and twelfth centuries, as can be seen from the church of the Virgin's Assumption at the Kievan Cave Monastery (built in the 1070s) and the churches dedicated to the Assumption and the *Pokrov* (Virgin's Protective Veil) by Prince Andrei Bogoliubskii in the north-east in the 1150s and 1160s. The dedication of these elite churches is an indication of the high standing of the cult of the Mother of God in Rus', as well as of Andrei's high ambition. Vladimir promoted the cult of St Basil, from whom he took his Christian name, dedicating a church to him where, only a few years before, 'the prince and the people had performed their sacrifices'.[84] Other much venerated saints in early Rus' included George, Demetrius, Andrew and Theodore, due in part to promotion by Byzantine churchmen, such as the Byzantine-born Metropolitan Ephraim of Pereiaslavl' who founded churches of St Andrew and St Theodore, while military saints' support was particularly welcome in the hazardous steppe frontier zone.[85] Rus' texts also extol indigenous saints such as Boris and Gleb and also Theodosius and other monks of the Kievan Cave Monastery.

Underpinning the cult of saints – literally so, in the case of church altars – were their relics and there is no reason to doubt that the Rus' maintained the Byzantine custom of depositing the relics of saints under or inside the altar of a church. For example, the relics of Sts Panteleimon, Acacius and Maccabees were deposited in a container with an inscription stating the

---

[83] Vodoff 2003, 45.   [84] *PVL*, 53; *RPC*, 117.
[85] For example, *PVL*, 88–9; *RPC*, 170. On the cult of military saints: White 2004.

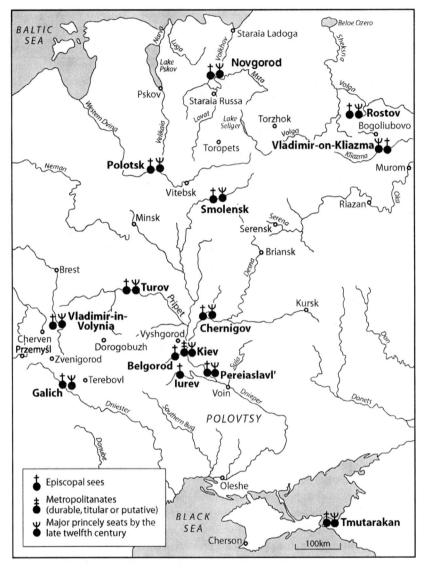

23. Episcopal sees, princely seats and other important towns in Rus' and the northern Black Sea region in the eleventh and twelfth centuries

saints' names by the altar of the church of St Saviour at Chernigov in the 1030s.[86] The relics of St Clement of Rome deposited in the Tithe-Church in Kiev were given such prominence that the church appeared, to the informant of the early eleventh-century chronicler Thietmar of Merseburg, to be dedicated to Clement, rather than the Mother of God.[87] Literary sources are not explicit concerning the import of relics from the Byzantine Christian world, but there is every reason to suppose that relics imported from Constantinople and the Holy Land were venerated among the Rus'. Many cross-*encolpia* of Byzantine type, and presumably once containing particles of the True Cross, have been found in Rus' centres, and by the late twelfth century a church dedicated to the holy mandylion of Edessa (the miraculous imprint of Christ's features on a cloth) stood in Novgorod; the church probably housed an icon representing the features on the cloth.[88]

There is little detailed evidence on how the Church envisaged that Christian Rus' society should function, since no formal ecclesiastical code of conduct or legislation seems to have been issued. The *Primary Chronicle* denounces *volkhvy* (wizards) with suggestive frequency, as also do several texts attributed to Rus' senior churchmen of the later eleventh and twelfth centuries, condemning unchristian practices linked to alternative powers.[89] In his responses to a series of questions posed by clergymen, the Byzantine-born Metropolitan John II censures unacceptable eating practices and dress, although he allows that even priests could wear furs 'because of the terrible cold and frost'. The laity's blithe indifference to Christian marriage ceremonies was one of the issues raised: 'You say that only boiars and princes get married with proper ceremony and blessing, while the common people do not, . . . tak[ing] wives as if by abduction, with much leaping and dancing and hooting.'[90]

Collections of 'Church Statutes', the oldest allegedly issued by Vladimir and by Iaroslav, date in their present form from the twelfth century or later still, and the composition dates of the supposed originals are uncertain. They lay down rules for the Church's income and list types of misbehaviour which came under its jurisdiction. It is clear that during the twelfth century, church jurisdiction expanded in matters such as divorce, sexual relations, adultery, incest, heresy and inheritance disputes. The Church's overall frame

---

[86] Kholostenko 1974, 199–202.

[87] Thietmar of Merseburg, *Chronicon*, 436–7. Ukhanova 2000, 67–8; 2003.

[88] Wolf 2003, 286–7.   [89] Metropolitan John II, *Canonical Responses*, cols. 7–18.

[90] Metropolitan John II, *Canonical Responses*, col. 18, tr. in Franklin and Shepard 1996, 230; Franklin and Shepard 1996, 229–30; on marriage customs as against the ceremony in church: Senyk 1993, 208–10.

of reference was provided by Byzantine canon law, itself a medley of texts and ad hoc arrangements, having as its centrepiece a sizable collection called the *Nomocanon of Fourteen Titles*.[91]

No definitive answer can be given to the question of how far Christian teaching and worship sank into Rus' society below the level of the princely family, its retainers and agents, given the scantiness and partisan nature of the evidence and the almost measureless expanses of the Rus' lands. One might expect that Christian observance and belief would be most entrenched in areas directly supervised by princes and their agents and receiving intensive pastoral care from bishops and priests: basically, a 250-kilometre or so radius around Kiev, the towns along the great north–south riverways and the fairly thickly populated lines of trade routes leading westwards to Przemyśl and Kraków. Metropolitan Ilarion in his sermon confirms this supposition, tacitly qualifying the geographical extent of regular worship in churches: his more fulsome descriptions are mostly set in 'cities', notably Kiev, where Iaroslav 'entrusted your [Vladimir's] people and city to the holy, all-glorious Mother of God'.[92] In contrast, Ilarion represents Vladimir as learning 'how devout are their [Byzantine] cities and villages'; this amplification, that life was prayerful in the Byzantine countryside as well as in the towns, does not feature in his descriptions of Rus' after the conversion.[93] Ilarion thus tacitly concedes that Rus' had yet to catch up with 'the pious land of the Greeks'.

The heterogeneous nature of the urban network's population was captured by Thietmar of Merseburg in 1018, when he described it as consisting of 'runaway slaves rushing hither and thither', and of Scandinavians. He further states that Kiev had more than 400 churches, corroborating Yahya of Antioch's emphasis on church-building in his account of the conversion.[94] The small number of eleventh-century stone churches known to us does not contradict this, as the vast majority of churches would have been wooden. Vladimir himself seems to have commissioned a wooden church at Vasil'ev, in thanksgiving for a close escape from marauding Pechenegs.[95] Although highly idealized, the *Life of Theodosius* depicts townspeople as dressing up in fine clothes to attend feast-day banquets and going to church regularly in Vasil'ev, to the south of Kiev, and in Kursk.[96] This scenario is

---

[91] Known in its Slavonic translation as the *Kormchaia kniga* ('Helmsman's Book'). Survey: Franklin and Shepard 1996, 230–6; Franklin 2002, 136–8, 148–52.

[92] 'Cities were graced by the cross' and 'the thunder of the Gospels resounded throughout all the cities': Ilarion, *Sermon*, 44–5, 50–1; Franklin 1991, 19, 24.

[93] Ilarion, *Sermon*, 44–5; Franklin 1991, 18.

[94] Thietmar of Merseburg, *Chronicon*, 474–5; Yahya of Antioch, *Histoire*, 423.

[95] *PVL*, 55–6; *RPC*, 121.   [96] *Life of Theodosius*, 356–63; Heppell, tr. *Paterik*, 27–31.

matched by archaeological evidence from Belgorod and Voyn, where some of the wealthier inhabitants wore small pectoral crosses made of bronze, marble or mother-of-pearl, and occasionally of silver.[97] How far down in society this apparently Christianized way of life reached is harder to judge. The lack of patently unchristian burial grounds near Kiev suggests observance of Christian norms: the dead were nailed down in wooden coffins, accompanied by non-Christian symbols (such as amulets and miniature axes) or Christian ones (such as pectoral or necklace crosses and stamped metal icons). These cult objects are quite often found together in the same grave, suggesting that princes and churchmen could only loosely police private beliefs and rituals and that ordinary people saw no contradiction between symbols of the cross and of, for example, the sun. Indeed, forms of religious devotion distinctive to Rus' seem to have been developing by the 1030s and 1040s, including the 'wandering folk', devotees who moved constantly in quest of the holy places. Such movements betoken at least outline acquaintance with Gospel stories on the part of lay persons, and the number of native-born priests in the Middle Dnieper region and towns along the riverways within a generation of Vladimir's conversion was probably considerable. The boy Theodosius is depicted as being baptized by a priest in Vasil'ev and subsequently helping the priest of his local church in Kursk in the 1030s or 1040s; these priests were most probably Rus'-born.[98]

There appears to have been some correlation between the distance from main riverways and how strictly Rus' funerary rites followed Byzantine Christian norms. Pagan burial grounds were abandoned in the larger towns, notably in Kiev, where the Tithe-Church was built over part of a pagan burial ground. At Novgorod, Perun's sanctuary was destroyed at the time of the conversion, while boat-burnings and other cremation rituals ceased at Gnezdovo's main burial ground from the end of the tenth century; pagan burial grounds were likewise abandoned at Pskov and, on the Upper Volga, at the town of Uglich.[99] A shift away from cremation occurred in outlying areas, as well as in towns and along major riverways.[100] However, raising barrows over inhumation graves persisted into the mid-eleventh century even at Gnezdovo, and until the thirteenth century in settlements further removed from princely and church supervision. The Church disapproved of such practices, seeing that burial rituals were a signal of one's religious

[97] An example of the latter: Putsko 1974, 209–14.
[98] *Life of Theodosius*, 354–5, 358–61; Heppell, tr. *Paterik*, 26, 29–30.
[99] Franklin and Shepard 1996, 173–4.
[100] Rusanova 1966, 6–27; for elsewhere in and around the Middle Dnieper region, Motsia 1990, 21–66.

affiliation. The *Primary Chronicle* claims that Princess Olga specifically proscribed the holding of a funeral feast in her honour, and that she was buried in a grave in Christian fashion, with no mention of a barrow.[101] In contrast to Olga's grave, barrows were raised over pagan princes such as Oleg and Olga's own husband, Igor.[102] The *Primary Chronicle* remarks of the pre-Christian era that 'whenever a death occurred, a feast was held over the corpse and a great pyre was constructed on which the deceased was laid and burned. After the bones were collected, they were put in a small urn and set up on a post by the roadside: this is what the Viatichi do even to this day.'[103] Excavations indicate that the Viatichi continued with pagan ritual, such as cremation, until the early twelfth century.[104]

However, rural settlements in the north may have been more closely acquainted with Christianity than was previously supposed. Recent excavations of villages near Lake Kubenskoe in the far north-east have revealed finds of crosses and other Christian symbols which are markedly greater than the scale of such finds in burial grounds.[105] Churchmen in pre-Mongol Rus' seem to have regarded the placing of crosses in graves with equanimity but showed concern that valuables such as metal icons might be dug up by robbers, disturbing the dead.[106] By the late twelfth century most villagers appear to have worn a cross-pendant in daily life, suggesting widespread veneration of the Christian cross as a personal talisman – and the adaptation of Christian rites to personal needs – even while some pre-Christian burial customs persisted. Fur traders and other entrepreneurs from the urban network were probably instrumental in bringing the rudiments of Christian observance to villages, together with the small crosses, cheap icons and other Christian symbols. There are no known resident priests for outlying clusters of rural settlements. The priests travelling with tribute-collecting agents may well have been the only form of pastoral care provided for the eleventh- and twelfth-century rural population, and they may periodically have carried out mass baptisms of infants, celebration of the liturgy and commemoration of the dead.

4. ROYAL POWER

Princes in the pre-Christian period, such as Vladimir, could fight their way to sole rule, dispatching other members of their kin and rivals. A

---

[101] *PVL*, 32; *RPC*, 86.   [102] *PVL*, 20, 27, 28; *RPC*, 69, 78, 80.   [103] *PVL*, 11; *RPC*, 57.

[104] Nikol'skaia 1981, 27, 37–41, 97–106. Survey of the advance of Christian ritual and increasing finds of small crosses and icons in the land of the Viatichi: Belen'kaia 1976, 88–96. She argues that the main diffusion point for Christian practices and observance among the Viatichi was Moscow. For the rural settlements of the Novgorodian Land: Musin 2002, 178–207.

[105] Makarov 2004, 263–72; Musin 2002, 178–84.   [106] Musin 2002, 73–9.

term meaning 'sole ruler' is occasionally used in eleventh-century contexts, being applied to Vladimir's son, Iaroslav, who effectively became 'sole ruler' (*samovlastets*) of the land of Rus' upon the death of his brother, Mstislav, in 1036.[107] But the periods when Rus' was under a sole ruler were relatively brief – Vladimir (*c.* 978–1015) and Iaroslav (1036–54) – and the term did not have particularly exalted, sacral or ideologically charged connotations; if anything, it had negative ones. There were no effective legal or ceremonial means for determining succession, leading to frequent scrambles for power among the descendants of Vladimir. Sviatopolk, one of the contenders during the struggle between Vladimir's sons after his death, was held responsible for the deaths of two of Vladimir's other sons, Boris and Gleb, and the hagiography recounting the 'martyrdom' of these 'princely saints' cast Sviatopolk as the villain of the piece: 'Sviatopolk the Accursed'. The political message of the cult of Boris and Gleb from the later eleventh century onwards was that princes should honour and respect the senior prince as a father, giving him a degree of deference, and that he should respect and love his fellow princes as brothers. In effect this was the consecration of a form of collective leadership of the princely clan. Monarchy was not extolled for its own sake, as a gift from God illustrated by the Old Testament Books of Kings.

A more neutral designation of pre-eminence was that of 'great prince' (*velikii kniaz*), used regularly of and (apparently) by such masterful figures as Andrei Bogoliubskii and his brother and successor as ruler in the north-east, Vsevolod 'Big Nest'.[108] This does not seem to have been a formal title denoting extra powers, and the term generally applied to males of princely stock was *kniaz*. Neither family feeling nor the role models of Boris and Gleb could prescribe how power should be shared in practice, and most princes expected to have their own 'throne', as if the land of Rus' were property to be divided up between all the family's members. At the so-called Council of Liubech (1097) – more aptly termed a meeting of the clan – senior princes tried to resolve succession squabbles by agreeing that the sons of the aforementioned triumvirate should bequeath to their children the throne-towns and other 'patrimony' which the triumvirs had themselves inherited from Iaroslav. As a result, Chernigov became established as the seat of Sviatoslav Iaroslavich's offspring, but Kiev remained a special, much sought-after, case and the forceful Vladimir Monomakh, discontented with Pereiaslavl' on the steppe frontier, took over Kiev upon the death of his elder brother Sviatopolk in 1113. Sviatopolk's descendants managed to establish themselves in lesser throne-towns to the west. Kiev was

---

[107] *PVL*, 66; *RPC*, 136.   [108] Dimnik 2004, 289–92, 297–302.

inherited by Monomakh's eldest son, Mstislav, and then by his next surviving son, Iaropolk. But after Iaropolk's death in 1139 Kiev was fair game for those whose father or grandfather had 'sat' there and Chernigov's princes, based nearby, vied with Monomakh's surviving sons, who themselves were at odds with their nephews.[109] The Rus' chronicles' blow-by-blow coverage of the struggles for Kiev makes it easy to disregard the more positive aspects of princely proliferation. Galich, in the south-west, Smolensk and, in the north-east, Rostov became seats of Monomakh's most vigorous descendants. Besides stepping up tribute and other fiscal exactions in the vicinity of their seats and creating a market for luxury goods, these princes patronized churchmen. Important throne-towns needed episcopal status, and it is no accident that the foundation charter laying down the revenues to be allocated to the new see of Smolensk dates from 1136, when Rostislav was establishing his rights to this city. Bishops built churches and trained priests and, with princely involvement, annals were kept under their auspices. By the later twelfth century, records of princely doings and church-building work were being kept at Galich and in the north-east as well as at Kiev and Novgorod. All these sees, even Novgorod, were ultimately under the jurisdiction of the metropolitan 'of *Rhōsia*' (the Byzantine Greek name for Rus') based in Kiev. In the later 1160s Andrei Bogoliubskii, intent on putting his dominions in the north-east on a par with the rest of Rus', tried to have the see of Vladimir-on-Kliazma designated as a separate metropolitanate. Sanction from Constantinople, however, was not forthcoming. The patriarch declared that there should be just one metropolitan for 'all *Rhōsia*'. Rus' remained a single unit within the Orthodox church hierarchy, its sees increasing more or less in proportion to the multiplication of major power points. And the vigour of Andrei's exertions to make his throne-town a centre of piety enjoying divine protection did much to promote regular Christian worship in what had been wayward recesses of Rus'.

Given the lack of institutionalized sole rulership, it is unsurprising that we find no unambivalent symbols or regalia of monarchy in pre-Mongol Rus', even though Rus' leaders were in close contact through their churchmen with Byzantium, which exalted the concept of the supreme ruler as God's representative on earth, and had elaborate ceremonial and iconography in glorification of 'autocracy'. Rus' princes wore Byzantine-style court vestments, including silks, but these were marks of high status, not specific authority symbols. We do not, therefore, find regalia in the sense of divinely charged instruments of sovereignty bestowed on a ruler in an ecclesiastical

---

[109] Dimnik 2003a, 13–26, 52–9, 72–8.

inauguration ritual definitively and irrevocably transforming his status. Equally, there was no regular use of, or depiction of the ruler as having, an orb, sceptre and crown, and there is no evidence in the pre-Mongol period of rites of coronation, anointing of the ruler by churchmen, or of a coronation-*ordo* in the style of western rulers. Although Vladimir's earliest coin designs appropriate the imperial symbols of Byzantine coins, these symbols did not endure. Coin-striking itself, although clearly intended to denote legitimate overlordship, did not take root among the Rus' as a visible statement of authority.

The trident symbol was a mark of princely authority, though not specifically of monarchy. Featured on some types of Vladimir's coins, use of the symbol proved rather more durable than coin-striking, and individual princes had their own variant forms of trident or fork on their seals in the eleventh and twelfth centuries. It would seem that possession of such a symbol was a mark of one's membership of the princely house, that is, the Rurikids. This retention of an essentially Khazar or Turkic symbol is consistent with the durability of the title of *khagan*, which was still in use in the mid-eleventh century: Ilarion in his thoroughly Christian *Sermon* apostrophizes both the deceased Vladimir and the living ruler Iaroslav as *khagan*.[110] This term was also still in unofficial use in the eleventh century, and is found on a graffito in Kiev's St Sophia, which refers to 'our *khagan*'.[111] The other main symbol of authority was the throne itself, which was not, in the eleventh century, located in a church. Thus the *Primary Chronicle* records simply that 'Iaroslav sat in Kiev on the throne of his father and grandfather.'[112] There seems to be a parallel here to practices in Scandinavia, where the heir to a king or a *jarl* was conducted to the high seat and there assumed full authority.[113] Princes, from the senior prince of Kiev downwards, were depicted wearing a particular kind of fur-edged cap and the (few) illuminations in manuscripts depicting Rus' princes show them wearing elaborate vestments similar to those of the Byzantine court. These cannot, however, be termed 'regalia'.

Besides the late eleventh-century Trier Psalter showing Iaropolk Iziaslavich, his wife and mother,[114] there are a few other extant representations of the ruling family. The most striking group portrait is the wall

[110] For example Ilarion, *Sermon*, 52–3; Franklin 1991, 26.
[111] Vysotsky 1966, 49–52.   [112] *PVL*, 63; *RPC*, 132.
[113] Turville-Petre 1964, 259. Seating oneself on the barrow of former princes or ancestors may have been a legitimizing rite among the Rus', as apparently in some Scandinavian societies: Androshchuk 2003.
[114] Kämpfer 1978, 116; Smirnova 2001, 5–21; Smorag Różycka 2003, 20 (fig. 1), 24–30, 57–73.

painting of Iaroslav, his wife Ingigerd and their sons and daughters in the cathedral church of St Sophia, painted in the later 1040s. Only the paintings of two of the sons and four of the daughters have survived, on the north and south walls respectively, but the drawing made by a Dutch artist in the seventeenth century gives us some idea of the appearance of the west wall. Iaroslav and Ingigerd were portrayed, most probably together with Christ.[115] Also worth noting is a manuscript illumination of Prince Sviatoslav Iaroslavich, together with his family, presenting Sviatoslav's *Izbornik of 1073* to Christ.[116] Another portrayal of a prince, enthroned and flanked by his young children, features in a monumental relief carving above a window on the exterior of the church built by Vsevolod ('Big Nest'), dedicated to St Dimitri (Demetrius) in Vladimir-on-Kliazma, around 1196. The interpretation of the figures around the prince has prompted scholarly controversy, but Vsevolod was most probably evoking some Old Testament theme to style himself as founder of a new branch of the ruling family.[117]

Group portraits of a prince and his wife and offspring are not peculiar to Rus'. They are to be found in, for example, fourteenth-century Serbian art, and Byzantine emperors were occasionally shown with their children rather than solely with their designated heir. Nonetheless, the group portraits of Rus' princes are further evidence of the prevalence of the sense of a ruling family, as against monarchy, and portrayals of individual princes by themselves are not central to Old Rus' art. Neither is the representation of a prince being crowned by Christ, the Mother of God or other heavenly powers. What does sometimes feature in pre-Mongol portrayals of Rus' princes is the surrounding of the prince's head with a nimbus. This distinction seems, however, normally to have been reserved for princes or princesses who were deceased.

In some ways, the construction of stone buildings, whether sacred or palatial, was a more telling expression of princely aspirations to pre-eminence and demonstration of their proximity to higher powers. Possession of superior technology was associated with the introduction of the new religion. Extensive use of masonry involving bricks and worked stone was new to Rus', as also was glass-making and the manufacture of cloisonné enamels. Glass-making, most probably introduced to Rus' at the time of the construction of Vladimir's Tithe-Church in the 990s, was learnt and further

[115] Lazarev 1966, 47–8, 52, 236 and illustrations nos. 30, 36 and 237, fig. 27; Kämpfer 1978, 111–16.
[116] Kämpfer 1978, 116, 119 and photo on 118, figs. 65, 66. The *Izbornik of 1073*, literally '[Book of] Excerpts', is a codex of a Slavic translation of a Greek collection of excerpts ('Florilegium'), copied for Sviatoslav in 1073.
[117] Kämpfer 1978, 130–2 and photo on 128, fig. 69; Brumfield 1993, 52–6.

developed by Rus' craftsmen, and eventually ceased to be an attribute of the prince or even of the elite. Mosaics and cloisonné enamels, however, remained expensive and elitist, if not princely.[118]

The clearest symbolism of all is probably the fact that Vladimir devoted massive resources to the construction of a large show-church, forming part of his new palace complex in Kiev. Both the church and the princely halls flanking it were constructed by Byzantine builders and decorated by Byzantine artists and craftsmen.[119] Also noteworthy is the fact that Iaroslav in the mid-eleventh century wished his principal city to be reminiscent of Constantinople, partaking of its spiritual properties, as if it were an icon. Iaroslav's personal association with the creation of a Christian city is shown by the fact that two of the main churches which he had built were dedicated to the patron saints of himself and his wife, Ingigerd (whose Christian name was Irene), respectively Sts George and Irene. Iaroslav also employed Byzantine craftsmen to build and decorate the centrepiece of his new town, the church of St Sophia, and its exterior appearance was – with its many cupolas – an attempt to imitate the great church of St Sophia built by Justinian 500 years earlier. Similarly, the Golden Gates of his new town were intended to be evocative of Constantinople's Golden Gates and presumably Iaroslav was aware that these in turn were supposed to evoke the Golden Gates of Jerusalem.[120]

A further example of a prince's reliance on a complex of buildings to create a new sacral point of power, making visible reference to a more established one, is Andrei Bogoliubskii's building programme in and around the town he wished to make the seat of a new metropolitanate, Vladimir-on-Kliazma. His church of the Intercession on the Nerl, built near his palace at Bogoliubovo in the mid-1160s and still standing today, was intended to demonstrate that Andrei's authority enjoyed divine protection. His town at Vladimir was equipped with monumental Golden Gates and Andrei clearly intended the layout of his newly sacred seat to mirror that of Kiev. A chronicler writing not long after Andrei's death recorded that his residence at Bogoliubovo was 'as far from Vladimir as is Vyshgorod from Kiev'.[121] In other words, Andrei Bogoliubskii had intended his palace complex at Bogoliubovo to play the part of Vyshgorod, famed as the resting place of Boris and Gleb, in relation to Andrei's new version of Kiev, at Vladimir-on-Kliazma. Andrei's brother Vsevolod 'Big Nest' likewise sought to establish

---

[118] Noonan 1988; Shchapova 1998, 73–86, 105–7, 132.
[119] Brumfield 1993, 10–11; Franklin and Shepard 1996, 164–5.
[120] Poppe 1981, 38–50; Brumfield 1993, 11–14; Franklin and Shepard 1996, 209–14.
[121] *Hypatian Chronicle*, col. 580; Brumfield 1993, 47–51; Franklin and Shepard 1996, 359–60.

himself as a pre-eminent prince with the help of monumental building-work.

As we have already seen, pleas made for the recognition of Prince Vladimir as a saint by the late eleventh century or earlier do not seem to have fallen on particularly receptive ears. In contrast, the cult of the princes Boris and Gleb, who perished at the hands of Sviatopolk in 1015, gained momentum from the later eleventh century onwards. The dating and the procedures for the recognition of the brothers as saints are controversial, a reflection partly of the incompleteness of our source materials and partly of the diversity of ways in which saints came to be recognized and their cults established in Byzantium: such variability can be expected to have extended a fortiori to candidates for veneration in newly converted lands, such as Rus'.

A strong case for an early dating of the development of the cult has been made by L. Müller.[122] This would place the veneration of Boris and Gleb as saints in the first half of the eleventh century, initiated under the auspices of Iaroslav. However, a no less strong case for putting back the formal institution of the cult to the generation following Iaroslav's death, when relations between the princes were fraught and civil war loomed, has been made by A. Poppe. In Poppe's reckoning, even the earliest extant texts about Boris and Gleb date from around 1072. The best known of these is a fairly firmly datable hagiographical work devoted to Boris and Gleb, written by Nestor around 1080, *The Lesson on the Life and Murder of the Holy Passion Sufferers Boris and Gleb and on their Miracles*. Other early texts about Boris and Gleb, some predating Nestor's *Lesson*, include the anonymous *Tale of the Passion and Encomium of the Holy Martyrs Boris and Gleb*, composed around 1072 and supplemented by *The Tale of the Miracles of the Holy Passion Sufferers of Christ Romanus and David* (Boris and Gleb), composed in 1072–3 and continued around 1111. The oldest *Office for the Holy Martyrs Romanus and David* was perhaps composed around 1084, but possibly much earlier; and finally there are the entries for the years 1015, 1072 and 1115 in the *Rus' Primary Chronicle*.[123] What seems clear is that full-scale veneration of the brothers, complete with a regularly observed feast day, only began in 1072 and from then onwards 'what had begun as a ruling dynasty's cult of its murdered innocents became common property, and the princes were venerated as passion sufferers at every level of society

---

[122] Müller 1995, 5–20.
[123] Poppe 2003, 133–68. Translations of the main sources: Hollingsworth 1992; further discussion in Podskal'sky 1996, 184–97, 376–80.

in Christian Rus".[124] By the time their sarcophagi were translated to a new stone church in Vyshgorod in 1115, Boris and Gleb had a strong track record for working miracles. So much so, that for three days a huge crowd of pilgrims, 'the rich and the humble, the healthy and the sick', thronged past, so as to be allowed to touch the 'noble coffins'.[125]

This was a cult of home-grown saints, which struck a number of chords in the sensibilities of Rus' Christians, besides serving to further dignify the status of the princely dynasty, which now counted martyrs in its ranks. If the dynamics of the process cannot readily be reconstructed, there is no doubt that the church housing their relics at Vyshgorod became a major centre of pilgrimage and they came to be regarded and depicted on icons as warrior saints, capable of giving supernatural protection to all the people of Rus', as well as being victims and martyrs. The princely family already enjoyed distinctive blood-right at the time of Vladimir's baptism, and his role as converter of his people and quasi-apostle endowed his descendants with virtually unchallengeable qualifications for hegemony. But it was the rollercoaster progress of the cult of Boris and Gleb that brought to Rus' political culture a particular blend of princely mystique, models for personal behaviour, national security and individual hopes of cures for physical ailments.

5. THE EFFECTS OF CHRISTIANIZATION

The nature of Rus' Christianity is hard to define: practices and attitudes in government, law and society varied enormously and the evidence available is often ambiguous, uneven and controversial. Penetrating behind the triumphalist rhetoric of change for the better purveyed by princes and churchmen is problematic, as is measuring change and assessing the extent to which it was directly due to princely adoption of Christianity. Even apparently straightforward issues of church organization, such as the number and location of bishoprics, are contentious.

Vladimir's baptism was intended to attach to his personal regime the majesty of a single, mighty God in a highly visible manner, making up for his 'legitimacy deficit'. Coin-striking was one effective means of achieving this, making use of new technologies associated with Christianity to portray the ruler in authority and demonstrate his joint rule with Christ on a medium that would reach virtually all those who mattered. Vladimir introduced

---

[124] Poppe 2003, 158.
[125] *Zhitiia Sviatykh Muchenikov*, 65; Hollingsworth 1992, 133; see also Poppe 2003, 167.

the striking of gold and silver coins to Rus' soon after his baptism. His earliest coin designs were modelled on Byzantine ones, and their symbolism clearly demonstrates Vladimir's aspirations to proximity to Christ, who is shown as the Ruler of All (*Pantokrator*). On the reverse sits Vladimir enthroned, wearing a Byzantine-style crown with pendants and holding a cross-topped sceptre. Later types of Vladimir's silver coins show a nimbus around his head and depict his throne more clearly, while the bust of Christ is replaced by Vladimir's trident-like symbol of personal authority. This visual, tangible message of God-given wealth and legitimate authority will have been obvious enough to those, mainly in Vladimir's employ, who received the silver and (much rarer) gold coins. Over 200 examples of the silver coins have been found as far afield as the island of Gotland and the Dnieper estuary, carried there, presumably, by Scandinavian and other warriors whom Vladimir had seen fit to reward or impress.[126] Although silver coins were struck by a few of Vladimir's successors in the eleventh century, notably by Iaroslav in Novgorod, Rus' lacked a monetary economy in the normal sense of that word. The Islamic and, from the late tenth century, western European silver coins in circulation were valued for their precious metal content and weight, not at face value. Vladimir could not transform the economic realities of exchange and production in Rus', and the only place where coins seem to have been issued by a prince out of mainly economic considerations was Tmutarakan on the Straits of Kerch. This princely seat lay well within the Byzantine trading zone.[127]

On most of Vladimir's silver coins a Slavonic legend – for example 'Vladimir on the throne and this is his silver!' – reinforces the image, assuming that those handling and seeing the coins would be at least familiar with, and perhaps able to read, it.[128] Slavonic was already spoken in elite circles, as well as among most of the traders, craftsmen and other free inhabitants of the urban network, and its use for the coin-legends further enhanced its status, making it the language of princely authority. Seemingly without any specific decision taken or decree formally issued by prince or metropolitan, Slavonic became the language of worship, once texts for use in religious services were widely available in Rus', probably mostly brought there by Bulgarians and other South Slavs, under the aegis of the Byzantine church authorities. This brought greater prestige and enrichment to Slavonic as a literary language, putting it on a pedestal above the speech of the Balts and Finns. This was not a foregone conclusion. Scandinavian

---

[126] Sotnikova and Spasski 1982, 66, 79–90.   [127] Shepard 2006.
[128] Sotnikova and Spasski 1982, 80, 97, 103.

runes and Arabic and Hebrew letters had been of practical use in tenth-century Kiev, and Vladimir's choice of Byzantine Christianity could have made Greek the paramount language of godly learning, the liturgy and the princely elite. The earliest phase of the Byzantine mission to Rus' most probably used Greek, and Greek inscriptions continued to help explain or simply signal images in churches and on portable icons.[129] Greek was also used on bishops' seals until the later twelfth century, and many seals of Constantinopolitan patriarchs and externally based Byzantine churchmen and monks have been found within the confines of the land of Rus'.[130] Greek was the language in which these churchmen wrote to one another and few Byzantine-born metropolitans could speak or write Slavonic. Metropolitan Nicephorus, early in the twelfth century, expressed regret that he had to 'stand speechless among you' for lack of knowledge of the language.[131] And yet save for the mid- and second half of the eleventh century when Greek-style princely seals were issued, mostly by princes connected with Tmutarakan,[132] the symbolic and the functional language of princely authority was Slavonic.

Vladimir is said by the *Primary Chronicle* to have lived in peace with rulers such as Bolesław of the Poles and István of the Hungarians,[133] and presumably this required the exchange of written messages, greetings and gifts. Articulate, knowledgeable emissaries were thus important in keeping up with, and being seen to keep up with, one's newly Christian neighbours, a high priority for would-be leaders of Scandinavian and Slav polities of the period of conversions. As with the first steps towards baptism and the bouts of coin-striking in the late tenth century, a degree of mutual comparison and emulation between potentates is very likely. Vladimir therefore had an additional incentive for encouraging his elite's education, besides gaining divine favour through their enlightenment and political benefit from bonding them together in a common faith under his aegis. One may therefore accept more or less at face value the *Primary Chronicle's* statement that the children of notable families were taken off to be instructed in 'book-learning', more or less synonymous with studying the Scriptures and gaining strength in the faith, while their mothers, 'still not strong in the faith . . . wept for them as if they were dead'.[134] The *Chronicle* portrays Iaroslav, Vladimir's son, as a keen reader, 'night and day': he gathered 'many scribes', who copied texts or translated them from Greek into

[129] Franklin and Shepard 1996, 315–16; Franklin 2002, 60–1, 103–5, 247; Vodoff 2003, 209–18.
[130] Ianin 1970, I, 44–59; Ianin and Gaydukov 1998, 27–38; Bulgakova 2004, 79–90, 215–16, 227–9.
[131] Dölker 1985, 2 and n. 2 (introduction).   [132] Shepard 2006.
[133] *PVL*, 56; *RPC*, 122.   [134] *PVL*, 53; *RPC*, 117.

Slavonic; and, 'having written many books, Iaroslav placed them in St Sophia'.[135]

Scraps of evidence indicating more widespread literacy among the laity, and a thirst for knowledge of the faith through letters and book-learning, begin to accumulate from the mid-eleventh century onwards. Some delay after the conversion is unsurprising, especially if much of the earliest worship, preaching and teaching was conducted in Greek, and if Vladimir's own educational ambitions were focused on his own and other 'notable families'. However, organizational measures seem to have been underway by the second quarter of the eleventh century, perhaps the most important stimulus being the need to train an indigenous clergy, equipping deacons and priests to conduct the readings and prayers of the liturgy and to consult and expound the Scriptures. This need was accentuated by the distance between Rus' and Byzantium – and from any other centre where prospective priests might gain a Christian education – and by the very size of the land of Rus'. Although churches with resident priests were mostly confined to the urban network until around 1200, there were now many towns, each with numerous churches linked to pious, well-to-do families, and therefore requiring a supply of adequately trained deacons and priests. According to Novgorodian chronicles, around 1030 the sons of the 'elders and priests' in the town were induced to become students by Prince Iaroslav.[136] This suggests that the education of priests and the sons of leading laymen often went hand in hand, and also that the priesthood almost immediately became heritable.

The diffusion of basic literacy – both writing and reading – among young laymen and trainee priests was facilitated by the relatively cheap writing materials available in Rus'. Eleventh- and twelfth-century urban society appears to have been familiar with books and writing implements, judging by the finds of styluses for writing on wax-covered boards or birchbark. Already in the opening years of the eleventh century, waxed wooden tablets were being used in Novgorod for writing out psalms and passages from the Apocalypse and apocryphal texts.[137] The availability of a corpus of vernacular writing and religious texts, combined with home-grown writing materials such as wax and birchbark, meant that by the twelfth century a sizable proportion of the population living in the urban network knew how to write. This is indicated by finds of birchbark letters in Novgorod, Staraia

[135] *PVL*, 66–7; *RPC*, 137–8; Franklin and Shepard 1996, 241–2; Turilov and Floria 2002, 438–9.
[136] *Novgorodskaia Chetvertaia Letopis'*, 113; *Sofiiskaia Pervaia Letopis'*, col. 176.
[137] Franklin 2002, 46–7; Turilov and Floria 2002, 434, 436.

Russa, Smolensk and other towns. The fur trade was facilitated by the participants' common adherence to Christianity, and by affordable means of corresponding about complex financial matters across vast distances. Letters from Smolensk and the Middle Dnieper region have been found in Novgorod. The traders and urban artisans soon took to the faith in distinctive ways, providing for their own personal and material needs. Business concerns such as accounts, lists of goods, commercial undertakings and disputes mingle in the letters with matters of marriage and divorce; they take for granted a calendar of saints' feast days and kissing the cross so as to reinforce oaths.[138] The townsfolk did not have to look to the princely elite for a lead or instruction.

Vladimir is depicted as consulting his retainers 'about the ordering of the land, about wars and about the law of the land', but the *Primary Chronicle* makes no claim for him or for Iaroslav, the new 'Solomon', as codifiers or promulgators of written law. There had long been some sense of property, rights to life and limb, and due legal process among the Rus'. Procedures for settling disputes and compensating infringement of rights inform the tenth-century Russo-Byzantine treaties. However, there is no evidence that the Rus' set down such procedures in writing for their own internal purposes, or that the princes had much role in determining what manner of laws there should be or in enforcing them. There was most probably an assortment of practical measures for resolving conflicts in the Rus' urban network, but nothing amounting to a law code. After the conversion, justice continued to be regarded by most Rus', whether members of the elite or ordinary town-dwellers, as essentially a bilateral matter of parleying and recompense for insult, loss or death. Indeed, the *Chronicle* highlights the limits of authority as conceived by the prince himself after his conversion. Vladimir was apparently urged by the bishops to take punitive action against the quantities of robbers at large, for 'you have been appointed by God to punish evil-doers'. Reportedly, Vladimir stopped exacting fines in compensation for offences (*viry*), but later he reverted to 'the ways of his father and grandfather'.[139] In other words, the 'new Constantine' of Rus' did not conceive of his role as God's agent as extending to the formulation or enforcement of a new code of law, thoroughly imbued with Christian values.

Nevertheless, a brief text was compiled under princely auspices in the mid-eleventh century, setting out some basic tenets and procedures for

---

[138] Franklin and Shepard 1996, 219, 282–9, 297–9; Franklin 2002, 120–7, 275–6.
[139] *PVL*, 56; *RPC*, 122.

dispute settlement. The 'Short *Pravda*' is attributed to Iaroslav, but some parts are expressly the work of his three elder sons, acting in concert after succeeding to his authority in 1054: a politic move after their father's death and the subsequent division of the Middle Dnieper region between the three, ensconced near one another at Chernigov and Pereiaslavl', as well as Kiev itself. The 'Short *Pravda*' consists mainly of practical provisions, rates of compensation varying according to the status of offender and offended.[140] Much attention is paid to the retribution to be meted out for injuries done to officials, traders and others under the protection of, or of keen financial concern to, the prince. There are similarly harsh sanctions for damage to princely possessions or chattels, which by the later eleventh century were substantial.

A considerably later version of the *Pravda*, known as the 'Extended *Pravda*', was still fairly compact and narrow in scope, essentially a list of compensation tariffs. Neither version offered a general model for correct, let alone avowedly Christian, behaviour, although the 'Extended *Pravda*' provided for resolution of civil disputes, inheritance, wardship and debt. Most acts of violence, theft and disputes were settled on the spot by the individuals concerned or by their kin or community, without reference to the procedures laid down in writing by the prince or enforced by his agents. Indeed, there is no hard evidence that copies of the 'Short' or 'Extended' versions of the *Pravda* were on hand to the governors and other representatives of princely authority. This holds true even in the towns, for whose property-owners, traders and craftsmen the clauses of the *Pravda* chiefly provide. The birchbark letters show that townsfolk generally expected to resolve disputes over business dealings or personal injury for themselves, drawing on agreed notions as to who, for example, could stand as a witness and how stolen goods should be retrieved. The 'land of Rus'' is, even in the twelfth century, best understood as an archipelago of largely self-regulating communities, each with its own esprit de corps, mutual guarantees and patron saints.[141] The princes and the Church presided and prayed over them, and their judicial courts were available – at a fee – to try and cope with disputes and other problems that defied bilateral, familial or communal resolution. But they did not operate under the canopy of an overarching ideology, a law code invoking divine sanction and moral rectitude for meting out justice.

In areas set back from the major riverways, the greater part of the pine-forest zone and the far north, princely governance amounted to little more

---

[140] Kaiser 1992, 14–19. Also Franklin 2002, 156–7.   [141] Dewey and Kleimola 1984, 180–91.

than the levying of tribute. Collected periodically by agents, this took the form of primary produce – wax, honey, slaves and, above all, furs – generally at an agreed rate of, for example, a black marten-skin per household. The loose mesh of princely governance away from the urban centres is illustrated by the tribute-collector Ian's inability to halt the *volkhvy* in the north-east around 1071: dependent on local cooperation, Ian had to agree to the *volkhvy* being tried before his prince, Sviatoslav, on the Middle Dnieper, rather than on the spot.[142] Meting out justice does not seem to have formed part of a tribute-collector's brief, and suppressing flagrantly unchristian behaviour was the most he could hope to accomplish. The literary sources hint at the extent to which churchmen in the north still looked to princely protection in the later eleventh century: even in Novgorod, the bishop owed his life to the prince's intervention when the populace led by a *volkhv* threatened to kill him.[143] A hundred or so years after Vladimir's conversion, the Church in Rus' was still in many ways a missionary Church, and clergymen could not yet count on communal support.

By the mid-twelfth century, new churches were built away from the main riverways, preachers of alternative beliefs no longer challenged Christianity openly, and greater numbers of priests and deacons provided pastoral care. However, bishoprics, churches and monasteries still depended heavily on revenue allocations and one-off gifts from princely benefactors, and they did not play a significant role in fiscal or other forms of princely governance, whether as institutions or as individual monks and senior clergymen.[144] Tithes of urban market-tolls and of the princely tribute paid by outlying populations probably made up the largest and most stable proportion of church income for much of the twelfth century. However, during this period the Church also began to acquire additional sources of income. These included produce or rents from its own landed estates (which became more extensive); and fees and fines (in tithes or even in toto) for the burgeoning assortment of offences now deemed to come within the Church's jurisdiction, and thus imposed by its own courts.[145]

Churchmen remained dependent on princely agents' cooperation for the enforcement of their rights and ultimately for protection of their own officials and their growing possessions. So, not surprisingly, the infrastructure of the established Church in the eleventh and twelfth centuries – the

---

[142] *PVL*, 75–8; *RPC*, 150–4.   [143] *PVL*, 154; *RPC*, 78.

[144] They also received gifts and other forms of patronage from many boiars and traders in Novgorod and, to a lesser extent, in other large towns: on Novgorod, see Dejevsky 1977, 400–1; 1984, 217–23.

[145] Survey in Franklin and Shepard 1996, 232, 236–7 with references to sources.

bishoprics, grand church buildings, monasteries and pilgrimage shrines – clung quite closely to the areas where the princes' presence and protection was palpable, essentially the urban network straddling the main riverways and trade routes. From the mid-twelfth century the establishment of sees, monasteries and churchmen in the north-east of Rus' registers the rising wealth and political clout of the princes who were establishing seats there, first and foremost Iuri Vladimirovich (d. 1157) and his son Andrei Bogoliubskii (d. 1174). Churchmen do not emerge as key administrators or counsellors at the princely court, nor did they cut powerful figures on the political stage. As in Byzantium, there were no ecclesiastical chancellors or keepers of the ruler's seal in pre-Mongol Rus'.

The exception to this rule, as to so many others, was Novgorod, whose senior churchmen had something resembling an independent power base, rooted in the community. The town was home to competing factions of wealthy local families and unruly town assemblies, and princes seldom managed to tap Novgorod's potentially lucrative tax-base for long, alluring as it was: the princes, often called in by one faction or another, lacked long-standing local ties and they rarely lasted for more than a few years, under pressure from boiars, townsfolk and other aspiring princes. In contrast, Novgorod's bishops at least had the advantage of continuity and connections, being mostly of local stock from the mid-twelfth century onwards. They tended to play a more active role in the town's politics and administration, coping with the interminable wrangling generated by the size of the huge conurbation, intensive trading, bitter rivalries and a very uncertain supply of basic necessities. From the twelfth century the bishops of Novgorod commonly styled themselves archbishops, issuing particularly grand seals, building spectacular churches (like other local grandees) and patronizing the keeping of annals. They were, in effect, second-in-rank after the metropolitans of Kiev. The title of archbishop was, however, no more than that: titular and neither regularly used nor universally accepted. So although the Novgorodian prelates were, from the mid-twelfth century, elected locally, not appointed by the metropolitan of Kiev, they continued to be his suffragans and had to be consecrated by him.[146]

We are ill-informed even on such basic matters of church organization in Rus' in the eleventh and twelfth centuries as the number of sees.[147] It is

[146] See Poppe 1970, 167, 169, 171–2, 175, 214; Dejevsky 1984, 208–17, 221–2; Franklin and Shepard 1996, 278–9, 355–7; Shchapov 1993, 34–6, 61–8, 133–4; Vodoff 2003, 79, 96–8, 219–28.

[147] Poppe examined the likely dates of the appearance of bishoprics. A map of bishoprics, table with basic information on each see and prosopographical list of the metropolitans is in Poppe's Appendix to the Russian version of Podskalsky 1982, i.e. Poppe 1996, 442–71; Poppe 1997, 341–55. A prosopographical list of bishops in Rus' is in Shchapov 1993, 229–39.

generally agreed that a metropolitan headed the Church in Rus', and that his see was in Prince Vladimir's main town of Kiev. It is overwhelmingly likely that this was the case from the time of Vladimir's conversion, and that the metropolitanate of '*Rhōsia*' came under the jurisdiction of the patriarch of Constantinople. The earliest Byzantine list of metropolitanates under the patriarchate to mention *Rhōsia* dates from the late eleventh century and the ranking order assigned to *Rhōsia* points to a late tenth-century date for the see's creation.[148] Although not invariably officially sponsored, these lists (known as *Notitiae*) tend to signal new creations and the list in question serves to corroborate the statement of Yahya of Antioch that Emperor Basil II sent to Rus' 'metropolitans and bishops who baptized the king and all the people of his country'.[149] The fact that no metropolitan of *Rhōsia*/Rus' features in Rus' sources before an entry in the *Rus' Primary Chronicle* for the year 1039 is not conclusive in itself. The *Primary Chronicle*'s coverage of the first fifty years or so following Vladimir's conversion is very patchy. Moreover, a Byzantine text mentions a certain Theophylact as in office as metropolitan of Rus' during the reign of Basil II, thus between *c.* 988 and 1025. There is no positive evidence to substantiate the theses advanced by some scholars regarding the existence of an independent archbishopric of Rus', or a Rus' church subordinate to the Bulgarian patriarchate of Ochrid.[150] In the mid-eleventh century, there were titular metropolitans at Chernigov and Pereiaslavl', beside the metropolitan at Kiev; this unusual arrangement most probably reflected the triumvirate of power among Iaroslav's elder sons at the time.[151] The question of where other sees were located is highly controversial, but the earliest well-attested bishops are mostly in the south, in Belgorod, Chernigov, Pereiaslavl' and Iurev, all close to Kiev. Others in the eleventh century lay along the main riverways further north, notably at Polotsk and Novgorod.[152] The number of episcopal sees rose during the twelfth century, although still situated along the riverways, and always based at princely seats such as Turov, Vladimir-in-Volynia, Smolensk and Rostov; in many ways the diffusion of episcopal sees mirrors the diffusion of princely power in twelfth-century Rus'.[153]

Monasteries, too, were largely urban phenomena in this period. Monks probably played a part in evangelization following Vladimir's conversion, as they did on other Byzantine missions. But the house which emerged as intellectually predominant was founded and inhabited by native Rus', the

---

[148] Darrouzès 1981, 343 (text); 122–7 (commentary).   [149] Yahya of Antioch, *Histoire*, 423.
[150] See Poppe 1979.   [151] See Poppe 1970, esp. 177–84 and 168–9, map.
[152] Poppe 1970, 174–6, 184–9; Senyk 1993, 82–94; Shchapov 1993, 35–45.
[153] Poppe 1970, 189–201; Shchapov 1993, 41–50.

Cave Monastery just outside Kiev. The founder, Anthony, had sought spiritual enlightenment on 'the Holy Mountain', almost certainly Athos, but his spiritual father instructed him: 'Go back to Rus' . . . and from you there will come to be many monks.'[154] Towards the mid-eleventh century the monastery attracted Theodosius, who is said to have preferred its simplicity to that of wealthier houses which he visited. Another intelligent and well-read associate of the monastery was Ilarion, who was appointed metropolitan of Rus' in 1051. An early thirteenth-century alumnus could boast that nearly fifty bishops had been former brethren of the Cave Monastery.[155] The Cave Monastery's self-aggrandizement rested on solid religious and cultural achievements. Nestor, eloquent composer of the *Life of Theodosius* and the *Lesson on . . . Boris and Gleb*, wrote there, and the monastery was an effective promoter of the cult of the murdered princes, advocating peaceful collaboration between princes, sharing rule over Rus'. The *Rus' Primary Chronicle* is, in its present form, essentially a product of the Cave Monastery, with Nestor probably playing a key role in its compilation, intermingling recent happenings in Kiev and the monastery itself with the broader themes of the origins and, in particular, the conversion of Rus'. The monastery's ties with the Byzantine world were not ignored: the 'book of the fathers' (*Paterik*) recording the lives of some of the monks states that the house was 'under the blessing of the Holy Mount', and a version of the monastic regulations (*Typikon*) of Constantinople's Studios Monastery was translated into Slavonic, probably at the behest of Theodosius in the early 1060s, together with other works intended to provide Rus' with a corpus of texts needed for everyday worship.[156]

6. CONCLUSION

It is not difficult to pick holes in the tapestry of enlightenment and transformation under princely leadership which works such as Ilarion's *Sermon on Law and Grace* and the *Rus' Primary Chronicle* have woven. A fair amount of adoption of Christian symbols, rites and baptism – Christianization – had been underway among the Rus' for some time before Vladimir's drastic measures of the 980s. Vladimir's own political position was secure, after he had eliminated serious rivals to his hegemony. But his attempt to organize an elaborate public cult focused on sacrifice does not seem to have carried conviction and he may in part have been reacting to the allure

---

[154] *PVL*, 68; *RPC*, 139–40.   [155] *Paterik*, ed. Likhachev *et al.*, 360–1; Heppell, tr. *Paterik*, 118–19.
[156] *Paterik*, ed. Likhachev *et al.*, 318–19; Heppell, tr. *Paterik*, 20–1; Turilov and Floria 2002, 439–40.

which monotheism exercised on some of his more significant subjects. Embracing the Byzantines' variant of Christianity was an attractive, but far from sole, option available to Vladimir. He gained quasi-apostolic prestige, and articulate advocates in the form of Rus' churchmen. Bishoprics were founded in his power base and a formal, lettered institution in the form of an Orthodox metropolitanate now highlighted his dominions. Only a generation or so after Vladimir's death in 1015 Christian religious culture was blossoming in the Middle Dnieper region, with Ilarion's *Sermon* its outstanding literary and theological achievement. In the later eleventh century annalistic recording of events was underway in the Cave Monastery and this came to full fruition in the form of the *Rus' Primary Chronicle*, a work celebrating the conversion and proclaiming the unity of the land of Rus'.

That unity was, however, under strain by the time the *Primary Chronicle* was composed in the early twelfth century. Christianization and conversion did not implant the theory or practice of monarchy. Seats of authority and lucrative catchment areas of tribute were divided, subdivided and fought over with each passing generation and although lip service was paid to the primacy of Kiev, the nature of that primacy was ill-defined and by the later twelfth century Andrei Bogoliubskii was vying with Kiev, attempting to institutionalize his parity with the aid of a separate metropolitan see in Vladimir-on-Kliazma. Andrei promoted a sophisticated politico-religious culture. But his mode of governance was quite rudimentary by contemporary western European standards; it did not entail regular recourse to the written word for the purpose of issuing commands or recording the settlement of disputes. Revenue came from the produce of landed estates, taxes on primary produce such as furs, wax and still, in the twelfth century, from slaves, or from tribute rendered by outlying peoples.

There was then, less of a transformation in the sphere of governance and dispute resolution than in the nature of belief, ritual and normative values and in new role models. But one should not draw too sharp a distinction between religious ideals observed strictly by monks and the faithful few on the one hand and the rough and tumble of everyday disputes and princely rivalries on the other. Conscience and unease at taking human life, even in vengeance, nagged at masterful princes, and while Monomakh had little compunction about killing a captive Polovtsian prince, he did write a letter breathing Christian forgiveness to his cousin Oleg, after Monomakh's son had been killed in battle against Oleg.[157] The cult of Boris and Gleb

---

[157] *PVL*, 105–6; *RPC*, 216–18.

conveyed diverse messages, offering basic Christian teachings about love of one's enemy in Russified guise, besides more specific role models for princes. The notion of heavenly princes, martyrs yet equipped to fend off the enemies of Rus', resonated with Christians who were virtually surrounded by non-Christians, whether Lithuanians to the north-west, Volga Bulgars to the east or Polovtsians in the southern steppes.

Feelings of 'us-ness' and 'otherness' do not lend themselves to precise calibration and they may well have fluctuated greatly across the vast expanses of Rus'. But awe for the powers of the cross engendered respect for those in possession of processional crosses or relics of the True Cross, in other words for bishops and princes, a hierarchy of faith and power. Professing that one was a Christian seems to have been virtually a badge of membership of Rus', and the wearing of crosses was apparently customary in rural settlements of north-east Rus' by the later twelfth century. These customs and cults did not necessarily translate into positive allegiance to individual princes and one's overall impression is of the limitations of the resources at the disposal of princes as, for better or for worse, they fought for one another's throne-towns or positions of hegemony. Nonetheless, the adoption of Christian rites, cults and symbols by so many population groups across a huge area forged ties transcending those of commercial exchange and tribute obligations. There was also some sense as to who shared these rightful beliefs and who remained ignorant pagans or worshipped falsely like the Muslims and (in churchmen's eyes) the Latins. This sense, now expressible in a written vernacular, contained the germs of nationhood.

REFERENCES

Adalbert, *Continuatio Reginonis*, ed. A. Bauer and R. Rau, in *Quellen zur Geschichte der Sächsischen Kaiserzeit*, Darmstadt, 1971.
Androshchuk, A. 2003, 'K istorii obriada intronizatsii drevnerusskikh kniazei ("Sidenie na kurganakh")', in Tolochko *et al.* 2003, 5–10.
Annales Bertiniani, ed. F. Grat, J. Vielliard and S. Clémencet, Paris (Société de l'histoire de France 470), 1964.
Artamonov, I. A. 2001, 'Formirovanie rodovykh nekropolei na Rusi v XI–XII vv.', in *Vostochnaia Evropa v drevnosti i srednevekov'e*, Moscow, 11–20.
Belen'kaia, D. A. 1976, 'Kresty i ikoni iz kurganov Podmoskov'ia', *Sovetskaia Arkheologiia* 4, 88–99.
Birnbaum, H. and M. Flier, eds. 1984, *Medieval Russian Culture*, Berkeley, Los Angeles and London (California Slavic Studies 12).
Brumfield, W. C. 1993, *A History of Russian Architecture*, Cambridge.
Bruno of Querfurt, *Epistola ad Henricum regem*, ed. J. Karwasińska, *MPH* n.s. IV/3, Warsaw, 1973, 97–106.

Bulgakova, V. 2004, *Byzantinische Bleisiegel in Osteuropa*, Wiesbaden (Mainzer Veröffentlichungen zu Byzantinistik 4).

Carver, M. ed. 2003, *The Cross Goes North: Processes of Conversion in Northern Europe, AD 300–1300*, York.

Chiat, M. J. and K. L. Reyerson, eds. 1988, *The Medieval Mediterranean: Cross-Cultural Contacts*, St Cloud (Medieval Studies at Minnesota 3).

Constantine VII, *De administrando imperio*, ed. G. Moravcsik and R. J. H. Jenkins, 2nd edn, Washington, DC, 1967.

Constantine VII, *De cerimoniis aulae byzantinae*, ed. I. I. Reiske, 2 vols., Bonn, 1829.

Darrouzès, J. 1981, *Notitiae episcopatuum ecclesiae Constantinopolitanae*, Paris.

Dejevsky, N. J. 1977, 'Novgorod: The Origins of a Russian Town', in *European Towns: Their Archaeology and Early History*, ed. M. W. Barley, London, 391–403.

Dejevsky, N. J. 1984, 'The Churches of Novgorod: The Overall Pattern', in Birnbaum and Flier 1984, 206–23.

Dewey, H. C. and A. E. Kleimola 1984, 'Russian Collective Consciousness: The Kievan Roots', *Slavonic and East European Review* 62, 180–91.

Dimnik, M. 2003a, *The Dynasty of Chernigov 1146–1246*, Cambridge.

Dimnik, M. 2003b, 'The Princesses of Chernigov (1054–1246)', *Mediaeval Studies* 65, 163–212.

Dimnik, M. 2004, 'The Title "Grand Prince" in Kievan Rus'', *Mediaeval Studies* 66, 253–312.

Dölker, A. ed. 1985, *Der Fastenbrief des Metropoliten Nikfor an den Fürsten Vladimir Monomakh*, Tübingen.

Dolukhanov, P. M. 1996, *The Early Slavs: Eastern Europe from the Initial Settlement to the Kievan Rus*, London.

DOP: Dumbarton Oaks Papers.

Düwel, K. *et al.* eds. 1987, *Untersuchungen zu Handel und Verkehr der vor- und frühgeschichtlichen Zeit in Mittel- und Nordeuropa*, IV, *Der Handel der Karolinger- und Wikingerzeit*, Abhandlungen der Akademie der Wissenschaften in Göttingen, philol.-hist. Klasse, 3 Folge, no. 156, Göttingen.

Featherstone, J. 2003, 'Olga's Visit to Constantinople in *De Cerimoniis*', *Revue des Études Byzantines* 61, 241–51.

Franklin, S. 1991, *Sermons and Rhetoric of Kievan Rus'*, Cambridge, MA.

Franklin, S. 2002, *Writing, Society and Culture in Early Rus, c. 950–1300*, Cambridge.

Franklin, S. and J. Shepard 1996, *The Emergence of Rus 750–1200*, London.

Gager, J. G. ed. 1992, *Curse Tablets and Binding Spells from the Ancient World*, New York and Oxford.

Golb, N. and O. Pritsak, eds. 1982, *Khazarian Hebrew Documents of the Tenth Century*, Ithaca and London.

Golubeva, L. A. 1997, 'Amulety', in Rybakov 1997, 153–65.

Heppell, M. tr. *The Paterik of the Kievan Caves Monastery*, Cambridge, MA, 1989.

Hollingsworth, P. tr. and intr. 1992, *The Hagiography of Kievan Rus'*, Cambridge, MA.

Hypatian Chronicle, PSRL, II, St Petersburg, 1908.

Ianin, V. L. 1970, *Aktovye pechati drevnei Rusi X–XVvv.*, 2 vols., Moscow.

Ianin, V. L. and P. G. Gaydukov 1998, *Aktovye pechati drevnei Rusi X–XVvv.*, Moscow.

Ibn Fadlan, *Risala*, ed. T. Lewicki, A. Kmietowicz and F. Kmietowicz, *Źródła arabskie do dziejów slowianszczyzny*, III, Wrocław, Warsaw, Cracow, Gdańsk and Łódź, 1985; tr. J. E. Montgomery in his 'Ibn Fadlān and the Rōsiyyah', *Journal of Arabic and Islamic Studies* 3, 2000, 1–25.

Ibn Khurradadhbih, *Kitāb al-Masalik wa 'l Mamalik*, ed. T. Lewicki, *Źródła arabskie do dziejów słówiańszczyzny*, I, Wrocław and Cracow, 1956.

Ibn Rusta, *Kitāb al-A'lāk an-nafīsa*, ed. T. Lewicki, *Źródła arabskie do dziejów słówiańszczyzny*, II.2, Wrocław, Warsaw, Cracow and Gdańsk, 1977; tr. G. Wiet, *Les Atours précieux*, Cairo, 1955.

Ilarion, *Sermon on Law and Grace*, in *Biblioteka literatury drevnei Rusi*, ed. D. S. Likhachev *et al.*, I, St Petersburg, 1997, 26–61.

Janin, R. 1969, *Le Siège de Constantinople et le patriarcat oecuménique*, vol. III, *Les églises et les monastères*, Paris.

Jansson, I. 1987, 'Communications between Scandinavia and Eastern Europe in the Viking Age: The Archaeological Evidence', in Düwel *et al.* 1987, 773–807.

JöB: Jahrbuch der österreichischen Byzantinistik.

Kaiser, D. H. ed. and tr. 1992, *The Laws of Rus' – Tenth to Fifteenth Centuries* (The Laws of Russia, Series I, Medieval Russia, vol. I), Salt Lake City.

Kämpfer, F. 1978, *Das russische Herrscherbild von den Anfängen bis zu Peter dem Grossen. Studien zur Entwicklung politischer Ikonographie im byzantinischen Kulturkreis*, Recklinghausen.

Kholostenko, N. V. 1974, 'Moshchenitsa Spasa chernigovskogo', in *Kul'tura srednevekovoi Rusi. Sbornik k 70-letiiu M. K. Kargera*, ed. A. N. Kirpichnikov and P. A. Rappoport, Leningrad, 199–202.

Korpela, J. 2001, *Prince, Saint and Apostle: Prince Vladimir Svjatoslavic of Kiev, his Posthumous Life, and the Religious Legitimization of the Russian Great Power*, Wiesbaden.

Kovalev, R. K. and H. M. Sherman, eds. 2001, *Festschrift for Thomas S. Noonan* (*Russian History/Histoire Russe*, 28/1–4), Pittsburgh, PA.

Lazarev, V. 1966, *Old Russian Murals and Mosaics from the XI to the XVI Century*, London.

Lenhoff, G. 1992, 'Canonization and Princely Power in Northeast Rus: The Cult of Leontii Rostovskij', *Die Welt der Slawen* 37, n.s. 16, 359–80.

Lidov, A. ed. 2000, *Relics in the Art and Culture of the Eastern Christian World* (*Relikvii v iskusstve i kulture vostochnokhristianskogo mira*), Moscow.

Lidov, A. ed. 2003, *Eastern Christian Relics* (*Vostochnokhristianskie relikvii*), Moscow.

Life of Theodosius, in *Biblioteka literatury drevnei Rusi*, ed. D. S. Likhachev *et al.*, I, St Petersburg, 1997, 352–433.

Likhachev, D. S. 1981, *The Great Heritage: The Classical Literature of Old Rus'*, Moscow.

Louis II, 'Epistola ad Basilium I', *MGH, Epistolae Karolini Aevi*, V, Berlin, 1928, 386–94.

Magdalino, P. 1987, 'Observations on the Nea Ekklesia of Basil I', *JöB* 37, 51–64.

Magdalino, P. 1988, 'Basil I, Leo VI and the Feast of the Prophet Elijah', *JöB* 38, 193–6.

Maguire, H. ed. 1995, *Byzantine Magic*, Washington, DC.

Makarov, N. A. 2004, 'Kresty-tel'nikiiz raskopok srednevekovykh selishch i problema khristianizatsii severnorusskoi derevni', *Istoricheskie Zapiski* 7/125, 251–74.

Malingoudis, J. 1994, *Die russisch-byzantinischen Verträge des 10. Jhds. aus diplomatischer Sicht*, Thessalonica.

Mango, C. 1959, *The Brazen House: A Study of the Vestibule of the Imperial Palace of Constantinople*, Copenhagen.

Mango, C. ed. 2002, *Oxford Illustrated History of Byzantium*, Oxford.

Metropolitan John II, *Canonical Responses*, no. 30, *Russkaia Istoricheskaia Biblioteka* VI, St Petersburg, 1880, cols. 1–20.

Mikhailov, K. A. 2001, 'Drevnerusskie kamernye pogrebeniia i Gnezdovo', *Arkheologicheskii sbornik. Trudy Gosudarstvennogo Istoricheskogo Muzeia* 124, 159–75.

Minorsky, V. tr. *Sharaf al-Zaman Tahir Marvazi on China, the Turks and India*, London, 1942.

Motsia, A. P. 1990, *Pogrebal'nye pamiatniki iuzhnorusskikh zemel' IX–XIII vv.*, Kiev.

Müller [Miuller], L. 1995, 'O vremeni kanonizatsii sviatykh Borisa i Gleba', *Russia Mediaevalis* 8/1, 5–20.

Müller-Wille, M. ed. 1997–8, *Rom und Byzanz im Norden. Mission und Glaubenswechsel im Ostseeraum während des 8.-14. Jahrhunderts*, 2 vols., Stuttgart.

Musin, A. E. 1998, 'Two Churches or Two Traditions: Common Traits and Peculiarities in Northern and Russian Christianity', in Müller-Wille 1997–8, II, 275–95.

Musin, A. E. 2002, *Khristianizatsiia novgorodskoi zemli v IX–XIV vv.*, St Petersburg.

Nazarenko, A. V. 2001, *Drevniaia Rus' na mezhdunarodnykh putiakh*, Moscow.

Nicholas I, Patriarch of Constantinople, *Letters*, ed. and tr. L. G. Westerink and R. J. H. Jenkins, Washington, DC, 1973.

Nikol'skaia, T. N. 1981, *Zemlia viatichei. K istorii naseleniia basseina verkhnei i srednei Oki v IX–XIII vv.*, Moscow.

The Nikonian Chronicle, I, *From the Beginning to the Year 1132*, tr. S. A. Zenkovsky and B. J. Zenkovsky, Princeton, 1984.

Nikonovskaia Letopis', PSRL, IX–XIII, St Petersburg, 1862; repr. Moscow, 1965.

Noonan, T. S. 1988, 'Technology Transfer between Byzantium and Eastern Europe: A Case Study of the Glass Industry in Early Russia', in Chiat and Reyerson 1988, 105–11.

Novgorodskaia Chetvertaia Letopis', PSRL, IV/1, Petrograd, 1915.

Novikova, G. L. 1992, 'Iron Neck-rings and Thor's Hammers Found in Eastern Europe', *Fornvännen* 87, 73–88.

Obolensky, D. 1989, 'Cherson and the Conversion of Rus': An Anti-Revisionist View', *Byzantine and Modern Greek Studies* 12, 244–56.

Obolensky, D. 1993, 'Byzantium, Kiev and Cherson in the Tenth Century', *Byzantinoslavica* 54, 108–14.

Paterik, in *Biblioteka literatury drevnei Rusi*, ed. D. S. Likhachev *et al.*, IV, St Petersburg, 1997, 296–489.

Petrukhin, V. I. 1995, *Nachalo etnokul'turnoi istorii Rusi IX–XI vekov*, Moscow.

Petrukhin, V. I. 2000, *Drevniaia Rus': Narod, Kniaz'ia, Religiia*, in *Iz istorii russkoi kul'tury*, I (*Drevniaia Rus'*), Moscow.

Petrukhin, V. I. 2002, 'Khristianstvo na Rusi vo vtoroi polovine X-pervoi polovine XI v.', in *Khristianstvo v stranakh vostochnoi, iugo-vostochnoi i tsentral'noi Evropy na poroge vtorogo tysiacheletiia*, ed. B. N. Floria, Moscow, 60–132.

Petrukhin, V. I. and T. A. Pushkina 1998, 'Old Russia: The Earliest Stages of Christianization', in Müller-Wille 1997–8, II, 247–58.

Photius, *Epistulae et Amphilochia*, I, ed. B. Laourdas and L. G. Westerink, Leipzig, 1983.

Podskalsky, G. 1982, *Christentum und theologische Literatur in der Kiever Rus' (988–1237)*, Munich.

Podskal'sky, G. 1996, *Khristianstvo i bogoslovskaia literatura v kievskoi Rusi (988–1237 gg.)*, St Petersburg (2nd edn in Russian of Podskal'sky 1982).

Poppe, A. 1970, 'L'Organisation diocésaine de la Russie aux XIe–XIIe siècles', *Byzantion* 40, 165–217, repr. Poppe 1982, no. 8.

Poppe, A. 1976, 'The Political Background to the Baptism of Rus: Byzantine–Russian Relations between 986–989', *DOP* 30, 197–244; repr. in Poppe 1982, no. 2.

Poppe, A. 1979, 'The Original Status of the Old-Russian Church', *Acta Poloniae Historica* 39, 5–45, repr. Poppe 1982, no. 3.

Poppe, A. 1981, 'The Building of the Church of St Sophia in Kiev', *Journal of Medieval History* 7, 15–66, repr. Poppe 1982, no. 4.

Poppe, A. 1982, *The Rise of Christian Russia*, London.

Poppe, A. 1996, 'Appendix', in Podskal'sky 1996, 442–97.

Poppe, A. 1997, 'The Christianization and Ecclesiastical Structure of Kyivan Rus' to 1300', *Harvard Ukrainian Studies* 21, 311–92.

Poppe, A. 2003, 'Losers on Earth, Winners from Heaven: The Assassination of Boris and Gleb in the Making of Eleventh-Century Rus', *Quaestiones Medii Aevii Novae* 8, 133–68.

Pritsak, O. 1970, 'An Arabic Text on the Trade Route of the Corporation of Ar-Rūs in the Second Half of the Ninth Century', *Folia Orientalia* 12, 241–59.

PSRL: Polnoe Sobranie Russkikh Letopisei.

Putsko, V. G. 1974, 'Grecheskaia nadpis' iz Voina', *Numizmatika i Epigrafika* 11, 208–14.

PVL: Povest' Vremennykh Let, ed. V. P. Adrianova-Peretts and D. S. Likhachev, rev. M. B. Sverdlov, St Petersburg, 1996.

RA: Rossiiskaia Arkheologiia.

RPC: *Russian Primary Chronicle*, tr. S. H. Cross and O. P. Sherbowitz-Wetzor, Cambridge, MA, 1953.

Rusanova, I. P. 1966, *Kurgany Polyan X–XIIvv. Svod Arkheologicheskikh Istochnikov*, EI-24, Moscow.

Rusanova, I. P. 1992, 'Kul'tovye mesta i iazycheskie sviatilishcha slavian VI–XIII vv.', *RA* 4, 50–67.

Rusanova, I. P. and B. A. Timoshchuk 1998, 'Religioznoe "dvoeverie" na Rusi v XI–XIII vv.', *Kul'tura Slavian i Rus'*, ed. I. S. Kukushkin *et al.*, Moscow, 144–63.

Russell, J. 1995, 'The Archaeological Context of Magic in the Early Byzantine Period', in Maguire 1995, 35–50.

Ryan, W. F. 1999, *The Bath-House at Midnight: An Historical Survey of Magic and Divination in Russia*, Stroud.

Rybakov, B. A. 1987, *Iazychestvo drevnei Rusi*, Moscow.

Rybakov, B. A. ed. 1997, *Drevniaia Rus'. Byt i kultura*, Moscow.

Sedov, V. V. 1982, *Vostochnye slaviane v VI–XIII vv.*, Moscow.

Sedov, V. V. 2002, *Slaviane. Istoriko-arkheologicheskoe issledovanie*, Moscow.

Senyk, S. 1993, *A History of the Church in Ukraine, I, To the End of the Thirteenth Century*, Rome (Orientalia Christiana Analecta 243).

Shchapov, I. N. 1993, *State and Church in Early Russia, 10th–13th Centuries*, New Rochelle, Athens and Moscow.

Shchapova, I. L. 1998, *Vizantiiskoe steklodelie. Ocherki istorii*, Moscow.

Shepard, J. 1986, 'A Cone-Seal from Shestovitsy', *Byzantion* 56, 252–74.

Shepard, J. 1992, 'Some Remarks on the Sources for the Conversion of Rus'', in *Le origini e lo sviluppo della cristianità slavo-bizantina*, ed. S. W. Swierkosz-Lenart, Rome, 59–95.

Shepard, J. 2002, 'Spreading the Word', in Mango 2002, 230–47.

Shepard, J. 2006, 'Closer Encounters with the Byzantine World: The Rus at the Straits of Kerch', in *Pre-Modern Russia and its World: Essays in Honor of Thomas S. Noonan*, ed. J. Tracy *et al.*, Wiesbaden, 15–77.

Shepard, J. forthcoming, 'The Coming of Christianity to Rus', in *Conversions Compared*, ed. W. Phillips *et al.*, Cambridge.

Smirnova, E. S. 2001, 'The Miniatures in the Prayer Book of Princess Gertrude: Program, Dates, Painters', *Russia Mediaevalis* 10/1, 5–21.

Smorag Różycka, M. 2003, *Bizantyńsko-ruskie miniatury Kodeksu Gertrudy*, Cracow.

Sofiiskaia Pervaia Letopis', PSRL, V, Leningrad, 1925.

Sotnikova, M. P. and I. G. Spasski 1982, *Russian Coins of the X–XI centuries AD*, Oxford (BAR International Series 136).

Staecker, J. 1999, *Rex regum et dominus dominorum*, Lund.

Staecker, J. 2003, 'The Cross Goes North: Christian Symbols and Scandinavian Women', in Carver 2003, 463–82.

Stalsberg, A. 2001, 'Scandinavian Viking-Age Boat Graves in Old Rus', in Kovalev and Sherman 2001, 359–401.

Theophanes Continuatus, *Chronographia*, ed. I. Bekker, Bonn, 1838.

Thietmar of Merseburg, *Chronicon*, ed. R. Holtzmann and W. Trillmich (*AQ* IX), Darmstadt, 2002.

Tolochko, O. 2002, 'All the Happy Families . . . The Rurikids in the Eleventh Century', in Urbańczyk 2002, 155–68.

Tolochko, P. P. ed. 1981, *Novoe v arkheologii Kieva*, Kiev.

Tolochko, P. P. *et al.* eds. 2003, *Druzhynni starozhytnosti tsentral'no-skidnoi Evropy VIII–IX st.*, Chernigov (Materialy mizhnarodnogo pol'ovogo arkheolohichnogo seminaru).

Turilov, A. A. and B. N. Floria 2002, 'Khristianskaia literatura u Slavian v seredine X–seredine XI v. i mezhslavianskie kul'turnye sviazi, in *Khristianstvo v stranakh vostochnoi, iugo-vostochnoi i tsentral'noi Evropy na poroge vtorogo tysiacheletiia*, ed. B. N. Floria, Moscow, 398–458.

Turville-Petre, G. 1964, *Myth and Religion of the North*, London.

Ukhanova, E. V. 2000, 'Moshchi sv. Klimenta Rimskogo i stanovlenie russkoi tserkvi v X–XI vekakh', in Lidov 2000, 67–8.

Ukhanova, E. V. 2003, 'Obretenie moshchei v vizantiiskoi tserkvi (po materialam slova Konstantina filosofa na obretenie moshchei sv. Klimenta Rimskogo)', in Lidov 2003, 132–50.

Urbańczyk, P. ed. 2002, *The Neighbours of Poland in the Eleventh Century*, Warsaw.

Uspensky, F. B. 2002a, 'Kogda byl kanonizirovan kniaz' Vladimir Sviatoslavich?', *Palaeoslavica* 10, 271–81.

Uspensky, F. B. 2002b, *Skandinavy, Variagi, Rus'. Istoriko-filologicheskie ocherki*, Moscow.

Vodoff, V. 2003, *Autour du mythe de la Sainte Russie: Christianisme, pouvoir et société chez les Slaves orientaux (Xe–XVIIe siècles)*, Paris.

Vysotsky, S. A. 1966, *Drevne-russkie nadpisi Sofii Kievskoi XI–XIV vv.*, I, Kiev.

Wamers, E. 1997, 'Hammer und Kreuz. Typologische Aspekte einer nordeuropäischen Amulettsitte aus der Zeit des Glaubenswechsels', in Müller-Wille 1997–8, I, 83–107.

White, M. 2004, 'Military Saints in Byzantium and Rus, 900–1200' (unpublished PhD thesis, University of Cambridge).

Wolf, G. 2003, 'The Holy Face and the Holy Feet: Preliminary Reflections before the Novgorod Mandylion', in Lidov 2003, 281–9.

Yahya ibn-Said of Antioch, *Histoire*, ed. and French tr. I. Kratchkovsky and A. Vasiliev, Paris, 1932; repr. Turnhout, 1988.

Zhitiia Sviatykh Muchenikov Borisa i Gleba i Sluzhby im, ed. D. I. Abramovich, Petrograd, 1916; partial reproduction with introduction by L. Müller, *Die altrussichen hagiographischen Erzählungen und liturgischen Dichtungen über die Heiligen Boris und Gleb*, Munich (Slavische Propyläen 14), 1967.

Index

Compiled by the authors with the assistance of Laura Napran

bishopric of, 231, 235, 237, 238, 242, 244, 245, 251, 252, 329
Castle, 216, 218, 225, 227, 232, 234, 237, 238, 239, 241, 246, 247, 248
chapter of, 248
church of, 239, 241, 247
Prandota, bishop of Kraków (1242–66), 293
pravda, 215
Premonstratensians, *see* monks and monasticism
Přemyslids (Přemyslid family), 214, 215, 218, 225, 226, 227, 228, 229, 232, 235–7, 238, 241, 242, 244, 246, 247, 248, 250, 252
Přemysl Oráč the ploughman, mythical Czech prince, 218, 240, 241
Přemysl Otakar I, Czech ruler (1192–3, 1197), and Czech king (1198–1230), 241
prepositi, 98
Pribina, Moravian magnate (d. c. 830), 221
Pribislav-Henry of Brandenburg (d. 1150), 66
Přibyslava, St Václav's sister (first half of tenth century), 235
priests, *see* ecclesiastics
prime-signing (*prima signatio*), 12, 129, 180, 386
Pripegala, Slav god, 307
Pripet, river, 372
Procopius of Caesarea (d. c. 562), 268
Procopius, saint, hermit and founder of Sázava monastery (d. 1053), 234, 235
proto-Slavs, 268
Prove, Slav god, 305, 306
Prüfening, 48
Prunwart, missionary (second half of tenth century), 328, 329
Prunwart, monk of Sankt-Gallen, missionary bishop (second half of tenth century), 331
Prussia, 33–4, 66, 268
Prussians, 63, 67, 289, 290, 294
Przemyśl (Peremyshl), 274, 295, 296, 386, 390
Castle Hill in, 285, 292
Pseudo-Isidore, 358
Pskov, 391
Pskov, lake, 369
Püspökladány-Eperjesvölgy, 328
Pyrzyce, 306

Quedlinburg, 16, 231, 328

Radim-Gaudentius, archbishop of Gniezno (1000–c. 1016), 282, 284, 289, 290, 293
Radla, associate of St Adalbert (d. after 1030), 284, 336
Radogošč (Rethra, Rethre, Rheda, Riedegost), 56, 59, 303, 304, 307
Radogost, Slav God, 306

Radulf (Ralph), bishop of Ribe (1162–71), 81, 93, 101
Rædwald, king of East Anglia (d. 617/25), 22
Ragnar Lodbrok, legendary Scandinavian king, 70
Ragnhild of Tälje, saint (early twelfth century), 188
raids, 11, 14, 34, 47, 77, 79, 324, 327, 328, 382
Ramsunds, 171
Ran, Scandinavian god, 168
Randers, 86
Rani, Rans, Rugians, 49, 59, 300, 304, 306, 307
Ratisbon, *see* Regensburg
Ravenna, 282, 290
Ravning Enge (Jylland), 82
Redars, 303
regalia, 146, 148, 167, 242, 289, 291–2, 349–50, 352, 394–5
coronation sword (*Szczerbiec*), 292
crown, 241, 349, 350, 395, 400
lance, 240, 349, 359
Lancea Regis (Lance of St Mauritius), 291, 349, 358
mantle, 349
orb, 349, 395
sceptre, 349–50, 395, 400
sword, 350
Regelinda, daughter of Bolesław Chrobry, wife of Hermann, margrave of Meissen (c. 989–?), 288
Regensburg, 224, 225, 228, 229, 231, 238, 249, 276, 336, 337, 355
bishopric of, 223, 227, 228, 234
Reginbrand, bishop of Århus (948–?), 81
Reginhar, bishop of Passau (ninth century), 221
Reichenau, 290
Reims, bishopric of, 109
Reinbern, bishop of Kołobrzeg (1000–?, d. c. 1013), 276, 282, 293, 294, 302
relics, 99, 100, 101, 131, 132, 138, 146, 169, 189, 228, 229, 230, 234, 235–8, 290, 337–8, 375, 387, 389, 399, 410
Reric, 77
Rethra, Rethre, *see* Radogošč
Reval, *see* Tallinn
Reynolds, Susan, 8
Rheda, *see* Radogošč
Rhineland, 107, 108, 199, 335, 355, 370
Rhōs, as guards of honour, 377
Rhōsia, metropolitanate of, 394, 407
Ribe, 77, 78, 79, 81, 94, 100, 101
bishopric of, 81, 84, 94
Richeza, wife of Mieszko II (1025–63), 289, 292
Riedegost, exact site not identified, *see* Radogošč
Riga, archbishopric of, 96